2nd Edition

Financial Accounting

FUNDAMENTALS, ANALYSIS AND REPORTING

2nd Edition

Financial Accounting

FUNDAMENTALS, ANALYSIS AND REPORTING

R. K. Arora

Professor

International Management Institute

New Delhi

WILEY

Financial Accounting

Second Edition

Author: R. K. Arora

Published by Wiley India Pvt. Ltd.,
Plot No. 382, 383 Shahabad Daulatpur, New Delhi-110042

Printed at: SDR Printers

First Edition: 2017
Second Edition: 2018
Reprint: 2026

ISBN: 978-81-265-7570-1
ISBN: 978-81-265-8668-4 (ebk)

Other Wiley Editorial Offices:
John Wiley & Sons, Inc. 111 River Street, Hoboken, NJ 07030, USA
Wiley-VCH Verlag GmbH, Boschstr. 12, 69469 Weinheim, Germany
John Wiley & Sons Australia, Ltd (ACN:009 673 081) at Level 4,600 Bourke St, Melbourne Victoria 3000
John Wiley & Sons Singapore Pte. Ltd, 134 Jurong Gateway Road, #04-307H, Singapore 600134
John Wiley & Sons Canada Ltd, 22 Worcester Road, Etobicoke, Ontario, Canada, M9W ILI
John Wiley & Sons, Ltd, New Era House, 8 Oldlands Way, Bognor Regis, West Sussex, PO22 9NQ, UK

www.wileyindia.com

Preface

The study of financial accounting is necessary for business managers, investors and many other users to take informed decisions and to make appropriate judgements. There are many excellent books available on the subject. However, I felt there was a need for a book that starts with simple and easy concepts and then gradually explains the difficult and complex ones. To this end, the book first explains the accounting concepts with reference to financial statements of non-corporate entities and only later moves to the more complex corporate financial statements.

Moreover, there have been important changes in the recent past that made it necessary to have a book that incorporates these changes. The first important change was the promulgation of the Companies Act, 2013. The new Act made many changes in the provisions related to corporate accounts and corporate financial statements. The other major change was the coming into effect, in a staggered manner, of the new Indian Accounting Standards (Ind AS) which marks a step towards convergence of the Ind AS with the International Financial Reporting Standards (IFRS). This book is based on the new provisions that form a part of the Companies Act, 2013 and the Ind AS.

The book is primarily written for graduate students of management. However, it should prove equally useful for undergraduate students of commerce (B. Com.) as well as students of professional courses, such as Chartered Accountancy (CA) and Cost and Management Accountancy (CMA).

Organization of the Book

The book comprises 13 chapters that provide the fundamentals, analysis and reporting of financial accounting.

1. Chapter 1, *Nature and Purpose of Accounting* introduces the readers to the basics of accounting and its uses.
2. Chapter 2, *Balance Sheet*, and Chapter 3, *Statement of Profit and Loss*, explain simple financial statements: balance sheet and statement of profit and loss for non-corporate entities.
3. Chapter 4, *Accounting Records and Systems* deals with the accounting records that a business needs to keep and the basics of recording transactions and events in accounting books.
4. The actual preparation of financial statements of non-corporate entities based on the summary of account balances is a part of Chapter 5, *Preparation of Financial Statements*. The adjustment entries made at the year-end to account for accruals and deferrals are also explained in this chapter.

5. Chapter 6, *Plant Assets and Intangible Assets*, describes in detail the accounting requirements related to Property, Plant and Equipment and intangible assets of a business and how a business entity should account for the consumption of these assets by way of depreciation and amortization.
6. Chapter 7, *Inventories: Accounting and Valuation* deals with the record-keeping for inventories, their valuation and physical verification.
7. In Chapter 8, *Corporate Financial Statements*, the knowledge acquired in relation to financial statements of non-corporate entities is applied to the preparation of financial statements of corporate entities. The specific requirements of the Companies Act, 2013 and the new Indian Accounting Standards with which companies have to comply with in preparing their financial statements are also covered in this chapter.
8. Chapter 9, *Financial Statements of Banking Companies* describes the special characteristics of banking companies: accounts, financial statements and certain specific transactions. The regulatory requirements relating to capital adequacy, provisioning for non-performing banking assets are also discussed in detail.
9. Besides corporate financial statements, annual reports of companies contain a plethora of other information like the directors' report, the auditor's report, management discussion and analysis, corporate governance report, etc. All these aspects of corporate financial reporting form a part of Chapter 10, *Understanding Corporate Annual Reports*.
10. Companies also need to present a third financial statement, *the cash flow statement*, as part of their annual accounts. This statement is meant to explain how the different business activities – operating, investing and financing – translate into the change in the cash available with the company. The method of preparing the cash flow statement and the related concepts are covered in Chapter 11, *Statement of Cash Flows*.
11. Chapter 12, *Analysis of Financial Statements* covers the analysis and interpretation of the financial statements from the perspective of investors, lenders and managers. A number of analytical tools such as common-size statements, trend ratios, financial ratios are described and illustrated in this chapter.
12. Chapter 13, *Financial Reporting Standards* presents the existing and the new accounting standards and how these accounting standards differ from International Financial Reporting Standards (IFRS).

Features of the Book

The chapters are written with the intent that they provide an easy and effective way of learning. For this purpose, the following pedagogical features have also been incorporated into the chapters:

Learning Objectives

Learning Objectives outline the learning goals highlighting the key concepts that would be discussed in the chapter.

LEARNING OBJECTIVES

After reading this chapter, you will be able to:

- Understand the relationship between profit and loss account and balance sheet.
- Prepare profit and loss account and balance sheet from the given trial balance without accounting for any adjustment entries.
- Understand how to make adjustments for accruals, deferrals and other items.
- Prepare profit and loss account and balance sheet after accounting for adjustment entries.
- Prepare closing entries and post-closing trial balance.

Exhibit 8.2

Balance sheet of Asian Paints Ltd. as on March 31, 2017

(Rupees in Millions)

	Notes	As on 31.03.2017	As on 31.03.2016
Assets			
Non-Current Assets			
Property, plant and equipment	2	25,120.1	25,329.7
Capital work-in-progress		2,197.6	927.9
Goodwill	3A	353.6	353.6
Other intangible assets	3B	573.1	606.6
Financial Assets			
Investments	4	14,545.5	13,196.4
Loans	5	702.7	610.7
Others Financial Assets	6	1980.5	305.4
Current tax assets (Net)	7	364.8	151.5
Other non-current assets	8	2003.9	350.1
		47,841.8	41,831.9
Current Assets			
Inventories	9	21,940.9	1,610.12
Financial assets			

Exhibits

Exhibits provide the real-world application of accounting concepts. These are excerpts from corporate annual reports.

Illustrations

Illustrations are easy-to-follow examples which help in explaining the accounting concepts and procedures.

Illustration 8.11

A company currently has a paid-up share capital of Rs. 2,000,000 (200,000 equity shares of Rs. 10 each) and a balance of Rs. 1,800,000 in Profit and Loss Account. The company decides to issue one bonus share for every four shares held by shareholders prior to the bonus distribution.

The company will issue 50,000 new shares as bonus shares by using Rs. 500,000 out of the balance in the Profit and Loss Account. Balance Sheet of the company prepared after the issue of bonus shares will show a paid-up share capital of Rs. 2,500,000 (250,000 equity shares of Rs. 10 each) and a balance of Rs. 1,300,000 in the Profit and Loss Account.

Summary – Review of Learning Objectives

1. **Understand the nature and purpose of balance sheet.** The balance sheet reveals the financial position of an entity. It is prepared on a particular date, and is true only on that date because even a single transaction will affect some of the assets or liabilities and, therefore, the owners' capital shown in the balance sheet drawn on that date. It is prepared only after the preparation of the profit and loss account as the net income revealed by the profit and loss account is added to the owners' capital. The two sides of the balance sheet must have the same total because capital is always equal to the difference between assets and liabilities, and the amount of capital is independently arrived at by the capital account. The non-agreement of the two sides indicates the presence of some error in preparation.

   Balance sheet is useful to both investors and lenders. Investors analyze the balance

Summary – Review of Learning Objectives

Summary – Review of Learning Objectives discusses the points mentioned in Learning Objectives as per the concepts mentioned in the chapter.

Glossary

Glossary provides definition/information regarding important key terms.

»

Glossary

- **Adjusted trial balance.** After posting of adjustment entries in the ledger, an adjusted trial balance is prepared that carries a summary of updated account balances.
- **Closing entries.** At the end of the accounting period, expense and revenue accounts are closed by transferring their balances to the profit and loss account. The profit and loss account is also closed by transferring the balance to the owners' capital or retained earnings (in the case of of the ending inventory is determined by taking a physical inventory count.
- **Operating profit** is calculated as gross profit minus operating expenses.
- **Operating expenses** are related to normal operations of the business and include administrative, selling and general expenses.
- **Net profit** is calculated by adjusting the operating profit for non-operating revenues, expenses, gains and losses.

Solved Problem

1. Table 2.3 shows the trial balance extracted from the books of Akhilesh as on March 31, 2015.

Table 2.3 Trial balance of Akhilesh as on March 31, 2015

	Debit Amount (Rs.)	Credit Amount (Rs.)
Debtors/Creditors	78,695	25,000
Net profit earned during the year		40,595
Cash in hand	6,900	
Capital		100,000
Property, plant and equipment	80,000	
	165,595	165,595

Prepare the balance sheet as on March 31, 2015 in both horizontal and vertical forms.

«

Solved Problems

Solved Problems help students understand how to solve numerical problems.

Multiple Choice Questions

Multiple Choice Questions help teachers as well as students to create a short and crisp understanding and evaluation of the concepts discussed in the chapter.

»

Multiple Choice Questions

1. Which one of the following financial statements is generally prepared first?
   - **a.** Income statement
   - **b.** Balance sheet
   - **c.** Cash flow statement
   - **d.** Statement of retained earnings
2. Which one of the following items is not reported in the income statement as an expense?
   - **a.** Salaries
   - **b.** Depreciation
   - **c.** Rent
   - **d.** Dividend

Rs. 5,00,000 during the year. What is the amount of cost of goods sold revealed by the firm's accounting information system?
   - **a.** Rs. 500,000
   - **b.** Rs. 600,000
   - **c.** Rs. 400,000
   - **d.** Rs. 520,000

5. Which one of the following items will not appear on a firm's income statement?
   - **a.** Rent expense
   - **b.** Salaries
   - **c.** Insurance expense
   - **d.** Purchase price of furniture

Answers to Multiple Choice Questions

1. (a)
2. (d)
3. (c)
4. (d)
5. (d)
6. (d)
7. (c)

«

Answers to Multiple Choice Questions

Answers to Multiple Choice Questions provide answers to all the multiple choice questions asked in a chapter.

Practice Problems

Practice Problems help students to revise the concepts learned.

Practice Problems

1. From the data drawn from the books of X (Table 2.6), prepare a balance sheet as on March 31, 2016 in both horizontal and vertical forms.

Table 2.6 X: Ledger balances as on March 31, 2016

Capital	2,400,000	Long-term debt	1,200,000
Debtors	160,000	Outstanding expenses	160,000
Prepaid expenses	80,000	Building	1,200,000
Equipment	400,000	Furniture	320,000
Patents	240,000	Investments	240,000
Cash	200,000	Creditors	200,000
Inventories	320,000	Land	800,000

In addition there are also *Instructor Resources*, which can be accessed by writing in to acadmktg@wiley.com

Suggestions for improvement of the book are welcome. These may kindly be sent to rkarora@imi.edu

Acknowledgements

I sincerely thank the following colleagues for their valuable feedback to improve the text.

Kanhaiya Singh	Professor, Fore School of Management, Delhi
Anil Kshatriya	Professor, Institute of Management Technology, Nagpur
Nitin Saxena	Assistant Professor, Institute of Technology & Science, Ghaziabad
K. H. Gokula Krishnan	Associate Professor, Dhruva College of Management, Hyderabad
Pawan Jain	Associate Professor, IMT, Nagpur

My special thanks to the editorial and production team of Wiley India and in particular to Meenakshi Sehrawat and Rupnarayan Das for their valuable support. I owe a lot to International Management Institute (IMI), New Delhi, for providing the necessary library and computing resources. Also, many thanks to my wife, Sangeeta and my sons, Ankit and Nikhil for their support and understanding.

I dedicate this work to my parents.

Suggestions for improvement of the book are welcome. These may kindly be sent to rkarora@imi.edu.

Ravinder Kumar Arora

About the Author

Ravinder Kumar Arora is Professor of Finance and Accounting at International Management Institute, New Delhi. He has a B.Com. degree with distinction from Panjab University; an MBA degree from University Business School, Chandigarh; and a doctorate from Indian Institute of Technology, Delhi. He is also a fellow member of the Institute of Cost Accounts of India and the Institute of Company Secretaries of India. He has nearly three and a half decades of industry, teaching and research experience. He has published his research in premier national and international journals.

Contents

Nature and Purpose of Accounting

1

LEARNING OBJECTIVES

After reading this chapter, you will be able to:

- Understand the role of accounting information in making economic decisions.
- Identify the users and uses of accounting information.
- Understand the sub-fields of accounting and their relevance.
- Explain different accounting terms.
- Describe the contents and the purpose of different financial statements.
- Understand the purpose of generally accepted accounting principles.

1.1 Introduction

Decision making is a part and parcel of carrying on a business. There are many stakeholders in a business enterprise. These include owners, managers, investors, lenders, customers, suppliers, labor unions and the government. All these stakeholders make some or the other kind of decision. For making decisions, the stakeholders need relevant economic information. "Accounting" provides the relevant economic information required by stakeholders.

1.2 Accounting

Accounting has been aptly defined by the American Accounting Association as:

> *Accounting is the process of identifying, measuring and communicating economic information to permit informed judgments and decisions by the users of accounts.*

This definition implies that there are certain users of accounts who need information for judgment and decision making, and accounting is a process of identifying users' information requirements and collecting, processing and communicating such information to the users.

1.3 Users and Uses of Accounting Information

Accounting information has both *internal and external users.* Internal users are managers in all areas of functional responsibility such as marketing, finance, human resources and general management. Marketing managers use accounting information to make decisions relating to pricing of products, sales promotion, etc. Finance managers use accounting information to decide on making new investments, raising funds, payment of dividends, etc. Human resources managers make decisions relating to pay revision, declaration of bonus, etc. on the basis of accounting information. General managers make decisions on the product-mix of the entity using accounting information. The type of reports generated by the accounting information system for use by managers include forecasts of income, projections of funds requirement and availability, comparison of financial results of alternative courses of action, etc.

External users of accounting information include investors, lenders, customers, suppliers, labor unions and the government. *Owners and investors* are interested in knowing whether the business would be able to provide a reasonable return on their investment and whether to continue with the investment inthe business, how to finance the expansion of business, etc. *Lenders* need information for determining the capacity of the business to pay interest and to repay loans in time. *Customers* want to know whether the business will continue producing the item they are using so that there are no problems relating to servicing of its products and associated warranties. *Suppliers* want to satisfy themselves about the ability of the business to make payments of their dues on time. *Labor unions* are interested in knowing whether the business will be able to pay increased wages and bonuses. *Government* wants to know whether the business is rightly determining its profit or loss and whether it is duly paying the taxes due from it.

1.4 Sub-Fields of Accounting

Information needed by managers and owners is more detailed, and the sub-field of accounting that generates this information is known as *managerial accounting.* Managers use managerial accounting information to set organizational goals, evaluate individual and departmental performances, make decisions relating to the introduction of new products or entering new markets, etc. Managerial accounting information need not be organized in a particular format. The presentation depends on the decision at hand. A major part of managerial accounting consists of information relating to the cost of products and services. Managerial accounting uses both historical information and projections for the future.

The other sub-field of accounting is called *financial accounting.* It relates to the preparation of financial statements for use by both managers and external stakeholders. Financial accounting reports present information about all activities of the business, be it *operating activities* (main revenue-producing activities); *investing activities* (activities involving purchase and sale of long-lived assets and investments); or *financing activities* (activities that change the amount and composition of financial resources). Financial accounting is basically historical in nature.

1.5 Accounting Terms

The following terms are commonly used in financial accounting and are of interest to different users of accounting information:

1.5.1 Asset

Assets are economic resources controlled by an entity whose cost (or fair value) at the time of acquisition could be objectively measured. A resource is an economic resource if it provides future cash flows to the entity. An asset can be: (i) cash or something convertible into cash (e.g. accounts receivable), (ii) goods expected to be sold and cash received from them and (iii) items to be used in future activities that will generate cash flows.

Land and building, plant and machinery, furniture and fixtures, inventories, debtors and cash balance are examples of assets.

1.5.2 Liability

Liabilities are claims to assets. A business raises financial resources from both its owners and outside parties. Both have claims to the assets of the entity. Liabilities are claims to assets of parties other than owners. Loans, debentures (bonds), creditors, unpaid expenses are examples of liabilities. Liabilities create negative future cash flows for the entity.

For example, a business has assets worth Rs. 10 million which are financed by owners' funds of Rs. 6 million and loans of Rs. 4 million. The loan of Rs. 4 million represents a claim to 40 percent of the assets and is termed as a liability of the business.

1.5.3 Capital/Owners' Equity

Capital (owners' equity) generally refers to the amount invested in an enterprise by the owners. It is also used to refer to the claim of owners to the assets of an enterprise. The claims of owners to assets are secondary to those of creditors and lenders.

Changes in owners' equity occurs when: (i) owners either invest in or withdraw cash or other assets from the business and (ii) the business either earns income from profitable operations or incurs losses from unprofitable operations.

1.5.4 Revenue

Revenue is the gross inflow of cash, receivables or other consideration arising during the course of ordinary activities of an enterprise from the sale of goods, rendering of services, and from the use by others of enterprise resources yielding interest, royalties and dividends.

1.5.5 Cost

Cost is a monetary measurement of the amount of resources used for some purpose. For example, an entity incurs a cost when it purchases an item of equipment.

1.5.6 Expense

All costs incurred by an entity are not expenses. An expense is that cost which relates to the operations of an accounting period (e.g. rent) or to the revenue earned during the period (cost of goods sold) or the benefits of which do not extend beyond that period. Expenses, thus, have a relation with the accounting period and represent that part of the cost of an asset or service that is consumed during the accounting period.

For example, a businessman dealing in televisions buys 1,000 television sets at a cost of Rs. 20 million during an accounting year. This amount of Rs. 20 million is a cost as it represents the amount of resource (cash) used. During this accounting period, the businessman sells only 800 televisions. The cost of 800 televisions, that is, Rs. 16 million is the expense of that accounting year as it represents the cost that corresponds to the revenue earned during the year from the sale of 800 televisions.

A business that prepares its accounts every calendar year (January–December) buys an yearly insurance cover on its assets on 1 April by paying a premium of Rs. 50,000. This amount of Rs. 50,000 is a cost as it represents the amount of resource (cash) used. However, the business will not enjoy the entire benefit of this cost in the accounting period that ends on 31 December. The benefit of the insurance cover extends to 31 March of the next accounting period. Only three-fourth of this cost relates to nine months of the current accounting period, that is, Rs. 37,500 will be treated as an expense of the current accounting period.

1.5.7 Goods

The term 'Goods' refers to the property in which the business deals. Goods are purchased by a business for resale and not for use in the business. For example, furniture acquired for resale by a furniture dealer will be treated as goods and furniture acquired by such a dealer for use in his/her office will be treated as an asset.

1.5.8 Debtors (Accounts Receivable)

Debtor refers to a person who owes money to the business for goods purchased from the business.

1.5.9 Creditors (Accounts Payable)

Creditor refers to the person to whom the business owes money for goods purchased by the business from that person.

1.5.10 Debits and Credits

The accounting system keeps a separate record for each item of assets, liabilities, income and expense. This record is called an *account.* An account has two sides, the left-hand side and the right-hand side. Accounting records are maintained using a *double-entry accounting system.* Under this system, debit and credit entries of equal amount are made to record every business transaction. Entering an amount on the left-hand side of the account is called *debiting the account* and entering an amount on the right-hand side of an account is called *crediting the account.* Accounting records are considered accurate only when the sum of all debits is equal to the sum of all credits.

1.6 Financial Statements

Information to users of accounting information is provided in the form of financial statements that arrange assets, liabilities, revenue and expenses in different ways. Every business enterprise generally prepares three financial statements: income statement, balance sheet and statement of cash flows.

1.6.1 Income Statement

The income statement (or the profit and loss account) reports the result of business operations during the accounting period. It matches the expenses for the accounting period with the revenues earned, and reports the resulting net income (profit or loss). The income statement is of particular use to investors, lenders and creditors. Investors use the past net income as a basis to predict the future net income and to make their investment decisions. Lenders to the business use information provided by the income statement to form an opinion about the ability of the business to repay loans and to pay interest on time. Creditors use the income statement to form an opinion about the ability of the business to pay their dues on time.

1.6.2 Balance Sheet

The balance sheet reports the financial position of the business at a particular point of time, generally at the end of the accounting period. It shows the amount of assets owned by the business and the claims on these assets. The claims on the assets belong to the providers of resources to buy the assets, i.e., the owners and creditors/lenders. As the business cannot spend more on buying assets than the resources it has, the following relationship (also called the *accounting equation*) always holds.

$$\text{Assets} = \text{Owners' Capital} + \text{Liabilities}$$

Creditors and lenders analyze the balance sheet to understand the ability of the business to repay their dues. The proportion of owners' capital in relation to outside liabilities also serves as an indicator of the financial strength of the business.

1.6.3 Statement of Cash Flow

The statement of cash flow provides information about the cash receipts and cash payments during an accounting period. Particularly, it shows the sources from which cash is received, the uses to which cash is put and the change in the cash balance during the accounting period.

The presentation of financial statements for external users depends on the type of business organization. A business can be organized as *sole-proprietorship* (having a single owner), a *partnership* (with two or more owners or partners) or a *company* (having a large number of owners or shareholders). Only companies are required by law to keep the prescribed set of books and to present their financial statements in the prescribed format. Other forms of business organization need to maintain their accounts in a manner that enables determination of their income for income tax purposes.

Normally, companies are required to prepare annual and quarterly financial statements. The quarterly financial statements are also known as *interim financial statements*. Certain business organizations are, however, not required to prepare interim financial statements for external reporting.

1.7 Generally Accepted Accounting Principles

Generally accepted accounting principles (GAAP) are a set of conventions, rules and procedures that define the accepted accounting practice at a particular time. These result from a broad agreement on the theory and practice of accounting at a particular time. The purpose of GAAP is to ensure that the information provided in the financial statements is reliable and understandable to the users. The users should be able to meaningfully compare the current performance of a business entity with its past performance and the performance of other business entities. The GAAP keep changing from time to time as the circumstances or the information needs of the users change.

In India, the sources of GAAP include the Companies Act, 2013, Indian accounting standards and the pronouncements of the accounting profession. A detailed account of the Indian GAAP is provided in Chapter 13 of the book.

Summary – Review of Learning Objectives

1. **Understand the role of accounting information in making economic decisions.** There are a number of stakeholders in a business who make some or the other kind of decision. For making these decisions, the stakeholders need relevant economic information. It is accounting that provides the relevant economic information required by the stakeholders.
2. **Identify the users and uses of accounting information.** Accounting information includes both internal and external users. Managers are internal users. Investors, lenders, customers, suppliers, labor unions and the government are external users.
3. **Understand the sub-fields of accounting and their relevance.** There are two sub-fields of accounting: managerial accounting and financial accounting. Managerial accounting generates detailed information for owners and managers. On the contrary, financial accounting relates to the preparation of financial statements for use by both managers and external stakeholders.
4. **Explain the meaning of different accounting terms.** For proper understanding of accounting, one needs to understand the meaning of important accounting terms such as asset, liability, owners' equity, revenue, cost, expense, debtors, creditors, etc.
5. **Describe the content and purpose of different financial statements.** The income statement reports the result of business operations during the accounting period. It matches the expenses for the accounting period with the revenues earned and reports the resulting net income (profit or loss). The balance sheet reports the financial position of the business at a particular point of time, generally at the end of the accounting period. It shows the amount of assets owned by the business and the claims on these assets. The statement of cash flows provides information about the cash receipts and cash payments during an accounting period.
6. **Understand the purpose of generally accepted accounting principles.** Generally accepted accounting principles (GAAP) are a set of conventions, rules and procedures that define the accepted accounting practice at a particular time. These result from a broad agreement on the theory and practice of accounting at a particular time.

Glossary

- **Accounting system** keeps a separate record for each item of assets, liabilities, income and expense. This record is called an *account*. An account has two sides, the left-hand side and the right-hand side.

- **Accounting** is the process of identifying, measuring and communicating economic information to permit informed judgments and decisions by the users of accounts.
- **Assets** are economic resources controlled by an entity whose cost (or fair value) at the time of acquisition could be objectively measured.
- **Capital/owners' equity** generally refers to an amount invested in an enterprise by the owners.
- **Cost** is a monetary measurement of the amount of resources used for some purpose.
- **Credit** results from entering an amount on the right-hand side of an account.
- **Creditors (accounts payable)** are persons to whom the business owes money for goods purchased by the business.
- **Debit** results from entering an amount on the left-hand side of an account.
- **Debtors (accounts receivable)** are persons who owe money to the business for goods purchased.
- **Expense** is the cost relating to the operations of an accounting period or to the revenue earned during the period or to the benefits of which do not extend beyond that period.
- **Financial accounting** is concerned with the preparation of financial statements for use by both managers and external stakeholders.
- **Goods** refer to the property in which the business deals.
- **Liability** is the financial obligation of an enterprise other than the owner's funds arising from events that have already happened.
- **Managerial accounting** provides detailed information needed by managers and owners for decision making.
- **Revenue** is the gross inflow of cash, receivables or other consideration arising during the course of ordinary activities of an enterprise from the sale of goods, rendering of services, and from the use by others of enterprise resources yielding interest, royalties and dividends.

Multiple Choice Questions

1. Which of the following is the most appropriate and modern definition of accounting?
   a. The information system that identifies, records and communicates the economic events of an organization to interested users.
   b. A means of collecting information.
   c. The interconnected network of subsystems necessary to operate a business.
   d. Electronic collection, organization, and communication of vast amounts of information.

2. The group of users of accounting information charged with achieving the goals of the business is its ________.
   a. auditors
   b. investors
   c. managers
   d. creditors

3. Which of the following groups use accounting information to determine whether the company can pay its obligations?
   a. Investors in common stock
   b. Marketing managers
   c. Creditors
   d. Chief Financial Officer

4. The common characteristic possessed by all assets is ________.
   a. long life
   b. great monetary value
   c. tangible nature
   d. future economic benefit

5. Expenses are incurred ________.
   a. only on rare occasions
   b. to produce assets
   c. to produce liabilities
   d. to generate revenues
6. The cost of assets consumed or services used is also known as ________.
   a. a revenue
   b. an expense
   c. a liability
   d. an asset
7. Resources owned by a business are referred to as ________.
   a. owners' equity
   b. liabilities
   c. assets
   d. revenues
8. The best definition of assets is the ________.
   a. cash owned by the company
   b. collection of resources belonging to the company and the claims on these resources
   c. owners' investment in the business
   d. resources belonging to a company that have future benefits
9. Debts and obligations of a business are referred to as ________.
   a. assets
   b. equities
   c. liabilities
   d. expenses
10. Which of the following financial statements is concerned with the financial position of a company at a point in time?
    a. Balance sheet
    b. Income statement
    c. Retained earnings statement
    d. Statement of cash flows
11. An income statement ________.
    a. summarizes the changes in retained earnings for a specific period of time
    b. reports the changes in assets, liabilities and stockholders' equity over a period of time
    c. reports the assets, liabilities and stockholders' equity at a specific date
    d. presents the revenues and expenses for a specific period of time
12. Which of the following groups uses accounting information to determine whether the company's net income will result in a stock price increase?
    a. Investors in common stock
    b. Marketing managers
    c. Creditors
    d. Chief Financial Officer
13. Which of the following groups use accounting information to determine whether a marketing proposal will be cost effective?
    a. Investors in common stock
    b. Marketing managers
    c. Creditors
    d. Chief Financial Officer
14. Which of the following would **not** be considered an external user of accounting data for a company?
    a. Income tax officer
    b. Management
    c. Creditors
    d. Customers
15. Which of the following would **not** be considered an internal user of accounting data for a company?
    a. The president of a company
    b. The controller of a company
    c. Creditor of a company
    d. Salesperson of a company

Review Questions

1. Define accounting.
2. How does managerial accounting differ from financial accounting?
3. How does an expense differ from a cost?
4. Who are the main users of accounting information and how do they use this information?
5. Define the terms revenue, asset and liability.
6. Name the three financial statements generated by the accounting information system and state the objectives of preparing these statements.
7. What are generally accepted accounting principles (GAAP)? What purpose do they serve?
8. What are the main sources of Indian GAAP?

Answers to Multiple Choice Questions

1. (a)
2. (c)
3. (c)
4. (d)
5. (d)
6. (b)
7. (c)
8. (d)
9. (c)
10. (a)
11. (d)
12. (a)
13. (b)
14. (b)
15. (c)

Balance Sheet

2

LEARNING OBJECTIVES

After reading this chapter, you will be able to:

- Understand the nature and purpose of a balance sheet.
- Understand the format and contents of a balance sheet.
- Explain the accounting principles that underlie the preparation of a balance sheet.

2.1 Introduction

Balance sheet is the first of three financial statements discussed in Chapter 1. In this chapter, the contents of the balance sheet of a sole proprietorship will be discussed. Corporate balance sheet will be discussed in Chapter 8.

2.2 Balance Sheet

A balance sheet reveals the financial position of an entity. It sets out the assets, liabilities and owners' capital of an entity as on a certain date. As explained in Chapter 1, assets are economic resources controlled by an entity which provide future cash flows to the entity. These economic resources are in the form of land and building, plant and machinery, furniture and fixtures, investments, inventories, receivables, cash balances, etc. Liabilities represent the claims of persons other than owners on these assets or the amount of money provided by them for acquisition of assets. Capital represents the claims of owners on the assets or the amount of money invested by the owners to acquire the assets.

It is prepared on a particular date and is true only on that date because even a single transaction will affect the assets or liabilities and, therefore, the owners' capital shown in the balance sheet drawn on that date. It is prepared only after preparing the profit and loss account as the net income revealed by the profit and loss account is added to the owners' capital. The two sides of the balance sheet must have the same total because capital is always equal to the difference between assets and liabilities, and the amount of capital is independently arrived at by the capital account. The non-agreement of the two sides indicates the presence of some error in the preparation.

Balance sheet is useful to both investors and lenders. Investors analyze the balance sheet to form an opinion about the financial strength of the business. Lenders use the balance sheet to understand the capacity of the entity to repay the borrowed money.

The balance sheet can be prepared in a horizontal or vertical form. In the horizontal form, there are two sides of a balance sheet: asset side and liability side. The assets are grouped under the heads non-current assets and current assets. The liability side shows the non-current and current liabilities below the owners' funds or owners' equity (capital, reserves and undistributed profits). The liability side of the balance sheet reflects the sources of funds, whereas the asset side reflects the uses of these funds.

Balance sheet of a typical non-corporate entity in horizontal form is presented in Table 2.1.

Table 2.1 Balance sheet of X as on March 31, 2016 (Horizontal form)

Liabilities and Capital		Amount (Rs.)	Assets		Amount (Rs.)
Capital		600,000	**Non-current assets**		
Long-term debt		300,000	Land	200,000	
Current liabilities			Building	300,000	
Creditors	50,000		Equipment	100,000	
Accrued expenses	40,000		Furniture	80,000	
		90,000	Patents	60,000	
					740,000
			Non-current investments		60,000
			Current assets		
			Cash	50,000	
			Debtors	40,000	
			Inventories	80,000	
			Prepaid expenses	20,000	
					190,000
		990,000			990,000

In the vertical form of the balance sheet, capital and liabilities are listed at the top. The vertical form of the balance sheet given in Table 2.1 is presented in Table 2.2.

Table 2.2 Balance sheet of X as on March 31, 2016 (Vertical form)

Sources of Funds

Capital and Liabilities	Rs.
Capital	600,000
Long-term debt	300,000

(Continued)

Table 2.2 (Continued)

Capital and Liabilities		Rs.
Current liabilities		
Creditors	50,000	
Accrued expenses	40,000	
		90,000
		990,000

Application of funds

Assets		Rs.
Fixed assets		
Land	200,000	
Building	300,000	
Equipment	100,000	
Furniture	80,000	
Patents	60,000	
		740,000
Non-current investments		60,000
Current assets		
Cash	50,000	
Debtors	40,000	
Inventories	80,000	
Prepaid expenses	20,000	
		190,000
		990,000

The various elements of the balance sheet are explained in the next section.

2.3 Assets

2.3.1 Non-Current Assets

Non-current assets include fixed assets and other long-term assets such as investments. Fixed assets are meant for a long-term use and are not acquired for the purpose of resale. Fixed assets are of two types: *tangible* and *intangible*. Tangible fixed assets have a physical existence while intangible assets do not. Goodwill, patents, copyrights, trademarks, brands, etc. are examples of intangible assets. Land, buildings, plant and machinery and furniture are examples of tangible fixed assets. Fixed assets are shown at their net value after accounting for accumulated depreciation.

2.3.2 Investments

Investments refer to money invested outside the business in the form of shares, bonds or other instruments. Investments made for a period of more than one year are called non-current investments. Investments made for a period of less than one year are called current investments or marketable securities. While non-current investments are referred to as non-current assets, short-term investments are included in current assets.

2.3.3 Current Assets

Current assets are either in the form of cash or are meant to be converted into cash or other current assets during the accounting period or the *operating cycle* of the business, whichever is longer. The operating cycle is the time period between two points. The first point is the time of payment by an entity for purchase of raw materials. The second point is the time of realization of cash from customers for sale of finished goods that are converted from the raw material. Cash, marketable securities, debtors (accounts receivable) and inventories of raw material and finished goods are examples of current assets. Current assets reflect the ability of the business to pay its short-term liabilities.

2.3.4 Order of Presentation of Assets

Assets can be presented either in the *order of permanence* or in the *order of liquidity*. In the former case, the asset used over the longest time period is listed first and the others are listed in that order. For example, Goodwill is listed first followed by Land, Buildings, Plant and Machinery, Furniture, Patents, Vehicles, Investments, Stocks, Debtors and Cash balance. In the latter case, exactly the reverse order is followed as liquidity refers to the ease with which an asset can be converted into cash. It must, however, be noted that there is no legal requirement relating to the order in which assets and liabilities may be presented in the case of non-corporate entities. However, in the case of a company, the order in which assets are to be shown is prescribed by the Companies Act, 2013. Companies have to prepare their financial statements in accordance with Schedule III of the Companies Act, 2013.

2.4 Liabilities

The liabilities to outsiders can either be short term or long term.

2.4.1 Long-Term Liabilities

Long-term liabilities include borrowings from banks or financial institutions for a period of more than one year. These may be secured or unsecured. In the case of secured loans, some assets of the firm serve as collateral for the loan. Long-term liabilities also include bonds and debentures, which generally have a maturity of more than one year.

2.4.2 Short-Term Liabilities

Short-term or current liabilities are those that must be settled within one year, for example, creditors (accounts payable), outstanding expenses, etc.

2.4.3 Owners' Capital or Owners' Equity

For a non-corporate entity, owners' capital consists of the capital originally contributed by the owner and adjusted for subsequent profits/losses and drawings (withdrawals of money or goods by owners for their personal use). In the case of a corporate entity, owners' capital or shareholders' equity consists of share capital, retained earnings, securities premium and other reserves.

2.5 Basic Concepts Underlying Preparation of Balance Sheet

In preparing the balance sheet, certain basic principles or concepts are followed. Every entity is expected to follow these concepts so that their financial statements provide reliable information, are consistent and comparable with those of other entities. These are:

1. Business entity concept
2. Money measurement concept
3. Going concern concept
4. Cost concept
5. Dual aspect concept

2.5.1 Business Entity Concept

Business entity concept requires that the business enterprise and the owners be treated as two independent entities. The affairs of the business should not be mixed up with personal affairs of the owners. The implication of the entity concept is that personal transactions of the owner are not recorded in the books of the business. This concept helps determine the profit or loss made by the business. Personal assets of the owner are also not included in determining the business assets. The business is liable to the owner for the capital investment made by the latter. Any amount withdrawn by the owner for personal use is treated as a reduction of the capital and not as an expense of the business.

2.5.2 Money Measurement Concept

Only those transactions that can be measured in terms of money are to be recorded in the books of accounts. Many aspects of business such as quality of management, level of customer satisfaction, etc., which cannot be expressed in terms of money, are not recorded. The reason for using this concept is that a common unit of measurement is needed for preparing the financial statements of business that report the operating results and financial position of the business. Money serves as a common denominator in which the value of different items such as a piece of land, a piece of equipment and raw material can be expressed. A further assumption made by accountants is that the value of money does not change with the passage of time. This is a limitation of this concept as it is well known that the purchasing power of money declines during periods of rising prices and rises during periods of falling prices.

2.5.3 Going Concern Concept

Financial statements are prepared on the assumption that the enterprise would continue to exist for an indefinite period of time. The enterprise has no intention of liquidating the business in the near future. Following the going concern concept, those expenditures which are expected to provide future benefits are treated as assets rather than expenses. For example, the expenditure on purchasing a machine is treated as a fixed asset. The cost of the machine is spread over its useful life in the form of depreciation which is set-off against revenue in the income statement of different accounting periods over the life of the machine. At the end of each accounting period, the value of the machine is shown at its acquisition cost minus accumulated depreciation, and value of the machine represents the cost applicable to its remaining useful life. In the absence of the going concern assumption, the cost of the machine shown in the books will have a different value (e.g. current market price). Similarly, the amount of prepaid expenses and inventories are carried forward at the end of an accounting period to be charged against the revenue of future periods. The going concern concept provides a sound basis for the measurement of income and motivates investors by ensuring the continuity of returns from investments.

An implicit assumption is made that the accounts have been prepared on a going concern basis. If this is not the case, then the fact has to be explicitly disclosed, and the basis on which accounts have been prepared also needs to be disclosed.

2.5.4 Cost Concept

The value of an asset shown in the balance sheet is the price paid for its acquisition and not its current market value. For example, a machine acquired for Rs. 100,000 is shown in the books at a value of Rs. 100,000. This value is easily determinable, objective and free from bias. Recording the assets at its current cost presents a problem because it may change every day. It may also not be easily determinable because exactly the same asset may not be available. Similarly, the realizable value of an asset can be known only when it is sold. Following the cost concept, an asset will not be shown in the books of accounts if the entity has not paid anything for acquiring the asset. For example, an entity can show goodwill as an asset in its balance sheet only when it has purchased that goodwill for a price.

The problem with using this concept is that it loses its relevance when inflation affects the price of an asset. For example, a piece of land purchased for Rs. 1 million ten years earlier may cost Rs. 5 million now. If the cost of the land is shown in the books at Rs. 1 million, the accounts will not reflect the true position of the capital used in the business. Secondly, this concept results in loss of comparability. Two assets acquired at different points of time at different costs may give equal cash flows. The old asset would appear to be more efficient as it is shown at a lower cost. However, a different conclusion may be drawn if the current cost of that machine is taken into account. Thirdly, many assets such as human assets do not have any acquisition cost. Such assets, though important to an organization, do not get recognized under the cost concept. Finally, when the cost principle is followed, the balance sheet does not reveal the current worth of the business.

In some cases, an exception is made to the cost principle. Highly liquid assets that are expected to be shortly converted into cash (e.g. short-term investments, accounts receivables, etc.) are shown at their *net realizable value* if it is less than the cost. The net realizable value is the amount expected to be realized when the asset is converted into cash. Similarly, a business may make investments in other enterprises that it intends to sell in the near future. Such investments are shown at their current market value in the balance sheet.

2.5.5 Dual Aspect Concept

Every transaction or event has two aspects. It affects two items of the accounting equation simultaneously in one of the following ways:

1. It increases one asset and decreases another asset; or
2. It increases an asset and a liability/capital simultaneously; or
3. It decreases one asset and increases another asset; or
4. It decreases an asset and simultaneously decreases a liability/capital; or
5. It increases one liability and decreases another liability; or
6. It decreases a liability and increases another liability.

For example, if a machine is purchased for cash, it results in an increase of one asset (machine) and decrease of another asset (cash). If the machine is purchased on credit, it results in an increase of an asset (machine) and increase of a liability (creditor).

The dual aspect concept leads to the basic accounting equation:

$$\text{Equity (Capital)} + \text{Liabilities} = \text{Assets}$$

which always holds true.

The basic accounting equation implies that the assets of a business are always equal to the claims of owners and outsiders to these assets. The owners' claims are termed as capital and outsiders' claims are termed as liabilities.

Summary – Review of Learning Objectives

1. **Understand the nature and purpose of balance sheet.** The balance sheet reveals the financial position of an entity. It is prepared on a particular date, and is true only on that date because even a single transaction will affect some of the assets or liabilities and, therefore, the owners' capital shown in the balance sheet drawn on that date. It is prepared only after the preparation of the profit and loss account as the net income revealed by the profit and loss account is added to the owners' capital. The two sides of the balance sheet must have the same total because capital is always equal to the difference between assets and liabilities, and the amount of capital is independently arrived at by the capital account. The non-agreement of the two sides indicates the presence of some error in preparation.

   Balance sheet is useful to both investors and lenders. Investors analyze the balance sheet to form an opinion about the financial strength of the business. Lenders use the balance sheet to form an opinion about the capacity of the entity to repay the borrowed money.

2. **Understand the format and contents of a balance sheet.** It sets out the assets, liabilities and owners' capital of an entity as on a certain date. The balance sheet can be prepared in a horizontal or vertical form. In the horizontal form, there are two sides: asset side and liability side. The assets are grouped under the heads fixed assets, investments and current assets. The liability side shows the long-term liabilities and current liabilities below the owners' funds or owners' equities (capital, reserves and undistributed profits). The liability side of the balance sheet reflects the sources of funds, while the asset side reflects the use of these funds. In the vertical form of the balance sheet, liabilities and capital are listed at the top.
3. **Explain the accounting principles that underlie the preparation of a balance sheet.** Only those transactions that can be measured in terms of money are to be recorded in the books of accounts (money measurement principle). The affairs of business are distinguished from the personal affairs of the owners (business entity concept). Financial statements are prepared on the assumption that the enterprise would continue to exist for an indefinite period of time. The enterprise has no intention of liquidating the business in the near future (going concern concept). The value of an asset is to be determined on the basis of its acquisition cost, which is the most objective basis (cost concept). Every transaction or event has two aspects. The impact of a transaction is such that the accounting equation:

   Assets = Liabilities + Owners' Capital

   always holds. For example, if as a result of a transaction, an asset increases, it has to be matched by a decrease of another asset, or an increase in a liability or owners' capital (dual aspect concept).

Glossary

- **Cost concept** is the concept by which the value of an asset is determined on the basis of its acquisition cost, which is the most objective basis.
- **Current assets** are assets that are either in the form of cash or are meant to be converted into cash or other current assets during the accounting period or operating cycle, whichever is longer.
- **Current liabilities** are liabilities that must be settled within one year.
- **Dual aspect concept** states that every transaction or event has two aspects. The impact of a transaction is such that the accounting equation: Assets = Liabilities + Owners' Capital always holds.
- **Entity concept** is a concept under which the affairs of business are distinguished from the personal affairs of the owners.
- **Fixed assets** are meant to be used for a long period and are not acquired for the purpose of resale.
- **Going concern assumption** assumes that the enterprise would continue to exist for an indefinite period of time. The enterprise has no intention of liquidating the business in the near future.
- **Intangible fixed assets** do not have a physical existence.

- **Investments** represent the money invested outside the business in the form of shares, bonds or other instruments.
- **Long-term liabilities** are borrowings from banks or financial institutions for a period of more than one year.
- **Money measurement concept** implies that only those transactions that can be measured in terms of money are recorded in the books of accounts.
- **Order of liquidity** refers to the presentation of assets on the balance sheet in a manner that the asset that is to be used over the shortest time period is listed first and the others are listed in that order.
- **Order of permanence** refers to the presentation of assets on the balance sheet in a manner that the asset that is to be used over the longest time period is listed first and the others are listed in that order.
- **Tangible fixed assets** have a physical existence.

Solved Problem

1. Table 2.3 shows the trial balance extracted from the books of Akhilesh as on March 31, 2015.

Table 2.3 Trial balance of Akhilesh as on March 31, 2015

	Debit Amount (Rs.)	Credit Amount (Rs.)
Debtors/Creditors	78,695	25,000
Net profit earned during the year		40,595
Cash in hand	6,900	
Capital		100,000
Property, plant and equipment	80,000	
	165,595	165,595

Prepare the balance sheet as on March 31, 2015 in both horizontal and vertical forms.

Solution:

Horizontal Form (Table 2.4)

Table 2.4 Balance sheet of Akhilesh as on March 31, 2015

Liabilities		Amount (Rs.)	Assets	Amount (Rs.)
Capital	100,000		Property, plant and equipment	80,000
Add: Net profit	40,595		Debtors	78,695
		140,595	Cash in hand	6,900
Creditors		25,000		
		165,595		165,595

Vertical Form (Table 2.5)

Table 2.5 Balance sheet of Akhilesh as on March 31, 2015

Sources of Funds

Capital and Liabilities		Rs.
Capital	100,000	
Add: Net profit	40,595	
		140,595
Current liabilities		
Creditors		25,000
		165,595

Application of Funds

Assets		Rs.
Fixed assets		
Property, plant and equipment		80,000
Current assets		
Debtors	78,695	
Cash	6,900	85,595
		165,595

Multiple Choice Questions

1. Sources of funds for an enterprise are reflected on the ______.
   a. income side of profit and loss account
   b. expense side of profit and loss account
   c. asset side of the balance sheet
   d. liability side of the balance sheet

2. The dual aspect concept means that ______.
   a. when a transaction is recorded in the accounting system, there are at least two effects on the accounting equation
   b. both parties to a transaction have to record the transaction
   c. both the income statement and the balance sheet are affected by the transaction
   d. one account increases and the other account decreases as a result of the transaction

3. Which of the following is incorrect about a company's balance sheet?
   a. It displays the sources and uses of cash.
   b. It displays the sources and uses of funds.
   c. It is an expansion of the basic accounting equation: Assets = Liabilities + Owners' Equity.
   d. It is also referred to as a statement of the financial position.

4. The going concern concept implies that ______.
   a. the business will continue to be profitable
   b. the business will continue to exist in the foreseeable future
   c. the owners are concerned about the success of the business
   d. all of the above

5. The balance sheet ______.
   a. summarizes the changes in retained earnings for a specific period of time
   b. reports the changes in assets, liabilities and owners' equity over a period of time
   c. reports the assets, liabilities and owners' equity at a specific date
   d. presents the revenues and expenses for a specific period of time
6. Given the following figures, what is the amount of owners' capital?

	Rs.		Rs.
Creditors	90,000	Machinery	100,000
Debtors	15,000	Bank loan	150,000
Buildings	200,000	Cash	45,000

   a. Rs. 400,000
   b. Rs. 360,000
   c. Rs. 500,000
   d. Rs. 120,000
7. Given the owners' capital of Rs. 150,000 and the following figures, what is the amount of cash?

	Rs.		Rs.
Creditors	90,000	Machinery	100,000
Debtors	15,000	Bank loan	150,000
Buildings	200,000	Cash	?

   a. Rs. 50,000
   b. Rs. 60,000
   c. Rs. 70,000
   d. Rs. 75,000

Review Questions

1. In what order are assets listed on a balance sheet of a sole proprietor?
2. At the instance of the management, you want to show the good quality of management in financial statements. As an accountant, which accounting concept will you be violating?
3. A company wants to:
   a. Treat goods drawn from the business by the owner as his/her personal expense.
   b. Ignore the increase in the price of some inventory items.

   State the accounting concept the company would need to follow in the above cases.
4. Why is a business treated as a separate entity for accounting purposes?
5. Name the two main forms in which a balance sheet can be prepared.
6. Why should the two sides of a balance sheet always match?
7. How are fixed assets different from current assets?
8. What are intangible fixed assets? Give some examples.
9. How is the going concern assumption applied in the presentation of financial statements?
10. State the problems that arise in the application of the cost concept to the preparation of balance sheet.
11. Why is it not possible for an asset to increase without affecting any other asset, liability or owners' capital?
12. Why is it necessary to prepare the profit and loss account before preparing the balance sheet?
13. What is the basic purpose of preparing a balance sheet?
14. Classify the following items as (i) non-current asset, (ii) current asset, (iii) long-term liability, (iv) current liability:
   (a) Goodwill
   (b) Land
   (c) Inventories
   (d) Accounts payable
   (e) Cash
   (f) Trademarks
   (g) Stock of raw material
   (h) Investment in 10-year bonds

Practice Problems

1. From the data drawn from the books of X (Table 2.6), prepare a balance sheet as on March 31, 2016 in both horizontal and vertical forms.

Table 2.6 X: Ledger balances as on March 31, 2016

Capital	2,400,000	Long-term debt	1,200,000
Debtors	160,000	Outstanding expenses	160,000
Prepaid expenses	80,000	Building	1,200,000
Equipment	400,000	Furniture	320,000
Patents	240,000	Investments	240,000
Cash	200,000	Creditors	200,000
Inventories	320,000	Land	800,000

2. From the balances extracted from the books of Naveen Brothers (Table 2.7), prepare the balance sheet as on March 31, 2016.

Table 2.7 Naveen Brothers: Ledger balances as on March 31, 2016

	Rs.		Rs.
Inventories	148,000	Plant and machinery	249,200
Furniture	26,800	Cash in hand	37,680
Capital	394,240	Accounts receivable	185,400
Accounts payable	92,840	Bank loan	160,000

Answers to Multiple Choice Questions

1. (d)
2. (a)
3. (a)
4. (b)
5. (c)
6. (d)
7. (d)

Statement of Profit and Loss

3

LEARNING OBJECTIVES

After reading this chapter, you will be able to:

- Understand the nature and purpose of statement of profit and loss.
- Understand the form and contents of statement of profit and loss.
- Explain the accounting principles that underlie the preparation of statement of profit and loss.

3.1 Introduction

The second financial statement, *the statement of profit and loss*, which measures the income of an entity during an accounting period will be discussed in this chapter. The basic concepts that underlie the preparation of this statement will also be explained.

3.2 Statement of Profit and Loss

Statement of profit and loss or the income statement is prepared to show the amount of profit earned or loss suffered by an entity during a period. It shows the various items of income and expenditure, grouped under different heads, relating to an accounting period. It is generally prepared in different sections. For a trading firm, the first section measures the *gross profit*, which is simply the difference between sales revenue and the cost of goods sold. In the next section, the *operating profit* is determined by deducting operating expenses from the gross profit. *Operating expenses* relate to the normal operating activities of the business such as administrative, selling and general expenses. Finally, the *net profit* is determined by adjusting *non-operating expenses* (such as interest expense, loss on sale of fixed assets) and *non-operating income* (such as interest income, profit on sale of fixed assets) from the operating profit.

In a manufacturing concern, the cost of goods sold also includes all expenses incurred in the factory for producing the goods – wages, power and fuel and rent of factory premises. A typical multi-step statement of profit and loss is presented in Exhibit 3.1.

Exhibit 3.1

Multi-Step Statement of Profit and Loss of A for the Year Ended March 31, 2016

Particulars	Amount (Rs.)
Net sales	5,000,000
Less: Cost of goods sold	3,800,000
Gross profit	1,200,000
Less: Selling, general and administrative expenses	400,000
Operating profit	800,000
Interest expense	(50,000)
Interest income	30,000
Net profit	780,000

Exhibit 3.2 provides an alternative form of the multi-step statement of profit and loss. The statement of profit and loss is prepared in two parts, the first part called the *trading account* and the second part called the *profit and loss account.* The trading account lists the components of cost of goods sold on two sides of the account. The cost of goods sold (Rs. 3,800,000 in Exhibit 3.1) is shown in the trading account in Exhibit 3.2.

Exhibit 3.2

Multi-Step Statement of Profit and Loss in Two Parts: Trading and Profit and Loss Account of A for the Year Ended March 31, 2016

		(Rs.)			(Rs.)
To Opening stock		350,000	By Sales	5,200,000	
Purchases	3,300,000		Less: Returns	200,000	5,000,000
Less: Returns	150,000				
		3,150,000	Closing stock		150,000
Wages		300,000			
Carriage on purchases		150,000			
Gross profit c/d		1,200,000			
		5,150,000			5,150,000

	(Rs.)		(Rs.)
To Depreciation	150,000	By Gross profit b/d	1,200,000
Insurance	40,000	Interest	30,000
Printing expenses	25,000		
Carriage on sales	27,000		
Salaries	1,30,000		
Interest	50,000		
Bad debts	28,000		
Net profit	780,000		
	1,230,000		1,230,000

From the trading account, the cost of goods sold, Rs. 3,800,000, can be worked out as follows:

Beginning inventory	350,000	
Add: Purchases (net of returns)	3,150,000	
Carriage on purchases	150,000	
Wages	300,000	
Cost of goods available for sale		3,950,000
Less: Ending inventory		150,000
Cost of goods sold		3,800,000

The selling, general and administrative expenses of Rs. 400,000 in Exhibit 3.1 are the sum of the following expenses:

	(Rs.)
Depreciation	150,000
Insurance	40,000
Printing expenses	25,000
Carriage on sales	27,000
Salaries	130,000
Bad debts	28,000
	400,000

When the form of the statement of profit and loss, as given in Exhibit 3.1, is used, the details of the cost of goods sold and of selling, general and administrative expenses are provided in separate schedules.

The operating profit is not specifically calculated as in Exhibit 3.2. However, the same can be worked out by using the figures of net profit, non-operating expenses and non-operating incomes as shown below:

	(Rs.)
Net profit	780,000
Add: Interest expense (Non-operating expense)	50,000
	830,000
Less: Interest income (Non-operating income)	30,000
Operating profit	800,000

Some firms, however, prepare a single-step statement of profit and loss, where all expenses are deducted from revenue to determine the net income. A single-step statement of profit and loss is presented in Exhibit 3.3. Here again, the details of the cost of goods sold and of selling, general and administrative expenses are provided in separate schedules.

Exhibit 3.3

Multi-Step Statement of Profit and Loss of A for the Year Ended March 31, 2016

Particulars	Amount (Rs.)
Revenues	
Net sales	5,000,000
Other income	30,000
	5,030,000
Expenses	
Cost of goods sold	3,800,000
Selling, general and administrative expenses	400,000
Interest expense	50,000
	4,250,000
Net profit	780,000
	5,030,000

The division of the statement of profit and loss under different sections provides more information to the users leading to better decision making. Comparison of current gross profit rate with past rates and that of other firms in the industry reveals the effectiveness of a firm's purchasing and pricing policies. Similarly, non-operating income may form a significant portion of the total income. External users of financial statements focus more on the operating income as they consider this income to be sustainable in the future and non-operating income to be non-recurring.

3.3 Basic Concepts

As in the case of balance sheet, certain basic principles or concepts are followed in the preparation of statement of profit and loss also to secure reliability, consistency and comparability with other entities. The basic concepts underlying the preparation of statement of profit and loss include: (i) accounting period, (ii) conservatism, (iii) realization, (iv) matching, (v) consistency, (vi) accrual and (vii) materiality.

3.3.1 Accounting Period Concept

A business is expected to have a long life, and its exact profit or loss can be determined only when the business is wound up. Measuring the performance over a long period of time loses value because no corrective steps can be taken to improve the performance if it is below the owner's expectations. To track the business performance and to measure its financial position from time to time, its life is divided into relatively small intervals of time, usually a year. The accounting period is called an *accounting year* or a *financial year*.

The adoption of accounting year for reporting purposes is also influenced by certain legal requirements. Under the law relating to companies, a company is required to submit annual reports to its shareholders. The law relating to taxation of income requires determination of annual taxable income. The accounting period usually adopted by a business is either a calendar year (January–December) or a financial year (April–March). Listed companies are also required to prepare quarterly income statements.

The adoption of the accounting period concept requires identification of transaction that relate to a specific accounting period. For some transactions, the identification is easy and straightforward. For many transactions, such as acquisition of a fixed asset that affect more than one accounting year, allocations have to be made to determine the consumption of the asset in a particular accounting period.

3.3.2 Conservatism Concept

In preparing financial statements of a business, an accountant should be conservative. He/she should apply that accounting treatment to a transaction that results in the lowest (most conservative) estimate of the income. He/she should not anticipate incomes and should provide for all possible losses. An income should be recognized only when it has been realized. Further, when there are many alternative values of an asset, an accountant should choose the method that leads to a lesser value. Following the conservatism concept, the rule 'cost or market value, whichever is lower' is followed in valuing inventories. Following this rule, the value of inventory is written down to its market value if it declines below its cost. However, the value of inventory is not revised upward if its market value goes above its cost. There are many other instances where conservatism is applied, for example, making provision for doubtful debts, marking investments to market to reflect their current market value, etc. The main objective behind applying the conservatism concept is that the income should never be overstated. Hence, there should be at least three qualitative characteristics of financial statements:

1. **Prudence:** Applying judgment about the possible future losses that are to be guarded and gains that are uncertain.
2. **Neutrality:** Unbiased outlook is required for identifying and recording such losses and for excluding uncertain gains.
3. **Faithful representation of alternative values.**

The above qualitative characteristics are absent when accountants deliberately attempt to understate income by matching future expenses with current income, making excessive provisions for anticipated losses, etc. This is done when the objective is to understate the current income and to overstate the future income. Such a practice presents a poor financial position of a business and undermines the confidence of prospective investors in that business.

3.3.3 Realization Concept

According to the realization concept, revenue should be recognized when it is realized. Revenue from sales or service transactions is considered to be realized only when certain requirements relating to performance (such as transfer of property or transfer of risks and rewards of ownership) are satisfied, and at the time of performance there is no significant uncertainty regarding the ultimate collection of revenue.

Revenue may be recognized even when the payment for a transaction is yet to be received. As a result, even credit sales are recognized by a business as revenue. For example, a business receives an order from a customer for the supply of a custom-made machine in the year 2013. The business supplies the machine to the customer in 2014 and the customer makes the payment in 2015. In this case, the condition for recognition of revenue is satisfied in the year 2014, and hence revenue should be recognized in 2014.

Another interpretation of realization concept: Any change in the value of goods is to be recorded only when the business realizes it, that is, when the goods are sold.

3.3.4 Matching Concept

To determine the income of an accounting period, revenues earned during the accounting period are matched with the expenses incurred to earn the revenues. The first step in the matching of revenues and expenses is to determine the revenue earned during an accounting period. After determining the revenue for an accounting period, all expenses incurred to earn that revenue are deducted from the revenue to determine the income of that accounting period. If the recognition of revenue is deferred on the basis that it is not yet earned, all expenses pertaining to such revenue must also be deferred. The question of matching arises because of accrual and accounting period concepts.

Example

X buys 500 chairs @ Rs. 1,000 each during the period 1.4.2014 to 31.3.2015. During the accounting period, he has paid Rs. 450,000 to the supplier of chairs. He sells 400 of these chairs @ Rs.1,200 each. His customers are yet to pay him Rs. 20,000 as on March 31, 2015. He hires an employee @ Rs. 1,000 per month. The salary of the employee for the month of March 2015 is yet to be paid.

Following the matching concept, X will recognize the revenue for the 400 chairs sold and treat the cost of 400 chairs as an expense. The balance 100 chairs will be shown as stock in hand. Accordingly, the revenue for the period will be Rs. 480,000, from which expenses of Rs. 400,000 on account of purchase cost of chairs and Rs. 12,000 on account of salary (for 12 months following the accrual concept) will be deducted. X will show a profit of Rs. 68,000 for the year.

The actual amount received from the customers and the actual amount paid to the supplier are not relevant for measuring profit or loss. What is relevant is the revenue earned and expenses incurred during the accounting period, irrespective of the amount received or paid.

It is easy to match those expenses to revenue that are directly associated with the earning of revenue. An example is the cost of goods sold. For some expenses, subjective judgement is required to apply the matching concept. An example is the cost of fixed assets, which provide benefits over a number of accounting periods. There are other expenses such as administrative expenses that cannot be associated with particular goods or services sold. Such expenses, known as 'period costs', are treated as expenses of the accounting period in which these are incurred. Expenses related to products or services are known as 'product costs'.

3.3.5 Consistency

Consistency implies that same accounting policies and procedures are followed by an enterprise in preparing its accounts from one accounting period to another. Accounting standards provide for equally acceptable accounting alternatives in respect of certain matters. For example, an enterprise can value its inventories using either the first-in-first-out (FIFO) method or the last-in-first-out (LIFO) method. Under the FIFO method, the cost of older inventories is used to determine the profit or loss, while the ending inventories represent the most recently purchased items. Under the LIFO method, the cost of most recently purchased items is used to determine the profit or loss and the ending inventories represent items purchased earlier in time. Change in the method from one accounting period to another can have a significant impact on the amount of expense recognized and the value of inventory in hand at the end of the accounting period.

Similarly, several alternative methods, such as the straight-line method, written-down-value method, sum-of-the-years-digits method, etc. are available to provide for depreciation on fixed assets. Again, change in the method of providing depreciation can have a significant impact on the amount of depreciation expense recognized and the value of fixed assets in hand at the end of the accounting period.

The consistency principle helps to achieve comparability of financial statements of an enterprise through time. It is not that the accounting policies, once adopted, cannot be changed. Accounting standards allow change in accounting policies under certain circumstances. Whenever a change is made, the accounting standards require that the enterprise should make a full disclosure of the change and also of the rupee effect of the change on the reported income and financial position of the enterprise.

3.3.6 Accrual Concept

Under the accrual concept, revenues are recognized when they are earned and expenses are recognized when the related goods or services are used. The timing of receipt of revenues and payment of expenses is immaterial. The accrual concept facilitates measurement of income for a particular accounting period. Applying appropriate tests, the revenue pertaining to an accounting period is recognized first. Then the expenses incurred to earn that revenue are recognized. Income for the accounting period is then determined as the difference between the revenue recognized and the matched expenses.

Example

X buys goods worth Rs. 500,000 paying Rs. 350,000 in cash and agreeing to pay Rs. 150,000 later. He sells these goods for Rs. 650,000. He receives Rs. 400,000 from his customers immediately and the rest will be paid by them later. X's revenue would be Rs. 650,000, his expense is Rs. 500,000 and his profit based on the accrual concept will be Rs. 150,000. Cash receipt of Rs. 500,000 and cash payment of Rs. 350,000 do not enter the calculation of profit.

The alternative to accrual accounting is the *cash basis accounting*. Revenue may not be realized in cash. Cash may be received simultaneously or before the revenue is created or after the revenue is created. The same is the case with expenses. Pure cash basis accounting is not appropriate for measuring the profitability of economic activities carried out during the accounting period.

X buys	Rs. 400,000
X's revenue =	Rs. 650,000
X's expense =	Rs. 500,000
X's profit based on the accural concept =	Rs. 150,000

3.3.7 Materiality

The term *materiality* refers to the relative importance of an item or event. An item or event is considered material if its knowledge is likely to affect the decisions of the users of financial statements. Accountants should ensure that all material items are properly reported in the financial statements. In determining the materiality of an item, they need to compare the value of information with the cost of providing such information. The value must exceed the cost. For immaterial items, accountants can use estimates instead of keeping detailed records and can also disregard certain accounting principles. Professional judgment is required to assess the materiality of an item.

For example, the cost of small value items such as stationery, lighting material may not be treated as an asset and may be written off as expenses. Ignoring the matching principle, utility bills may be charged as expenses when bills are received rather than when services are rendered.

Summary – Review of Learning Objectives

1. **Understand the nature and purpose of statement of profit and loss:** Statement of profit and loss or the income statement is prepared to show the amount of profit earned or loss suffered during a period. It shows the various items of income and expenditure, grouped under different heads, relating to an accounting period.
2. **Understand the form and contents of statement of profit and loss:** Statement of profit and loss is generally prepared in different sections. For a trading firm, the first section measures the gross profit, which is simply the difference between sales revenue and the cost of goods sold. In the next section, the operating profit is determined by deducting operating expenses from the gross profit. Operating expenses relate to the normal operating activities of the business such as administrative, selling and general expenses. Finally, the net profit is determined by adjusting non-operating expenses (such as interest expense, loss on sale of fixed assets) and non-operating income (such as interest income, profit on sale of fixed assets) from the operating profit.

   In a manufacturing concern, the cost of goods sold also includes all expenses incurred in the factory for producing goods such as wages, power and fuel and rent of factory premises.
3. **Explain the accounting principles that underlie the preparation of statement of profit and loss:** To track the business performance and to measure its financial position from time to time, its life is divided into relatively small intervals of time, usually a year. The accounting period is called an accounting year or a financial year (accounting period concept).

   In preparing financial statements of a business, an accountant should be conservative. He/she should not anticipate incomes and should provide for all possible losses (conservatism concept).

   Revenue should be recognized when it is realized (realization concept).

   To determine the income of an accounting period, revenues earned during the accounting period are matched with the expenses incurred to earn these revenues (matching concept).

   The same accounting policies and procedures are followed by an enterprise in preparing its accounts from one accounting period to another (consistency).

   Revenues are recognized when these are earned and expenses are recognized when these are incurred. The timing of receipt of revenues and payment of expenses is immaterial (accrual concept).

   Accountants should ensure that all material items are properly reported in financial statements. An item or event is considered material if its knowledge is likely to affect the decisions of the users of financial statements.

Glossary

- **Accounting period** is a small interval of time, usually a year out of the life of business, determined to track the business performance and to measure its financial position.
- **Accrual basis of accounting** implies that revenues are recognized when these are earned and expenses are recognized when these are incurred. The timing of receipt of revenues and payment of expenses is immaterial.
- **Consistency** means that the same accounting policies and procedures are followed by an enterprise in preparing its accounts from one accounting period to another.

- **Conservatism** is the non-anticipation of incomes and making provision for all possible losses.
- **Cost of goods sold** is the cost of that part of goods available for sale (beginning inventory + purchases), which is sold during the accounting period. It is calculated as the cost of goods available for sale minus the cost of ending inventories.
- **Gross profit** is simply the difference between sales revenue and the cost of goods sold.
- **Matching** refers to revenues earned during an accounting period matched with the expenses incurred to earn these revenues to determine the income of an accounting period.
- **Materiality** implies that accountants should ensure that all material items are properly reported in financial statements. An item or event is considered material if its knowledge is likely to affect the decisions of the users of financial statements.
- **Net profit** is determined by adjusting non-operating expenses (such as interest expense, loss on sale of fixed assets) and non-operating income (such as interest income, profit on sale of fixed assets) from the operating profit.
- **Operating expenses** relate to the normal operating activities of the business such as administrative, selling and general expenses.
- **Operating profit** is determined by deducting operating expenses from the gross profit.
- **Realization** implies that revenue should be recognized only when it is realized.

Solved Problem

1. Table 3.1 gives the trial balance extracted from the books of Akhilesh as on March 31, 2015.

Table 3.1 Trial balance of Akhilesh as on March 31, 2015

	Debit Amount (Rs.)	Credit Amount (Rs.)
Purchases and sales	60,000	127,000
Returns	1,000	750
Rent, rates and taxes	10,000	
Freight on sales	1,200	
Manufacturing wages	10,000	
Discount	425	800
Provision for doubtful debts		525
Salaries	7,550	
Debtors/Creditors	45,000	25,000
Printing and advertising	2,000	
Opening stock	30,000	
Cash in hand	6,900	
Property, plant and equipment	80,000	
Capital		100,000
	254,075	254,075

Stock at the end is Rs. 34,220. Prepare trading and profit and loss account for the year ended March 31, 2015.

Solution: Table 3.2 shows the trading and profit and loss account of Akhilesh for the year ended March 31, 2015.

Table 3.2 Trading and profit and loss account of Akhilesh for the year ended March 31, 2015

Particulars		Amount (Rs.)	Particulars		Amount (Rs.)
To Opening stock		30,000	By sales	127,000	
Purchases	60,000		Less: Returns	1,000	
Less: Returns	750				126,000
		59,250	Closing stock		34,220
Manufacturing wages		10,000			
Gross profit c/d		60,970			
		160,220			160,220
To Salaries		7,550	By gross profit b/d		60,970
Rent, rates and taxes		10,000	Discount		800
Printing and advertising		2,000			
Freight on sales		1,200			
Discount		425			
Net profit transferred to capital account		40,595			
		61,770			61,770

Multiple Choice Questions

1. What is the underlying concept that supports the immediate recognition of an estimated loss?
   a. Substance over form
   b. Consistency
   c. Matching
   d. Conservatism

2. An enterprises follows the written-down-value method of depreciating machinery year after year due to ______.
   a. comparability
   b. convenience
   c. consistency
   d. all of the above

3. A purchased goods for Rs. 1,500,000 and sold 4/5th of the goods for Rs. 1,800,000 and met expenses amounting to Rs. 250,000 during the year 2015. He counted the net profit as Rs. 350,000. Which of the accounting concepts was followed by him?
   a. Entity
   b. Periodicity
   c. Matching
   d. Conservatism

4. A businessman purchased goods for Rs. 2,500,000 and sold 80% of such goods during the accounting year ended March 31, 2016.

The market value of the remaining goods was Rs. 400,000. He valued the closing stock at Rs. 500,000. He violated the concept of ______.

a. money measurement
b. conservatism
c. cost
d. periodicity

5. The determination of expenses for an accounting period is based on the principle of ______.

a. objectivity
b. materiality
c. matching
d. periodicity

6. The income statement shows ______.

a. cash balance at the end of the period
b. contributions by the owner during the period
c. revenues earned during the period
d. profit earned or loss incurred during the period

7. Which of the following statements is incorrect?

a. Net income is reported by an entity for a period of time
b. Net income increases the owner's capital
c. Net income is equal to revenue minus expenses
d. Net income is equal to revenue minus the sum of expenses and drawings

Review Questions

1. What is the purpose of preparing the statement of profit and loss?
2. Describe the various ways in which the statement of profit and loss can be presented.
3. Why is an accounting period chosen to prepare the statement of profit and loss?
4. Explain the conservative approach for preparing financial statements.
5. When should an entity recognize revenue?
6. What does the term 'matching' mean in the context of preparation of statement of profit and loss?
7. Explain the term 'consistency' in the preparation of financial statements.
8. When are incomes and expenses recognized following the accrual assumption?
9. As an accountant, which accounting concept will you be violating in the following circumstances?
   a. The management wants to show higher revenues by treating orders received from customers as sales although no goods have been supplied to them.
   b. To show higher profitability in the current year, the management wants you to adopt a depreciation method that would lead to a lower depreciation charge.
10. A company wants to:
   a. Record expected losses arising out of default by some debtors.
   b. Keep on following the straight-line method of charging depreciation year after year.
   c. Treat sales made as revenue only when the goods have been supplied to customers.
   d. Calculate profit by deducting expenses incurred, which is not paid during the accounting year.

State the accounting concept the company would need to follow in each of the above cases.

Practice Problems

1. From the following information, calculate the value of cost of goods sold.

Beginning inventory	1,400,000
Purchases	12,600,000
Ending inventory	600,000

2. From the following information, calculate the amount of gross profit.

Beginning inventory	1,400,000
Purchases	13,200,000
Ending inventory	600,000
Purchases returns	600,000
Carriage on purchases	600,000
Wages	1,200,000
Sales	20,800,000
Sales returns	800,000

3. From the balances extracted from the books of Naveen Brothers, prepare the trading and profit and loss account for the year ended March 31, 2016.

	(Rs.)		(Rs.)
Opening stock	50,000	Purchase returns	55,200
Sales	472,000	Salaries	30,000
Depreciation	26,680	Discount allowed	13,120
Commission received	8,440	Wages	63,560
Insurance	15,200	Sales returns	66,360
Carriage on purchases	19,240	Purchases	347,160
Printing expenses	12,000	Bad debts	7,200
Carriage on sales	8,000		

Closing stock as on March 31, 2016 is Rs. 148,000.

Answers to Multiple Choice Questions

1. (d)
2. (c)
3. (c)
4. (b)
5. (c)
6. (d)
7. (d)

Accounting Records and Systems

4

LEARNING OBJECTIVES

After reading this chapter, you will be able to:

- Understand the accounting process that leads to the preparation of financial statements.
- Analyze the effect of accounting transactions on the basic accounting equation.
- Understand the use of an account in the process of building accounting records.
- Understand the rules of debit and credit in recording business transactions in relevant accounts.
- Understand how a journal is maintained and the concept of subsidiary books.
- Understand the posting of entries in the ledger.
- Understand how trial balance is extracted and its purpose.

4.1 Introduction

An enterprise must have a proper accounting system for recording the effect of economic events such as purchase of raw materials, sale of goods, acquisition and disposal of assets, etc. The final step in the accounting process is the preparation of financial statements. Financial statements, however, are not prepared after every transaction. A continuous sequence of steps (called *accounting cycle*) is followed to record, classify and summarize business transactions in accounting records. The data in these accounting records is then used to prepare financial statements. Accounting records are also used for several other purposes.

4.2 Steps in the Accounting Cycle

The accounting cycle consists of the following steps:

1. Analysis of transactions in terms of their effect on assets, liabilities and owners' capital.
2. Accounts are prepared for each item of assets, liabilities, revenues and expenses using the rules of debit and credit. These accounts are maintained in a record called *ledger*. Entries can be made directly into the ledger or another intermediate record called *journal*. In some cases, the journal is subdivided into a number of journals called *subsidiary books*.

3. Closing balances of all accounts are transferred to a statement called *trial balance*.
4. At the end of the accounting period, some *adjustment entries* are made and an adjusted trial balance is prepared.
5. Financial statements are prepared using the information in the adjusted trial balance.
6. Certain closing entries are passed and an after-closing trial balance is prepared.

This chapter covers the accounting cycle up to the stage of preparation of trial balance. The remaining steps are covered in the next chapter.

4.3 Analysis of Accounting Transactions

An accounting transaction occurs when an economic event causes a change in the assets, liabilities or owners' capital. Examples of economic events are purchase of an item of equipment, payment of salaries to employees. Appointment of a manager is not an economic event as no change occurs in the assets, liabilities or owners' capital as a result of this event.

All accounting transactions are analyzed in terms of their effect on assets, liabilities and owners' capital. Since the basic accounting equation provides a relationship between assets, liabilities and owners' capital, the accounting transactions can be analyzed using the basic accounting equation.

Since the accounting equation must balance, each transaction has a dual effect on the accounting equation. An increase in an asset must be matched by a decrease in another asset, or an increase in a liability or an increase in owners' capital. On purchase of furniture, either the cash balance will be reduced or a liability to the supplier will increase. Alternatively, only a part of the cost of furniture may be paid in cash and the balance reflected as an increase in liabilities.

Illustration 4.1

Consider the following transactions pertaining to A's business:

1. Started business with cash Rs. 300,000.
2. Purchased goods for cash Rs. 120,000.
3. Purchased goods on credit Rs. 60,000.
4. Purchased furniture for cash Rs. 20,000.
5. Deposited Rs. 50,000 in the bank account.
6. Sold goods costing Rs. 15,000 for Rs. 18,000, on credit.
7. Sold goods costing Rs. 30,000 for Rs. 36,000, in cash.
8. Paid rent Rs. 10,000 and salaries Rs. 20,000.
9. Withdrew Rs. 15,000 from the bank account to pay for private expenses.
10. Received cash against goods sold on credit Rs. 18,000.

Each transaction can be analyzed in the following manner:

- **Transaction 1:** The business received cash of Rs. 300,000; it is an asset to the business. The business owes this amount to A, the proprietor, and therefore, it also represents the capital of the business. Capital of Rs. 300,000 is equal to assets of Rs. 300,000.

- **Transaction 2:** Purchase of goods for cash increases goods (an asset) and reduces cash (another asset). The accounting equation remains the same as after transaction 1.
- **Transaction 3:** Purchase of goods on credit increases goods (an asset) and simultaneously increases creditors (a liability). The sum of liabilities and capital is now Rs. 360,000 matched by assets of Rs. 360,000.
- **Transaction 4:** Purchase of furniture for cash increases an asset (furniture) and reduces another asset (cash). The accounting equation remains the same as after transaction 3.
- **Transaction 5:** Deposit of cash in the bank account increases one asset (balance in the bank account) and reduces another asset (cash). The accounting equation remains the same as after transaction 4.
- **Transaction 6:** Sale of goods costing Rs. 15,000 for Rs. 18,000 on credit decreases an asset (goods) by Rs. 15,000 and increases another asset (debtors) by Rs. 18,000. The difference of Rs. 3,000 between the two amounts is profit. The profit belongs to the proprietor and increases his/her business capital. After this transaction, the liabilities are Rs. 60,000, capital is Rs. 3,03,000 and assets are Rs. 363,000.
- **Transaction 7:** Sale of goods costing Rs. 30,000 for Rs. 36,000 on cash basis decreases an asset (goods) by Rs. 30,000, increases another asset (cash) by Rs. 36,000 and also increases the capital by the amount of profit (Rs. 6,000). After this transaction, the liabilities are Rs. 60,000, capital is Rs. 309,000 and assets are Rs. 369,000.
- **Transaction 8:** Payment of rent Rs. 10,000 and salaries Rs. 20,000 decreases an asset (cash) by Rs. 30,000 and also decreases capital by Rs. 30,000. After this transaction, the liabilities are Rs. 60,000, capital is Rs. 279,000 and assets are Rs. 339,000.
- **Transaction 9:** Withdrawal of Rs. 15,000 from the bank account for meeting private expenses decreases one asset (bank balance) and also reduces capital by Rs. 15,000. After this transaction, the liabilities are Rs. 60,000, capital is Rs. 264,000 and assets are Rs. 324,000.
- **Transaction 10:** Receipt of cash against goods sold on credit increases one asset (cash) and reduces another asset (debtors) by the same amount. The accounting equation remains the same as after transaction 9.

The accounting equation after different transactions can be presented as in Table 4.1.

Table 4.1 Accounting equation for different transactions

No.	Transaction	Assets (Rs.)	=	Liabilities (Rs.)	+	Capital (Rs.)
1.	Started business with cash Rs. 300,000	300,000				300,000
2.	Purchased goods for cash Rs. 120,000	300,000				300,000
3.	Purchased goods on credit Rs. 60,000	360,000		60,000		300,000
4.	Purchased furniture for cash Rs. 20,000	360,000		60,000		300,000
5.	Deposited Rs. 50,000 in the bank account	360,000		60,000		300,000
6.	Sold goods costing Rs. 15,000 for Rs. 18,000, on credit	363,000		60,000		303,000

(Continued)

Table 4.1 (Continued)

No.	Transaction	Assets (Rs.)	=	Liabilities (Rs.)	+	Capital (Rs.)
7.	Sold goods costing Rs. 30,000 for Rs.36,000, in cash	369,000		60,000		309,000
8.	Paid rent Rs. 10,000 and salaries Rs. 20,000	339,000		60,000		279,000
9.	Withdrew Rs. 15,000 from the bank account to pay for private expenses	324,000		60,000		264,000
10.	Received cash against goods sold on credit Rs. 18,000	324,000		60,000		264,000

The simple accounting equation in Illustration 4.1 can be expanded to show the effect of business transactions on specific assets and liabilities.

Illustration 4.2

Consider the following transactions pertaining to A's business:

1. Started business with cash Rs. 400,000.
2. Purchased equipment for cash Rs. 150,000.
3. Purchased goods on credit Rs. 100,000.
4. Took a loan of Rs. 50,000 from bank.
5. Deposited Rs. 50,000 in the bank account.
6. Sold goods costing Rs. 50,000 for Rs. 65,000, on credit.
7. Sold goods costing Rs. 50,000 for Rs. 70,000, in cash.
8. Paid rent Rs. 8,000 and salaries Rs. 18,000.
9. Withdrew Rs. 25,000 from the bank account to pay for private expenses.
10. Received cash against goods sold on credit Rs. 65,000.

The detailed accounting equation after each transaction is presented in Table 4.2.

Table 4.2 Accounting equations after each transaction

	Assets					Liabilities			
Transaction	Debtors	Cash	Inventories	Equipment	=	Creditors	Bank Loan	+	Capital
1.		400,000							400,000
2.		250,000		150,000					400,000
3.		250,000	100,000	150,000		100,000			400,000
4.		300,000	100,000	150,000		100,000	50,000		400,000

(Continued)

Table 4.2 (Continued)

	Assets					Liabilities		
Transaction	Debtors	Cash	Inventories	Equipment	=	Creditors	Bank Loan	+ Capital
5.		300,000	100,000	150,000		100,000	50,000	400,000
6.	65,000	300,000	50,000	150,000		100,000	50,000	415,000
7.	65,000	370,000	0	150,000		100,000	50,000	435,000
8.	65,000	344,000	0	150,000		100,000	50,000	409,000
9.	65,000	319,000	0	150,000		100,000	50,000	384,000
10.	0	384,000	0	150,000		100,000	50,000	384,000

4.4 Accounting Records

4.4.1 Account

The accounting system keeps a separate record for each item that appears in the financial statement. This record is called an account. The account for any item records increases and decreases in that item as a result of business transactions and determines the balance of that item at any time after one or more transactions affecting that item have taken place.

For example, a person starts a business with say Rs. 50,000. In this case, his/her capital is Rs. 50,000 and assets in the form of cash are also Rs. 50,000. Transactions entered into by the firm will either increase the cash balance (e.g., transactions such as sales for cash and collections from customers, etc.) or decrease the cash balance (e.g., payment for goods purchased, salaries, rent, etc.). The cash balance can be changed with every transaction by erasing the old amount and entering the new amount for each transaction. This is quite cumbersome and time consuming. Instead, it is convenient if all the transactions that lead to an increase or decrease in cash are collected together in the cash account. The new cash balance can be calculated by adding the sum of increases to the starting balance and then subtracting the sum of decreases.

An account has a title and two columns. It resembles the English letter 'T' and is called a 'T Account'. The left-hand side of the account is called the debit side and the right-hand side is called the credit side. An illustration of an account is shown in Table 4.3.

Table 4.3 Simple form of an account

Cash			
Debit Side	**(Rs.)**	**Credit Side**	**(Rs.)**
Starting balance	40,000	Decreases	8,000
Increases	4,400		2,000
	2,000		4,000

(Continued)

Table 4.3 (Continued)

Cash			
Debit Side	(Rs.)	Credit Side	(Rs.)
	1,000		1,500
	300		
	47,700		15,500
New balance	32,200		

What we have done is to put the increase of cash on the left-hand side and the decrease on the right-hand side. The proper form of an account is as given in Table 4.4.

Table 4.4 An account in a proper form

Date	Particulars	Reference	Amount	Date	Particulars	Reference	Amount

Note: Reference indicates the source of information.

An alternative form of an account is given in Table 4.5.

Table 4.5 Alternate form of an account

Date	Particulars	Reference	Dr. Amount (Rs.)	Cr. Amount (Rs.)	Balance Amount (Rs.)

Note: Dr. denotes debit and Cr. denotes credit.

4.4.1.1 Classification of Accounts

Accounts can be classified into the following categories: (i) asset accounts, (ii) liability accounts, (iii) capital accounts, (iv) expense accounts and (v) income accounts.

4.4.1.2 Rules for Debit and Credit

Accounting records are maintained using a *double-entry accounting system*. Under this system, debit and credit entries of equal amount are made to record every transaction. Entering a transaction on the left-hand side of an account is known as *debiting the account* and entering a transaction on the right-hand side is called *crediting the account*. The rules of debit and credit differ with the account type, and are as follows:

(a) Increases in assets are debits; decreases in assets are credits.
(b) Increases in liabilities are credits; decreases in liabilities are debits.
(c) Increases in owners' capital are credits; decreases in owners' capital are debits.
(d) Expenses and losses are debits; incomes and gains are credits.

Accounts can also be classified into the following categories:

1. **Personal accounts:** These accounts relate to persons. Accounts of customers, suppliers, lenders and bankers fall in this category. The capital account of the owners is also a personal account.
2. **Real accounts:** These accounts relate to assets of the firm such as land, building, investments, fixed deposits, cash balance, etc.
3. **Nominal accounts:** These accounts relate to expenses, revenues, losses and gains. Salaries paid, interest paid, commission received are examples of nominal accounts. Nominal accounts are temporary only as their net result is reflected as profit or loss, which is transferred to the capital account.

For this alternative classification of accounts, the following rules of debit and credit are followed:

1. For personal accounts, debit the receiver and credit the giver.
2. For real accounts, debit what comes in and credit what goes out.
3. For nominal accounts, debit all expenses and losses and credit all incomes and gains.

Illustration 4.3

A, after starting business on January 1, 2016, with cash of Rs. 100,000, entered into the following transactions:

Jan 3: Purchased machinery for Rs. 50,000
Jan 5: Paid rent for the shop Rs. 2,000
Jan 31: Paid salary to employee Rs. 3,000
Jan 31: Received commission Rs. 15,000

These transactions can be analyzed in terms of accounts involved (assets, liabilities, expenses, incomes) and debit/credit rules as in Table 4.6.

Table 4.6 Analysis of transactions

Date (2016)	Particulars	Accounts Involved	Type of Account	Effect	Debit (Rs.)	Credit (Rs.)
Jan 1	Rs. 100,000 cash	Cash	Asset	Increased	100,000	
	invested in business	A's capital	Capital	Increased		100,000
Jan 3	Purchased machinery	Machinery	Asset	Increased	50,000	
	for Rs. 50,000	Cash	Asset	Decreased		50,000
Jan 5	Paid rent for the shop	Rent	Expense	Increased	2,000	
	Rs. 2,000	Cash	Asset	Decreased		2,000
Jan 31	Paid salary to employee	Salary	Expense	Increased	3,000	
	Rs. 3,000	Cash	Asset	Decreased		3,000
Jan 31	Received commission	Cash	Asset	Increased	15,000	
	Rs. 15,000	Commission	Income	Increased		15,000

The transactions in Table 4.6 can be analyzed in terms of the alternative classification of accounts involved (personal, real, nominal) and debit/credit rules as in Table 4.7.

Table 4.7 Analysis of transactions using alternative classification of accounts

Date (2016)	Particulars	Accounts involved	Type of Account	Effect	Debit (Rs.)	Credit (Rs.)
Jan 1	Rs. 100,000 cash invested in business	Cash	Real	Comes in	100,000	
		A's Capital	Personal	Giver		100,000
Jan 3	Purchased machinery for Rs. 50,000	Machinery	Real	Comes in	50,000	
		Cash	Real	Goes out		50,000
Jan 5	Paid rent for the shop Rs. 2,000	Rent	Nominal	Expense	2,000	
		Cash	Real	Goes out		2,000
Jan 31	Paid salary to employee Rs. 3,000	Salary	Nominal	Expense	3,000	
		Cash	Real	Goes out		3,000
Jan 31	Received commission Rs. 15,000	Cash	Real	Comes in	15,000	
		Commission	Nominal	Income		15,000

Based on Tables 4.6 and 4.7, the 'T' form accounts in Table 4.8 can be prepared.

Table 4.8 Ledger accounts

Date	Particulars	Reference	Amount (Rs.)	Date	Particulars	Reference	Amount (Rs.)
Cash account							
	Increases (Dr.)				Decreases (Cr.)		
Jan 1	A's Capital		100,000	Jan 3	Machinery		50,000
Jan 31	Commission		15,000	Jan 5	Rent		2,000
				Jan 31	Salary		3,000
A's capital account							
	Decreases (Dr.)				Increases (Cr.)		
				Jan 1	Cash		100,000
Machinery account							
	Increases (Dr.)				Decreases (Cr.)		
Jan 3	Cash		50,000				
Rent account							
	Increases (Dr.)				Decreases (Cr.)		
Jan 5	Cash		2,000				

(Continued)

Table 4.8 (Continued)

Date	Particulars	Reference	Amount (Rs.)	Date	Particulars	Reference	Amount (Rs.)
Salary account							
	Increases (Dr.)				Decreases (Cr.)		
Jan 31	Cash		3,000				
Commission account							
	Decreases (Dr.)				Increases (Cr.)		
				Jan 31	Cash		15,000

4.4.2 Journal and Ledger

The accounting record where all the accounts are kept together is called the *ledger.* It is also referred to as the *principal book*. Though accounts can be written directly in the ledger, it is common to use two records for the purpose. These are the journal and the ledger.

4.4.2.1 Journal

Transactions are first entered in this record to show the accounts to be debited and credited. Journal is also called a subsidiary book. Transactions are entered in a chronological order in the journal. The debit and credit amounts recorded in the journal are subsequently transferred to the relevant accounts in the ledger at convenient intervals.

4.4.2.2 Entering Transactions into the Journal

The journal is prepared in the following manner (Table 4.9).

Table 4.9 Format of journal

Date	Particulars	L.F.	Dr. Amount	Cr. Amount

1. In the first column, the date of the transaction is entered. At the top, the year is written and below the year, the month and the date are written.
2. In the second column, the names of the accounts involved are written. The account to be debited is written first with the word 'Dr.' (which stands for debit). It is written towards the end of the column. In the next line, a little space is left, then the word 'To' is written, after which the name of the account to be credited is written. In the next line, 'narration' is written which refers to the explanation for the entry being made and the necessary details relating thereto. It starts with the words 'Being'.

3. In the third column, L.F. refers to 'Ledger Folio', which is the page of the ledger containing the account in which the entry is written up or posted.
4. The fourth column refers to the debit amount. In this column, the amounts to be debited are entered.
5. In the fifth column, the amounts to be credited are entered.

The process of entering the transactions in the journal is called *journalizing.*

Illustration 4.4

A has entered into the following transactions during January 2016.

Date (2016)		(Rs.)
Jan 1	A started business with cash	100,000
Jan 3	Deposited cash into the bank	75,000
Jan 4	Purchased stationary	500
Jan 5	Purchased goods for cash	20,000
Jan 7	Purchased goods from B on credit	25,000
Jan 8	Sold goods for cash	15,000
Jan 9	Sold goods to C on credit	18,000
Jan 10	Drew cash from bank	10,000
Jan 15	Paid to B	24,500
	Discount allowed by B	500
Jan 20	Received cash from C	17,700
	Discount allowed to C	300
Jan 31	Paid salary	2,000

The above transactions will appear in A's journal as shown in Table 4.10.

Table 4.10 Journal of A

Date (2016)	Particulars		L.F.	Dr. Amount (Rs.)	Cr. Amount (Rs.)
Jan 1	Cash account	Dr.		100,000	
	To Capital account				100,000
	(being the amount invested by A in his/her business)				

(Continued)

Table 4.10 (Continued)

Date (2016)	Particulars		L.F.	Dr. Amount (Rs.)	Cr. Amount (Rs.)
Jan 3	Bank account	Dr.		75,000	
	To Cash account				75,000
	(being the amount deposited in bank)				
Jan 4	Stationery account	Dr.		500	
	To Cash account				500
	(being stationery purchased for cash)				
Jan 5	Purchases account	Dr.		20,000	
	To Cash account				20,000
	(being goods purchased for cash)				
Jan 7	Purchases account	Dr.		25,000	
	To B's account				25,000
	(being goods purchased from B on credit)				
Jan 8	Cash account	Dr.		15,000	
	To Sales account				15,000
	(being goods sold for cash)				
Jan 9	C's account	Dr.		18,000	
	To Sales account				18,000
	(being goods sold to C on credit)				
Jan 10	Cash account	Dr.		10,000	
	To Bank account				10,000
	(being cash withdrawn from bank)				
Jan 15	B's account	Dr.		25,000	
	To Cash account				24,500
	To Discount account				500
	(being cash paid to B and discount allowed by him/her)				
Jan 20	Cash account	Dr.		17,700	
	Discount account	Dr.		300	
	To C's account				18,000
	(being cash received from C and discount allowed to him/her)				
Jan 30	Salaries account	Dr.		2,000	
	To Cash account				2,000
	(being the amount paid for salary)				

4.4.2.3 Posting Entries into the Ledger

Entries are posted into the ledger from the journal. The transfer of journal entry amounts to the ledger is called *posting*. The journal shows the account to be debited and the account to be credited along with the amounts involved. A ledger account has two sides: the debit side on the left and the credit side on the right. For the account, which is to be debited, the entry will be made on the left-hand side of the account. The date of the transaction will be entered in the date column and the particulars in the particulars column of the account. The particulars will be preceded by the word 'To'.

For the account to be credited, the entry will be made on the right-hand side of the account. The particulars will be preceded by the word 'By'.

Finding the Balance in a Ledger Account

To find the balance in an account at the end of the accounting period or at any other time, the two sides of the account are totaled and the difference between the two is calculated. This difference represents the balance in the account. The balance is a credit balance when the total of the credit side of the account is greater than the total of the debit side. If the total of the debit side is greater, the balance in the account is a debit balance. The credit balance is written on the debit side as 'To balance c/d', where c/d stands for 'carried down'. Similarly, a debit balance is written on the credit side as 'By balance c/d'. The totals of the two sides are now equal and are written on the two sides opposite each other. After determining the total, the credit balance is written on the credit side as 'By balance b/d', where b/d stands for brought down. It represents the starting balance of the next accounting period. Similarly, the debit balance is written on the debit side as 'To balance b/d' in the next period.

The revenue and expense accounts are not balanced, but their amounts are transferred to the profit and loss account. This is the reason these accounts are also referred to as *temporary accounts*, while asset and liability accounts are referred to as *permanent accounts*.

The posting of transactions given in Illustration 4.4 and the balancing of ledger accounts is shown in Tables 4.11.

Table 4.11 Posting of transactions into ledger accounts

Ledger

Cash Account

Dr. **Cr.**

Date	Particulars	Amount (Rs.)	Date	Particulars	Amount (Rs.)
2016 Jan 1	To Capital A/c	100,000	2016 Jan 3	By Bank A/c	75,000
8	To Sales A/c	15,000	4	By Stationary A/c	500
10	To Bank A/c	10,000	5	By Purchases A/c	20,000
20	To C's A/c	17,700	15	By B's A/c	24,500
			31	By Salaries A/c	2,000
				By Balance c/d	20,700
		142,700			142,700
Feb 1	To Balance b/d	20,700			

Capital account

Dr. Cr.

Date	Particulars	Amount (Rs.)	Date	Particulars	Amount (Rs.)
2016 Jan 31	To Balance c/d	100,000	2016 Jan 1	By Cash A/c	100,000
		100,000			100,000
			Feb 1	By Balance b/d	100,000

Bank account

Dr. Cr.

Date	Particulars	Amount (Rs.)	Date	Particulars	Amount (Rs.)
2016 Jan 3	To Cash A/c	75,000	2016 Jan 10	By Cash A/c	10,000
			31	By Balance c/d	65,000
		75,000			75,000
Feb 1	To Balance b/d	65,000			

Stationary account

Dr. Cr.

Date	Particulars	Amount (Rs.)	Date	Particulars	Amount (Rs.)
2016 Jan 4	To Cash	500			

Purchases account

Dr. Cr.

Date	Particulars	Amount (Rs.)	Date	Particulars	Amount (Rs.)
2016 Jan 5	To Cash A/c	20,000			
Jan 7	To B's A/c	25,000			

Sales account

Dr. Cr.

Date	Particulars	Amount (Rs.)	Date	Particulars	Amount (Rs.)
2016			2016 Jan 8	By Cash A/c	15,000
			9	By C's A/c	18,000

B's account

Dr. Cr.

Date	Particulars	Amount (Rs.)	Date	Particulars	Amount (Rs.)
2016 Jan 15	To Cash A/c	24,500	2016 Jan 7	By Purchases A/c	25,000
	To Discount A/c	500			
		25,000			25,000

C's account

Dr. Cr.

Date	Particulars	Amount (Rs.)	Date	Particulars	Amount (Rs.)
2016 Jan 9	To Sales A/c	18,000	2016 Jan 20	By Cash A/c	17,700
				By Discount A/c	300
		18,000			18,000

Discount account

Dr. Cr.

Date	Particulars	Amount (Rs.)	Date	Particulars	Amount (Rs.)
2016 Jan 20	To C's Account	300	2016 Jan 15	By B's A/c	500

Salaries account

Dr. Cr.

Date	Particulars	Amount (Rs.)	Date	Particulars	Amount (Rs.)
2016 Jan 31	To Cash	2,000			

4.4.3 Subsidiary Books

Most of the transactions in a business relate to receipts and payments of cash, purchase of goods and sale of goods. Instead of routing these transactions through the journal, these transactions are recorded in separate records meant for each class of transactions. These books are called subsidiary books or books of prime entry because transactions are first recorded in these books before these are posted into the ledger. The following subsidiary books are commonly used in a business:

1. Cash book to record receipts and payments of cash and also receipts into and payments out of the bank.
2. Purchases book to record credit purchases of goods which a business deals in or of materials and stores required for production.

3. Sales book to record the credit sales of goods in which the firm deals.
4. Purchases returns book to record the returns of purchased goods and materials to suppliers.
5. Sales returns book to record return of goods by customers.
6. Bills receivable book to record bills of exchange or promissory notes received from other parties.
7. Bills payable book to record bills of exchange or promissory notes issued to other parties.
8. Journal proper to record those transactions that cannot be recorded in any of the above mentioned subsidiary books.

Subsidiary books are maintained because they offer many advantages such as division of work, specialization, saving of time, availability of separate information for each class of transactions and easy detection and correction of errors.

4.5 Trial Balance

After the transactions are posted in the ledger, a statement showing the accounts with debit and credit balances separately is prepared. This statement is called the *trial balance*. It serves as a summary of the contents of the ledger. It has two columns. The debit balances are listed in the left-hand column and the credit balances are listed in the right-hand column.

The trial balance is prepared on a particular date, which is mentioned at the top of the trial balance. The general format of the trial balance is shown in Table 4.12.

Table 4.12 Trial balance as on ___________

S. No.	Ledger Account	L.F.	Debit Balance (Rs.)	Credit Balance (Rs.)

The totals of the debit and credit balances must agree if there are no arithmetical errors in the accounting process because under the double-entry system all debits and credits taken together must be equal. Instead of using balances of ledger accounts, the trial balance may be prepared using the totals of the debit and credit sides of all ledger accounts.

The trial balance agreement implies that the accounting work is free from clerical errors, even though other errors may still be present. Some entries may have been omitted or posted to the wrong ledger account, but on the correct side. Mistakes in posting on the debit side may have been offset by mistakes in posting on the credit side.

If the debit and credit totals of the trial balance do not agree, one or more of the following errors might have been committed:

1. A debit amount is posted as a credit amount or vice-versa.
2. Arithmetic mistakes in determining account balances.
3. Error in carrying the amount from the ledger account to the trial balance or listing the account balance in the wrong column of the trial balance.
4. Errors in calculating totals of the trial balance.

The work of preparing financial statements starts after establishing the agreement of the trial balance. This is because it is desirable to ensure that the total of accounts with debit balances is equal to the total of accounts with credit balances. Preparation of financial statements becomes difficult in the absence of an agreed trial balance.

For the ledger accounts prepared in Table 4.11, the trial balance (using balances) is shown in Table 4.13.

Table 4.13 Trial balance as on January 31, 2016

S. No.	Ledger Account	L.F.	Debit Balance (Rs.)	Credit Balance (Rs.)
1.	Cash account		20,700	
2.	Capital account			1,00,000
3.	Bank account		65,000	
4.	Stationary account		500	
5.	Purchases account		45,000	
6.	Sales account			33,000
7.	Discount account			200
8.	Salaries account		2,000	
	Total		133,200	133,200

Summary – Review of Learning Objectives

1. **Understand the accounting process that leads to the preparation of financial statements.** The accounting process starts with the analysis of transactions in terms of their effect on assets, liabilities and owners' capital. Then, either the transactions are entered into a record called journal or they are directly entered into the ledger account. In doing so, certain rules of debit and credit are followed. If the transactions are first recorded in the journal, they are subsequently posted to the ledger. In the ledger, an account is maintained for individual assets, liabilities, revenues and expenses. At the end of the accounting period, balances of all accounts are transferred to a statement called the trial balance, and some adjustment entries and closing entries are made in the accounts. Financial statements are then prepared using the information in the trial balance, adjustment and closing entries.
2. **Analyze the effect of business transactions on the basic accounting equation.** All accounting transactions are analyzed in terms of their effect on assets, liabilities and owners' capital. Since the basic accounting equation provides the relationship between assets, liabilities and owners' capital, the accounting transactions can be analyzed using the basic accounting equation. Since the accounting equation must balance, each transaction has a dual effect on the accounting equation. Increase in an asset must be matched by a decrease in another asset, or increase in a liability or increase in owners' capital.
3. **Understand the use of an account in the process of building accounting records.** An account is a convenient way of finding

the balance of an item at any time after one or more transactions affecting that item have taken place. An account has two columns. It resembles the English letter 'T' and is called a *T Account.* The left-hand side of the account is called the debit side and the right-hand side is called the credit side. Increases in the account are entered on one side and decreases on the other. The difference in the amounts on the two sides represents the balance in the account.

4. **Understand the rules of debit and credit in recording business transactions in relevant accounts.** Entering a transaction on the left-hand side of an account is known as *debiting the account* and entering a transaction on the right-hand side is called *crediting the account.* The rules of debit and credit differ with the account type. Increases in assets are debits; decreases in assets are credits. Increases in liabilities are credits; decreases in liabilities are debits. Increases in the owners' capital are credits; decreases in the owners' capital are debits. Expenses and losses are debits; incomes and gains are credits.

   An alternative classification of accounts is personal accounts, real accounts and nominal accounts. For personal accounts, the receiver is debited and the giver is credited. For real accounts, what comes in is debited and what goes out is credited. For nominal accounts, all expenses and losses are debited and all incomes and gains are credited.

5. **Understand how a journal is maintained and the concept of subsidiary books.** A journal has five columns. The first column carries the date of the transaction is entered. In the second column, the names of the accounts involved are written. The third column L.F. refers to ledger folio which is the page of the ledger containing the account in which the entry is written up or posted. The fourth column refers to the debit amount, the word 'Dr.' represents debit. In the fifth column, the amounts to be credited are entered. Sometimes, a journal is subdivided according to the nature of transactions. The parts of the journal are called subsidiary books.

6. **Understand the posting of entries in the ledger.** On the basis of entries made in the journal, accounts are prepared. The record, which contains the accounts, is called *ledger.* A ledger account has two sides, debit side on the left and credit side on the right. For the account, which is to be debited, the entry will be made on the left-hand side of the account. For the account that is to be credited, the entry will be made on the right-hand side of the account. To find the balance in an account at the end of the accounting period or at any other time, the two sides of the account are totaled and the difference between the two is calculated. This difference represents the balance in the account. The balance is a credit balance when the total of the credit side of the account is larger than the total of the debit side. If the total of the debit side is greater, the balance in the account is a debit balance.

7. **Understand how trial balance is extracted and its purpose.** The closing balances of all ledger accounts are transferred to a statement called the trial balance. It serves as a summary of the contents of the ledger. Debit and credit balances are shown in different columns. The totals of the debit and credit balances must agree if there are no arithmetical errors in the accounting process because under the double-entry system, all debits and credits taken together, must be equal.

Glossary

- **Account** is a two-column format, resembling the English alphabet 'T', used to record accounting transactions.
- **Accounting transaction** occurs when an economic event causes a change in the assets, liabilities or owners' capital.

- **Double-entry accounting system** requires debit and credit entries of equal amount to record every transaction.
- **Journal** is an accounting record in which transactions are entered as they occur.
- **Ledger** is an accounting record with separate accounts for each account classification in which transactions are posted from the journal.
- **Nominal accounts** relate to expenses, revenues, losses and gains.
- **Personal accounts** relate to persons. An account of customers, suppliers, lenders and bankers fall in this category .The capital account of the owners is also a personal account.
- **Real accounts** relate to assets of the firm such as land, building, investments, fixed deposits, cash balance, etc.
- **Subsidiary books** are records used to enter special types of transactions such as purchase and sale of goods, receipts and payments of cash, etc. Such transactions may otherwise be recorded in the journal.
- **Trial balance** is the statement that shows the closing balances of all ledger accounts separately for debit and credit balances.

Solved Problem

1. Journalize the following transactions, post them in the ledger and extract the trial balance.

2016			
Jan 1	Assets:	Cash in hand	12,600
		Cash at bank	462,000
		Stock of goods	520,000
		M	134,000
	Liabilities:	N	77,600
		Ram	60,000
Jan 2	Received cheque from M in full settlement		132,000
Jan 3	Sold goods to D		28,000
Jan 4	Sold goods to J for cash		42,000
Jan 5	Bought goods from Ram		80,000
Jan 6	Bought goods from C by cheque		126,000
Jan 7	D returns goods, not being up to standard		5,000
	Traveling expenses paid to salesmen		3,000
Jan 13	Returned goods to Ram (not being up to specification)		6,000
Jan 15	Paid for furniture by cheque		14,000
Jan 16	Goods used personally by proprietor		1,000
Jan 18	D paid by cheque		23,000
Jan 29	Paid telephone charges		4,600
Jan 31	Paid salaries		6,000
	Paid rent		3,000
	Bank charges		1,000
	Drawn from bank for personal use		5,000

Solution: The journal entries relating to the above transactions are given in Table 4.14. The ledger posting of these transactions is presented in Table 4.15 and the trial balance extracted from the ledger accounts appears in Table 4.16.

Table 4.14 Journal

Date (2016)	Particulars		L.F.	Dr. Amount (Rs.)	Cr. Amount (Rs.)
Jan 1	Cash account	Dr.		12,600	
	Bank account	Dr.		462,000	
	Opening stock	Dr.		520,000	
	M	Dr.		134,000	
	To N				77,600
	To Ram				60,000
	To Capital account				991,000
	(being last year's balances brought forward; capital is the difference between assets and liabilities)				
Jan 2	Bank account	Dr.		132,000	
	Discount account	Dr.		2,000	
	To M				134,000
	(being cheque received from M in full settlement of account)				
Jan 3	D	Dr.		28,000	
	To Sales account				28,000
	(being goods sold to D on credit)				
Jan 4	Cash account	Dr.		42,000	
	To Sales account				42,000
	(being goods sold for cash)				
Jan 5	Purchases account	Dr.		80,000	
	To Ram				80,000
	(being goods purchased from Ram on credit)				
Jan 6	Purchases account	Dr.		126,000	
	To Bank account				126,000
	(being goods purchased, payment made by cheque)				
Jan 7	Sales returns account	Dr.		5,000	
	To D				5,000
	(being goods returned by D)				
Jan 7	Traveling expenses account	Dr.		3,000	
	To Cash account				3,000
	(being traveling expenses paid to salesmen)				

(*Continued*)

Table 4.14 (Continued)

Date (2016)	Particulars		L.F.	Dr. Amount (Rs.)	Cr. Amount (Rs.)
Jan 13	Ram	Dr.		6,000	
	To Purchases returns				6,000
	(being goods returned to Ram)				
Jan 15	Furniture account	Dr.	.	14,000	
	To Bank				14,000
	(being furniture purchased, payment made by cheque)				
Jan 16	Drawings account	Dr.		1,000	
	To Purchases account				
	(being goods withdrawn by the proprietor for personal use)				1,000
Jan 18	Bank account	Dr.		23,000	
	To D				23,000
	(being cheque received from D)				
Jan 29	Telephone expenses	Dr.		4,600	
	To Cash				4,600
	(being payment of telephone expenses)				
Jan 31	Salaries account	Dr.		6,000	
	Rent account	Dr.		3,000	
	To Cash				9,000
	(being payment of salaries and rent)				
Jan 31	Bank charges	Dr.		1,000	
	Drawings account	Dr.		5,000	
	To Bank				6,000
	(being bank charges debited by bank, and the withdrawal from bank for personal use of the proprietor)				

Table 4.15 Ledger

Ledger

Cash Account

Dr. Cr.

Date	Particulars	Amount (Rs.)	Date	Particulars	Amount (Rs.)
2016 Jan 1	To Balance b/d	12,600	2016 Jan 7	By Traveling exp	3,000
Jan 4	To Sales A/c	42,000	Jan 29	By Telephone exp	4,600

(Continued)

Table 4.15 (Continued)

Cash Account

Dr. Cr.

Date	Particulars	Amount (Rs.)	Date	Particulars	Amount (Rs.)
			2016 Jan 31	By Salaries A/c	6,000
			Jan 31	By Rent A/c	3,000
			Jan 31	By Balance c/d	38,000
		54,600			54,600
Feb 1	To Balance b/d	38,000			

Bank Account

Dr. Cr.

Date	Particulars	Amount (Rs.)	Date	Particulars	Amount (Rs.)
2016 Jan 1	To Balance b/d	462,000	2016 Jan 6	By Purchases	126,000
Jan 2	To M	132,000	Jan 15	By Furniture A/c	14,000
Jan 18	To D	23,000	Jan 31	By Bank charges	1,000
			Jan 31	By Drawings	5,000
			Jan 31	By Balance c/d	471,000
		617,000			617,000
Feb 1	To Balance b/d	471,000			

Opening Stock Account

Dr. Cr.

Date	Particulars	Amount (Rs.)	Date	Particulars	Amount (Rs.)
2016 Jan 1	To Balance b/d	520,000			

M's Account

Dr. Cr.

Date	Particulars	Amount (Rs.)	Date	Particulars	Amount (Rs.)
2016 Jan 1	To Balance b/d	134,000	2016 Jan 2	By Bank A/c	132,000
				By Discount A/c	2,000
		134,000			134,000

N's Account

Dr. Cr.

Date	Particulars	Amount (Rs.)	Date	Particulars	Amount (Rs.)
2016 Jan 31	To Balance c/d	77,600	2016 Jan 1	By Balance b/d	77,600
		77,600			77,600

Ram's Account

Dr. Cr.

Date	Particulars	Amount (Rs.)	Date	Particulars	Amount (Rs.)
2016 Jan 13	To Purchases returns	6,000	2016 Jan 5	By Balance b/d	60,000
Jan 31	To Balance c/d	134,000	Jan 5	By Purchases	80,000
		140,000			140,000
			Feb 1	By balance b/d	134,000

Capital Account

Dr. Cr.

Date	Particulars	Amount (Rs.)	Date	Particulars	Amount (Rs.)
2016 Jan 31	To Balance c/d	991,000	2016 Jan 1	By Balance b/d	991,000
		991,000			991,000
			Feb 1	By Balance b/d	991,000

D's Account

Dr. Cr.

Date	Particulars	Amount (Rs.)	Date	Particulars	Amount (Rs.)
2016 Jan 3	To Sales	28,000	2016 Jan 7	By Sales returns	5,000
			Jan 18	By Bank A/c	23,000
		28,000			28,000

Discount Account

Dr. Cr.

Date	Particulars	Amount (Rs.)	Date	Particulars	Amount (Rs.)
2016 Jan 2	To M's Account	2,000			

Sales Account

Dr. Cr.

Date	Particulars	Amount (Rs.)	Date	Particulars	Amount (Rs.)
2016			2016 Jan 3	By D	28,000
			Jan 4	By Cash	42,000

Purchases Account

Dr. Cr.

Date	Particulars	Amount (Rs.)	Date	Particulars	Amount (Rs.)
2016 Jan 5	To Ram	80,000	2016 Jan 16	By Drawings A/c	1,000
6	To Bank	126,000			

Sales Returns Account

Dr. Cr.

Date	Particulars	Amount (Rs.)	Date	Particulars	Amount (Rs.)
2016 Jan 7	To D's Account	5,000			

Traveling Expenses Account

Dr. Cr.

Date	Particulars	Amount (Rs.)	Date	Particulars	Amount (Rs.)
2016 Jan 7	To Cash	3,000			

Purchases Returns Account

Dr. Cr.

Date	Particulars	Amount (Rs.)	Date	Particulars	Amount (Rs.)
			2016 Jan 13	By Ram's A/c	6,000

Furniture Returns Account

Dr. Cr.

Date	Particulars	Amount (Rs.)	Date	Particulars	Amount (Rs.)
2016 Jan 15	To Bank account	14,000	2016 Jan 31	By Balance c/d	14,000
		14,000			14,000

Drawings Account

Dr. Cr.

Date	Particulars	Amount (Rs.)	Date	Particulars	Amount (Rs.)
2016 Jan 16	To Purchases account	1,000	2016 Jan 31	By Balance c/d	6,000
Jan 31	To Bank account	5,000			
		6,000			6,000

Telephone Expenses Account

Dr. Cr.

Date	Particulars	Amount (Rs.)	Date	Particulars	Amount (Rs.)
2016 Jan 29	To Cash	4,600			

Salaries Account

Dr. Cr.

Date	Particulars	Amount (Rs.)	Date	Particulars	Amount (Rs.)
2016 Jan 31	To Cash	6,000			

Rent Account

Dr. Cr.

Date	Particulars	Amount (Rs.)	Date	Particulars	Amount (Rs.)
2016 Jan 31	To Cash	3,000			

Bank Charges Account

Dr. Cr.

Date	Particulars	Amount (Rs.)	Date	Particulars	Amount (Rs.)
2016 Jan 31	To Bank	1,000			

Table 4.16 Trial balance as on January 31, 2016

S. No.	Ledger Account	L.F.	Debit Balance (Rs.)	Credit Balance (Rs.)
1.	Cash		38,000	
2.	Bank		471,000	

(Continued)

Table 4.16 (Continued)

S. No.	Ledger Account	L.F.	Debit Balance (Rs.)	Credit Balance (Rs.)
3.	Opening stock		520,000	
4.	N			77,600
5.	Ram			134,000
6.	Capital			991,000
7.	Discount		2,000	
8.	Sales			70,000
9.	Purchases		205,000	
10.	Sales returns		5,000	
11.	Traveling expenses		3,000	
12.	Purchases returns			6,000
13.	Furniture		14,000	
14.	Drawings		6,000	
15.	Telephone expenses		4,600	
16.	Salaries		6,000	
17.	Rent		3,000	
18.	Bank charges		1,000	
	Total		1,278,600	1,278,600

Multiple Choice Questions

1. 'A' purchased a car for Rs. 500,000, making a down payment of Rs. 100,000 and signing a Rs. 400,000 bill payable due in 3 months. As a result of this transaction ______.
   a. total assets increased by Rs. 500,000
   b. total liabilities increased by Rs. 400,000
   c. total assets increased by Rs. 400,000
   d. total assets increased by Rs. 400,000 with corresponding increase in liabilities by Rs. 400,000

2. Capital brought in by the proprietor is an example of ______.
   a. increase in asset and increase in liability
   b. increase in liability and decrease in asset
   c. increase in asset and decrease in liability
   d. increase in one asset and decrease in another asset

3. A transaction results in a Rs. 90,000 decrease in both assets and liabilities. The transaction could have been a ______.
   a. repayment of bank loan of Rs. 90,000
   b. collection from debtors of Rs. 90,000
   c. purchase of an item of equipment for Rs. 90,000
   d. sale of an item of equipment for Rs. 90,000

4. Select the best answer:
   (i) Rent account is a ______.
   (a) nominal account
   (b) personal account
   (c) asset account

(ii) Salary outstanding account is a ______.
(a) personal account
(b) nominal account
(c) real account

(iii) Bank account is a ______.
(a) real account
(b) personal account
(c) nominal account

(iv) The account of a limited company is a ______.
(a) real account
(b) nominal account
(c) personal account

(v) Debit means ______.
(a) decrease in capital
(b) increase in capital
(c) increase in liability

(vi) Credit means ______.
(a) increase in an asset
(b) increase in an expenditure
(c) increase in liability

(vii) Loss on account of fire is a ______.
(a) real account
(b) nominal account
(c) personal account

5. Indicate which alternative in each of the following cases is considered to be correct:

(i) The liabilities of a firm are Rs. 30,000. The capital of the proprietor is Rs. 70,000. The total assets are ______.
(a) Rs. 70,000
(b) Rs. 100,000
(c) Rs. 40,000

(ii) The assets of the business as on March 31, 2015 are worth Rs. 500,000 and its capital is Rs. 350,000. Its liabilities on that date shall be ______.
(a) Rs. 850,000
(b) Rs. 150,000
(c) Rs. 350,000

(iii) The accounting equation states that ______.
(a) Capital = Assets + Liabilities
(b) Capital + Liabilities = Assets
(c) Assets + Liabilities = Capital

(iv) Purchase of furniture for cash ______.
(a) increases total assets
(b) keeps total assets unchanged
(c) decreases total assets

(v) The owners' equity (i.e., capital) shall stand increased by ______.
(a) proprietor's drawings
(b) purchasing furniture on credit
(c) profit earned during the accounting year

(vi) If the total assets of a business are Rs. 1,300,000 and the owners' equity is Rs. 800,000, the liabilities will be ______.
(a) Rs. 5,00,000
(b) Rs. 21,00,000
(c) Rs. 3,00,000

(vii) If the owners' equity of a business is Rs. 700,000 and liabilities are Rs. 400,000, the total assets of the business would be ______.
(a) Rs. 3,00,000
(b) Rs. 11,00,000
(c) Rs. 7,00,000

6. In the case of balance sheet accounts ______.
a. decreases in asset accounts are recorded by debits
b. increases in asset accounts are recorded by credits
c. decreases in liability accounts are recorded by debits
d. increases in liability accounts are recorded by debits

7. A trial balance in which total debits are equal to total credits provides a ______.
a. proof that no transaction has been omitted from being recorded
b. proof that posting has been done in proper ledger accounts
c. proof that posting has been done on the correct sides of ledger accounts

d. proof that the balances of the ledger accounts have been correctly extracted

8. Which of the following statements relating to revenue and expense accounts is not correct?
a. Revenue accounts have debit balances.
b. Expense accounts have debit balances.
c. Expenses are recorded as debits in ledger accounts.
d. Revenues are recorded as credits in ledger accounts.

9. Indicate the incorrect answer in the accounting cycle.
a. Transactions are first recorded in the journal.
b. Transactions are posted after they are journalized.
c. The trial balance is prepared from the ledger.
d. The trial balance is prepared from the journal.

10. Indicate the incorrect answer.
a. Drawings are withdrawals by the owners from the business.
b. Drawings decrease the net income.
c. Drawings decrease the owners' capital.
d. Drawings are not treated as business expense.

11. The left-hand side of an account is ______.
a. blank
b. a description of the account
c. the debit side
d. the balance of the account

12. A debit to an asset account indicates ______.
a. an error
b. that a credit was made to a liability account
c. a decrease in the asset
d. an increase in the asset

13. The normal balance of any account is written on the ______.
a. left side
b. right side
c. side which has a higher total
d. side which has a lower total

14. The double-entry system requires that each transaction must be recorded ______.
a. in at least two different accounts
b. in two sets of books
c. in a journal and in a ledger
d. first as a revenue and then as an expense

15. A revenue account ______.
a. is increased by debits
b. is decreased by credits
c. has a normal balance of a debit
d. is increased by credits

16. The usual sequence of steps in the transaction recording process is ______.
a. journalize, analyze, post to the ledger
b. analyzc, journalize, post to the ledger
c. journalize, post to the ledger, analyze
d. post to the ledger, journalize, analyze

Review Questions

1. Following is the list of various accounts. Find the assets, liabilities, capital, revenue or expense accounts:
(i) Machinery
(ii) Bank
(iii) Sales
(iv) Unsold stock
(v) Bank overdraft
(vi) Ram (customer)
(vii) Purchases
(viii) Cash
(ix) Interest received
(x) Mohan (Proprietor)

2. Classify the following under personal, real and nominal accounts:
(i) Stock
(ii) Loan
(iii) Bank loan

(iv) Capital
(v) Drawings
(vi) Furniture
(vii) Cash
(viii) Bank
(ix) Ram (a purchaser)

3. On which side, the increase in the following accounts will be recorded. Also, mention the nature of account:
   (i) Furniture
   (ii) Mohan (Proprietor)
   (iii) Salary
   (iv) Purchases
   (v) Sales
   (vi) Interest paid
   (vii) Sohan (Creditor)
   (viii) Ram (Debtor)

4. Fill in the blanks by putting 'debit' or 'credit' as you deem fit:
   (i) When furniture is purchased, _____ the furniture account.
   (ii) When rent is paid, _____ the cash account.
   (iii) When payment is made to the supplier, _____ the supplier's account.
   (iv) Cash received on account of dividend should be _____ to dividend account.
   (v) Loss on account of fire should be _____ to loss due to fire account.
   (vi) Furniture purchased on credit, should be _____ to the supplier's account.
   (vii) A decrease in furniture account will be _____ to that account.
   (viii) An increase in owner's capital will be _____ to that account.
   (ix) A decrease in supplier's account will be _____ to that account.
   (x) An increase in rent paid account will be _____ to that account.

5. Following transactions took place during January 2016. You are required to fill in the blanks by using the words "Debit' or 'Credit' as the case may be. Also, mention the nature of accounts.
   (i) Ram started business with Rs. 200,000. The cash account should be _____ and capital account should be _____.
   (ii) He purchased goods for cash Rs. 30,000. Purchases account should be _____ and cash account should be _____.
   (iii) He paid salaries Rs. 5,000. Cash account should be _____ and salaries account should be _____.
   (iv) Sold goods to M on credit Rs. 20,000. Sales account should be _____ and M's account should be _____.
   (v) Furniture purchased for cash Rs. 10,000. Furniture account should be _____ and cash account should be _____.
   (vi) Took loan from Bank Rs. 50,000. Bank loan account should be _____ and cash account should be _____.
   (vii) Received interest from N Rs. 500. Interest account should be _____ and cash account should be _____.
   (viii) Printing and Stationery purchased for office use.
   Printing and stationery account should be _____ and cash account should be _____.
   (ix) Rent paid to landlord Rs. 2,000. Cash account should be _____ and rent account should be _____.
   (x) Received cash from M Rs. 15,000. Cash account should be _____ and M's account should be _____.

6. You are given a number of accounts below. State which of them will show a debit balance and which will show a credit balance.
   (i) Carriage
   (ii) Machinery
   (iii) Sales
   (iv) Cash
   (v) Ram (a debtor)
   (vi) Rent

(vii) Sales returns
(viii) Bad debts
(ix) Capital
(x) Purchases returns
(xi) Discount allowed
(xii) Repairs
(xiii) Purchases
(xiv) Commission received

7. Name the steps involved in the accounting cycle.
8. What are the two alternative ways in which accounts can be classified?

Practice Problems

1. Show the accounting equation on the basis of the transactions shown in Table 4.17. Determine the profit/loss for the month from the accounting equation and verify the same by preparing an income statement.

Table 4.17 Transactions done by Anil

		(Rs.)
1.	Anil started business with cash	600,000
2.	He purchased land for	90,000
3.	He purchased goods from Sunil on credit	100,000
4.	He paid carriage	15,000
5.	He sold to Shyam on credit goods costing Rs. 24,000 for	30,000
6.	He received rent from tenants	10,000
7.	Purchased stationery for cash	10,000
8.	Received interest in cash	15,000
9.	Introduced fresh capital	50,000
10.	Goods destroyed by fire	5,000

2. A has entered into the transactions shown in Table 4.18 during January 2016.

Table 4.18 Transactions done by A

2016		(Rs.)
Jan 1	A started business with cash	200,000
Jan 3	Deposited cash into the bank	75,000
Jan 5	Purchased goods for cash	50,000
Jan 7	Purchased goods from B on credit	30,000
Jan 8	Sold goods for cash (cost Rs. 40,000)	48,000
Jan 9	Sold goods to C on credit (cost Rs. 20,000)	24,000
Jan 10	Drew cash from bank	15,000
Jan 15	Paid to B	25,000
	Discount allowed by B	1,000

(Continued)

Table 4.18 (Continued)

2016		(Rs.)
Jan 16	Purchased furniture by cheque	10,000
Jan 20	Received cash from C	18,000
	Discount allowed to C	1,000
Jan 31	Paid salary	5,000
Jan 31	Paid rent	2,000

You are required to present the above transactions in the form of accounting equation using separate columns for cash and bank.

3. Journalize the transactions shown in Table 4.19, post them in the ledger and extract the trial balance.

Table 4.19 Transactions

2016			(Rs.)
Jan 1	Assets:	Cash	6,300
		Cash in bank	231,000
		Stock of goods	260,000
		Mohan & Co.	67,000
	Liabilities:	Marathi & Co.	38,800
		Ram	30,000
Jan 2	Received cheque from Mohan & Co. in full settlement		66,000
Jan 3	Sold goods to Dass		14,000
Jan 4	Sold goods to Jaichand		14,000
	Carriage paid		350
	Sold goods to Govind for cash		31,200
Jan 5	Bought goods from Ram		40,000
Jan 6	Bought goods from Chatterjee		63,000
Jan 7	Dass returns goods, not being up to standard		1,000
	Traveling expenses paid to salesmen		1,470
	Goods sold for cash		8,000
Jan 8	Paid for stationary		660
Jan 13	Returned goods to Chatterjee (not being up to specification)		3,000
	Chatterjee admits claim for damage of goods		1,000
Jan 15	Paid for furniture by cheque		7,000
Jan 16	Goods used personally by proprietor		500
Jan 17	Goods sold to Mohan & Co.		50,000

(Continued)

2016		(Rs.)
Jan 18	Dass paid by cheque	13,000
Jan 20	Cheque received from Jaichand	14,400
Jan 22	Bank advises Jai Chand's cheque returned unpaid	
Jan 23	Sold goods for cash	8,000
Jan 24	Cash deposited with bank	20,000
Jan 27	Cheque sent to Chatterjee (discount allowed Rs. 500)	58,500
Jan 29	Paid telephone charges	2,300
Jan 31	Paid salaries	6,000
	Paid rent	3,000
	Bank charges	1,000
	Drawn from bank for personal use	5,000
	Received claim from Mohan & Co. for defects in goods supplied to them; claim admitted	1,500

4. From the following balances extracted from the ledger of N, prepare a trial balance as on March 31, 2016 (Table 4.20).

Table 4.20 Ledger of N

Account Head	Amount (Rs.)	Account Head	Amount (Rs.)
Capital	75,00,000	Building	9,40,000
Plant	15,00,000	Stock (1.4.2015)	12,50,000
Cash in hand	2,500	Cash at bank	5,75,000
Commission received	1,75,000	Rates and taxes	30,000
Discount allowed	55,000	Discount received	45,000
Purchase return	50,000	Sundry creditors	2,50,000
Interest received	30,000	Sales	62,50,000
Repairs	1,25,000	Sundry debtors	15,00,000
General expenses	3,00,000	Rent	62,500
Wages	5,00,000	Purchases	48,00,000
Furniture	1,20,000	Carriage and freight	75,000
Sales returns	90,000	Delivery van	5,00,000
Loan advanced	6,00,000	Traveling expenses	50,000
Office salaries	6,25,000	Drawings	6,00,000

5. Your accountant has submitted to you the trial balance given in Table 4.21.

Table 4.21 Trial balance

Name of Account	Debit (Rs.)	Credit (Rs.)
Capital		76,700
Cash		300
Purchases	89,900	
Sales		1,10,600
Cash at bank	8,850	
Furniture	2,250	
Equipment	15,000	
Lighting and heating	650	
Bills receivables		8,250
Sales returns		300
Salaries	10,750	
Creditors		18,900
Debtors	57,000	
Opening stock (1.4.2005)	30,000	
Printing expenses	2,250	
Bills payable	18,750	
Insurance	1,900	
Discount received	4,450	
Discount allowed		2,000
Total	2,41,750	2,17,050

You will notice that the total of debit and credit balances in the trial balance does not match. You are required to draft the trial balance correctly.

Answers to Multiple Choice Questions

1. (d)
2. (a)
3. (a)
4. (i)→(a), (ii)→(a), (iii)→(b), (iv)→(c), (v)→(a), (vi)→(c), (vii)→(b)
5. (i)→(b), (ii)→(b), (iii)→(b), (iv)→(b), (v)→(c), (vi)→(a), (vii)→(b)
6. (c)
7. (c)
8. (a)
9. (d)
10. (b)
11. (c)
12. (d)
13. (d)
14. (a)
15. (d)
16. (b)

Preparation of Financial Statements

5

LEARNING OBJECTIVES

After reading this chapter, you will be able to:

- Understand the relationship between profit and loss account and balance sheet.
- Prepare profit and loss account and balance sheet from the given trial balance without accounting for any adjustment entries.
- Understand how to make adjustments for accruals, deferrals and other items.
- Prepare profit and loss account and balance sheet after accounting for adjustment entries.
- Prepare closing entries and post-closing trial balance.

5.1 Introduction

Financial statements here refer to the profit and loss account and the balance sheet. The contents and formats of these statements have already been explained in Chapters 2 and 3. In Chapter 4, the steps in the accounting cycle, leading to the preparation of the trial balance were discussed. In this chapter, we will discuss the remaining steps in the accounting cycle, which involve preparation of adjusted trial balance, preparation of financial statements, passing of closing entries and preparation of post-closing trial balance. The steps discussed in this chapter focus on financial statements of a sole proprietor. The preparation of financial statements for corporate entities is discussed in Chapter 8.

Profit and loss account or revenue account is prepared to show the amount of profit earned or loss suffered during a period. The balance sheet shows the amount of assets and liabilities of the business at the close of an accounting period. These two statements are closely related to each other.

5.2 Relationship Between Profit and Loss Account and Balance Sheet

Both the profit and loss account and the balance sheet are interrelated. A cost relating to the operations of an accounting period or to the revenue earned during the period whose benefits do not extend beyond that period is treated as an expense and is shown in the profit and loss account. Any cost or a part of the cost whose benefits extend beyond the accounting period is treated as an asset and shown in the balance sheet. For example, a part of the cost of a machine that is depreciation for an accounting period is shown in the profit and loss account while the remaining cost of the machine is shown as an asset in the balance sheet. It is important that the parts of a cost to be charged in the profit and loss account and the part to be shown in the balance sheet are properly determined so that both the statements show the correct scenario. For this purpose, the matching principle is followed.

The profit earned during an accounting period and retained in the business (net profit minus drawings) forms part of the owners' capital in the balance sheet.

5.3 Preparation of Profit and Loss Account

In this section, the various elements of a multi-step profit and loss account, as described in Chapter 3, are discussed.

5.3.1 Gross Profit

Gross profit is the difference between the sales revenue and the cost of goods sold. The cost of goods sold in the case of a trading firm consists of purchases (adjusted for increase or decrease in stocks) and all other expenses incurred in bringing the goods to their present location and condition. Examples of such expenses are freight paid on purchases, cartage, octroi and customs duty. In a manufacturing concern, the cost of goods sold also includes all expenses incurred in the factory for producing goods such as wages, power and fuel and rent of factory premises.

5.3.2 Sales Revenue

Revenue recognition principles govern the time at which a firm recognizes earning of sales revenue. The total sales revenue for an accounting period is taken from the sales account in which day-to-day sales transactions are entered on the basis of sales invoices.

5.3.3 Sales Returns and Allowances

Sales returns are that part of sales revenue that represents the value of goods returned by customers as they were not in accordance with the specifications, or damaged or defective. Sometimes, instead of returning such goods, customers retain these goods and are given an allowance to compensate them for change in specification, damage or defect.

Sales returns and allowances are a counter revenue account to sales revenue and are shown as a deduction from the sales revenue in the profit and loss account.

5.3.4 Sales Tax

Sales tax is shown as a deduction from gross sales. It is an indirect tax that the seller recovers from the customer and deposits it with the government.

Net sales figure is calculated as follows:

Gross sales		____
Less: sales returns	____	
sales tax	____	
	____	____
Net sales		____

5.3.5 Cost of Goods Sold

The following items form part of the calculation of cost of goods sold.

1. **Beginning inventory:** The beginning inventory of an accounting period is the closing inventory of the previous accounting period. This figure is taken from the trial balance.
2. **Purchases:** The total purchases figure for the accounting period is taken from the purchases account in which day-to-day purchase transactions are entered on the basis of purchase invoices. Purchases are shown at net value after deducting any *trade discount* allowed by the supplier for purchasing a quantity of merchandise in excess of a specified amount. Sometimes, suppliers also give *allowances* by way of reduction in the invoice price for goods that do not meet the quality standards of the purchaser. Such allowances are also deducted from the purchase price.
3. **Purchases returns:** The cost of purchased items that is returned to sellers is accumulated in the purchases returns account and is shown as a deduction from the purchases figure in the profit and loss account.
4. **Freight on purchases:** Freight on purchase of inventory items is a part of purchase cost and is added to the purchase price of the goods for calculation of cost of goods sold.
5. **Wages:** Wages paid to workers in stores and warehouses also form a part of cost of goods sold. However, wages paid in relation to an item of fixed assets is added to the cost of that asset.
6. **Ending inventory:** Unsold goods at the end of an accounting period constitute the ending inventory. There is no account that provides the value of the ending inventory. Two alternative systems are available to ascertain the value of ending inventory. These are given as follows:
   (a) ***Perpetual inventory system:*** Under perpetual inventory system, a detailed record of each inventory purchase and sale is maintained. The inventory that should be on hand is available perpetually from these records.
   (b) ***Periodic inventory system:*** Under the periodic inventory system, no detailed records of inventory on hand are maintained. The value of the ending inventory is determined by taking a physical inventory count.

The cost of goods sold for any time period is readily available from the perpetual inventory system records. However, under the periodic inventory system, the cost of goods sold is calculated as follows:

Beginning inventory	____
Add: Purchases	____
Freight in	____
Wages	____
Cost of goods available for sale	____

Less: Ending inventory	____
Cost of goods sold	____

As both the opening stock and purchases appear on the debit side of the trading account, the closing stock is shown on the credit side of the trading account. The amount of closing stock is also shown as an asset in the balance sheet to complete the double entry.

If the closing stock appears in the trial balance, it implies that the amount of purchases during the accounting period has already been reduced by the closing stock. In such a case, the closing stock will not be shown on the credit side of the trading account. It will only be shown as an asset in the balance sheet.

5.3.6 Operating Profit

The operating profit is calculated as gross profit minus operating expenses. Operating expenses are related to normal operations of the business and include administrative, selling and general expenses.

Administrative expenses include salaries paid to office employees, rent of office building, lighting expenses, legal expenses, postage and telephone charges, audit fee, etc. Selling and distribution expenses include salesmen's salaries and commission, advertisement expenses, packing expenses, warehousing expenses, freight and carriage on sales, export duties, expenses on running and maintenance of delivery vehicles, insurance expenses, bad debts, etc. General expenses include maintenance costs, security expenses, etc.

5.3.7 Net Profit

Net profit is calculated by adjusting the operating profit for non-operating revenues, non-operating expenses, gains and losses. Non-operating items are not related to the main business operations and include such items as interest income, dividend income, interest expense, profit or loss on disposal of fixed assets, etc.

5.3.8 Income Tax

For companies, income tax is treated as a separate business expense. In the case of sole-proprietorship, income tax is treated as a personal expense and is adjusted in the owners' capital account.

5.3.9 Drawings

Drawings represent the money or goods withdrawn by the proprietor for his/her personal use. These also include the cost of office facilities such as car used for personal purpose of the proprietor. The amount of drawings is not a business expense, but is adjusted against the capital of the proprietor.

5.4 Preparation of Balance Sheet

Assets, liabilities and owners' equities are arranged either in a horizontal or vertical format, as described in Chapter 2.

Illustration 5.1

From the balances extracted from the books of Naveen Brothers for the year ended March 31, 2016 (Table 5.1), prepare a trading and profit and loss accounts, and balance sheet.

Table 5.1 Balances from the books of Naveen Brothers for the year ended March 31, 2016

	(Rs.)		(Rs.)
Opening stock	50,000	Plant and machinery	249,200
Sales	472,000	Purchase returns	55,200
Depreciation	26,680	Cash in hand	37,680
Commission received	8,440	Salaries	30,000
Insurance	15,200	Accounts receivable	185,400
Carriage on purchases	12,000	Discount allowed	13,120
Furniture	26,800	Wages	63,560
Printing expenses	19,240	Sales returns	66,360
Carriage on sales	8,000	Bank overdraft	160,000
Capital	369,120	Purchases	347,160
Accounts payable	92,840	Bad debts	7,200

Closing stock as on March 31, 2016 is Rs. 148,000.

Solution: See Tables 5.2 and 5.3.

Table 5.2 Trading and profit and loss accounts of Naveen Brothers for the year ended March 31, 2016

		(Rs.)			(Rs.)
To Opening stock		50,000	By Sales	472,000	
Purchases	347,160		Less: Returns	66,360	
Less: Returns	55,200				405,640
		291,960	Closing stock		148,000
Wages		63,560			
Carriage on purchases		12,000			
Gross profit c/d		136,120			
		553,640			553,640
To Depreciation		26,680	By gross profit b/d		136,120
Insurance		15,200	Commission		8,440
Printing expenses		19,240			
Carriage on sales		8,000			

(Continued)

Table 5.2 (Continued)

	(Rs.)		(Rs.)
Salaries	30,000		
Discount	13,120		
Bad debts	7,200		
Net profit	25,120		
	144,560		144,560

Table 5.3 Balance sheet of Naveen Brothers as on March 31, 2016

Liabilities		(Rs.)	Assets	(Rs.)
Capital	369,120		Plant and machinery	249,200
Add: Net profit	25,120		Furniture	26,800
		394,240	Closing stock	148,000
Accounts payable		92,840	Accounts receivable	185,400
Bank overdraft		160,000	Cash	37,680
		647,080		647,080

5.5 Adjustment Entries

Some business activities affect revenues and expenses of more than one accounting period. Some adjustments are required at the end of the accounting period to ensure proper measurement of income for an accounting period and to give a true picture of the state of affairs of the business at the end of the accounting period. Adjustment entries apply both the realization and matching principles to transactions affecting two or more periods.

Adjustment entries affect both the income statement and the balance sheet. This is because the adjustment entries relate to recognition of revenue and expenses causing a change in the owners' capital. As already known, the basic accounting equation always holds. Therefore, a change in the owners' capital is accompanied by a change in assets or liabilities.

These adjustments usually relate to the following:

1. Adjustments needed to convert assets into expenses:
   (a) Prepaid expenses
   (b) Depreciation and amortization
2. Adjustments needed to convert liabilities into revenue:
   (a) Income received in advance or unearned income

3. Adjustments needed to accrue unpaid expenses and uncollected revenue:
   (a) Outstanding expenses
   (b) Outstanding or accrued income
4. Adjustments needed to account for expected future expenses:
   (a) Provision for bad debts

5.5.1 Prepaid Expenses

For some items such as insurance and rent, payments are made in advance. These payments may benefit more than one accounting period, and there may be some unexpired part of such expenditure at the end of the accounting year. At the time of payment, such expenditure is treated as an asset. The adjusting entry treats the part of the asset consumed during the accounting period as an expense and the remaining part is shown as an asset in the balance sheet.

To account for such expenses, the prepaid expenses account is debited and the relevant expense account is credited. The effect of this entry is that the amount of expense for the accounting period is reduced, and an asset account in the form of prepaid expenses account is created. The prepaid portion of the expense is deducted from the amount of such expenses actually paid during the accounting year and the remaining amount is shown on the debit side of the trading account or the profit and loss account. To complete the dual effect, the amount of prepaid expenses is shown on the asset side of the balance sheet.

Prepaid expenses appearing in the trial balance imply that the amount of expenses during the accounting period has already been reduced by the prepaid expenses. In such a case, the prepaid expenses will not be deducted from the amount of expenses paid when shown in the trading account or profit and loss account. These will only be shown as an asset in the balance sheet.

Illustration 5.2

A firm pays an annual insurance premium of Rs. 48,000 on January 1, 2015. The accounting year of the firm ends on March 31, 2015. Only a part of the benefit of this expense (3/12) is consumed in the current accounting year and the remaining benefit (9/12) is used in the next accounting year.

Therefore, only Rs. 12,000 out of Rs. 48,000 paid pertains to the accounting year ended on March 31, 2015 and the remaining amount of Rs. 36,000 is treated as a prepaid expense. In the profit and loss account, Rs. 36,000 will be shown as deduction from Rs. 48,000 and the net debit will be Rs. 12,000. The prepaid amount of Rs. 36,000 will be shown as an asset in the balance sheet.

5.5.2 Depreciation and Amortization

Depreciation is the charge for the consumption of property, plant and equipment, and *amortization* is a charge for the expiry of benefits from intangible assets, such as goodwill, patents, etc. Depreciation and amortization convert the consumed part of the asset during the accounting year into an expense.

There are two alternative ways of accounting for depreciation. In the first method, depreciation (amortization) account is debited and the related asset account is credited. Depreciation (amortization) account is transferred to the profit and loss account and it appears on the debit side of the profit and loss account. The value of the asset in the balance sheet is reduced by the amount of depreciation provided during the accounting period. Under this method, depreciation (amortization) amount for the accounting year is shown as a deduction from the written-down value (net of depreciation) of items of property, plant and equipment and items of intangible assets as at the beginning of the accounting year in the balance sheet.

In the second method, depreciation (amortization) account is debited and provision for depreciation (amortization) account (or accumulated depreciation account) is credited. Depreciation (amortization) account is transferred to the debit of profit and loss account. Under this method, items of property, plant and equipment and items of intangible assets are shown at their original cost. Depreciation (amortization) charged from year to year is accumulated in the provision for depreciation account (or accumulated depreciation account). In the balance sheet, the provision for depreciation account (or accumulated depreciation account) is shown as a deduction from the original cost of assets.

When there is provision for depreciation account (or accumulated depreciation account), it appears at its beginning of the year value in the trial balance along with the asset account at its original cost. When there is no provision for depreciation account (or accumulated depreciation account), there is no depreciation account in the trial balance, and the assets are shown at their written-down value.

When the depreciation account is given in the trial balance, it means that the value of the asset has already been reduced by the amount of depreciation for the current accounting year. In such a case, depreciation (amortization) account is transferred to the profit and loss account, and it appears on the debit side of the profit and loss account. The value of the asset in the balance sheet is not reduced by the amount of depreciation provided during the accounting period.

The topic of depreciation and amortization of assets is covered in greater detail in Chapter 6.

Illustration 5.3

In the books of A, the net value (written-down value) of property, plant and equipment at the beginning of the accounting year is Rs. 192,000. The original cost of assets was Rs. 300,000 and a total depreciation of Rs. 108,000 was charged on these assets till the beginning of the year. Depreciation is charged at 20% on the written-down value of assets.

The depreciation for the current accounting year is Rs. 38,400 (20% of Rs. 192,000). This amount is debited to the profit and loss account. When there is provision for depreciation (accumulated depreciation) account, the balance in the account is increased by Rs. 38,400 to Rs. 146,400.

The disclosure in the balance sheet will be as follows (Tables 5.4 and 5.5):

Method 1: When there is no provision for depreciation (accumulated depreciation) account.

Table 5.4 Balance sheet

Liabilities	Assets	(Rs.)	(Rs.)
	Property, plant and equipment	192,000	
	Less: Depreciation	38,400	
			153,600

Method 2: When there is provision for depreciation (accumulated depreciation) account.

Table 5.5 Balance sheet

Liabilities	Assets	(Rs.)	(Rs.)
	Property, plant and equipment	300,000	
	Less: Provision for depreciation (accumulated depreciation)	146,400	
			153,600

5.5.3 Income Received in Advance or Unearned Income

Sometimes, a firm receives an advance payment for goods to be supplied or for services to be rendered in future. For example, subscriptions may be received in advance by publishers of a magazine or insurance premium may be received in advance by an insurance company. Such receipts cannot be treated as revenue until the related goods have been supplied or the services have been rendered. Till such time, these receipts are treated as liabilities. The purpose of the adjustment entry is to transfer that part of the liability to revenue that has been earned during the accounting period.

Part of the payment received, which has not been earned at the end of the accounting year, is known as income received in advance or unearned income. To account for such income, relevant income account is debited and the income received in advance account is credited. The effect of this entry is that the amount of income for the accounting period is reduced and a liability account in the form of income received in advance is created. Income received in advance is shown as deduction from the related head of income in the profit and loss account and recognized as a liability in the balance sheet.

If the unearned income appears in the trial balance, it implies that the amount of income earned during the accounting period has already been reduced by the unearned income. In such a case, the unearned income will not be deducted from the amount of income earned when shown in the trading account or profit and loss account. This will only be shown as a liability in the balance sheet.

Illustration 5.4

An insurance company receives an annual premium of Rs. 50,000 on an insurance policy whose coverage period extends till the mid of the next accounting year.

The insurance company will show Rs. 25,000 as an unearned income by way of deduction from the premium income of Rs. 50,000. The unearned income of Rs. 25,000 will also be shown as a liability in the balance sheet.

5.5.4 Outstanding (Accrued) Expenses

Outstanding expenses are expenses that are not paid till the end of the accounting year. For example, salaries payable to the employees of the firm in the last month of the year are paid in the first month of the next accounting period. These expenses relate to the previous accounting year and should be part of that year's expense.

To account for such expenses, the relevant expense account is debited and the outstanding expenses account is credited. The effect of this entry is that the amount of expense for the accounting period is increased and a liability account in the form of outstanding expenses account is created. The unpaid amount of expenses is added to the amount of such expenses actually paid during the accounting year, and the total amount is shown on the debit side of the trading account or the profit and loss account. To complete the dual effect, the amount of outstanding expenses is shown on the liability side of the balance sheet.

If the outstanding expenses appear in the trial balance, it implies that the amount of expenses paid during the accounting period has already been increased by the outstanding expenses. In such a case, the outstanding expenses will not be added to the amount of expenses paid when shown in the trading account or profit and loss account. These will only be shown as a liability in the balance sheet.

Illustration 5.5

A firm has a monthly salary expense of Rs. 100,000. For the accounting year ended on March 31, 2015, it has paid Rs. 1,100,000 during the year on account of salary. The salary for the month of March 2015 is paid in April 2015.

The salary expense for the accounting year ended on March 31, 2015 debited in the profit and loss account will be Rs. 1,200,000 (Rs. 1,100,000 paid plus Rs. 100,000 outstanding). Rs. 100,000 will also be shown as a liability in the balance sheet.

5.5.5 Outstanding or Accrued Income

Sometimes interest on securities or deposits is earned, and it is accumulated over time, but is not due for collection by the firm till the end of the accounting year. The firm may be entitled to receive dividends declared on its investments, which are not received by the firm during the accounting year. A firm may have rendered services, which have not been billed and collected by the end of the accounting year. All these are examples of accrued or outstanding income. Such incomes must be accounted for to report the correct amount of income.

To account for such an income, the accrued income account is debited, and the relevant income account is credited. The effect of this entry is that the amount of income for the accounting period is increased and an asset account in the form of accrued income is created. In the profit and loss account, the amount of the relevant income actually received during the accounting year is increased by the amount of accrued income, and the amount of accrued income is shown as an asset in the balance sheet.

If the accrued income appears in the trial balance, it implies that the amount of income earned during the accounting period has already been increased by the accrued income. In such a case, the accrued income will not be added to the amount of income earned when shown in the trading account or profit and loss account. This will only be shown as an asset in the balance sheet.

Illustration 5.6

A firm has invested Rs. 100,000 in debentures of a company that bear 14% interest. The interest is paid on June 30 and December 31 every year. The accounting period of the firm ends on March 31.

The firm is entitled to receive Rs. 7,000 every six months on June 30 and December 31. As on March 31, the firm earns an interest for only 3 months out of the period of 6 months between December 31 and June 30. The firm will show Rs. 3,500 (50% of Rs. 7,000) as an accrued interest income in the profit and loss account for the year ended on March 31 by debiting accrued interest and crediting interest account. The accrued interest of Rs. 3,500 will be shown as an asset in the balance sheet.

When the firm receives Rs. 7,000 on June 30 next year, it will debit cash account by Rs. 7000, credit accrued interest by Rs. 3,500 and credit interest account by Rs. 3,500.

5.5.6 Provision for Bad and Doubtful Debts

Bad debts are losses that result from debts that default on their obligation to pay. Bad debts account is debited and the debtors account is credited. The balance in the bad debts account is transferred to the debit of the profit and loss account. The balance in the debtors account is reduced by the amount of bad debts. When the amount of bad debts is given in the trial balance, it means that the balance of debtors (accounts receivable) account has already been reduced by the amount of bad debts. No further adjustment is required in the amount of debtors when it is carried to the balance sheet.

There are some debts that have not yet become bad but their recovery is uncertain. As the amount of bad debts is uncertain, a provision is created for bad and doubtful debts by debiting the profit and loss account and crediting the provision for bad and doubtful debts account. If there is any balance in the provision account at the beginning of the accounting year, the same is reduced from the amount of provision to be maintained at the end of the accounting year and only the remaining amount is debited to the profit and loss account.

If the amount of provision to be maintained at the end of the accounting year is less than the balance in the provision account at the beginning of the year, the difference is credited to the profit and loss account.

In the balance sheet, the provision for bad and doubtful debts is shown as deduction from the balance in the debtors account.

Illustration 5.7

The trial balance of a firm shows a balance of Rs. 100,000 in the debtors account and a balance of Rs. 8,000 in the bad debts account. The firm wants to create a provision for bad and doubtful debts equal to 5% of the balance in the debtors account.

In this case, the balance of Rs. 8,000 in the bad debts account will be transferred to the debit side of the profit and loss account. The profit and loss account will be further debited by Rs. 5,000 (5% of Rs. 100,000) by giving credit to provision for bad and doubtful debts. The entries in the balance sheet appear as shown in Table 5.6.

Table 5.6 Balance sheet

Liabilities	Assets	(Rs.)	(Rs.)
	Debtors	100,000	
	Less: Provision for bad and doubtful debts	5,000	
			95,000

Illustration 5.8

The following balances appear in the trial balance of a firm as on March 31, 2015.

	(Rs.)
Bad debts	8,000
Debtors	100,000
Provision for bad and doubtful debts (as on April 1, 2014)	5,000

It is proposed to maintain a provision of 10% on debtors for bad and doubtful debts.

In this case, Rs. 8,000 of bad debts will be debited to the profit and loss account. The required provision is Rs. 10,000 (10% of Rs. 100,000). The existing provision is Rs. 5,000. An additional provision of Rs. 5,000 will be created by debiting the profit and loss account and crediting the provision for bad and doubtful debts.

5.6 Adjusted Trial Balance

After posting of adjustment entries in the ledger, an adjusted trial balance is prepared that carries a summary of updated account balances.

Illustration 5.9

From the trial balance given in Table 5.7, prepare trading and profit and loss accounts for the year ended March 31, 2015 and balance sheet on that date.

Table 5.7 Trial balance as on March 31, 2015

	Debit Amount (Rs.)	Credit Amount (Rs.)
Purchases and sales	550,000	1,040,000
Sales returns	30,000	

(*Continued*)

Table 5.7 (Continued)

	Debit Amount (Rs.)	Credit Amount (Rs.)
Purchase returns		18,000
Freight on purchases	24,800	
Wages and salaries	117,200	
Miscellaneous expenses	4,400	
Rent		26,000
Insurance	4,000	
Audit fees	2,400	
Debtors/creditors	226,600	128,600
Printing and advertising	11,000	
Commission		2,000
Opening stock	72,000	
Cash in hand	25,600	
Cash at bank	53,600	
Bank loan		40,000
Interest on loan	3,000	
Capital		500,000
Drawings	30,000	
Property, plant and equipment	600,000	
	1,754,600	1,754,600

Adjustments:

(i) Stock at the end: Rs. 1,20,000.
(ii) Depreciate property, plant and equipment by 10%.
(iii) Commission earned, but not received amounts to Rs. 800.
(iv) Rent received in advance Rs. 2,000.
(v) Interest on bank loan @ 15 % p.a. is unpaid for the last six months.
(vi) Make a provision of 5% for bad debts.

For Illustration 5.9, the adjusted trial balance and the adjustments made in the original trial balance are as follows:

1. Depreciation account is debited by Rs. 60,000 (10% of Rs. 600,000) and property, plant and equipment account is credited by Rs. 60,000, reducing the balance in that account to Rs. 540,000.
2. Commission outstanding account is debited by Rs. 800 and the commission account is credited, increasing the commission income from Rs. 2,000 to Rs. 2,800.

3. Rent income is debited by Rs. 2,000, reducing the rent income from Rs. 26,000 to Rs. 24,000. Rent received in advance account is credited by Rs. 2,000.
4. Interest on loan is increased by Rs. 3,000 (Rs. 40,000 × 15% × 6/12), increasing the interest expense from Rs. 3,000 to Rs. 6,000. Outstanding interest account is credited by Rs. 3,000.

Closing stock and provision for bad debts are not reflected in the adjusted trial balance (Table 5.8) because their double entry takes place in the trading and profit and loss accounts. For closing stock, the journal entry is to debit the closing stock and to credit the trading account or profit and loss account. For bad debts provision, profit and loss account is debited and provision for bad debts is credited.

Table 5.8 Adjusted trial balance

	Debit Amount (Rs.)	Credit Amount (Rs.)
Purchases and sales	550,000	1,040,000
Sales returns	30,000	
Purchase returns		18,000
Freight on purchases	24,800	
Wages and salaries	117,200	
Miscellaneous expenses	4,400	
Rent		24,000
Insurance	4,000	
Audit fees	2,400	
Debtors/creditors	226,600	128,600
Printing and advertising	11,000	
Commission		2,800
Opening stock	72,000	
Cash in hand	25,600	
Cash at bank	53,600	
Bank loan		40,000
Interest on loan	6,000	
Capital		500,000
Drawings	30,000	
Property, plant and equipment	540,000	
Depreciation	60,000	
Commission outstanding	800	
Rent received in advance		2,000
Outstanding interest		3,000
	1,758,400	1,758,400

The financial statements prepared on the basis of adjusted trial balance are presented in Tables 5.9 and 5.10.

Table 5.9 Trading and profit and loss account for the year ended on March 31, 2015

Particulars		Amount (Rs.)	Particulars		Amount (Rs.)
To Opening stock		72,000	By Sales	1,040,000	
Purchases	550,000		Less: Returns	30,000	
Less: Returns	18,000				1,010,000
		532,000	Closing stock		120,000
Wages & salaries		117,200			
Freight on purchases		24,800			
Gross profit c/d		384,000			
		1,130,000			1,130,000
To Insurance		4,000	By gross profit b/d		384,000
Audit fee		2,400	Rent	26,000	
Printing and advertising		11,000	Less: Received		
Interest on loan	3,000		in advance	2,000	
Add: Outstanding	3,000				24,000
		6,000	Commission	2,000	
Depreciation		60,000	Add: Outstanding	800	
Provision for bad debts		11,330			2,800
Miscellaneous expenses		4,400			
Net profit		311,670			
		410,800			410,800

Table 5.10 Balance sheet as on March 31, 2015

Liabilities		Amount (Rs.)	Assets		Amount (Rs.)
Capital	500,000		Property, plant and equipment	600,000	
Add: Net profit	311,670		Less: Depreciation	60,000	
					540,000

(Continued)

Table 5.10 (Continued)

Liabilities		Amount (Rs.)	Assets		Amount (Rs.)
	811,670		Debtors	226,600	
Less: Drawings	30,000		Less: Provision for bad debts	11,330	
		781,670			215,270
Bank loan	40,000				
Add: Outstanding			Closing stock		120,000
interest	3,000		Cash in hand		25,600
		43,000	Cash at bank		53,600
Creditors		128,600	Commission outstanding		800
Rent received in advance		2,000			
		955,270			955,270

5.6.1 Closing Entries

Revenue and expenses accounts are temporary accounts as these are not carried forward to the next accounting year. At the end of the accounting period, these accounts are closed by transferring their balances to the profit and loss account. Revenue accounts have credit balances. To close these accounts, they are debited with a corresponding credit to the profit and loss account, the amount being equal to the balance in the account. Similarly, expense accounts are credited with a corresponding debit to the profit and loss account.

After the balances in revenue and expense accounts have been transferred to the profit and loss account, the balance in the profit and loss account will either show the net profit (when the sum of credit balances is more than the sum of debit balances) or the net loss (when the sum of debit balances is more than the sum of credit balances).

The profit and loss account is also closed by transferring the balance to the owners' capital or retained earnings (in the case of companies).

5.6.2 Post-Closing Trial Balance

The post-closing trial balance is prepared after closing the revenue and expense accounts. This trial balance consists of only those accounts that appear in the balance sheet. The purpose of preparing this trial balance is to check the accuracy in posting of closing entries. It also serves as the starting point for recording transactions in the next accounting period.

Summary – Review of Learning Objectives

1. **Understand the relationship between profit and loss account and balance sheet.** Both the profit and loss account and balance sheet are interrelated. A cost relating to the operations of an accounting period or to the revenue earned during the period whose benefits do not extend beyond that period is shown in the profit and loss account. On the contrary, any cost or a part of the cost whose benefit extends beyond the accounting period is shown in the balance sheet.
2. **Prepare profit and loss account and balance sheet from the given trial balance, without accounting for any adjustment entries.** First, the gross profit is determined by deducting the cost of goods sold from the sales revenue. Sales revenue is measured based on the revenue recognition policy, and adjustments are made for sales returns, sales allowances and sales tax. Cost of goods sold is determined on the basis of beginning inventory, purchases (net of returns), direct expenses (freight, wages, etc.) and ending inventory figures. Inventory can be measured using either the periodic or perpetual inventory system.

   Operating profit is calculated as gross profit minus operating expenses. Operating expenses are related to normal business operations and includes administrative, selling and general expenses. Net profit is calculated by adjusting the operating profit for non-operating revenues, expenses, gains and losses.

   Income-tax and drawings are treated as personal expenses of the owner and are, therefore not shown in the profit and loss account. These are adjusted in the owners' capital in the balance sheet.

   For the preparation of balance sheet, the assets and liabilities are grouped under the heads non-current assets and current assets on the asset side. The liability side shows the non-current liabilities and current liabilities below the owners' funds or owners' equities (capital, reserves and undistributed profits). The assets can be presented either in the order of permanence or in the order of liquidity.
3. **Understand how to make adjustments for accruals, deferrals and other items.** Some business activities affect revenues and expenses of more than one accounting period. Some adjustments are required at the end of the accounting period to ensure proper measurement of income for an accounting period and to give a true picture of the state of affairs of the business at the end of the accounting period. Adjustment entries apply both the realization and matching principles to transactions affecting two or more periods. Adjustments are usually made relating to outstanding expenses, prepaid expenses, outstanding or accrued income, income received in advance or unearned income, depreciation and amortization, and provision for bad debts.
4. **Prepare profit and loss account and balance sheet after accounting for adjustment entries.** The amounts in the trial balance get adjusted with the amount of adjustments made. Following the same principles that apply in the absence of adjustments, the profit and loss account and the balance sheet are prepared on the basis of the adjusted trial balance.
5. **Prepare closing entries and post-closing trial balance.** At the end of the accounting period, revenue and expense accounts are closed by transfer to profit and loss account. The balance in the profit and loss account is transferred to owners' capital account or retained earnings account. Thereafter, post-closing trial balance is prepared that consists of only balance sheet accounts. This trial balance is prepared to check the accuracy in posting of closing entries and to serve as the starting point for recording transactions in the next accounting period.

Glossary

- **Adjusted trial balance.** After posting of adjustment entries in the ledger, an adjusted trial balance is prepared that carries a summary of updated account balances.
- **Closing entries.** At the end of the accounting period, expense and revenue accounts are closed by transferring their balances to the profit and loss account. The profit and loss account is also closed by transferring the balance to the owners' capital or retained earnings (in the case of companies).
- **Cost of goods sold** is equal to the cost of goods available for sale (beginning inventory + net purchases + direct expenses) minus ending inventory.
- **Gross profit** is the difference between the sales revenue and the cost of goods sold.
- **Perpetual inventory system** keeps a detailed record of each inventory purchase and sale. The inventory that should be on hand is available perpetually from these records.
- **Periodic inventory system** does not keep a detailed record of inventory on hand. The value of the ending inventory is determined by taking a physical inventory count.
- **Operating profit** is calculated as gross profit minus operating expenses.
- **Operating expenses** are related to normal operations of the business and include administrative, selling and general expenses.
- **Net profit** is calculated by adjusting the operating profit for non-operating revenues, expenses, gains and losses.
- **Order of permanence.** Assets are presented in the balance sheet in such a manner that the asset that is to be used over the longest time period is listed first and the others are listed in that order.
- **Order of liquidity.** Assets are presented in the balance sheet in an order that is the reverse of the order of permanence.
- **Post-closing trial balance.** The post-closing trial balance is prepared after closing the revenue and expense accounts. This trial balance consists of only those accounts that appear in the balance sheet.

Solved Problems

1. The review problems given in this section have been solved without first preparing the adjusted trial balance. Students may, however, test their knowledge by preparing the adjusted trial balance.

   The trial balance extracted from the books of Akhilesh as on March 31, 2015 is given in Table 5.11.

Table 5.11 Trial balance from the books of Akhilesh as on March 31, 2015

	Debit Amount (Rs.)	Credit Amount (Rs.)
Purchases and sales	60,000	127,000
Returns	1,000	750
Rent, rates and taxes	10,000	
Freight on sales	1,200	
Manufacturing wages	10,000	

(*Continued*)

Table 5.11 (Continued)

	Debit Amount (Rs.)	Credit Amount (Rs.)
Discount	425	800
Provision for doubtful debts		525
Salaries	7,550	
Debtors/creditors	45,000	25,000
Printing and advertising	2,000	
Opening stock	30,000	
Cash in hand	6,900	
Capital		100,000
Property, plant and equipment	80,000	
	254,075	254,075

Prepare trading and profit and loss accounts for the year ended March 31, 2015 and the balance sheet on that date after taking into account the following adjustments:

(a) Stock at the end Rs. 34,220.
(b) Depreciate property, plant and equipment by 10%.
(c) Provision for doubtful debts to be kept at Rs. 500.
(d) The proprietor has taken goods worth Rs. 5,000 for personal use and additionally distributed goods worth Rs. 1,000 as samples.
(e) Purchase of equipment worth Rs. 920 was passed through Purchases Book.

Solution: See Tables 5.12 and 5.13.

Table 5.12 Trading and profit and loss accounts of Akhilesh for the year ended March 31, 2015

Particulars		Amount (Rs.)	Particulars		Amount (Rs.)
To Opening stock		30,000	By Sales	127,000	
Purchases	60,000		Less: Returns	1,000	
Less: Returns	750				126,000
	59,250		Closing stock		34,220
Less: Drawings	5,000				
	54,250				
Less: Samples (advertisement)	1,000				
	53,250				
Less: Equipment purchased	920				
		52,330			

(*Continued*)

Table 5.12 (Continued)

Particulars	Amount (Rs.)	Particulars	Amount (Rs.)
Manufacturing wages	10,000		
Gross profit c/d	67,890		
	160,220		160,220
To Salaries	7,550	By gross profit b/d	67,890
Rent, rates and taxes	10,000	Discount	800
Printing and advertising	3,000	Provision for doubtful debts (525–500)	25
Freight on sales	1,200		
Depreciation (Refer WN)	8,092		
Discount	425		
Net profit transferred to capital account	38,448		
	68,715		68,715

Table 5.13 Balance sheet of Akhilesh as on March 31, 2015

Liabilities		Amount (Rs.)	Assets		Amount (Rs.)
Capital	100,000		Property, plant and equipment	80,920	
Add: Net profit	38,448		Less: Depreciation	8,092	
	138,448				72,828
Less: Drawings	5,000		Debtors	45,000	
		133,448	Less: Provision for bad debts	500	
Creditors		25,000			44,500
			Closing stock		34,220
			Cash in hand		6,900
		158,448			158,448

Working Note:

Depreciation:	(Rs.)
Value of property, plant and equipment in trial balance	80,000
Add: Purchase of equipment passed through purchases book	920
	80,920
Depreciation @ 10%	8,092

2. From the trial balance of K. Krishna (Table 5.14), prepare trading and profit and loss accounts for the year ended March 31, 2015 and the balance sheet on that date.

Table 5.14 Trial balance of K. Krishna as on March 31, 2015

	Debit Amount (Rs.)	Credit Amount (Rs.)
Purchases and sales	90,000	140,400
Traveling expenses	800	
Provision for doubtful debts		2,000
Freight on purchases	2,000	
Salaries	9,000	
Miscellaneous expenses	1,000	
Rent	3,400	
Insurance (includes premium of Rs. 300 paid up to 30.9.2015)	400	
Manufacturing wages	12,500	
Debtors/creditors	29,500	20,000
Commission		700
Opening stock	40,000	
Cash in hand	2,500	
Cash at bank	5,800	
10% Bank loan (taken on 1.10.2014)		10,000
Capital		50,000
Drawings	6,000	
Property, plant and equipment	20,200	
	223,100	223,100

Adjustments:

(i) Stock at the end Rs. 38,000.
(ii) Depreciate property, plant and equipment by 10%.
(iii) Manufacturing wages include Rs. 800 paid for erection of new machinery on April 1, 2014.
(iv) Write off Rs. 500 as bad debts and maintain the provision for doubtful debts at 5% on debtors.

Solution: See Tables 5.15 and 5.16.

Table 5.15 Trading and profit and loss accounts of K. Krishna for the year ended March 31, 2015

Particulars	Amount (Rs.)	Particulars	Amount (Rs.)
To Opening stock	40,000	By Sales	140,400
Purchases	90,000	Closing stock	38,000

(Continued)

Table 5.15 (Continued)

Particulars		Amount (Rs.)	Particulars	Amount (Rs.)
Manufacturing wages	12,500			
Less: For machinery	800			
		11,700		
Freight on purchases		2,000		
Gross profit c/d		34,700		
		178,400		178,400
To Rent		3,400	By gross profit b/d	34,700
Salaries		9,000	Commission	700
Miscellaneous expenses		1,000	Provision for bad debts (2,000 – 1,450) (W.N.2)	550
Outstanding interest on Loan		500		
Insurance	400			
Less: Prepaid	150			
		250		
Bad debts		500		
Traveling expenses		800		
Depreciation (W.N.1)		2,100		
Net profit		18,400		
		35,950		35,950

Table 5.16 Balance sheet of K. Krishna as on March 31, 2015

Liabilities		Amount (Rs.)	Assets		Amount (Rs.)
Capital	50,000		Property, plant and equipment	20,200	
Add: Net profit	18,400		Add: Erection expenses	800	
	68,400			21,000	
Less: Drawings	6,000		Less: Depreciation	2,100	
		62,400			18,900
Bank loan	10,000		Debtors	29,500	
Add: Outstanding interest	500		Less: Bad debts	500	
		10,500		29,000	
Creditors		20,000	Less: Provision for bad debts	1,450	
					27,550

(*Continued*)

Table 5.16 (Continued)

Liabilities	Amount (Rs.)	Assets	Amount (Rs.)
		Closing stock	38,000
		Cash in hand	2,500
		Cash at bank	5,800
		Prepaid insurance	150
	92,900		92,900

Working Note:

1. Depreciation	(Rs.)
Value of property, plant and equipment in the trial balance	20,200
Add: Erection expenses	800
	21,000
Depreciation @ 10%	2,100

2. Provision for bad debts	(Rs.)
Debtors	29,500
Less: Bad debts	500
	29,000
Provision (5%)	1,450

3. The trial balance extracted from the books of Kanshi Ram as on March 31, 2015 is given in Table 5.17.

Table 5.17 Trial balance from the books of Kanshi Ram as on March 31, 2015

	Debit Amount (Rs.)	Credit Amount (Rs.)
Purchases and sales	1,595,000	2,310,000
Freight on purchases	25,000	
Wages (11 months up to 28.2.2015)	66,000	
Discount		15,000
Postage, telegrams, telephones	12,000	
Salaries	140,000	
Debtors/creditors	250,000	300,000
Printing and stationery	18,000	
Opening stock	75,000	

(Continued)

Table 5.17 (Continued)

	Debit Amount (Rs.)	Credit Amount (Rs.)
Cash at bank	150,000	
Capital		800,000
Property, plant and equipment	840,000	
Drawings	60,000	
Miscellaneous expenses	30,000	
Investments	100,000	
Bad debts	15,000	
Provision for bad debts		8,000
Commission on sales	45,000	
Interest on investments		12,000
Insurance (up to 31.07.2015)	24,000	
	3,445,000	3,445,000

Prepare trading and profit and loss accounts for the year ended March 31, 2015 and the balance sheet on that date after taking into account the following adjustments:

(a) Stock at the end Rs. 225,000.
(b) Machinery worth Rs. 45,000 purchased on October 1, 2014 was shown as purchases. Freight paid on the machinery was Rs. 5,000, which is included in freight on purchases.
(c) Commission on sales is payable @ 2.5%.
(d) Investments were sold at 10% profit, and the entire sales proceeds were taken as sales.
(e) Write off bad debts Rs. 10,000 and create a provision for doubtful debts at 5% of debtors.
(f) Depreciate property, plant and equipment by 10%.

Solution: See Tables 5.18 and 5.19.

Table 5.18 Trading and profit and loss accounts of Mr. Kanshi Ram for the year ended March 31, 2015

Particulars		Amount (Rs.)	Particulars		Amount (Rs.)
To Opening stock		75,000	By Sales	2,310,000	
Purchases	1,595,000		Less: Sale of investments	110,000	
Less: Purchase of machine	45,000				2,200,000
		1,550,000	Closing stock		225,000

(*Continued*)

Table 5.18 (Continued)

Particulars		Amount (Rs.)	Particulars	Amount (Rs.)
Wages	66,000			
Add: Outstanding	6,000			
		72,000		
Freight on purchases	25,000			
Less: For machinery	5,000			
		20,000		
Gross profit c/d		708,000		
		2,425,000		2,425,000
To Postage, telegrams, telephones		12,000	By gross profit b/d	708,000
Salaries		140,000	Interest on investment	12,000
Miscellaneous expenses		30,000	Profit on sale of investment	10,000
Printing and stationery		18,000	Discount	15,000
Commission on sales	45,000			
Add: Outstanding	10,000			
		55,000		
Insurance	24,000			
Less: Prepaid	8,000			
		16,000		
Bad debts	15,000			
Add: Further written off	10,000			
		25,000		
Provision for doubtful debts (W.N.2)	12,000			
Less: Old provision	8,000			
		4,000		
Depreciation (W.N.1)		89,000		
Net profit		356,000		
		745,000		745,000

Table 5.19 Balance sheet of Mr. Kanshi Ram as on March 31, 2015

Liabilities		Amount (Rs.)	Assets		Amount (Rs.)
Capital	800,000		Property, plant and equipment (W.N.1)	890,000	
Add: Net profit	356,000		Less: Depreciation	89,000	
	1,156,000				801,000
Less: Drawings	60,000		Debtors	250,000	
		1,096,000	Less: Bad debts	10,000	
Creditors		300,000		240,000	
Outstanding expenses			Less: Provision for bad debts	12,000	
Wages	6,000				228,000
Commission	10,000		Closing stock		225,000
		16,000	Cash at bank		150,000
			Prepaid insurance		8,000
		1,412,000			1,412,000

Working Notes:

1. Depreciation	(Rs.)
Value of property, plant and equipment in the trial balance	840,000
Add: Item of machinery wrongly shown as purchases	45,000
Add: Freight on purchase of machinery wrongly shown as freight on purchases	5,000
	890,000
Depreciation @ 10%	89,000

2. Provision for bad debts	(Rs.)
Debtors	250,000
Less: Bad debts	10,000
	240,000
Provision (5%)	12,000

4. From the balances extracted from the books of Karan and the additional information (Table 5.20), prepare the trading and profit and loss accounts for the year ended March 31, 2015 and also show the balance sheet as on that date.

Table 5.20 Trial balance of Karan as on March 31, 2015

	Debit Amount (Rs. in '000)	Credit Amount (Rs. in '000)
Purchases and sales	903	1,372
Returns	22	13
Direct expenses	75	
Bank overdraft		400
Postage, telegrams, telephones	25	
Salaries	90	
Debtors/creditors	240	450
Opening stock	625	
Cash in hand	35	
Capital		300
Property, plant and equipment	380	
Drawings	45	
Fire insurance premium	20	
Investments	110	
Interest		5
Commission		30
	2,570	2,570

Additional information:

(a) Closing stock on March 31, 2015 is valued at Rs. 6,50,000. Goods worth Rs. 5,000 are reported to have been taken away by the proprietor for his/her personal use at home during the year.

(b) Interest on investments Rs. 5,000 is yet to be received while Rs. 10,000 of the commission received is yet to be earned.

(c) Rs. 5,000 of the fire insurance premium paid is in respect of the quarter ending June 30, 2015.

(d) Salaries Rs. 10,000 for March, 2010 and bank overdraft interest estimated at Rs. 20,000 are yet to be recorded as outstanding charges.

(e) Depreciation is to be provided on property, plant and equipment @ 10% per annum.

(f) Make a provision for doubtful debts @ 5% of trade debtors.

Solution: See Tables 5.21 and 5.22.

Table 5.21 Trading and profit and loss accounts of Karan for the year ended March 31, 2015

Particulars		Amount (Rs. in '000)	Particulars		Amount (Rs. in '000)
To Opening stock		625	By Sales	1,372	
Purchases	903		Less: Returns	22	
Less: Returns	13				1,350

(Continued)

Table 5.21 (Continued)

Particulars		Amount (Rs. in '000)	Particulars		Amount (Rs. in '000)
	890		Closing stock		650
Less: Drawings	5				
		885			
Direct expenses		75			
Gross profit c/d		415			
		2,000			2,000
To Salaries	90		By gross profit b/d		415
Add: Outstanding	10		Interest on investment	5	
		100	Add: Outstanding	5	
Postage, telegrams, and telephone		25			10
Fire insurance	20		Commission	30	
Less: Prepaid	5		Less: Received in advance	10	
		15			20
Depreciation		38			
Interest on overdraft		20			
Provision for bad debts		12			
Net profit transferred to capital account		235			
		445			445

Table 5.22 Balance sheet of Karan as on March 31, 2015

Liabilities		Amount (Rs. in '000)	Assets		Amount (Rs. in '000)
Capital	300		Property, plant and equipment	380	
Add: Net profit	235		Less: Depreciation	38	
	535				342
Less: Drawings	50		Investments		110
		485	Debtors	240	
Creditors		450	Less: Provision for bad debts	12	228
Bank overdraft	400		Closing stock		650
Add: Outstanding interest	20		Cash in hand		35
		420	Outstanding interest on investment		5

(Continued)

Table 5.22 (Continued)

Liabilities	Amount (Rs. in '000)	Assets	Amount (Rs. in '000)
Outstanding salaries	10	Prepaid insurance	5
Commission received in advance	10		
	1,375		1,375

Multiple Choice Questions

1. Which one of the following financial statements is generally prepared first?
   a. Income statement
   b. Balance sheet
   c. Cash flow statement
   d. Statement of retained earnings

2. Which one of the following items is not reported in the income statement as an expense?
   a. Salaries
   b. Depreciation
   c. Rent
   d. Dividend

3. A firm uses a perpetual inventory system. The inventory at the beginning of the year was Rs. 100,000. It purchased inventory costing Rs. 500,000 and sold inventory costing Rs. 525,000 during the year. What is the value of the ending inventory revealed by the firm's accounting information system?
   a. Rs. 50,000
   b. Rs. 100,000
   c. Rs. 75,000
   d. Rs. 60,000

4. A firm uses a periodic inventory system. The inventory at the beginning of the year was Rs. 100,000 and at the end of the year it was Rs. 80,000. It purchased inventory costing Rs. 5,00,000 during the year. What is the amount of cost of goods sold revealed by the firm's accounting information system?
   a. Rs. 500,000
   b. Rs. 600,000
   c. Rs. 400,000
   d. Rs. 520,000

5. Which one of the following items will not appear on a firm's income statement?
   a. Rent expense
   b. Salaries
   c. Insurance expense
   d. Purchase price of furniture

6. A firm received a rental income of Rs. 50,000 during a year. It, however, wrongly recorded it as a rental expense. What is the effect of this error on the firm's income?
   a. −50,000
   b. +50,000
   c. +100,000
   d. −100,000

7. The charge for the expiry of benefits from intangible assets is called ______.
   a. depreciation
   b. depletion
   c. amortization
   d. none of the above

Review Questions

1. How is gross profit measured?
2. What are allowances in relation to sales revenue?
3. How is sales tax treated in accounts?
4. How is the cost of goods sold calculated?
5. What expenses are classified as operating expenses?
6. Define operating profit.
7. State any five adjustment entries made in the preparation of financial statements at the end of the accounting period.
8. Differentiate between the terms depreciation and amortization.

Practice Problems

1. On March 31, 2015, the trial balance shown in Table 5.23 was extracted from the books of Prakash, a trader.

Table 5.23 Trial balance from the books of Prakash as on March 31, 2015

	Debit Amount (Rs.)	Credit Amount (Rs.)
Purchases and sales	1,664,580	2,102,430
Freight on purchases	29,290	
Interest on loan	3,000	
Loan on mortgage		95,000
Sales returns	78,210	
Salaries	90,970	
Debtors/creditors	269,820	130,150
Freight on sales	24,040	
Opening stock	68,390	
Cash at bank	35,550	
Capital		280,000
Property, plant and equipment	220,000	
Drawings	30,000	
General expenses	34,890	
Rates and taxes	28,000	
Bad debts	5,250	
Provision for bad debts		7,100
Advertising	32,640	
Discount		5,500
Insurance	910	
Cash in hand	20,500	

(Continued)

Table 5.23 (Continued)

	Debit Amount (Rs.)	Credit Amount (Rs.)
Purchase returns		13,460
Rent received		2,400
	2,636,040	2,636,040

Prepare trading and profit and loss accounts for the year ended March 31, 2015 and a balance sheet as on that date after making the following adjustments:

(a) Depreciate property, plant and equipment @ 10%.
(b) Interest on loan @ 6% per annum is due for 6 months.
(c) Prepaid insurance on March 31, 2015 was Rs. 150.
(d) On March 31, 2015, the outstanding expenses were:
  (i) Salaries Rs. 7,500
  (ii) Rates and taxes Rs. 3,500
(e) Provision for bad debts to be maintained @ 5% on sundry debtors.
(f) Manager's commission to be provided @ 10% on net profit after charging such commission.
(g) Stock on March 31, 2015 was Rs. 62,500.

2. The trial balance of Arman as on March 31, 2015 is given in Table 5.24.

Table 5.24 Trial balance of Arman as on March 31, 2015

	Debit Amount (Rs.)	Credit Amount (Rs.)
Purchases and sales	2,600,000	3,100,000
Freight on purchases	46,000	
Goodwill (at cost)	200,000	
Salaries	55,000	
Debtors/creditors	400,000	200,000
Discount	2,000	
Opening stock	450,000	
Cash at bank	58,000	
Capital		800,000
Furniture	100,000	
Drawings	60,000	
General expenses	5,000	
Rent	24,000	
Bad debts	16,000	
Provision for bad debts		9,000
Advertising	50,000	

(Continued)

Table 5.24 (Continued)

	Debit Amount (Rs.)	Credit Amount (Rs.)
Commission		13,000
Insurance	4,000	
Cash in hand	52,000	
	4,122,000	4,122,000

Adjustments:

(a) Stock on March 31, 2015 was valued at Rs. 530,000.
(b) Salaries paid so far for 11 months only.
(c) Unexpired insurance included in the figure of Rs. 4,000 appearing in the trial balance is Rs. 1,000.
(d) Commission earned but not yet received amounting to Rs. 1,220 is to be recorded in books of account.
(e) Provision for bad debts is to be brought up to 3% of sundry debtors.
(f) Manager is to be allowed a commission of 10% of net profits after charging such commission.
(g) Furniture is depreciated @ 10% per annum.
(h) Only one-fourth of advertising expenses are to be written off.

Prepare trading and profit and loss accounts for the year ended March 31, 2015 and a balance sheet as on that date.

3. The trial balance of Arman as on March 31, 2015 is given in Table 5.25.

Table 5.25 Trial balance of Arman as on March 31, 2015

	Debit Amount (Rs.)	Credit Amount (Rs.)
Purchases and sales	140,000	230,000
Freight on purchases	1,200	
Freight on sales	2,000	
Loan		30,000
Purchase return		2,600
Sales return	4,200	
Salaries	11,000	
Debtors/creditors	86,000	43,000
Rent	5,500	
Opening stock	62,000	
Cash at bank	2,600	
Capital		162,000
Property, plant and equipment	117,400	
Drawings	12,000	
Interest on loan	2,700	

(Continued)

Table 5.25 (Continued)

	Debit Amount (Rs.)	Credit Amount (Rs.)
Rates and taxes	2,100	
Provision for bad debts		3,000
Printing and stationery	1,800	
Electric charges	1,200	
Bad debts	2,000	
Discount	2,400	1,600
General expenses	3,000	
Bank charges	1,600	
Motor car expenses	2,400	
Insurance	3,600	
Cash in hand	5,500	
	472,200	472,200

Prepare the trading and profit and loss accounts for the year ended March 31, 2015 and the balance sheet as on that date after making the following adjustments:

(a) Provide depreciation on property, plant and equipment @ 10%.
(b) Value of stock at the close of the year was Rs. 44,000.
(c) Provision for bad debts is to be maintained at 5% of sundry debtors.
(d) Insurance premium includes Rs. 2,000 paid towards proprietor's life insurance policy and the balance of the insurance charges covers the period from July 1, 2014 to June 30, 2015.

4. The trial balance extracted from the books of Shri Ram Prasad as on March 31, 2015 is given in Table 5.26.

Table 5.26 Trial balance from the books of Ahri Ram Prasad as on March 31, 2015

	Debit Amount (Rs.)	Credit Amount (Rs.)
Purchases and sales	800,000	1,403,700
Returns	42,400	28,200
Freight on purchases	23,100	
Wages	62,800	
Freight on sales	169,400	
Discount		1,900
Postage and telephones	8,200	
Salaries	98,700	
Debtors/creditors	633,100	189,200

(Continued)

Table 5.26 (Continued)

	Debit Amount (Rs.)	Credit Amount (Rs.)
Printing and stationery	6,600	
Opening stock	114,600	
Cash at bank	124,000	
Capital		1,000,000
Property, plant and equipment	355,000	
Drawings	176,000	
Office expenses	13,400	
Cash in hand	22,100	
Bad debts	14,000	
Provision for bad debts		32,400
Rates and insurance	13,000	
Rent		21,000
	2,676,400	2,676,400

Prepare trading and profit and loss accounts for the year ended March 31, 2015 and the balance sheet on that date after taking into account the following adjustments:

(a) Depreciate property, plant and equipment @ 10%.
(b) Write off further bad debts of Rs. 5,700.
(c) Prepaid insurance on March 31, 2015 was Rs. 2,400.
(d) On March 31, 2015, the outstanding salaries were Rs. 5,799.
(e) Provision for bad debts to be maintained @ 6% on sundry debtors.
(f) Rent receivable is Rs. 2,000.
(g) Stock on March 31, 2015 was Rs. 142,900.

5. From the balances and adjustments for the year ending on March 31, 2015 given in Table 5.27, prepare trading and profit and loss accounts and a balance sheet.

Table 5.27 Trial balance as on March 31, 2015

	Debit Amount (Rs.)	Credit Amount (Rs.)
Purchases and sales	1,302,950	1,805,000
Returns	24,000	1,950
Repairs	16,750	
Wages	225,250	
Interest on loan	6,000	
Discount	8,000	5,300

(Continued)

Table 5.27 (Continued)

	Debit Amount (Rs.)	Credit Amount (Rs.)
Freight on purchases	5,000	
Salaries	80,000	
Debtors/creditors	300,000	303,050
Sales tax	8,000	
Opening stock	400,000	
Cash at bank	95,000	
Capital		375,000
Property, plant and equipment	160,000	
Office expenses	1,250	
Cash in hand	5,000	
Bad debts	23,100	
Insurance	10,000	
Rent	20,000	
Loan (12% p.a.) as on 1.4.2014		200,000
	2,690,300	2,690,300

Adjustments:

(a) Wages include Rs. 20,000 for erection of new machinery installed on April 1, 2014.
(b) Depreciate property, plant and equipment @ 5%.
(c) Write off further bad debts of Rs. 4,000.
(d) On March 31, 2015, the outstanding salaries were Rs. 8,000.
(e) Make a provision of 5% on debtors for doubtful debts.
(f) Stock on March 31, 2015 was Rs. 409,250.
(g) Annual rent is paid up to June 30, 2015.
(h) Unexpired insurance is Rs. 3,000.

6. From the trial balance of Ram Gopal & Sons as on March 31, 2015 given in Table 5.28, prepare trading and profit and loss accounts for the year ending March 31, 2015 and the balance sheet on that date.

Table 5.28 Trial balance of Ram Gopal & Sons as on March 31, 2015

	Debit Amount (Rs.)	Credit Amount (Rs.)
Purchases and sales	480,000	960,000
Returns	20,000	24,000
Wages	96,000	
Interest on loan	44,000	
Discount	10,000	

(*Continued*)

Table 5.28 (Continued)

	Debit Amount (Rs.)	Credit Amount (Rs.)
Freight on purchases	24,000	8,000
Salaries	120,000	
Debtors/creditors	180,000	80,000
Commission	16,000	
Opening stock	100,000	
Cash at bank	50,000	
Capital		700,000
Property, plant and equipment	968,000	
Advertisement	30,000	
Cash in hand	24,000	
Provision for doubtful debts		24,000
Drawings	50,000	
Taxes and insurance	24,000	
Loan (10% p.a.) as on 1.4.2014		440,000
	2,236,000	2,236,000

Adjustments:

(a) Outstanding wages and salaries were Rs. 10,000 and Rs. 8,000, respectively on March 31, 2015.
(b) Depreciate property, plant and equipment @ 10%.
(c) Provision for doubtful debts is to be maintained at 10% on debtors.
(d) Stock on March 31, 2015 was Rs. 92,000.

7. The trial balance of X for the year ending March 31, 2015 is given in Table 5.29.

Table 5.29 Trial balance of X for the year ending March 31, 2015

	Debit Amount (Rs.)	Credit Amount (Rs.)
Purchases and sales	547,500	1,545,000
Returns	20,000	12,500
Commission		37,500
Interest	11,800	
Bad debts	12,500	
Salaries	330,000	
Debtors/creditors	380,000	250,000
Opening stock	346,000	
Cash at bank	65,000	
Capital		1,250,000

(Continued)

Table 5.29 (Continued)

	Debit Amount (Rs.)	Credit Amount (Rs.)
Property, plant and equipment	1,439,000	
Advertisement	45,000	
Provision for doubtful debts		20,000
General expenses	78,200	
Taxes and insurance	125,000	
Bank overdraft		285,000
	3,400,000	3,400,000

Stock on March 31, 2015 was valued at Rs. 32,500. Depreciate property, plant and equipment @ 10%. Interest of Rs. 8,500 is payable on bank overdraft. Salary Rs. 30,000 and tax Rs. 12,000 are outstanding. Insurance prepaid is Rs. 10,000 and one-third of commission received is in advance. Furniture purchased Rs. 10,000 in April, 2014 is included in purchases. Write off Rs. 10,000 as further bad debts and provision for bad debts is to be made at 5% on debtors.

8. From the trial balance of Mrs. Gaurav Singh as on March 31, 2015 (Table 5.30), and additional information given, prepare trading and profit and loss accounts for the year ending March 31, 2015 and a balance sheet on that date.

Table 5.30 Trial balance of Mrs. Gaurav Singh as on March 31, 2015

	Debit Amount (Rs.)	Credit Amount (Rs.)
Purchases and sales	4,000,000	7,000,000
Wages and salaries	250,000	
Interest on loan	24,000	
Freight on purchases	80,000	
Debtors/creditors	900,000	620,000
Commission		134,000
Opening stock	500,000	
Cash at bank	196,000	
Capital		3,712,000
Property, plant and equipment	5,310,000	
Bad debts recovered		64,000
Drawings	500,000	
Taxes and insurance	170,000	
Loan (10% p.a.) as on 1.4.2014		400,000
	11,930,000	11,930,000

Additional information:

(a) Outstanding wages and salaries were Rs. 100,000 and insurance prepaid is Rs. 40,000.
(b) Depreciate property, plant and equipment @ 10%. Plant included a machine purchased for Rs. 308,000 on September 30, 2014.
(c) Goods costing Rs. 80,000 were taken by the proprietor for her personal use but no entry was made in the books of accounts.
(d) Stock on March 31, 2015 was Rs. 400,000.

9. The trial balance of Banerjee on March 31, 2015 is given in Table 5.31.

Table 5.31 Trial balance of Banerjee as on March 31, 2015

	Debit Amount (Rs.)	Credit Amount (Rs.)
Purchases (adjusted)	2,100,000	
Sales		3,850,000
Freight on purchases	12,000	
Freight on sales	20,000	
Loan @ 18% p.a. taken on 1.4.2014		250,000
Purchase return		25,000
Sales return	15,000	
Wages	453,000	
Salaries	390,000	
Debtors/creditors	600,000	373,500
Stock as on March 31, 2015	450,000	
Cash at bank	160,000	
Capital		1,150,000
Property, plant and equipment	1,320,000	
Commission		15,000
Bad debts	12,000	
Discount	7,500	12,000
General expenses	154,000	
Insurance	15,000	
Expenses payable		33,000
	5,708,500	5,708,500

Prepare the trading and profit and loss accounts for the year ended March 31, 2015 and the balance sheet as on that date after making the following adjustments:

(a) Provide depreciation on property, plant and equipment @ 10%.
(b) Create a provision for bad debts at 2% of sundry debtors.
(c) Insurance premium includes Rs. 2,500 paid in advance.

10. From the trial balance of Shishir as on March 31, 2015 (Table 5.32) and additional information given, prepare profit and loss account for the year ending March 31, 2015 and a balance sheet on that date.

Table 5.32 Trial balance of Shishir as on March 31, 2015

	Debit Amount (Rs.)	Credit Amount (Rs.)
Trading profits		1,172,000
Salaries	140,000	
Interest on loan to Manoj		10,000
Printing and stationery	20,000	
Debtors/creditors	250,000	457,000
Discount	15,000	
Stock as on March 31, 2015	740,000	
Cash at bank	250,000	
Capital		2,000,000
Property, plant and equipment	1,660,000	
Provision for bad debts		48,000
Drawings	100,000	
Insurance	30,000	
Loan (10% p.a.) to Manoj as on 1.10.2014	400,000	
Bad debts	6,000	
Office Rent	26,000	
Cash in hand	105,000	
Outstanding wages as on 31.3.2015		5,000
Insurance claim received for loss of goods		50,000
	3,742,000	3,742,000

Additional information:

(a) Outstanding salaries were Rs. 7,000 and insurance prepaid is Rs. 4,000.

(b) Depreciate property, plant and equipment @ 10%. A machine was purchased for Rs. 150,000 on December 31, 2014 on credit for which no entry has been made in the books.

(c) Provision for doubtful debts is to be maintained at 5% on debtors.

11. From the figures extracted from the books of Govind (Table 5.33), you are required to prepare trading and profit and loss accounts for the year ending March 31, 2015 and a balance sheet on that date after making the necessary adjustments.

Table 5.33 Trial balance of Govind as on March 31, 2015

	Debit Amount (Rs.)	Credit Amount (Rs.)
Shri Govind's capital		2,288,000
Shri Govind's drawings	132,000	
Purchases	1,100,000	
Purchases returns		11,000
Salaries	132,000	
Office expenses	27,500	
Interest on loan to Krishna		11,000
Printing and stationery	15,400	
Debtors/creditors	292,600	495,000
Discount	13,200	
Stock as on April 1, 2014	385,000	
Cash at bank	292,600	
Sales		2,314,400
Property, plant and equipment	1,727,000	
Provision for doubtful debts		8,800
Wages	352,000	
Insurance	17,600	
Gas and fuel	29,700	
Loan (10% p.a.) to Krishna as on 1.10.2014	440,000	
Bad debts	6,600	
Office rent	28,600	
Cash in hand	26,400	
Freight	99,000	
Factory lighting	11,000	
	5,128,200	5,128,200

Adjustments:

1. Stock on March 31, 2015 was valued at Rs. 726,000.
2. A new machine was installed during the year costing Rs. 154,000, but it was not recorded in the books as no payment was made for it. Wages Rs. 11,000 paid for the erection were debited to the wages account.
3. Of the sundry debtors, Rs. 6,600 are bad and should be written off.
4. Maintain a provision of 5% on sundry debtors for doubtful debts.
5. The manager is entitled to a commission of 10% of the net profit after charging such commission.
6. Depreciate property, plant and equipment @ 10%.

12. From the trial balance of Hari (Table 5.34) and additional information, prepare trading and profit and loss accounts for the year ending March 31, 2015 and a balance sheet on that date after making the necessary adjustments.

Table 5.34 Trial balance of Hari as on March 31, 2015

	Debit Amount (Rs.)	Credit Amount (Rs.)
Capital		1,000,000
Drawings	240,000	
Purchases	1,500,000	
Purchases returns		50,000
Salaries	300,000	
Office expenses	120,000	
Interest earned		40,000
Printing and stationery	80,000	
Debtors/creditors	2,000,000	1,200,000
Stock as on April 1, 2014	500,000	
Sales		3,210,000
Furniture	200,000	
Provision for doubtful debts		60,000
Wages	200,000	
Insurance	120,000	
Sales return	100,000	
Bad debts	70,000	
Rent	150,000	
Provision for depreciation		20,000
	5,580,000	5,580,000

Adjustments:

1. Stock on March 31, 2015 was valued at Rs. 600,000.
2. Maintain a provision of 5% on sundry debtors for doubtful debts.
3. Depreciate furniture @ 10% on original cost.
4. Salaries for the month of March 2015 amounting to Rs. 30,000 were not paid. However, salaries included Rs. 20,000 paid in advance.
5. Insurance prepaid is Rs. 20,000.
6. Provide for outstanding office expenses Rs. 80,000.
7. Stock used for private purpose Rs. 60,000.

13. From the figures extracted from the books of Ganguli (Table 5.35), you are required to prepare trading and profit and loss accounts for the year ending March 31, 2015 and a balance sheet on that date after making the necessary adjustments.

Table 5.35 Trial balance of Ganguli as on March 31, 2015

	Debit Amount (Rs.)	Credit Amount (Rs.)
Ganguli's capital account		540,500
Drawings	50,000	
Purchases	1,215,500	
Purchase returns		29,000
Salaries	46,500	
General expenses	19,600	
Interest	4,500	7,250
Printing and stationery	17,000	
Debtors/creditors	120,000	74,000
Discount	37,700	14,950
Stock as on April 1, 2014	234,000	
Cash on hand	1,900	
Sales		1,448,000
Furniture as on 1.4.2014	9,000	
Investments (at 5%) as on 1.4.2014	25,000	
Audit fees	3,500	
Fire insurance premium	3,000	
Deposits at 10% as on 1.4.2014	150,000	
Loan (12% p.a.) from Dena Bank (1.4.2014)		100,000
Traveling expenses	11,650	
Rent	28,500	
Freight	93,000	
Advertising	56,000	
Postage	4,350	
Cash with Traders Bank Ltd.	40,000	
Sales returns	43,000	
	2,213,700	2,213,700

Adjustments:

1. Stock on March 31, 2015 was valued at Rs. 393,000. This includes goods returned by customers on March 31, 2015 of value Rs.15,000 for which no entry has been passed in the books.
2. Purchases include furniture purchased on January 1, 2005 for Rs. 10,000.
3. Maintain a provision of 5% on sundry debtors for doubtful debts.
4. Depreciate furniture @ 10% p.a.

14. From the figures extracted from the books of Krishna (Table 5.36), you are required to prepare trading and profit and loss accounts for the year ending March 31, 2015 and a balance sheet on that date after making the necessary adjustments.

Table 5.36 Trial balance of Krishna as on March 31, 2015

	Debit Amount (Rs.)	Credit Amount (Rs.)
Capital		473,900
Drawings	20,000	
Purchases	1,570,000	
General expenses	19,900	
Loan from Ram		25,000
Bad debts	1,000	
Debtors/creditors	95,000	290,000
Investments	65,000	
Stock as on April 1, 2014	273,500	
Cash on hand	3,350	
Sales		1,850,000
Property, plant and equipment	315,000	
Dividends		5,350
Wages	100,000	
Provision for bad debts		16,000
Rent and rates	8,500	
Discount	6,300	
Freight	11,200	
Income tax	10,250	
Cash at bank	162,000	
Interest		750
	2,661,000	2,661,000

Adjustments:

1. Stock on March 31, 2015 was valued at Rs. 150,000.
2. Accrued dividend is Rs. 1,350. Outstanding wages are Rs. 4,500. Rates paid in advance are Rs. 1,000.
3. Write off further bad debts of Rs. 3,000 and maintain a provision of 20% on sundry debtors for doubtful debts.
4. Depreciate property, plant and equipment @ 10% p.a.
5. Provide for interest at 12% p.a. due on loan taken on 1.6.2014.
6. Income tax paid has to be treated as drawings.

Answers to Multiple Choice Questions

1. (a)
2. (d)
3. (c)
4. (d)
5. (d)
6. (d)
7. (c)

Plant Assets and Intangible Assets

6

LEARNING OBJECTIVES

After reading this chapter, you will be able to:

- Understand the meaning of property, plant and equipment.
- Determine the cost of property, plant and equipment.
- Explain the revaluation of property, plant and equipment.
- Account for retirements and disposal of property, plant and equipment.
- Explain the concept of depreciation.
- Compute periodic depreciation using different methods.
- Understand the legal provisions related to accounting of property, plant and equipment.
- Explain impairment of property, plant and equipment.
- Understand the meaning of intangible assets.
- Understand how intangible assets are recognized and measured.
- Account for internally generated intangible assets.
- Understand how to determine the amortization amount in respect of intangible assets.
- Account for research and development expenses.
- Account for goodwill.

6.1 Introduction

Some assets held by a business are long-term in nature. These are called non-current assets. Some non-current assets are called plant assets and include property, plant and equipment and capital work-in-progress. Other types of non-current assets include goodwill, other intangible assets, and intangible assets under development. Under the new IFRS converged accounting standards, Ind AS 16 deals with accounting for property, plant and equipment and Ind AS 38 contains provisions relating to accounting and amortization of intangible assets.

Ind AS 16 defines property, plant and equipment as tangible items that (i) are held for use in the production or supply of goods or services, for rental to others, or for administrative purposes and (ii) are expected to be used during more than one period.

Intangible fixed assets are assets without any physical existence. Examples include patents, copyrights and software licenses.

This chapter deals with the (i) accounting for property, plant and equipment and depreciation of these assets; and (ii) accounting for intangible assets and amortization of such assets.

6.2 Accounting for Property, Plant and Equipment

The principal issues in accounting for property, plant and equipment are the recognition of such assets, the determination of their carrying amounts and the knowledge of their depreciation charges and impairment losses. Section 123 of the Companies Act, 2013 and Ind AS 16 provide the necessary guidance for this purpose.

6.2.1 Recognition of Cost of Property, Plant and Equipment

The cost of an item of property, plant and equipment is recognized as an asset if, and only if: (a) it is probable that future economic benefits associated with the item will flow to the entity and (b) the cost of the item can be measured reliably.

6.2.2 Elements of Cost

The cost of an item of property, plant and equipment comprises:

1. Its purchase price, including import duties and non-refundable purchase taxes, after deducting trade discounts and rebates.
2. Any costs directly attributable to bringing the asset to the location, and conditions necessary for it to be capable of operating in the manner intended by the management.
3. The initial estimate of the costs that may arise out of an obligation to dismantle and remove the item and restore the site on which it is located.

Examples of directly attributable costs are:

1. Costs of employee benefits arising directly from the construction or acquisition of the item of property, plant and equipment.
2. Costs of site preparation.
3. Initial delivery and handling costs.
4. Installation and assembly costs.

5. Costs of testing whether the asset is functioning properly, after deducting the net proceeds from selling any items produced while bringing the asset to that location and condition (such as samples produced when testing an equipment).
6. Professional fees.

Some items of property, plant and equipment acquired for safety or environmental reasons, although not directly increasing the future economic benefits of any particular existing item of property, plant and equipment, may be necessary for an entity to obtain economic benefits from other assets in future. Such items of property, plant and equipment qualify for recognition as assets. For example, the equipment installed by a chemical manufacturer to control environmental pollution is recognized as an asset because without it the entity is unable to manufacture and sell chemicals.

The cost of parts of some items of property, plant and equipment that need to be replaced at regular intervals (e.g., lining of a furnace, seats of an aircraft) is included in the cost of that item of property, plant and equipment. Similarly, the cost of major inspections for faults (e.g., of an aircraft), even though no part is replaced, is included in the cost.

6.2.2.1 Costs not Forming Part of the Cost of Property, Plant and Equipment

Some costs are not considered as forming part of the cost of property, plant and equipment. Examples of such costs are:

1. Costs of opening a new facility.
2. Costs of introducing a new product or service (including costs of advertising and promotional activities).
3. Costs of conducting business in a new location or with a new customer (including costs of staff training).
4. Administration and other general overhead costs.
5. Costs incurred when an item capable of operating in the manner intended by the management is yet to be put into use or is operated at less than full capacity;
6. Initial operating losses, such as those incurred when demand for an item's output builds up.
7. Costs of relocating or reorganizing part or all of an entity's operations.
8. Costs of the day-to-day servicing of the item.

Illustration 6.1 Acquisition cost

A company purchases land for building a factory by paying Rs. 8,500,000. For acquiring the land, the company pays a brokerage fee of Rs. 300,000 and a legal fee of Rs. 100,000. The company has to spend Rs. 550,000 for demolishing the old building on the land and for leveling the land. The rubble from the old building realizes Rs. 200,000. The cost of acquisition of the land is estimated as Rs. 9,250,000, and is calculated as follows:

	(Rs.)
Purchase price	8,500,000
Brokerage fee	300,000
Legal expenses	100,000

(Continued)

	(Rs.)
Demolishing expenses of old building and leveling cost	550,000
Realization from sale of rubble	(200,000)
Total cost of acquisition	9,250,000

6.2.3 Self-Constructed Assets

In arriving at the cost of self-constructed property, plant and equipment, costs of construction that relate directly to the specific asset and costs that are attributable to the construction activity in general and can be allocated to the specific asset are included. If an entity makes similar assets for sale in the normal course of business, the cost of the asset is usually the same as the cost of constructing an asset for sale. Therefore, any internal profits are eliminated in arriving at such costs. Similarly, the cost of abnormal amounts of wasted material, labor or other resources incurred in self-constructing an asset is not included in the cost of the asset.

6.2.4 Borrowing Costs

Borrowing costs incurred for an item of property, plant and equipment are included as a component of the cost of such item in accordance with Ind AS 23. The core principle is that borrowing costs directly attributable to the acquisition, construction or production of a qualifying asset form part of the cost of that asset.

Borrowing costs include interest and other costs that an entity incurs when borrowing funds. These include interest expenses calculated using the effective interest method, finance charges in respect of finance leases and exchange differences arising from foreign currency borrowings.

A qualifying asset is an asset that necessarily takes a substantial period of time to get ready for its intended use or sale. Depending on the circumstances, qualifying assets may include inventories, manufacturing plants, power generation facilities, intangible assets, investment properties and bearer plants.

Borrowing costs eligible for inclusion as part of the cost of an asset are those that are directly attributable to the acquisition, construction or production of a qualifying asset. The costs are considered directly attributable if they could have been avoided if the expenditure on the qualifying asset had not been made.

Capitalization of borrowing costs should commence from the date when the entity first meets all of the following conditions: (i) it incurs expenditures for the asset; (ii) it incurs borrowing costs; and (iii) it undertakes activities that are necessary to prepare the asset for its intended use or sale. However, capitalization of borrowing costs should be suspended during extended periods in which the entity suspends the active development of a qualifying asset. An entity should cease capitalizing borrowing costs when all the activities necessary to prepare the qualifying asset for its intended use or sale are complete.

6.2.5 Property, Plant and Equipment Acquired for a Consolidated Price (Basket Purchases)

Where several assets are purchased for a consolidated price, the consideration is apportioned to the various assets on a fair basis, as determined by competent valuers.

Illustration 6.2 Basket purchases

A company buys a building along with the land on which it is located. The company pays a lump sum amount of Rs. 5,000,000 to the seller. The company wants to apportion the lump sum consideration between land and building. It seeks the advice of an expert valuer. According to the valuer, the cost of land would be Rs. 600,000 and that of the building Rs.5,400,000 if they had been purchased separately. The cost at which the company should record the land and the building in its books of account is determined as given in Table 6.1.

Table 6.1 Allocation of cost of land and building

	Valuer's Estimate (Rs.)	Percentage (%)	Apportioned Cost (Rs.)
Land	600,000	10	500,000
Building	5,400,000	90	4,500,000
Total	6,000,000	100	5,000,000

6.2.6 Assets Acquired in Exchange

When an item of property, plant and equipment is acquired in exchange for another asset, its cost is measured at fair value, provided: (a) the exchange transaction has commercial substance or (b) the fair value of either the asset received or the asset given up is reliably measurable.

To determine whether an exchange transaction has commercial value, the extent to which its future cash flows are expected to change as a result of the transaction are considered. An exchange transaction has commercial value if:

1. the configuration (risk, timing and amount) of cash flows of the asset received differs from the configuration of cash flows of the asset transferred; or
2. the change in value of the entity's operations as a result of the exchange (measured by post-tax cash flows) is significant relative to the fair value of the assets exchanged.

The fair value of an asset can be reliably measured if comparable market transactions exist. In other cases, the fair value of an asset is reliably measurable if: (a) the variability in the range of reasonable fair value measurements is not significant for that asset or (b) the probabilities of the various estimates within the range can be reasonably assessed and used when measuring the fair value.

If an entity is able to measure reliably the fair value of either the asset received or the asset given up, then the fair value of the asset given up is used to measure the cost of the asset received unless the fair value of the asset received is clearly evident.

It may also be appropriate to consider the fair market value of the asset acquired if this is clearly evident. Fair market value is the price that would be agreed to in an open and unrestricted market between knowledgeable and willing parties dealing at arm's length who are fully informed and are not under any compulsion to transact.

An alternative accounting treatment that is sometimes used for an exchange of assets, particularly similar assets, is to record the asset acquired at the net book value of the asset given up. In each case, an adjustment is made for any balancing receipt or payment of cash or other consideration.

When a fixed asset is acquired in exchange for shares or other securities in the enterprise, it is usually recorded at its fair market value, or the fair market value of the securities issued, whichever is clearly evident.

6.2.7 Expenditure on Repairs and Improvements

Expenditure on normal repairs is not added to the cost of property, plant and equipment. Only expenditure that increases the future benefits from the existing asset beyond its previously assessed standard of performance is included in the gross book value, for example, an increase in capacity. The cost of an addition or extension to an existing asset, which is of a capital nature and which becomes an integral part of the existing asset, is usually added to its gross book value.

6.2.8 Property, Plant and Equipment Acquired on Hire Purchase Basis

In the case of assets acquired on hire purchase terms, although the legal ownership does not vest in the enterprise, such assets are recorded at their cash value, which, if not readily available, is calculated by assuming an appropriate rate of interest. They are shown in the balance sheet, with an appropriate narration to indicate that the enterprise does not have full ownership thereof.

6.2.9 Property, Plant and Equipment Acquired Jointly with Others

Where an enterprise owns assets jointly with others (otherwise than as a partner in a firm), the extent of its share in such assets, the proportion in the original cost, accumulated depreciation and written-down value (WDV) are stated in the balance sheet. Alternatively, the *pro rata* cost of such jointly owned assets is grouped together with similar fully owned assets. Details of such jointly owned assets are indicated separately in the fixed assets register.

6.3 Revaluation of Property, Plant and Equipment

An entity can choose either the cost model or the revaluation model as its accounting policy, and apply the policy to an entire class of property, plant and equipment.

Under the cost model, an item of property, plant and equipment is carried at its cost minus any accumulated depreciation and any accumulated impairment loss.

Under the revaluation model, the asset is carried at a revalued amount, being its fair value at the date of the revaluation minus accumulated depreciation and accumulated impairment loss. Revaluations are to be made with sufficient regularity to ensure that the carrying amount does not differ materially from the fair value at the end of the reporting period.

The items within a class of property, plant and equipment are revalued simultaneously to avoid selective revaluation of assets and the reporting of amounts in the financial statements that are a combination of costs and values at different dates.

A class of property, plant and equipment is a grouping of assets of a similar nature and use in an entity's operations. The following are examples of separate classes: (a) land; (b) land and buildings; (c) machinery; (d) ships; (e) aircraft; (f) motor vehicles; (g) furniture and fixtures; (h) office equipment and (i) bearer plants.

If an asset's carrying amount is increased as a result of a revaluation, the increase is credited to equity under the heading of revaluation surplus. However, if an increase reverses a previous revaluation decrease in the same asset and that decrease was recognized in profit or loss, the increase shall be recognized in profit or loss.

If an asset's carrying amount is decreased as a result of a revaluation, the decrease shall be recognized in profit or loss. However, the decrease shall be charged to revaluation surplus if there is any credit balance existing in the revaluation surplus in respect of that asset.

The revalued amounts of fixed assets are presented in financial statements either by restating both the gross book value and accumulated depreciation so as to give a net book value equal to the net revalued amount, or by restating the net book value by adding therein the net increase on account of revaluation.

On revaluation of a class of assets, the net book value of that class cannot be greater than the recoverable amount of assets of that class. The net book value is the gross book value net of accumulated depreciation.

Illustration 6.3 Revaluation of property, plant and equipment

A company purchased a plant on April 1, 2009 for Rs. 10 million with an estimated useful life of 10 years, and depreciated it using the straight-line method. On April 1, 2014, valuation by experts suggested that the current purchase price of a similar plant is Rs. 15 million. The company decided to revalue the plant on April 1, 2014. The amount the company will transfer to the revaluation surplus and the depreciation expense for the financial year 2014–15 is determined as follows:

	(Rs.)
Cost	10,000,000
Less: Accumulated depreciation (Rs. 10,000,000 × 5/10)	5,000,000
Written-down value	5,000,000
Current value	15,000,000
Less: Accumulated depreciation (Rs. 15,000,000 × 5/10)	7,500,000
Written-down value	7,500,000

The company will debit Rs. 5,000,000 (15,000,000 – 10,000,000) to the plant account, credit Rs. 2,500,000 (7,500,000 – 5,000,000) to the accumulated depreciation account and credit Rs. 2,500,000 (7,500,000 – 5,000,000) to the revaluation surplus.

The depreciation expense for the year 2014–15 will be Rs. 1,500,000 (Rs. 7,500,000/5).

6.4 Retirements and Disposals

An item of property, plant and equipment is eliminated from the financial statements on disposal. Items of property, plant and equipment that have been retired from active use and are held for disposal are stated at the lower of their net book value and net realizable value, and are shown separately in the financial statements. Any expected loss is recognized immediately in the profit and loss statement.

In historical cost financial statements, gains or losses arising on disposal are generally recognized in the profit and loss statement.

On disposal of a previously revalued item of fixed asset, the difference between the net disposal proceeds and the net book value is normally charged or credited to the profit and loss statement except that, to the extent such a loss is related to an increase which was previously recorded as a credit to the revaluation reserve and which has not been subsequently reversed or utilized, it is charged directly to that account. The amount standing in revaluation reserve following the retirement or disposal of an asset which relates to that asset may be transferred to the general reserve.

Illustration 6.4 Disposal of property, plant and equipment

A logistics company sold a car for Rs. 250,000. The company had purchased the car 3 years back for Rs. 1,000,000 and had depreciated it using the diminishing balance method, assuming its useful life to be 5 years and a residual value of Rs. 77,760. The gain or loss on sale is calculated as follows:

	(Rs.)
Original cost	1,000,000
Rate of written-down value depreciation = $1 - (77{,}760/1{,}000{,}000)^{(1/5)}$ = 0.40 or 40%	
Depreciation for year 1 = Rs. 1,000,000 × 40%	400,000
Depreciation for year 2 = (Rs. 1,000,000 – 400,000) × 40%	240,000
Depreciation for year 3 = (Rs. 1,000,000 – 400,000 – 240,000) × 40%	144,000
Accumulated depreciation year 3 = (400,000 + 240,000 + 144,000)	784,000
Book value at the end of year 3 = (Rs. 1,000,000 – 784,000)	216,000
Selling price	250,000
Profit on sale (Rs. 250,000 – 216,000)	34,000

6.4.1 Tax Treatment of Profit/Loss on Disposal

Under the Income Tax Act, 1961, fixed assets are grouped into blocks. A block of asset is a group of assets that have the same depreciation rates within the asset classes of buildings, furniture, machinery and plant, ships and intangible assets. A company need not, therefore, keep a record of each item of asset. All additions and disposals are adjusted within the block of assets.

For tax purposes, a profit on disposal of an asset will arise only when the sale proceeds from the asset are more than the depreciable amount of the block to which the asset belongs. A loss will arise only when the entire block is disposed off and the sale proceeds from disposal are less than the depreciable amount of the block.

6.5 Depreciation

Depreciation is defined as the diminution in the value or utility of an asset, due to natural wear and tear, exhaustion of the subject matter, effluxion of time, accident and obsolescence through technology and market changes.

It is essential to calculate depreciation on assets to accurately determine the profit or loss made by a business because the loss in value of an asset for carrying on a business is an essential element of business expenditure. Further, the true financial position of a business can be ascertained only when the value of fixed assets is adjusted for depreciation. Depreciation also draws attention to the fact that a certain amount should be retained by a business out of the gross revenue, for replacement of assets used up in the course of business. It should be noted, however, that depreciation by itself does not create funds required for replacement of assets, simply because it is a non-cash expense and does not require any cash outflow.

Depreciation accounting involves allocation of the depreciable amount of an asset on a systematic basis over its useful life. The *useful life* is (a) the period over which an asset is expected to be available by an entity; or (b) the number of production or similar units expected to be obtained from the asset by an entity.

Depreciable amount of an asset is its cost minus the residual value.

The *residual value* of an asset is the estimated amount that an entity would obtain from the disposal of the asset, after deducting the estimated costs of disposal, if the asset were already of the age and in the condition expected at the end of its useful life.

The residual value and the useful life of an asset should be reviewed at each financial year-end, and if expectations differ from previous estimates, the change(s) should be accounted for as a change in an accounting estimate.

The following factors are considered in determining the useful life of an asset:

1. **Expected usage of the asset.** Usage is assessed with reference to the asset's expected capacity or physical output.
2. **Expected physical wear and tear,** which depends on operational factors such as the number of shifts for which the asset is to be used and the repair and maintenance program, and the care and maintenance of the asset while idle.
3. **Technical or commercial obsolescence** arising from changes or improvements in production, or from a change in the market demand for the product or service output of the asset.
4. Legal or similar limits on the use of the asset, such as the expiry dates of related leases.

Depreciation is recognized even if the fair value of the asset exceeds its carrying amount, as long as the asset's residual value does not exceed its carrying amount. The residual value of an asset may increase to an amount equal to or greater than the asset's carrying amount. If it does, the asset's depreciation charge is zero unless and until its residual value subsequently decreases to an amount below the asset's carrying amount.

Depreciation of an asset begins when it is available for use, that is, when it is in the location and condition necessary for it to be capable of operating in the manner intended by the management. Depreciation of an asset ceases when it is classified as held for sale (or included in a disposal group that is classified as held for sale). Therefore, depreciation does not cease when the asset becomes idle or is retired from active use unless the asset is fully depreciated. However, under usage methods of depreciation the depreciation charge can be zero while there is no production.

Except for some land assets such as quarries and landfill sites, land has an indefinite life. It is, therefore, not depreciated. However, building property has a limited useful life and is, therefore, depreciated. It becomes necessary to treat land and buildings as separate assets, and to segregate the cost of acquisition of land and buildings whenever these are purchased by paying a single sum.

6.6 Depreciation Methods

A variety of depreciation methods can be used to allocate the depreciable amount of an asset on a systematic basis over its useful life. The depreciation method used shall reflect the pattern in which the asset's future economic benefits are expected to be consumed by the entity. These methods include the straight-line method, the diminishing balance method, sum of the years' digits method and the units of production method.

6.6.1 Straight-Line Method

According to this method, an equal amount is provided every year during the useful life of an asset so as to reduce the cost of the asset to zero or to its residual value at the end of its useful life.

$$\text{Straight-line depreciation} = \frac{\text{Cost of an asset} - \text{Residual value}}{\text{Useful life of the asset}}$$

Illustration 6.5 Straight-line depreciation

Suppose an asset costs Rs. 105,000, has a useful life of 10 years and a residual value of Rs. 5,000 at the end of 5 years. The depreciation to be charged every year using the straight-line method will be Rs. 20,000 determined as follows:

$$\text{Straight-line depreciation} = \frac{105{,}000 - 5{,}000}{5} = \text{Rs. } 20{,}000$$

The depreciation schedule shown in Table 6.2 presents the year-wise depreciation expense, end-of year accumulated depreciation and end-of-year book value of the asset.

Table 6.2 Depreciation schedule: straight-line method

Year	Cost (Rs.)	Annual Depreciation (Rs.)	Year-end Accumulated Depreciation (Rs.)	Year-end Book Value (Rs.)
1	105,000	20,000	20,000	85,000
2	105,000	20,000	40,000	65,000
3	105,000	20,000	60,000	45,000
4	105,000	20,000	80,000	25,000
5	105,000	20,000	100,000	5,000

The straight-line depreciation schedule is graphically shown in Figure 6.1. The annual depreciation over the years is a horizontal straight line.

Straight-line depreciation results in a constant charge over the useful life if the asset's residual value does not change. It is based on the assumption that the asset provides equal utility every year over its lifetime and entails an equal amount of expense every year. This may, however, not hold in all cases. The asset capacity used may vary from year to year and the expense of maintenance and repair may become higher as the asset becomes old. This method is suitable for assets whose wear and tear does not depend on its usage, for example, office furniture, buildings, warehouses, etc.

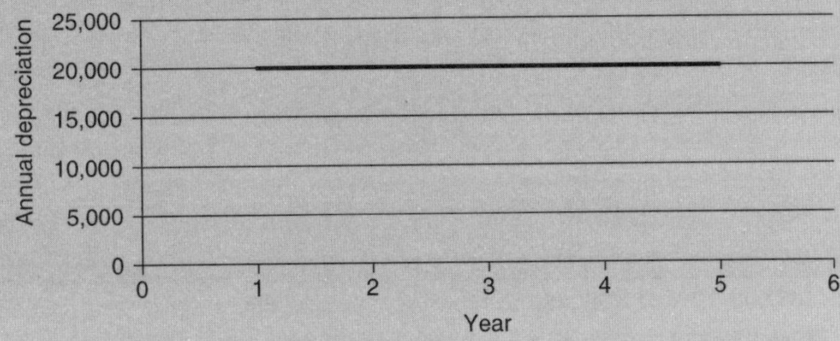

Figure 6.1 Straight-line depreciation.

6.6.2 Diminishing Balance (Written-Down Value) Method

According to this method, a fixed percentage of the diminishing value of the asset is charged as depreciation each year so as to reduce the asset to its residual value at the end of its useful life. This is an accelerated method of charging depreciation as the depreciation charge is higher during the initial years of the life of the asset and it decreases from year to year. The rate of depreciation using this method can be determined using the following formula:

$$\text{Depreciation rate} = 1 - n\sqrt{\frac{\text{Residual value}}{\text{Original cost}}}$$

where n is the useful life in years.

Managers choose the declining balance method when they think that the utility of the asset is likely to decline with time or the asset is likely to lose value due to technological changes.

The charge to revenue in this method is uniform from year to year as depreciation is higher in initial years but expenses on repairs and maintenance is lower. In the later years, the charge for depreciation is lower but the expense on repairs and maintenance is higher. However, in this method, the value of the asset can never be completely extinguished even after writing off all the installments with the result that over the life of the asset, full depreciation may not be provided.

Under the tax laws, companies are allowed to use only the WDV method as the motive is to provide incentive to businesses to recover their investment in an accelerated manner and to quickly replace the assets.

Illustration 6.6 Diminishing balance (written-down value) depreciation

Using the information as provided in Illustration 6.5, the WDV depreciation rate is found to be 45.61%, and is calculated as follows:

$$\text{Depreciation rate} = 1 - \sqrt[5]{\frac{5{,}000}{105{,}000}} = 0.4560 \text{ or } 45.60\%$$

The corresponding depreciation schedule is given in Table 6.3.

Table 6.3 Depreciation schedule: diminishing balance method

Year	Cost (Rs.)	Annual Depreciation (Rs.)	Year-end Accumulated Depreciation (Rs.)	Year-end Book Value (Rs.)
1	105,000	47,880	47,880	57,120
2	105,000	26,047	73,927	31,073
3	105,000	14,169	88,096	16,904
4	105,000	7,708	95,804	9,196
5	105,000	4,193	99,997	5,003*

*Different from Rs. 5,000 due to rounding off of the depreciation rate.

The WDV depreciation schedule is graphically shown in Figure 6.2. The graph is a downward sloping curve, indicating decreasing amounts of annual depreciation over the years.

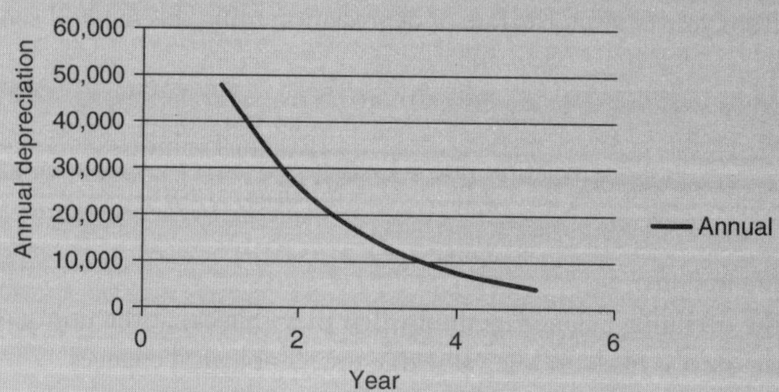

Figure 6.2 Written-down value depreciation.

6.6.3 Sum of the Years' Digits Method

Like the WDV method, the sum of the years' digits method is an accelerated method of charging depreciation. The depreciation charge is higher in the initial years of the life of an asset. According to this method, the fraction of the asset's cost minus the residual value, which is charged as depreciation every year, is determined by using the following formula:

$$\text{Fraction of the asset's cost minus the residual value} = \frac{\text{The number of years of remaining life of the asset (including the present year)}}{\text{Sum of all digits of the life of the asset (in years)}}$$

For example, if the estimated life of an asset is 5 years; the sum of all the digits from 1 to 5 is 15. In the first year, the depreciation charged will be 5/15 of the asset's cost minus the residual value; in the second year the fraction will be 4/15 and so on.

This method is a variation of the diminishing balance method and has the same advantages and limitations as that of the diminishing balance method. However, this method is not being currently followed in India.

Illustration 6.7 Sum of the Years' Digits depreciation

Considering Illustration 6.5, the annual depreciation for each of the 5 years will be as follows:

$$\text{Depreciation for year } 1 = \text{Rs. } 100{,}000 \times 5/15 = \text{Rs. } 33{,}333$$
$$\text{Depreciation for year } 2 = \text{Rs. } 100{,}000 \times 4/15 = \text{Rs. } 26{,}667$$
$$\text{Depreciation for year } 3 = \text{Rs. } 100{,}000 \times 3/15 = \text{Rs. } 20{,}000$$
$$\text{Depreciation for year } 4 = \text{Rs. } 100{,}000 \times 2/15 = \text{Rs. } 13{,}333$$
$$\text{Depreciation for year } 5 = \text{Rs. } 100{,}000 \times 1/15 = \text{Rs. } 6{,}667$$

The depreciation schedule under the sum of the years' digits method is given in Table 6.4.

Table 6.4 Depreciation schedule: sum of the years' digits method

Year	Cost (Rs.)	Annual Depreciation (Rs.)	Year-end Accumulated Depreciation (Rs.)	Year-end Book Value (Rs.)
1	105,000	33,333	33,333	71,667
2	105,000	26,667	60,000	45,000
3	105,000	20,000	80,000	25,000
4	105,000	13,333	93,333	11,667
5	105,000	6,667	100,000	5,000

The sum of the years' depreciation schedule is shown in Figure 6.3. The graph is a linear downward sloping curve, indicating an equal decrease in the amount of annual depreciation every year.

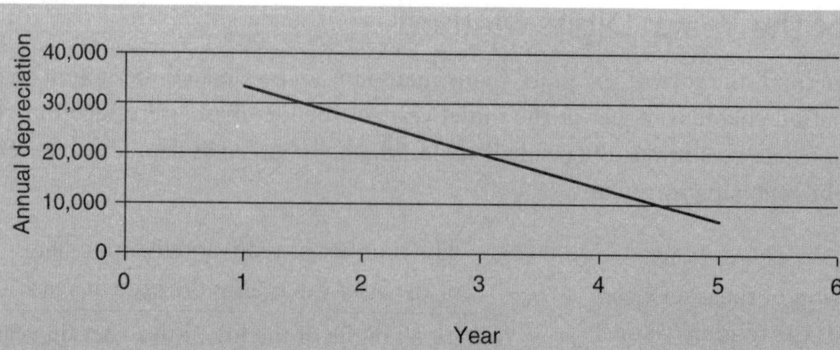

Figure 6.3 Sum of the years' digits depreciation.

6.6.4 Production Units Method

According to the production units method, the useful life of an asset is expressed in terms of the total units of production or the expected use of the asset. Using this method, depreciation is charged on the basis of the number of units produced during a period. The per unit depreciation rate is calculated on the basis of estimated total production. This method is well-suited to factory machinery. The life of the machinery can be expressed either in terms of units of production or in terms of machine hours. The method can also be used for delivery vehicles (miles driven) and airplanes (flying hours). Depreciation for a period, using this method, is calculated as:

$$\text{Depreciation for the period} = \text{Depreciable amount} \times \frac{\text{Production for the period/Hours worked}}{\text{Estimated total production/Total hours}}$$

This method cannot be used for assets such as buildings or furniture because it is difficult to measure activity levels for these assets.

Illustration 6.8 Depreciation using the production unit method

A company acquired a new machine for Rs. 1,000,000 to produce a special product. The useful life of the machine was estimated to be 5 years, after which it was expected to be sold at Rs. 100,000. During its useful life, the machine was expected to produce 90,000 units. The year-wise estimated production is as given in Table 6.5.

Table 6.5 Estimated year-wise production

Year	Production (units)
1	6,250
2	12,500
3	15,000
4	25,000
5	31,250

The year-wise depreciation is calculated as follows:

Depreciation for year 1 = Rs. 900,000 × 6,250/90,000 = Rs. 62,500

Depreciation for year 2 = Rs. 900,000 × 12,500/90,000 = Rs. 125,500

Depreciation for year 3 = Rs. 900,000 × 15,000/90,000 = Rs. 150,000

Depreciation for year 4 = Rs. 900,000 × 25,000/90,000 = Rs. 250,000

Depreciation for year 5 = Rs. 900,000 × 31,250/90,000 = Rs. 312,500

The depreciation schedule under the production unit method is given in Table 6.6.

The units of production depreciation schedule is graphically presented in Figure 6.4. The graph is a linear upward sloping curve that indicates an increase in depreciation expense proportionate to the number of units produced every year.

Table 6.6 Depreciation schedule: production unit method

Year	Cost (Rs.)	Annual Depreciation (Rs.)	Year-end Accumulated Depreciation (Rs.)	Year-end Book Value (Rs.)
1	1,000,000	62,500	62,500	937,500
2	1,000,000	125,000	187,500	812,500
3	1,000,000	150,000	337,500	662,500
4	1,000,000	250,000	587,500	412,500
5	1,000,000	312,500	900,000	100,000

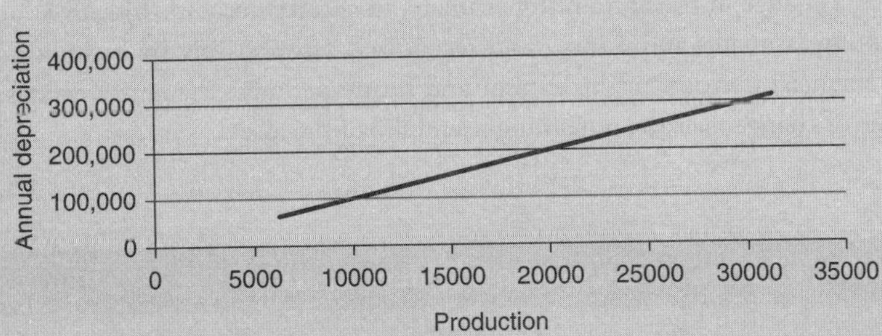

Figure 6.4 Units of production depreciation.

6.6.5 Choice of Method of Depreciation

As discussed, a variety of depreciation methods can be used to allocate the depreciable amount of an asset on a systematic basis during its useful life. The entity should select a method that closely reflects the expected pattern of consumption of the future economic benefits embodied in the asset.

The straight-line method is simple, but it fails to match the cost of consumption of the asset with the revenue when the use of the asset is not uniform over the life of the asset. It may result in the overstatement of profit and the value of the asset in the initial years of the life of the asset when it is used more intensively.

The diminishing balance method is more consistent with the life cycle cost of most assets as depreciation is higher in the initial years but expenses on repairs and maintenance is lower. In the later years, depreciation is lower but the expense on repairs and maintenance is higher. The charge to revenue under this method is uniform from year to year. The units of production method provides for a better matching of costs and revenues for most types of equipment. However, it requires additional record-keeping. In most cases, companies adopt the same method of depreciation as is used by other companies in the same industry.

Thus, the nature of industry, type of equipment, objective of the management are some of the factors that influence the choice of the method of depreciation. Practically, companies may not use the same method of depreciation for all depreciable assets as the following excerpt (Exhibit 6.1) from the annual report of Grasim Industries for the year 2013–14 shows.

Exhibit 6.1

Grasim Industries: Accounting Policies for Depreciation

"Depreciation/Amortization charge is provided on fixed assets on written-down-value method in respect of fixed assets of Viscose Staple Fibre Division (excluding Power Plants), Nagda, Engineering Division, Nagda, and Corporate Finance Division, Mumbai, and on Straight-line Method in respect of other assets."

6.6.6 Change in the Method of Depreciation

The depreciation method applied to an asset should be reviewed at least at each financial year-end. If there has been a significant change in the expected pattern of consumption of the future economic benefits embodied in the asset, the method should be changed to reflect the changed pattern. Such a change should be accounted for as a change in the accounting estimate, in accordance with Ind AS 8 "accounting policies changes in accounting estimates and errors," and recognized prospectively by including it in the financial performance and financial position in the current and future periods. The entity expenses the depreciable amount at the time of change over the remaining useful life of the asset.

Illustration 6.9 Change in the method of depreciation

A company bought a truck for Rs. 2,500,000. It estimated its useful life as 8 years and a residual value of Rs. 250,000. The company followed the straight-line method of depreciation for the first 4 years and then decided to change the depreciation method to diminishing value. The depreciation that the company will charge in the fifth year, assuming there is no change in the residual value, is calculated below.

Depreciable amount (Rs. 2,500,000 – Rs. 250,000)	Rs. 2,250,000
Annual straight-line depreciation (Rs. 2,250,000/8)	281,250
Accumulated depreciation for 4 years (Rs. 281,250 × 4)	1,125,000

Written-down value at the end of 4 years (Rs. 2,250,000 – 1,125,000)	1,125,000
Rate of written-down value depreciation $[1 - (250{,}000/1{,}125{,}000)^{0.25}]$	31.34%
Depreciation charge for the fifth year (1,125,000 × 31.34%)	352,575

Some instances of the statements contained in the financial statements of companies that have changed the method of depreciation are given in Exhibit 6.2.

Exhibit 6.2

Accounting for Change in the Method of Depreciation

Jet Airways' unaudited results for the quarter ended June 30 2008 state *"Depreciation on Narrow Body Aircraft was hitherto provided on Written-Down Value Method. Based on the usage of such Aircraft, the industry practice followed in domestic and international markets, the Company, in order to reflect a more appropriate preparation/presentation of financial statements, has changed the method of depreciation on such Aircraft to Straight Line Method and the surplus arising from retrospective computation aggregating Rs. 92,377 lac (excluding adjustment to revaluation reserve) has been accounted and disclosed under Exceptional Item. Consequently, charge on account of depreciation for the current quarter is lower by Rs. 3,472 lac."*

Cairn India Limited's unaudited results for the quarter ended on June 30, 2014 contains the note: *"With the implementation of Schedule II of the Companies Act 2013 from 1 April 2014, the Company has changed the method of depreciation on some of its oil and gas assets from 'Straight Line' method to the 'Unit of Production' method so as to be in compliance with the requirements of 'Guidance Note on Accounting for Oil and Gas Producing Activities (Revised 2013)' issued by the Institute of Chartered Accountants of India. As prescribed under Accounting Standard 6, 'Depreciation Accounting', the change has been made with retrospective effect and the additional charge due to the same for the period up to 31 March 2014, net of tax credit of 227.08 crores, has been disclosed as an exceptional item. Further, the depreciation charge for the current quarter is higher and the profit after tax is lower by 47.26 crores and 31.20 crores, respectively due to the aforementioned change."*

6.6.7 Component Depreciation

One of the main features of the Companies Act, 2013 relates to the provision of component-wise depreciation. Each part of an item of property, plant and equipment with a cost that is significant in relation to the total cost of the item shall be depreciated separately. For example, it may be appropriate to depreciate separately the chassis and engine of a bus, whether owned or subject to a finance lease. This is because the chassis is expected to have a relatively longer life than that of the engine. Some parts may be grouped in determining the depreciation charge when these have the same useful lives and depreciation methods.

6.6.8 Revisions in the Useful Life and Residual Value

An entity needs to review the estimated useful life and residual value of an asset on each reporting date. The estimates may change due to new developments such as unexpected changes in technology or damage to the asset. Such a change shall be accounted for as a change in the accounting estimate, in accordance with Ind AS 8 "Accounting Policies, Changes in Accounting Estimates and Errors", to be recognized prospectively by including it in the financial performance and financial position in the current and future periods. The entity expenses the depreciable amount at the time of change over the remaining useful life of the asset.

Exhibit 6.3

Indian Hotels Company Limited: Revision in Useful Lives of Tangible Assets

The audited results of the Indian Hotels Company Limited for the quarter ended on June 30, 2014 state *"During the quarter ended June 30, 2014, the Company has reassessed the useful lives of its tangible fixed assets. On and from April 1, 2014, the revised useful lives, as assessed by Management, match those specified in Part C of Schedule II to the Companies Act, 2013, for all classes of assets, other than end-user computers, electrical installation and equipment, plant and machinery and select items of furniture. Management believes that the revised useful lives of the assets reflect the periods over which these assets are to be used. As a result of the change, the change on account of Depreciation for the quarter ended June 30, 2014, is lower by Rs. 18 lakhs as compared to the useful lives estimated in earlier periods."*

Illustration 6.10 Revision in the useful life and residual value

On April 1, 2015, XYZ Ltd. decided to change the estimated useful lives and residual values of some depreciable assets as given in Table 6.7.

Table 6.7 Old and proposed useful lives and residual values of depreciable assets

Asset	Date of Acquistion	Cost (Rs.)	Accumulated Depreciation	Useful Life (years)		Residual Value (Rs.)	
			31.3.2015	Old	Proposed	Old	Proposed
Building	1.4.2007	35,000,000	6,500,000	40	48	2,500,000	1,750,000
Equipment	1.4.2010	6,000,000	1,150,000	25	20	250,000	1,800,000

The company follows the straight-line method of depreciation. The depreciation expense for the year 2015 is calculated based on new values.

Type of Asset

	Building (Rs.)	Equipment (Rs.)
Cost	35,000,000	6,000,000
Less: Accumulated depreciation	6,500,000	1,150,000

(Continued)

	Building (Rs.)	Equipment (Rs.)
Book value, 1/4/15	28,500,000	4,850,000
Less: Salvage value	1,750,000	180,000
Depreciable cost (1)	26,750,000	4,670,000
Revised remaining useful life in years (2)	40*	15**
	*(48 – 8)	**(20 – 5)
Revised annual depreciation (1) ÷ (2)	668,750	311,333

6.6.9 Treatment of Depreciation Charge in Accounts

The depreciation charge for each period shall be recognized in profit or loss. However, sometimes, the future economic benefits embodied in an asset are absorbed in producing other assets. In this case, the depreciation charge constitutes part of the cost of the other asset and is included in its carrying amount. For example, the depreciation of manufacturing plant and equipment is included in the costs of conversion of inventories. Similarly, depreciation of property, plant and equipment used for development activities may be included in the cost of an intangible asset.

6.6.10 Legal Provisions Relating to Depreciation

6.6.10.1 Under the Companies Law

Schedule XIV of the Companies Act, 1956 specified the minimum rates of depreciation to be provided by a company. However, Schedule II of the Companies Act, 2013 requires systematic allocation of the depreciable amount of an asset over its useful life. It specifies the useful life and residual value of various tangible assets. For this purpose, Schedule II divides companies into two categories:

1. For a prescribed class of companies, the useful lives should normally be in accordance with the schedule. However, if a prescribed company uses a different useful life, it should disclose a justification for doing so. The prescribed class of companies includes those whose financial statements are required to comply with accounting standards prescribed under Companies Act, 2013.
2. For other companies, the useful life and the residual value applied should not be higher than that specified in Schedule II.

The residual value of an asset is often insignificant, but it should generally be not more than 5% of the original cost of the asset.

Useful lives of important assets are provided in Table 6.8.

Table 6.8 Useful lives of assets under the Companies Act, 2013

Nature of Assets	Useful Life (Years)
Buildings	
Buildings (other than factory buildings) RCC frame structure	60

(Continued)

Table 6.8 (Continued)

Nature of Assets	Useful Life (Years)
Buildings (other than factory buildings) other than RCC frame structure	30
Factory buildings	30
Others (including temporary structure, etc.)	3
Plant and Machinery	
Plant and machinery other than continuous process plant not covered under specific industries	15
Continuous process plant for which no special rate has been prescribed	8
Plant and machinery used in mines and quarries	8
Refineries	25
Pipelines	30
Plant and machinery used in generation, transmission and distribution of power (other than wind power)	40
Wind power generation plant	22
Plant and machinery used in the manufacture of pharmaceuticals and chemicals	20
Plant and machinery used in salt works	15
Furniture and fittings	
General furniture and fittings	10
Furniture and fittings used in hotels, restaurants and boarding houses, schools, colleges and other educational institutions, libraries; welfare centers; meeting halls, cinema houses; theatres and circuses; and furniture and fittings let out on hire for use on the occasion of marriages and similar functions.	8
Motor Vehicles	
Motor cycles, scooters and other mopeds	10
Motor buses, motor lorries, motor cars and motor taxies used in a business of running them on hire	6
Motor buses, motor lorries and motor cars other than those used in a business of running them on hire, motor tractors, harvesting combines and heavy vehicles, electrically operated vehicles including battery powered or fuel cell powered vehicles	8
Aircraft or Helicopters	20

Depreciation on Assets Used for a Part of the Financial Year

Where, during any financial year, any addition has been made to any asset, or where any asset has been sold, discarded, demolished or destroyed, depreciation shall be calculated on such assets on a *pro rata* basis from the date of such addition or, as the case may be, up to the date on which such asset has been sold, discarded, demolished or destroyed.

Disclosures

Companies are required to disclose the depreciation methods used and the useful lives of assets for computing depreciation, if they are different from the life specified in Schedule II.

Useful Life for Parts

The useful life specified in Schedule II is for the whole asset. Where cost of a part of the asset is significant to the total cost of the asset and useful life of that part is different from the useful life of the remaining asset, useful life of that significant part shall be determined separately.

Extra-Shift Depreciation

The useful lives of assets used on a shift-basis have been specified in the schedule based on their single shift working. Except for assets in respect of which no extra shift depreciation (NESD) is permitted, if an asset is used for any time during the year for double shift, the depreciation will increase by 50% for that period and in case of the triple shift the depreciation shall be calculated on the basis of 100% for that period.

6.6.10.2 Under the Income-Tax Laws

The Income Tax Act, 1961 allows companies to claim depreciation on WDV at the prescribed rates. While companies compute depreciation for financial reporting purposes using rates of depreciation prescribed by Company Law, they can use higher rates of depreciation provided under the Tax Laws to compute their taxable income. Higher rates of depreciation are generally allowed under the tax laws to provide an incentive for more investment in businesses (Table 6.9).

Table 6.9 Rates of depreciation under the Income Tax Act, 1961

Block of Assets	Rate of Depreciation % (WDV)
Building	
General	5
Purely temporary erections such as wooden structures	100
Furniture and Fittings	10
Machinery and Plant	
General	15
Motor cars	15
Aeroplanes	40
Containers made of glass or plastic used as re-fills	50
Books	100
Ships	20
Intangible Assets	
Know-how, patents, copyrights, trademarks, licenses, franchises or any other business or commercial rights of similar nature	25

6.7 Impairment of Assets

Impairment of assets is a sudden or unexpected decline in the expected future benefits from an asset such as factory, vehicle or property. This might result from physical damage to the asset, changes in law or obsolescence resulting from technological innovation. Impairment is different from depreciation. Depreciation accounting involves allocation of the depreciable amount of an asset on a systematic basis over its useful life.

According to Ind AS 36 "Impairment of assets", an *impairment loss* is the amount by which the carrying amount of an asset or a cash-generating unit exceeds its recoverable amount. The *recoverable amount* of an asset or a cash-generating unit is the higher of its fair value minus costs to sell and its value in use. *Fair value minus costs to sell* is the amount that can be obtained from the sale of an asset or cash-generating unit in an arm's length transaction between knowledgeable, willing parties, minus the costs of disposal. *Value in use* is the present value of future cash flows expected to be derived from an asset or cash-generating unit.

A *cash-generating unit* is the smallest identifiable group of assets that generates cash inflows that are largely independent of cash inflows from other assets or groups of assets. For example, a mining entity owns a private railway to support its mining activities. The private railway could be sold only for a scrap value as it does not generate cash inflows that are largely independent of cash inflows from other assets of the mine. Therefore, the entity estimates the recoverable amount of the cash-generating unit to which the private railway belongs, that is, the mine as a whole.

An entity is required to assess at the end of each reporting period whether there is any indication that an asset may be impaired. If any such indication exists, the entity shall estimate the recoverable amount of the asset. If it is not possible to estimate the recoverable amount of the individual asset, an entity shall determine the recoverable amount of the cash-generating unit to which the asset belongs (the asset's cash-generating unit). In assessing whether there is any indication that an asset may be impaired, an entity shall consider both external and internal sources of information.

External sources of information include significant decline in market value; significant adverse change in technology, market, economic or legal environment; increase in market interest rates and market capitalization of the entity falling below the carrying amount of the net assets of the entity. Internal sources of information include evidence of obsolescence or physical damage of an asset; the asset becoming idle, plans to discontinue or restructure the operation to which an asset belongs, plans to dispose of an asset before the previously expected date and reassessing the useful life of an asset as finite rather than indefinite; and internal reports showing that the economic performance of an asset is, or will be, worse than expected.

If the recoverable amount of an asset is less than its carrying amount, the carrying amount of the asset shall be reduced to its recoverable amount. This reduction is an impairment loss. An impairment loss shall be recognized immediately in profit or loss, unless the asset is carried at a revalued amount After the recognition of an impairment loss, the depreciation (amortization) charge for the asset shall be adjusted in future periods to allocate the asset's revised carrying amount minus its residual value (if any), on a systematic basis over its remaining useful life.

An impairment loss recognized in an earlier period may be reversed in a subsequent period. For this purpose, an entity shall assess at the end of each reporting period whether there is any indication that an impairment loss recognized in prior periods for an asset may no longer exist or may have decreased. If any such indication exists, the entity shall estimate the recoverable amount of that asset and recognize a reversal of an impairment loss in profit or loss, unless the asset is carried at a revalued amount.

6.8 Intangible Assets

Ind AS 26 "Intangible Assets" and Ind AS 38 "Intangible Assets" contain provisions relating to accounting of intangible assets. Intangible assets are distinguished as those assets that are purchased and acquired in a business combination, generated internally, and received as government grants.

6.8.1 Definition of Intangible Asset

An intangible asset is an identifiable non-monetary asset without physical substance. Monetary assets are money held and assets to be received in fixed or determinable amounts of money. The definition of an intangible asset requires an intangible asset to be identifiable to distinguish it from goodwill.

An asset is identifiable if it either: (a) is separable, i.e. is capable of being separated or divided from the entity and sold, transferred, licensed, rented or exchanged, either individually or together with a related contract, identifiable asset or liability, regardless of whether the entity intends to do so; or (b) arises from contractual or other legal rights, regardless of whether those rights are transferable or separable from the entity or from other rights and obligations.

Entities frequently expend resources, or incur liabilities, on the acquisition, development, maintenance or enhancement of intangible resources such as scientific or technical knowledge, design and implementation of new processes or systems, licences, intellectual property, market knowledge and trademarks (including brand names and publishing titles). Common examples of items encompassed by these broad headings are computer software, patents, copyrights, motion picture films, customer lists, mortgage servicing rights, fishing licences, import quotas, franchises, customer or supplier relationships, customer loyalty, market share and marketing rights.

Any item listed above is considered an intangible asset only when it satisfies the definition of an intangible asset. Otherwise, expenditure to acquire it or generate it internally is recognised as an expense when it is incurred. However, if the item is acquired in a business combination and cannot be recognized as an intangible asset, it forms part of the goodwill recognised at the acquisition date.

Schedule III of the Companies Act, 2013 requires the following classification of intangible assets to be presented in a company's balance sheet:

1. Goodwill
2. Brands/trademarks
3. Computer software
4. Mastheads and publishing titles
5. Mining rights
6. Copyrights, patents and other intellectual property rights, services and operating rights
7. Recipes, formulae, models, designs and prototypes
8. Licenses and franchise
9. Others (specify nature)

6.8.2 Recognition of Intangible Assets

An intangible asset is recognised if and only if: (a) it is probable that the expected future economic benefits that are attributable to the asset will flow to the entity and (b) the cost of the asset can be measured reliably.

The future economic benefits flowing from an intangible asset may include revenue from the sale of products or services, cost savings, or other benefits resulting from the use of the asset by the entity. For example, the use of intellectual property in a production process may reduce future production costs rather than increase future revenues. The following is an example of policy relating to recognition of intangibles:

> *"Cost of Right of Way for laying pipelines is capitalised as Intangible Asset and is amortised over a period of 99 years. Technical know-how or licence fee relating to production process and process design are recognized as Intangible Assets. Cost of Software directly identified with hardware is capitalised along with the cost of hardware. Application software is capitalised as Intangible Asset."*
>
> (Source: Hindustan Petroleum Corporation Limited Annual Report 2015–16)

6.8.3 Measurement of Intangible Assets

An intangible asset is to be measured initially at cost. This cost comprises: (a) its purchase price, including import duties and non-refundable purchase taxes, after deducting trade discounts and rebates; and (b) any directly attributable cost of preparing the asset for its intended use. Examples of directly attributable costs are: (a) costs of employee benefits arising directly from bringing the asset to its working condition; (b) professional fees arising directly from bringing the asset to its working condition; and (c) costs of testing whether the asset is functioning properly.

If an intangible asset is acquired in a business combination, the cost of that intangible asset is its fair value at the acquisition date.

In some cases, an intangible asset may be acquired free of charge, or for nominal consideration, by way of a government grant. This may happen when a government transfers or allocates to an entity intangible assets such as airport landing rights, licences to operate radio or television stations, import licences or quotas or rights to access other restricted resources. In such a case, an entity recognises both the intangible asset and the grant initially at fair value.

When one or more intangible assets are acquired in exchange for a non-monetary asset or assets, or a combination of monetary and non-monetary assets, the cost of such an intangible asset is measured at fair value.

The cost of an internally generated intangible asset comprises all directly attributable costs necessary to create, produce, and prepare the asset to be capable of operating in the manner intended by management. Examples of directly attributable costs are: (a) costs of materials and services used or consumed in generating the intangible asset; (b) costs of employee benefits arising from the generation of the intangible asset; (c) fees to register a legal right; and (d) amortization of patents and licences that are used to generate the intangible asset. Exhibit 6.4 reports how Reliance India Limited measures its intangible assets.

Exhibit 6.4

Measurement of Intangible Assets

Reliance Industries Limited

Intangible assets are stated at cost of acquisition net of recoverable taxes less accumulated amortization/depletion and impairment loss, if any. The cost comprises purchase price, borrowing costs, and any cost directly attributable to bringing the asset to its working condition for the intended use and net charges on foreign exchange contracts and adjustments arising from exchange rate variations attributable to the intangible assets.

(Source: Reliance Industries Limited Annual Report 2015–16)

Wipro Limited

Intangible assets acquired separately are measured at cost of acquisition. Intangible assets acquired in a business combination are measured at fair value as at the date of acquisition. Following initial recognition, intangible assets are carried at cost less accumulated amortization and impairment losses, if any.

(Source: Wipro Limited Annual Report 2015–16)

Lupin Limited

Intangible assets are carried at cost less accumulated amortization and impairment losses, if any. The cost of an intangible asset comprises its purchase price, including any import duties and other taxes (other than those subsequently recoverable from the taxing authorities), and any directly attributable expenditure on making the asset ready for its intended use.

(Source: Lupin Limited Annual Report 2015–16)

Hindustan Unilever Limited

Intangible assets are stated at acquisition cost, net of accumulated amortization and accumulated impairment losses, if any.

(Source: Hindustan Unilever Limited Annual Report 2015–16)

6.9 Internally Generated Intangible Assets

Internally generated brands, mastheads, publishing titles, customer lists and items similar in substance cannot be recognized as intangible assets. Similarly, internally generated goodwill cannot be recognized as an asset.

6.10 Amortization of Intangible Assets

Amortization means allocation of the depreciable amount of an intangible asset with a finite useful life on a systematic basis over its useful life. Amortization begins when the asset is available for use, i.e. when it is in the location, and when the condition necessary for it to be capable of operating in the manner intended by the management is fulfilled. Amortization ceases at a date earlier than the date the asset is classified as held for sale (or included in a disposal group that is classified as held for sale) in accordance with Ind AS 105 "Non-Current Assets Held for Sale" and the date that the asset is derecognized.

The amortization method used is based on the pattern in which the asset's future economic benefits are expected to be consumed by the entity. If that pattern cannot be determined reliably, the straight-line method is to be used. The amortization charge for each period is recognised in profit or loss unless it is allowed to be included in the carrying amount of another asset. Exhibit 6.5 carries the accounting policies of prominent Indian companies relating to amortization of intangible assets.

Exhibit 6.5

Amortization of Intangible Assets

Hindustan Petroleum Corporation Limited

Intangible assets other than application software and cost of right of way are amortized on a straight line basis over a period of ten years or life of the underlying plant/facility, whichever is earlier.

(Source: Hindustan Petroleum Corporation Limited Annual Report 2015–16)

Reliance Industries Limited

Intangible assets are amortised as follows:

Particulars	Amortization/Depletion
Technical know-how	Over the useful life of the underlying assets
Computer software	Over a period of 5 years
Development rights	Depleted in proportion of oil and gas production achieved vis-a-vis the proved reserves (net of reserves to be retained to cover abandonment costs as per the production sharing contract and the Government of India's share in the reserves, where applicable) considering the estimated future expenditure on developing the reserves as per technical evaluation.
Others	Over the period of agreement of right to use, provided that in case of jetty, the aggregate amount amortised to date is not less than the aggregate rebate availed by the Company.

(Source: Reliance Industries Limited Annual Report 2015–16)

NLC Limited

Computer Software Application Software acquired for an amount more than Rs. 10 lakh are capitalised as intangible assets and amortised over a period of 5 years.

(Source: NLC Limited Annual Report 2015–16)

Hindustan Unilever Limited

Intangible assets are amortised on the straight line basis as per rates mentioned below:

Asset class	
Goodwill	25%
Brands/trademarks	25%
Computer software	20%

(Source: Hindustan Unilever Limited Annual Report 2015–16)

Godrej Consumer Products Limited

Intangible assets are amortised on straight line basis as follows:

1. Software license is amortised over a period of 6 years.
2. SAP licenses acquired pursuant to the Scheme of the Amalgamation of the erstwhile Godrej Household Products Limited (GHPL) with the Company are amortised over a period of 4 years. The cost of SAP licenses incurred for certain subsidiaries are being recovered from respective subsidiaries.
3. Trademarks acquired are amortised equally over the best estimate of their useful life not exceeding a period of 10 years, except in the case of Goodknight, HIT, Kinky, Soft & Gentle and Pamela Grant & Milleofiori brands where the brands are amortised equally over a period of 20 years. In accordance with the Court order approving the Scheme of Amalgamation of the erstwhile GHPL with the Company, an amount equivalent to the amortization of the Goodknight and HIT brands at the end of each financial year is directly debited to the balance in the General Reserve Account.
4. Goodwill is amortised over a period of 5 years.
5. Technical know-how is depreciated over a period of 10 years. Residual value is estimated to be immaterial by management and hence has been considered at Re. 1.

It is estimated that the impact on depreciation and amortization of the difference in expected useful lives between the holding company and subsidiaries is not material.

(Source: Godrej Consumer Products Limited Annual Report 2015–16)

6.11 Useful Life of Intangible Assets

An entity needs to assess whether the useful life of an intangible asset is finite or indefinite and, if finite, the length of, or number of production or similar units constituting, that useful life.

An intangible asset shall be regarded by the entity as having an indefinite useful life when, based on an analysis of all of the relevant factors, there is no foreseeable limit to the period over which the asset is expected to generate net cash inflows for the entity.

An intangible asset with an indefinite useful life cannot be amortised.

The accounting policy of Wipro Limited relating to determination of useful life of intangible assets is shown in Exhibit 6.6.

Exhibit 6.6

Wipro Limited: Determination of Useful Lives of Intangible Assets

The amortization of an intangible asset with a finite useful life reflects the manner in which the economic benefit is expected to be generated and is included in selling and marketing expenses in the consolidated statements of income. The estimated useful life of amortizable intangibles are reviewed and where appropriate are adjusted, annually. The estimated useful lives of the amortizable intangible assets for the current and comparative periods are as follows:

Category	Useful life
Customer-contract intangibles	5 to 10 years
Technical know-how, patents, trademarks and	3 to 10 years

(Source: Wipro Limited Annual Report 2015–16)

6.12 Residual Value of Intangible Assets

The residual value of an intangible asset with a finite useful life is assumed to be zero unless:

1. there is a commitment by a third party to purchase the asset at the end of its useful life or
2. there is an active market for the asset and
   (a) residual value can be determined by reference to that market and
   (b) it is probable that such a market will exist at the end of the asset's useful life.

6.13 Research and Development Expenditure

Research and development activities are directed to the development of knowledge. Research is original and planned investigation undertaken with the prospect of gaining new scientific or technical knowledge and understanding. Development is the application of research findings or other knowledge to a plan or design for the production of new or substantially improved materials, devices, products, processes, systems or services before the start of commercial production or use.

An entity is required to disclose the aggregate amount of research and development expenditure recognised as an expense during the period.

To assess whether an internally generated intangible asset meets the criteria for recognition, an entity classifies the generation of the asset into: (a) a research phase and (b) a development phase.

6.13.1 Research Phase

An entity cannot recognize an intangible asset arising from research (or from the research phase of an internal project). In the research phase of an internal project, an entity cannot demonstrate that an intangible asset exists that will generate probable future economic benefits. Therefore, this expenditure is recognized as an expense when it is incurred. Examples of research activities are:

1. Activities aimed at obtaining new knowledge.
2. The search for, evaluation and final selection of, applications of research findings or other knowledge.
3. The search for alternatives for materials, devices, products, processes, systems or services.
4. The formulation, design, evaluation and final selection of possible alternatives for new or improved materials, devices, products, processes, systems or services.

6.13.2 Development Phase

An intangible asset arising from development (or from the development phase of an internal project) can be recognized if and only if an entity can demonstrate all of the following:

1. The technical feasibility of completing the intangible asset so that it will be available for use or sale.
2. Its intention to complete the intangible asset and use or sell it.
3. Its ability to use or sell the intangible asset.
4. How the intangible asset will generate probable future economic benefits.
5. The availability of adequate technical, financial and other resources to complete the development and to use or sell the intangible asset.
6. Its ability to reliably measure the expenditure attributable to the intangible asset during its development.

In the development phase of an internal project, an entity can, in some instances, identify an intangible asset and demonstrate that the asset will generate probable future economic benefits. This is because the development phase of a project is further advanced than the research phase. Examples of development activities are:

1. The design, construction and testing of pre-production or pre-use prototypes and models.
2. The design of tools, jigs, moulds and dies involving new technology.
3. The design, construction and operation of a pilot plant that is not of a scale economically feasible for commercial production.
4. The design, construction and testing of a chosen alternative for new or improved materials, devices, products, processes, systems or services.

Exhibit 6.7 carries the accounting policies of prominent Indian companies relating to accounting of research and development costs.

Exhibit 6.7

Accounting for Research and Development Costs

Lupin Limited
Expenditure on research and development eligible for capitalization are carried as intangible assets under development where such assets are not yet ready for their intended use.

Research and development: Revenue expenditure pertaining to research is charged to the Consolidated Statement of Profit and Loss. Development costs of products are also charged to the Consolidated Statement of Profit and Loss in the year it is incurred, unless a product's technological feasibility has been established, in which case such expenditure is capitalised. These costs are charged to the respective heads in the Statement of Profit and Loss in the year it is incurred. The amount capitalised comprises of expenditure that can be directly attributed or allocated on a reasonable and consistent basis for creating, producing and making the asset ready for its intended use. Fixed assets utilised for research and development are capitalised and depreciated in accordance with the policies stated for tangible fixed assets and intangible assets.

Expenditure on in-licensed development activities, whereby research findings are applied to a plan or design for the production of new or substantially improved products and processes, is capitalised, if the cost can be reliably measured, the product or process is technically and commercially feasible and the Group has sufficient resources to complete the development and to use and sell the asset.

Impairment of assets: The carrying values of assets/cash generating units at each balance sheet date are reviewed for impairment.

(Source: Lupin Limited Annual Report 2015–16)

NLC Limited

Research and development (internally generated projects):

1. Expenditure incurred during the phase of research is charged to revenue.
2. Expenditure incurred during the phase of development is capitalised with respect to each project and amortised over its useful life.

(Source: NLC Limited Annual Report 2015–16)

Hindustan Unilever Limited

Revenue expenditure pertaining to research is charged to the Statement of Profit and Loss. Development costs of products are also charged to the Statement of Profit and Loss unless a product's technical feasibility and other criteria as set out in paragraph 44 of AS 26 – 'Intangible Assets' have been established, in which case such expenditure is capitalised. The amount capitalised comprises expenditure that can be directly attributed or allocated on a reasonable and consistent basis to creating, producing and making the asset ready for its intended use. Fixed assets utilised for research and development are capitalised and depreciated in accordance with the policies stated for tangible assets.

(Source: Hindustan Unilever Limited Annual Report 2015–16)

6.14 Goodwill

In some cases, expenditure is incurred to generate future economic benefits, but it does not result in the creation of an intangible asset that meets the recognition criteria. Such expenditure is often described as contributing to internally generated goodwill. Internally generated goodwill is not recognised as an asset because it is not an identifiable resource (i.e. it is not separable nor does it arise from contractual or other legal rights) controlled by the entity that can be measured reliably at cost.

Goodwill can be recognised in a business combination. Any item acquired in a business combination that cannot be recognised as an intangible asset forms part of the amount recognised as goodwill at the acquisition date. Goodwill represents the future economic benefits arising from such item. The future economic benefits may result from synergy between the identifiable assets acquired and such items.

Illustration 6.11

Mars Limited places a value of Rs. 2,000,000 on the business of Venus Ltd. It acquires Venus Limited paying a consideration of Rs. 2,000,000. On takeover, the assets and liabilities taken over are valued at Rs.3,000,000 and Rs. 1,200,000, respectively. Based on these values, the net assets are worth Rs. 1,800,000, while the consideration paid is Rs. 2,000,000. The difference of Rs. 2,00,000 is attributable to intangible assets that cannot be recognized. Mars Limited can recognize this amount of Rs. 200,000 as goodwill.

Wipro Limited's policy related to recognition and impairment of goodwill is shown in Exhibit 6.8.

Exhibit 6.8

Wipro Limited: Accounting for Goodwill

The goodwill arising on acquisition of a group of assets is not amortised and is tested for impairment if indicators of impairment exist.

Goodwill is tested for impairment at least annually and when events occur or changes in circumstances indicate that the recoverable amount of the cash generating unit is less than its carrying value. The recoverable amount of cash generating units is higher of value-in-use and fair value less cost to sell. The calculation involves use of significant estimates and assumptions which includes turnover and earnings multiples, growth rates and net margins used to calculate projected future cash flows, risk-adjusted discount rate, future economic and market conditions.

In accounting for business combinations, judgment is required in identifying whether an identifiable intangible asset is to be recorded separately from goodwill. Additionally, estimating the acquisition date fair value of the identifiable assets acquired, and liabilities and contingent consideration involves management judgment. These measurements are based on information available at the acquisition date and are based on expectations and assumptions that have been deemed reasonable by management. Changes in these judgments, estimates, and assumptions can materially affect the results of operations.

Business combinations are accounted for using the purchase (acquisition) method. The cost of an acquisition is measured as the fair value of the assets transferred, liabilities incurred or assumed and equity instruments issued at the date of exchange by the Company. Identifiable assets acquired and liabilities and contingent liabilities assumed in a business combination are measured initially at fair value at the date of acquisition. Transaction costs incurred in connection with a business acquisition are expensed as incurred. The cost of an acquisition also includes the fair value of any contingent consideration measured as at the date of acquisition. Any subsequent changes to the fair value of contingent consideration classified as liabilities, other than measurement period adjustments, are recognized in the consolidated statement of income.

The excess of the cost of an acquisition over the Company's share in the fair value of the acquiree's identifiable assets, liabilities and contingent liabilities is recognized as goodwill. If the excess is negative, a bargain purchase gain is recognized immediately in the statement of income.

(Source: Wipro Limited Annual Report 2015–16)

Summary – Review of Learning Objectives

1. **Understand the meaning of property, plant and equipment.** Ind AS 16 "Property, Plant and Equipment" defines property, plant and equipment as tangible items that: (a) are held for use in the production or supply of goods or services, for rental to others, or for administrative purposes and (b) are expected to be used during more than one period.

2. **Determine the cost of property, plant and equipment.** The cost of an item of property, plant and equipment comprises its purchase price, including import duties and non-refundable purchase taxes, after deducting trade discounts and rebates. It also includes any costs directly attributable to bringing the asset to the location and conditions necessary

for it to be capable of operating in the manner intended by the management and the costs that arise out of an obligation to dismantle and remove the item and restoring the site on which it is located.

3. **Explain revaluation of property, plant and equipment.** An entity can choose either the cost model or the revaluation model as its accounting policy and shall apply that policy to an entire class of property, plant and equipment. Under the cost model, an item of property, plant and equipment is carried at its cost minus any accumulated depreciation and any accumulated impairment loss. Under the revaluation model, the asset is carried at a revalued amount, its fair value at the date of the revaluation minus the accumulated depreciation and accumulated impairment loss. Revaluations are to be made with sufficient regularity to ensure that the carrying amount does not differ materially from the fair value at the end of the reporting period.
4. **Account for retirements and disposal of property, plant and equipment.** An item of property, plant and equipment is eliminated from the financial statements on disposal. Items of property, plant and equipment that have been retired from active use and are held for disposal are stated at a value lower than their net book value and net realizable value and are shown separately in the financial statements. Any expected loss is recognized immediately in the profit and loss statement. In historical cost financial statements, gains or losses arising from disposal are generally recognized in the profit and loss statement.
5. **Explain the concept of depreciation.** Depreciation is defined as the diminution in the value or utility of an asset, due to natural wear and tear, exhaustion of the subject matter, effluxion of time, accident and obsolescence through technology and market changes. Depreciation accounting involves allocation of the depreciable amount of an asset on a systematic basis over its useful life. Depreciable amount of an asset is its cost minus the residual value.
6. **Compute periodic depreciation using different methods.** A variety of depreciation methods can be used to allocate the depreciable amount of an asset on a systematic basis over its useful life. The depreciation method used shall reflect the pattern in which the asset's future economic benefits are expected to be consumed by the entity. These methods include the straight-line method, the diminishing balance method, sum of the years' digits method and the units of production method.
7. **Understand the legal provisions related to accounting of property, plant and equipment.** Schedule II of the Companies Act, 2013 requires a systematic allocation of the depreciable amount of an asset over its useful life. It specifies the useful life and residual value of various tangible assets. The Income Tax Act, 1961 allows companies to claim depreciation on WDV basis at the prescribed rates. While companies compute depreciation for financial reporting purposes using rates of depreciation prescribed by Company Law, they can also use higher rates of depreciation provided under the Tax Laws to compute their taxable income. Higher rates of depreciation are generally allowed under the tax laws to provide an incentive for more investment in businesses.
8. **Explain impairment of property, plant and equipment.** An impairment loss is the amount by which the carrying amount of an asset or a cash-generating unit exceeds its recoverable amount. The recoverable amount of an asset or a cash-generating unit is the higher of its fair value minus costs to sell and its value in use. An entity is required to assess at the end of each reporting period whether there is any indication that an asset may be impaired. If any such indication exists, the entity shall estimate the recoverable amount of the asset.

If the recoverable amount of an asset is less than its carrying amount, the carrying amount of the asset shall be reduced to its recoverable amount.

9. **Understand the meaning of intangible assets.** An intangible asset is an identifiable non-monetary asset without physical substance.
10. **Understand how intangible assets are recognized and measured.** An intangible asset is recognised if and only if: (a) it is probable that the expected future economic benefits that are attributable to the asset will flow to the entity and (b) the cost of the asset can be measured reliably. An intangible asset is to be measured initially at cost. Intangible assets acquired in a business combination, free of cost or in exchange of monetary and non-monetary assets are measured at fair value.
11. **Account for internally generated intangible assets.** Internally generated brands, mastheads, publishing titles, customer lists and items similar in substance cannot be recognised as intangible assets. Similarly, internally generated goodwill cannot be recognised as an asset.
12. **Understand how to determine the amortization amount in respect of intangible assets.** Amortization means allocation of the depreciable amount of an intangible asset with a finite useful life on a systematic basis over its useful life. The amortization method used is based on the pattern in which the asset's future economic benefits are expected to be consumed by the entity. If that pattern cannot be determined reliably, the straight-line method is to be used. An intangible asset with an indefinite useful life cannot be amortised. The residual value of an intangible asset with a finite useful life is generally assumed to be zero.
13. **Account for research and development expenses.** To assess whether an internally generated intangible asset meets the criteria for recognition, an entity classifies the generation of the asset into: (a) a research phase and (b) a development phase. An entity cannot recognize an intangible asset arising from research. Therefore, expenditure on research is recognized as an expense when it is incurred. An intangible asset arising from development (or from the development phase of an internal project) can be recognized if and only if an entity is able to demonstrate that the development meets some requirements.
14. **Account for goodwill.** Internally generated goodwill cannot be recognised as an asset. Goodwill can be recognised in a business combination. Any item acquired in a business combination that cannot be recognised as an intangible asset forms part of the amount recognised as goodwill at the acquisition date.

Glossary

- **Basket purchase** is the purchase of several assets for a consolidated price. The consideration is apportioned to various assets on a fair basis, as determined by competent valuers.
- **Cash-generating unit** is the smallest identifiable group of assets that generates cash inflows that are largely independent of cash inflows from other assets or groups of assets.
- **Component depreciation** is a system where each part of an item of property, plant and equipment with a cost that is significant in relation to the total cost of the item is depreciated separately.
- **Depreciable amount** of an asset is its cost minus residual value.
- **Depreciation** is the diminution in the value or utility of an asset, due to natural wear and tear,

exhaustion of the subject matter, effluxion of time, accident and obsolescence through technology and market changes.

- **Diminishing balance (written-down value) method** is a method of charging depreciation whereby a fixed percentage of the diminishing value of the asset is charged as depreciation each year so as to reduce the asset to its residual value at the end of its useful life.
- **Fair value minus costs to sell** is the amount obtainable from the sale of an asset or cash-generating unit in an arm's length transaction between knowledgeable, willing parties, minus the costs of disposal.
- **Impairment of assets** is a sudden or unexpected decline in the expected future benefits from an asset such as factory, vehicle or property. This might result from physical damage to the asset, changes in law or obsolescence resulting from technological innovation.
- **Production unit's method** is a method of charging depreciation, whereby depreciation is charged on the basis of number of units produced during a period.
- **Property, plant and equipment** are tangible items that: (a) are held for use in the production or supply of goods or services, for rental to others or for administrative purposes; and (b) are expected to be used during more than one period.
- **Recoverable amount** of an asset or a cash-generating unit is the higher of its fair value minus costs to sell and its value in use.
- **Residual value** of an asset is the estimated amount that an entity would currently obtain from the disposal of the asset, after deducting the estimated costs of disposal, if the asset were already of the age and in the condition expected at the end of its useful life.
- **Straight-line method** is a method of charging depreciation, whereby an equal amount is provided every year during the useful life of the asset so as to reduce the cost of the asset to zero or to its residual value at the end of its useful life.
- **Useful life** is (a) the period over which an asset is expected to be available by an entity; or (b) the number of production or similar units expected to be obtained from the asset by an entity.
- **Value in use** is the present value of the future cash flows expected to be derived from an asset or cash-generating unit.

Solved Problem

1. A company acquired a machine on October 1, 2013 at a cost of Rs. 210,000 and spent Rs. 15,000 on its installation. The company writes off depreciation at 10% per annum. The books are closed on 31st March every year. Calculate the accumulated depreciation and the book value of the machine as on March 31, 2015 when: (a) the company uses the straight-line method of charging depreciation and (b) the company uses the WDV method of charging depreciation.

Solution:

	(Rs.)
Purchase price	210,000
Installation cost	15,000
Depreciable amount	225,000

(*Continued*)

	(Rs.)
Straight-line method	
Depreciation (Oct 1, 2013–March 31, 2014) (Rs. 225,000 × 10% × 0.5)	11,250
Depreciation (2014–15) (Rs. 225,000 × 10%)	22,500
Accumulated depreciation	33,750
Book value (Rs. 225,000 – Rs. 33,750)	191,250
WDV method	
Depreciation (Oct. 1, 2013–March 31, 2014) (Rs. 225,000 × 10% × 0.5)	11,250
Depreciation (2014–15) (Rs. (225,000 – 11,250) × 10%)	21,375
Accumulated depreciation	32,625
Book value (Rs. 225,000 – 32,625)	192,375

Multiple Choice Questions

1. A company purchased a piece of land for Rs. 17,500,000. It paid a commission of Rs. 1,250,000 and spent Rs. 1,750,000 for demolishing an old building on the land. At what cost would the company record the land in its books?
   a. Rs. 19,250,000
   b. Rs. 17,500,000
   c. Rs. 18,750,000
   d. Rs. 20,500,000

2. A company purchases a new delivery van for Rs. 1,000,000. It pays taxes of 12.5% on the purchase price, Rs. 11,000 on safety tests and Rs. 60,000 on painting the name of the company on the van. The annual license fee is Rs. 6,000. At what cost will the company record the van?
   a. Rs. 1,202,000
   b. Rs. 1,196,000
   c. Rs. 1,125,000
   d. Rs. 1,136,000

3. When can the borrowing costs be included in the acquisition cost of a non-current asset?
   a. During the construction period of a self-constructed asset.
   b. When the asset is purchased on credit.
   c. When the asset acquisition is financed by a long-term loan.
   d. When it is a part of a basket purchase.

4. A company purchased equipment costing Rs. 4,500,000, and paid transportation charges of Rs. 210,000. Further, Rs. 600,000 was spent on installing the equipment. The equipment is expected to have a useful life of 5 years and a residual value of Rs. 900,000. What would be the annual depreciation charge under the straight-line method?
   a. Rs. 1,062,000
   b. Rs. 882,000
   c. Rs. 738,000
   d. Rs. 720,000

5. A company charges a depreciation of Rs. 70,000 per month on a machine using the straight-line method. The machine was acquired for Rs. 9,000,000 and is expected to have a salvage value of Rs. 600,000 at the end of its useful life. What is the annual rate of depreciation?
   a. 12%
   b. 2%

c. 8%
d. 10%

6. A company purchased factory equipment on September 1, 2014 for Rs. 4,800,000. The useful life of the equipment is 10 years, and it is estimated that the equipment will have a salvage value of Rs. 300,000 at the end of its useful life. How much depreciation would the company charge on the equipment on March 31, 2015 using the straight-line method?
   a. Rs. 450,000
   b. Rs. 262,500
   c. Rs. 225,000
   d. Rs. 187,500

7. A company's records show a depreciation expense of Rs. 250,000 on an equipment for the current year and a balance of Rs. 1,250,000 in the accumulated depreciation account at the end of the year. The cost of the equipment was Rs. 3,750,000. The salvage value was estimated at Rs. 750,000 at the end of its useful life. The company charges depreciation on a straight-line basis. What is the remaining useful life of the equipment?
   a. 15 years
   b. 12 years
   c. 5 years
   d. 7 years

8. A machine purchased for Rs. 2,250,000 has an estimated salvage value of Rs. 450,000. If the machine's value is depreciated at the rate is 20% using the declining balance method, the second year depreciation will be ______.
   a. Rs. 450,000
   b. Rs. 288,000
   c. Rs. 360,000
   d. Rs. 300,000

9. After using an equipment for 2 years, a company revises its total useful life as 6 years from the original estimate of 8 years. The cost of the equipment was Rs. 3500,000 and its estimated salvage value Rs. 700,000. The equipment was depreciated using the straight-line method. With the revision in the useful life, how much depreciation should the company charge in the third year?
   a. Rs. 525,000
   b. Rs. 466,650
   c. Rs. 700,000
   d. Rs. 350,000

10. A company sells a machine for Rs. 4,000,000 on March 31, 2015. The machine was acquired 6 years earlier for Rs. 12,000,000. The company has been depreciating the machine on a straight-line basis assuming its useful life to be 10 years and a salvage value of Rs. 2,000,000. The company should recognize a
    a. Rs. 2,000,000 loss on disposal
    b. Rs. 2,000,000 gain on disposal
    c. Rs. 4,000,000 loss on disposal
    d. Rs. 4,000,000 gain on disposal

Review Questions

1. What are the main features of non-current assets?
2. What costs are included in the acquisition cost of an item of property, plant and equipment?
3. What costs are not included in the acquisition cost of property, plant and equipment?
4. How would you determine the cost of a self-constructed property, plant and equipment?
5. How should borrowing costs be treated in determining the cost of property, plant and equipment?
6. On what basis is the single consideration paid for acquiring more than one item of property, plant and equipment apportioned among different items?

7. What kind of expenditure incurred on repairs or improvement of property, plant and equipment is allowed to be capitalized?
8. How is fair market value of an asset defined?
9. How would you account for an increase or decrease in an asset's carrying amount as a result of a revaluation?
10. How is the loss or gain on the sale of an item of property, plant and equipment determined?
11. Why do we need to depreciate property, plant and equipment?
12. Why do we not depreciate land?
13. How do we determine the amount of depreciation to be provided for an asset?
14. At the time of buying a piece of equipment, a company estimated its useful life to be 10 years. However, it later decided to depreciate the asset over a period of 6 years only. Why would the company do so?
15. What factors should a company take into consideration when deciding on the method of charging depreciation?
16. Should a company stop depreciating a non-current asset if its current market value is more than its purchase price?
17. On what basis does a company determine the useful life of an asset?
18. When an addition is made to an existing item of property, plant and equipment, over what period should this addition be depreciated?
19. How do we determine the loss from impairment of an asset?
20. How is a cash-generating unit defined?

Practice Problems

1. A company acquired a machine on October 1, 2013 at a cost of Rs. 140,000 and spent Rs. 10,000 on its installation. The company writes off depreciation at 10% per annum. The books are closed on 31 March every year. Calculate the accumulated depreciation and the book value of the machine as on 31 March, 2015 when: (a) the company uses straight-line method of charging depreciation, (b) the company uses written-down value method of charging depreciation.
2. ABC Ltd. purchased a machine for Rs. 1,00,000 which has a useful life of 10 years and a residual value of Rs. 12,000. The machine was put to use on 1.4.2008. The company uses the sum of the years' digits method for charging depreciation. Calculate the accumulated depreciation and the book value of the machine as on 31 March, 2014.
3. A firm purchased on April 1, 2012 certain machinery for Rs. 58,200 and spent Rs. 1,800 on its erection. On September 1, 2012 another machine was acquired for Rs. 20,000. On September 1, 2013 the machinery purchased on April 1, 2012, having become obsolete was auctioned for Rs. 38,600 and on the same date fresh machinery was purchased for Rs. 40,000.

   Depreciation is charged at 10% per annum on the WDV. Calculate: (a) the profit or loss on the sale of machine, (b) the accumulated depreciation, gross value and net value of machinery as on March 31, 2014.
4. A company's plant and machinery account on March 31, 2014 and the corresponding depreciation provision account, broken down by year of purchase are as given in Table 6.10.

Table 6.10

Year of Purchase	Plant & Machinery at Cost	Depreciation Provision
2001–02	20,000	20,000
2002–03	30,000	30,000

(Continued)

Table 6.10 (Continued)

Year of Purchase	Plant & Machinery at Cost	Depreciation Provision
2004–05	1,00,000	95,000
2005–06	70,000	59,500
2012–13	50,000	7,500
2013–14	30,000	1,500

Depreciation is at the rate of 10% per annum on cost. It is assumed that all purchases and sales occur on 30 September in the relevant year.

During 2014–15, the following transactions took place:

1. Purchase of plant and machinery amounting to Rs. 150,000.
2. Plant that had been purchased in 2001–02 for Rs. 17,000 was scrapped.
3. Plant that had been bought in 2004–05 for Rs. 9,000 was sold for Rs. 500.
4. Plant that had been bought in 2005–06 for Rs. 24,000 was sold for Rs. 1,500.

Calculate the provision for depreciation of plant and machinery for the year ending March 31, 2015.

5. A firm purchased on April 1, 2013 certain machinery for Rs. 52,380 and spent Rs. 1,620 on its erection. On the same date, another machinery was acquired for Rs. 19,000. On October 1, 2014, the first machinery purchased on April 1, 2013 having become obsolete was auctioned for Rs. 28,600 and on the same date fresh machinery was purchased at a cost of Rs. 40,000.

   Depreciation was provided annually on 31st March at the rate of 10% on the WDV. In 2014, however, the firm changed this method of providing depreciation and adopted the method of providing 5% per annum depreciation on the original cost.

   Calculate the amount of depreciation expense for the year 2014–15.

6. M&M company commenced business on April 1, 2010, when they purchased plant and equipment for Rs. 700,000. They adopted a policy of (i) charging depreciation at 15% per annum on diminishing balance basis and (ii) charging full year's depreciation on additions.

   Over the years, their purchase of plant has been as given in Table 6.11.

   Table 6.11 Amount spent on purchase of plant

Date	Amount (Rs.)
1-8-2011	150,000
30-9-2014	200,000

   On April 1, 2014, it was decided to change the method and rate of depreciation to 10% on straight-line basis. Calculate the depreciation on plant and equipment for the year ending March 31, 2015.

7. M/s. M& Co. purchased a machine on April 1, 2009 for Rs. 2,000,000. The estimated useful life was 10 years and scrap value at the end was estimated at Rs. 200,000. On April 1, 2014, the WDV of the machine was revalued up by 20%, useful life was re-estimated at 13 years and residual value at Rs. 280,000. The company follows the WDV method of charging depreciation. Calculate the provision for depreciation for the year ended March 31, 2015.
8. On April 1, 2012, A bought a new computer system for Rs. 2,40,000. The new computer was estimated to have a useful life of 5 years with an estimated salvage value of Rs. 20,000 at the end of 5 years. A has asked you to help him decide which depreciation method should be selected for the new computer. The methods being considered are straight-line method, written-down value method and sum of the years' digits' method. Assuming that A closes his books on 31st March each year,
   (i) Prepare a schedule showing depreciation for the years ending March 31, 2012, 2013 and 2014 for each of the three methods.

(ii) For each of the three methods, compute the asset book value reported on the balance sheet.

(iii) Which method would maximize the income for three years (2012–2014) and which method would minimize the income for the same period?

9. The Accounting Policy related to depreciation appearing in the financial statements of a company engaged in steel production reads:

"For financial reporting purposes, the company uses the units-of-production method of depreciating its steel rolling mills and the straight-line method for other plants and equipment. Annual straight-line depreciation rates for financial reporting purposes are as follows: Buildings 2.5%–10%, Machinery and Equipment 5%–33%. For tax purposes, depreciation is computed using the written-down value method."

(i) How does the company decide on the method of charging depreciation?

(ii) The company is using different depreciation methods for its steel rolling mills and other items of plant. Is it in violation of the principle of consistency?

(iii) What factors does the company consider in determining the useful lives of different assets?

(iv) Why does the company use written-down value method for tax purposes?

10. A company buys land for a new project. The purchase price is Rs. 8,500,000. The broker who consummates the deal is paid a commission of 4% of the purchase price. The company has to pay a legal fee of Rs. 100,000 to get the land registered in its name. The land is uneven and the company spends Rs. 200,000 on leveling it. Determine the cost at which the land will be recorded in the books of the company.

11. X purchases a car service facility for Rs. 12,000,000. Had X purchased various items separately, the land would have cost Rs. 3,000,000, the building Rs. 7,500,000 and the equipment Rs. 5,250,000. How should X apportion the total cost of Rs. 12,000,000 among land, building and equipment?

12. The accounting records of a company shows the following items of expenditure incurred on the construction of a new plant during the year ended on March 31, 2015.

	(Rs.)
Cost of land	1,58,300,000
Legal expenses	350,000
Brokerage	1,050,000
Land survey cost	200,000
Cost of removing grass	250,000
Cost of leveling land	210,000
Foundation digging	1,730,000
Architect's fee	350,000
Cost of building construction	35,500,000
Landscaping cost	590,000
Cost of equipment	49,450,000
Cost of transporting equipment	2,765,000
Installation cost	8,810,000
Testing cost	1,105,000

The company sold the grass removed from the land for Rs. 100,000. Two of the company's employees drawing an annual salary of Rs. 2,400,000 and Rs. 2,100,000, respectively, were involved full time for a period of six months in the construction of the plant. Determine the amount at which the company would capitalize different assets.

13. A college acquired a piece of land with some buildings constructed on it for Rs. 90 million. For acquiring the land, the college borrowed an amount of Rs. 30 million at 8% per annum. The college demolished the old buildings at a cost of Rs. 50,00,000 and spent Rs. 50 million on constructing a new building. It borrowed another sum of Rs. 25 million at 10% per annum. It took

the college 6 months to make the building ready for use. At what amount will the college record the cost of land and building?

14. X purchases land and a building for Rs. 50,000,000. Had X purchased the various items separately, the land would have cost Rs. 24,000,000, and the building Rs. 36,000,000. How much of the purchase price should X apportion to the land and the building?
15. X acquires a second-hand truck for Rs. 1,700,000 and spends Rs. 3,50,000 on its overhaul to make it ready for his use. He estimates that the useful life of the truck will be 4 years and that he would be able to sell the truck for Rs. 150,000 at the end of 4 years. He decides to depreciate the truck using the straight-line method. At the end of 2 years, X sells the truck for Rs. 1,200,000. Determine the gain or loss made by X on the sale of the truck.
16. A transport company estimates the useful life of a truck at 150,000 kilometers. It acquires a truck costing Rs. 5,000,000 and estimates its residual value to be Rs. 500,000. The company depreciates the truck on a mileage basis. The truck is used for 30,000 kilometers in the first year, 50,000 kilometers in the second year and 60,000 kilometers in the third year. Calculate the depreciation expense for each of the three years.
17. A company's plant and machinery account on March 31, 2014 and corresponding depreciation provision account, broken down by year of purchase are as given in Table 6.12.

Table 6.12 Plant and machinery as on March 31, 2014

Year of Purchase	Plant and Machinery at Cost	Depreciation Provision
2001–02	400,000	400,000
2002–03	600,000	600,000
2004–05	2,000,000	1,900,000
2005–06	1,400,000	1,190,000
2012–13	1,000,000	150,000
2013–14	600,000	30000

Depreciation is at the rate of 10% per annum on cost. It is assumed that all purchases and sales occur on 30 September in the relevant year.

During 2014–15, the following transactions took place:

1. Purchase of plant and machinery for Rs. 3,000,000.
2. Plant that had been purchased in 2001–02 for Rs. 340,000 was scrapped.
3. Plant that had been bought in 2004–05 for Rs. 180,000 was sold for Rs. 10,000.
4. Plant that had been bought in 2005–06 for Rs. 480,000 was sold for Rs. 30,000.

Calculate the provision for depreciation of plant and machinery for the year ended March 31, 2015.

18. An oil company acquires a drilling rig for Rs. 100 million. The company estimates that the rig can extract 200,000 barrels of oil and will have a residual value of Rs. 12.96 million at the end of its useful life of 4 years. The drill is expected to extract 65,000 barrels in the first year, 50,000 barrels in the second year, 45,000 barrels in the third year and 40,000 barrels in the fourth year.

    Compute depreciation for each year under the straight-line, diminishing balance and units of production methods.
19. A company purchased a textile weaving machine for Rs. 10 million. The machine has an expected useful life of 6 years and a residual value of Rs. 1 million. The company uses the straight-line

method for charging depreciation. At the end of year 5, the company spends Rs. 2.5 million on a major overhaul of the machine. The company expects the machine to last another 2 years after which it will have a residual value of Rs. 1.5 million. How much depreciation will the company charge in year 6 and year 7?

20. On April 1, 2014, a company's records showed the following information regarding a piece of equipment:

Equipment (original cost)	Rs. 900,000
Residual value estimated at the time of acquisition	200,000
Accumulated depreciation (on straight-line basis for 3 years)	300,000

What was the company's estimate of the useful life of the equipment?

21. On April 1, 2014, a company's records showed the following information regarding a piece of equipment:

Equipment (original cost)	Rs. 1,000,000
Residual value estimated at the time of acquisition	77,760
Estimated useful life	5 years

Calculate the amount of accumulated depreciation on the equipment at the end of 3 years from the date of purchase if the company follows the diminishing balance method of depreciation.

22. On April 1, 2014, a company's records showed the following information regarding a piece of equipment:

Equipment (original cost)	Rs. 1,000,000
Residual value estimated at the time of acquisition	200,000
Accumulated depreciation (on the basis of production units for 2 years)	480,000
Units produced–Year 1: 65,000; Year 2: 55,000	

What was the company's estimate of the production capacity of the equipment?

23. On April 1, 2015, XYZ Ltd. decided to change the estimated useful lives and salvage values of some depreciable assets as given in Table 6.13. The company follows the straight-line method of depreciation. Calculate the depreciation expense for the year 2015 based on the new values.

24. XYZ Ltd. depreciates buildings on straight-line basis and equipment on diminishing balance basis. On April 1, 2015 it decided to change the method of depreciating equipment to straight-line method and estimated the useful life to 48 years. There is no change in the residual values estimated originally. Other details relating to these assets are as given in Table 6.14.

Table 6.13 XYZ Ltd.: Proposed useful lives and residual values of building and equipment

Asset	Date of Acquisition	Cost (Rs.)	Accumulated Depreciation 31.3.2015	Useful Life (Years) Old	Useful Life (Years) Proposed	Residual Value (Rs.) Old	Residual Value (Rs.) Proposed
Building	1.4.2009	35,000,000	6,500,000	30	36	2,500,000	1,750,000
Equipment	1.4.2011	6,000,000	1,150,000	20	25	250,000	1,800,000

Table 6.14 Details of building and equipment as on March 31, 2015

Asset	Date of Acquisition	Cost (Rs.)	Accumulated Depreciation 31.3.2015	Useful Life (Years)	Residual Value (Rs.)
Building	1.4.2007	35,000,000	6,500,000	40	2,500,000
Equipment	1.4.2014	6,000,000	2,822,400	5	250,000

Calculate the depreciation expense for the year 2015 based on the new values.

25. On April 1, 2014, a company decides to revalue a building at Rs. 4,800,000. The building was purchased for Rs. 2,400,000 on April 1, 2008. The useful life of the building was estimated to be 30 years at the time of purchase. The company charged depreciation on straight-line basis.

Calculate the amount the company will transfer to revaluation surplus and the depreciation expense for the financial year 2014–15.

26. On April 1, 2014, a company decides to revalue a building at Rs. 7,200,000. The building was purchased for Rs. 3,600,000 on April 1, 2004. The useful life of the building was estimated to be 40 years at the time of purchase. The company charged depreciation on straight-line basis.

Calculate the amount the company will transfer to revaluation surplus and the depreciation expense for the financial year 2014–15.

Answers to Multiple Choice Questions

1. (d)
2. (b)
3. (a)
4. (b)
5. (d)
6. (b)
7. (d)
8. (c)
9. (a)
10. (a)

Inventories: Accounting and Valuation

7

LEARNING OBJECTIVES

After reading this chapter, you will be able to:

- Define inventories.
- Describe the different types of inventories maintained by manufacturing, merchandising and service companies and the reasons thereof.
- Explain the objectives of inventory accounting.
- Explain the effect of errors on inventory measurement.
- Explain and use the periodic and perpetual inventory systems.
- Determine the quantity of inventory.
- Identify the amount to be included in the cost of inventories.
- Compute the inventory value using different inventory costing methods.
- Explain the significance of the consistency principle.
- Report inventory at the lower-of-cost or market value.
- Apply the retail and gross-profit methods of estimating inventory values.
- Explain the accounting treatment of inventories.
- Explain the disclosures in financial statements relating to inventories.

7.1 Introduction

Inventories are part of current assets, as defined in Chapter 6, and represent the second largest asset category for manufacturing companies, next only to plant and equipment. The general proportion of inventories to total assets varies between 15% and 30%. Therefore, the efficient management of inventories assumes significant importance.

In this chapter, the meaning of inventories and their cost, the systems of inventory record keeping and different cost flow assumptions in the context of determination of cost of inventories is discussed.

7.2 Inventories

Indian Accounting Standard (Ind AS) 2 "Inventories" defines inventories as follows:

Inventories are assets: (a) held for sale in the ordinary course of business, (b) in the process of production for such sale or (c) in the form of materials or supplies to be consumed in the production process or in the rendering of services.

This definition includes three types of inventories: (a) Finished goods or completed units ready for sale, for example, completely built up motorcycles held by Bajaj Auto Ltd. (b) Work-in-process or units in the process of production but not yet complete. When the units are completed, work-in-process inventories become finished goods inventories. (c) Raw material or items purchased for processing to produce finished goods, for example, engines, carburetors and other parts to be used in producing motorcycles. When these items are used, they become part of work-in-process inventory.

In addition, manufacturing companies keep inventory of supplies such as lubricants, coolants, cleaning items such as sandpapers, cotton waste and also spare parts for machines and equipment.

While manufacturing companies carry all these types of inventories, merchandising firms such as wholesale and retail businesses hold only finished goods as they generally do not carry out any processing activity other than repackaging large lots into smaller packages in some cases.

Service companies also maintain inventories, but the type of inventories carried depends on the nature of the service.

7.3 Reasons for Keeping Inventories

By keeping raw materials inventory, a firm can delink its purchasing and production activities. Work-in-process inventories are required because it takes time to complete a process/operation and to move products from one stage to another. Finished goods inventory decouples the firm's production and marketing activities and facilitates efficient servicing of customer demands.

7.4 Objectives of Inventory Accounting

The main objective of inventory management is to maintain an optimum level of inventories, making a tradeoff between benefits and costs of keeping inventories. Benefits of large inventories include economies in purchasing and production and quick filling of customer orders. Costs include storage, handling, insurance, obsolescence and required return on capital tied up in an inventory.

The objectives of inventory accounting are as follows:

1. To match the cost of goods sold, an expense, with the revenue earned from the sale of those goods in an accounting period, and to measure the cost of inventory on hand at the end of the period, which is an asset. This function of inventory accounting enables preparation of periodic financial statements and tax returns.
2. To facilitate decisions regarding the timing and size of manufacturing or purchase orders.
3. To provide information that facilitates a check on theft or wastage of inventories.

Determination of profit or loss for an accounting period calls for matching sales revenue with the cost of goods sold. Sales revenue in an accounting period is the product of units sold and the selling price per unit. Cost of goods sold is the same number of units multiplied by per unit cost. Cost of goods sold is determined in two steps. Goods produced or purchased during an accounting period are added to the *beginning inventory*. The resulting sum is *goods available for sale* during the period. The *ending inventory* or cost of goods unsold at the end of the period is deducted from goods available for sale to arrive at the *cost of goods sold*. Thus, cost of goods sold is that part of goods available for sale that is sold during an accounting period. Cost of goods sold is shown as a deduction from the sales revenue in the income statement to derive the amount of gross profit. The ending inventory is shown in the balance sheet as part of current assets.

7.5 Effects of Inventory Misstatements

It is important to value the ending inventory correctly because any error in measuring the ending inventory will lead to an inaccuracy in cost of goods sold, gross profit, net profit, current assets and equity of an entity and make the financial statements of the entity less credible. A higher value of ending inventory lowers the cost of goods sold and increases the gross profit, net income, current assets and shareholders' equity. There is a reverse effect when the value of the ending inventory is lower.

The misstatement can occur because of mistakes in the accounting process. The amount of ending inventory can also be deliberately overstated or understated by including end-of-the-year sales and purchase transactions in the wrong accounting year. The manipulation could be motivated by a desire to obtain higher bank financing or employee incentives or to create a better perception of the company's prospects among market participants.

The misstatement in inventory value affects the financial statements of the current period and the next period. This is because the ending inventory of one period becomes the beginning inventory of the next period. If the ending inventory is overvalued in one period, it will result in overstatement of profit for that period and understatement of profit for the next period. Even though the effect on income before taxes is offset over two accounting periods, misstatement of inventory violates the matching principle and distorts the financials of each year.

7.6 Systems for Keeping Inventory Records

There are two systems for determining the value of ending inventory and the cost of goods sold: the periodic inventory system and the perpetual inventory system.

In the *periodic inventory system*, the ending inventory is found by a physical count and the cost of goods sold is obtained by deducting the cost of inventory from the cost of goods available for sale. Under the periodic inventory system, all purchases are debited to a purchase account which is closed by transfer to the trading account (income statement/cost of goods sold).

In the *perpetual inventory system*, inventory balances are determined after each receipt and issue. Under this method, physical inventory is taken to check the accuracy of accounting records. Cost of goods sold can be ascertained directly from the accounting records.

7.6.1 Comparison of Periodic and Perpetual Inventory Systems

1. The periodic inventory system is simple and less expensive. On the contrary, the perpetual inventory system is costlier due to additional record keeping.
2. The periodic inventory system is based on physical verification. Frequent physical counting may be required for the preparation of quarterly financial statement, leading to the disruption of normal operations. Under the perpetual inventory system, as information on inventory and cost of goods sold is continuously available, an income statement can be prepared without taking a physical inventory at any time interval. The accuracy of the underlying perpetual inventory records can be checked by an annual or semi-annual physical inventory.
3. Under the periodic inventory system, the difference between the goods available for sale and the goods on hand is assumed to be the cost of goods sold. This assumption is not necessarily correct because some of the goods may have been pilfered, lost, thrown away or overlooked when the physical inventory was taken. This is the inventory shrinkage. In the perpetual inventory system, an actual count of goods on hand can be used as a check on the accuracy of inventory records. Shrinkage can thus be separately identified rather than being included in the cost of goods sold.
4. The periodic inventory system does not provide any information that can help in exercising inventory control. Perpetual inventory system helps determine the reorder quantity and reorder level depending on demand. This helps avoid both stock-outs and excess inventories of various items carried by the firm.

7.6.2 Merchandising and Manufacturing Business

A merchandising company has one inventory account. The cost of goods available for sale is divided into the cost of goods sold and closing inventory by using either the periodic inventory system or the perpetual inventory system. Manufacturing companies have three types of inventories: material inventory, work-in-process inventory and finished goods inventory. To account for these, a periodic inventory system as in case of merchandising business may be used. If perpetual inventory system is followed, it is called Product Costing System. In such a system, the cost of each product is accumulated as it flows through the production process. The information for passing the entries is obtained directly from the cost records. Figure 7.1 presents the typical cost flows in a manufacturing environment.

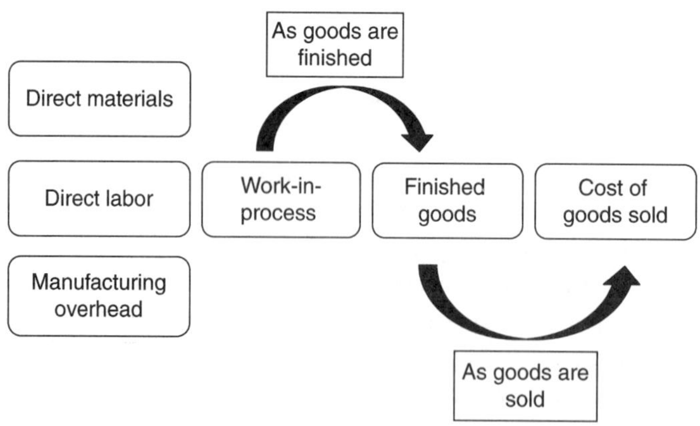

Figure 7.1 Cost flow in a manufacturing concern.

7.7 Cost of Inventories

The cost of inventories shall comprise all costs of purchase, costs of conversion and other costs incurred in bringing the inventories to their present location and condition.

1. **Costs of purchase:** The costs of purchase of inventories comprise the purchase price, import duties and other taxes (other than those subsequently recoverable by the entity from the taxing authorities), and transport, handling and other costs directly attributable to the acquisition of finished goods, materials and services. Trade discounts, rebates and other similar items are deducted in determining the costs of purchase.
2. **Costs of conversion:** The costs of conversion of inventories include costs directly related to the units of production, such as direct labor. They also include a systematic allocation of fixed and variable production overheads that are incurred in converting materials into finished goods. Fixed production overheads are those indirect costs of production that remain relatively constant regardless of the volume of production, such as depreciation and maintenance of factory buildings and equipment, and the cost of factory management and administration. Variable production overheads are those indirect costs of production that vary directly, or nearly directly, with the volume of production, such as indirect materials and indirect labor.
3. **Allocation of production overheads:** The allocation of fixed production overheads to the costs of conversion is based on the normal capacity of the production facilities. Normal capacity is the production expected to be achieved on an average over a number of periods or seasons under normal circumstances, taking into account the loss of capacity resulting from planned maintenance. The actual level of production may be used if it approximates the normal capacity. The amount of fixed overhead allocated to each unit of production is not increased as a consequence of low production or idle plant. Unallocated overheads are recognized as an expense in the period in which they are incurred. In periods of abnormally high production, the amount of fixed overhead allocated to each unit of production is decreased so that inventories are not measured above cost. Variable production overheads are allocated to each unit of production on the basis of the actual use of the production facilities.
4. **Joint and by-products:** A production process may result in more than one product being produced simultaneously. This is the case, for example, when joint products are produced or when there is a main product and a by-product. When the costs of conversion of each product are not separately identifiable, they are allocated between the products on a rational and consistent basis. The allocation may be based, for example, on the relative sales value of each product either at the stage in the production process when the products become separately identifiable, or on completion of production. Most by-products, by their nature, are immaterial. When this is the case, they are often measured at net realizable value, and this value is deducted from the cost of the main product. As a result, the carrying amount of the main product is not materially different from its cost.
5. **Other costs:** These are included in the cost of inventories only to the extent that they are incurred in bringing the inventories to their present location and condition. For example, it may be appropriate to include non-production overheads or costs of designing products for specific customers in the cost of inventories.

6. **Exclusions:** Examples of costs excluded from the cost of inventories and recognized as expenses in the period in which they are incurred are as follows:
   (a) abnormal amounts of wasted materials, labor or other production costs;
   (b) storage costs, unless necessary in the production process before a further production stage;
   (c) administrative overheads that do not contribute to bringing inventories to their present location and condition; and
   (d) selling costs.
7. **Borrowing costs:** These are included in the cost of inventories in limited circumstances mentioned in Ind AS 23 "Borrowing Costs."

   An entity may purchase inventories on deferred settlement terms. When the arrangement effectively contains a financing element, that element, for example, a difference between the purchase price for normal credit terms and the amount paid, is recognized as an interest expense over the period of financing.
8. **Inventories of service providers:** In the case of service providers, to the extent that service providers have inventories, they measure them at the costs of their production. These costs consist primarily of the labor and other costs of personnel directly engaged in providing the service, including supervisory personnel, and attributable overheads. Labor and other costs relating to sales and general administrative personnel are not included, but are recognized as expenses in the period in which they are incurred. The cost of inventories of a service provider does not include profit margins or non-attributable overheads that are often factored in the prices charged by service providers.
9. **Agricultural produce:** Inventories comprising agricultural produce that an entity has harvested from its biological assets are measured on initial recognition at their fair value minus costs to sell at the point of harvest.

7.8 Inventory Costing Methods

When the per unit cost of one or more items in the inventory changes during the accounting period, what items are treated as sold or remaining in the inventory becomes important as the choice can materially affect the profit or loss figure and the resulting tax liability of an entity. There are four generally accepted inventory costing methods that provide alternative ways of assigning the cost of goods available for sale between inventory and cost of goods sold. These methods are as follows:

1. Specific identification method
2. First-in-first-out method (FIFO)
3. Last-in-first-out method (LIFO)
4. Weighted average cost method

7.8.1 Specific Identification Method

This method identifies the individual items that remain in the inventory or are sold as coming from a specific purchase. The cost of each item sold is individually identified and recorded as cost of goods sold. Therefore, this method is used when it is possible to ascertain the actual cost of each item sold, for example, in the case of automobiles, expensive jewelry and custom-made furniture. The major advantage of the specific identification method is that it tracks the actual physical flow of goods available for sale. This method becomes unsatisfactory when a large number of similar items are sold as it is easy to affect the cost of goods sold and the value of ending inventory by choosing from among the several available costs. To avoid such manipulation, we use one of the other three methods. These three methods are based on the assumption that inventory costs follow a certain flow, that is, they assume a sequence in which goods are used or sold. This assumed sequence may be different from the actual sequence in which goods are used or sold or the *physical flow*.

It may be impractical to use the actual physical flow because many items are indistinguishable from one another. It may also be inappropriate to use the actual physical flow as management may be able to manipulate the net income through specific identification of items sold.

7.8.2 First-In-First-Out Method

This method assumes that the oldest goods are sold first, and that the most recently purchased goods are in the ending inventory. This method allocates the oldest unit costs to the cost of goods sold and the newest unit costs to the ending inventory.

Under the FIFO method, the value of the ending inventory is close to its current market value as it consists of items valued at the most recent costs. In times of rising prices, FIFO leads to higher reported net incomes as the cost of the oldest cheapest unit is matched with its current higher price. FIFO does not, therefore, correctly match costs and revenues.

Many companies select accounting methods with the objective of maximizing, in the near term, the amount of income reported to shareholders. Because under inflationary conditions which have been prevalent over a long period of time, the costs of inventories increase and FIFO reports a lower cost of goods sold. Many companies prefer FIFO for increasing the reported income.

7.8.3 Last-In-First-Out Method

Under this method, the cost of goods sold is based on the most recent purchases resulting in more realistic reported profit. However, the ending inventory may be valued at amounts prevailing several years ago which, in an era of inflation, are far below the current costs.

In periods of inflation, LIFO results in lower income than does FIFO or average cost, and thus results in lower income taxes. If the physical size of the inventory remains constant or grows, LIFO reduces the taxable income indefinitely. Only if the LIFO layers are stripped off in future years, the LIFO taxable income may exceed the taxable income under FIFO. These tax advantages of LIFO, which improve a company's cash flow, lead many companies to select the LIFO method.

The above arguments suggest that more and more companies should use the LIFO method, but it is not the case due to the following reasons:

1. Some countries do not permit LIFO. Therefore, companies having overseas operations cannot adopt LIFO.
2. Although the economy may, as a whole be experiencing inflation, the prices of specific items in a company's inventory may not necessarily be increasing, for example, calculators and computers.
3. LIFO results in lower reported earnings and thus may result in lower stock prices, which may not be acceptable to the board of directors who are supposed to protect shareholders' interests.

In a year when the physical size of the inventory increases above the amount in hand at the beginning of the year, with LIFO, the inventory account is increased by the additional quantity valued at the costs existing during the year. During a period of growth, the inventory account will consist of a number of layers, a new layer being added each year. If the physical inventory should subsequently decrease in size, these layers are in effect stripped off taking the most recently added layer first.

This process can have a peculiar effect on the income statement. If the inventory is decreased to the extent that several layers are stripped off, then the inventory items would be moving into the cost of goods sold at costs established for several years. If there has been a constant inflation during the interim, such a decrease in inventory can result in a significant increase in the reported income. Some people assert that in a recession, some companies deliberately eat into their LIFO inventories to increase the reported income in a lean year. Many countries do not permit the use of LIFO for this reason.

7.8.4 Weighted Average Cost Method

The weighted average cost method uses the weighted average unit cost of goods available for sale to value both the cost of goods sold and the ending inventory.

In the case of the periodic inventory system, the average is calculated for the whole period. It is a weighted average; each unit cost is weighted by the number of units. In the perpetual inventory system, a new average unit cost is calculated after each purchase.

The weighted average cost method is suitable when there are substantial price fluctuations because the unit cost is affected by all the purchase prices during the accounting period.

Real World Insight

The majority of Indian companies follow the weighted average cost method to determine the cost of raw materials, stores and supplies as the following excerpts from the financial statements of the well-known Indian companies for the year ended March 31, 2014 show.

1. **Asian Paints.** In determining the cost of raw materials, packing materials, stock-in trade, stores, spares, components and consumables, *weighted average cost method* is used.
2. **Bajaj Auto.** Stores, packing material and tools are valued at cost arrived at on *weighted average basis.*
3. **BHEL.** In respect of raw material, components, loose tools, stores and spares cost means *weighted average cost.*
4. **Hero MotoCorp.** The basis of determining cost for various categories of inventories are as follows: stores and spares, loose tools, raw materials and components – *weighted average cost.*
5. **Jindal Steel.** Raw materials and stores and spares are valued at lower of cost, computed on *weighted average basis* or net realizable value.
6. **Larsen & Toubro.** Raw materials, components, construction materials, stores and spares, and loose tools at lower of *weighted average cost* or net realizable value.
7. **Mahindra & Mahindra.** Raw materials and bought out components are valued at the lower-of-cost or net realizable value. The cost is determined on the basis of the *weighted average method.*
8. **Reliance Industries.** The cost of raw materials, process chemicals, stores and spares, packing materials, trading and other products are determined on a *weighted average basis.*
9. **Tata Motors.** The cost of raw materials and consumables are ascertained on a *moving weighted average/monthly moving weighted average basis.*

There are some **exceptions** also.

1. **Colgate Palmolive India Ltd.** Inventories of raw and packing materials, work-in-progress and finished goods are valued at lower-of-cost and net realizable value. The cost of work-in-progress and finished goods includes materials, labor and manufacturing overheads, and other costs incurred in bringing the inventories to their present location. This cost is determined using the *standard cost method* that approximates the actual cost.
2. **Hawkins Cookers Limited.** Raw materials are valued at lower of *weighted average cost* and estimated net realizable value. Materials other than raw materials are valued on the basis of *first-in, first-out.*

7.9 Inventory Costing Under the Periodic Inventory System

The cost of ending inventory is the product of units in the ending inventory and the unit cost. Units in the ending inventory are determined by the physical count under the periodic inventory system. The unit costs are determined by using one of the costing methods discussed before.

Illustration 7.1 Inventory costing methods under periodic system

The following particulars are given in respect of a stores' item by a company:

Date (2015)			(Rs.)
January 1	Beginning inventory	100 units @ Rs. 30 per unit	3,000
January 1	Purchases	200 units @ Rs. 31 per unit	6,200
January 12	Purchases	400 units @ Rs. 32 per unit	12,800
January 23	Purchases	300 units @ Rs. 34 per unit	10,200
	Goods available for sale	1,000 units	32,200

Inventory at the end of January 2015 is 300 units.

The purpose of inventory costing is to divide the cost of goods available for sale (Rs. 32,200) between the 700 units consumed and 300 units in the ending inventory. The division depends on the method of inventory costing: specific identification, FIFO, LIFO and weighted average cost adopted for the purpose.

Specific identification method: This method can be used when the units in the ending inventory can be identified with specific purchases. Suppose the ending inventory comprises of 100 units each from the purchases made on January 1, 12 and 23. The assignment of cost under the specific identification method will be as follows:

Periodic Inventory System: Specific Identification Method

Ending inventory	100 units @ Rs. 31	Rs. 3,100
	100 units @ Rs. 32	Rs. 3,200

(Continued)

	100 units @ Rs. 34	Rs. 3,400
		Rs. 9,700
Cost of goods sold	(Rs. 32,200 – Rs. 9,700)	Rs. 22,500

FIFO method: The units in the ending inventory are assumed to be out of the most recent purchases, that is, the purchases made on January 23. The cost of ending inventory and the cost of goods sold are worked out as follows:

Periodic Inventory System: FIFO Method

Ending inventory	300 units @ Rs. 34 per unit	Rs. 10,200
Cost of goods sold	(Rs. 32,200 – Rs. 10,200)	Rs. 22,000

LIFO method: The units in the ending inventory are assumed to be out of the earliest purchases, that is, 100 units of the beginning inventory and 200 units purchased on January 1. The cost of the ending inventory and the cost of goods sold are worked out as follows:

Periodic Inventory System: LIFO Method

Ending inventory	100 units @ Rs. 30 per unit	Rs. 3,000
	200 units @ Rs. 31 per unit	Rs. 6,200
		Rs. 9,200
Cost of goods sold	(Rs. 32,200 – Rs. 9,200)	Rs. 23,000

Weighted average cost method: Under the weighted average cost method, the average cost of goods available for sale is used to value the ending inventory. This average cost is calculated by dividing the total cost of goods available for sale by the total number of units available for sale. The cost of the ending inventory and the cost of goods sold are worked out as follows:

Periodic Inventory System: Weighted Average Cost Method

$$\text{Average unit cost} = \frac{\text{Cost of goods available for sale}}{\text{Units available for sale}}$$

$$= \frac{\text{Rs. } 32,200}{1,000} = \text{Rs. } 32,20$$

Ending inventory	300 units @ Rs. 32.20 per unit	Rs. 9,660
Cost of goods sold	(Rs. 32,200 – Rs. 9,660)	Rs. 22,540

7.10 Inventory Costing Under the Perpetual Inventory System

Under the perpetual inventory system, the cost of goods sold is accumulated by transferring costs from the inventory account to the cost of goods sold account as goods are sold or issued. The balance in the inventory account is the cost of the ending inventory.

Illustration 7.2 Inventory costing methods under perpetual system

The following particulars are given in respect of a stores item by a company:

Date (2015)		
January 1	Opening stock	100 units @ Rs. 30 per unit
January 1	Purchases	200 units @ Rs. 31 per unit
January 10	Issued for production	100 units
January 12	Purchases	400 units @ Rs. 32 per unit
January 15	Issued for production	200 units
January 18	Issued for production	200 units
January 23	Purchases	300 units @ Rs. 34 per unit
January 31	Issued for production	200 units

Under the specific identification method, the cost of the ending inventory and the cost of goods sold are the same under the perpetual inventory system as under the periodic system as the ending inventory comprises the same identified units.

With the FIFO and LIFO methods, the units and cost of inventory are updated after each transaction. The FIFO and the LIFO methods are applied as given in Tables 7.1 and 7.2.

Table 7.1 Perpetual inventory system: FIFO method

	Receipts			Issues			Balance		
Date (2015)	Units	Rate (Rs.)	Amount (Rs.)	Units	Rate (Rs.)	Amount (Rs.)	Units	Rate (Rs.)	Amount (Rs.)
1-Jan							100	30	3,000
1-Jan	200	31	6,200				100	30	3,000
							200	31	6,200
10-Jan				100	30	3,000	200	31	6,200
12-Jan	400	32	12,800				200	31	6,200
							400	32	12,800
15-Jan				200	31	6,200	400	32	12,800
18-Jan				200	32	6,400	200	32	6,400
23-Jan	300	34	10,200				200	32	6,400
							300	34	10,200
31-Jan				200	32	6,400	300	34	10,200
Cost of goods sold						22,000			

The cost of the ending inventory and the cost of goods sold are the same as under the periodic inventory system. This always happens under the FIFO method as the units in the ending inventory are from the last purchases in both the cases (Table 7.2).

Table 7.2 Perpetual inventory system: LIFO method

	Receipts			Issues			Balance		
Date (2015)	Units	Rate (Rs.)	Amount (Rs.)	Units	Rate (Rs.)	Amount (Rs.)	Units	Rate (Rs.)	Amount (Rs.)
1-Jan							100	30	3,000
1-Jan	200	31	6,200				100	30	3,000
							200	31	6,200
10-Jan				100	31	3,100	100	30	3,000
							100	31	3,100
12-Jan	400	32	12,800				100	30	3,000
							100	31	3,100
							400	32	12,800
15-Jan				200	32	6,400	100	30	3,000
							100	31	3,100
							200	32	6,400
18-Jan				200	32	6,400	100	30	3,000
							100	31	3,100
23-Jan	300	34	10,200				100	30	3,000
							100	31	3,100
							300	34	10,200
31-Jan				200	34	6,800	100	30	3,000
							100	31	3,100
							100	34	3,400
Cost of goods sold						22,700			

The value of stock as on January 31, 2015 under LIFO is Rs. 9,500 comprising 100 units @ Rs. 30,100 units @ Rs. 31 and 100 units @ Rs. 34. The cost of goods sold is Rs. 22,700. These figures are different from those computed under the periodic inventory system. The reason being the cost of goods available for sale is not the same. Under a periodic system, the pool of costs is the goods available for sale for the entire period, whereas under a perpetual system, the pool is the goods available for sale up to the date of sale.

The weighted average cost method produces values of ending inventory and cost of goods sold under the perpetual inventory system that are different from those under the periodic inventory system.

This is because the average cost under the periodic system is based on all goods available for sale during the period and under the perpetual system, the average is computed after each purchase (Table 7.3).

Table 7.3 Perpetual inventory system: weighted average cost method

Date (2015)	Receipts			Issues			Balance		
	Units	Rate (Rs.)	Amount (Rs.)	Units	Rate (Rs.)	Amount (Rs.)	Units	Rate (Rs.)	Amount (Rs.)
1-Jan							100	30	3,000
1-Jan	200	31	6,200				300	30.67	9,200
10-Jan				100	30.67	3,067	200	30.67	6,133
12-Jan	400	32	12,800				600	31.56	18,933
15-Jan				200	31.56	6,312	400	31.56	12,621
18-Jan				200	31.56	6,312	200	31.56	6,309
23-Jan	300	34	10,200				500	33.02	16,509
31-Jan				200	33.02	6,604	300	33.02	9,906
Cost of goods sold						22,295			

7.11 Comparison of Alternative Inventory Costing Methods

Table 7.4 shows how different inventory costing methods affect financial statements. The gross profit is calculated assuming sales revenue of Rs. 30,000. Managers consider trend in prices and the effect of different inventory costing methods on financial statements, income taxes, cash flows among other factors in choosing a particular inventory costing method. Inventory costing methods have an effect on both the income statement (gross profit) and the balance sheet (value of ending inventory).

Table 7.4 Comparison of alternative inventory costing methods

Method	Cost of Goods Sold		Gross Profit		Ending Inventory	
	Periodic (Rs.)	Perpetual (Rs.)	Periodic (Rs.)	Perpetual (Rs.)	Periodic (Rs.)	Perpetual (Rs.)
Specific identification	22,500	22,500	7,500	7,500	9,700	9,700
FIFO	22,000	22,000	8,000	8,000	10,200	10,200
LIFO	23,000	22,700	7,000	7,300	9,200	9,500
Weighted average cost	22,540	22,295	7,460	7,705	9,660	9,906

In this example, the material prices were found to be rising. Under these circumstances, the FIFO method shows the highest valuation of ending inventory while the LIFO method shows the lowest valuation. The weighted average method, which is best suited to conditions of fluctuating prices shows a valuation that lies between the above two valuations, both under the periodic and perpetual inventory systems. The gross profit figures also show a similar pattern.

The LIFO method matches revenues with current costs, and is therefore the most suitable method for income statement. However, the LIFO method does not accurately reflect the value of ending inventory on the balance sheet. On the contrary, the FIFO method presents a realistic value of ending inventory on the balance sheet but is not a suitable method for the income statement.

When prices are declining, the LIFO method results in a higher gross profit and a higher value of ending inventory than that under the FIFO method. As there is a significant variation in the amount of gross profit under these two methods during periods of fluctuating prices, these are not well suited for the financial statements of a company during such periods. The weighted average cost method is ideally suited in such times.

7.12 The Consistency Principle

A company is free to adopt any one of the cost flow assumptions discussed earlier. The consistency principle requires that once a company has chosen a particular method, it should continue using the same method. Consistency principle facilitates comparison of financial statements of an entity over successive time periods. Following the consistency principle does not mean that the entity can never change the inventory costing method. An entity can change the inventory costing method only if the change is required by an accounting standard or it results in a better presentation of financial statements. When an entity decides to change the method of costing inventories, it should disclose the change and the effect of the change on its net income. The following excerpt from the financial statements of Lanco Industries Ltd. (name subsequently changed to Srikalahasthi Pipes Ltd.) for the year 2003–04 states the circumstances requiring the change in the method of valuing inventories and the financial impact of the change.

> *"Schedule 20, Note 2: Lanco Kalahasthi Castings Limited (LKCL) which merged with the company during the year 2003–04 was following weighted average method of valuation while the company was following the FIFO method. With the objective to follow a uniform method and to make more appropriate presentation of financial statements, the method of calculating cost in respect of raw material, stores and spares has been changed to weighted average method instead of FIFO method followed previously. Consequently, the value of such items of inventory as at March 31, 2004 is lower by Rs. 194.31 lakhs with a corresponding effect on the profits for the year."*

7.13 Lower-of-Cost or Market Value

FIFO, LIFO and other methods are used to determine the cost of inventory on hand. But for financial reporting purposes, the principle is lower-of-cost or market value (net realizable value).

The net realizable value is the estimated selling price in the normal course of business minus the estimated costs of completion and the estimated costs necessary to make the sale.

The cost of inventories may not be recoverable if those inventories are damaged, if they have become wholly or partially obsolete, or if their selling prices have declined. The cost of inventories may also not be recoverable if the estimated costs of completion or the estimated costs to be incurred to make the sale have increased. The practice of writing inventories down below the cost to net realizable value is consistent with the view that assets should not be carried in excess of amounts expected to be realized from their sale or use.

Inventories are usually written down to net realizable value item by item. In some circumstances, however, it may be appropriate to group similar or related items. This may be the case with items of inventory relating to the same product line that have similar purposes or end uses, are produced and marketed in the same geographical area and cannot be practicably evaluated separately from other items in that product line. It is not appropriate to write inventories down on the basis of a classification of inventory, for example, finished goods, or all the inventories in a particular operating segment. Service providers generally accumulate costs in respect of each service for which a separate selling price is charged. Therefore, each such service is treated as a separate item.

Estimates of net realizable value are based on the most reliable evidence available at the time the estimates are made of the amount the inventories are expected to realize. These estimates take into consideration fluctuations of price or cost directly relating to events occurring after the end of the period to the extent that such events confirm conditions existing at the end of the period.

Estimates of net realizable value also take into consideration the purpose for which the inventory is held. For example, the net realizable value of the quantity of inventory held to satisfy firm sales or service contracts is based on the contract price. If the sales contracts are for less than the inventory quantities held, the net realizable value of the excess is based on general selling prices. Provisions may arise from firm sales contracts in excess of inventory quantities held or from firm purchase contracts. Such provisions are dealt with under Ind AS 37, *Provisions, Contingent Liabilities and Contingent Assets.*

Materials and other supplies held for use in the production of inventories are not written down below cost if the finished products in which they will be incorporated are expected to be sold at or above cost. However, when a decline in the price of materials indicates that the cost of the finished products exceeds the net realizable value, the materials are written down to net realizable value. In such circumstances, the replacement cost of the materials may be the best available measure of their net realizable value.

A new assessment is made of the net realizable value in each subsequent period. When the circumstances that previously caused inventories to be written down below cost no longer exist or when there is clear evidence of an increase in the net realizable value because of changed economic circumstances, the amount of the write-down is reversed (i.e., the reversal is limited to the amount of the original write-down) so that the new carrying amount is the lower-of-cost and the revised net realizable value. This occurs, for example, when an item of inventory that is carried at the net realizable value, because its selling price has declined, is still on hand in a subsequent period and its selling price has increased.

Illustration 7.3 Lower-of-cost or market rule

A dealer of mobile handsets has the following handsets in inventory as on March 31, 2015 (Table 7.5).

Table 7.5 Inventory at hand as on March 31, 2015

Item	Quantity	Cost per Unit (Rs.)	Market Price per Unit as on March 31, 2015 (Rs.)
Nokia	50	10,000	9,800
Samsung	70	8,800	9,000
Sony	100	12,000	11,500
Motorola	80	7,500	7,600

Following the lower-of-cost or market value, the value of inventory to be reported in the financial statements of the dealer for the year ended March 31, 2015 will be Rs. 2,856,000 as worked out in Table 7.6.

Table 7.6 Valuation of Inventory at hand as on March 31, 2015

Item	Quantity	Cost per Unit (Rs.)	Market Price per Unit (Rs.)	Lower-of-Cost or Market per Unit (Rs.)	Total Lower of Cost or Market (Rs.)
Nokia	50	10,000	9,800	9,800	490,000
Samsung	70	8,800	9,000	8,800	616,000
Sony	100	12,000	11,500	11,500	1,150,000
Motorola	80	7,500	7,600	7,500	600,000
			Value of inventory		2,856,000

7.14 Determining Inventory Quantities

Determination of inventory quantity at the end of the accounting period is necessary under the periodic inventory system and under the perpetual inventory system. Under the periodic inventory system, inventory quantity serves to determine the inventory at hand and the cost of goods sold. Under the perpetual inventory system, inventory quantity is required to check the correctness of inventory records and to determine shrinkage in inventory due to wastage and theft.

Companies generally take the physical inventory at the end of the accounting period. Taking a physical inventory is a formidable task as each item of inventory needs to be counted, measured or weighed. Whenever physical inventory is taken during the financial year, companies have to suspend all operations for one or two days. For the year-end inventory valuation physical stock taking it is often not possible to carry out stock taking on the closing day. It is carried out a few days later or sometimes even a few days earlier. In such a case, the actual value of the stock must be so adjusted as to relate it to the end of the year concerned. For doing so, it is necessary to take into account the goods that have come in (purchases and sales returns) and those that have gone out (sales and purchases returns) during the interval between the close of the year and the date of actual stock taking. Further, the adjustment of all the goods must be on the basis of cost. Later, a value is put on each item. The principle of cost or market price, whichever is lower, is applied either for inventory as a whole or item by item.

Illustration 7.4 Physical inventory

Suppose a firm that closes its books on March 31, carried out the stock taking on April 7 next year and the actual stock value was Rs. 400,000. During the period April 1–7, purchases amounted to Rs. 80,000 and sales Rs. 125,000. The gross margin on sales is 20%. The stock on March 31, would be Rs. 420,000 as shown below:

	(Rs.)
Stock ascertained on April 7	400,000
Less: Purchases during the period April 1–7	80,000
	320,000
Add: Cost of goods sold during the period Rs. 125,000 × 80/100	100,000
	420,000

Another important aspect of determining the inventory quantity is to add the inventory owned by the company, which is not at the company premises. These include goods in transit, goods sent on consignment and goods sent out for job-work. Similarly, inventory quantity at the company's premises may include items not owned by it, for example, goods received on consignment. These need to be deducted from the physical inventory. A key issue here is the determination of ownership of inventory.

7.14.1 Goods in Transit

Goods in transit are goods on board a truck, train, plane or ship at the end of the accounting period. These include goods purchased by the company not yet received and goods sold by the company not yet delivered. These goods are included in the inventory of the company that has the legal title to the goods. Legal title depends on the terms of sale of goods.

If the terms are *free on board (FOB) shipping point*, the buyer becomes the owner when the public carrier accepts the goods from the seller.

If the terms are *FOB destination*, the seller remains the owner till the goods reach the buyer.

7.14.2 Goods on Consignment

The title of goods on consignment lies with the consignor though the goods are in the possession of the consignee. Such goods should be included in the inventory of the consignor. The same rule applies to goods sent out by a company for some job-work, such as finishing, painting, etc.

7.15 Valuing Inventories by Estimation

Sometimes, it becomes necessary to estimate the value of the ending inventory. Commonly used methods to estimate the value of the ending inventory are the standard cost method, retail method and the gross-profit method.

7.15.1 Standard Cost Method

According to Ind AS 2 "Inventories", the standard cost method may be used for convenience if the results approximate cost. Standard costs take into account the normal levels of materials and supplies, labor efficiency and capacity utilization. They should be regularly reviewed and, if necessary, revised in the light of current conditions.

7.15.2 Retail Method

The retail method is used by retail stores. Normally, an entity would need the cost of ending inventory to prepare financial statements. Under the retail method, the physical inventory is measured at retail prices rather than at cost as most retail stores have price tags attached to products. The retail value of the inventory is reduced to cost by using the ratio of cost to sales.

To apply the retail method, the records must show the beginning inventory at cost and at retail prices. They should also show the purchases made during the period at cost and at retail prices. The sum of the beginning inventory and purchases provides the value of goods available for sale at cost and at retail. The estimated retail value of the ending inventory is calculated by deducting the sales for the period from the retail value of goods available for sale. The retail value of the ending inventory is then converted to cost using the ratio of cost to retail.

Illustration 7.5 Retail method

A retail store has a beginning inventory of Rs. 2,000,000 and a retail value of Rs. 2,750,000. The values of purchase during the period at cost are Rs. 5,500,000 and at retail are Rs. 7,250,000. Sales during the period are Rs. 8,000,000. The ending inventory at cost is Rs. 1,500,000, which is calculated as follows:

	Cost (Rs.)	Retail (Rs.)
Beginning inventory	2,000,000	2,750,000
Add: Purchases during the period	5,500,000	7,250,000
Goods available for sale	7,500,000	10,000,000
Ratio of cost to retail price = 7,500,000/10,000,000 = 75%		
Less: Sales during the period		8,000,000
Estimated ending inventory at retail		2,000,000
Estimated ending inventory at cost (2,000,000 × 75%)		1,500,000

7.15.3 Gross-Profit Method

This method is used to estimate the value of the ending inventory when the retail prices of the beginning inventory and purchases are not available. It is also a useful method for estimating the amount of inventory lost or destroyed by fire, theft or other reasons. Insurance companies also use this method to verify insurance claims.

Cost of goods available for sale is calculated by adding the cost of the beginning inventory and the cost of purchases during the period. The cost of goods sold is calculated by deducting the gross margin from the sales value. The cost of goods sold is then deducted from the cost of goods available for sale to estimate the cost of ending inventory.

Illustration 7.6 Gross-profit method

A store has a beginning inventory of Rs. 2,500,000 at cost. The cost of purchases during the period is Rs. 14,500,000. Sales during the period are Rs. 20,000,000. The gross-profit margin is 30% on sales. The cost of the ending inventory is Rs. 3,000,000 calculated as follows:

	(Rs.)	(Rs.)
Beginning inventory at cost		2,500,000
Add: Purchases at cost		14,500,000
Goods available for sale		17,000,000
Less: Estimated cost of goods sold		
Sales at selling price	20,000,000	
Less: gross margin (30%)	6,000,000	
		14,000,000
Estimated cost of ending inventory		3,000,000

7.16 Recognition of Inventories as an Expense

When inventories are sold, the carrying amount of the inventories is recognized as an expense in the period in which the related revenue is recognized.

The amount of any write-down of inventories to net realizable value and all losses of inventories are recognized as an expense in the period the write-down or loss occurs.

The amount of any reversal of any write-down of inventories, arising from an increase in net realizable value, is recognized as a reduction in the amount of inventories recognized as an expense in the period in which the reversal occurs.

Some inventories may be allocated to other asset accounts, for example, inventory used as a component of self-constructed property, plant or equipment. Inventories allocated to another asset in this way are recognized as an expense during the useful life of that asset.

7.17 Disclosure

In accordance with Ind AS 2 "Inventories", an entity is required to make the following disclosures relating to inventories in its financial statements:

1. The accounting policies adopted in measuring inventories, including the cost formula used.
2. The total carrying amount of inventories and the carrying amount in classifications appropriate to the entity.
3. The carrying amount of inventories carried at fair value minus costs to sell.
4. The amount of inventories recognized as an expense during the period.
5. The amount of any write-down of inventories recognized as an expense in the period.
6. The amount of any reversal of any write-down that is recognized as a reduction in the amount of inventories recognized as an expense in the period.
7. The circumstances or events that lead to the reversal of a write-down of inventories.
8. The carrying amount of inventories pledged as security for liabilities.

The disclosures relating to the accounting policy and carrying amount of inventories by Asian Paints Limited are presented in Exhibit 7.1.

Exhibit 7.1

Asian Paints Limited: Accounting Policy Relating to Inventories

1. Raw materials, work in progress, finished goods, packing materials, stores, spares, components, consumables and stock-in-trade are carried at the lower-of-cost and net realisable value. However, materials and other items held for use in production of inventories are not written down below cost if the finished goods in which they will be incorporated are expected to be sold at or above the cost. The comparison of cost and net realisable value is made on an item-by-item basis. Damaged, unserviceable and inert stocks are valued at net realizable value.
2. In determining cost of raw materials, packing materials, stock-in-trade, stores, spares, components and consumables, weighted average cost method is used. Cost of inventory comprises all costs of purchase, duties, taxes (other than those subsequently recoverable from tax authorities) and all other costs incurred in bringing the inventory to their present location and condition.
3. Cost of finished goods and work-in-progress includes the cost of raw materials, packing materials, an appropriate share of fixed and variable production overheads, excise duty as applicable and other costs incurred in bringing the inventories to their present location and condition. Fixed production overheads are allocated on the basis of normal capacity of production facilities.

Carrying Amount of Inventories **(Rs. in Crores)**

Inventories (At lower of cost and net realizable value)		As on March 31, 2016	As on March 31, 2015
(a)	Raw materials	455.11	496.72
	Raw materials-in-transit	79.23	44.79
		534.34	541.51
(b)	Packing materials	40.13	35.63
(c)	Finished goods	775.99	1,008.49
	Finished goods-in-transit	2.42	1.04
		778.41	1,009.53
(d)	Work-in-progress	64.47	91.90
(e)	Stores, spares and consumables	57.75	52.63
(f)	Stock-in-trade (acquired for trading)	134.52	70.32
	Stock-in-trade (acquired for trading) in-transit	0.50	0.66
		135.02	70.98
	Total	1,610.12	1,802.18

(Rs. in Crores)

Stock of work in progress	As on March 31, 2016	As on March 31, 2015
Paints, Enamels and Varnishes	62.80	89.01
Others	1.67	2.89
Total	64.47	91.90

(Source: Asian Paints Annual Report 2015–16)

Summary – Review of Learning Objectives

1. **Define inventories.** Inventories are assets: (a) held for sale in the ordinary course of a business, (b) in the process of production for such sale or (c) in the form of materials or supplies to be consumed in the production process or in the rendering of services.
2. **Describe the different types of inventories maintained by manufacturing, merchandising and service companies and the reasons thereof.** Manufacturing companies carry inventories of finished goods, work-in-process, raw materials and supplies. Merchandising firms carry inventories of finished goods only.

   The type of inventories carried by service companies depends on the nature of the service. Raw materials inventory delinks purchasing and production activities of a firm. Work-in-process inventories are required because it takes time to complete a process/operation and to move products from one stage to another. Finished goods inventory decouples the firm's production and marketing activities, and facilitates efficient servicing of customer demands.
3. **Explain the objectives of inventory accounting.** Inventory accounting provides information for the preparation of periodic financial statements, tax returns and for exercising control over inventories.
4. **Explain the effect of errors on inventory measurement.** Errors in measuring the ending inventory lead to an inaccuracy in cost of goods sold, gross profit, net profit, current assets and equity of an entity and make the financial statements of the entity less credible.
5. **Explain and use the periodic and perpetual inventory systems.** In the periodic inventory system, the ending inventory is found by a physical count, and the cost of goods sold is obtained by deducting the cost of inventory from the cost of goods available for sale. Under the perpetual inventory system, inventory balances are determined after each receipt and issue. Under this method, physical inventory is taken to check the accuracy of accounting records. Cost of goods sold can be ascertained directly from the accounting records.
6. **Determine the quantity of inventory.** Physical inventory is taken during the financial year and at the year end. For the year-end inventory valuation, physical stock is carried out a few days later or sometimes even a few days earlier. In such a case, the actual value of the stock must be so adjusted for sales and purchases during the intervening period as to relate it to the end of the year concerned. Goods in transit and goods on consignment also require adjustment.

7. **Identify the amounts that should be included in the cost of inventories.** The cost of inventories shall comprise all costs of purchase, costs of conversion and other costs incurred in bringing the inventories to their present location and condition.
8. **Compute inventory value using different inventory costing methods.** There are four generally accepted inventory costing methods that provide alternative ways of assigning the cost of goods available for sale between inventory and cost of goods. These methods are specific identification method, first-in-first-out method (FIFO), last-in-first-out method (LIFO) and weighted average cost method.
9. **Explain the significance of the consistency principle.** The consistency principle requires that once a company has chosen a particular method, it should continue using the same method. Consistency principle facilitates comparison of financial statements of an entity over successive time periods.
10. **Report inventory at the lower-of-cost or market value.** Inventory costing methods are used to determine the cost of inventory on hand. But for balance sheet reporting purposes, the principle is lower-of-cost or market value (net realizable value). The net realizable value is estimated as the selling price in the normal course of business minus the estimated costs of completion and the estimated costs necessary to make the sale.
11. **Apply the retail and the gross-profit methods for estimating inventory values.** Sometimes, it becomes necessary to estimate the value of the ending inventory because the cost of the ending inventory is difficult to determine, but the sales value is available. Two commonly used methods to estimate the value of the ending inventory are the retail method and the gross-profit method.
12. **Accounting treatment of inventories.** The carrying amount of inventories is recognized as an expense at the time of their sale. The amount of write-down of inventories to realizable value and losses of inventories are recognized as an expense in the period the write-down or loss occurs. The amount of any reversal of any write-down of inventories is reduced from the amount of inventories recognized as an expense in the period in which the reversal occurs.
13. **Disclosure requirements.** The disclosure requirements relate to accounting policies, carrying amount, inventories expensed, write-downs, reversal of write-downs, etc.

Glossary

- **Consistency principle** requires that once a company has chosen a particular method, it should continue using the same method.
- **Cost of inventories** comprise all costs of purchase, costs of conversion and other costs incurred in bringing the inventories to their present location and condition.
- **First-in, first-out (FIFO) method** is an inventory costing method that assumes that the oldest goods are sold first and that the most recently purchased goods are in the ending inventory. This method allocates the oldest unit costs to the cost of goods sold and the newest unit costs to the ending inventory.
- **Gross-profit method** is a method of inventory estimation in which the cost of goods sold is calculated by deducting the gross margin from the sales value. The cost of goods sold is then deducted from the cost of goods available for sale to estimate the cost of the ending inventory.
- **Inventories** are assets: (a) held for sale in the normal course of a business; or (b) in the process

of production for such sale; or (c) in the form of materials or supplies to be consumed in the production process or in the rendering of services.

- **Last-in, first-out (LIFO) method** is an inventory costing method that assumes that the cost of goods sold comprises the cost of the most recent purchases.
- **Lower-of-cost or market rule** is a rule under which an inventory is reported at lower-of-cost or market value (net realizable value) in the financial statements.
- **Net realizable value** is the estimated selling price in the normal course of business minus the estimated costs of completion and the estimated costs necessary to make the sale.
- **Periodic inventory system** is a system of keeping inventory records in which the ending inventory is found by a physical count and the cost of goods sold is obtained by deducting the cost of inventory from the cost of goods available for sale.
- **Perpetual inventory system** is a system of keeping inventory records in which inventory balances are determined after each receipt and issue. Under this method, physical inventory is taken to check the accuracy of accounting records.
- **Retail method** is a method of inventory estimation used by retail stores in which the retail value of the inventory is reduced to cost by using the ratio of cost to sales.
- **Specific identification method** is an inventory costing method in which the cost of each item in the ending inventory is individually identified as coming from a specific purchase.
- **Weighted average cost method** is an inventory costing method in which the weighted average unit cost of goods available for sale is used to value both the cost of goods sold and the ending inventory.

Solved Problem

1. The following information is provided by a dealer in computer chips. The dealer follows a periodic method of accounting for inventory.

January 1	Beginning inventory 750 chips @ Rs. 1,550 per chip
Purchases:	
January 10	1,000 chips @ Rs. 1,750 per chip
January 20	1,650 chips @ Rs. 1,875 per chip
Sales:	
January 15	900 chips @ Rs. 3,000 each
January 25	1,950 chips @ Rs. 3,250 each

(a) Assuming that the dealer uses the FIFO cost flow assumption, calculate the cost of goods sold and the gross profit.

(b) Assuming that the dealer uses the LIFO cost flow assumption, calculate the cost of goods sold and the gross profit.

(c) Which cost flow assumption should the dealer choose?

Solution:

(a) FIFO method

Cost of goods available for sale

January 1	Beginning inventory	750 @ Rs. 1,550	Rs. 1,162,500
January 10	Purchase	1,000 @ Rs. 1,750	1,750,000
January 20	Purchase	1,650 @ Rs. 1,875	3,093,750
		3,400	Rs. 6,006,250
Goods available for sale		3,400	
Units sold		2,850	
Ending inventory		550 @ Rs. 1,875	Rs. 1,031,250
Cost of goods available for sale		Rs. 6,006,250	
Ending inventory		–Rs. 1,031,250	
Cost of goods sold		4,975,000	
Sales revenue			
January 15	900 @ Rs. 3,000	Rs. 2,700,000	
January 25	1,950 @ Rs. 3,250	Rs. 6,337,500	
	2850	Rs. 9,037,500	
Gross profit: Rs. 9,037,500 – Rs. 4,975,000 = Rs. 4,062,500			

(b) LIFO method

Cost of goods available for sale	Rs. 6,006,250
Ending inventory 550 @ Rs. 1,550	852,500
Cost of goods sold	Rs. 5,153,750
Gross profit: Rs. 9,037,500 – Rs. 5,153,750 = Rs. 3,883,750.	

(c) The choice of inventory method depends on the company's objectives. The FIFO method would result in a higher income, but the LIFO method would reduce income taxes and provide better matching of current sales revenue with current costs.

Multiple Choice Questions

1. If goods are shipped FOB destination, who has the legal title to the goods while these are in transit?
a. The seller
b. The buyer
c. The carrier
d. None of the above

2. Which of the following should not be included in the physical inventory of a company?
a. Goods held on consignment from another company.
b. Goods in transit from another company shipped FOB shipping point.

c. Goods shipped on consignment to another company.
d. All of the above

3. What is the purpose of taking a physical inventory under the perpetual inventory system?
   a. To determine the accuracy of the perpetual inventory records.
   b. To determine cost of goods sold for the accounting period.
   c. To compute inventory ratios.
   d. All of the above

4. The LIFO inventory method assumes that the cost of the latest units purchased is ______.
   a. the last to be allocated to the cost of goods sold
   b. the first to be allocated to the ending inventory
   c. the first to be allocated to the cost of goods sold
   d. not allocated to the cost of goods sold or the ending inventory

5. A company has made the following four inventory purchases in January:

		(Rs.)
January 5	300 units	39,000
January 12	400 units	58,500
January 16	400 units	63,000
January 25	300 units	49,500

The physical inventory on January 31 is 400 units. What is the value of the ending inventory under the LIFO inventory method?

   a. Rs. 51,675
   b. Rs. 53,625
   c. Rs. 66,375
   d. Rs. 65,475

6. A company has made the following four inventory purchases in January:

		(Rs.)
January 5	300 units	39,000
January 12	400 units	58,500
January 16	400 units	63,000
January 25	300 units	49,500

The physical inventory on January 31 is 400 units. What is the value of the ending inventory under the FIFO inventory method?
   a. Rs. 65,250
   b. Rs. 63,625
   c. Rs. 64,750
   d. Rs. 65,475

7. A company has made the following four inventory purchases in January:

		(Rs.)
January 5	300 units	39,000
January 12	400 units	58,500
January 16	400 units	63,000
January 25	300 units	49,500

The physical inventory on January 31 is 400 units. What is the value of the ending inventory under the weighted average cost inventory method?
   a. Rs. 61,675
   b. Rs. 60,000
   c. Rs. 66,375
   d. Rs. 65,475

8. A company has made the following four inventory purchases in January:

		(Rs.)
January 5	300 units	39,000
January 12	400 units	58,500
January 16	400 units	63,000
January 25	300 units	49,500

The physical inventory on January 31 is 400 units. Which inventory method results in the highest gross profit for January?

a. The FIFO method
b. The LIFO method
c. The average cost method
d. Cannot be determined

9. The following purchases have been made by a company:

400 units at Rs. 250
600 units at Rs. 275

The average unit cost for inventory is ______.

a. Rs. 250
b. Rs. 262.50
c. Rs. 265
d. Rs. 275

10. Which of the following is not an inventory costing method?

a. FIFO
b. Specific identification
c. Average cost
d. Lower-of-cost or market

11. Which of the following is a cost flow assumption used in costing an inventory?

a. Lower-of-cost or market
b. Periodic
c. Perpetual
d. Average cost

12. A company reports the following inventory transactions during 2014:

March 1, 2014	Purchase	100 units @ Rs. 900
May 14, 2014	Purchase	125 units @ Rs. 940
July 1, 2014	Purchase	80 units @ Rs. 980

The company sold 250 units at Rs. 1,260 each. The company follows a periodic inventory system and pays tax at the rate of 40%. What is the company's gross profit using LIFO?

a. Rs. 236,400
b. Rs. 232,000
c. Rs. 78,600
d. Rs. 83,000

13. A company reports the following inventory transactions during 2014:

March 1, 2014	Purchase	100 units @ Rs. 900
May 14, 2014	Purchase	125 units @ Rs. 940
July 1, 2014	Purchase	80 units @ Rs. 980

The company sold 250 units at Rs. 1,260 each. The company follows a periodic inventory system and pays tax at the rate of 40%. What is the company's gross profit using FIFO?

a. Rs. 236,400
b. Rs. 232,000
c. Rs. 78,600
d. Rs. 83,000

14. In periods of rising prices, the inventory method which results in the inventory value on the balance sheet that is closest to the current cost is the

a. FIFO method
b. LIFO method
c. Average cost method
d. All of the above

15. In a period of declining prices, which of the following inventory methods generally results in the lowest balance sheet figure for an inventory?

a. Average cost method
b. LIFO method
c. FIFO method
d. None of the above

Review Questions

1. What types of assets qualify to be called inventories?
2. Why does a firm need to maintain inventories?
3. What are the main objectives of inventory accounting?
4. There is an overstatement of the ending inventory by Rs. 250,000 by a company as on March 31, 2013. State the effect of this error on the net income of the year ended March 31, 2013, next year and the combined net income of two years.
5. What are the advantages of using a perpetual inventory system?
6. A company that follows the perpetual inventory system need not take the year-end physical inventory. Do you agree?
7. A company is able to take the physical inventory on April 7, 2015 while its accounting year ends on March 31, 2015. What adjustments would the company need to make to the physical inventory figure determined on April 7, 2015 to arrive at the physical inventory figure as on March 31, 2015?
8. Company X has dispatched goods to company Y on FOB destination terms on March 28, 2015. As on March 31, 2015, the goods are in transit. Which of the two companies should include these goods in its ending inventory as on March 31, 2015?
9. A company receives a shipment of goods with a listed price of Rs. 150,000. The supplier allows a discount of 5% on the listed price. The company pays freight charges of Rs. 3,750 for the shipment. At what cost should the company include these goods in the inventory?
10. State one advantage and one disadvantage of the specific identification method of inventory costing.
11. Are the costs of the ending inventory the same under the periodic and perpetual inventory systems when one adopts the FIFO or LIFO cost flow assumption?
12. Why does the weighted average cost of the ending inventory different under the periodic inventory system and the perpetual inventory system?
13. Identify the inventory cost flow assumption in the following cases:
    - **(a)** In a period of rising prices, the cost of inventory reported in the balance sheet is close to its current cost.
    - **(b)** In a period of falling prices, the cost of inventory reported in the balance sheet is considerably above its current cost.
    - **(c)** The cost flow matches the physical flow of merchandise.
    - **(d)** The unit cost is determined by dividing the cost of goods available for sale by the total units available for sale.
14. In times of rising prices, under which of the two cost flow assumptions: FIFO and LIFO, is the reported net income higher and why?
15. Which accounting principle ensures that financial statements of a company are comparable over time?
16. Under which of the cost flow assumptions, that is, specific identification, FIFO, LIFO and average cost, can the lower-of-cost or market basis of accounting be used?
17. Under what circumstances can a company use the retail inventory method to determine the cost of inventory?

Practice Problems

1. Based on the following information, calculate cost of goods sold and the cost of ending inventory under FIFO, LIFO and weighted average method.

	Purchase	Sales	Stock
December 31, 2009			200 units @ Rs. 5
January 25, 2010	170 units @ Rs. 6		
January 29, 2010		150 units	
May 28, 2010	190 units @ Rs. 7		
June 7, 2010		230 units	
November 20, 2010	150 units @ Rs. 8		
December 15, 2010		100 units	

2. Specialty Store uses a periodic inventory system but needs to determine the approximate amount of inventory at the end of each month without taking a physical inventory. The store has provided the following data:

	Cost Price (Rs.)	Retail Selling Price (Rs.)
Inventory of merchandise, June 30	6,00,000	10,00,000
Purchases during July	4,44,000	8,00,000
Goods available for sale during July	10,44,000	18,00,000
Net sales during July		12,00,000

   (i) Estimate the cost of goods sold and the cost of July 31 inventory using the retail method of evaluation.
   (ii) Was the cost of inventory, as a percentage of sales price, higher or lower in July than it was in June? Explain.

3. Inventory accounting is based on certain cost flow assumptions and techniques for estimating the cost of goods sold and the ending inventory. For each of the statements given here, indicate the cost flow assumption or the technique used:
   (i) A pattern of transferring unit costs from the inventory account to the cost of goods sold that may parallel the physical flow of merchandise.
   (ii) The only flow assumption in which all units of merchandise are assigned the same per unit cost.
   (iii) The method used to record the cost of goods sold when each unit in the inventory is unique.
   (iv) The most conservative of the flow assumptions during a period of sustained inflation.
   (v) The flow assumption that provides the most current valuation of inventory in the balance sheet.
   (vi) A technique for estimating the cost of goods sold and the ending inventory that is based on the relationship between the cost and sales price during the current accounting period.

4. Two identical companies A and B reported a net income of Rs. 6,00,000 and Rs. 5,50,000, respectively. An analyst attributes the higher profit of company A to its use of FIFO method of valuing inventory as against the LIFO method by company B under business conditions attended by rising prices. Do you agree with the analyst? Explain.

5. Trans Retail Ltd. provides the following information relating to the accounting year ended March 31, 2014:

	(Rs.)
Goods purchased at list price	5,000,000
Trade discount 10% and sales tax 12%	
Freight charges	260,000
Sales during the year	6,000,000
Ending inventory at selling price	625,000

Find the cost of ending inventory using the retail method.

6. Global Retails provide the following information relating to the accounting year ended March 31, 2014:

	(Rs.)
Cost of goods purchased	3,000,000
Sales during the year	3,000,000
Ending inventory at selling price	750,000

Find the cost of the ending inventory using the retail method.

7. The following information is available from the accounting records of a company for the accounting year ended March 31, 2015.

	(Rs.)
Stock as on 1-4-2014	285,000
Purchases	1,525,000
Manufacturing expenses	300,000
Selling expenses	121,000
Administrative expenses	60,000
Financial charges	43,000
Sales	2,490,000

At the time of valuing stock as on March 31, 2015, a sum of Rs. 35,000 was written off on a particular item which was originally purchased for Rs. 100,000 and was sold during the year for Rs. 90,000. Except for this item, the gross profit earned during the year was 20% on sales. Ascertain the value of stock as on March 31, 2015 and also the profit for the year.

8. From the following information, find the value of stock as on March 31, 2015.
   (i) Cost of physical stock on March 31, 2015 was Rs. 320,000.
   (ii) Cost of stock held as consignee was Rs. 160,000.
   (iii) Stock was expected to realize the normal selling price of 150% of cost except for the following:
      (a) Goods costing Rs. 20,000 were damaged and an expenditure of 10% of the normal selling price is necessary to realize the normal selling price of goods.
      (b) Goods costing Rs. 15,000 were damaged beyond repair and were expected to realize Rs. 2,000 only.

9. A trader prepared his accounts on March 31 every year. Due to some unavoidable reasons, no inventory could be taken till April 15, 2015, the date on which the total cost of goods in the warehouse came to Rs. 50,000. The following facts were established between March 31 and April 15, 2015.
   (i) Sales Rs. 41,000
   (ii) Purchases Rs. 5,034
   (iii) Sales return Rs. 1,000

   Goods are sold by the trader at a profit of 20% on sales. You are required to ascertain the value of inventory as on March 31, 2015.

10. A company carries out a physical count of inventory on March 31, 2015. The value of the inventory is determined as Rs. 6,500,000. The management suspects that some employees have been involved in pilfering the inventory. Given the following information, find the estimated cost of the pilfered inventory.

	(Rs.)
Beginning inventory on April 1, 2014	12,000,000
Purchases during the year	68,000,000
Sales during the year	96,000,000

The company earns a gross profit of 25% on sales.

11. The following information is available from the records of X Ltd. as on March 31, 2015.

	(Rs.)
Beginning inventory on April 1, 2014	2,400,000
Purchases during the year	4,800,000
Sales during the year	6,000,000

The records show that on October 1, 2014, goods worth Rs. 900,000 were destroyed by fire. The company sells goods at a gross margin of 25% on sales. Find the cost of the ending inventory of the company.

12. The following information has been extracted from the books of ABC Ltd.

	Purchase	Sales	Stock
January 1, 2015			1500 units @ Rs. 42
January 5, 2015		1,000 units	
January 8, 2015	2,000 units @ Rs. 48		
January 15, 2015		1,500 units	
January 20, 2015	1,000 units @ Rs. 46		

The company has been following the FIFO method of valuing inventories. However, it has decided to change to the LIFO method with effect from January 1, 2015. Determine the change in the value of inventory as on January 31, 2015 due to the change in method.

13. A company carried out a physical inventory check on April 6, 2015 for the purpose of preparing its financial statements for the year ended March 31, 2015. The value of the inventory based on physical check was determined as Rs. 525,000. The following transactions were recorded from April 1, 2015 to April 6, 2015.

(i) Goods costing Rs. 75,000 were sold.

(ii) Goods received on consignment valued at Rs. 60,000 were included in the value of inventory.

(iii) Goods purchased before March 31, 2015 amounting to Rs. 15,000 were returned to suppliers.

(iv) Goods valued at Rs. 90,000 were purchased and accounted for before March 31, 2015, but were not received until April 6, 2015.

Determine the value of inventories held by the company as on March 31, 2015.

14. A company carries out a physical count of inventory on March 31, 2015. The value of the inventory is determined as Rs. 6,270,000. The management suspects that some employees have been involved in pilfering the inventory. Given the following information, find the estimated cost of the pilfered inventory and the cost of goods sold during the year.

	(Rs.)
Beginning inventory on April 1, 2014	4,500,000
Purchases during the year	13,500,000
Sales during the year	15,000,000

The company earns a gross profit of 25% on sales.

15. A dealer in cameras has the following items in inventory as on March 31, 2015 (Table 7.7).

Table 7.7 Details of inventory as on March 31, 2015

Item	Quantity	Cost per Unit (Rs.)	Market Price per Unit as on March 31, 2015 (Rs.)
Nikon	10	8,500	7,900
Canon	14	7,250	7,600
Minolta	24	6,250	5,700
Yashica	20	6,000	6,750

Calculate the value of inventory to be reported in the balance sheet of the dealer as on March 31, 2015.

16. A company reported the following figures of cost of goods sold for the last two years.

	2013 (Rs.)	2014 (Rs.)
Beginning inventory	1,000,000	1,500,000
Purchases	8,200,000	8,750,000
Cost of goods available for sale	9,200,000	10,250,000
Less: Ending inventory	1,500,000	1,850,000
Cost of goods sold	7,700,000	8,400,000

The accounting staff of the company has committed two errors:

1. Ending inventory for 2013 has been overstated by Rs. 100,000.
2. Ending inventory for 2014 has been understated by Rs. 250,000.

You are required to calculate the correct cost of goods sold for 2013 and 2014.

17. The following information is provided by a dealer in computer chips. The dealer follows a periodic method of accounting for inventory. He carries only one type of chip and all chips are identical. He codes every batch of chips and marks its purchase price.

January 1	Beginning inventory 750 chips @ Rs. 1,550 per chip
Purchases:	
January 10	1,000 chips @ Rs. 1,750 per chip
January 20	1,650 chips @ Rs. 1,875 per chip
Sales:	
January 15	900 chips @ Rs. 3,000 each
January 25	1,950 chips @ Rs. 3,250 each

How can the dealer, using the specific identification cost flow assumption, maximize and minimize his gross profit by specifically selecting the chips to sell on January 15 and January 25?

18. Based on the following information, prepare an income statement in columnar form under FIFO, LIFO and weighted average method. Assume other expenses as Rs. 1,000 and the income tax rate as 40%. The company follows the perpetual inventory system.

	Purchase	Sales	Stock
December 31, 2009			200 units @ Rs. 5
January 25, 2010	170 units @ Rs. 6		
January 29, 2010		150 units	
May 28, 2010	190 units @ Rs. 7		
June 7, 2010			230 units
November 20, 2010	150 units @ Rs. 8		
December 15, 2010		100 units	

Answers to Multiple Choice Questions

1. (a)
2. (a)
3. (a)
4. (c)
5. (b)
6. (a)
7. (b)
8. (a)
9. (c)
10. (d)
11. (d)
12. (c)
13. (d)
14. (a)
15. (c)

Corporate Financial Statements

8

LEARNING OBJECTIVES

After reading this chapter, you will be able to:

- Explain the books of account companies are required to keep and the financial statements they are required to prepare.
- Explain the form and contents of corporate financial statements.
- Prepare corporate financial statements.

8.1 Introduction

All business transactions carried out by a business are summarized at the end of the accounting period in the form of financial statements. The three basic financial statements prepared by all business entities are the income statement (statement of profit and loss), the balance sheet and the cash flow statement. The income statement reveals the financial performance of the entity during the accounting period in terms of profit or loss made by the entity. The balance sheet conveys the financial position of the entity on the last date of the accounting period in terms of what the entity owns (assets) and what it owes (liabilities). The cash flow statement shows how the balance of cash and cash equivalents has changed during the accounting period due to inflows and outflows of cash. The financial statements provide necessary information to investors, lenders and other stakeholders in the business to take informed decisions.

There is no fundamental difference in the manner in which financial statements are prepared by companies and non-company entities, such as sole owners and partnerships. All entities follow the same basic principles. Some special features of company financial statements are as follows:

1. Companies have to follow the requirements of the Companies Act and other applicable laws in preparing their financial statements.
2. Financial statements of companies are published for use by interested parties; these are public documents.
3. Financial statements of companies carry comparative figures of the previous accounting period.

This chapter explains the statutory provisions relating to the books of accounts to be maintained by companies; form and contents of financial statements (balance sheet and statement of profit and loss); and year-end accounting adjustment entries, some of which are specifically applicable to companies. Many solved problems are provided to facilitate understanding. The statement of cash flow is covered in Chapter 11.

8.2 Books of Accounts to Be Kept by a Company

Section 128(1) of the Companies Act, 2013 requires every company to prepare and keep at its registered office books of account and other relevant books and papers and financial statements for every financial year, which give a true and fair view of the state of affairs of the company, including that of its branch office or offices, if any, and explain the transactions effected both at the registered office and its branches. Such books shall be kept on an accrual basis and according to the double entry system of accounting.

According to Section 2(13) of the Companies Act, 2013, "books of account" include records maintained in respect of:

1. all sums of money received and expended by a company and matters in relation to which the receipts and expenditure take place;
2. all sales and purchases of goods and services by the company;
3. assets and liabilities of the company; and
4. the items of cost as may be prescribed under Section 148 in the case of a company which belongs to any class of companies specified under that section.

8.3 Financial Statements

Section 129 of the Companies Act, 2013 requires that at every annual general meeting of a company, the Board of Directors of the company shall lay before such meeting the financial statements for the financial year.

According to Ind AS 1 *Presentation of Financial Statements*, a complete set of financial statements comprises:

1. a balance sheet as on the end of the period;
2. a statement of profit and loss for the period;
3. statement of changes in equity for the period;
4. a statement of cash flows for the period;
5. notes, comprising a summary of significant accounting policies and other explanatory information;
6. comparative information in respect of the preceding period; and
7. a balance sheet as on the beginning of the preceding period if the company has applied an accounting policy retrospectively, or made a retrospective restatement of items in its financial statements, or has reclassified items in its financial statements.

In the case (7), a company would need to prepare three balance sheets, one for the current period, second for the preceding period and the third at the beginning of the preceding period.

Section 129 of the Companies Act, 2013 further requires that the financial statements shall give a true and fair view of the state of affairs of the company or companies, comply with the accounting standards notified under Section 133 and shall be in the form or forms as may be provided for different class or classes of companies in Schedule III.

8.3.1 Consolidated Financial Statements

Where a company has one or more subsidiaries, it shall also prepare a consolidated financial statement of the company and of all the subsidiaries. Where a company is required to prepare Consolidated Financial Statements, that is, consolidated balance sheet, consolidated statement of changes in equity and consolidated statement of profit and loss, the company shall follow the same requirements of Schedule III as are applicable to a company in the preparation of balance sheet, statement of changes in equity and statement of profit and loss.

In addition, the consolidated financial statements are required to disclose the information as per the requirements specified in the applicable Indian Accounting Standards notified under the Companies (Indian Accounting Standards) Rules 2015, including the following, namely:

(i) Allocation of profit or loss for the period as attributable to 'non-controlling interest' and to 'owners of the parent' in the statement of profit and loss. Similarly, allocation of 'total comprehensive income' (TCI) for the period is allocated as attributable to 'non-controlling interest' and to 'owners of the parent' needs to be presented in the statement of profit and loss.
The allocation of 'TCI' is also required to be made in the statement of changes in equity.

(ii) In the Balance Sheet and in the Statement of Changes in Equity, within equity, 'Non-controlling interests' is required to be shown separately from the equity of the 'owners of the parent'.

(iii) Investments accounted for using the equity method.
Consolidated financial statement will cover all subsidiaries, associates and joint ventures (whether Indian or foreign). An entity is also required to disclose the list of subsidiaries or associates or joint ventures which have not been consolidated in the consolidated financial statements along with the reasons of not consolidating.

Further, the following additional information is required to be disclosed in the consolidated financial statements.

Name of the entity in the group	Net Assets, i.e., total assets minus total liabilities		Share in profit or loss		Share in other comprehensive income		Share in total comprehensive income	
	As % of consol. net assets	Amount	As % of consol. profit or loss	Amount	As % of consol. other comp. income (OCI)	Amount	As % of consol. total comp. income (TCI)	Amount
Parent								
Subsidiaries								
Indian								
1								
2								
3								

(Continued)

Name of the entity in the group	Net Assets, i.e., total assets minus total liabilities		Share in profit or loss		Share in other comprehensive income		Share in total comprehensive income	
	As % of consol. net assets	Amount	As % of consol. profit or loss	Amount	As % of consol. other comp. income (OCI)	Amount	As % of consol. total comp. income (TCI)	Amount
Foreign								
1								
2								
3								
Non-controlling interest in all subsidiaries								
Associates (Investment as per the equity method)								
Indian								
1								
2								
3								
Foreign								
1								
2								
3								
Joint Ventures (Investment as per the equity method)								
Indian								
1								
2								
3								
Foreign								
1								
2								
3								
Total								

The additional information relating to subsidiaries, associates and joint ventures provided by Asian Paints Limited for the year ended 31st March, 2017, is presented in Exhibit 8.1.

Exhibit 8.1

Disclosure of Additional Information pertaining to the Parent Company, Subsidiaries and Associates in the consolidated financial statements of Asian Paints Limited for the year ended 31st March, 2017

(Rupees in Millions)

Name of the entity in the group	Net Assets, i.e., total assets minus total liabilities		Share in profit or loss		Share in other comprehensive income		Share in total comprehensive income	
	As % of consol. net assets	Net Assets	As % of consol. profit or loss	Profit/ (Loss)	As % of consol. other comp. income	OCI	As % of consol. total comp. income	TCI
Parent								
Asian Paints Limited	87.1	69,506.0	89.2	17,981.5	1811.1	13,904.0	95.7	19,731.9
Indian Subsidiaries								
Direct Subsidiaries								
Asian Paints Ind. Coating	0.1	83.8	(0.1)	(22.0)	(1.2)	(0.9)	(0.1)	(22.9)
Maxbhumi Developers Ltd.	0.0	(17.2)	0.0	(2.3)	0.0	—	0.0	(2.3)
Sleek International Pvt. Ltd.	(0.2)	(131.0)	(0.5)	(103.2)	2.3	1.8	(0.5)	(101.4)
Asian Paints PPG Pvt. Ltd.	0.3	276.0	0.5	93.7	2.1	1.6	0.5	95.3

(Continued)

Name of the entity in the group	Net Assets, i.e., total assets minus total liabilities		Share in profit or loss		Share in other comprehensive income		Share in total comprehensive income	
	As % of consol. net assets	Net Assets	As % of consol. profit or loss	Profit/ (Loss)	As % of consol. other comp. income	OCI	As % of consol. total comp. income	TCI
Foreign Subsidiaries								
Direct Subsidiaries								
Asian Paints (Nepal) Pvt. Ltd.	0.7	568.7	1.0	199.0	0.4	0.3	1.0	199.3
Asian Paints (Int.) Ltd.	1.7	1,350.9	(0.2)	(13.9)	0.0	—	(0.1)	(13.9)
Indirect Subsidiaries								
Samoa Paints Limited	0.0	8.0	0.0	9.7	0.0	—	0.0	9.7
Asian Paints (South Pacific)	0.4	309.2	0.6	115.8	0.0	—	0.6	115.8
Asian Paints (Tonga) Ltd.	0.0	15.4	0.0	3.1	0.0	—	0.0	3.1
Asian Paints (SI) Limited	0.1	48.0	0.2	33.6	0.0	—	0.2	33.6
Asian Paints (Vanuatu) Ltd.	0.0	5.6	0.0	9.1	0.0	—	0.0	9.1
Asian Paints (Middle East)	0.4	282.3	0.3	64.7	(0.6)	(0.5)	0.3	64.2
Asian Paints (Bangladesh)	0.4	318.0	0.3	65.8	0.0	0.0	0.3	65.8
SCB Chemicals S.A.E.	0.4	347.0	1.1	220.9	0.0	—	1.1	220.9

(*Continued*)

Name of the entity in the group	Net Assets, i.e., total assets minus total liabilities		Share in profit or loss		Share in other comprehensive income		Share in total comprehensive income	
	As % of consol. net assets	Net Assets	As % of consol. profit or loss	Profit/ (Loss)	As % of consol. other comp. income	OCI	As % of consol. total comp. income	TCI
Asian Paints (Lanka) Ltd.	0.0	(8.1)	0.1	17.3	1.5	1.1	0.1	18.4
Berger International Pvt. Ltd.	0.2	138.3	(0.6)	(123.6)	0.0	—	(0.6)	(123.6)
Berger Paints Singapore Pte	(0.4)	(329.7)	(0.1)	(18.2)	0.0	—	(0.1)	(18.2)
Berger Paints Bahrain W.L.L	0.5	430.1	0.9	188.2	(1.2)	(0.9)	0.9	187.3
Berger Paints Emirates Ltd.	0.8	641.1	1.0	192.5	3.9	3.0	1.0	195.4
Nirvana investments Ltd.	0.0	19.7	0.0	—	0.0	—	0.0	0.00
Enterprise Paints Ltd.	(0.2)	(182.3)	0.0	—	0.0	—	0.0	0.00
Universal Paints Ltd.	0.0	32.6	0.0	—	0.0	—	0.0	0.00
Lewis Berger (Overseas Holdings) Ltd.	0.1	51.7	0.0	(1.3)	0.0	—	0.0	(1.3)
Berger Paints Jamaica Ltd.	0.1	78.1	0.4	81.4	12.3	9.5	0.4	90.9
Berger Paints Trinidad Ltd.	0.1	48.0	(0.1)	(24.8)	34.5	26.5	0.0	1.7
Berger Paints Barbados Ltd.	0.5	384.8	0.3	68.7	0.0	—	0.3	68.7

(Continued)

Name of the entity in the group	Net Assets, i.e., total assets minus total liabilities		Share in profit or loss		Share in other comprehensive income		Share in total comprehensive income	
	As % of consol. net assets	Net Assets	As % of consol. profit or loss	Profit/ (Loss)	As % of consol. other comp. income	OCI	As % of consol. total comp. income	TCI
Kadisco Paint and Adhesive Industry Share Company	0.1	93.0	0.8	164.9	(2.7)	(2.0)	0.8	162.9
PT Asian Paints Indonesia	(0.2)	(163.6)	(0.6)	(117.9)	0.0	—	(0.6)	(117.9)
PT Asian Paints Color Indonesia	(0.1)	(92.3)	(0.4)	(83.6)	0.0	—	(0.4)	(83.6)
Minority Interest in all Subsidiaries	4.7	3,754.50	3.8	768.2	(668.2)	(513.0)	1.3	255.2
Associates Company Indian								
PPG Asian Paints Pvt. Ltd.	2.4	1,910.9	2.0	395.1	(7.4)	(5.7)	1.9	389.4
Foreign currency translation reserve	0.0	—	0.0	—	(1086.9)	(834.4)	(4.1)	(834.4)
Total	100.0	79,777.5	100.0	20162.4	100.0	76.8	100.0	20,239.2

Schedule III of the Companies Act, 2013 which provides the form of Financial Statements is given as follows:

Schedule III
Part I – Balance Sheet

Name of the Company ____________
Balance Sheet as on ____________
(Rupees in ____________)

Particulars	**Note No.**	**Figures as on the end of the current reporting period**	**Figures as on the end of the previous reporting period**
1	2	3	4
Assets			
1. **Non-current assets**			
(a) Property, plant and equipment			
(b) Capital work-in-progress			
(c) Investment property			
(d) Goodwill			
(e) Other intangible assets			
(f) Intangible assets under development			
(g) Biological assets other than bearer plants			
(h) Financial assets			
(i) Investments			
(ii) Trade receivables			
(iii) Loans			
(iv) Others (to be specified)			
(i) Deferred tax assets (net)			
(j) Other non-current assets			
2. **Current assets**			
(a) Inventories			
(b) Financial assets			
(i) Investments			
(ii) Trade receivables			
(iii) Cash and cash equivalents			
(iv) Bank balances other than (iii) above			
(v) Loans			
(vi) Others (to be specified)			

(c) Current tax assets (net)
(d) Other current assets

Total Assets

Equity and Liabilities

Equity
(a) Equity share capital
(b) Other equity

Liabilities

1. Non-current liabilities
(a) Financial liabilities
(i) Borrowings
(ii) Trade payables
(iii) Other financial liabilities (other than those specified in item (b), to be specified)
(b) Provisions
(c) Deferred tax liabilities (net)
(d) Other non-current liabilities

2. Current liabilities
(a) Financial liabilities
(i) Borrowings
(ii) Trade payables
(iii) Other financial liabilities (other than those specified in item (c))
(b) Other current liabilities
(c) Provisions
(d) Current tax liabilities (net)

Total Equity and Liabilities

For reference, the balance sheet of Asian Paints as on March 31, 2017 is presented in Exhibit 8.2.

Exhibit 8.2

Balance sheet of Asian Paints Ltd. as on March 31, 2017

(Rupees in Millions)

	Notes	As on 31.03.2017	As on 31.03.2016
Assets			
Non-Current Assets			
Property, plant and equipment	2	25,120.1	25,329.7
Capital work-in-progress		2,197.6	927.9
Goodwill	3A	353.6	353.6
Other intangible assets	3B	573.1	606.6
Financial Assets			
Investments	4	14,545.5	13,196.4
Loans	5	702.7	610.7
Others Financial Assets	6	1980.5	305.4
Current tax assets (Net)	7	364.8	151.5
Other non-current assets	8	2003.9	350.1
		47,841.8	41,831.9
Current Assets			
Inventories	9	21,940.9	1,610.12
Financial assets			
Investments	4	13,154.0	1,477.00
Trade receivables	10	9,946.3	759.06
Cash and cash equivalents	11A	613.4	76.75
Other balances with banks	11B	1,439.3	84.03
Loans	5	135.5	9.65
Other financial assets	6	4,744.3	306.27
Assets classified as held for sale	12	5.7	0.96
Other current assets	8	2319.4	217.92
		54,298.8	45,417.6
Total Assets		102,140.6	87,249.5

(Continued)

	Notes	As on 31.03.2017	As on 31.03.2016
Equity and Liabilities			
Equity			
Equity share capital	13	959.2	959.2
Other equity	14	68,550.6	58,298.1
		69,509.8	59,257.3
Liabilities			
Non-Current Liabilities			
Financial liabilities			
Borrowings	15	103.8	292.7
Other financial liabilities	16	23.1	16.8
Provisions	17	1,098.4	942.3
Deferred tax liabilities (Net)	18C	2,611.7	2,171.7
Other non-current liabilities	19	36.5	18.2
		3,873.5	3441.7
Current Liabilities			
Financial liabilities			
Borrowings	15	268.3	—
Trade payables			
Due to micro and small enterprises	20	265.9	179.5
Due to others	20	16,446.7	13,152.0
Other financial liabilities	16	8,798.0	8,234.7
Other current liabilities	19	2,063.2	1,982.3
Provisions	17	362.00	363.5
Current tax liabilities (Net)	21	553.2	638.00
		28,757.3	24,550.5
Total Equity and Liabilities		102,140.6	87,249.5

(*Source:* Asian Paints Annual Report 2016–17)

8.3.2 Statement of Changes in Equity

The statement of changes in equity is prepared in two parts. Part A depicts the changes in equity share capital and part B depicts changes in other equity.

Statement of Changes in Equity

Name of the Company ___________

Statement of changes in Equity for the period ended ___________

(Rupees in ___________)

A. Equity Share Capital

Balance at the Beginning of the Reporting Period	Changes in Equity Share Capital during the Year	Balance at the end of the Reporting Period

The statement of changes in equity share capital of Asian Paints Limited is presented in Exhibit 8.3.

Exhibit 8.3

Statement of Changes in Equity Share Capital of Asian Paints Ltd. for the Year ended 31st March, 2017

(Rupees in Millions)

Equity Share Capital	As on 31.03.2017	As on 31.03.2016
Balance at the beginning of the reporting year	959.2	959.2
Changes in equity share capital during the year	—	—
Balance at the end of the reporting year	959.2	959.2

Part B of the statement of changes in equity requires the following information to be presented.

B. Other Equity

	Share Application Money Pending Allotment	Equity Component of Compound Financial Instruments	Reserves and Surplus				Debt Instruments through Other Comprehensive Income	Equity Instruments through Other Comprehensive Income	Effective Portion of Cash Flow Hedges	Revaluation Surplus	Exchange Difference on Translating the Financial Statements of a Foreign Operation	Other Items of Other Comprehensive Income (Specify Nature)	Money Received against Share Warrants	Total
			Capital Reserve	Securities Premium Reserve	Other Reserves (Specify Nature)	Retained Earnings								
Balance at the beginning of the reporting period														
Changes in accounting policy or prior period errors														
Total comprehensive income for the year														
Dividends														
Transfer to Retained Earnings														
Any other change (to be specified)														
Balance at the end of the reporting period														

The statement of changes in other equity of Asian Paints Limited is presented in Exhibit 8.4.

Exhibit 8.4

Statement of Changes in Other Equity of Asian Paints Ltd. for the Year ended 31st March, 2017

(Rupees in Millions)

Other Equity	Reserves and Surplus: Capital Reserve	Capital Redemption Reserve	General Reserve	Retained Earnings	Debt Instruments through OCI	Equity Instruments through OCI	Total
Balance as on 1st April, 2016 (A)	*	5.0	36,667.4	21,815.5	8.7	(198.5)	58,298.1
Additions during the year							
Profit for the year				18,031.0			18,031.0
Items of OCI for the year, net of tax							
Remeasurement benefit of defined benefit plans				53.8			53.8
Net fair value gain on investment in equity instruments through OCI						1,307.6	1,307.6
Net fair value gain on investment in debt instruments through OCI					29.0		29.0

(Continued)

	Reserves and Surplus						
Other Equity	Capital Reserve	Capital Redemption Reserve	General Reserve	Retained Earnings	Debt Instruments through OCI	Equity Instruments through OCI	Total
Total Comprehensive Income for the year 2016-17(B)	—	—	—	18,084.8	29.0	1,307.6	19,421.4
Reductions during the year							
Dividends				(7,625.6)			(7,625.6)
Income tax on dividend				(1,543.3)			(1,543.3)
Transfer to General Reserve			5,000.0	(5,000.0)			—
Total (C)	—	—	5,000.0	(14,168.9)	—	—	(9,168.9)
Balance as on 31st March, 2016 (A+B+C)	*	5.0	41,667.4	25,731.4	37.7	1,109.1	68,550.6

*₹5,000/-

Each component of the balance sheet is discussed in detail in the following sections.

8.4 Assets

Assets are economic resources controlled by an entity whose cost (or fair value) at the time of acquisition could be objectively measured. A resource is an economic resource if it provides future cash flows to the entity. Control of an asset is generally associated with its ownership. However, an entity may control an asset without being its legal owner. For example, in a finance lease transaction, the lessor is the legal owner of the asset but the risks and rewards of ownership are passed on by the lessor to the lessee. The lessee, being in control of the asset for a major part of its life, is allowed to report the asset in its balance sheet. An asset can be: (i) cash or something convertible into cash (e.g. accounts receivable), (ii) goods expected to be sold and cash received from them and (iii) items to be used in future activities that will generate cash flows.

A basic classification of assets is between current assets and non-current assets. An asset is classified as *current* when it satisfies any of the following criteria:

1. It is expected to be realized in, or is intended for sale or consumption in, the company's normal operating cycle. An *operating cycle* is the time between the acquisition of assets for processing and their realization in cash or cash equivalents. Where the normal operating cycle cannot be identified, it is assumed to have duration of 12 months.
2. It is held primarily for the purpose of being traded.
3. It is expected to be realized within 12 months after the reporting date.
4. It is cash or cash equivalent unless it is restricted from being exchanged or used to settle a liability for at least 12 months after the reporting date.

All other assets are classified as *non-current.*

8.4.1 Non-Current Assets

Non-current assets are further classified as:

1. Property, plant and equipment
2. Capital work-in-progress
3. Investment property
4. Goodwill
5. Other intangible assets
6. Intangible assets under development
7. Biological assets other than bearer plants
8. Financial assets
   (a) Investments
   (b) Trade receivables
   (c) Loans
   (d) Others (to be specified)
9. Deferred tax assets (net)
10. Other non-current assets

8.4.1.1 Property, Plant and Equipment

Ind AS 16 defines property, plant and equipment as tangible items that (i) are held for use in the production or supply of goods or services, for rental to others, or for administrative purposes and (ii) are expected to be used during more than one period.

The following classification is required to be given in respect of property, plant and equipment

1. Land
2. Buildings
3. Plant and equipment
4. Furniture and fixtures
5. Vehicles
6. Office equipment
7. Bearer plants
8. Others (specify nature)

Any item of property, plant and equipment that is held under lease by a company needs to be separately specified. Companies are also required to show a reconciliation of the gross and net carrying amounts of each class of assets at the beginning and end of the reporting period showing additions, disposals, acquisitions through business combinations and other adjustments. Depreciation and impairment losses/reversals related to these assets are to be disclosed separately.

If a company reduces the value of assets on a reduction of its capital or increases the value of assets on revaluation of assets, the company will have to show the reduced or increased figure and also the amount and date of the reduction or increase in every balance sheet for the first 5 years subsequent to the date of such reduction or increase.

8.4.1.2 Capital Work-in-Progress

Capital work-in-progress is the amount invested in constructing a tangible non-current asset that is not yet complete and ready for its intended use. Amounts paid as advance to suppliers of such assets also fall under this head.

8.4.1.3 Investment Property

Investment property is that property that is held by a company for long-term rental income or capital appreciation or both and that is not occupied by the group. Companies are required to show a reconciliation of the gross and net carrying amounts of each class of property at the beginning and end of the reporting period showing additions, disposals, acquisitions through business combinations, and other adjustments and the related depreciation and impairment losses or reversals shall be disclosed separately.

8.4.1.4 Goodwill

Goodwill, as explained in Chapter 6, is recognized in a business combination. Companies are also required to show a reconciliation of the gross and net carrying amount of goodwill at the beginning and end of the reporting period showing additions, impairments, disposals and other adjustments.

8.4.1.5 Other Intangible Assets

Other intangible assets are shown under the following classification:

1. Brands/trademarks
2. Computer software
3. Mastheads and publishing titles
4. Mining rights
5. Copyrights, patents and other intellectual property rights, services and operating rights
6. Recipes, formulae, models, designs and prototypes
7. Licenses and franchise
8. Others (specifying nature)

In a manner similar to that for tangible assets, companies are required to show reconciliation of gross and net carrying amount at the beginning and end of reporting period for each class of other intangible assets. The reconciliation should show additions, disposals, acquisitions through business combinations and other adjustments. The related amortization and impairment losses or reversals need to be disclosed separately.

Provisions relating to disclosure of reduction or increase pursuant to reduction of capital or revaluation of assets are similar to those for tangible assets.

8.4.1.6 Intangible Assets under Development

Intangible assets under development represent amounts invested in the development of an intangible asset such as computer software before it is developed and becomes ready for its intended use.

8.4.1.7 Biological Assets other than Bearer Plants

As per *Ind AS-41 Agriculture*, a biological asset is a living animal or plant. Examples of biological assets are sheep, trees in a timber plantation, dairy cattle, cotton plants, tea bushes, oil palms, fruit trees, etc. Some plants, for example, cotton plants, tea bushes, oil palms, fruit trees, grape vines, usually meet the definition of a bearer plant. However, the produce growing on bearer plants, such as, cotton, tea leaves, oil palm fruit, fruits, grapes, are biological assets other than bearer plants.

For these biological assets, a reconciliation of the carrying amounts of each class of assets at the beginning and end of the reporting period showing additions, disposals, acquisitions through business combinations and other adjustments is required to be disclosed separately.

8.4.1.8 Financial Assets

According to Ind AS 32 *Financial Instruments: Presentation*, a financial asset is any asset that is:

1. Cash or,
2. An equity instrument of another entity or,
3. A contractual right: (i) to receive cash or another financial asset from another entity; or (ii) to exchange financial assets or financial liabilities with another entity under conditions that are potentially favorable to the entity or,
4. A contract that will or may be settled in the entity's own equity instruments and is: (i) a non-derivative for which the entity is or may be obliged to receive a variable number of the entity's own equity instruments; or (ii) a derivative that will or may be settled other than by the exchange of a fixed amount of cash or another financial asset for a fixed number of the entity's own equity instruments.

Financial assets are further classified as:

1. Investments
2. Trade receivables
3. Loans
4. Others (to be specified)

8.4.1.8.1 Investments

Investments are amounts of money invested outside the business in stocks, other securities, firms, subsidiary companies and other assets. Non-current investments are long term in nature and are not expected to be sold within a year.

These are required to be classified as:

1. Investments in Equity Instruments;
2. Investments in Preference Shares;

3. Investments in Government or trust securities;
4. Investments in debentures or bonds;
5. Investments in Mutual Funds;
6. Investments in partnership firms; or
7. Other investments (specify nature).

For each of the above types of investments, companies need to provide details of names of the bodies corporate that are (i) subsidiaries, (ii) associates, (iii) joint ventures, or (iv) structured entities, in whom investments have been made and the nature and extent of the investment so made in each such body corporate

Partly paid investments are required to be disclosed separately. Similarly, if a company has made investments in partnership firms, it has to disclose separately names of the firms, their partners, total capital and the shares of each partner.

Further, companies are also required to disclose:

1. Aggregate amount of quoted investments and market value thereof;
2. Aggregate amount of unquoted investments; and
3. Aggregate amount of impairment in value of investments.

8.4.1.8.2 Trade Receivables

A receivable is classified as a *trade receivable* if it is in respect of the amount due on account of goods sold or services rendered in the normal course of business.

Trade receivables are required to be further classified as:

1. Secured, considered good;
2. Unsecured considered good; and
3. Doubtful.

Separate disclosure is required for:

1. Allowance for bad and doubtful debts.
2. Debts due by directors or other officers of the company or any of them either severally or jointly with any other person or debts due by firms or private companies respectively in which any director is a partner or a director or a member

8.4.1.8.3 Loans

Loans include loans extended by a company to its officers, directors or outside parties

Loans are required to be further classified as:

1. Security deposits,
2. Loans to related parties (giving details thereof), and
3. Other loans (specifying their nature).

Further sub-classification of the above types of loans is required as:

1. Secured, considered good,
2. Unsecured, considered good, and
3. Doubtful.

Separate disclosure is required for:

1. Allowance for bad and doubtful debts.
2. Debts due by directors or other officers of the company or any of them either severally or jointly with any other person or debts due by firms or private companies respectively in which any director is a partner or a director or a member

8.4.1.8.4 Other Financial Assets

Some examples of other financial assets are:

1. Bank deposits with more than 12 months of original maturity
2. Subsidy receivable from government
3. Term deposits kept as margin money by the bank against guarantees given by the bank
4. Cash and bank balances not available for immediate use, for example, balance in the account representing unpaid dividend
5. Value of derivative financial instruments

8.4.1.8.5 Deferred Tax Assets

Deferred tax assets and deferred tax liabilities are netted off against each other. An amount against deferred tax assets will appear in the balance sheet when the amount of deferred tax assets exceed the amount of deferred tax liabilities.

8.4.1.8.6 Other Non-Current Assets

Other non-current assets are required to be classified as:

1. Capital advances and
2. Advances other than capital advances.

Capital advances are moneys given as advance for procurement of non-current assets and the company does not expect to realize these in the next 12 months or within the normal operating cycle.

Advances other than capital advances should be further classified as:

1. Security deposits,
2. Advances to related parties (giving details thereof) and
3. Other advances (specifying nature).

Examples of advances other than capital advances include security deposits with port, customs and other statutory authorities.

A separate disclosure is required for advances to directors or other officers of the company or any of them either severally or jointly with any other persons or advances to firms or private companies respectively in which any director is a partner or a director or a member.

Advances in the nature of financial assets are discussed under 'Other Financial Assets'.

(iii) Others (specify nature).

8.4.2 Current Assets

Current assets are liquid assets of the company that are held either in the form of cash or can be easily converted into cash within one accounting period, usually a year. Schedule III of the Companies Act, 2013 classifies current assets in the following manner:

1. Inventories
2. Financial Assets
   (a) Investments
   (b) Trade receivables
   (c) Cash and cash equivalents
   (d) Bank balances other than (c) above
   (e) Loans
   (f) Others (to be specified)
3. Current tax assets (net)
4. Other current assets

8.4.2.1 Inventories

Inventories are assets held for sale in the ordinary course of business; in the process of production for such sale; or in the form of materials or supplies to be consumed in the production process or in the rendering of services. Inventories encompass goods purchased and held for resale; for example, merchandise purchased by a retailer and held for resale, computer software held for resale, or land and other property held for resale. Inventories also encompass finished goods produced, or work in progress being produced by the enterprise and include materials, maintenance supplies, consumables and loose tools awaiting use in the production process.

For financial reporting, inventories are classified as:

1. Raw materials
2. Work-in-progress
3. Finished goods
4. Stock-in-trade (in respect of goods acquired for trading)
5. Stores and spares
6. Loose tools
7. Others (specify nature)

Companies also have to disclose goods-in-transit under the relevant sub-head of inventories and the mode of valuation. The schedule of inventories appearing in the annual report of Asian Paints for the year 2016–17 is reproduced in Exhibit 8.5.

8.4.2.2 Investments

Current investments are short-term securities that are easily convertible into cash. Companies usually invest liquid assets in excess of transaction cash needs in such securities to generate better returns. In a company's balance sheet, current investments are required to be classified as:

1. Investments in equity instruments
2. Investment in preference shares
3. Investments in government or trust securities

Exhibit 8.5

Inventories of Asian Paints as on March 31, 2017

Inventories (at lower of cost and net realizable value)	Rs. in Millions As on March 31, 2017	As on March 31, 2016
(a) Raw materials	5,167.8	4,551.1
Raw materials-in-transit	811.6	792.3
	5,979.4	5,343.4
(b) Packing materials	363.2	401.3
(c) Work-in-progress	748.0	664.7
(d) Finished goods	12,315.0	7,759.9
Finished goods-in-transit	18.0	24.2
	12,333.0	7,784.1
(e) Stock-in-trade (acquired for trading)	1,824.1	1,345.2
Stock-in-trade (acquired for trading)	29.7	5.0
	1,853.8	1,350.2
(f) Stores, spares and consumables	661.0	577.5
Stores, spares and consumables in transit	2.5	—
	663.5	577.5
Total	21,940.9	16,101.2

4. Investments in debentures or bonds
5. Investments in mutual funds
6. Investments in partnership firms
7. Other investments (specify nature)

For each of the above types of investments, companies need to provide details of names of the bodies corporate that are (i) subsidiaries, (ii) associates, (iii) joint ventures, or (iv) structured entities, in whom investments have been made and the nature and extent of the investment so made in each such body corporate.

Further, companies are also required to disclose:

(a) Aggregate amount of quoted investments and market value thereof;
(b) Aggregate amount of unquoted investments; and
(c) Aggregate amount of impairment in value of investments.

8.4.2.3 Trade Receivables

Trade receivables are required to be further classified as:

1. Secured, considered good;
2. Unsecured considered good; and
3. Doubtful.

Separate disclosure is required for:

1. Allowance for bad and doubtful debts. Trade receivables are reported in the balance sheet at their net realizable value. An allowance or provision is made for expected loss from bad and doubtful debts. This allowance or provision is disclosed separately under the relevant heads to reflect the net realizable value of trade receivables.
2. Debts due by directors or other officers of the company or any of them either severally or jointly with any other person or debts due by firms or private companies respectively in which any director is a partner or a director or a member

Trade receivables reported by Asian Paints as on March 31, 2017 are presented in Exhibit 8.6.

8.4.2.4 Cash and Cash Equivalents

Cash and cash equivalents include cash in hand, cheques and drafts in hand pending their deposit in the bank account, and balance in bank accounts (current accounts and time deposit accounts).

Companies need to separately disclose:

1. Balances with Banks (of the nature of cash and cash equivalents);
2. Cheques, drafts on hand;

Exhibit 8.6

Trade receivables of Asian Paints as on March 31, 2017

	Rs. in Millions	
Trade Receivables	**As on March 31, 2017**	**As on March 31, 2016**
(a) Secured, considered good	—	—
(b) Unsecured, considered good	9,946.3	7,590.6
(c) Unsecured, considered doubtful	126.3	101.2
	10,072.6	7,691.8
Less: Allowance for unsecured doubtful debts	(126.3)	(101.2)
Total	9,946.3	7,590.6

3. Cash on hand; and
4. Others (specify nature).

Further, separate disclosures are required regarding

1. Earmarked balances with banks (for example, for unpaid dividend)
2. Balances with banks to the extent held as margin money or security against the borrowings, guarantees, other commitments.
3. Repatriation restrictions, if any, in respect of cash and bank balances

The schedule of cash and bank balances appearing in the annual report of Asian Paints for the year 2016–17 is reproduced in Exhibit 8.7.

8.4.2.5 Loans

Loans are required to be further classified as:

1. Security deposits;
2. Loans to related parties (giving details thereof) and
3. Other loans (specifying their nature).

Exhibit 8.7

Cash and bank balances of Asian Paints as on March 31, 2017

Cash and Bank Balances	Rs. in Millions			
	Non-Current		Current	
	As on March 31, 2017	As on March 31, 2016	As on March 31, 2017	As on March 31, 2016
A. Cash and Cash Equivalents				
(a) Balances with banks				
(i) Current accounts			222.2	21.3
(ii) Cash credit account			83.0	64.2
(iii) Deposits with original maturity of less than 3 months			—	435.1
(b) Cheques, drafts on hand			307.9	246.3
(c) Cash on hand			0.3	0.6
Total			613.4	767.5

(Continued)

Cash and Bank Balances	Rs. in Millions			
	Non-Current		Current	
	As on March 31, 2017	As on March 31, 2016	As on March 31, 2017	As on March 31, 2016
B. Other Bank Balances				
(a) Term deposit with original maturity of more than 3 months but less than 12 months			1,323.8	758.0
(b) Unpaid dividend and sales proceeds of fractional bonus shares account			115.5	82.3
(c) Term deposit held as margin money against bank guarantee and other commitments	0.5	0.1		
	0.5	0.1	1,439.3	840.3
Amount included under the head Non-Current assets	0.5	0.1	—	—
Total	—	—	1,439.3	840.3

Further sub-classification of the above types of loans is required as:

1. Secured, considered good;
2. Unsecured, considered good; and
3. Doubtful.

Separate disclosure is required for:

1. Allowance for bad and doubtful debts.
2. Debts due by directors or other officers of the company or any of them either severally or jointly with any other person or debts due by firms or private companies respectively in which any director is a partner or a director or a member

8.4.2.6 Other Current Assets

This is an all-inclusive heading, which incorporates current assets that do not fit into any other asset categories. Other current assets are to be classified as:

1. Advances other than capital advances classified as:
   (a) Security deposits;
   (b) Advances to related parties (giving details thereof);
   (c) Other advances (specify nature).
   Advances to directors or other officers of the company or any of them either severally or jointly with any other persons or advances to firms or private companies respectively in which any director is a partner or a director or a member should be separately stated.
2. Others (specifying nature)
   Some examples of other current assets are:
   (a) Advances to suppliers
   (b) Advances to employees
   (c) Export benefits receivable
   (d) Prepaid expenses

8.5 Equity

Equity generally refers to the amount invested in an enterprise by the owners (shareholders). These are also used to refer to the claim of owners to the assets of an enterprise. The claims of owners to assets are secondary to those of creditors and lenders. These are also called the *residual claims* as owners get only what is left after all obligations to outsiders have been paid. Changes in equity occur when (i) new shares are issued by the company or existing shares are bought back and (ii) the business earns income from profitable operations or incurs losses from unprofitable operations of business. Equity is divided into two parts: equity share capital and other equity.

8.5.1 Equity Share Capital

The capital of a company is divided into small units called *shares*. Companies can have two classes of share capital, equity share capital and preference share capital. Equity shares or ordinary shares are the basic types of equity shares. These shares have the usual rights of ownership: right to vote, right to receive dividend and a residual claim on the assets of the company in the case of liquidation. For each class of equity share capital, companies are required to disclose:

1. The number and amount of shares authorized.
2. The number of shares issued, subscribed and fully paid, and subscribed but not fully paid.
3. Par value per share.
4. A reconciliation of the number of shares outstanding at the beginning and at the end of the reporting period.
5. The rights, preferences and restrictions attached to each class of shares, including restrictions on the distribution of dividends and the repayment of capital.
6. Shares in respect of each class in the company held by its holding company or its ultimate holding company, including shares held by subsidiaries or associates of the holding company or the ultimate holding company in aggregate.

7. Shares in the company held by each shareholder holding more than 5% shares specifying the number of shares held.
8. Shares reserved for issue under options and contracts/commitments for the sale of shares/disinvestment, including the terms and amounts.
9. For the period of 5 years immediately preceding the date as on which the balance sheet is prepared:
   (a) An aggregate number and class of shares allotted as fully paid up pursuant to contract(s) without payment being received in cash.
   (b) An aggregate number and class of shares allotted as fully paid up by way of bonus shares.
   (c) An aggregate number and class of shares bought back.
10. Terms of any securities convertible into equity/preference shares issued along with the earliest date of conversion in descending order, starting from the farthest such date.
11. Calls unpaid (showing the aggregate value of calls unpaid by directors and officers).
12. Forfeited shares (amount originally paid up).

8.5.2 Preference Shares

Preference shares have a preference over equity shares in the matter of payment of dividend and repayment of capital at the time of liquidation. Preference shares are entitled to a fixed rate of dividend and normally do not carry any voting rights. The holders of preference shares do not have a guarantee that they will receive the fixed dividend. It is only when the board of directors declare a dividend that the company has an obligation to pay dividend to its shareholders. In such a case, dividend is first paid to holders of preference shares.

Preference shares may be cumulative or non-cumulative. In the case of cumulative preference shares, the dividend if not declared in a particular year gets accumulated and is required to be paid in a subsequent year before any dividend is paid on equity shares. Preference shares do not normally carry any voting power. But they get voting power if the company fails to pay dividend on such shares for a specified time period.

Two other common classifications of preference shares are redeemable and irredeemable preference shares, and convertible and non-convertible preference shares. Holders of redeemable preference shares have a right to sell their shares back to the company at an agreed-upon price. Irredeemable preference shares are perpetual in nature. Indian companies are allowed to issue only redeemable preference shares. Convertible preference shares carry a right that allows holders to convert their preference shares into equity shares at a specified ratio. An excerpt related to share capital from the annual report of Asian Paints Limited as on March 31, 2017 is shown in Exhibit 8.8.

Preference shares including premium received on issue is to be classified and presented as 'Equity' or 'Liability' in accordance with the requirements of the relevant Indian Accounting Standards. Accordingly, the disclosure and presentation requirements in this regard applicable to the relevant class of equity or liability shall be applicable *mutatis mutandis* to the preference shares. For instance, redeemable preference shares shall be classified and presented under 'non-current liabilities' as 'borrowings' and the disclosure requirements in this regard applicable to such borrowings shall be applicable *mutatis mutandis* to redeemable preference shares.

8.5.2.1 Authorized Share Capital

Authorized share capital is the value of shares that the company is authorized to issue by its Memorandum of Association. The companies are governed by the provisions of their constitution which is known as Memorandum of Association. Authorized capital is the maximum capital which a company can issue without altering the capital clause of the Memorandum of Association for an increase in its authorized capital.

Exhibit 8.8

Share capital of Asian Paints Limited as on March 31, 2017

Share Capital	Rs. in Millions	
	As on March 31, 2017	As on March 31, 2016
Authorized:		
995,000,000 Equity shares of the par value of Rs. 1 each	995.0	995.0
50,000 11% Redeemable Cumulative Preference shares of Rs. 100 each	5.0	5.0
	1,000.0	1,000.0
Issued Subscribed and Paid-up Capital		
959,197,790 Equity shares of Rs. 1 each fully paid up	959.2	959.2
	959.2	959.2

8.5.2.2 Issued, Subscribed and Paid-Up Capital

Issued capital is the nominal or face value of shares which are offered by the company to the public for subscription. It cannot be more than the authorized capital. *Subscribed capital* is the nominal value of shares taken up by the public. Subscribed capital is equal to issued capital if all the shares offered to the public are taken up by the public. However, sometimes all the shares that are offered to the public for subscription may not be taken up by the public. In such a case, only that part of the issued capital that is subscribed by the public is called subscribed capital. Sometimes, companies do not require subscribers of its shares to pay the whole face value of shares upfront. Some part of the face value is payable by shareholders later as and when the company makes the necessary calls on them. That part of the subscribed capital that has been called up by the company is called *called-up capital*. Paid-up capital is that part of the called-up capital which has been paid up by the shareholders. If all the called-up capital has been received, paid-up capital is equal to the called-up capital. That part of the called-up capital that has not yet been received is called *calls in arrear or calls unpaid*.

8.5.2.3 Par Value

Par value (also called face value or nominal value) represents the legal capital per share. The shareholders' funds cannot be reduced below the par value of share capital except by losses suffered by the company or by special legal action. The company is not allowed to declare a dividend that will reduce the shareholders' funds below the par value of share capital. Majority of companies in India have par value of Rs. 10 per share. Others have Rs. 5 or Rs. 2 or Rs. 1 as par value of a share.

Illustration 8.1

Mars Limited issues 5,000 equity shares of Rs. 10 each at Rs. 20. The whole amount of Rs. 20 is payable at the time of application. The transaction will be recorded in the following manner:

	(Rs.)	
Bank (Dr.)	100,000	
To equity share capital		50,000
To securities premium		50,000

8.5.2.4 Issue of Shares for Consideration Other than Cash

A company may issue shares for consideration other than cash. This may happen when a company pays for purchase of fixed assets in the form of shares or when a company acquires another business and pays either the full or part of purchase consideration by way of its own shares. When a company issues shares for cash, it debits cash account and credits share capital account. When a company pays for assets by way of shares, it debits the vendor or the seller and credits share capital account.

Illustration 8.2

Mars Limited buys a piece of equipment priced at Rs. 60,000. The vendor agrees to accept 300 shares with a par value of Rs. 10 each as consideration for the sale of equipment. These transactions will be recorded as follows:

	(Rs.)	
Equipment (Dr.)	60,000	
To Vendor		60,000
Vendor (Dr.)	60,000	
To equity share capital		30,000
To securities premium		30,000

8.5.2.5 Issue of Bonus Shares

Bonus shares are the shares allotted to existing equity shareholders without any consideration being received in cash or in kind. When a company issues bonus shares, it converts its accumulated profits and other reserves into share capital. A company can issue bonus shares only if so permitted by its Articles of Association and in accordance with the guidelines issued by SEBI. The bonus shares can be issued only out of free reserves built out of genuine profits or securities premium collected in cash. A company cannot issue bonus shares using revaluation reserves and unless the existing partly paid shares, if any, are made fully paid-up.

Illustration 8.3

The balance sheet of Mars Limited as on March 31, 2016 reports the following shareholders' funds:

	Rs. in Millions
Equity share capital (1 million shares of Rs. 10 each)	10
Securities premium	4
General reserves	3
Surplus	5

The company decides to issue bonus shares in the ratio of 1:2 by capitalizing the securities premium and general reserves. The transaction will be recorded as follows:

	Rs. in Millions	
Securities premium (Dr.)	4	
General reserves (Dr.)	1	
To equity share capital		5

After the bonus issue, the shareholders' funds will appear as follows:

	Rs. in Millions
Equity share capital (1.5 million shares of Rs. 10 each)	15
General reserves	2
Surplus	5

8.5.2.6 Buyback of Shares

In a buyback of shares, a company buys its shares from the market or from existing shareholders and cancels such shares. A company generally decides to buy back its shares when it feels that the shares are undervalued and the company has surplus cash. The buyback of shares results in the reduction of its paid-up share capital and its cash balance. The excess of price paid by the company over the par value of shares bought back is drawn from the company's reserves.

Illustration 8.4

Mars Limited has 50,000 shares of Rs. 10 each and a balance of Rs. 500,000 in the general reserves. The company decides to buy back 10,000 shares at Rs. 30. The transaction will be recorded as follows:

	(Rs.)	
Equity share capital (Dr.)	100,000	
General reserves (Dr.)	200,000	
To Bank		300,000

After the buyback, the equity share capital will get reduced by Rs. 100,000, reserves will get reduced by Rs. 200,000 and the bank balance will get reduced by Rs. 300,000.

8.5.2.7 Forfeited Shares

If a shareholder fails to pay the amount due on call by the last date fixed for payment, the Board of Directors, if so empowered by the Articles of Association, may proceed to forfeit the shares on which the call money is due. The Articles of Association of the company lay down the procedure for forfeiting shares. On forfeiture, share capital account is debited with the amount called up. Calls-in-arrear account is credited with the amount unpaid and shares forfeited account is credited with the amount paid up on these shares.

Illustration 8.5

Mars Limited has the following capital structure:

	(Rs.)
Issued share capital (100,000 shares of Rs. 10 each)	1,000,000
Subscribed and called-up capital (1,00,000 shares of Rs. 10 each, Rs. 6 called up)	600,000
Paid-up capital	597,000
Calls-in-arrear	3,000

A shareholder holding 1,000 shares has failed to pay the call money of Rs. 3 per share. The company has decided to forfeit these 1,000 shares after giving the necessary notice to the defaulting shareholder. The transaction will be recorded as follows:

	(Rs.)	
Equity share capital (Dr.)	6,000	
To calls-in-arrear		3,000
To shares forfeited account		3,000

After the forfeiture of shares, the capital structure of the company will appear as follows:

	(Rs.)
Issued share capital (100,000 shares of Rs. 10 each)	1,000,000
Subscribed and called-up capital (99,000 shares of Rs. 10 each, Rs. 6 called up)	594,000
Paid-up capital	594,000
Shares forfeited	3,000

8.6 Other Equity

Other equity comprises of:

1. Share application money pending allotment
2. Equity component of compound financial instruments
3. Capital reserve
4. Securities premium reserve
5. Other Reserves
6. Retained earnings
7. Debt instruments through other comprehensive income
8. Equity instruments through other comprehensive income
9. Effective portion of cash flow hedges
10. Revaluation surplus
11. Exchange difference on translating financial statements of foreign operations
12. Other items of other comprehensive income
13. Money received against share warrants

Companies need to disclose, under each of these heads, additions and deductions since last balance sheet.

The balance of 'Other Equity', after adjusting negative balance of retained earnings, if any, shall be shown under the head 'Other Equity' even if the resulting figure is in the negative.

8.6.1 Share Application Money Pending Allotment

When a company issues its equity shares to the public to raise funds, it receives the application money from the applicants. However, the equity shares are allotted to the applicants on a later date. It is only on allotment of shares, that the application money gets transferred to the equity share capital.

Share application money pending allotment is to be classified into equity or liability in accordance with relevant Indian Accounting Standards. Share application money to the extent not refundable shall be shown under the head 'Equity' and share application money to the extent refundable shall be separately shown under 'Other financial liabilities'.

8.6.2 Equity Component of Compound Financial Instruments

Compound instruments contain both equity and liability components. An example of a compound instrument is a bond that pays a fixed coupon and is convertible into a fixed number of shares of the issuer. The liability component of this instrument consists of the liability to pay coupons and to repay the principal as long as the bond is not converted. The equity component comprises of the written call option that grants the holder of the bond the right to convert the bond into a fixed number of shares of the issuer.

The liability and equity component of a compound instrument are required to be accounted separately. The equity component is shown as part of 'Other Equity' and the liability component is shown as a financial liability. The separation between the liability and the equity component is done when the instrument is first recognized. For this purpose, the fair value of the liability component is calculated. This fair value becomes the liability component of the instrument. Then the fair value of the liability component is deducted from the total fair value of the instrument and the resulting residual value is accounted for as the equity component of the instrument.

8.6.3 Capital Reserve

It is a reserve created as a result of capital profits. Capital profits are profits other than those earned from normal business operations. These include profit on sale of fixed assets, profit prior to incorporation, premium on issue of shares, premium on issue of debentures, profit on purchase of business, profit on redemption of debentures, surplus arising out of revaluation of fixed assets and grant (of capital nature) received by the company. Premium on issue of shares and revaluation profits are required to be shown separately. Capital reserve is not available for distribution of dividend. However, it may be used to issue bonus shares and setting off of capital losses.

8.6.4 Securities Premium Reserve

When shares are issued at a price higher than the par value, it is called an issue of shares at a premium. Excess of issue price over face value is called the securities premium. It is a capital profit for the company and this profit has to be credited to a separate account called the *securities premium reserve.*

There are no restrictions on issue of shares at a premium. But there are restrictions on the ways securities premium reserve can be used. Securities premium reserve can only be used for:

1. Issue of fully paid bonus shares to the members of the company; or
2. Writing off the preliminary expenses of the company; or
3. Writing off the expenses of, or the commission paid or discount allowed on issue of shares or debentures of the company; or
4. Providing for the premium payable on the redemption of any redeemable preference shares or debentures.

8.6.5 Other Reserves

Other reserves may include reserves, such as capital redemption reserve, debenture redemption reserve, general reserve, etc.

8.6.5.1 Capital Redemption Reserve

If a company has issued redeemable preference shares, it can redeem these shares out of its profits that would otherwise be available for dividend or out of proceeds of a fresh issue of shares made for the purpose of the redemption. Both sources can be used simultaneously.

To the extent the shares are redeemed out of profits, capital redemption reserve account must be credited debiting the profit and loss account, general reserve or other accounts showing profits otherwise available for distribution of dividends. Capital redemption reserve account can be used for the issue of fully paid bonus shares to the members of the company. Otherwise, it must be kept intact unless sanctioned by the court.

8.6.5.2 *Debenture Redemption Reserve*

Companies that issue debentures with maturity of more than 18 months have to create a debenture redemption reserve to meet the requirement of funds for redemption of debentures. The reserve is created out of the statement of profit and loss. Companies are required to create debenture redemption reserve equal to 50% of the amount of debenture issue before debenture redemption commences. Withdrawal from debenture redemption reserve is permitted only after 10% of the debenture liability has actually been redeemed by the company. Debenture redemption reserve is treated as a part of general reserve for issue of bonus shares.

8.6.6 Retained Earnings

A part of the profit earned by a company may be distributed as dividend. The remaining profit is retained within the business and gets accumulated year after year and appears as retained earnings in the balance sheet. The balance in retained earnings gets depleted when the company uses the amount in this account to issue bonus shares, for redemption of preference shares or for redemption of debentures.

8.6.7 Instruments through Other Comprehensive Income or through Profit or Loss

In respect of financial assets, such as equity or debt investments, a business can decide at inception to determine the fair value of such assets as Fair Value through Other Comprehensive Income (FVTOCI) or as Fair Value through Profit or Loss (FVTPL). In the first case, the gains and losses are recognized in OCI and accumulated in other equity. In the second case, the gains and losses are recognized in profit and loss and become part of retained earnings.

8.6.8 Debt Instruments through Other Comprehensive Income

This represents the cumulative gains and losses arising on the revaluation of debt instruments measured at fair value through other comprehensive income that have been recognized in other comprehensive income, net of amounts reclassified to profit or loss when such assets are disposed of and impairment losses on such instruments.

8.6.9 Equity Instruments through Other Comprehensive Income

This represents the cumulative gains and losses arising on the revaluation of equity instruments measured at fair value through other comprehensive income, under an irrevocable option, net of amounts reclassified to retained earnings when such assets are disposed of.

8.6.10 Effective Portion of Cash Flow Hedges

A cash flow hedge is an arrangement to manage the risk of changes in cash flows associated with a recognized asset or liability or a probable forecast transaction. The cash flows from an investment in a foreign bond that receives cash flows denominated in foreign currency are uncertain as they depend on foreign currency rates.

An issue of floating rate bonds involves uncertain cash flows that depend on the level of a benchmark interest rate. The holder of the foreign bond may hedge the cash flow uncertainty by entering into a currency swap. The issuer of a floating rate bond may hedge the cash flow uncertainty by entering into an interest-rate swap.

An effective hedge is the one in which the change in the cash flow is exactly offset by the change in the value of the hedging instrument. If the change in the value of the hedging instrument is more or less than the change in the cash flow, the extra change is referred to as the portion of the hedge that is not effective.

Gains or losses (effective) are reported in equity. Gains or losses (ineffective) are reported in the income statement.

8.6.11 Revaluation Surplus

Revaluation surplus arises when items of property, plant and equipment are valued at their fair value instead of their book value. A credit is given to the revaluation surplus when the value of an item of property, plant and equipment is written up on revaluation. The amount of credit is the difference between the fair value and the book value of the item of property, plant and equipment. A company cannot distribute its revaluation surplus as dividend to shareholders.

If the fair value of an item of property, plant and equipment is found to be less than its book value, this decrease is charged to the statement of profit and loss. However, if this decrease relates to an asset whose value was written up earlier by credit to revaluation surplus, the decrease is charged against the revaluation surplus. Similarly, if an increase in the value of an item of property, plant and equipment is related to a previous decrease that was charged to the statement of profit and loss, such increase is also credited in the statement of profit and loss to the extent it offsets the previous decrease.

When a previously revalued asset is disposed of, the difference between the sale price and the book value of the asset is charged or credited to the statement of profit and loss. However, if there is a loss on sale and the loss relates to a previous increase that was credited to revaluation surplus, the loss is charged to revaluation surplus, provided the earlier credit to the revaluation surplus has not been subsequently reversed or utilized.

8.6.12 Share Options Outstanding

Many companies offer stock options to their employees as a measure of motivation. These options (also called employee stock options) entitle the employees to subscribe to the company's shares at a discount to their market price. A vesting period and an exercise period are associated with these options. Employees get the right to subscribe in the vesting period on satisfaction of vesting requirements and the right can be actually exercised during the exercise period that starts after the vesting period. The accounting value of the options granted is determined using either the option pricing methodology or the difference between the market price of the share at the time of grant and the exercise price. The accounting value is treated as employee compensation. The accounting value is credited to *employee stock options outstanding account* by debit to *deferred employee compensation expense account.* The deferred employee compensation expense account is amortized on a straight line basis over the vesting period debiting employee compensation account by the amortized amount in each period. Employee stock options outstanding account is debited with the accounting value of options exercised and of any options that have lapsed either due to employees failure to satisfy vesting conditions or to exercise the options. The balance in this account is shown under the head *reserves and surplus* in the balance sheet.

Illustration 8.6

Suppose a company grants 1000 options to its employees on 1.4.2015 when the market price of the company's share is Rs. 140. Employees can exercise the option paying Rs. 40 per share. The vesting period is 2 years and the maximum exercise period is 1 year. A total of 900 options are exercised on 30.6.2017 and 100 options lapse at the end of the exercise period. The following accounting entries will be made.

1.4.2015	Deferred employee compensation expense	Dr.	Rs. 100,000	
	To employee stock options outstanding			Rs. 100,000
	(Grant of 1,000 options at accounting value of Rs. 100 each)			
31.3.2016	Employee compensation expense	Dr.	Rs. 50,000	
	To deferred employee compensation expense			Rs. 50,000
	(Amortization of deferred compensation over 2 years on straight line basis)			
31.3.2017	Employee compensation expense	Dr.	Rs. 50,000	
	To deferred employee compensation expense			Rs. 50,000
	(Amortization of deferred compensation over 2 years on straight line basis)			
30.6.2017	Cash account	Dr.	Rs. 36,000	
	Employee stock options account		Rs. 90,000	
	To share capital			Rs. 9,000
	To securities premium			Rs. 117,000
	(Exercise of 900 options at exercise price of Rs. 40 and accounting value of Rs. 100)			
1.4.2018	Employee stock options account	Dr.	Rs. 10,000	
	To employee compensation expense			Rs. 10,000
	(Reversal of debit to employee compensation expense on lapse of 100 vested options at the end of exercise period)			

8.6.13 Money Received Against Share Warrants

Share warrant is an option issued by the company that gives the warrant holder a right to subscribe to equity shares at a predetermined price on or after a predetermined period. Some companies may decide to issue share warrants instead of shares if the current share price is not attractive enough. If the issuer issues shares right away, it will get the current price. By issuing warrants, it can raise capital right away while deferring the issue of shares. This allows the issuer to take advantage of future appreciation in the share price. The warrant holder partly pays the premium for the option which he has purchased and partly pays the price of the share that will get allotted to him when he exercises the option. The money so received forms part of other equity in the balance sheet.

8.7 Liabilities

Liabilities are claims to assets. A business raises financial resources from both its owners and outside parties. Both have claims to the assets of the entity. Liabilities are claims to assets of parties other than owners. Liabilities are classified as current liabilities and non-current liabilities. According to Schedule III of the Companies Act, 2013, a liability shall be classified as *current* when it satisfies any of the following criteria:

1. It is expected to be settled in the company's normal operating cycle. An *operating cycle* is the time between the acquisition of assets for processing and their realization in cash or cash equivalents. Where the normal operating cycle cannot be identified, it is assumed to have a duration of 12 months.
2. It is held primarily for the purpose of being traded.
3. It is due to be settled within 12 months after the reporting date.
4. The company does not have an unconditional right to defer settlement of the liability for at least 12 months after the reporting date. Terms of a liability that could, at the option of the counterpart, result in its settlement by the issue of equity instruments do not affect its classification.

Liabilities other than those classified as current are classified as *non-current liabilities*.

8.7.1 Non-Current Liabilities

Non-current liabilities are long-term in nature. These usually arise from major expenditures such as acquisition of non-current assets or acquisition of another business. Large amounts are generally involved in relatively few transactions related to non-current liabilities. Schedule III further classifies current liabilities in the following manner:

1. Financial liabilities
   - (a) Borrowings
   - (b) Trade payables
   - (c) Other financial liabilities (other than those specified in item (b), to be specified)
2. Provisions
3. Deferred tax liabilities (net)
4. Other non-current liabilities

8.7.1.1 Financial Liabilities

According to Ind AS 32 *Financial Instruments: Presentation*, a financial liability is any liability that is:

1. a contractual obligation
   - (a) to deliver cash or another financial asset to another entity or
   - (b) to exchange financial assets or financial liabilities with another entity under conditions that are potentially unfavorable to the entity; or

2. a contract that will or may be settled in the entity's own equity instruments and is:
   (a) a non-derivative for which the entity is or may be obliged to deliver a variable number of the entity's own equity instruments or
   (b) a derivative that will or may be settled other than by the exchange of a fixed amount of cash or another financial asset for a fixed number of the entity's own equity instruments.

For this purpose, rights, options or warrants to acquire a fixed number of the entity's own equity instruments for a fixed amount of any currency are equity instruments if the entity offers the rights, options or warrants pro rata to all of its existing owners of the same class of its own non-derivative equity instruments.

Apart from the aforesaid, the equity conversion option embedded in a convertible bond denominated in foreign currency to acquire a fixed number of the entity's own equity instruments is an equity instrument if the exercise price is fixed in any currency.

Also for these purposes, the entity's own equity instruments do not include:

1. puttable financial instruments that are classified as equity instruments in accordance with this standard.
2. instruments that impose on the entity an obligation to deliver to another party a pro rata share of the net assets of the entity only on liquidation and are classified as equity instruments in accordance with this standard.
3. instruments that are contracts for the future receipt or delivery of the entity's own equity instruments.

As an exception, an instrument that meets the definition of a financial liability is classified as an equity instrument if it has all the features and meets the conditions specified in the standard.

8.7.1.1.1 Borrowings

Borrowings having a maturity of more than 1 year are considered as non-current liability. These may take one of the following forms:

1. Bonds or debentures
2. Term loans
   (a) From banks
   (b) From other parties
3. Deferred payment liabilities
4. Deposits
5. Loans from related parties
6. Long-term maturities of finance lease obligations
7. Liability component of compound financial instruments
8. Other loans and advances (specify nature)

Bonds or Debentures

When a large loan is split into small transferable units, these are called bonds or debentures. These are interest-bearing instruments which are generally sold to the investing public but may also be sometimes placed privately with financial institutions. Debentures may carry a fixed rate or a floating rate of interest. Some bonds (called zero-coupon bonds) do not pay any interest but are issued at a discount to their par value. Debentures may be short-term, medium-term or long-term. These may be secured by a charge on the assets of the company or may be unsecured. Some debentures, called convertible debentures, carry an option to convert the debentures into shares. Other types of debentures may be non-convertible or partly-convertible debentures. Callable debentures carry a call option exercisable by the issuer whereby the issuer can redeem the debentures before maturity at the stated price. Puttable debentures provide an option to the holder to seek redemption before maturity at a predetermined price. A major advantage of debentures is that these are flexible instruments that offer a wider choice to issuers with regard to maturity, security, interest rates and other features.

Illustration 8.7

Mars Limited issues 10,000 12% debentures of Rs. 100 each on January 1, 2015. Interest on these debentures is payable semi-annually on June 30 and December 31 every year. The debentures will be redeemed at par by the company on December 31, 2017. The following entries will be recorded at the time of issue, payment of interest and redemption of debentures:

January 1, 2015				
	Bank	Dr.	Rs. 1,000,000	
	To 12% Debentures			Rs. 1,000,000
June 30, 2015				
	Debenture interest	Dr.	Rs. 60,000	
	To Bank			Rs. 60,000
	This entry will be repeated every six months till June 30, 2017.			
December 31, 2017				
	12% Debentures	Dr.	Rs. 1,000,000	
	Debenture interest	Dr.	Rs. 60,000	
	To Bank			Rs. 1,060,000

Term Loans

Term loans are a form of long-term debt finance provided to companies by banks and financial institutions for setting up new projects or for expansion and modernization. These are generally secured by the assets that are financed by such loans. These loans can be in domestic currency or in foreign currencies. Interest on term loans is payable at quarterly or half-yearly intervals. A moratorium of 1–2 years is given by the lenders for repayment of principal. In some cases, financial institutions impose some restrictive conditions on the borrowers to safeguard their interest. Important restrictions relate to additional borrowings by the company or limit on the amount of dividend the company may pay.

Deferred Payment Liabilities

Deferred payment liabilities are current obligations to pay for which the payment is deferred to a future period or periods. The time for payment should be more than one year from the date of creation of the obligation. For example, a company may buy a costly piece of equipment on deferred payment basis. The company does not pay the price of the equipment immediately but at some agreed upon future date or dates. The total payment to be made by the company may include an element of interest also. The company should capitalize the asset in its books at its fair value and not at its invoice price. It should account for the interest element separately in a systematic manner.

Deposits

Companies are allowed to accept deposits from public as well as its employees. These deposits can have a maturity ranging from 6 months to 3 years. Deposits with a maturity of more than one year are considered as long-term borrowings. These deposits are unsecured. Deposits are a convenient source of finance for companies as these are unsecured and do not carry any restrictive covenants. However, companies can raise only limited amounts of funds through deposits.

Finance Lease Obligations

A lease is a contract whereby the owner of an asset (the lessor) grants to another party (the lessee), the exclusive right to use the asset in return for the payment of rent. Operating leases are for a time shorter than the economic life of the asset. Financial leases are for terms that approach the economic life of the asset. In a finance lease, the lessee acquires most of the economic benefits and risks associated with the leased property.

With a finance lease, the lessee reports the value of the leased property on the asset side of the balance sheet. The amount reflected is the present value of minimum lease payments over the lease period. If the fair value of the leased property is lower than the present value of the minimum lease payments, then the fair value would be shown. The associated lease obligation would be shown on the liability side of the balance sheet with the present value of payments due within one year being reflected as current liabilities.

The lease obligation gets reduced by the principal component in lease payments. The interest component in each lease payment is treated as an expense and is charged to the statement of profit and loss. The leased asset is depreciated on a systematic basis.

Illustration 8.8

Mars Limited signs an agreement with First Leasing Limited to lease a piece of equipment. The term of the lease is 3 years and the lease agreement is non-cancellable. The fair value of the equipment is Rs. 1,000,000. A lease rental of Rs. 416,340 is payable at the end of each of the three years. The lessor is known to charge interest at a rate of 12% on the lease. Mars Limited depreciates the equipment using the straight-line method.

The break-up of the lease payments between principal and interest components is shown below:

Year	Beginning Balance of Lease Obligation (A) Rs.	Lease Payment (B) Rs.	Interest (12% of A) (C) Rs.	Principal (D = B – C) Rs.	Ending Balance of Lease Obligation (E = A – D) Rs.
1	1,000,000	416,349	120,000	296,349	703,651
2	703,651	416,349	84,438	331,911	371,740
3	371,740	416,349	44,609	371,740	0

The following entries are made to account for the transaction:

At the inception of the lease:

Leased equipment	Dr.	Rs. 1,000,000	
To Finance lease obligation			Rs. 1,000,000

At the end of first year

Interest expense	Dr.	Rs. 120,000	
Finance lease obligation	Dr.	Rs. 296,349	
To Bank			Rs. 416,349
Depreciation on leased equipment	Dr.	Rs. 333,333	
To accumulated depreciation on leased equipment			Rs. 333,333

At the end of second year

Interest expense	Dr.	Rs. 84,438	
Finance lease obligation	Dr.	Rs. 331,911	
To Bank			Rs. 416,349
Depreciation on leased equipment	Dr.	Rs. 333,333	
To accumulated depreciation on leased equipment			Rs. 333,333

At the end of third year

Interest expense	Dr.	Rs. 44,609	
Finance lease obligation	Dr.	Rs. 371,740	
To Bank			Rs. 416,349
Depreciation on leased equipment	Dr.	Rs. 333,333	
To accumulated depreciation on leased equipment			Rs. 333,333

Disclosures Required by Schedule III in Respect of Borrowings

Companies need to classify all borrowings as secured and unsecured and to specify the nature of security separately for each type of borrowing. Further, where loans have been guaranteed by directors or others, the aggregate amount of such loans under each head also requires disclosure.

In respect of bonds/debentures, the rate of interest and particulars of redemption or conversion need to be disclosed. The bonds/debentures are to be stated in descending order of maturity or conversion, starting from farthest redemption or conversion date, as the case may be. Where bonds/debentures are redeemable by installments, the date of maturity for this purpose is reckoned as the date on which the first installment becomes due. If the company has power to issue any redeemed bonds/debentures, the company has to disclose particulars of such instruments.

In the case of term loans and other loans, the company needs to state the terms of their repayment. If the company has been in continuous default on the date of the balance sheet in respect of repayment of loans and interest, the company needs to specify the period and amount of continuing default. The schedule of long-term borrowings appearing in the annual report of Asian Paints for the year 2015–16 is shown in Exhibit 8.9.

Exhibit 8.9

Borrowings of Asian Paints as on March 31, 2017

	Rs. in Millions			
	Non-Current		Current	
Long-Term Borrowings	As on March 31, 2017	As on March 31, 2016	As on March 31, 2017	As on March 31, 2016
Secured				
(i) Term loans				
From other parties				
Loan taken from National Skill				
Development Corporation	—	0.6	—	—
(ii) Deferred payment liabilities:				
Loan from State of Haryana	103.8	70.3	19.8	—
Unsecured				
(i) Deferred payment liability:				
Sales tax deferment scheme – State of Andhra Pradesh	—	221.8	—	64.4
(ii) Loans repayable on demand from banks (bank overdraft)	—	—	268.3	—
Amount included under the head "Other financial liabilities"	—	—	(19.8)	(64.4)
Total 3	103.8	292.7	268.3	—

8.7.1.1.2 Trade Payables

A payable is classified as a *trade payable* if it is in respect of the amount due on account of goods purchased or services received in the normal course of business.

8.7.1.1.3 Other Financial Liabilities

Some examples of non-current other financial liabilities are:

1. Retention money relating to capital expenditure
2. Deposits from contractors or dealers
3. Amounts payable under derivative contracts

8.7.1.2 Provisions

A provision is an amount set aside from a company's profits to meet an expected liability or for the decrease in the value of an asset, but the amount of the liability is uncertain and requires estimation. Important liabilities for which provisions are required are employee pensions and product warranties. Schedule III of the Companies Act, 2013 requires provisions to be classified as provision for employee benefits and other provisions, specifying their nature. Exhibit 8.10 presents the item of Provisions, as it appears in the balance sheet of Asian Paints Limited as on March 31, 2017

Exhibit 8.10

Provisions in the Balance Sheet of Asian Paints Limited as on March 31, 2017

	Rs. in Millions			
	Non-Current		Current	
Provisions	As on March 31, 2017	As on March 31, 2016	As on March 31, 2017	As on March 31, 2016
(a) **Provision for employee benefits**	1,039.1	907.8	134.8	120.0
Provision for compensated absences	15.5	18.8	3.5	2.1
Provision for gratuity				4.0
Provision for pension	43.8	15.7	1.4	1.3
Provision for post-retirement medical and other benefits	1,098.4	942.3	139.7	127.4
(b) **Others**				
Provision for excise				
Provision for Central Sales			5.8	9.6
Tax/VAT			216.5	226.5
	—	—	222.3	236.1
Total	1,098.4	942.3	362.0	363.5

8.7.1.3 Deferred Tax Liabilities

These arise due to difference between the profit as per statement of profit and loss and the taxable income calculated under the Income Tax Act. There are two kinds of differences: permanent differences and timing differences.

Permanent differences arise out of incomes that are exempt from tax or out of expenses that are disallowed for tax purposes. These differences are not reversed in subsequent accounting periods. Timing differences arise because deduction for some expenses is allowed for tax purposes only when these are actually paid. Another reason is difference in rates of depreciation under the Companies Act and the Income Tax Act. These differences are reversed in the subsequent periods.

A deferred tax liability is created when the tax on accounting income is more than the tax payable under the Income Tax Act. This happens when accounting income is more than taxable income. A deferred tax asset is created when the tax on accounting income is less than the tax payable under the Income Tax Act. This happens when accounting income is less than the taxable income.

Deferred tax assets and deferred tax liabilities are netted off against each other. An amount against deferred tax liabilities will appear in the balance sheet when the amount of deferred tax liabilities exceeds the amount of deferred tax assets. The schedule of deferred tax liabilities appearing in the annual report of Asian Paints for the year 2016-17 is shown in Exhibit 8.11.

Exhibit 8.11

Deferred tax liabilities of Asian Paints as on March 31, 2017

	Rs. in Millions	
Deferred Tax Liabilities (Net)	As on March 31, 2017	As on March 31, 2016
Deferred Tax Liabilities		
Difference between written down value/capital work in progress of fixed assets as per the books of accounts and Income Tax Act, 1961.	(2,950.0)	(2,519.5)
Expense claimed for tax purpose on payment basis	(103.0)	(87.9)
Provision for expense allowed for tax purpose on payment basis	533.4	454.6
Allowance for doubtful debts and advances	3.8	3.8
Voluntary Retirement Scheme (VRS) expenditure (allowed in Income tax over 5 years)	50.6	67.9
Difference in carrying value and tax base of investments in debt instruments measured at FVTOCI	18.5	16.8
Remeasurement benefit of the defined benefit plans through OCI	(37.5)	(9.1)
Difference in carrying value and tax base of investments measured at FVTPL	(127.5)	(98.3)
Net deferred tax (liability)	(2,611.7)	(2,171.7)
Net Deferred tax expense/(benefit) for the year	(440.0)	(404.5)

8.7.1.4 Other Non-Current Liabilities

Other long-term liabilities include liabilities other than those mentioned under specific heads. These are further classified as:

1. Advances
2. Others

Examples of other non-current liabilities are:

1. Deferred income arising from government grants
2. Annuity payable to VRS optees
3. Advances from customers
4. Sales tax deferment loan from state government

8.7.2 Current Liabilities

We have already defined current liabilities as those liabilities which satisfy the requirements specified by Schedule III of the Companies Act, 2013. Schedule III further classifies current liabilities in the following manner:

1. Financial Liabilities
   (a) Borrowings
   (b) Trade payables
   (c) Other financial liabilities (other than those specified in item (c)
2. Other current liabilities
3. Provisions
4. Current Tax Liabilities (Net)

8.7.2.1 Borrowings

Borrowings shown under the head 'current liabilities' represent short-term borrowings. These are to be classified as:

1. Loans repayable on demand
   (a) from banks
   (b) from other parties
2. Loans and advances from related parties
3. Deposits
4. Other loans and advances (specify nature)

Borrowings are to be sub-classified as secured and unsecured specifying the nature of security for secured borrowings. Separate disclosure is required for loans guaranteed by directors or others and the period and amount of default as on the balance sheet date in repayment of loans and interest.

8.7.2.2 Other Financial Liabilities

Other current financial liabilities are required to be classified as:

1. Current maturities of long-term debt;
2. Current maturities of finance lease obligations;
3. Interest accrued;
4. Unpaid dividends;
5. Application money received for allotment of securities to the extent refundable and interest accrued thereon;
6. Unpaid matured deposits and interest accrued thereon;
7. Unpaid matured debentures and interest accrued thereon and
8. Others (specify nature).

8.7.2.2.1 Current Maturities of Long-Term Debt and Finance Lease Obligations

Long-term debt and finance lease obligations are classified as non-current liabilities. To present a better picture of a company's short-term fund requirement, that portion of long-term debt and finance lease obligations that matures for payment in the next 12 months is classified as current liability.

8.7.2.2.2 Accrued Interest

Interest payable on a company's borrowings accrues with time but becomes payable or due on specified dates which are usually at six-month time intervals. On the date of the balance sheet, some interest might have accrued but not yet become due, while some interest might also have become due. The former is known as *interest accrued but not due* and the latter is known as *interest accrued and due.*

Illustration 8.9

A company has a borrowing of Rs. 1 million bearing an interest rate of 10% per annum. The interest is payable semi-annually on June 30 and December 31. During the year ended March 31, 2017, the company would need to make interest payments amounting to Rs. 50,000 each on June 30, 2016 and December 31, 2016. These two payments represent interest accrued and due. If the company has made these two payments, no amount would be shown in the balance sheet prepared on March 31, 2017 as *interest accrued and due* under the head *other current financial liabilities*. However, if on March 31, 2017, the company is yet to pay the interest due on December 31, 2015, Rs. 50,000 will appear as *interest accrued and due* under the head *other current financial liabilities.*

In addition, interest of Rs. 25,000 for the period of 3 months from January 2017 to March 2017 has accrued as on March 31, 2017 though it is not yet due for payment. This amount will be shown as *interest accrued but not due* under the head *other current financial liabilities.*

8.7.2.2.3 Application Money Due for Refund

Share application money includes advances towards allotment of share capital. A company may get application money in excess of the share capital it intends to issue. In such a case, the excess application money received by the company has to be refunded to the applicants. Share application money, not exceeding the issued capital and to the extent not refundable, is shown under the head. *Equity* and share application money to the extent refundable that is, the amount in excess of subscription or in case the requirements of minimum subscription are not met, is to be separately shown under *other current liabilities*. Other financial liabilities, both non-current and current, of Asian Paints Limited as on March 31, 2017 are presented in Exhibit 8.12.

Exhibit 8.12

Other Financial Liabilities of Asian Paints Limited as on March 31, 2017

	Rs. in Millions			
	Non-Current		Current	
Other Financial Liabilities	As on March 31, 2017	As on March 31, 2016	As on March 31, 2017	As on March 31, 2016
(a) Current maturities of long-term debt			19.8	64.4
(b) Investor education and protection fund				
(i) Unpaid/unclaimed dividend			115.1	81.9
(ii) Unclaimed amount of sale proceeds of fractional coupons of bonus shares issued in earlier years			0.4	0.4
			115.5	82.3
(c) Others				
Retention monies relating to capital expenditure	23.1	16.8	295.9	464.9
Payable towards capital expenditure			407.4	774.0
Payable towards services received			2,055.1	1,962.7
Payable towards stores, spares and consumables			379.3	163.7
Payable to employees			1,301.7	1,240.5
Payable towards other expenses			4,198.9	3,482.2
Forward exchange contract (net)			24.4	
	23.1	16.8	8,662.7	8,088.0

8.7.2.3 Other Current Liabilities

These are classified as:

(a) revenue received in advance;
(b) other advances (specify nature) and
(c) others (specify nature)

8.7.2.3.1 Revenue Received in Advance

Sometimes, a company receives an advance payment for goods to be supplied or for services to be rendered in future. For example, subscriptions may be received in advance by publishers of a magazine or insurance premia may be received in advance by an insurance company. Such receipts cannot be treated as revenue until the related goods have been supplied or the services have been rendered. Till such time, these receipts are treated as current liabilities.

8.7.2.4 Provisions

Like long-term provisions, short-term provisions are classified as provision for employee benefits and others, specifying the nature of other provisions.

8.8 Contingent Liabilities and Commitments

A contingent liability is: (a) a possible obligation that arises from past events and whose existence will be confirmed only by the occurrence or non-occurrence of one or more uncertain future events not wholly within the control of the entity; or (b) a present obligation that arises from past events but is not recognized because: (i) it is not probable that an outflow of resources embodying economic benefits will be required to settle the obligation; or (ii) the amount of the obligation cannot be measured with sufficient reliability.

A contingent liability is not a real liability but a potential liability that depends on an uncertain future event. A company is not required to recognize a contingent liability. It needs to just disclose the contingent liability in *notes to accounts*. If the possibility of an outflow of resources embodying economic benefits is remote, no disclosure is required.

Companies need to classify contingent liabilities as:

1. Claims against the company not acknowledged as debt, e.g. tax demands disputed by the company.
2. Guarantees**:** Liability against a guarantee arises only when the party in respect of which the company has stood guarantor, defaults.
3. Other money for which the company is contingently liable.

Companies might also have made some commitments which may give rise to an obligation only on the happening of a future uncertain event. Companies need to classify such commitments as:

1. Estimated amount of contracts remaining to be executed on capital account and not provided for
2. Uncalled liability on shares and other investments partly paid
3. Other commitments

8.8.1 Statement of Profit and Loss

The Statement of Profit and Loss includes:

1. Profit or loss for the period and
2. Other Comprehensive Income for the period.

The sum of (1) and (2) above is 'Total Comprehensive Income'.

The form of Statement of Profit and Loss is provided by Part II of Schedule III to the Companies Act, 2013. The provisions of Part II apply to the income and expenditure account, in like manner as they apply to the Statement of Profit and Loss.

Part II – Form of Statement of Profit and Loss

Name of the Company ______________
Statement of Profit and Loss for the period ended ______________ (Rupees in ______________)

	Particulars	**Note No.**	**Figures for the current reporting period**	**Figures for the previous reporting period**
I	Revenue from operations	xxx		
II	Other income	xxx		
III	Total revenue (I + II)	xxx		
IV	Expenses:	xxx		
	Cost of materials consumed			
	Purchases of stock-in-trade			
	Changes in inventories of finished goods, work-in-progress and stock-in-trade			
	Employee benefits expense			
	Finance costs			
	Depreciation and amortization expense			
	Other expenses			
	Total expenses (IV)			
V	Profit/(loss) before exceptional items and tax (I – IV)	xxx		
VI	Exceptional items	xxx		
VII	Profit/(loss) before tax (V – VI)	xxx		
VIII	Tax expense:	xxx		
	(1) Current tax			
	(2) Deferred tax			

IX	Profit (loss) for the period from continuing operations (VII – VIII)	xxx
X	Profit (loss) from discontinued operations	xxx
XI	Tax expense of discontinued operations	xxx
XII	Profit (loss) from discontinued operations (after tax) (X – XI)	xxx
XIII	Profit (loss) for the period (IX + XII)	xxx
XIV	Other Comprehensive Income	xxx
	A (i) Items that will not be reclassified to profit or loss	
	(ii) Income tax relating to items that will not be reclassified to profit or loss	
	B (i) Items that will be reclassified to profit or loss	
	(ii) Income tax relating to items that will be reclassified to profit or loss	
XV	Total Comprehensive Income for the period (XIII + XIV) (Comprising Profit (Loss) and Other Comprehensive Income for the period)	xxx
XVI	Earnings per equity share (for continuing operations)	xxx
	(1) Basic	
	(2) Diluted	
XVII	Earnings per equity share (for discontinued operations)	xxx
	(1) Basic	
	(2) Diluted	
XVIII	Earnings per equity share (for discontinued & continuing operations)	xxx
	(1) Basic	
	(2) Diluted	

For reference, the statement of profit and loss of Asian Paints for the year ended March 31, 2017 is presented in Exhibit 8.13.

Exhibit 8.13

Statement of Profit and Loss of Asian Paints Ltd. for the year ended 31st March, 2017

(Rupees in Millions)

		Year 2016–17	Year 2015–16
Revenue from Operations			
Revenue from sale of products (including excise duty)	22A	141,545.4	131,323.2
Revenue from sale of services	22B	75.9	126.3
Other operating revenues	22C	1,983.0	1,872.3
Other income	23	3,009.0	2,494.3
Total Income (I)		146,613.3	135,816.1
Expenses			
Cost of materials consumed	24A	67,374.5	58,659.4
Purchases of stock-in-trade	24B	6,465.3	5,244.2
Changes in inventories of finished goods, stock-in-trade and work-in-progress	24C	(5,155.8)	1,945.1
Excise duty		17,133.2	15,018.5
Employee benefits expense	25	7,428.3	6,668.3
Other expenses	26	23,644.4	21,017.0
Total (II)		116,889.9	108,552.5
Earning before Interest, Tax, Depreciation and Amortization		29,723.4	27,263.6
Finance costs	27	188.6	234.0
Depreciation and amortization expense	28	2,954.3	2,345.1
Profit before Exceptional Items and Tax		26,580.5	24,684.5
Exceptional items	45	—	653.5
Profit before Tax		26,580.5	24,031.0
Tax Expense	18		
(1) Current tax		8,172.2	7,437.4
(2) (Excess)/Short tax provision for earlier years		(36.0)	(33.3)
(3) Deferred tax		413.3	398.8
Total tax expense		8,549.5	7,802.9
Profit before Tax		18,031.0	16,228.1

(Continued)

		Year 2016–17	Year 2015–16
Other Comprehensive Income (OCI)			
A. Items that will not be reclassified to Statement of Profit and Loss			
(a) (i) Remeasurement benefit of defined benefit plans		82.2	26.3
(ii) Income tax expense on remeasurement benefit of defined benefit plans		(28.4)	(9.1)
(b) Net fair value gain/(loss) on investments in equity instruments through OCI		1,307.6	(198.5)
B. Items that will be reclassified to Statement of Profit and Loss			
(a) (i) Net fair value gain on investments in debt instruments through OCI		27.3	5.3
(ii) Income tax benefit on net fair value gain on investments in debt instruments through OCI		1.7	3.4
Total Other Comprehensive Income (A + B)		1,390.4	(172.6)
Total Comprehensive Income for the Year		19,421.4	16,055.5
Earnings per equity share (Face value of Rs. 1 each)	42		
(1) Basic (in Rs.)		18.80	16.92
(2) Diluted (in Rs.)		18.80	16.92
Significant accounting policies and key accounting estimates and Judgements	1		
See accompanying notes to the financial statements	2-49		

(Source: Asian Paints Annual Report 2016–17)

The various components of the statement of profit and loss are discussed in detail in the following sections.

8.9 Revenue from Operations

Revenue is the gross inflow of economic benefits during the period arising during the ordinary activities of an entity when those inflows result in increases in equity, other than increases relating to contributions from equity participants.

A company has to disclose revenue from operations under the following heads in the notes:

1. Sale of products (including excise duty or goods and services tax)
2. Sale of services
3. Other operating revenues

Other operating revenue is the revenue arising from activities which are incidental to the main revenue earning activities of the company, e.g. revenue from sale of scrap by a manufacturing company or revenue from sale of waste paper or packaging material by a merchandising company.

Excise duty (goods and services tax) is an indirect tax payable by a company to the government.

A finance company is required to report the revenue from operations under the following heads:

1. Interest
2. Other financial services

The schedule of revenue from sale of goods and services appearing in the annual report of Asian Paints for the year 2016–17 is reproduced in Exhibit 8.14.

Exhibit 8.14

Revenue from sale of goods and services of Asian Paints for the year 2016–17

	Rs. in Millions	
Revenue from Operations	Year 2016–17	Year 2015–16
(A) Revenue from Sale of Products (Including Excise Duty)		
Home market (net of returns)	159,338.0	147,252.8
Exports	637.0	491.0
Turnover	159,975.0	147,743.8
Less: Discounts	18,429.6	16,420.6
Total	141,545.4	131,323.2
(B) Revenue from Sale of Services		
Revenue from home solutions operations	47.0	96.9
Color consultancy income	28.9	29.4
Total	75.9	126.3
(C) Other Operating Revenues		
Processing and service income	530.7	451.7
Scrap sales	86.1	78.5
Subsidy from state government	1,366.2	1,342.1
Total	1,983.0	1,872.3

8.9.1 Revenue Recognition

There are two interrelated issues associated with revenue recognition: quantum of revenue and timing of recognition. Revenue is recognized using the accrual principle.

According to Ind AS 18 'Revenue', revenue is to be measured at the fair value of the consideration received or receivable taking into account the amount of any trade discounts and volume rebates allowed by the entity. The fair value is the amount for which an asset could be exchanged, or a liability settled, between knowledgeable, willing parties in an arm's length transaction.

When the inflow of cash is deferred, the fair value may be less than the amount of cash receivable. For example, an entity may provide interest free credit to the buyer or accept a note receivable bearing a below-market interest rate from the buyer as consideration for the sale of goods.

When the arrangement effectively constitutes a financing transaction, the fair value of the consideration is determined by discounting all future receipts using an imputed rate of interest. The difference between the fair value and the nominal amount of the consideration is recognized as interest revenue.

Revenue from the sale of goods is recognized when all the following conditions have been satisfied:

1. The entity has transferred to the buyer the significant risks and rewards of ownership of the goods;
2. The entity retains neither continuing managerial involvement to the degree usually associated with ownership nor effective control over the goods sold;
3. The amount of revenue can be measured reliably;
4. It is probable that the economic benefits associated with the transaction will flow to the entity and
5. The costs incurred or to be incurred in respect of the transaction can be measured reliably.

Revenue from the rendering of services is recognized by reference to stage of completion of the transaction at the end of the reporting period. The recognition occurs only when the outcome of the transaction can be estimated reliably. This occurs when all the following conditions are satisfied:

1. The amount of revenue can be measured reliably.
2. It is probable that the economic benefits associated with the transaction will flow to the entity.
3. The stage of completion of the transaction at the balance sheet date can be measured reliably.
4. The costs incurred for the transaction and the costs to complete the transaction can be measured reliably.

Interest income is recognized using the effective interest method as set out in Ind AS 39. The effective interest rate is the rate that exactly discounts estimated future cash payments or receipts through the expected life of the financial instrument or, when appropriate, a shorter period to the net carrying amount of the financial asset or financial liability Income from royalties is recognized on accrual basis in accordance with the substance of the relevant agreement. Income from dividends is recognized when the owner's right to receive payment is established.

Under Ind AS 11, 'Construction Contracts', in the case of construction contracts, when the outcome of a construction contract can be estimated reliably, contract revenue and contract costs associated with the construction contract are recognized as revenue and expenses respectively by reference to the stage of completion of the contract activity at the end of the reporting period. An expected loss on the construction contract is recognized as an expense immediately.

With effect from April 1, 2018, Ind AS 115 'Revenue from Contracts with Customers' will replace Ind AS 11 'Construction Contracts' and Ind AS 18 'Revenue'. Ind AS 115 is applicable to all contracts with customers (including those with non-monetary asset). It adopts a five-step model which makes revenue recognition more scientific and transparent.

Ind AS 115 defines revenue as income arising during an entity's ordinary activities. The term income is defined as increases in economic benefits in the form of inflows or enhancements of assets or decreases of liabilities that result in an increase in equity (except capital contributions).

The five steps involved in revenue recognition process under Ind AS 115 are:

1. Identify the contract with a customer.
2. Identify the separate performance obligations in the contract.
3. Determine the transaction price.
4. Allocate the transaction price to the separate performance obligations.
5. Recognize revenue when (or as) each performance obligation is satisfied.

Revenue is recognized by an entity when (or as) the entity satisfies a performance obligation by transferring a promised asset to a customer. Further, an asset is transferred when (or as) the customer obtains control of that asset. A customer obtains control when it has the ability to direct the use of and obtain the benefits from the good or service.

The accounting policy of Asian Paints Limited relating to revenue recognition for the year ended on March 31, 2017 is presented in Exhibit 8.15.

Exhibit 8.15

Asian Paints: Accounting Policy for Revenue Recognition

Revenue is recognized when it is probable that economic benefits associated with a transaction flows to the Company in the ordinary course of its activities and the amount of revenue can be measured reliably. Revenue is measured at the fair value of the consideration received or receivable, net of returns, trade discounts and volume rebates allowed by the Company.

Revenue includes only the gross inflows of economic benefits, including excise duty, received and receivable by the Company, on its own account. Amounts collected on behalf of third parties such as sales tax and value added tax are excluded from revenue.

Sale of products: Revenue from sale of products is recognized when the Company transfers all significant risks and rewards of ownership to the buyer, while the Company retains neither continuing managerial involvement nor effective control over the products sold.

Rendering of services: Revenue from services is recognized when the stage of completion can be measured reliably. Stage of completion is measured by the services performed till Balance Sheet date as a percentage of total services contracted.

Interest, royalties and dividends: Interest income is recognized using effective interest method. Royalty income is recognized on an accrual basis in accordance with the substance of the relevant agreement. Dividend income is recognized when the right to receive payment is established.

(Source: Annual reports of Asian Paints for the year ended March 31, 2017)

8.10 Other Income

In addition to income from its regular operating activities, a company may also generate income from other sources such as income from rent, dividend, interest, gain or loss on sale of assets or investments. Interest income earned by a finance company is part of its operating revenue.

Companies are required to report other income classified as:

1. interest Income;
2. dividend Income and
3. other non-operating income (net of expenses directly attributable to such income).

The schedule of other income appearing in the annual report of Asian Paints for the year 2016–17 is reproduced in Exhibit 8.16.

Exhibit 8.16

Schedule of Other Income of Asian Paints for the Year 2016–17

	Rs. in Millions	
Other Income	**Year 2016–17**	**Year 2015–16**
(a) Interest Income		
Investment in debt instruments measured at fair value through OCI	55.7	40.2
Other Financial instruments carried at amortized cost	159.7	75.1
(b) Dividend Income	215.4	115.3
Dividends from quoted equity investments measured at fair value through OCI	148.7	47.7
Dividends from subsidiary companies	50.8	30.5
Dividends from mutual fund investments measured at FVTPL	569.6	624.8
	769.1	703.0
(c) Other Non-Operating Income		
(i) Insurance claims received	2.9	4.2
(ii) Royalty received		
– From subsidiaries and associate	401.2	428.2
– From Others	1.7	1.8
	402.9	430.0
(iii) Others	766.0	588.0
	1,171.8	1,022.2

(Continued)

Other Income	Rs. in Millions Year 2016–17	Year 2015–16
(d) Other Gains and Losses		
Net gain arising on financial assets measured at FVTPL	522.0	456.1
Gain on sale of financial assets measured at FVTPL	154.5	70.3
Net foreign exchange gain	168.3	23.7
Net gain on sale of property, plant and equipment	7.9	103.7
	852.7	653.8
Total	3,009.0	2,494.3

8.11 Expenses

Expenses are matched with revenue to determine the profit or loss made by a business during an accounting period. An expense is that cost which relates to the operations of an accounting period (e.g. rent) or to the revenue earned during the period (cost of goods sold) or the benefits of which do not extend beyond that period. Expenses, thus, have a relation with the accounting period and represent that part of the cost of an asset or service that is consumed during the accounting period. Companies are required to report expenses under the following heads:

1. Cost of materials consumed
2. Purchases of stock-in-trade
3. Changes in inventories of finished goods, work-in-progress and stock-in-trade
4. Employee benefits expense
5. Finance costs
6. Depreciation and amortization expense
7. Other expenses

8.11.1 Cost of Materials Consumed

The purpose of the statement of profit and loss is to calculate profit or loss made by a business during the accounting period. This is achieved by matching expenses and revenue. The first step in this direction is matching of revenue with cost of goods sold. Cost of goods sold represents aggregation of expenses directly related to earning of revenue, i.e. the direct costs of goods that have been sold. This comprises cost of materials consumed and other manufacturing and merchandising cost. Cost of goods sold is calculated as cost of goods available for sale adjusted for change in the inventory of finished goods.

The first element of cost of goods available for sale is the cost of materials consumed. Companies purchase materials that serve as an input to the manufacturing process in anticipation of sales. All the materials purchased may not get consumed during the accounting period. Cost of materials consumed results from subtracting the cost of ending raw material inventory from the sum of the cost of beginning raw material inventory and the cost of raw material purchased during the accounting period.

Cost of material consumed = Beginning inventory of materials + Material purchased
– Ending inventory of materials

8.11.2 Purchases of Stock-in-Trade

Many companies do not manufacture all the items that they sell. They also engage in merchandising transaction and purchase of finished goods for resale. The cost of purchase of such items is reported under this head. Purchase of stock-in-trade is the second element of the cost of goods sold.

8.11.3 Changes in Inventories of Finished Goods, Work-in-Progress and Stock-in-Trade

Computation of cost of goods sold requires adjustment for the cost of different types of inventory items at the beginning and end of the accounting period. Manufacturing companies usually carry three types of inventory items: inventory of materials, work-in-process and finished goods.

The inventory adjustment for raw materials is done when the cost of material consumed is calculated. Work-in-process inventory represents inventory of semi-finished goods. As these semi-finished items get finished, there is a change in the work-in-process inventory. This change reflects addition to the cost of goods available for sale.

Cost of goods available for sale = Cost of materials consumed + Direct manufacturing cost
+ Purchase of stock-in-trade + Change in inventory of work- in-process

All goods produced and purchased by a company may not be sold. Some part of manufactured and purchased goods may end up in inventory at the end of the accounting period. A part of the goods sold may come from the inventory of finished goods carried over from the previous year. Cost of goods available for sale need to be adjusted for change in the inventory of finished goods to calculate cost of goods sold.

Cost of goods sold = Cost of goods available for sale
+ Change in inventory of finished goods and stock-in-trade

8.11.4 Employee Benefits Expense

Under this head, companies have to show separately expenses incurred on:

1. Salaries and wages
2. Contribution to provident and other funds
3. Share based payments to employees
4. Staff welfare expenses

8.11.5 Finance Costs

Finance costs are costs related to the borrowings of the company. These costs are to be reported under the following classification:

1. interest;
2. dividend on redeemable preference shares;
3. exchange differences regarded as an adjustment to borrowing costs and
4. other borrowing costs (specifying nature).

8.11.6 Depreciation and Amortization Expenses

Most of the items of property, plant and equipment have limited useful life. The cost of an item of property, plant and equipment needs to be appropriated on a systematic basis over its useful life. This process of appropriation is called *depreciation* in relation to tangible assets and *amortization* in relation to intangible assets. The appropriation is based upon the *matching principle*.

8.11.7 Other Expenses

Expenditure on each of the following items is required to be shown separately:

1. Consumption of stores and spare parts
2. Power and fuel
3. Rent
4. Repairs to buildings
5. Repairs to machinery
6. Insurance
7. Rates and taxes, excluding taxes on income

The schedule of other expenses appearing in the annual report of Asian Paints for the year 2016–17 is reproduced in Exhibit 8.17.

Exhibit 8.17

Schedule of Other Expenses of Asian Paints for the Year 2016–17

	Rs. in Millions	
Other Expenses	**Year 2016–17**	**Year 2015–16**
Consumption of stores, spares and consumables	426.6	458.8
Power and fuel	879.8	950.7
Processing charges	1,003.9	935.0

(Continued)

Other Expenses	Rs. in Millions Year 2016–17	Year 2015–16
Repairs and maintenance		
Building	121.7	146.0
Machinery	210.1	221.4
Other assets	530.7	456.5
	862.5	823.9
Rent	1,955.6	1,561.3
Rates and taxes	424.6	385.2
Water charges	46.2	42.2
Insurance	68.9	68.8
Printing, stationery and communication expenses	478.2	413.2
Travelling expenses	1,009.5	922.0
Donations	24.9	23.0
Corporate social responsibility expenses	478.4	344.4
Commission to non-executive directors	36.5	36.6
Directors' siting fees	6.5	8.0
Payment to auditors	22.5	13.2
Electricity expenses	95.8	85.7
Bank charges	34.4	36.0
Information technology expenses	447.4	368.2
Legal and professional expenses	373.6	304.0
Training and recruitment	456.1	378.0
Freight and handling charges	8,294.1	7,162.3
Advertisement expenses	5,165.0	4,658.4
Bad debts written off	21.1	19.8
Allowance for doubtful debts and advances(net)	25.1	33.4
Security expenses	275.3	266.0
Miscellaneous expenses	731.9	718.9
Total	23,644.4	21,017.0

A Company is required to disclose by way of notes, additional information regarding aggregate expenditure and income on the following items:

1. **Employee Benefits expense** showing separately
   - **(a)** salaries and wages,
   - **(b)** contribution to provident and other funds,
   - **(c)** share based payments to employees,
   - **(d)** staff welfare expenses.
2. **Depreciation and Amortization Expense:** Most of the items of property, plant and equipment have limited useful life. The cost of an item of property, plant and equipment needs to be appropriated on a systematic basis over its useful life. This process of appropriation is called *depreciation* in relation to tangible assets and *amortization* in relation to intangible assets. The appropriation is based upon the *matching principle*.
3. Any item of income or expenditure which exceeds one per cent of the revenue from operations or Rs. 10,00,000, whichever is higher,
   - **(a)** any item that is considered material for Preparation of financial statements of a company;
   - **(b)** interest income;
   - **(c)** interest expense;
   - **(d)** dividend income;
   - **(e)** net gain or loss on sale of investments;
   - **(f)** net gain or loss on foreign currency transaction and translation (other than considered as finance cost);
   - **(g)** **payments to the auditor** as
     - **(i)** auditor,
     - **(ii)** for taxation matters,
     - **(iii)** for company law matters,
     - **(iv)** for other services,
     - **(v)** for reimbursement of expenses;
   - **(h)** in case of companies covered under section 135 of the Companies Act, 2013, amount of expenditure incurred on corporate social responsibility activities. These companies have net worth of Rs. 500 crore or more, or turnover of Rs. 1,000 crore or more or a net profit of Rs. 5 crore or more during any financial year
   - **(i)** details of items of **exceptional nature**

Exceptional items are those items that occur during the ordinary course of the business but need to be disclosed due to their size or incidence. Examples are profit/loss on disposal of surplus properties or profit/loss on disposal of business/subsidiary. Profit before tax is calculated after deducting exceptional items from profit before exceptional items and tax.

8.12 Profit Before Exceptional Items and Tax

Profit before exceptional items and tax is the difference between total revenue and total expenses.

8.13 Exceptional Items

Exceptional items are those items that occur during the ordinary course of the business but need to be disclosed due to their size or incidence. Examples are:

1. Profit/loss on disposal of surplus properties
2. Profit/loss on disposal of business/subsidiary.
3. Impairment loss on non-current assets of subsidiary companies
4. Restructuring costs
5. Impairment loss on investments
6. Employee separation cost

The purpose of reporting exceptional items separately is to allow users of financial statements to assess the ability of the business to generate income from its regular operating activities.

Profit before tax is calculated after deducting exceptional expenses from profit before exceptional items and tax.

8.14 Tax Expense

A company is required to pay income tax on the income earned during an accounting period. The tax is calculated in accordance with the provisions of the Income Tax Act, 1961. The tax expense is calculated separately for continuing operations and discontinued operations. A detailed treatment of income tax expense is provided later in this chapter.

8.15 Profit (Loss) for the Period from Continuing Operations

Profit (loss) for the period from continuing operations is calculated after deducting tax expense from profit before tax. It measures the profit/loss from ongoing operations and helps in making predictions about a company's future earnings.

8.16 Discontinued Operations

If the company has decided to discontinue a line of activity or has entered into a contract to sell a segment of the business, the results of such line of activity or segment are shown separately in the statement of profit and loss. This enables the users of financial statements to better evaluate the performance of the company's continuing operations.

8.17 Profit (Loss) for the Period

Profit (loss) for the period is the sum of profit (loss) from continuing operations and profit (loss) from discontinued operations.

8.18 Other Comprehensive Income

The performance of a company is reported in the statement of profit and loss and other comprehensive income. Profit or loss is the total of income less expenses, excluding the components of other comprehensive income'. Other comprehensive income (OCI) comprises items of income and expense (including reclassification adjustments) that are not recognized in profit or loss as required or permitted by different accounting standards. Thus, other comprehensive income comprises those items that are not reported on the statement of profit and loss but have an effect on the balance sheet amount of equity.

The components of other comprehensive income include:

1. Changes in revaluation surplus;
2. Actuarial gains and losses on defined benefit plans;
3. Gains and losses arising from translating the financial statements of a foreign operation;
4. Gains and losses on remeasuring available-for-sale financial assets;
5. The effective portion of gains and losses on hedging instruments in a cash flow hedge.

Reclassification adjustments are amounts reclassified to profit or loss in the current period that were recognized in other comprehensive income in the current or previous periods.

For example, gains realized on the disposal of available-for-sale financial assets are included in profit or loss of the current period. These amounts may have been recognized in other comprehensive income as unrealized gains in the current or previous periods. Those unrealized gains must be deducted from other comprehensive income in the period in which the realized gains are reclassified to profit or loss to avoid including them in TCI twice.

Schedule III of the Companies Act, 2013 divides such items into two categories: (i) Items that will not be reclassified to profit or loss and (ii) Items that will be reclassified to profit or loss.

1. Items that will not be reclassified to profit or loss:
   (a) Changes in revaluation surplus;
   (b) Re-measurements of the defined benefit plans;
   (c) Equity Instruments through other comprehensive Income;
   (d) Fair value changes relating to own credit risk of financial liabilities designated at fair value through profit or loss;
   (e) Share of other comprehensive income in Associates and Joint Ventures, to the extent not to be classified into profit or loss; and
   (f) Others (specify nature).

   Items that are not be reclassified to profit or loss are adjusted with retained earnings.
2. Items that will be reclassified to profit or loss:
   (a) Exchange differences in translating the financial statements of a foreign operation;
   (b) Debt Instruments through other comprehensive income;
   (c) The effective portion of gains and loss on hedging instruments in a cash flow hedge;
   (d) Share of other comprehensive income in Associates and Joint Ventures, to the extent to be classified into profit or loss; and
   (e) Others (specify nature).

8.19 Earnings per Share

Earnings per share (EPS) of equity share capital is an important accounting statistic widely used by existing and prospective equity shareholders of the company. Companies are required by accounting standards to present the EPS on the face of the statement of profit and loss to improve performance comparisons between different entities in the same reporting period and between different reporting periods for the same entity.

8.19.1 Basic Earnings per Share

An entity is required to calculate basic earnings per share amounts for profit or loss attributable to ordinary equity holders of the entity and, if presented, profit or loss from continuing operations attributable to those equity holders.

Basic earnings per share shall be calculated by dividing profit or loss attributable to ordinary equity holders of the entity (the numerator) by the weighted average number of ordinary shares outstanding (the denominator) during the period.

$$\text{Basic EPS} = \frac{\text{Profit or loss (profit or loss from continuing operations) Attributable to ordinary equity holders}}{\text{Weighted average number of ordinary shares outstanding}}$$

The objective of basic earnings per share information is to provide a measure of the interests of each ordinary share of an entity in the performance of the entity over the reporting period.

For calculating the amounts attributable to ordinary equity holders of the entity, the profit or loss from continuing operations attributable to the entity is adjusted for the after-tax amounts of preference dividends, differences arising on the settlement of preference shares, and other similar effects of preference shares.

The weighted average number of ordinary shares outstanding during the period is the number of ordinary shares outstanding at the beginning of the period, adjusted by the number of ordinary shares bought back or issued during the period multiplied by a time-weighting factor. The time-weighting factor is the number of days that the shares are outstanding as a proportion of the total number of days in the period.

For example, if the number of ordinary shares outstanding is 100,000 during the first nine months of the accounting year and 150,000 during the last three months, the weighted average number of ordinary shares outstanding during the accounting year is 112,500 ($100{,}000 \times 9/12 + 150{,}000 \times 3/12$).

8.19.2 Diluted Earnings per Share

Companies are also required to report diluted earnings per share in addition to basic earnings per share. The purpose of reporting the diluted earnings per share is to inform investors about the potential dilution that might occur in the earnings per share.

For the purpose of calculating diluted earnings per share, profit or loss attributable to ordinary equity holders of the entity and the weighted average number of shares outstanding is adjusted for the effects of all dilutive potential ordinary shares.

A potential ordinary share is a financial instrument or other contract that may entitle its holder to ordinary shares. Examples of potential ordinary shares are:

1. Financial liabilities or equity instruments, including preference shares, that are convertible into ordinary shares.
2. Options and warrants.
3. Shares that would be issued upon the satisfaction of conditions resulting from contractual arrangements, such as the purchase of a business or other assets.

Dilution is a reduction in earnings per share or an increase in loss per share resulting from the assumption that convertible instruments are converted, that options or warrants are exercised, or that ordinary shares are issued upon the satisfaction of specified conditions.

Except when potential ordinary shares are issued during the current accounting period, these are assumed to be converted into ordinary shares at the beginning of the accounting period. For potential ordinary shares that are issued during the current accounting period, the date of conversion is assumed to be the date of issue.

If in the previous example, the company had 50,000 stock options outstanding at the beginning of the accounting period entitling the holders of the option to get one ordinary share, the weighted average number of ordinary shares outstanding during the accounting year for the purpose of calculating the diluted EPS will be 162,500 (150,000 × 9/12 + 200,000 × 3/12).

8.20 Income Taxes

8.20.1 Advance Tax

Under the Income Tax laws, income earned by an assessee during an accounting year (called the Previous Year) is chargeable to income tax in the Assessment Year. Assessment Year is a period of 12 months, starting April 1 and ending March 31 next. Previous Year is the financial year immediately preceding the Assessment Year. For example, for the Assessment Year 2016–17, the Previous Year is 2015–16.

Even though the income of the Previous Year is taxable during the Assessment Year, assesses have to pay taxes as they earn, that is, in advance. Whenever a company makes advance payment of income tax, it debits Advance Income Tax Account and credits Bank Account.

Income tax paid in advance is shown as tax asset (current or non-current) in the balance sheet

8.20.2 Provision for Tax

At the end of each accounting year, a company calculates its taxable income and income tax liability in accordance with the Income Tax Act. The company makes a provision for income tax by debiting Profit and Loss Account and crediting provision for Income Tax Account.

Provision for tax is shown as 'current tax liability' in the balance sheet.

8.20.3 Accounting for Actual Income Tax Liability on Assessment

If the assessed income tax liability is more than the provision made, the difference is debited from the Statement of Profit and Loss and credited to the Provision for Income Tax Account. If the assessed income tax liability is less than the provision made, the difference is credited to the Statement of Profit and Loss and debited from the Provision for Income Tax Account.

8.20.4 Closing the Advance Income Tax Account

After the income tax assessment for a year is completed, the Advance Income Tax Account is transferred to the Provision for Income Tax Account, debiting the provision for Income Tax Account and crediting the Advance Income Tax Account.

8.20.5 Payment of the Balance Amount of Income Tax

The balance in the Provision for Income Tax Account represents the balance tax payable. It may be paid immediately by debiting the provision for Income Tax and crediting the Bank Account. Alternatively, the balance in the provision for Income Tax Account may be transferred to the liability for Taxation Account and shown as a current liability in the balance sheet.

Illustration 8.10

The trial balance of Complex Ltd. as on March 31, 2017 is given in Table 8.1.

Table 8.1 Trial balance of Complex Ltd. as on March 31, 2017

Particulars	Dr. (Rs.)	Cr. (Rs.)
Advance payment of income tax	220,000	
Provision for income tax for the year ended 31.3.2016		120,000

The following information is given:

1. Advance payment of income tax includes Rs. 140,000 for 2015–16.
2. Actual tax liability for 2015–16 amounts to Rs. 152,000 and no effect for the same has so far been given in accounts.
3. Provision for income tax has to be made for 2016–17 for Rs. 140,000 for current tax and Rs. 20,000 for deferred tax.

You are required to prepare: (a) Provision for Income Tax Account; (b) Advance Payment of Income Tax Account; (c) Liability for Taxation Account and also show how the relevant items will appear in the Statement of Profit and Loss and Balance Sheet of the company.

Solution See Tables 8.2–8.8.

Table 8.2 Provision for Income Tax (2015–16) account in the books of Complex Ltd.

Date	Particulars	(Rs.)	Date	Particulars	(Rs.)
31.3.2017	To advance payment of income tax A/c	140,000	1.4.2016	By balance b/d	120,000
31.3.2017	To liability for taxation A/c	12,000	31.3.2017	By profit & loss A/c	32,000
		152,000			152,000

Table 8.3 Provision for Income Tax (2016–17) (current tax) account

Date	Particulars	(Rs.)	Date	Particulars	(Rs.)
31.3.2017	To balance c/d	140,000	31.3.2017	By profit & loss A/c	140,000

Table 8.4 Provision for Income Tax (2016–17) (deferred tax) account

Date	Particulars	(Rs.)	Date	Particulars	(Rs.)
31.3.2017	To balance c/d	20,000	31.3.2017	By profit & loss A/c	20,000

Table 8.5 Advance payment of Income Tax account

Date	Particulars	(Rs.)	Date	Particulars	(Rs.)
1.4.2016	To balance b/d	220,000	31.3.2017	By provision for income tax (2015–16) A/c	140,000
			31.3.2017	By balance c/d	80,000
		220,000			220,000

Table 8.6 Liability for taxation account

Date	Particulars	(Rs.)	Date	Particulars	(Rs.)
31.3.2017	To balance c/d	12,000	31.3.2017	By provision for income tax A/c	12,000

Table 8.7 Statement of Profit and Loss for the year ended March 31, 2017

Profit before tax	—
Tax Expense	
Current tax	140,000
Deferred tax	20,000

Table 8.8 Balance sheet of Complex Ltd. as on March 31, 2016

Liabilities	(Rs.)
Current Assets	
Current tax assets	80,000
Non-Current Liabilities	
Deferred tax liability	20,000
Current Liabilities	
Current tax liability	152,000

8.21 Dividend

Dividend is the distribution of profits by a company to its shareholders. Companies generally pay two types of dividends: interim dividend and final dividend.

8.21.1 Interim Dividend

Interim dividend is paid by a company during a financial year. Section 123(3) of the Companies Act, 2013 provides that the Board of Directors of a company may declare interim dividend during any financial year out of the surplus in the profit and loss account and out of profits of the financial year in which such interim dividend is sought to be declared.

However, in case the company has incurred loss during the current financial year up to the end of the quarter immediately preceding the date of declaration of interim dividend, such interim dividend shall not be declared at a rate higher than the average dividends declared by the company during the immediately preceding three financial years.

8.21.2 Final Dividend

At every annual general meeting of the company, the shareholders consider for approval any dividend that the directors propose to pay to the shareholders for a financial year. This dividend is generally known as the final dividend. The declaration of the final dividend is also subject to the requirements of Section 123 of the Companies Act, 2013.

Section 123(1) of the Companies Act, 2013 provides that no dividend shall be declared or paid by a company for any financial year except:

1. out of the profits of the company for that year arrived at after providing for depreciation in accordance with the provisions of sub-section (2), or out of the profits of the company for any previous financial year or years arrived at after providing for depreciation in accordance with the provisions of that sub-section and remaining undistributed, or out of both; or
2. out of money provided by the Central Government or a State Government for the payment of dividend by the company in pursuance of a guarantee given by that Government.

Provided that a company may, before the declaration of any dividend in any financial year, transfer such percentage of its profits for that financial year as it may consider appropriate to the reserves of the company.

Provided further that where, owing to inadequacy or absence of profits in any financial year, any company proposes to declare dividend out of the accumulated profits earned by it in previous years and transferred by the company to the reserves, such declaration of dividend shall not be made except in accordance with such rules as may be prescribed.

Provided also that no dividend shall be declared or paid by a company from its reserves other than from the free reserves.

Section 123(2) provides that for the purposes of clause 1 of sub-section(1) of Section 123, depreciation shall be provided in accordance with the provisions of Schedule II of the Companies Act, 2013.

Section 123(6) provides that a company which fails to comply with the provisions of sections 73 and 74 shall not, so long as such failure continues, declare any dividend on its equity shares. Section 73 of the Companies Act, 2013 deals with the acceptance of deposits from public by companies and Section 74 deals with the repayment of such deposits.

8.21.3 Accounting Treatment of Dividends

All dividends paid by the company are shown as deduction from the "Retained Earnings" under "Reserves and Surplus" in the balance sheet.

8.21.4 Dividend Distribution Tax

Currently, Indian companies have to pay a dividend distribution tax of 15% + surcharge 10% + education cess 3% (total 16.995%) on any dividend declared and paid by them. Therefore, companies have to also deduct dividend distribution tax on dividend paid from 'Retained Earnings'.

8.22 Preliminary Expenses

Preliminary expenses are those expenses that are incurred during the formation of the company but before it commences business. Under the Income Tax Act, 1961, these expenses are allowed to be written off in five equal installments, starting with the previous year in which the company commences business.

Whenever a part of preliminary expenses is written off, these are debited to the profit and loss account or deducted from the Securities Premium Account under "Reserves and Surplus" in the balance sheet. The outstanding balance in the Preliminary Expenses Account can be shown under "Other Current Assets" to the extent it is to be written off in the next 12 months. The remaining amount can be shown as "Other Non-Current Assets".

8.23 Discount on Issue of Shares or Debentures

The amount of discount on issue of shares or debentures can be written off over a number of years. The portion that is written off in a year is debited to the profit and loss account or deducted from Securities Premium Account and the remaining balance can be shown under Other Current Assets/Other Non-Current Assets depending on whether the amount will be amortized in the next 12 months or thereafter.

8.24 Capitalization of Profits

When a company accumulates a significant amount of reserves, it may decide to capitalize a part of the reserves (convert reserves into share capital). The purpose is to reward the shareholders and to show a realistic relationship between capital and profits. Capitalization of profits results in a reduction in the amount of reserves and an increase in the amount of paid-up share capital of the company.

Capitalization of profits may be done in two ways:

1. By making partly paid shares as fully paid and/or
2. By issuing unissued shares as fully paid bonus shares to the existing shareholders.

For making partly paid shares fully paid up, a company may use the amount for the time being, standing to the credit of any of the company's reserve accounts, or to the credit of the profit and loss account, or otherwise available for distribution.

For issuing bonus shares, securities premium account and capital redemption reserve account can also be used in addition to the amounts mentioned above.

Illustration 8.11

A company currently has a paid-up share capital of Rs. 2,000,000 (200,000 equity shares of Rs. 10 each) and a balance of Rs. 1,800,000 in Profit and Loss Account. The company decides to issue one bonus share for every four shares held by shareholders prior to the bonus distribution.

The company will issue 50,000 new shares as bonus shares by using Rs. 500,000 out of the balance in the Profit and Loss Account. Balance Sheet of the company prepared after the issue of bonus shares will show a paid-up share capital of Rs. 2,500,000 (250,000 equity shares of Rs. 10 each) and a balance of Rs. 1,300,000 in the Profit and Loss Account.

8.25 Preparing Profit and Loss Account and Balance Sheet

Illustration 8.12

The trial balance of P.K. Limited as on March 31, 2017 is given in Table 8.9.

Table 8.9 Trial balance of P.K. Limited as on March 31, 2017

Particulars	Rs. in Millions	Particulars	Rs. in Millions
Raw materials inventory (1.4.2016)	107	Equity share capital	20
Work-in-process inventory (1.4.2016)	13	General reserve	733

(Continued)

Particulars	Rs. in Millions	Particulars	Rs. in Millions
Inventory of stock-in-trade (1.4.2016)	27	Retained earnings	436
Inventory of finished goods	175	Long-term loans from banks	2
Purchase of raw materials	1126	Retention money relating to capital expenditure	1
Land	180	Provision for employee pension	22
Building	230	Deferred tax liability	43
Plant and equipment	714	Advances from customers	1
Furniture and fixtures	5	Payable for services received	176
Vehicles	1	Short-term loans from banks	5
Goodwill	8	Provision for income tax	13
Computer software	17	Trade payables	321
Long-term investments	341	Revenue from sale of products (including GST)	2,831
Short-term investments	278	Revenue from sale of services (including GST)	2
Cash at hand	2	Scrap sales	40
Trade receivables	200	Interest income	60
Deposits with banks with maturity of more than 12 months	10		
Loans	3		
Royalty receivable	95		
Advances to employees	40		
Balances with government	26		
Advance tax paid	3		
GST paid	348		
Purchases of stock–in-trade	129		
Salaries and wages	130		
Contribution to provident fund	18		
Repairs and maintenance	75		
Rent	180		
Insurance	50		
Advertisement	168		
Interest expense	7		
	4,706		4,706

Additional Information:

1. Stock on March 31, 2017 (in Rs. Millions): Raw materials 120, Work-in-process 15, Finished goods 247, Stock-in-trade 37.
2. Provision for tax: Current tax 301, deferred tax 8.
3. Depreciation to be charged on Building 4%, Plant and equipment 15%, Furniture 10%, Vehicles 20%.

From the trial balance given in Table 8.9, the Profit and Loss account and the Balance Sheet can be prepared in the manner shown in Tables 8.10–8.12.

Table 8.10 Statement of Profit and Loss account of P.K. Limited for the year ended March 31, 2017

Particulars	Note No.	Rs. in Millions
Revenue from sale of products		2,831
Revenue from sale of services		2
Other operating revenue (scrap sales)		40
Other income (interest)		60
Total income		2,933
Cost of materials consumed	1	1,113
Purchase of stock-in-trade		129
Changes in inventories of finished goods, work-in-process and stock-in-trade	2	(84)
GST		348
Employee benefit expenses	3	148
Other expenses	4	473
		2,127
Earnings before interest, tax, depreciation and amortization		806
Finance cost		7
Depreciation and amortization	5	117
Profit before exceptional items and tax		682
Tax expense		
Current tax		301
Deferred tax		8
Total tax expense		309
Profit after tax		373

Table 8.11 Balance sheet of P.K. limited as on March 31, 2017

Particulars	Note No.	Rs. in Millions
Assets		
Non-Current Assets		
Property, plant and equipment	6	1,013
Goodwill		8
Other intangible assets (computer software)		17
Financial Assets		
Investments		341
Loans		3
Other financial assets (bank deposits with maturity of more than 12 months)		10
Current tax assets		3
Current Assets		
Inventories	7	419
Financial assets		
Investments		278
Trade receivables		200
Cash and cash equivalents		2
Other financial assets (royalty receivable)		95
Other current assets	8	66
Total		2,455
Equity and Liabilities		
Equity		
Equity share capital		20
Other equity	9	1,542
Liabilities		
Non-Current Liabilities		
Financial liabilities		
Borrowings		2
Other financial liabilities (retention money relating to capital expenditure)		1
Provisions (for employee pension)		22
Deferred tax liabilities	10	51
Other non-current liabilities	11	177

(Continued)

Particulars	Note No.	Rs. in Millions
Current Liabilities		
Financial liabilities		
Borrowings		5
Trade payables		321
Current tax liabilities	12	314
Total		2,455

Table 8.12 Notes to accounts

		Rs. in Millions	Rs. in Millions
1. Cost of materials consumed			
Beginning inventory		107	
Add: Purchases		1,126	
		1,233	
Less: Ending inventory		120	1,113
2. Changes in inventories			
Finished goods			
Beginning inventory	175		
Less: Ending inventory	247		
		(72)	
Work-in-process			
Beginning inventory	13		
Less: Ending inventory	15		
		(2)	
Stock-in-trade			
Beginning inventory	27		
Less: Ending inventory	37		
		(10)	(84)
3. Employee benefit expenses			
Salaries and wages		130	
Contribution to provident fund		18	148
4. Other expenses			
Repairs and maintenance		75	
Rent		180	

(Continued)

		Rs. in Millions	Rs. in Millions
Insurance		50	
Advertisement		168	473
5. Depreciation and amortization			
Building		9.2	
Plant and equipment		107.1	
Furniture and fixtures		0.5	
Vehicles		0.2	117
6. Property, plant and equipment			
Land			180
Building		230.0	
Less: Depreciation		9.2	220.8
Plant and equipment		714.0	
Less: Depreciation		107.1	606.9
Furniture and fixtures		5.0	
Less: Depreciation		0.5	4.5
Vehicles		1.0	
Less: Depreciation		0.2	0.8
			1,013.0
7. Inventories			
Raw materials		120	
Work-in-process		15	
Finished goods		247	
Stock-in-trade		37	419
8. Other current assets			
Advances to employees		40	
Balances with government		26	66
9. Other equity			
General reserve			
Retained earnings		733	
Beginning balance	436		
Add: Profits during the year	373		
		809	1,542
10. Deferred tax liabilities			
Beginning balance		43	
Addition during the year		8	51

(Continued)

	Rs. in Millions	Rs. in Millions
11. Other non-current liabilities		
Advances from customers	1	
Payable for services received	176	177
12. Current tax liabilities		
Provision for tax at the beginning of the year	13	
Add: Provision made during the year	311	314

Summary – Review of Learning Objectives

1. **Explain requirements relating to corporate books of account and financial statements.** Companies Act, 2013 requires every company to prepare and keep books and papers and financial statements for every financial year, which give a true and fair view of the state of affairs of the company. The books are required to keep records of all sums of money received and expended; all sales and purchases of goods and services by the company; assets and liabilities of the company; and cost information in certain cases.
2. **Explain the form and contents of corporate financial statements.** Financial statements of a company include the balance sheet; profit and loss account; cash flow statement; statement of changes in equity, if applicable and explanatory notes annexed to these statements. Financial statements are required to give a true and fair view of the state of affairs of the company or companies, comply with the notified accounting standards and shall be in the form or forms as may be provided for different class or classes of companies in Schedule III. Where a company has one or more subsidiaries, it shall also prepare a consolidated financial statement of the company and of all the subsidiaries in the same form and manner as that of its own.
3. **Prepare corporate financial statements.** The starting point for the preparation of financial statement is a statement called the Trial Balance, which is a summary of ending balances of all the accounts maintained by a company. These accounts can be classified into asset accounts, liabilities accounts, income accounts and expense accounts. Income and asset accounts are carried to the Profit and Loss account. The net result of the Profit and Loss account represents the net profit or loss made by the business during the accounting period. Asset and Liability accounts are transferred to the Balance Sheet along with the net result of the Profit and Loss account.

Glossary

- **Current asset** is an asset that is expected to be realized in, or is intended for sale or consumption in, the company's normal operating cycle; held primarily for the purpose of being traded; expected to be realized within 12 months after the reporting date; or is cash or cash equivalent unless it is restricted from being exchanged or used to settle a liability for at least 12 months after the reporting date.

- **Current liability** is a liability that is expected to be settled in the company's normal operating cycle; it is held primarily for the purpose of being traded; it is due to be settled within 12 months after the reporting date; or the company does not have an unconditional right to defer settlement of the liability for at least 12 months after the reporting date.
- **Financial statement** in relation to a company includes a balance sheet as on the end of the financial year; a profit and loss account for the financial year; cash flow statement for the financial year; a statement of changes in equity, if applicable and related explanatory notes.
- **Non-current asset** is an asset other than a current asset.
- **Non-current liability** is a liability other than a current liability.
- **Operating cycle** is the time between the acquisition of assets for processing and their realization in cash or cash equivalent. Where the normal operating cycle cannot be identified, it is assumed to have a duration of 12 months.
- **Other comprehensive income** (OCI) comprises those items that are not reported on the statement of profit and loss but have an effect on the balance sheet amounts.
- **Trade payable** is a payable in respect of the amount due on account of goods purchased or services received in the normal course of a business.
- **Trade receivable** is a receivable in respect of the amount due on account of goods sold or services rendered in the normal course of a business.

Solved Problems

1. The trial balance of India Airtel Limited as on March 31, 2017 is given in Table 8.13.

Table 8.13 Trial balance of India Airtel Limited as on March 31, 2017

Particulars	Rs. in Millions	Particulars	Rs. in Millions
Securities premium	21,436	Advances to suppliers	6,200
Dividend paid (including tax)	1,309	Capital advances	207
Short-term borrowings	15,424	Other long-term advances	7,766
Current maturities of long-term loans	6,690	Software	3,267
Network operating expenses	29,072	Bandwidth	5,683
Land	180	Equity share capital	3,997
Building	1,631	General reserve	5,416
Plant and equipment	178,893	Retained earnings	200,721
Furniture and fixtures	360	Long-term loans from banks	100,684
Vehicles	56	IT expenses	951

(Continued)

Particulars	Rs. in Millions	Particulars	Rs. in Millions
Office equipment	946	Provision for employee pension	724
Computer	5,201	Deferred tax assets	724
Capital work-in-progress	2,363	Advances from customers	4,614
Licenses	162,420	Payable for services received	51
Long-term investments	91,908	Trade payables	2,302
Short-term investments	278	Revenue from sale of services	124,553
Cash at hand	2,017	Interest income	4,684
Trade receivables	6,424	Accumulated depreciation:	
Deposits with banks with maturity of more than 12 months	111	Building	501
Loans	2,078	Plant and equipment	84,039
Business promotion expenses	341	Furniture and fixture	286
Advances to employees	40	Vehicles	47
Sales commission	4,391	Office equipment	580
Salaries and wages	2,946	Computer	4,093
Contribution to provident fund	135	Accumulated amortization:	
Legal and professional fee	1,977	Software	2,026
Bad debts written off	66	Bandwidth	2,134
Provision for doubtful debts	1,470	Licenses	12,883
Advertisement	1,440		
Interest expense	10,509		
Access charges	33,372		
License fee/Spectrum charge	31,154		

Additional Information:

1. Depreciation to be charged (in Rs. Million): Building 57, Plant and equipment 12,878, Furniture and fixtures 22, Vehicles 4, Office equipment 109, and Computer 397.
2. Intangible assets to be amortized as follows (Rs. in Millions): Software 473, Bandwidth 378, and Licenses 7,648.
3. Legal and professional fee is prepaid to the extent of Rs. 392 million.

Prepare the profit and loss account for the year ended March 31, 2017, and the Balance Sheet as on that date.

Solution: See Tables 8.14–8.16.

Table 8.14 Statement of Profit and Loss account of India Airtel Limited for the year ended March 31, 2017

Particulars	Note No.	Rs. in Millions
Revenue from sale of services		124,553
Other income (interest)		4,684
Total income		129,237
Network operating expenses		29,072
Access charges		33,372
License fee/spectrum charges		31,154
Employee benefit expenses	1	3,081
Other expenses	2	10,244
		106,923
Earnings before interest, tax, depreciation and amortization		22,314
Finance cost		10,509
Depreciation and amortization	3	21,966
Loss before tax		10,161
Tax expense		
Deferred tax		2,841
Loss for the year		13,002

Table 8.15 Balance sheet of India Airtel Limited as on March 31, 2017

Particulars	Note No.	Rs. in Millions
Assets		
Non-Current Assets		
Property, plant and equipment	4	84,254
Capital work-in-progress		2,363
Intangible assets	5	145,828
Other non-current assets	7	7,973
Financial Assets		
Investments		91,908
Loans		2,078
Current Assets		
Financial Assets		
Investments		278
Trade receivables		6,424
Cash and cash equivalents		2,016

(Continued)

Particulars	Note No.	Rs. in Millions
Other financial assets (Royalty receivable)		111
Other current assets	6	6,632
Total		349,865
Equity and Liabilities		
Equity		
Equity share capital		3,997
Other equity	8	213,262
Liabilities		
Non-Current Liabilities		
Financial liabilities		
Borrowings		100,684
Other financial liabilities		6,690
Provisions (for employee pension)		724
Deferred tax liabilities	9	2,117
Other non-current liabilities	10	4,614
Current Liabilities		
Financial liabilities		
Borrowings		15,424
Trade payables		2,302
Other current liabilities		51
Total		349,865

Table 8.16 Notes to accounts

		Rs. in Millions	Rs. in Millions
1. Employee Benefit Expenses			
Salaries and wages		2,946	
Contribution to provident fund		135	3,081
2. Other Expenses			
Business promotion expenses			
Sales commission		341	
Legal and professional fee	1,977	4,391	
Less prepaid	392		
Bad debts		1,585	

(Continued)

	Rs. in Millions	Rs. in Millions
Provision for doubtful debts	66	
Advertisement	1,470	
IT expenses	1,440	
	951	10,244
3. Depreciation and Amortization		
Building	57	
Plant and equipment	12,878	
Furniture and fixtures	22	
Vehicles	4	
Office equipment	109	
Computer	397	
Software	473	
Bandwidth	378	
Licenses	7,648	21,966
4. Property, Plant and Equipment		
Land		180
Building	1,631	
Less: Depreciation	558	1,073
Plant and equipment	178,893	
Less: Depreciation	96,917	81,976
Furniture and fixtures	360	
Less: Depreciation	308	52
Vehicles	56	
Less: Depreciation	51	5
Office equipment	946	
Less: Depreciation	689	257
Computer	5,201	
Less: Depreciation	4,490	711
		84.254
5. Intangible Assets		
Licenses	162,420	
Less: Amortization	20,531	141,889
Software	3,267	
Less: Amortization	2,499	768

(Continued)

	Rs. in Millions	Rs. in Millions
Bandwidth	5,683	
Less: Amortization	2,512	3,171
		145,828
6. Other Current Assets		
Advances to employees	40	
Prepaid expenses	392	
Advances to suppliers	6,200	6,632
7. Other Non-Current Assets		
Capital advances	207	
Other long-term advances	7,766	7,973
8. Other Equity		
Securities premium		21,436
General reserve		5,416
Retained earnings		
Beginning balance	200,721	
Less: Loss during the year	13,002	
	187,719	
Less: Dividend	1,309	186,410
		213,262
9. Deferred Tax Liabilities		
Beginning balance	(724)	
Addition during the year	2,841	2,117
10. Other Non-Current Liabilities		
Advances from customers		4,614

2. On March 31, 2015, the balances given in Table 8.17 appeared in the books of Balaji Auto Ltd.

Table 8.17 Balances in the books of Balaji Auto Ltd.

Particulars	Rs. in Millions	Particulars	Rs. in Millions
Raw materials inventory (1.4.2016)	2,719	Interest receivable on investment	384
Work-in-process inventory (1.4.2016)	426	Valuation gains on derivative hedging instruments	2,245
Inventory of traded goods (1.4.2016)	163	Deferred tax liability	3,136
Inventory of finished goods (1.4.2016)	3,843	Advances from customers	5,576

(Continued)

Particulars	Rs. in Millions	Particulars	Rs. in Millions
Purchase of raw materials	129,590	Payable for services received	176
Land	75	Short-term loans from banks	5
Building	8,225	Provision for income tax	157
Plant and equipment	18,230	Trade payables	22,358
Furniture and fixtures	419	Revenue from sale of products (including GST)	226,949
Vehicles and aircrafts	6,386	Interest and dividend income	12,220
Technical know-how	1,340	Purchase of traded goods	13,825
Capital advances	1,147	Water pumps and reservoirs	168
Long-term investments	86,810	Computers and IT equipment	826
Short-term investments	60,501	Dies and Jigs	6,432
Cash and cash equivalents	2,798	Office equipment	460
Security deposits	240	Capital work-in-progress	106
Deposits with banks with maturity of more than 12 months	2	Dividend paid	1,447
Loans	297	Tax on dividend	295
Trade receivable	9,533	Cash flow hedging reserve	2,003
Short-term loans and advances	10,963	Cost of hedging reserve	647
Balances with government	1,482	Sales tax deferral	1,199
Advance tax paid	3,999	Provision for employee benefits	781
GST paid	13,214	Annuity payable to VRS optees	73
Other bank balances	139	Unclaimed dividend	139
Salaries and wages	8,273	Employee benefits payable	2,130
Contribution to provident fund	1,700	Accumulated Depreciation:	
Repairs and maintenance	1,211	Buildings	2,314
Expenses on CSR activities	950	Water pumps and reservoirs	101
Packing material	2,449	Plant and equipment	10,293
Advertisement	3,953	Computers and IT equipment	599
Misc. expenses	2,999	Dies and jigs	4,433
Interest expense	14	Furniture and fixtures	228
Equity share capital	2,894	Office equipment	323
General reserve	36,636	Vehicles and aircrafts	3,217
Retained earnings	68,493		
Long-term loans from banks	2		

After taking into account the following information, prepare the company's balance sheet as on March 31, 2017 and its statement of profit and loss account for the year then ended.

1. Stock on March 31, 2017 (in Rs. Millions): Raw materials 2,393, Work-in-process 398, Finished goods 4,308, Traded goods 153.
2. Provision for tax: Current tax 1,456, deferred tax 50
3. An amount of Rs. 3,830 million is transferred to general reserve
4. Depreciation to be charged on Building 279, Plant and equipment 847, Furniture and fixtures 40, Vehicles and aircrafts 686, Water pumps and reservoirs 11, Dies and jigs 482, Computers and IT equipment 113 and Office equipment 58
5. Miscellaneous expenses include Rs. 100 million spent on erection of plant and equipment.

Solution: See Tables 8.18-8.20.

Table 8.18 Statement of Profit and Loss account of Balaji Auto Ltd. for the year ended March 31, 2017

Particulars	Note No.	Rs. in Millions
Revenue from sale of products		226,949
Other income (interest)		12,220
Total income		239,169
Cost of materials consumed	1	129,916
Purchase of traded goods		13,825
Changes in inventories of finished goods, work-in-process and traded goods	2	(427)
GST		13,214
Employee benefit expenses	3	9,973
Other expenses	4	11,462
		177,963
Earnings before interest, tax, depreciation and amortization		61,206
Finance cost		14
Depreciation and amortization	5	2,516
Profit before exceptional items and tax		58,676
Tax expense		
Current tax		1,456
Deferred tax		50
Total tax expense		1,506
		57,170
Profit after tax		
Other Comprehensive Income		
Items that will be reclassified to profit and loss		
Valuation gains on derivative hedging instruments (net of tax)		2,245
Total comprehensive income for the year		59,415

Table 8.19 Balance sheet of Balaji Auto Ltd. as on March 31, 2015

Particulars	Note No.	Rs. in Millions
Assets		
Non-Current Assets		
Property, plant and equipment	6	17,297
Capital work-in-progress		106
Other intangible assets		1,340
Financial Assets		
Investments		86,810
Loans		297
Other financial assets (bank deposits with maturity of more than 12 months)		2
Current tax assets		3,999
Other non-current assets	8	2,629
Current Assets		
Inventories	7	7,252
Financial assets		
Investments		60,501
Trade receivables		9,533
Cash and cash equivalents		2,798
Other balances with banks		139
Other financial assets	9	624
Other current assets		10,963
Total		204,290
Equity and Liabilities		
Equity		
Equity share capital		2,894
Other equity	10	164,158
Liabilities		
Non-Current Liabilities		
Financial liabilities		
Borrowings		2
Sales tax deferral		1,199
Provisions (for employee benefits)		781
Deferred tax liabilities	11	3,186
Other non-current liabilities (advances from customers)		5,576

(Continued)

Particulars	Note No.	Rs. in Millions
Current Liabilities		
Financial liabilities		
Borrowings		5
Trade payables		22,358
Other financial liabilities	12	2,445
Current tax liabilities	13	1,613
Other current liabilities		73
Total		204,290

Table 8.20 Notes to accounts

		Rs. in Millions	Rs. in Millions
1. Cost of Materials Consumed			
Beginning inventory		2,719	
Add: Purchases		129,590	
		132,309	
Less: Ending inventory		2,393	129,916
2. Changes in Inventories			
Finished goods			
Beginning inventory	3,843		
Less: Ending inventory	4,308		
Work-in-process		(465)	
Beginning inventory	426		
Less: Ending inventory	398		
Traded goods		28	
Beginning inventory	163		
Less: Ending inventory	153		
		10	(427)
3. Employee Benefit Expenses			
Salaries and wages		8,273	
Contribution to provident fund		1,700	9,973
4. Other Expenses			
Repairs and maintenance		1,211	
Expenses on CSR activities		950	
Packing material		2,449	
Miscellaneous expenses		2,899	
Advertisement		3,953	11,462

(Continued)

	Rs. in Millions	Rs. in Millions
5. Depreciation and Amortization		
Building	279	
Plant and equipment	847	
Furniture and fixtures	40	
Vehicles and aircrafts	686	
Water pumps and reservoirs	11	
Computers and IT equipment	113	
Dies and jigs	482	
Office equipment	58	2,516
6. Property, Plant and Equipment		
Land		75
Building	8,225	
Less: Depreciation	2,593	5,632
Plant and equipment	18,330	
Less: Depreciation	11,140	7,190
Furniture and fixtures	419	
Less: Depreciation	268	151
Vehicles and aircraft	6,386	
Less: Depreciation	3,903	2,483
Water pumps and reservoirs	168	
Less: Depreciation	112	56
Computers and IT equipment	826	
Less: Depreciation	712	114
Dies and jigs	6,432	
Less: Depreciation	4,915	1,517
Office equipment	460	
Less: Depreciation	381	79
		17,297
7. Inventories		
Raw materials	2,393	
Work-in-process	398	
Finished goods	4,308	
Traded goods	153	7,252
8. Other Non-Current Assets		
Capital advances	1,147	
Balances with government	1,482	2,629

(*Continued*)

		Rs. in Millions	Rs. in Millions
9. Other Financial Assets (Current)			
Interest receivable on investments		384	
Security deposit		240	624
10. Other Equity			
General reserve	36,636		
Add: Transfer from general reserve	3,830		
Retained earnings		40,466	
Beginning balance	68,493		
Add: Profits during the year	57,170		
	125,663		
Less: Transfer to general reserve	3,830		
	121,833		
Less: Dividend paid	1,447		
Tax on dividend	295		
		120,091	
Cash flow hedging reserve	2,003		
Less: Cost of hedging reserve	647		
		1,356	
Other comprehensive income (net of tax)		2,245	164,158
11. Deferred Tax Liabilities			
Beginning balance		3,136	
Addition during the year		50	3,186
12. Other Financial Liabilities (Current)			
Payable for services received		176	
Unclaimed dividend		139	
Employee benefit payable		2,130	2,445
13. Current Tax Liabilities			
Provision for tax at the beginning of the year		157	
Add: Provision made during the year		1,456	1,613

3. The trial balance of Rama Pharmaceutical Limited as on 31.3.2017 is given in Table 8.21.

Table 8.21 Trial balance of Rama Pharmaceuticals Limited as on March 31, 2017

Particulars	Rs. in Millions	Particulars	Rs. in Millions
Raw materials inventory (1.4.2016)	5,065	Equity share capital	829
Work-in-process inventory (1.4.2016)	6,402	General reserve	18,947
Inventory of stock-in-trade (1.4.2016)	1,374	Retained earnings	27,843
Inventory of finished goods	2,444	Long-term loans from banks	4,852
Purchase of raw materials	18,933	Receivables from subsidiary companies	187
Land	1,283	Provision for employee pension	623
Building	11,512	Deferred tax assets	635
Plant and equipment	22,248	Advances from customers	238
Furniture and fixtures	227	Payable to statutory authorities	230
Vehicles	47	Short-term loans from banks	18,699
Goodwill	323	Provision for income tax	1,826
Copyrights and patents	801	Trade payables	7,787
Long-term investments	18,028	Revenue from sale of products (including GST)	95,868
Short-term investments	12,991	Sale of spent chemicals	206
Cash and cash equivalents	668	Scrap sales	711
Trade receivables	44,054	Interest income	534
Deposits with banks with maturity of more than 12 months	13	Office equipment	612
Loans	1,932	Capital work-in-progress	5,400
Claims receivable	581	Product related intangibles	7,142
Interest accrued but not due	69	Technical know-how	86
Balances with government	7,290	Security deposits	449
Advance tax paid	2,892	Capital advances	372
GST paid	870	Derivative financial instruments	220
Purchases of stock-in-trade	6,715	Prepaid expenses	347
Salaries and wages	15,192	Advances to suppliers	798
Contribution to provident fund	1,002	Share-based payment reserve	906
Critical trial expenses	2,525	Capital reserve	267
Consumption of stores	4,544	Securities premium	20,021

(Continued)

Particulars	Rs. in Millions	Particulars	Rs. in Millions
Legal and professional expenses	4,129	Deferred revenue	411
Power and fuel	2,963	Payable to subsidiaries	3,672
Interest expense	572	Accrued expenses	5,132
Fair value gain on financial instruments through profit and loss	677	Share –based payment expenses	372
		Dividend income	3,199
		Foreign-exchange gain	831

You are required to prepare the Statement of Profit and Loss for the year ended 31.3.2017 and the balance sheet as on that date after taking into account the following:

1. Stock on March 31, 2017 (in Rs. Millions): Raw materials 5,822 Work-in-process 6,039, Finished goods 2,428, Stock-in-trade 1,734.
2. Provision for tax: Current tax 1,826, deferred tax (222).
3. Depreciation to be charged (in Rs. Millions) on Building 607, Plant and equipment 5,193, Furniture and fixtures 94, Office equipment 403, and vehicles 19.
4. Intangible assets to be amortized as follows: (in Rs. Millions) Technical know-how 9, Product related intangibles 771, Copyrights and patents 65.
5. Salaries of Rs. 100 Million are unpaid at the end of the year.
6. Interest on investments of Rs. 100 Million is due but not received.

Solution: See Tables 8.22–8.24.

Table 8.22 Statement of Profit and Loss of Rama Pharmaceuticals Limited for the year ended March 31, 2017

Particulars	Note No.	Rs. in Millions
Revenue from sale of products		95,868
Other operating revenue	1	917
Other income	2	5341
Total income		102,126
Cost of materials consumed	3	18,176
Purchase of stock-in-trade		6,715
Changes in inventories of finished goods, work-in-process and stock-in-trade	4	19
GST		870
Employee benefit expenses	5	16,666
Other expenses	6	14,161
		56,607

(Continued)

Particulars	Note No.	Rs. in Millions
Earnings before interest, tax, depreciation and amortization		45,519
Finance cost		572
Depreciation and amortization	7	7,161
Profit before exceptional items and tax		37,786
Tax expense		
Current tax		1,826
Deferred tax		(222)
Total tax expense		1,604
Profit after tax		36,182

Table 8.23 Balance sheet of Rama Pharmaceuticals Limited as on March 31, 2017

Particulars	Note No.	Rs. in Millions
Assets		
Non-Current Assets		
Property, plant and equipment	8	29,613
Capital work-in-progress		5,400
Goodwill		323
Other intangible assets	9	7,184
Financial Assets		
Investments		18,028
Loans		1,932
Other financial assets	10	462
Deferred tax assets		857
Current tax assets		2,892
Other non-current assets (capital advances)		372
Current Assets		
Inventories	11	16,023
Financial assets		
Investments		12,991
Trade receivables		44,054
Cash and cash equivalents		668
Other financial assets	12	1,157
Other current assets	13	8,435
Total		150,391

(Continued)

Particulars	Note No.	Rs. in Millions
Equity and Liabilities		
Equity		
Equity share capital		829
Other equity	14	104,166
Liabilities		
Non-Current Liabilities		
Financial		
Borrowings		4,852
Provisions (for employee pension)		623
Other non-current liabilities (deferred revenue)		411
Current Liabilities		
Financial liabilities		
Borrowings		18,699
Trade payables		7,787
Other financial liabilities	15	8,904
Current tax liabilities	17	3,652
Other current liabilities	16	468
Total		150,391

Table 8.24 Notes to accounts

	Rs. in Millions	Rs. in Millions
1. Other Operating Revenue		
Sale of spent chemicals	206	
Scrap sales	711	917
2. Other Income		
Fair value gain on financial instruments through profit and loss	677	
Interest income	634	
Dividend income	3,199	
Foreign exchange gain	831	5,341
3. Cost of Materials Consumed		
Beginning inventory	5,065	
Add: Purchases	18,933	
	23,998	18,176
Less: Ending inventory	5,822	

(Continued)

		Rs. in Millions	Rs. in Millions
4. Changes in inventories			
Finished goods			
Beginning inventory	2,444		
Less: Ending inventory	2,428		
Work-in-process		16	
Beginning inventory	6,402		
Less: Ending inventory	6,039		
Stock-in-trade		363	
Beginning inventory	1,374		
Less: Ending inventory	1,734		
		(360)	19
5. Employee Benefit Expenses			
Salaries and wages		15,292	
Contribution to provident fund		1,002	
Share-based payment expenses		372	16,666
6. Other Expenses			
Critical trial expenses		2,525	
Consumption of stores		4,544	
Legal and professional expenses		4,129	
Power and fuel		2,963	14,161
7. Depreciation and Amortization			
Building		607	
Plant and equipment		5,193	
Furniture and fixtures		94	
Office equipment		403	
Vehicles		19	
Technical know-how		9	
Product related intangibles		771	
Copyrights and patents		65	7,161
8. Property, Plant and Equipment			
Land			1,283
Building		11,512	
Less: Depreciation		607	10,905
Plant and equipment		22,248	
Less: Depreciation		5,193	17,055

(*Continued*)

	Rs. in Millions	Rs. in Millions
Furniture and fixtures	227	
Less: Depreciation	94	133
Vehicles	47	
Less: Depreciation	19	28
Office equipment	612	
Less: Depreciation	403	209
		29,613
9. Intangible Assets		
Copyrights and patents	801	
Less: Amortization	65	736
Product-related intangibles	7,142	
Less: Amortization	771	6,371
Technical know-how	86	
Less: Amortization	9	77
		7,184
10. Other Financial Assets (Non-Current)		
Deposits with banks with a maturity of more than 12 months	13	
Security deposits	449	462
11. Inventories		
Raw materials	5,822	
Work-in-process	6,039	
Finished goods	2,428	
Stock-in-trade	1,734	16,023
12. Other Financial Assets (Current)		
Claims receivable	581	
Interest accrued but not due	69	
Interest accrued and due	100	
Derivative financial instruments	220	
Receivables from subsidiary companies	187	1,157
13. Other Current Assets		
Advances to suppliers	798	
Prepaid expenses	347	
Balances with statutory authorities	7,290	8,435

(Continued)

		Rs. in Millions	Rs. in Millions
14. Other Equity			
Capital reserve		267	
General reserve		18,947	
Securities premium		20,021	
Share-based payment reserve		906	
Retained earnings			
Beginning balance	27,843		
Add: Profits during the year	36,182		
		64,025	104,166
15. Other Financial Liabilities (Current)			
Due to subsidiary companies		3,672	
Accrued expenses		5,132	
Unpaid salaries		100	8,904
16. Other Current Liabilities			
Advances from customers		238	
Payable to statutory authorities		230	468
17. Current Tax Liabilities			
Provision for tax at the beginning of the year		1,826	
Add: Provision made during the year		1,826	3,652

Multiple Choice Questions

1. On a balance sheet, short-term investments are shown as
   a. an intangible fixed asset
   b. a tangible fixed asset
   c. a current asset
   d. a current liability

2. A current asset is
   a. a recently purchased asset
   b. an asset used in manufacturing a product or rendering of a service
   c. an item shown in the statement of profit and loss
   d. expected to be converted to cash or used in the business within a year or operating cycle of the business

3. An intangible asset
   a. has a value due to the rights provided by such asset to its owner
   b. has no value because it has no physical existence
   c. is converted into a tangible asset during the operating cycle
   d. cannot be shown on the balance sheet because it has no physical existence

4. Which of the following is not considered an asset?
   a. Equipment
   b. Interest
   c. Accounts receivable
   d. Cash

5. In the balance sheet, copyrights are shown under the head ______.
   a. Other intangible assets
   b. Current liabilities
   c. Tangible assets
   d. Current assets
6. Two main classifications of liabilities on a balance sheet are
   a. short-term liabilities and long-term liabilities
   b. present liabilities and future liabilities
   c. tangible liabilities and intangible liabilities
   d. current liabilities and non-current liabilities
7. Which of the following would not be classified as a long-term liability?
   a. Current maturities of long-term debt
   b. Debentures
   c. Bonds
   d. Finance lease obligations
8. Which of the following will be classified as a current liability?
   a. Debentures
   b. Accounts payable
   c. Finance lease obligations
   d. Bonds
9. Land is classified on the balance sheet as
   a. a current asset
   b. a non-current asset
   c. an intangible asset
   d. a long-term investment
10. A company issues 300,000 equity shares of Rs. 10 face value at Rs. 15 per share. The company will show in its balance sheet
    a. Equity share capital of Rs. 3,000,000
    b. Equity share capital of Rs. 4,500,000
    c. Equity share capital of Rs. 3,000,000 and securities premium of Rs. 1,500,000
    d. Equity share capital of Rs. 3,000,000 and retained earnings of Rs. 1,500,000.

Review Questions

1. A debt that is payable within a year is a current liability. Do you agree? Explain.
2. What are the requirements relating to the presentation of non-current liabilities in financial statements?
3. What are the two major components of equity?
4. What restrictions are placed on a company's desire to pay dividends?
5. How do you account for depreciation of fixed assets in financial statements?
6. What is the difference between *interest accrued and due* and *interest accrued but not due*?
7. How are the terms *previous year* and *assessment year* defined under the Income Tax Act, 1961?
8. At what rate can a company pay interim dividend if the company has incurred loss during the current financial year up to the end of the quarter immediately preceding the date of declaration of interim dividend?
9. Can a company pay dividend out of its accumulated profits? Explain.
10. What is the effect of capitalization of profits by a company on its financial statements?
11. State the two ways in which a company can capitalize its profits.
12. Name the broad heads under which assets and liabilities are classified in the form of a balance sheet prescribed by Schedule III to the Companies Act, 2013.
13. What liabilities are classified as current liabilities?
14. What assets are classified as non-current assets?
15. How would you define an operating cycle?
16. What receivable is classified as trade receivable?
17. What kind of a reserve is called a fund?

Practice Problems

1. From the trial balance and additional information of Sam & Nam Limited (Table 8.25), prepare the Statement of Profit and Loss for the year ended March 31, 2017 and a Balance Sheet on that date.

Table 8.25 Trial balance of Sam & Nam Limited as on March 31, 2017

Particulars	Rs. in Millions	Particulars	Rs. in Millions
Raw materials inventory (1.4.2016)	6,609	Equity share capital	1,866
Inventory of construction material (1.4.2016)	1,179	General reserve	137,073
Work-in-process inventory (1.4.2016)	6,770	Retained earnings	77,103
Inventory of stock-in-trade (1.4.2016)	1,598	Long-term loans from banks	71,343
Inventory of finished goods	1,617	Receivables from subsidiary companies	20,479
Purchase of raw materials	73,029	Provision for employee pension	10,874
Purchase of construction material	189,430	Deferred tax assets	2,852
Purchase of stock-in-trade	13,908	Advances from customers	126,229
Sub-contracting charges	167,706	Revenue from construction	584,984
Land	3,623	Short-term loans from banks	23,348
Building	20,963	Trade payables	240,318
Plant and equipment	44,602	Revenue from manufacturing and trading (including GST)	57,310
Furniture and fixtures	1,180	Receivables under derivative contracts	2,831
Vehicles	1,540	Interest income	5,393
Computers	2,199	Office equipment	913
Specialized software	495	Capital work-in-progress	3,025
New product design and development	878	Investment property	3,967
Long-term investments	197,768	Capital advances	661
Short-term investments	69,821	Technical know-how	272
Cash and cash equivalents	22023	Other long-term advances	21,089
Trade receivables	199,200	Fixed deposits with banks	16,000
Cash and bank not available for immediate use	2,236	Prepaid expenses	347
Loans	36,891	Advances to suppliers	798

(Continued)

Particulars	Rs. in Millions	Particulars	Rs. in Millions
Claims receivable	2,892	Unbilled revenue	80,276
Interest accrued but not due	870	Capital reserve	105
GST paid	5,775	Securities premium	8,319
Salaries and wages	45,548	Dividend paid	18,427
Contribution to provident fund	7,963	Advances to subsidiaries	19,662
Hire charges	10,151	Dividend income	10,651
Engineering and consulting fee	9,863	Debenture redemption reserve	4,065
Travel expenses	10,399		
Power and fuel	10,415		
Interest expense	13,180		
Loss on re-measurement of the defined benefit plan	80		
Payable under derivative contracts	494		
Financial guarantees given	14,059		
Unclaimed dividend	466		

Additional Information:

1. Stock on March 31, 2017 (in Rs. Millions): Raw materials 5,932, Construction material 616, Work-in-process 6,418, Finished goods 2,215, Stock-in-trade 1,697.
2. Provision for tax (in Rs. Millions): Current tax 16,752, deferred tax (3,711).
3. Depreciation to be charged (in Rs. Millions) on Building 919, Plant and equipment 7,671, Furniture and fixtures 232, Office equipment 296, Computers 739 and Vehicles 328.
4. Intangible assets to be amortized as follows: (in Rs. Millions) Technical know-how 36, New product design and development 230, Specialized software 153,

2. From the trial balance and additional information of Bira Motors Limited (Table 8.26), prepare the Statement of Profit and Loss for the year ended March 31, 2017 and a Balance Sheet on that date.

Table 8.26 Trial balance of Bira Motors Limited as on March 31, 2017

Particulars	Rs. in Millions	Particulars	Rs. in Millions
Raw materials inventory (1.4.2016)	3,887	Equity share capital	399
Work-in-process inventory (1.4.2016)	279	General reserve	26,458
Inventory of finished goods	1,660	Retained earnings	61,465
Purchase of raw materials	189,823	Deferred tax liabilities	4,143
Security deposits	252	Security deposits from dealers	624
Advance tax paid	3,319	Provision for employee benefits	159

(Continued)

Particulars	Rs. in Millions	Particulars	Rs. in Millions
Prepayment for land leases	2,469	Balances with government (long-term)	1,870
Land	799	Advances from customers	783
Building	17,348	Provision for warranties	595
Plant and equipment	27,327	Statutory dues	1,064
Furniture and fixtures	258	Trade payables	32,473
Vehicles	273	Revenue from sale of products	303,288
Data processing equipment	785	Receivables under derivative contracts	46
Computer software	852	Interest income	1,569
Product design and development	753	Office equipment	230
Long-term investments	35,048	Capital work-in-progress	2,707
Short-term investments	45,409	Balances with government (short-term)	3,792
Cash and cash equivalents	154	Capital advances	2,158
Trade receivables	15,619	Advances to suppliers	876
Balance in earmarked bank accounts	900	Fixed deposits with banks	314
Long-term loans (Dr.)	231	Prepaid expenses	458
Short-term loans (Dr.)	217	Government incentive receipts	3,055
Capital creditors	2,003	Share options outstanding	13
Income from services	2,118	Capital reserve	105
Salaries and wages	12,076	Securities premium	9
Contribution to provident fund	1,089	Dividend paid	18,427
Staff welfare expenses	795	Deferred revenue	2,695
Packing and forwarding expenses	9,584	Dividend income	418
Advertisement	7,675	Gain on investments carried at fair value through profit or loss	1793
Power and fuel	1,126		
Interest expense	61		
Loss on re-measurement of the defined benefit plan	1,408		
Profit on sale of investments	1,379		
Rates and taxes	2,194		
Unclaimed dividend	900		
GST paid	23,711		
Miscellaneous expenses	9,249		

Additional Information:

1. Stock on March 31, 2017 (in Rs. Millions): Raw materials 4,224, Work-in-process 319, Finished goods 988
2. Provision for tax (in Rs. Millions): Current tax 10,821, deferred tax 1,993
3. Depreciation to be charged (in Rs. Millions) on Building 475, Plant and equipment 3,628, Furniture and fixtures 30, Office equipment 51, Data processing equipment 215 and Vehicles 44
4. Intangible assets to be amortized as follows: (in Rs. Millions) Computer software 128, Product design and development 357

3. From the trial balance and additional information of Hindustan Consumer Products Limited (Table 8.27), prepare the Statement of Profit and Loss for the year ended March 31, 2017 and a Balance Sheet on that date.

Table 8.27 Trial balance of Hindustan Consumer Products Limited as on March 31, 2017

Particulars	Rs. in Millions	Particulars	Rs. in Millions
Raw materials inventory (1.4.2016)	9,070	Equity share capital	2,160
Work-in-process inventory (1.4.2016)	3,540	General reserve	21,870
Inventory of finished goods	12,060	Retained earnings	22,060
Purchase of raw materials	113,350	Deferred tax assets	1,600
Purchase of stock-in-trade	41,660	Securities Premium	1,160
Security deposits	1,140	Provision for employee benefits	1,050
Land	900	Provision for statutory dues	3,800
Building	11,100	Balances with Statutory authorities (long-term)	370
Plant and equipment	26,800	Payable to employees	2,070
Furniture and fixtures	370	Advances from customers	700
Computer software	120	Capital redemption reserve	60
Know-how and design	590	Statutory dues	5,580
Brands and trademarks	3,110	Unpaid dividend	1,140
Long-term investments	2,560	Trade payables	53,740
Short-term investments	35,190	Revenue from sale of products	338,950
Cash and cash equivalents	5,720	Payables under derivative contracts	670
Trade receivables	9,280	Interest income	2,620
Long-term loans (Dr.)	980	Office equipment	450
Advance tax paid	3,110	Capital work-in-progress	2,030
Receivables from group companies	3,060	Contingent consideration	710

(Continued)

Particulars	Rs. in Millions	Particulars	Rs. in Millions
Income from services	5,130	Capital advances	330
Salaries and wages	13,300	Profit on sale of surplus assets	2,410
Contribution to provident fund	990	Fixed deposits with banks	9,850
Staff welfare expenses	1,910	Prepaid expenses	2,520
Carriage and freight expenses	14,570	Government incentive receivable	3,010
Advertisement	34,700	Employee stock options reserve	300
Power and fuel	2,570	Capital reserve	40
Interest expense	220	Dividend income	1,780
Loss on re-measurement of the defined benefit plan	210	Gain on investments carried at fair value through profit or loss	860
Royalty	10,440	Dividend paid (including tax)	42,540
Bank balance (unpaid dividend)	1,140		
GST paid	23,970		
Miscellaneous expenses	23,100		
Provision for restructuring	3,870		
Scrap sales	790		
Gain in fair value of debt instruments carried through other comprehensive income	10		

Additional Information:

1. Stock on March 31, 2017 (in Rs. Millions): Raw materials 8,790, Work-in-process 2,050, Finished goods 12,140
2. Provision for tax (in Rs. Millions): Current tax 18,650, deferred tax 410
3. Depreciation to be charged (Rs. Millions) on Building 350, Plant and equipment 2,570 Furniture and fixtures 40, Office equipment 70
4. Intangible assets to be amortized as follows: (in Rs. Millions) Computer software 60, know-how and design 60

4. From the trial balance and additional information of Alliance Industries Limited (Table 8.28), prepare the Statement of Profit and Loss for the year ended March 31, 2017 and a Balance Sheet on that date.

Table 8.28 Trial balance of Alliance Industries Limited as on March 31, 2017

Particulars	Rs. in Millions	Particulars	Rs. in Millions
Raw materials inventory (1.4.2016)	142,850	Interest accrued on investment	1,760
Work-in-process inventory (1.4.2016)	28,710	Securities premium	490,800

(Continued)

Particulars	Rs. in Millions	Particulars	Rs. in Millions
Inventory of traded goods (1.4.2016)	680	Deferred tax liability	247,660
Inventory of finished goods (1.4.2016)	75,950	Long-term borrowings	787,230
Purchase of raw materials	1,661,900	Prepaid expenses (long-term)	14,230
Land	380,840	Short-term borrowings	225,800
Building	78,530	Provision for decommissioning of assets	21,180
Plant and equipment	885,260	Trade payables	681,610
Furniture and fixtures	1,370	Revenue from sale of products (including GST)	2,649,090
Vehicles	2,530	Purchase of traded goods	51,610
Ships and aircrafts	1,340	Security deposits	31,960
Development rights	89,240	Technical know-how fee	12,050
Capital advances	11,920	Capital work-in-progress	1,282,830
Long-term investments	1,405,440	Dividend paid	60,390
Short-term investments	519,060	Tax on dividend	12,200
Cash and cash equivalents	17,540	Capital creditors (short-term)	376,140
Short-term loans	49,000	Current maturities of long-term debt	61,430
Long-term loans	104,180	Statutory dues	168,970
Trade receivable	54,720	Provision for employee benefits	12,680
Balances with government	34,360	Unclaimed dividend	2,410
GST paid	230,160	Income from sale of services	1,320
Salaries and wages	38,890	Interest accrued on borrowings	3,700
Contribution to provident fund	5,450	Interest income	35,350
Repairs and maintenance	11,480	Dividend income	2,710
Consumption of stores	50,350	Gain on sale of investments	49,030
Power and fuel	101,500	Remeasurement of defined benefit plans (net of tax)	280
Warehousing and distribution	55,520	Gain on debt instruments through OCI (net of tax)	21,640
Misc. expenses	79,780	Capital reserve	2,910
Interest expense	27,230	Debenture redemption reserve	11,170
Equity share capital	32,510	Other Comprehensive Income	50,210
General reserve	1,460,000		
Retained earnings	228,500		
Software	1,600		
Advance income tax	9,920		

Additional Information:

1. Stock on March 31, 2017 (in Rs. Millions): Raw materials 162,250, Work-in-process 48,370, Finished goods 92,080, Traded goods 550
2. Provision for tax: Current tax 83,330, deferred tax 10,190
3. Depreciation to be charged on Building 3,920, Plant and equipment 71,430, Furniture and fixtures 290, Vehicles 1160, Ships and aircrafts 110
4. Intangible assets to be amortized as follows: (in Rs. Millions) Software 720, Technical know-how fee 1,650, and Development rights 9,830

5. From the trial balance and additional information of Saturn Pharma Limited (Table 8.29), prepare the Statement of Profit and Loss for the year ended March 31, 2017 and a Balance Sheet on that date.

Table 8.29 Trial balance of Saturn Pharma Limited as on March 31, 2017

Particulars	Rs. in Millions	Particulars	Rs. in Millions
Raw materials inventory (1.4.2016)	7,644	Security deposits (long-term)	378
Work-in-process inventory (1.4.2016)	7,229	Investment in derivatives not designated as hedges	612
Inventory of stock-in-trade (1.4.2016)	440	Capital advances	2,918
Inventory of finished goods	5,621	Balances with government	1,183
Purchase of raw materials	22,519	Short-term loans	138
Land	1,960	Export incentives receivable	2,659
Building	11,466	Prepaid expenses	327
Plant and equipment	27,463	Advances to suppliers	8,241
Furniture and fixtures	697	Equity share capital	2,399
Vehicles	364	General reserve	57,373
Office equipment	461	Retained earnings	126,353
Product-related intangibles	129	Long-term borrowings	7,606
Computer software	525	Capital reserve	30,660
Capital work-in-progress	10,533	Securities premium	11,895
Investment in equity of subsidiaries	192,442	Interest accrued on long-term loans	7
Long-term investments	1,068	Provision for employee pension	2,444
Short-term investments	400	Provision for product related claims	8,884
Cash at hand	1,508	Short-term borrowings	40,540
Trade receivables	27,257	Advances from customers	353
Balances held in earmarked accounts	130	Current maturities of LT debt	12,319
Long-term loans	49	Product settlement claims	14,299

(Continued)

Particulars	Rs. in Millions	Particulars	Rs. in Millions
Deferred tax assets	7,517	Statutory dues	1,385
Advance tax paid	17,826	Trade payables	20,942
GST paid	1,092	Revenue from sale of products and services (including GST)	78,067
Purchases of stock-in-trade	12,365	Dividend income	2,041
Salaries and wages	13,663	Interest income	229
Contribution to provident fund	1,198	Rental income	189
Repairs and maintenance	2,110	Gain on sale of investments	2,685
Consumption of stores	4,279		
Selling and distribution expenses	4,556		
Professional and legal charges	3,811		
Freight charges	1,601		
Misc. expenses	11,421		
Interest expense	2,236		
Remeasurement of defined benefit plans	(600)		
Equity instruments through OCI	(34)		

Additional Information:

1. Stock on March 31, 2017 (in Rs. Millions): Raw materials 7,318, Work-in-process 8,403, Finished goods 6,053, Stock-in-trade 462.
2. Provision for tax: Current tax 25.
3. Depreciation to be charged on Building 368, Plant and equipment 3,136, Furniture and fixtures 124, Vehicles 60, and Office equipment 118.
4. Intangible assets to be amortized as follows: (in Rs. Millions) Computer Software 149, Product related intangibles 21.
5. Miscellaneous expenses include Rs. 200 million spent on installation of plant and equipment.

6. From the trial balance and additional information of Triton Motors Limited (Table 8.30), prepare the Statement of Profit and Loss for the year ended March 31, 2017 and a Balance Sheet on that date.

Table 8.30 Trial balance of Triton Motors Ltd. as on March 31, 2017

Particulars	Rs. in Millions	Particulars	Rs. in Millions
Raw materials inventory (1.4.2016)	14,308	Goodwill	991
Work-in-process inventory (1.4.2016)	4,885	Computer software	740
Inventory of finished goods (1.4.2016)	28,967	Product development	35,699

(Continued)

Particulars	Rs. in Millions	Particulars	Rs. in Millions
Purchase of raw materials	277,348	Capital work-in-progress	18,709
Purchase of stock-in-trade	39,460	Advance tax paid	8,541
Land	45,749	Dividend paid (including tax)	730
Building	24,501	Investment in subsidiaries	147,789
Plant and equipment	116,688	Deferred tax liability	980
Furniture and fixtures	1,164	Short-term borrowings	53,755
Vehicles	725	Liability under financial guarantees	20,451
Computers	1,155	Liability toward employee separation	1,280
Technical know-how	2,254	Provision for warranties	7,076
Capital advances	5,588	Trade payables	70,152
Long-term investments	5,284	Revenue from sale of products (including GST)	480,185
Short-term investments	24,009	Interest and dividend income	8,512
Cash and cash equivalents	1,884	Revenue from sale of services	3,680
Deposits with banks with maturity of more than 12 months	977	Current maturities of LT debt	5,224
Loans (long-term)	3,896	Statutory liabilities	7,990
Trade receivable	21,280	Securities premium	192,139
Loans (short-term)	2,314	Provision for employee benefits	6,109
Staff welfare expenses	3,711	Interest accrued on borrowings	4,497
GST paid	47,364	Deferred revenue:	4,281
Salaries and wages	29,914	Remeasurement of defined benefit plans (net of tax)	102
Contribution to provident fund	1,960	Gain on equity instruments through OCI	738
Freight and handling	15,419	Other operating revenue	7,138
Contract processing charges	15,224	Profit on sale of investments	1,177
Stores consumed	5,791	Equity share capital	6,792
Publicity expenses	8,484	Debenture redemption reserve	10,859
IT expenses	7,624	Retained earnings	24,227
Misc. expenses	34,432	Long-term borrowings	139,984
Interest expense	15,902		
Advances to suppliers	2,361		

(Continued)

Particulars	Rs. in Millions	Particulars	Rs. in Millions
Balances with government	24,338		
Prepaid expenses (long-term)	4,345		
Impairment of investment in subsidiary companies	1,232		
Employee separation costs	676		
Derivative financial instruments	2,916		

Additional Information:

1. Stock on March 31, 2017 (in Rs. Millions): Raw materials 15,112, Work-in-process 8,157, Finished goods 28,210.
2. Provision for tax: Current tax 445, deferred tax 147
3. Depreciation to be charged on Building 1,056, Plant and equipment 15,670, Furniture and fixtures 107, Vehicles 107, and Computers 26
4. Intangible assets to be amortized as follows: (in Rs. Millions) Computer software 268, Technical know-how 332, and Product development 10,360
5. Interest of Rs. 100 million on investments is due but not received

7. From the trial balance and additional information of Advanced Software Limited (Table 8.31), prepare the Statement of Profit and Loss for the year ended March 31, 2017 and a Balance Sheet on that date.

Table 8.31 Trial balance of Advanced Software Systems Limited as on March 31, 2017

Particulars	Rs. in Millions	Particulars	Rs. in Millions
Securities premium	22,080	Advances to suppliers	870
Dividend paid (including tax)	6,980	Capital advances	5,620
Cost of technical subcontractors	48,090	Capital reserve	540
Cost of software packages	12,350	Share options outstanding	1,200
Land	17,520	Equity share capital	11,480
Building	43,330	General reserve	110,870
Plant and equipment	9,750	Retained earnings	383,440
Furniture and fixtures	6,060	Cash flow hedge reserve	390
Vehicles	130	Equity instruments through OCI	(50)
Office equipment	4,090	Payable for acquisition of business	400
Computers	16,910	Deferred income	420
Capital work-in-progress	12,470	Deferred tax assets	3,460
Long-term investments	153,340	Advances from customers	250
Short-term investments	96,430	Payable to employees	25,460

(Continued)

Particulars	Rs. in Millions	Particulars	Rs. in Millions
Security deposits	810	Trade payables	2,690
Rental deposits	1,350	Revenue from software services	592,570
Cash and cash equivalents	191,530	Interest income	25,300
Trade receivables	109,600	Unpaid dividend:	170
Advance tax paid	54,540	Accrued expenses	20,130
Loans (long-term)	50	Retention money	1,530
Loans (short-term)	3,100	Contingent consideration	450
Restricted deposits	13,090	Capital creditors	2,570
Unbilled revenue	32,000	Unearned revenue	13,200
Interest accrued but not due	5,140	Deferred rent	20
Receivables under derivative contracts	3,800	Withholding taxes	10,270
Salaries and wages	301,110	Provision for post-sales client support and warranties	3,500
Contribution to provident fund	7,260	Revenue from software products	320
Consultancy and professional fee	5,380	Dividend income	230
Repairs and maintenance	10,730	Gain on investments through profit or loss	1,110
Branding and marketing expenses	2,760	Foreign currency gain on derivative contracts	5,510
Operating lease payments	2,840	Foreign currency loss on translation of other assets/liabilities	(1,530)
Miscellaneous expenses	35,470		
Loss on re-measurement of defined benefit plans	(420)		
Loss on equity instruments through OCI	(50)		
Travel expenses	16,380		
Fair value changes on cash flow hedges	290		

Additional Information:

1. Depreciation to be charged (in Rs. Million): Building 2,270, Plant and equipment 2,500, Furniture and fixtures 1,620, Vehicles 40, Office equipment 1,110, and Computers 5,720
2. Provision for tax (in Rs. Million): Current tax 50,680, deferred tax 520
3. Prepaid miscellaneous expenses are Rs. 8,210 Million

8. From the trial balance and additional information of Superior Tobacco Company Limited (Table 8.32), prepare the Statement of Profit and Loss for the year ended March 31, 2017 and a Balance Sheet on that date.

Table 8.32 Trial balance of Superior Tobacco Company Ltd. as on March 31, 2017

Particulars	Rs. in Millions	Particulars	Rs. in Millions
Raw materials inventory (1.4.2016)	48,888	Interest accrued but not due	4,740
Work-in-process inventory (1.4.2016)	1,805	Prepaid expenses (short-term)	6,106
Inventory of traded goods (1.4.2016)	3,464	Deferred tax liability	18,717
Inventory of finished goods (1.4.2016)	27,448	Advances from customers	6,684
Purchase of raw materials	117,506	Equity instruments through OCI	4,936
Purchase of stock-in-trade	35,666	Retention money payable towards plant and equipment	92
Land	15,965	Deferred revenue	147
Building	42,458	Trade payables	25,512
Plant and equipment	91,318	Revenue from sale of products (including GST)	536,724
Furniture and fixtures	419	Interest and dividend income	19,860
Vehicles	995	Revenue from sale of services	17,761
Know-how	241	Prepaid expenses (long-term)	6,484
Capital advances	10,565	Computer software	825
Long-term investments	84,855	Trademarks	3,308
Short-term investments	100,998	Office equipment	185
Cash and cash equivalents	1,582	Capital work-in-progress	34,913
Security deposits	9,653	Dividend paid	68,401
Deposits with banks with maturity of more than 12 months	25,332	Tax on dividend	13,335
Loans (long-term)	58	Cash flow hedging reserve	64
Trade receivable	22,075	Share options outstanding	15,647
Loans (short-term)	34	Securities premium	56,860
Share-based payments to employees	4,503	Provision for employee benefits	1,732
Staff welfare expenses	1,596	Capital reserve	25
GST paid	153,598	Unpaid dividend	1,574
Long-term loans from banks	180	Earmarked balances with banks:	1,577

(Continued)

Particulars	Rs. in Millions	Particulars	Rs. in Millions
Salaries and wages	14,872	Remeasurement of defined benefit plans (net of tax)	(280)
Contribution to provident fund	1,403	Gain on equity instruments through OCI	1,300
Freight and handling	13,370	Statutory liabilities	24,828
Contract processing charges	13,216		
Power and fuel	10,503		
Rent	8,087		
Rates and taxes	10,569		
Misc. expenses	15,904		
Interest expense	230		
Equity share capital	12,147		
General reserve	165,553		
Retained earnings	118,909		
Current maturities of long-term debt	78		

Additional Information:

1. Stock on March 31, 2017 (in Rs. Millions): Raw materials 48,738, Work-in-process 1,728, Finished goods 20228, Stock-in-trade 4,351.
2. Provision for tax: Current tax 52,857, deferred tax 164.
3. Depreciation to be charged on Building 1,206, Plant and equipment 8,054, Furniture and fixtures 659, Vehicles 151, and Office equipment 46.
4. Intangible assets to be amortized as follows: (in Rs. Millions) Computer software 208, Know-how 31, and trademarks 24.
5. Unpaid salaries and wages at the end of the year are Rs. 2,000 Million.

9. From the trial balance and additional information of Crest Motors Limited (Table 8.33), prepare the Statement of Profit and Loss for the year ended March 31, 2017 and a Balance Sheet on that date.

Table 8.33 Trial balance of Crest Motors Limited as on March 31, 2017

Particulars	Rs. in Millions	Particulars	Rs. in Millions
Raw materials inventory (1.4.2016)	17,343	Interest accrued but not due (Dr.)	21
Work-in-process inventory (1.4.2016)	1,643	Receivables from related parties (short-term)	1,129
Inventory of traded goods (1.4.2016)	2,480	Deferred tax liability	4,640
Inventory of finished goods (1.4.2016)	8,136	Advances from customers	9,392

(Continued)

Particulars	Rs. in Millions	Particulars	Rs. in Millions
Purchase of raw materials	422,634	Prepaid expenses (long-term)	3,929
Land	19,564	Short-term loans from banks	4,838
Building	17,529	Provision for warranties	156
Plant and equipment	113,310	Trade payables	83,673
Furniture and fixtures	1,287	Revenue from sale of products (including GST)	761,408
Vehicles	1,165	Purchase of traded goods	44,821
Lump sum royalty and engineering support fee	3,732	Security deposits	238
Capital advances	4,043	Deferred revenue	11,050
Long-term investments	262,147	Amounts paid under litigation	8,086
Short-term investments	20,137	EDP equipment	1,000
Cash and cash equivalents	181	Capital work-in-progress	12,523
Short-term loans	25	Dividend paid	10,573
Long-term loans	3	Tax on dividend	2,162
Trade receivable	11,982	Capital creditors (short-term)	8,308
Short-term claims receivable	5,471	Dealer deposits	4,719
Balances with government	9,917	Statutory dues	8,859
GST paid	92,314	Provision for employee benefits	63
Salaries and wages	20,772	Unclaimed dividend	8
Contribution to provident fund	2,538	Income from sale of services	4,806
Repairs and maintenance	1,706	Sale of scrap	3,830
Consumption of stores	2,241	Rental income	2,818
Power and fuel	5,172	Interest income	372
Advertisement and sales promotion	13,832	Dividend income	129
Royalty	38,480	Gain on sale of investments	22,024
Misc. expenses	25,797	Foreign exchange gains	273
Interest expense	894	Remeasurement of defined benefit plans (net of tax)	(158)
Equity share capital	1,510	Gain on equity instruments through OCI (net of tax)	2,361
General reserve	38,462		
Retained earnings	230,512		
Equity instruments through OCI	6,909		
Effective portion of gain/ (loss) on hedging instrument in a cash flow hedge (net of tax)	(47)		

Additional Information:

1. Stock on March 31, 2017 (in Rs. Millions): Raw materials 13,681, Work-in-process 1,546, Finished goods 12,811, Traded goods 2,591
2. Provision for tax: Current tax 23,317, deferred tax 2,719
3. Depreciation to be charged on Building 955, Plant and equipment 22,921, Furniture and fixtures 222, Vehicles 113, EDP equipment 392.
4. Rental income of Rs. 200 million has been received in advance.

Answers to Multiple Choice Questions

1. (c)
2. (d)
3. (a)
4. (b)
5. (a)
6. (d)
7. (a)
8. (b)
9. (b)
10. (c)

Financial Statements of Banking Companies

9

LEARNING OBJECTIVES

After reading this chapter, you will be able to:

- Understand the banking business and the functions performed by a banking company.
- Understand the legal provisions relating to capital, reserves, liquidity norms, dividend payments and disposal of non-banking assets that apply to banking companies.
- Understand the main characteristics of a bank's system of accounting.
- Understand the formats in which banks are required to prepare their financial statements.
- Understand the capital adequacy requirements that banks are required to follow.
- Understand the norms followed by banks for income recognition and the basis for classification of advances into standard, sub-standard and loss assets.
- Understand the techniques of classifying a bank's investments and make provision for their depreciation.
- Understand some transactions specific to the banking business.

9.1 Introduction

A bank is a financial institution that helps channelize the savings of households and others into productive means by lending to those in need of money. Banks are essential for a nation's development as they maintain the flow of money through the economy.

In India, banks and their activities are regulated by the Banking Regulation Act, 1949 (the Act, hereinafter). The Reserve Bank of India (RBI) is the apex institution that regulates the banking activities in India.

The term "Banking" is defined by Section 5(b) of the Act. Banking means accepting deposits of money from public for the purpose of lending. These deposits are repayable on demand and can be withdrawn by cheque, draft or otherwise.

9.2 Types of Banks

There are two main categories of commercial banks in India.

1. Scheduled commercial banks
2. Scheduled co-operative banks

Scheduled banks are those banks that have been included in the Second Schedule to Reserve Bank of India (RBI) Act, 1934. Except for some small and tiny urban co-operative banks, currently, there are no non-scheduled commercial banks in India. Banks included in the schedule satisfy certain requirements.

Scheduled commercial banks are further divided into five types:

1. Nationalized bank (e.g., State Bank of India, Punjab National Bank)
2. Development bank (e.g., Export Import Bank of India, National Bank for Agriculture and Rural Development)
3. Regional rural bank (e.g., Gramin Bank)
4. Foreign bank (e.g., Citibank, Standard Chartered Bank)
5. Private sector bank (e.g., HDFC Bank, ICICI Bank)

Similarly, scheduled co-operative banks are divided into two types: scheduled state co-operative bank and scheduled urban co-operative bank.

9.3 Accounting System of Banks

The accounting system of banks is quite different from the usual merchandizing and manufacturing businesses. Banks have to keep their customers' accounts up-to-date and have to check these regularly for accuracy. This is to ensure that a customer does not get paid anything more than the balance in his/her account and that a cheque should not get dishonored due to a mistake in the balance of a customer's account. A bank cannot afford to post entries into ledgers from the day book after a gap as is the practice with other businesses. All transactions of the bank are entered into the ledgers as soon as they take place.

Most of the banks operate on Core Banking Solutions (CBS) framework, which involves maintenance of accounts on huge capacity servers that allows instant updation of customer accounts through vouchers, debit cards, internet banking, etc.

The following are the main features of a bank's accounting system.

9.3.1 Slip System of Posting

Under this system, used in the case of banking companies, entries in the personal ledgers are made directly from vouchers instead of being posted from the day book. Pay-in- slips (used by customers at the time of making deposits) and cheques are used as slips, which form the basis of most of the transactions directly recorded in the customer accounts. As the slips are mostly filled by the customers themselves, this system saves a lot of time and labor of the bank staff.

The vouchers entered into different personal ledgers are summarized on summary sheets every day, totals of which are posted to different control accounts maintained in the general ledger.

9.3.2 Double Voucher System

In a bank, two vouchers are prepared for every transaction not involving cash—one debit voucher and another credit voucher. This system is called the double voucher system. The vouchers are sent to different clerks who make entries in books under their charge.

9.4 Legal Provisions

Important provisions of the Banking Regulation Act, 1949 that affect the functioning of banking companies are discussed in this section.

9.4.1 Forms of Business in Which Banking Companies may Engage

Section 6 of the Act specifies the forms of business in which banking companies may engage. In addition to the business of banking, banking company may engage in any one or more of the following forms of business, namely:

1. Borrowing, raising or taking up of money; lending or advancing of money either upon or without security; drawing, making and dealing in other ways in bills of exchange, *hundis* promissory notes and other instruments and securities.
2. Acting as agents for any Government or local authority or any other person or persons.
3. Contracting for public and private loans and negotiating and issuing the same.
4. Effecting, insuring, guaranteeing, underwriting, participating in managing and carrying out of any issue, public or private, of State, municipal or other loans or of shares, stock, debentures or debenture stock of any company, corporation or association and lending of money for the purpose of any such issue.
5. Carrying on and transacting every kind of guarantee and indemnity business.
6. Managing, selling and realizing any property that may come into the possession of the company in satisfaction or part satisfaction of any of its claims.
7. Acquiring and holding, and generally dealing with any property or any right, title or interest in any such property which may form the security or part of the security for any loans or advances or which may be connected with any such security.
8. Undertaking and executing trust.
9. Undertaking the administration of estates as executor, trustee or otherwise.
10. Establishing and supporting or aiding in the establishment and support of association, institutions, funds, trusts, etc.
11. Acquisition, construction, maintenance and alteration of any building or works necessary or convenient for the purposes of the company.
12. Selling, improving, managing, developing, exchanging, leasing, mortgaging, disposing of or turning into account or otherwise dealing with all or any part of the property and rights of the company.
13. Acquiring and undertaking the whole or any part of the business of any person or company.
14. Doing all such other things as are incidental or conducive to the promotion or advancement of the business of the company.
15. Any other forms of business which the Central Government may specify.

9.4.2 Restrictions on Payment of Dividend

A banking company cannot pay any dividend on its shares until all its capitalized expenses (including preliminary expenses, organization expenses, share-selling commission, brokerage, amounts of losses incurred and any other item of expenditure not represented by tangible assets) have been completely written off.

However, a banking company may pay dividends on its shares without writing off:

1. The depreciation, if any, in the value of its investments in approved securities in any case where such depreciation has not actually been capitalized or otherwise accounted for as a loss.
2. The depreciation, if any, in the value of its investments in shares, debenture or bonds (other than approved securities) in any case where adequate provision for such depreciation has been made to the satisfaction of the auditor of the banking company.
3. The bad debts, if any, in any case where adequate provision for such debts has been made to the satisfaction of the auditor of the banking company.

9.4.3 Prohibition of Trading

A banking company cannot directly or indirectly deal in the buying or selling or bartering of goods, except in connection with the realization of security given to or held by it. However, it may buy, sell or barter goods for others in connection with bills of exchange received for collection or negotiation.

9.4.4 Disposal of Non-Banking Assets

A banking company can hold any immovable property, only for its own use. Any other immovable property acquired by a bank (e.g., from a loan defaulter) has to be disposed of within 7 years from the acquisition thereof. The banking company may, within the period of 7 years as aforesaid, deal or trade in any such property for the purpose of facilitating the disposal thereof. The RBI may in any particular case extend the aforesaid period of 7 years by such period not exceeding 5 years.

9.4.5 Reserve Funds

Every banking company incorporated in India is required to create a reserve fund and to transfer at least 25% of its profit to the reserve fund before declaring its dividend. If any banking company makes any appropriation from the reserve fund or share premium account, it has to report to the RBI the reasons for such appropriation within 21 days.

9.4.6 Cash Reserve

Banks are required to maintain a minimum percentage of their net demand and time liabilities (NDTL) as cash reserve with itself or as a balance in a current account with the RBI or as a net balance in current account. This ratio is known as *cash reserve ratio*. The RBI keeps changing this ratio from time to time. The ratio, effective from the fortnight beginning February 9, 2013 is 4%.

9.4.7 Liquidity Norms

In addition to the cash reserve ratio, banking companies have to comply with another ratio known as the statutory liquidity ratio (SLR). SLR relates to holding liquid assets in the form of *cash, gold and unencumbered approved securities* at the close of business on any day and valued at a price not exceeding the current market price of these assets. The purpose of SLR is to ensure that banks are able to meet the cash requirements of its depositors at all times. RBI revises the SLR from time to time. As of January 7, 2017, the ratio is 20.50%.

9.5 Income Recognition

A major part of banks' income comes from two sources:

1. Interest on loans and advances to customers.
2. Discount and commission on money transfers, bills of exchange, letters of credit, letters of guarantee, etc.

The recognition of interest income depends on the classification of loans and advances into performing and non-performing assets (NPA). The income earned on performing assets is recognized as it is earned. On the contrary, for NPA, the income is recognized when it is actually received.

Illustration 9.1

A commercial bank provides the details of its interest income for the year ended March 31, 2015 (Table 9.1).

Table 9.1 Interest income for the year ended March 31, 2015

(Rs. in Millions)

	Performing Assets		Non-Performing Assets	
	Interest Earned	Interest Received	Interest Earned	Interest Received
Term loans	60.0	40.0	37.5	2.5
Cash credits and overdrafts	375.0	310.0	75.0	6.0
Bills purchased and discounted	75.0	75.0	50.0	10.0

Calculate the income to be recognized by the bank for the year ended March 31, 2015.

Solution: Income to be recognized is as follows:

(Rs. in Millions)

Term loans	(60.0 + 2.5)	62.5
Cash credits and overdrafts	(375.0 + 6.0)	381.0
Bills purchased and discounted	(75.0 + 10.0)	85.0
		528.5

9.6 Format of Financial Statements

The formats of financial statements of banking companies are specified by Schedule III of the Banking Regulation Act, 1949. Form A relates to the balance sheet and Form B relates to profit and loss account. The Act also specifies Schedules 1–16 containing details of items appearing in the balance sheet and profit and loss account. Banks may add two more schedules, Schedule 17 for notes on accounts and Schedule 18 for Accounting Policies for a better understanding of the financial statements. The formats of the balance sheet and the profit and loss account are given as follows.

Form "A"

Form of Balance Sheet

Balance Sheet of __________ (here enter the name of the banking company) as on March 31, (year)

(000's omitted)

Capital and Liabilities	**Schedule**	**As on 31.3..... (Current Year)**	**As on 31.3.... (Previous Year)**
Capital	1		
Reserves and surplus	2		
Deposits	3		
Borrowings	4		
Other liabilities and provisions	5		
Total			
Assets			
Cash and balances with RBI	6		
Balances with banks and money at call and short notice	7		
Investments	8		
Advances	9		
Fixed assets	10		
Other assets	11		
Total			
Contingent liabilities	12		
Bills for collection			

Schedule 1 – Capital

	As on 31.3….. (Current Year)	As on 31.3…. (Previous Year)
I. For Nationalized Banks		
Capital (fully-owned by Central Government)		
II. For Banks Incorporated Outside India		
Capital		
(i) (The amount brought in by banks by way of start-up capital as prescribed by RBI should be shown under this head)		
(ii) Amount of deposit kept with RBI under Section 11(2) of the Banking Regulation Act, 1949		
Total		
III. For Other Banks		
Authorized Capital		
(…… shares of Rs. ……each)		
Issued Capital		
(…… shares of Rs. ……each)		
Subscribed Capital		
(…… shares of Rs. ……each)		
Called-up Capital		
(…… shares of Rs. ……each)		
Less: Calls unpaid		
Add: Forfeited shares		

Schedule 2 – Reserves and Surplus

	As on 31.3…. (Current Year)	As on 31.3…. (Previous Year)
I. Statutory reserves		
Opening balance		
Additions during the year		
Deductions during the year		

II. Capital reserves		
Opening balance		
Additions during the year		
Deductions during the year		
III. Share premium		
Opening balance		
Additions during the year		
Deductions during the year		
IV. Revenue and other reserves		
Opening balance		
Additions during the year		
Deductions during the year		
V. Balance in profit and loss account		
	------------------	------------------
Total (I, II, III, IV and V)	------------------	------------------

Schedule 3 – Deposits

	As on 31.3….. (Current Year)	As on 31.3…. (Previous Year)
A. I. Demand deposits		
(i) From banks		
(ii) From others		
II. Saving bank deposits		
III. Term deposits		
(i) From banks		
(ii) From others		
	------------------	------------------
Total (I, II and III)	------------------	------------------
B. (i) Deposits of branches in India		
(ii) Deposits of branches outside India		
	------------------	------------------
Total		
	------------------	------------------

Schedule 4 – Borrowings

	As on 31.3….. (Current Year)	As on 31.3…. (Previous Year)
I. Borrowings in India		
(i) Reserve Bank of India		
(ii) Other banks		
(iii) Other institutions and agencies		
II. Borrowings outside India		
Total (I and II)		

Secured borrowings included in I & II above – Rs.

Schedule 5 – Other Liabilities and Provision

	As on 31.3….. (Current Year)	As on 31.3…. (Previous Year)
I. Bills payable		
II. Inter-office adjustments (net)		
III. Interest accrued		
IV. Others (including provisions)		
Total		

Schedule 6 – Cash and Balances with Reserve Bank of India

	As on 31.3….. (Current Year)	As on 31.3…. (Previous Year)
I. Cash in hand (including foreign currency notes)		
II. Balances with Reserve Bank of India		
(i) in Current account		
(ii) in Other accounts		
Total (I and II)		

Schedule 7 – Balances with Banks and Money at Call and Short Notice

	As on 31.3….. (Current Year)	As on 31.3…. (Previous Year)
I. In India		
(i) Balances with banks		
(a) in Current accounts		
(b) in Other deposit accounts		
(ii) Money at call and short notice		
(a) with banks		
(b) with other institutions		
Total [(i) and (ii)]		
II. Outside India		
(i) in current accounts		
(ii) in other deposit accounts		
(iii) Money at call and short notice		
Total [(i), (ii) and (iii)]		
Grand Total (I and II)		

Schedule 8 – Investments

	As on 31.3….. (Current Year)	As on 31.3…. (Previous Year)
I Investment in India in		
(i) Government securities		
(ii) Other approved securities		
(iii) Shares		
(iv) Debentures and bonds		
(v) Subsidiaries and/or joint ventures		
(vi) Others (to be specified)		
Total		

II Investment outside India in		
(i) Government securities (including local authorities)		
(ii) Subsidiaries and/or joint ventures		
(iii) Others (to be specified)		
	-------------------	-------------------
Total		
	-------------------	-------------------
	-------------------	-------------------
Grand Total (I and II)	============	===========

Schedule 9 – Advances

	As on 31.3….. (Current Year)	As on 31.3…. (Previous Year)
A (i) Bills purchased and discounted		
(ii) Cash credits, overdrafts and loans repayable on demand		
(iii) Term loans		
	-------------------	-------------------
Total		
	-------------------	-------------------
B (i) Secured by tangible assets		
(ii) Covered by bank/government guarantees		
(iii) Unsecured		
	-------------------	-------------------
Total		
	-------------------	-------------------
C I. Advances in India		
(i) Priority sector		
(ii) Public sector		
(iii) Banks		
(iv) Others		
	-------------------	-------------------
Total		
	-------------------	-------------------

II. Advances outside India
(i) Due from banks
(ii) Due from others
(a) Bills purchased and discounted
(b) Syndicated loans
(c) Others

Total		
Grand Total (CI and II)		

Schedule 10 – Fixed Assets

	As on 31.3….. (Current Year)	As on 31.3…. (Previous Year)
I. Premises		
At cost on 31 March of the preceding year		
Additions during the year		
Deductions during the year		
Depreciation to date		
II. Other fixed assets (including furniture and fixtures)		
At Cost on 31 March of the preceding year		
Additions during the year		
Deductions during the year		
Depreciation to date		
Total (I and II)		

Schedule 11 – Other Assets

	As on 31.3….. (Current Year)	As on 31.3…. (Previous Year)
I Inter-office adjustments (net)		
II Interest accrued		
III Tax paid in advance/tax deducted at source		
IV Stationery and stamps		
V Non-banking assets acquired in satisfaction of claims		
VI Others @		

Total		

@ In case there is any unadjusted balance of the loss, the same may be shown under this item with appropriate footnote.

Schedule 12 – Contingent Liabilities

		As on 31.3..... (Current Year)	As on 31.3.... (Previous Year)
I	Claims against the bank not acknowledged as debt		
II	Liabilities for partly paid investments		
III	Liability on account of outstanding forward exchange contracts		
IV	Guarantees given on behalf of constituents		
	(a) In India		
	(b) Outside India		
V	Acceptances, endorsements and other obligations		
VI	Other items for which the bank is contingently liable		
	Total		

Form "B"

Form of Profit and Loss Account

Profit and Loss Account for the Year Ended March 31, (Year)

(000's omitted)

		Schedule No.	Year ended on 31.3..... (Current Year)	Year ended on 31.3.... (Previous Year)
I.	**Incomc**			
	Interest earned	13		
	Other income	14		
		Total		
II.	**Expenditure**			
	Interest expended	15		
	Operating expenses	16		

Provisions and contingencies		
	----------	----------
Total		
	----------	----------
III. Profit/loss		
Net profit/loss (–) for the year		
Profit/loss (–) brought forward		
	----------	----------
Total		
	----------	----------
IV. Appropriations		
Transfer to statutory reserves		
Transfer to other reserves		
Transfer to government/proposed dividend		
Balance carried over to balance sheet		
	----------	----------
Total		
	----------	----------

Schedule 13 – Interest Earned

	Year ended on 31.3. (Current Year)	Year ended on 31.3. (Previous Year)
I. Interest/discount on advances/bills		
II. Income on investments		
III. Income on balances with Reserve Bank of India and other inter-bank funds		
IV. Others		
	----------	----------
Total		
	----------	----------

Schedule 14 – Other Income

	Year ended on 31.3. (Current Year)	Year ended on 31.3. (Previous Year)
I. Commission, exchange and brokerage		
II. Profit on sale of investments		
Less: Loss on sale of investments		
III. Profit on revaluation of investments		
Less: Loss on revaluation of investments		

		Year ended on 31.3. (Current Year)	Year ended on 31.3. (Previous Year)
IV.	Profit on sale of land, building and other assets *Less*: Loss on sale of land, building and other assets		
V.	Profit on exchange transactions *Less*: Loss on exchange transactions		
VI.	Income earned by way of dividends, etc., from subsidiaries/companies and/or joint ventures abroad/in India		
VII.	Miscellaneous income		
	Total		

Note: Under items II–V, loss figures may be shown in brackets.

Schedule 15 – Interest Expended

		Year ended on 31.3. (Current Year)	Year ended on 31.3. (Previous Year)
I.	Interest on deposits		
II.	Interest on Reserve Bank of India/ Inter-bank borrowings		
III.	Others		
	Total		

Schedule 16 – Operating Expenses

		Year ended on 31.3. (Current Year)	Year ended on 31.3. (Previous Year)
I.	Payments to and provisions for employees		
II.	Rent, taxes and lighting		
III.	Printing and stationery		
IV.	Advertisement and publicity		
V.	Depreciation on bank's property		
VI.	Director's fees, allowances and expenses		
VII.	Auditor's fees, allowances and expenses (including Branch Auditors)		
VIII.	Law charges		
IX.	Postages, telegrams, telephones, etc.		
X.	Repairs and maintenance		

XI. Insurance		
XII. Other expenditure		
	--------------------	------------------
Total		
	--------------------	------------------

Notes to Accounts and Accounting Policies

To facilitate a better understanding of the information contained in the financial statements, banks should disclose accounting policies relating to key areas of operation and the notes to accounts. Notes to Accounts may be added as Schedule 17 and the Significant Accounting Policies as Schedule 18. A sample of significant accounting policies appearing in the financial statements of HDFC Bank Ltd. for the year ended 31 March, 2014 is reproduced here (Exhibit 9.1).

Exhibit 9.1

HDFC Bank Limited: Extracts from the Annual Report for the Year Ended 31 March, 2014

Significant Accounting Policies

Advances

Classification

Advances are classified as performing and non-performing based on the RBI guidelines and are stated net of bills rediscounted, specific provisions, interest in suspense for non-performing advances, claims received from Export Credit Guarantee Corporation, provisions for funded interest term loan classified as non-performing advances and provisions in lieu of diminution in the fair value of restructured assets. Interest on non-performing advances is transferred to an interest suspense account and not recognized in the Statement of Profit and Loss until received.

Provisioning

Specific loan loss provisions in respect of non-performing advances are made based on the management's assessment of the degree of impairment of wholesale and retail advances, subject to the minimum provisioning level prescribed by the RBI.

The specific provision levels for retail NPAs are also based on the nature of product and delinquency levels. Specific loan loss provisions in respect of non-performing advances are charged to the Statement of Profit and Loss and included under Provisions and Contingencies.

Recoveries from bad debts written-off are recognized in the Statement of Profit and Loss and included under Other Income. In relation to non-performing derivative contracts, as per the extant RBI guidelines, the bank makes provision for the entire amount of overdue and future receivables relating to positive marked to market value of the said derivative contracts.

The bank maintains general provision for standard assets, including credit exposures computed as per the current marked to market values of interest rate and foreign exchange derivative contracts, and gold at levels stipulated by RBI from time to time. In the case of overseas branches, general provision on standard advances is maintained at the higher of levels stipulated by the respective overseas regulator or RBI. Provision for standard assets is included under Other Liabilities.

Provisions made in excess of these regulatory requirements or provisions which are not made with respect to specific NPAs are categorized as floating provisions. Creation of floating provisions is considered by the bank up to a level approved by the Board of Directors. In accordance with the RBI guidelines and as per the policy approved by the Board, floating provisions are not reversed by credit to Statement of Profit and Loss. Floating provisions are used only for contingencies under extraordinary circumstances wherein these are used for making specific provisions for impaired accounts. Floating provisions have been included under Other Liabilities.

Further to the provisions required to be held according to the asset classification status, provisions are held for individual country exposures (other than for home country exposure). Countries are categorized into risk categories as per the Export Credit Guarantee Corporation of India Ltd. (ECGC) guidelines, and provisioning is done in respect of that country where the net funded exposure is 1% or more than the bank's total assets.

In addition to the above, the bank on a prudential basis makes provisions on advances or exposures which are not NPAs, but has reasons to believe on the basis of the extant environment or specific information, the possible slippage of a specific advance or a group of advances or exposures or potential exposures. These are classified as contingent provisions and included under Other Liabilities.

The bank considers a restructured account as one where the bank, for economic or legal reasons relating to the borrower's financial difficulty, grants to the borrower concessions that the bank would not otherwise consider. Restructuring would normally involve modification of terms of the advance/securities, which would generally include, among others, alteration of repayment period/repayable amount/the amount of installments/rate of interest (due to reasons other than competitive reasons). Restructured accounts are classified as such by the bank only upon approval and implementation of the restructuring package. Necessary provision for diminution in the fair value of a restructured account is made. Restructuring of an account is done at a borrower level.

Fixed Assets and Depreciation

Fixed assets are stated at cost minus accumulated depreciation, as adjusted for impairment, if any. Cost includes cost of purchase and all expenditure such as site preparation, installation costs and professional fees incurred on the asset before it is ready for use. Subsequent expenditure incurred on assets put to use is capitalized only when it increases the future benefit/functioning capability from/of such assets.

Depreciation is charged over the estimated useful life of the fixed asset on a straight-line basis. The rates of depreciation are not lower than the rates prescribed in Schedule XIV of the Companies Act, 1956.

Transactions Involving Foreign Exchange

Foreign currency income and expenditure items of domestic operations are translated at the exchange rates prevailing on the date of transaction. Income and expenditure items of integral foreign operations (representative offices) are translated at the weekly average closing rates and of non-integral foreign operations (foreign branches) at the monthly average closing rates.

Foreign currency monetary items of domestic and integral foreign operations are translated at the closing exchange rates notified by Foreign Exchange Dealers' Association of India (FEDAI) as at the balance sheet date, and the resulting net valuation profit or loss arising due to a net open position in any foreign currency is recognized in the Statement of Profit and Loss.

Both monetary and non-monetary foreign currency assets and liabilities of non-integral foreign operations are translated at closing exchange rates notified by FEDAI at the balance sheet date, and the resulting profit/loss arising from exchange differences are accumulated in the Foreign Currency Translation Account until remittance or the disposal of the net investment in the non-integral foreign operations in accordance with AS-11.

Foreign exchange spot and forward contracts outstanding as at the balance sheet date and held for trading, are revalued at the closing spot and forward rates, respectively as notified by FEDAI and at interpolated rates for contracts of interim maturities. The contracts for longer maturities, that is, greater than 1 year are revalued using MIFOR (Mumbai Interbank Forward Offer Rate) and contracts with USD–INR currency pair are valued using USD LIBOR (London Interbank Offered Rate) rates. For other currency pairs, the forward points (as published by FEDAI) are extrapolated. The resulting profit or loss on valuation is recognized in the Statement of Profit and Loss.

Foreign exchange forward contracts, not intended for trading, are entered to establish the amount of reporting currency required or available at the settlement date of a transaction. They are outstanding at the balance sheet date, and are effectively valued at the closing spot rate. The premia or discount arising at the inception of such forward exchange contract is amortized as expense or income over the life of the contract.

Currency future contracts are marked to market daily using the settlement price on a trading day, which is the closing price of the respective future contracts on that day. While the daily settlement price is computed on the basis of the last half an hour weighted average price of such contract, the final settlement price is taken as the RBI reference rate on the last trading day of the future contract or as may be specified by the relevant authority from time to time. All open positions are marked to market based on the settlement price and the resultant marked to market profit/loss is daily settled with the exchange.

Contingent liabilities on account of foreign exchange contracts, currency future contracts, guarantees, letters of credit, acceptances and endorsements are reported at the closing rates of exchange notified by FEDAI as at the balance sheet date.

For reference, the balance sheet, profit and loss account, and cash flow statement of State Bank of India for the year 2015–16 are given in Exhibits 9.2, 9.3 and 9.4.

Exhibit 9.2

Balance Sheet of State Bank of India as on March 31, 2016

(000's omitted)

	Schedule No.	As on 31.03.2016 (Current Year) (Rs.)	As on 31.03.2015 (Previous Year) (Rs.)
Capital and liabilities			
Capital	1	776,27,77	746,57,31
Reserves & surplus	2	143498,15,83	127691,65,34
Deposits	3	1730722,43,61	1576793,24,50
Borrowings	4	224190,58,61	205150,29,26
Other liabilities and provisions	5	159875,57,46	137698,03,57
Total		2259063,03,28	2048079,79,98
Assets			
Cash and balances with Reserve Bank of India	6	129629,32,53	115883,84,35
Balances with banks and money at call and short notice	7	37838,33,12	38871,93,86
Investments	8	477097,27,65	481758,74,78
Advances	9	1463700,41,75	1300026,39,29
Fixed assets	10	10389,27,72	9329,16,42
Other assets	11	140408,40,51	102209,71,28
Total		2259063,03,28	2048079,79,98
Contingent liabilities	12	971956,00,58	1000627,25,78
Bills for collection	-	92211,64,83	92795,24,84
Significant accounting policies	17		
Notes to accounts	18		

Schedules referred to above form an integral part of the Balance Sheet

(Source: SBI, Annual Report 2015–16)

Exhibit 9.3

Profit and Loss Account of State Bank of India for the Year Ended on March 31, 2016

(000's omitted)

	Schedule No.	Year ended on 31.03.2016 (Current Year) (Rs.)	Year ended on 31.03.2015 (Previous Year) (Rs.)
I. Income			
Interest earned	13	163685,30,61	152397,07,42
Other income	14	28158,36,01	22575,89,26
Total		191843,66,62	174972,96,68
II. Expenditure			
Interest expended	15	106803,49,21	97381,82,36
Operating expenses	16	41782,36,65	38053,87,14
Provisions and contingencies		33307,15,39	26435,69,98
Total		181893,01,25	161871,39,48
III. Profit			
Net profit for the year		9950, 65,37	13101,57,20
Profit brought forward		32,48	32,48
Total		9950,97,85	13101,89,68
IV. Appropriations			
Transfer to statutory reserve		2985,19,61	4029,07,98
Transfer to capital reserve		345,27,46	105,50,44
Transfer to revenue and other reserves		4267,35,10	5889,05,56
Dividend for the previous year paid during the year (including tax on dividend)		80	—
Dividend for the current year		2018,32,20	2648,17,28
Tax on dividend for the current year		334,51,00	429,75,94
Balance carried over to balance sheet		31,68	32,48
Total		9950,97,85	13101, 89,68
Basic earnings per share		12.98	17.55
Diluted earnings per share		12.93	17.55
Significant accounting policies	17		
Notes to accounts	18		

Schedules referred to above form an integral part of the profit & loss account

(Source: SBI, Annual Report 2015–16)

Exhibit 9.4

Cash Flow Statement of State Bank of India for the Year Ended on March 31, 2016

Particulars	Year ended on 31.03.2016 (Current Year) (Rs.)	Year ended on 31.03.2015 (Previous Year) (Rs.)
Cash flow from operating activities:		
Net profit before taxes	13774,05,74	19313,96,20
Adjustments for:		
Depreciation on fixed assets	1700,30,45	1116,49,32
(Profit)/Loss on sale of fixed assets (Net)	16,69,37	42,74,99
(Profit)/Loss on revaluation of investments (Net)	151,67,43	0
(Profit)/Loss on sale of investments subsidiaries/Joint ventures/Associates	(108,00,00)	0
Provision for diminution in fair value & Non performing assets	26984,14,36	17908,05,50
Provision on standard assets	2157,54,91	2435,37,49
Provision for investment depreciation/(appreciation)	149,55,88	(590,07,29)
Other provisions including provision for contingencies	192,49,87	469,95,29
Income from investment in subsidiaries, Joint ventures, Associates	(475,82,57)	(677,03,43)
Interest paid on capital instruments	3722,80,38	3822,78,30
	48265,45,82	43842,26,37
Adjustments for:		
Increase/(Decrease) in deposits	153929,19,11	182384,74,02
Increase/(Decrease) in borrowings other than capital instruments	12902,76,40	22057,84,75
(Increase)/Decrease in investments other than investments In Subsidiaries/Joint ventures/Associates	5954,00,84	(80924,33,06)
(Increase)/Decrease in advances	(190658,16,81)	(108105,72,87)
Increase/(Decrease) in other liabilities	23446,33,07	34437,35,30
(Increase)/Decrease in other assets	(34583,68,76)	(61812,21,44)
Reduction in FCTR on disposal of investments in non-integral operations	(873,92,35)	0

(Continued)

Particulars		Year ended on 31.03.2016 (Current Year) (Rs.)	Year ended on 31.03.2015 (Previous Year) (Rs.)
		18381,97,32	31879,93,07
Tax refund/(Taxes paid)		(7185,42,60)	(4258,90,17)
Net cash generated from/(used in) operating activities	A	11196,54,72	27621,02,90
Cash flow from investing activities			
(Increase)/Decrease in investments in subsidiaries/Joint ventures/Associates		(1593,77,02)	(1444,77,30)
Profit/(Loss) on sale of investments in subsidiaries/Joint ventures /Associates		108,00,00	0
Dividend received from subsidiaries/Joint ventures/ Associates		475,82,57	677,03,43
(Increase)/Decrease in fixed assets		(2738,42,72)	(2490,36,07)
Net cash generated from/(used In) investing activities	B	(3748,37,17)	(3238,09,94)
Cash flow from financing activities			
Proceeds from issue of equity shares including share premium		5384,49,57	0
Share application money pending allotment received during the year		0	2970,00,00
Issue/(redemption) of capital instruments		5902,84,20	(200,00,00)
Interest on capital instruments		(3722,80,38)	(3822,78,30)
Dividends paid including tax thereon		(3058,65,86)	(1236,33,43)
Net cash generated from/ (used in) financing activities	C	4505,87,53	(2289,11,73)
Effect of exchange fluctuation on translation reserve	D	757,82,36	132,33,71
Net increase/(decrease) in cash & cash equivalents (A + B + C + D)		12711,87,44	22206,14,94
Cash and cash equivalents at beginning of the year		154755,78,21	132549,63,27
Cash and cash equivalents at end of the year		167467,65,65	154755,78,21
Note:			
Components of cash & cash equivalents as at:		31.03.2016	31.03.2013
Cash & balance with RBI		129629,32,53	115883,84,35
Balances with banks and money at call & short notice		37838,33,12	38871,93,86
Total		167467,65,65	154755,78,21

(Source: SBI, Annual Report 2015–16)

Illustration 9.2

The figures given in Table 9.2 are extracted from the books of KLM Bank Ltd. as on March 31, 2015.

Table 9.2 Extracted values from the books of KLM Bank Ltd. as on March 31, 2015

	Rs.
Interest and discount received	3,800,160
Interest paid on deposits	2,295,360
Issued and subscribed capital	1,000,000
Salaries and allowances	250,000
Director's fees and allowances	35,000
Rent and taxes paid	100,000
Postage and telegram	65,340
Statutory reserve fund	800,000
Commission, exchange and brokerage	190,000
Rent received	72,000
Profit on sale of investment	225,800
Depreciation on assets	40,000
Statutory expenses	38,000
Preliminary expenses	30,000
Auditor's fee	12,000

The following further information is given:

1. A customer to whom a sum of Rs. 1 million was advanced has become insolvent and only 55% is expected to be recovered from his estate.
2. There were also other debts for which a provision of Rs. 200,000 is required.
3. Rebate on bills discounted as on 31.03.2014 was Rs. 15,000 and as on 31.03.2015 was Rs. 20,000.
4. Income tax of Rs. 200,000 is to be provided.

The Director's desire to declare a 5% dividend.

Prepare the profit and loss account of KLM Bank Ltd. for the year ended March 31, 2015 and also show how the profit and loss account will appear in the balance sheet if the opening balance was NIL as on March 31, 2014.

Solution: See Table 9.3.

Table 9.3 Profit and loss account for the year ended March 31, 2015 for KLM Bank Ltd.

Particulars	Schedule	Amount (Rs.)
I. Income		
Interest earned	13	3,795,160
Other income	14	487,800
Total		4,282,960
II. Expenditure		
Interest expended	15	2,295,360
Operating expenses	16	570,340
Provisions and contingencies (450,000 + 200,000 + 200,000)		850,000
Total		3,715,700
III. Profits/Losses		
Net profit/loss (–) for the year		567,260
Profit/Loss (–) brought forward		-
		567,260
IV. Appropriations		
Transfer to statutory reserve (25% of Rs. 567,260)		141,815
Proposed dividend		50,000
Balance carried over to the balance sheet		375,445
		567,260

Profit and loss account balance of Rs. 375,445 will appear under the head "reserves and surplus" in Schedule 2 of the balance sheet.

Schedule 13 – Interest earned

	(Rs.)
Interest/discount on advances/bills (Refer W.N.)	3,795,160
	3,795,160

Schedule 14 – Other income

	(Rs.)
Commission, exchange and brokerage	190,000
Profit on sale of investments	225,800
Rent received	72,000
	487,800

Schedule 15 – Interest expended

	(Rs.)
Interest on deposits	2,295,360

Schedule 16 – Operating expenses

	(Rs.)
Payments to and provision for employees – Salaries, and allowances	250,000
Rent, taxes paid	100,000
Depreciation on assets	40,000
Director's fee, allowances and expenses	35,000
Auditor's fee	12,000
Statutory (law) expenses	38,000
Postage and telegrams	65,340
Preliminary expenses	30,000
	570,340

Working Note:

Interest Earned

	(Rs.)
Interest and discount received	3,800,160
Add: Rebate on bills discounted on 31.3.2014	15,000
Less: Rebate on bills discounted on 31.3.2015	(20,000)
	3,795,160

9.7 Classification of Advances and Provisioning

Banks have to classify their advances into two broad groups:

1. Performing assets
2. Non-performing assets

Performing assets are also called Standard Assets. Standard asset is one which does not disclose any problems and which does not carry more than the normal risk attached to the business.

An asset becomes non-performing when the bank does not receive income from it for a certain period. A bank should classify an account as NPA if the interest due and charged during any quarter is not serviced fully within 90 days from the end of the quarter.

NPAs are classified into three groups: (i) sub-standard assets, (ii) doubtful assets and (iii) loss assets.

A sub-standard asset is one which has been classified as NPA for a period not exceeding 12 months. In the case of term loans, those in which installments of principal are overdue for a period exceeding 1 year should be treated as sub-standard. In other words, such an asset will have well-defined credit weaknesses that jeopardize the liquidation of the debt and is characterized by the distinct possibility that the bank will sustain some loss, if deficiencies are not corrected.

A doubtful asset is one which has remained non-performing for a period exceeding 18 months. In the case of term loans, those in which installments of principal have remained overdue for a period exceeding 18 months should be treated as doubtful. A loan classified as doubtful has all the weaknesses inherent in that classified as sub-standard with added characteristic that the weaknesses make collection or liquidation in full, on the basis of currently known facts, conditions and values, highly questionable and improbable.

A loss asset is one in which loss has been identified by the bank or internal or external auditors or the RBI inspectors but the amount has not been written off, wholly or partly.

The classification of advances should be done taking into account: (i) the degree of well-defined credit worthiness and (ii) the extent of dependence on collateral security.

This classification is meant for the purpose of computing the amount of provision to be made in respect of advances and not for the purpose of presentation of advances in the balance sheet.

9.7.1 Provisions

Taking into account the time lag between an asset becoming sub-standard/doubtful and turning into a loss asset, RBI has directed banks to make provision against all assets, that is, loans and advances as given in Table 9.4.

Table 9.4 Provisions against advances

Category of Advances	Rate of Provisioning (%)
Standard Advances	
(a) direct advances to agricultural and SME	0.25
(b) advances to commercial real estate (CRE) Sector	1.00
(c) all other loans and advances not included in (a) and (b) above	0.40
Sub-Standard Advances	
(a) secured exposures	15
(b) unsecured exposures	25
(c) unsecured exposures in respect of infrastructure loan accounts where certain safeguards such as escrow accounts are available	20
Doubtful Advances	
(a) unsecured portion	100
(b) secured portion	
(i) doubtful up to 1 year	25

(Continued)

Table 9.4 (Continued)

Category of Advances	Rate of Provisioning (%)
(ii) doubtful greater than 1 year and up to 3 years	40
(iii) doubtful greater than 3 years	100
Loss Advances	100

Illustration 9.3

From the following details of advances of X Bank Limited, calculate the amount of provisions to be made in profit and loss account for the year ended March 31, 2015:

Asset Classification	(Rs. in Millions)
Standard	6,000
Sub-standard	4,400
Doubtful	
For 1 year	1,800
For 2 years	1,200
For 3 years	800
For more than 3 years	600
Loss assets	1,600

Solution: See Table 9.5.

Table 9.5 Provisions on various performing and non-performing assets

Asset Classification	Amount (Rs. in Millions)	Provision (%)	Amount of Provision (Rs. in Millions)
Standard	6,000	0.40	24
Sub-standard	4,400	15.00	660
Doubtful			
1 year	1,800	25.00	450
2 years	1,200	40.00	480
3 years	800	40.00	320
More than 3 years	600	100.00	600
Loss assets	1,600	100.00	1,600
			4,134

9.7.2 Provisioning for Advances Covered by ECGS/ DICGC Guarantee

In the case of advances guaranteed by Export Credit Guarantee Corporation (ECGC) and Deposit Insurance Credit Guarantee Corporation (DICGC), provision is required to be made only for the balance amount of advance outstanding in excess of the amount guaranteed by the corporations. If the bank also holds a security in respect of such advances, the realizable value of the security should be deducted from the outstanding balance before off-setting the ECGC/DICGC guarantee. According to the RBI, banks that follow a more stringent provisioning method for such advances can continue to do so.

Illustration 9.4

Rajatapeeta Bank Ltd. had extended the following credit lines to a Small Scale Industry, which had not paid any Interest since March, 2009.

	Term Loan	Export Loan
Balance outstanding on 31.03.2014	Rs. 35 Million	Rs. 30 Million
DICGC/ECGC cover	40%	50%
Securities held	Rs. 15 Million	Rs. 10 Million
Realizable value of securities	Rs. 10 Million	Rs. 8 Million

Compute the necessary provisions to be made for the year ended March 31, 2015.

Solution:

	Term Loan (Rs. in Millions)	Export Credit (Rs. in Millions)
Balance outstanding on 31.3.2014	35.0	30.0
Less: Realizable value of securities	10.0	8.0
	25.0	22.0
Less: DICGC cover @ 40%	10.0	
ECGC cover @ 50%		11.0
Unsecured balance	15.0	11.0
Required provision:		
100%* for unsecured portion	15.0	11.0
100% for secured portion	10.0	8.0
Total provision required	25.0	19.0

9.8 Classification of Investments

Banks are required to maintain a certain minimum level of liquid assets defined by the SLR. RBI issues directions to banks relating to the type of securities they can invest in for this purpose. The investment portfolio of a bank would normally consist of both approved securities (predominantly government securities) and other securities (shares, debentures, bonds, etc.). Banks are required to classify their entire investment portfolio into three categories: held-to-maturity (HTM), held-for-trading (HFT) and available-for-sale (AFS).

9.8.1 Held-to-Maturity

Securities acquired by banks with the intention to hold them up to maturity should be classified as "held-to-maturity." Investments under the HTM category should not exceed 25% of the total investment of the bank. However, a bank has the discretion to hold less than 25% under this category. Certain specified securities are not included while calculating the 25% limit for HTM securities.

9.8.2 Held-for-Trading

Securities acquired by banks with the intention to trade by taking advantage of short-term price/interest rate movements should be classified as held-for-trading (HFT)/maturity.

9.8.3 Available-for-Sale

Securities which do not fall within the above two categories should be classified as "available-for-sale" (AFS).

Banks are free to decide the amount of investment under HFT and AFS categories. The criteria applied to decide the amount of investment in a category include the objective of making the investment, forecast of market variables, tax considerations, capital position, manpower skills and risk-management capabilities. HFT securities have to be sold within 90 days. Profit or loss on sale of investments in both the categories is transferred to the profit and loss account.

9.9 Capital Adequacy Norms

Banks are exposed to various types of risks in the process of performing their banking functions. These risks include market risk, credit risk, operational risk and liquidity risk, among others. Banks need to have sufficient capital to absorb any losses arising out of their exposure to these risks. Adequate capital with banks protects depositors against unforeseen contingencies and promotes stability and efficiency of financial system.

Recognizing the need for a stable and sound International Banking System, The Basel Committee on Banking Supervision (BCBS) published the first Basel Capital Accord (popularly known as Basel I framework) in July 1988 that adopted minimum capital adequacy standards based on risk assets ratio for both the balance sheet and off-balance sheet system. The main objectives of the Basel Committee were:

1. to stop reckless lending by banks, thereby strengthening the soundness and stability of the banking system; and
2. to put banks from different countries on a more even competitive footing.

In April 1992, the RBI decided to introduce a risk asset ratio system for banks (including foreign banks) in India as a capital adequacy measure. In 2004, BCBS published Basel II guidelines which were the refined, reformed and more complex version of Basel I. While Basel I focused only on credit risk, Basel II included market and operational risks besides credit risk. Basel III released in December 2010 lay more focus on quality, consistency and transparency of the capital base. India adopted Basel I guidelines in 1999, while Basel II guidelines were implemented in phases by 2009. The Basel III capital regulations will be implemented in India in phases starting April 1, 2013. It is expected to be fully implemented by March 31, 2018.

Under Basel II norms, all Indian scheduled commercial banks (excluding regional rural banks) and foreign banks operating in India are required to maintain a minimum capital adequacy ratio (CAR). The CAR is defined as follows:

$$\text{CAR} = \frac{\text{Capital funds}}{\text{Risk weighted assets} + \text{Off-balance sheet items}} \times 100$$

Capital fund consists of Tier I and Tier II capital. The ratio is specified by the RBI from time to time and is currently 9%.

9.9.1 Tier I Capital

It is generally referred to as the core capital which absorbs losses without requiring a bank to cease operations, and thus provides more protection to bank depositors.

The elements of Tier I capital include:

1. Paid-up capital (ordinary shares), statutory reserves and other disclosed free reserves, including share premium, if any.
2. Perpetual Non-Cumulative Preference Shares (PNCPS) eligible for inclusion as Tier I capital, subject to laws in force from time to time.
3. Innovative Perpetual Debt Instruments (IPDI) eligible for inclusion as Tier I capital.
4. Capital reserves representing surplus arising out of sale proceeds of assets.

The sum of these components is *reduced by*:

(a) Intangible assets
(b) Current and brought forward losses
(c) **Deferred tax assets (DTA):** The reason for deducting DTA is that it results in an increase in Tier I capital of a bank without any tangible asset being added to the banks' balance sheet.

9.9.2 Tier II Capital

The elements of Tier II capital are less permanent in nature or are less readily available than those comprising Tier I capital. These include:

(i) undisclosed reserves and cumulative perpetual preference assets
(ii) revaluation reserves
(iii) general provisions and loss reserves
(iv) hybrid capital instruments
(v) subordinated debt
(vi) investment reserve account

9.9.2.1 Undisclosed Reserves

They can be included in capital, if they represent accumulations of post-tax profits and are not encumbered by any known liability and should not be routinely used for absorbing normal loss or operating losses.

9.9.2.2 Revaluation Reserves

Revaluation reserves arise on revaluation of assets. It would be prudent to consider revaluation reserves at a discount of 55% while determining their value for inclusion in Tier II capital. Such reserves will have to be reflected on the face of the balance sheet as revaluation reserves.

9.9.2.3 General Provisions and Loss Reserves

Such reserves can be included in Tier II capital if they are not attributable to the actual diminution in value or identifiable potential loss in any specific asset and are available to meet unexpected losses. Adequate care must be taken to see that sufficient provisions have been made to meet all known losses and foreseeable potential losses before considering general provisions and loss reserves to be part of Tier II capital. General provisions/loss reserves will be admitted up to a maximum of 1.25% of total risk weighted assets. "Floating Provisions" held by banks, which are general in nature and not made against any identified assets, may be treated as a part of Tier II capital within the overall ceiling of 1.25% of total risk weighted assets. Excess provisions which arise on sale of NPAs would be eligible Tier II capital subject to the overall ceiling of 1.25% of total risk weighted assets.

9.9.2.4 Hybrid Debt Capital Instruments

These instruments have features of both debt and equity instruments. When such instruments are able to support losses on an ongoing basis without triggering liquidation, they may be included in Tier II capital. At present the following instruments have been recognized and placed under this category:

1. Debt capital instruments eligible for inclusion as Upper Tier II capital.
2. Perpetual Cumulative Preference Shares (PCPS)/Redeemable Non-Cumulative Preference Shares (RNCPS)/Redeemable Cumulative Preference Shares (RCPS) as part of Upper Tier II Capital.

9.9.2.5 Subordinated Debt

Banks can raise, with the approval of their Boards, rupee-subordinated debt as Tier II capital, subject to the specified terms and conditions.

9.9.2.6 Investment Reserve Account

In the event of provisions created on account of depreciation in the AFS or HFT categories being found to be in excess of the required amount in any year, the excess should be credited to the profit and loss account and an equivalent amount (net of taxes, if any and net of transfer to statutory reserves as applicable to such excess provision) should be appropriated to an Investment Reserve Account in Schedule 2 – "reserves & surplus" under the head "revenue and other reserves" in the balance sheet. This would be eligible for inclusion under Tier II capital within the overall ceiling of 1.25% of total risk weighted assets prescribed for general provisions/loss reserves.

9.9.3 Deductions from Tier I and Tier II Capital

9.9.3.1 *Equity/Non-Equity Investments in Subsidiaries*

The investments of a bank in the equity and non-equity capital instruments issued by a subsidiary, which are reckoned towards its regulatory capital as per norms prescribed by the respective regulator, should be deducted at 50% each from Tier I and Tier II capitals of the parent bank, while assessing the capital adequacy of the bank on a "solo" basis, under the Basel I Framework.

Credit Enhancements Pertaining to Securitization of Standard Assets

1. **Treatment of first loss facility:** The first loss credit enhancement provided by the originator shall be reduced from the capital funds and the deduction capped at the amount of capital that the bank would have been required to hold for the full value of assets, had they not been securitized. The deduction shall be made at 50% from Tier I and 50% from Tier II capital.
2. **Treatment of second loss facility:** The second loss credit enhancement provided by the originator shall be reduced from the capital funds to the full extent. The deduction shall be made 50% from Tier I and 50% from Tier II capital.
3. **Treatment of credit enhancements provided by third party:** In case the bank acts as a third party service provider, the first loss credit enhancement provided by it shall be reduced from the capital to the full extent as indicated in point (1) above.
4. **Underwriting by an originator:** Securities issued by SPVs and devolved/held by banks in excess of 10% of the original amount of issue, including secondary market purchases, shall be deducted 50% from Tier I capital and 50% from Tier II capital.
5. **Underwriting by third party service providers:** If the bank has underwritten securities issued by SPVs devolved and held by banks which are below investment grade, the same will be deducted from capital at 50% from Tier I and 50% from Tier II.

9.9.4 Limit for Tier II Elements

Tier II elements should be limited to a maximum of 100% of total Tier I elements for the purpose of compliance with the norms.

9.9.5 Capital Funds of Foreign Banks Operating in India

For foreign banks operating in India, "capital funds" would include two components, that is, Tier I capital and Tier II capital.

1. **Elements of Tier I capital:** The elements of Tier I capital include:
   - **(a)** Interest-free funds from head office kept in a separate account in Indian books, specifically for the purpose of meeting the capital adequacy norms.
   - **(b)** Innovative instruments eligible for inclusion as Tier I capital.
   - **(c)** Statutory reserves kept in Indian books.
   - **(d)** Remittable surplus retained in Indian books which is not repatriable so long as the bank functions in India.

2. **Elements of Tier II capital:** The elements of Tier II capital include:
   (a) Elements of Tier II capital as applicable to Indian banks.
   (b) Head office (HO) borrowings raised in foreign currency (for inclusion in Upper Tier II Capital) subject to the specified terms and conditions.

Illustration 9.5

A commercial bank has the following capital funds:

	(Rs. in Millions)
Equity share capital	1440
Statutory reserve	840
Capital reserve (arising from sale)	75
Revaluation reserve	40
Intangible assets	10
Deferred tax assets	5
Perpetual cumulative preference shares	3

Classify the capital funds into Tier I Capital and Tier II Capital.

Solution:

Tier I Capital

		(Rs. in Millions)
Equity share capital		1,440
Statutory reserve		840
Capital reserve (arising from sale)		75
		2,355
Less:		
Intangible assets	10	
Deferred tax assets	5	
		15
		2,340

Tier II Capital

Revaluation reserve	40	
Less: Discount (55%)	22	
		18
Perpetual cumulative preference shares		3
		21

9.9.6 Risk-Adjusted Assets

To calculate the risk-adjusted assets for the purpose of calculating the CAR, each asset is multiplied by a risk weight. Off balance sheet items are first multiplied by credit conversion factors and then by the relevant risk weights. The risk weights assigned to different assets depend on the susceptibility of the assets to risks. Cash balances, being not risky at all, attract zero risk weight. Some advances, which are backed by counter-guarantees, also have a lesser risk weight compared to other advances.

Table 9.6 presents some important weights for ascertaining CAR.

Table 9.6 Risk weights for determination of CAR

Asset	Risk Weight (%)
Cash and balances with RBI	0
Balances in current account with other banks	20
Investment in Government securities	0
Other investments	100
Loans and advances guaranteed by Government	0
Other loans and advances	100
Bank premises, furniture and fittings	100
All off-balance sheet items such as letters of credit, bills accepted, etc.	100

Illustration 9.6

A commercial bank has capital funds of Rs. 45,126 million in the form of Tier I and Tier II capital. The details of the bank's assets are as given in Table 9.7.

Table 9.7 Details of assets

	(Rs. in Millions)
Cash balance with RBI	240
Balances with other banks	625
Investment in Government securities	1,425
Other investments	39,125
Loans and advances guaranteed by Government	6,410
Other loans and advances	260,125
Premises, furniture	6,840
Other assets	10,060
Letters of credit	185,125

Compute the risk-adjusted assets and risk-weighted assets ratio.

Solution: See Table 9.8.

Table 9.8 Risk-adjusted assets

Asset	Amount (Rs. in Millions)	Risk Weight (%)	Risk-Weighted Amount (Rs. in Millions)
Cash balance with RBI	240	0	0
Balances with other banks	625	20	125
Investment in Government securities	1,425	0	0
Other investments	39,125	100	39,125
Loans and advances guaranteed by Government	6,410	0	0
Other loans and advances	260,125	100	260,125
Premises, furniture	6,840	100	6,840
Other assets	10,060	100	10,060
Letters of credit (credit conversion factor 100%)	185,125	100	185,125
			501,400

$$\text{Risk-weighted assets ratio} = \frac{\text{Capital funds}}{\text{Risk-weighted assets}} \times 100$$

$$= \frac{45,126}{501,400} \times 100 = 9\%$$

9.10 Some Special Transactions

9.10.1 Acceptances, Endorsements and Other Obligations

Credit of a bank is more acceptable than that of its customers. Hence, a bank is often requested by a customer to accept or endorse a bill of exchange on its behalf or give a guarantee of repayment of a loan raised by the customer. Suppose A makes a purchase from B and wants credit. B is willing to extend credit, provided he/she is satisfied that on the due date, payment will be forthcoming. To assure B, A can do one of the following:

1. He/she may request his/her bank to stand as a guarantor.
2. He/she may send a promissory note in favor of the bank, and the bank may then endorse it in favor of B.
3. He/she may request the bank to send its own acceptance to B.

Guarantee and endorsement are on the same footing and will stand cancelled when A makes the payment. If A does not pay, the bank will pay to B, and debit A's account. In case the bank accepts a bill of exchange, the bank will have to pay to B, recovering the amount from A. In this case "acceptances on behalf of customers" will equal "customer's liability for acceptances."

To safeguard its interests, the bank may require the customer to deposit a security for an appropriate amount against a guarantee, or an acceptance or endorsement by the bank on behalf of the customer. A record of the guarantee given or the particulars of the bill accepted or endorsed and the particulars of the security collected from the customer will have to be recorded in different registers.

Outstanding amounts of acceptances, endorsements and other obligations at the end of the year have to be shown as contingent liabilities in Schedule 12 of the balance sheet of the bank.

9.10.2 Bills for Collection

A bank receives a large number of bills receivable for collection on the due dates of the bills. The bank keeps these bills with itself till maturity and, on realization, credits the amounts to the clients concerned. Similarly, businessmen who sell goods to outstation customers hand over documentary bills to the bank to be handed over to the purchasers on payment of the concerned bills. In this case also the amounts collected for the documentary bills are credited to the clients who submit such bills. The bank keeps a systematic record of all such bills in a separate register, which is called Bills for Collection Register. The total amount of bills lying with the bank for collection at the end of the year is shown separately at the foot of the balance sheet of the bank.

9.10.3 Bills Purchased and Discounted

A bank may straightaway purchase or discount a bill. In this case, the bank reduces the amount of the bill by discount charges and credits the balance amount to the customer account. The discount charged is credited to the discount account and the full amount of the bill is debited to the discounted bills account. On the due date of the bill, the bank collects the bill from the drawee and gets its payment. At the end of the year, the outstanding amount of all such bills is shown as bills purchased and discounted in Schedule 9 of the balance sheet.

9.10.3.1 Rebate on Bills Discounted

The bank credits the discount on all bills discounted by it to discount account. The bank earns the full amount of the discount income when the bill matures. Some of the discounted bills may mature after the close of the accounting year. The portion of the discount that relates to the period falling after the close of the accounting year is called "rebate on bills discounted."

The amount of rebate on bills discounted is deducted from the discount income in the profit and loss account (Schedule 13) and is shown as a liability under "other liabilities and provisions" in Schedule 15.

Illustration 9.7

On March 31, 2014, Uncertain Bank Ltd. had a balance of Rs. 90 million in "rebate on bills discounted" account. During the year ended March 31, 2015, Uncertain Bank Ltd. discounted bills of exchange of Rs. 40 billion, charging an interest at 18% per annum the average period of discount being for 73 days. Of these, bills of exchange of Rs. 6 billion were due for realization from the acceptors/customers after March 31, 1998, the average period outstanding after March 31, 1998 being 36.5 days.

What is the income of the bank from discount for the year ended March 31, 2015 and the rebate on bills discounted on that date?

Solution: The income of the bank from discount for the year ended March 31, 2015 and the rebate on bills discounted on that date will be calculated as follows:

Rebate on bills discounted as on April 1, 2014	Rs. 90 million
Add: Discount charged during the year ended March 31, 2015	
Rs. 40,000 million × 0.18 × 73/365	Rs. 1,440 million
	Rs. 1,530 million
Less: Rebate on bills discounted as on March 31, 2015	
Rs. 6000 million × 0.18 × 36.5/365	Rs. 108 million
Discount income for the year ended March 31, 2015	Rs. 1,422 million

Summary – Review of Learning Objectives

1. **Understand the banking business and the functions performed by a banking company.** Banking means accepting deposits of money from public for the purpose of lending. These deposits are repayable on demand and can be withdrawn by cheque, draft or otherwise. Besides banking, banks perform many other functions such as acting as agents, trustees, underwriters, executors, etc.
2. **Understand the legal provisions relating to capital, reserves, liquidity norms, dividend payments and disposal of non-banking assets that apply to banking companies.** Banks need to have a minimum capital to carry on the business of banking; have to transfer 25% of their profits to reserves before they can pay dividend; have to meet statutory liquidity and cash reserve requirement; and cannot acquire immovable property except for their own use.
3. **Understand the main characteristics of a bank's system of accounting.** The accounting system of banks is quite different from the usual merchandizing and manufacturing businesses. Banks have to keep their customers' accounts up-to-date and have to check these regularly for accuracy. Entries in the personal ledgers are made directly from vouchers (slips) instead of being posted from the day book. Two vouchers are prepared for every transaction not involving cash—one debit voucher and another credit voucher. This system is called the double voucher system.
4. **Understand the formats in which banks are required to prepare their financial statements.** The formats of financial statements of banking companies are specified by the Third Schedule of the Banking Regulation Act, 1949. Form A relates to the balance sheet and Form B to profit and loss account. The Act also specifies Schedules 1–16 containing details of items appearing in the balance sheet and profit and loss account. Banks may add two more schedules, Schedule 17 for Notes on Accounts and Schedule 18 for Accounting Policies for a better understanding of the financial statements.
5. **Understand the capital adequacy requirements that banks are required to follow.** Under Basel II norms, all Indian scheduled commercial banks (excluding regional rural banks) and foreign banks operating in India are required to maintain a minimum CAR. CAR is the ratio of capital funds to risk-weighted assets (including off-balance sheet items). Capital fund consists of

Tier I and Tier II capital. The ratio is specified by RBI from time to time and is currently 9%.

6. **Understand the norms followed by banks for income recognition and the basis of classification of advances into standard, sub-standard and loss assets.** Recognition of interest income depends on the classification of loans and advances into performing and non-performing assets. Income earned on performing assets is recognized as it is earned. For non-performing assets (NPA), income is recognized when it is actually received.

   Performing assets are also called Standard Assets. Standard asset is one which does not disclose any problems and which does not carry more than the normal risk attached to the business.

   An asset becomes non-performing when the bank does not receive income from it for a certain period. A bank should classify an account as NPA if the interest due and charged during any quarter is not serviced fully within 90 days from the end of the quarter.

   Non-Performing Assets are classified into three groups: (i) sub-standard assets, (ii) doubtful assets and (iii) loss assets.

   Classification of advances is meant for the purpose of computing the amount of provision to be made in respect of advances

7. **Understand the techniques of classifying a bank's investments and make provision for their depreciation.** Banks are required to classify their entire investment portfolio into three categories: held-to-maturity, available-for-sale and held-for-trading. Securities acquired by banks with the intention to hold them up to maturity should be classified as "held-to-maturity." Investments under this category should not exceed 25% of the total investments of the bank. Securities acquired by banks with the intention to trade should be classified as held-for-trading/-maturity. Securities which do not fall within the above two categories should be classified as "available-for-sale." Banks are free to decide on the amount of investment under "held-for-trading" and "available-for-sale" categories.

8. **Understand some transactions specific to the business of banking.** "Acceptances, endorsements and other obligations" bills accepted or endorsed by the bank on behalf of its customers and guarantees for repayment of loans raised by the customers. Outstanding amounts of acceptances, endorsements and other obligations at the end of the year have to be shown as contingent liabilities.

   A bank receives a large number of bills receivable for collection on the due dates of the bills. The total amount of the bills lying with the bank for collection at the end of the year is shown separately at the foot of the balance sheet of the bank.

   A bank may purchase or discount a bill earning discount income straightaway. At the end of the year, the outstanding amount of all such bills is shown as Bills Purchased and Discounted in Schedule 9 of the balance sheet. Some of the discounted bills may mature after the close of the accounting year. The portion of the discount that relates to the period falling after the close of the accounting year is called "rebate on bills discounted." The amount of rebate on bills discounted is deducted from the Discount income in the Profit and Loss Account (Schedule 13) and is shown as a liability under "other liabilities and provisions" in Schedule 15.

Glossary

- **Available-for-sale investments** are securities which are neither held-to-maturity investments nor held-for-trading investments.
- **Banking** means accepting deposits of money from public for the purpose of lending. These

deposits are repayable on demand and can be withdrawn by cheque, draft or otherwise.

- **Capital adequacy ratio** is the ratio of capital funds to the risk-weighed assets where capital funds consist of Tier I and Tier II capital.
- **Cash reserve ratio** is the minimum percentage of a bank's Net Demand and Time Liabilities (NDTL) that it needs to keep as cash reserve with itself or as balance in a current account with the Reserve Bank of India or as net balance in current accounts.
- **Doubtful asset** is one which has remained non-performing for a period exceeding 18 months.
- **Held-for-trading investments** are securities acquired by banks with the intention to trade by taking advantage of short-term price/interest rate movements.
- **Held-to-maturity investments** are securities acquired by banks with the intention to hold them up to maturity.
- **Non-performing asset** is an asset from which the bank does not receive the interest due and charged during any quarter fully within 90 days from the end of the quarter.
- **Rebate on bills discounted** is the portion of discount that relates to the period falling after the close of the accounting year.
- **Scheduled banks** are those banks which have been included in the Second Schedule to Reserve Bank of India (RBI) Act, 1934.
- **Statutory liquidity ratio (SLR)** is the percentage of liquid assets that a bank needs to keep in the form of Cash, Gold and Unencumbered Approved Securities at the close of business on any day.
- **Sub-standard asset** is one which has been classified as non-performing for a period not exceeding 12 months.

Solved Problems

1. A commercial bank provides the details (Table 9.9) of its interest income for the year ended March 31, 2015.

Table 9.9 Details of interest income for the year ended March 31, 2015

(Rs. in Millions)

	Performing Assets		Non-Performing Asset	
	Interest Earned	Interest Received	Interest Earned	Interest Received
Term loans	240	160	150	20
Cash credits and overdrafts	900	530	225	35
Bills purchased and discounted	350	275	175	18

Calculate the income to be recognized by the bank for the year ended March 31, 2015.

Solution: Income to be recognized is as follows:

		(Rs. in Millions)
Term loans	(240 + 20)	260
Cash credits and overdrafts	(900 + 35)	935
Bills purchased and discounted	(350 + 18)	368
		1,563

2. From the information given in Table 9.10, prepare the Profit and Loss account for the year ended and the balance sheet of Saraswati Bank as on March 31, 2015 giving the relevant schedules.

Table 9.10 Trial balance of Saraswati Bank as on March 31, 2015

Particulars	Dr. (Rs. in Millions)	Cr. (Rs. in Millions)
Share capital		95.00
Employee security deposits		3.71
Statutory reserve		70.0
Commission and brokerage		12.65
Profit and Loss account		3.25
Fixed deposit account		11.53
Savings deposit account		7.50
Current accounts		48.50
Borrowings from other banks		38.60
Cash in hand and with RBI	37.50	
Cash with other banks	23.20	
Money at call	13.00	
Gold	7.60	
Silver	1.00	
Constituent liabilities for acceptances and endorsements	28.25	28.25
Government securities	47.20	
Premises	32.50	
Furniture	2.50	
Term loan	90.50	
Other investments	27.81	
Interest accrued on investments	12.31	
Bills for collection	21.75	21.75
Interest		31.00
Bills discounted	6.25	
Interest	3.98	
Discounts		21.00
Rents		0.30
Audit fees	2.50	
Depreciation reserve (furniture)		0.10
Salaries	10.60	
Rent, rates and taxes	6.00	

(Continued)

Table 9.10 (Continued)

Particulars	Dr. (Rs. in Millions)	Cr. (Rs. in Millions)
Miscellaneous income		1.95
Depreciation reserve (building)		0.51
Director's fees	0.50	
Postage	0.65	
Loss on sale of investments	10.00	
Branch adjustments	10.00	
	395.60	395.60

Additional Information

	(Rs. in Millions)
(a) Rebate on bills discounted to be provided	2.00
(b) Depreciation for the year	
Premises	2.50
Furniture	0.50

(c) Included in the current accounts ledger are accounts overdrawn to the extent of Rs. 1.25 Million.

Solution: See Tables 9.11 and 9.12.

Table 9.11 Balance sheet of Saraswati Bank as on 31 March, 2015

(Rs. in Millions)

	Schedule	31.3.2015	31.3.2014
Capital and Liabilities			
Share capital	1	95.00	
Reserves and surplus	2	100.92	
Deposits	3	68.78	
Borrowings	4	38.60	
Other liabilities and provisions	5	5.71	
		309.01	
Assets			
Cash and balances with RBI	6	37.50	
Balances with banks and money at call and short notice	7	36.20	
Investments	8	83.61	
Advances	9	98.00	
Fixed assets	10	31.39	
Other assets	11	22.31	
		309.01	

(Continued)

Table 9.11 (Continued)

(Rs. in Millions)

	Schedule	31.3.2015	31.3.2014
Contingent liabilities	12	28.25	
Bills for collection		21.75	

Table 9.12 Profit and loss account for the year ended March 31, 2015

Particulars	Schedule	Amount (Rs. in Millions)
I. Income		
Interest earned	13	50.00
Other income	14	4.90
Total		54.90
II. Expenditure		
Interest expended	15	3.98
Operating expenses	16	23.25
Provisions and contingencies (740 + 460)		—
Total		27.23
III. Profits/Losses		
Net profit/loss (–) for the year		27.67
Profit/Loss (–) brought forward		3.25
		30.92
IV. Appropriations		
Transfer to statutory reserve (25% of Rs. 30.67 million)		7.73
Balance carried over to balance sheet		23.19
		30.92

For schedules, see Tables 9.13–9.28.

Table 9.13 Schedule 1 – Share capital

	(Rs. in Millions)
Authorized capital	—
Issued, subscribed and paid up capital	
3.96 million shares of Rs. 10 each	39.6

Table 9.14 Schedule 2 – Reserves and surplus

Statutory reserve		
Opening balance	70.00	
Additions during the year	7.73	
		77.73
Balance in Profit and Loss account		23.19
		100.92

Table 9.15 Schedule 3 – Deposits

	(Rs. in Millions)
Demand deposits	49.75
Savings bank deposits	7.50
Fixed deposits	11.53
	68.78

Table 9.16 Schedule 4 – Borrowings

	(Rs. in Millions)
Borrowings in India	
Other banks	38.60

Table 9.17 Schedule 5 – Other liabilities and provisions

	(Rs. in Millions)
Rebate on bills discounted	2.00
Employee security deposits	3.71
	5.71

Table 9.18 Schedule 6 – Cash and balances with RBI

	(Rs. in Millions)
Cash in hand and with RBI	37.50

Table 9.19 Schedule 7 – Balances with banks and money at call and short notice

	(Rs. in Millions)
In India	
(i) Balances with banks	
(a) in current accounts	23.20
(ii) Money at call and short notice	13.00
	36.20

Table 9.20 Schedule 8 – Investments

	(Rs. in Millions)
Investments in India in	
(i) Government securities	47.20
(ii) Others – Gold	7.60
– Silver	1.00
– Shares (assumed)	27.81
	83.61

Table 9.21 Schedule 9 – Advances

	(Rs. in Millions)
A (i) Term Loans	91.75
(ii) Bills purchased and discounted	6.25
	98.00
B (i) Secured by tangible assets	
(ii) Secured by bank/government guarantees	
(iii) Unsecured	

Table 9.22 Schedule 10 – Fixed assets

	(Rs. in Millions)
1. Premises	
At cost on March 31, 2014	31.99
Depreciation to date	2.50
	29.49

(Continued)

Table 9.22 (Continued)

	(Rs. in Millions)
2. Other Fixed Assets	
Furniture at cost on March 31, 2014	2.40
Depreciation to date	0.50
	1.90
Total (1 + 2)	31.39

Table 9.23 Schedule 11 – Other assets

	(Rs. in Millions)
Branch adjustment	10.00
Interest accrued	12.31
	22.31

Table 9.24 Schedule 12 – Contingent liabilities

	(Rs. in Millions)
Acceptances and endorsements	28.25

Table 9.25 Schedule 13 – Interest earned

	(Rs. in Millions)
Interest/discount on advances, bills (31.00 + 21.00 – 2.00)	50.00

Note: Interest on non-performing assets is recognized on receipt basis.

Table 9.26 Schedule 14 – Other income

	(Rs. in Millions)
Commission, exchange and brokerage	12.65
Miscellaneous income	1.95
Rent	0.30
Loss on sale of investment	(10.00)
	4.90

Table 9.27 Schedule 15 – Interest expended

	(Rs. in Millions)
Interest on deposits	3.98

Table 9.28 Schedule 16 – Operating expenses

	(Rs. in Millions)
Payments to and provision for employees – Salaries, bonus, allowances and PF	10.60
Rent, rates and taxes	6.00
Depreciation	3.00
Director's fee, allowances and expenses	0.50
Auditor's fees and expenses	2.50
Postage, telegrams, telephones, etc.	0.65
	23.25

3. From the details of advances of a commercial bank (Table 9.29), calculate the amount of provisions to be made in profit and loss account.

Table 9.29 Classification of advances

	(Rs. in Millions)
Asset classification	
Standard (Value of security Rs. 6,000 Million)	7,000
Sub-standard	3,000
Doubtful:	
For less than 1 year (Realizable value of security Rs. 500 Million)	1,000
For more than 1 year, but less than 3 years (Realizable value of security Rs. 300 Million)	500
For more than 3 years (No security)	300

Solution: See Table 9.30.

Table 9.30 Statement showing provisions on various performing and non-performing assets

Asset Classification	Amount (Rs. in Millions)	Provision %	Amount of Provision (Rs. in Millions)
Standard	7,000	0.40	28
Sub-standard	3,000	15.00	450
Doubtful			
Less than 1 year			
On secured portion	500	25.00	125
On unsecured portion	500	100.00	500

(Continued)

Table 9.30 (Continued)

Asset Classification	Amount (Rs. in Millions)	Provision %	Amount of Provision (Rs. in Millions)
More than 1 year, but less than 3 years			
On secured portion	300	40.00	120
On unsecured portion	200	100.00	200
More than 3 years (unsecured)	300	100.00	300
		Total Provision	1,723

4. Bidisha Bank Ltd. had extended the credit lines given in Table 9.31 to a small scale industry which had not paid any interest since March, 2008.

Table 9.31 Bidisha Bank Ltd.: Details of advances and security in respect of a non-paying small scale industry

	Term Loan	Export Loan
Balance Outstanding on 31.03.2014	Rs. 70 Million	Rs. 60 Million
DICGC/ECGC cover	50%	40%
Securities held	Rs. 30 Million	Rs. 25 Million
Realizable value of securities	Rs. 20 Million	Rs. 15 Million

Compute necessary provisions to be made for the year ended March 31, 2015.

Solution: See Table 9.32.

Table 9.32 Computation of provision in respect of advances

	Term Loan Rs. in Millions)	Export Credit (Rs. in Millions)
Balance outstanding on 31.3.2014	70.0	60.0
Less: Realizable value of securities	20.0	15.0
	50.0	45.0
Less: DICGC cover @ 50%	25.0	
ECGC cover @ 40%		18.0
Unsecured balance	25.0	27.0
Required provision:		
100%* for unsecured portion	25.0	27.0
100% for secured portion	20.0	15.0
Total provision required	45.0	42.0

*Since the advance is doubtful for more than 3 years.

5. The particulars are extracted from the books of Sound Bank Ltd. for the year ending March 31, 2015.

	(Rs.)
1. Interest and discount	19,662,400
2. Rebate on bills discounted (balance on 1-4-2014)	65,040
3. Bills discounted and purchased	6,745,400

It is ascertained that proportionate discount not yet earned on the bills discounted, which will mature during 2014–15 amounted to Rs. 92,760.

Calculate the amount of interest and discount income earned by the bank earned in the year ended March 31, 2015.

Solution:

	(Rs.)
Rebate on bills discounted as on April 1, 2014	65,040
Add: Interest and discount charged during the year ended March 31, 2015	19,662,400
	19,727,440
Less: Rebate on bills discounted as on March 31, 1994	92,760
Interest and discount income for the year ended March 31, 2015	19,634,680

Multiple Choice Questions

1. Hybrid capital instruments form part of _______ capital.
   (a) Tier I
   (b) Tier II
   (c) Paid up
   (d) Preference share

2. The provision to be made on Standard Assets for the current year is _______.
   (a) 0.25%
   (b) 0.40%
   (c) 0.30%
   (d) 0.35%

3. The percentage of profits that a bank is required to transfer to reserve funds as per Banking Regulation Act is _______%.
   (a) 25
   (b) 30
   (c) 20
   (d) 50

4. Select the incorrect statement in respect of "Financial Statements of Banks."
   (a) A banking company is not required to prepare financial statements in accordance with Schedule III of the Companies Act, 2013.
   (b) The Act prescribes special forms of balance sheet and profit and loss account for the preparation of its final accounts.
   (c) These are set out in form A and form B of the first schedule to the Banking Regulation Act, 1949.
   (d) Form A gives the format of a balance sheet and form "B" gives the format of a profit and loss account.

5. The financial statement of a bank consists of _______ schedules.
   (a) 18
   (b) 16
   (c) 17
   (d) 15

6. Liability for partially paid investments in respect of banking companies is grouped under the head _______.
   (a) investments
   (b) other assets
   (c) other liabilities and provisions
   (d) contingent liabilities

7. The investment under "held to maturity" should not exceed _______ of bank's total investment.
   (a) 25%
   (b) 75%
   (c) 5%
   (d) None of the above

8. Acceptances, endorsements and guarantees are shown as _______.
   (a) other assets
   (b) contingent liabilities
   (c) advances
   (d) other liabilities and provisions

9. Advances given to a staff by a bank as an employer should be included in _______.
   (a) other assets
   (b) advances
   (c) investments
   (d) none of the above

10. Investments, advances, fixed assets and other assets are part of Schedule Nos. _______, respectively.
    (a) 6, 7, 8, 9
    (b) 7, 8, 9, 10
    (c) 8, 9, 10, 11
    (d) 9, 10, 11, 12

Review Questions

1. How is the term "Banking" defined under the Banking Regulation Act, 1949?
2. Name the two main categories of commercial banks in India.
3. What type of bank is known as "Scheduled Commercial Bank" in India?
4. Why do banks need to enter all transactions into the ledgers as soon as they take place?
5. Explain the slip system of posting followed by the banks.
6. What are the legal provisions relating to the holding of immovable property by an Indian bank for its own use?
7. Explain the terms "cash reserve ratio" and "statutory liquidity ratio."
8. Name the two main sources of a bank's income.
9. Name the two broad groups into which banks classify their advances.
10. Explain performing assets and non-performing assets.
11. Which assets are classified by banks as "Standard Assets", "Sub-standard Assets" and "Loss Assets"?
12. Why do banks classify advances into different categories?
13. Name the three categories into which banks are required to classify their investment portfolio.
14. What types of investments are classified as "Held to Maturity", "Held for Trading" and "Available for Sale"?
15. Are there any restrictions on the amount of investment a bank can make under "Held for Trading" and "Available for Sale" categories?
16. What is "Rebate on Bills Discounted" and why do banks need to calculate it?

17. Name the funding sources that banks can include in Tier I and Tier II capital.
18. How is Capital Adequacy Ratio (CAR) calculated?
19. What is the limit imposed on the elements of Tier II capital in relation to Tier I capital?
20. What are "Hybrid Debt Capital Instruments"? Give examples of such instruments that are allowed to be included in Tier II capital.

Practice Problems

1. From the information in Table 9.33, you are required to prepare Profit and Loss Account of Zee Bank Ltd. for the year ended March 31, 2015.

Table 9.33 Zee Bank Ltd.: Extracts from books of account for the year ended March 31, 2015

	(Rs.)		(Rs.)
Interest and discount	4,400,000	Interest expended	1,360,000
Other income	125,000	Operating expenses	1,331,000
Income on investment	5,000	Interest on balance with RBI	25,000

Additional Information:

(a) Rebate on bills discounted to be provided Rs. 15,000.
(b) Make tax provision @ 35%.
(c) Profit and Loss Account (Cr.) Rs. 40,000.
(d) Classification of advances.

	(Rs.)
Standard assets	2,500,000
Sub-standard assets	560,000
Doubtful assets not covered by security	255,000
Doubtful assets covered by security	
For 1 year	25,000
For 2 years	50,000
For 3 years	100,000
For 4 years	75,000
Loss Assets	100,000

2. In Table 9.34, an extract from the Trial Balance of T.K. Bank Limited as on December 31, 2014 is given.

Table 9.34 Trial balance of T.K. Bank Limited as on December 31, 2014

Particulars	Debit (Rs.)	Credit (Rs.)
Bills discounted	1,264,000	
Rebate on bills discounted (1.1.2011)		8,340
Discount received for the year		85,912

An analysis of the bills discounted is shown in Table 9.35.

Table 9.35 T. K. Bank: Analysis of bills discounted as on December 31, 2014

Amount Rs.	Due Date in 2015	Rate of Discount (% p.a.)
140,000	March 6	5.0
436,000	March 12	4.5
282,000	March 26	6.0
406,000	April 6	4.0

Show how the relevant items will appear in the bank's profit and loss account for the year ended December 31, 2014 and the bank's balance sheet as on December 31, 2014.

3. How will you disclose the following Ledger balances in the Final Accounts of DVD Bank?

	(Rs. in Millions)
Current accounts	70
Savings accounts	50
Fixed deposits	70
Cash credits	60
Term loans	50
Bills discounted and purchased	80

Additional Information:

1. Included in the current accounts ledger are accounts overdrawn to the extent of Rs. 25 million.
2. One of the cash credit accounts of Rs. 1 million (including an interest of Rs. 0.1 million) is doubtful.
3. 60% of term loans are secured by Government guarantees, 20% of cash credits are unsecured, other portion is secured by tangible assets.

4. From the information in Table 9.36, find the amount of provisions to be shown in the Profit and Loss Account of Zenith Bank.

Table 9.36 Zenith Bank: Classification of assets

	(Rs. in Millions)
Standard	1,000
Sub-standard	640
Doubtful: for 1 year	320
: for 2 years	180
: for 3 years	90
: for more than 3 years	110
Loss assets	300

5. A commercial bank has capital funds and assets as given in Table 9.37. Segregate the capital funds into Tier I and Tier II capitals. Find the risk-adjusted assets and risk-weighted assets ratio.

Table 9.37 Details of capital funds and assets

	(Rs. in Millions)
Equity share capital	5,000
Statutory reserve	2,700
Capital reserve (of which Rs. 160 million were due for revaluation of assets and the balance due for sale)	780
Cash balances with RBI	100
Balance with other banks	180
Other investments	360
Loans and advances:	
Guaranteed by the Government	165
Others	56,750
Premises, furniture and fixtures	780
Off-balance sheet items:	
Guarantees and other obligations	8,000
Acceptances, endorsements and LCs	48,000

6. From the information given in Table 9.38, prepare the Profit and Loss Account for Jawahar Bank Limited for the year ended March 31, 2015. Also give the necessary schedules.

Table 9.38 Jawahar Bank Limited: Extracts from books of account for the year ended March 31, 2015

	(Rs. in '000)
Interest earned on term loans	17.26
Interest earned on term loans classified as NPA	4.52
Interest received on term loans classified as NPA	2.04
Interest on cash credits and overdrafts	38.54
Interest earned but not received on cash credit and overdraft treated as NPA	8.39
Interest on deposits	27.20
Commission	1.97
Profit on revaluation of investments	2.76
Income from investments	15.53
Salaries, bonus and allowances	18.75
Rent, taxes and lighting	1.70
Printing and stationery	0.75
Director's fees, allowances	1.33
Law charges	0.22
Repairs and maintenance	0.18
Insurance	0.30

Additional information:

Make necessary provision for risk assets:

(i) Sub-standard	15.00
(ii) Doubtful for 1 year	7.00
(iii) Doubtful for 2 years	2.40
(iv) Loss assets	0.65
Investments	37.00

Bank should not keep more than 25% of its investments as "held for maturity" investment. The market value of rest of its 75% investments is Rs. 900,00 as on March 31, 2015.

7. An extract from the trial balance of Engco Bank Limited as on March 31, 2015 is given in Table 9.39.

Table 9.39 Extract from the trial balance of Engco Bank Limited as on March 31, 2015

Particulars	Amount (Rs.)
Bills discounted	2,442,250
Rebate on bills discounted (not due on 31.3.2014)	60,610
Discount received for the year	610,800

An analysis of the bills discounted is shown in Table 9.40.

Table 9.40 Engco Bank: Analysis of bills discounted as on March 31, 2015

Amount	Due Date in 2015
375,000	April 15
490,000	May 6
245,000	June 1
368,000	June 20
485,000	July 4

The rate of discount is 12% per annum. You are required to:
(i) Calculate rebate on bills discounted as on March 31, 2015.
(ii) Determine the amount of discount to be credited to the Profit and Loss account.

8. A commercial bank has the following capital funds and assets (Table 9.41). Segregate the capital funds into Tier I and Tier II capitals. Find the risk-adjusted assets and risk-weighted assets ratio.

Table 9.41 Details of capital funds and assets

	(Rs. in Millions)
Paid up equity share capital	7,500
Statutory reserve	1,500
Share premium	1,500
Capital reserve (of which capital funds Rs. 400 million were due to revaluation of assets and balance due to sale)	900
Cash balances with RBI	600
Claims on banks	1,700
Other investments	23,000
Loans and advances:	
Guaranteed by the Government	4,000
Granted to staff of bank, fully secured by super-annuation	500
Benefits and mortgage of flat/house	
Other loans and advances	61,700
Premises, furniture and fixtures	39,250
Intangible assets	150
Off-balance sheet items:	
Acceptances, endorsements and LCs, guarantees and other obligations	15,500

9. The information given in Table 9.42 is available in the books of X Bank Limited as on March 31, 2015.

Table 9.42 X Bank Limited: Extracts from books of accounts for the year ended on March 31, 2015

	(Rs.)
Bills discounted	13,705,000
Rebate on bills discounted (1.4.2014)	221,600
Discount received	1,056,650

An analysis of the bills discounted is shown in Table 9.43.

Table 9.43 X Bank Limited: Analysis of bills discounted as on March 31, 2015

Amount (Rs.)	Due Date	Rate of Discount
1,825,000	05-06-2015	12%
5,000,000	12-06-2015	12%
2,820,000	25-06-2015	14%
4,060,000	06-07-2015	16%

Calculate the rebate on bills discounted as on 31.03.2015 and the discount income to be credited to the Profit and Loss Account.

10. From the information given in Table 9.44, find the amount of provisions to be shown in the Profit and Loss Account of STP Bank Ltd.

Table 9.44 STP Bank Ltd.: Details of assets

	(Rs. in Millions)
Assets	
Standard	3,000
Sub-standard	2,000
Doubtful: for 1 year (secured)	800
: for 2 years and 3 years (secured)	250
: for more than 3 years (secured by mortgage of plant and machinery, Rs. 50 million)	200
Loss assets	170

11. A loan account remains out of order as on the date of balance sheet of a bank. The account has been classified as doubtful asset (up to 3 years). Details of the account are as follows:

Outstanding	Rs. 724,000
ECGC Cover	30% of outstanding (subject to a maximum of Rs. 150,000)
Value of security	
As per valuation on the date of grant of loan	Rs. 225,000
As per realizable value as on the date of balance sheet	Rs. 175,000

Calculate the necessary provision to be made by the bank as per the applicable rate.

12. A commercial bank has the following capital funds and assets (Table 9.45). Segregate the capital funds into Tier I and Tier II capitals. Find the risk-adjusted assets and risk-weighted assets ratio. State your observations on the risk-weighted asset ratio.

Table 9.45 Details of capital funds and assets

	(Rs. in Millions)
Paid up equity share capital	4,000
Statutory reserve	2,500
Capital reserve (of which capital funds Rs. 180 million were due to revaluation of assets and balance due to sale)	860
Cash balances with RBI	120
Balances with other banks	200
Other investments	400
Loans and advances:	
Guaranteed by the Government	145
Other loans and advances	56,450
Premises, furniture and fixtures	740
Intangible assets	–
Off-balance sheet items:	
Guarantees and other obligations	7,000
Acceptances, endorsements and LCs	49,000

13. Based on the following information, calculate the provision to be made by the bank as on March 31, 2015.

Outstanding balance	Rs. 2,000,000
ECGC cover	50%
Period for which advance has remained doubtful as on 31.3.2015	More than 3 years
Value of security held	Rs. 750,000

14. Based on the following information, calculate the provision to be made by the bank as on March 31, 2015.

Outstanding balance	Rs. 2,000,000
ECGC cover	50%
Period for which advance has remained doubtful as on 31.3.2015	More than 3 years
Value of security held (realizable value only 80%)	Rs. 750,000

15. From the information given in Table 9.46, prepare a balance sheet of ABC Bank as on March 31, 2015 giving the relevant schedules.

Table 9.46 ABC Bank: Trial balance as on March 31, 2015

Particulars	Dr. (Rs. in Millions)	Cr. (Rs. in Millions)
Share capital (3.96 million shares of Rs. 10 each)		39.6
Statutory reserve		46.2
Net profit before appropriation		30.0
Profit and Loss account		82.4
Fixed deposit account		103.4
Savings deposit account		90.0
Current accounts	5.6	104.0
Bills payable		1.0
Cash credits	162.4	
Borrowings from other banks		21.7
Cash in hand	32.0	
Cash with RBI	7.5	
Cash with other banks	31.2	
Money at call	42.2	
Gold	11.5	
Government securities	22.2	
Premises	31.1	
Furniture	14.0	
Term loan	158.6	
	518.3	518.3

Additional Information:

	(Rs.)
Bills for collection	900,000
Acceptances and endorsements	700,000
Claims against the bank not acknowledged as debt	100,000
Depreciation charges – Premises	200,000
– Furniture	100,000

50% of term loans are secured by Government guarantees; 10% of cash credit is unsecured. The cash reserve ratio is 4% and the SLR is 23%.

16. An extract from the books of DTC Bank Ltd. as on March 31, 2015 is given in Table 9.47.

Table 9.47 Extract from the books of DTC Bank Ltd. as on March 31, 2015

	(Rs. in '000)
Interest and discount received	10,225
Interest paid on deposits	4,110
Interest on balances with RBI	885
Salaries and allowances	4,275
Director's fees and allowances	1,060
Rent and taxes paid	895
Postage and telegram	310
Profit on sale of investments	610
Commission, exchange and brokerage	3,560
Interest to RBI	735
Income from investment	560
Depreciation on assets	490
Printing and stationery	1,060
Advertisement and publicity	490
Auditor's fee	550
Law charges	760
Insurance	260
Repairs and maintenance	330

Additional information:

1. The following items are already adjusted with interest and discount:

	(Rs. in '000)
Tax provision	740
Provision for doubtful debts	460
Loss on sale of investment	60
Rebate on bills discounted	275

2. Appropriations:
   25% of profit is transferred to statutory reserves
   5% of profit is transferred to revenue reserve

Prepare the Profit and Loss account of DTC Bank Ltd. for the year ended 31.03.2015 and also give the necessary schedules.

17. From the information given in Table 9.48, prepare the Profit and Loss account of Lakshmi Bank Limited for the year ended March 31, 2015. Also give the necessary schedules.

Table 9.48 Extracts from books of account of Lakshmi Bank Limited for the year ended March 31, 2015

	(Rs. in '000)
Interest earned on term loans	7,700
Interest earned on term loans classified as NPA	3,750
Interest received on term loans classified as NPA	1,250
Interest on cash credits	9,100
Interest earned on cash credits classified as NPA	4,100
Interest received on cash credits classified as NPA	2,000
Interest on overdrafts	3,750
Interest earned on overdrafts classified as NPA	2,250
Interest received on overdrafts classified as NPA	500
Interest on deposits	13,600
Interest on balance with RBI	750
Commission on remittances and transfers	375
Commission on letters of credit	590
Commission on Government business	410
Profit on sale of land and building	135
Loss on exchange transactions	260
Salaries, bonus and allowances	6,200
Auditor's fees and allowances	600
Printing and stationery	700
Director's fees, allowances	1,250
Payment to provident fund	1,400
Repairs and maintenance	250
Postage, telegrams, telephones	400

Additional Information:

Make necessary provision on risk assets:

	(Rs. in '000)
Standard	150,000
Sub-standard	56,000

(Continued)

	(Rs. in '000)
Doubtful assets not covered by security	10,000
Doubtful assets covered by security for 1 year	2,500
Loss assets	10,000
Investments	137,500

Bank should not keep more than 25% of its investments as "held for maturity" investment. The market value of rest of its 75% investments is Rs. 98,750 as on March 31, 2015.

18. A commercial bank provides the following details of its interest income for the year ended March 31, 2015.

(Rs. in Millions)

	Performing Assets		Non-Performing Asset	
	Interest Earned	Interest Received	Interest Earned	Interest Received
Term loans	120	80	75	5
Cash credits and overdrafts	750	620	150	12

Calculate the income to be recognized by the bank for the year ended March 31, 2015.

19. From the details of advances of X Bank Limited given in Table 9.49, calculate the amount of provisions to be made in profit and loss account for the year ended March 31, 2015.

Table 9.49 X Bank Limited: Classification of assets as on March 31, 2015

Asset Classification	(Rs. in Millions)
Standard	4,000
Sub-standard	2,000
Doubtful:	
For up to 1 year	900
For up to 3 years	400
For more than 3 years	300
Loss assets	500

20. The following is an extract from the trial balance of Dream Bank Ltd. as on March 31, 2015:

Rebate on bills discounted as on 1.4.2014	68,259 (Cr.)
Discount received	1,70,156 (Cr.)

An analysis of bills discounted is shown in Table 9.50.

Table 9.50 Extracts from trial balance of Dream Bank Ltd. as on March 31, 2015

Amount (Rs.)	Due Date
2,80,000	June 1, 2015
8,72,000	June 8, 2015
5,64,000	June 21, 2015
8,12,000	July 1, 2015
6,00,000	July 5, 2015

You are required to find the amount of discount to be credited to the Profit and Loss account for the year ending March 31, 2015. The rate of discount may be taken at 10% per annum.

Answers to Multiple Choice Questions

1. (b)
2. (b)
3. (a)
4. (c)
5. (c)
6. (d)
7. (a)
8. (b)
9. (a)
10. (c)

Understanding Corporate Annual Reports

10

LEARNING OBJECTIVES

After reading this chapter, you will be able to:

- Understand the information provided in the annual reports of companies.
- Understand the topics to be covered under Notes to Accounts that form part of financial statements of a company.
- Understand the contents of Directors' Report, Independent Auditors' Report, Corporate Governance Report, Management Discussion and Analysis and Business Responsibility Report.
- Understand the difference between a Clean Audit Report and a Modified Audit Report.
- Understand the different kinds of modifications in Independent Auditors' Report.
- Understand the requirements of Indian Accounting Standards relating to disclosure of information pertaining to Operating Segments and transactions with Related Parties.
- Understand the Value Added Statement and the Economic Value Added Statement that are provided voluntarily by many companies as part of their annual reports.

10.1 Introduction

Annual reports published by companies contain a plethora of information, in addition to bare financial statements. The additional information provided by annual reports can be of great use in assessing the financial performance, financial position and future prospects of the company. Typically, annual reports include detailed notes to accounts and significant accounting policies, directors' report, auditors' report, corporate governance report, management discussion and analysis report, business responsibility report, segment data, related party disclosures, value added statement, etc. Companies include this additional information in their annual reports to comply with the requirements of the Companies Act, Accounting Standards and Listing Agreement with stock exchanges. Many entities also present reports and statements such as environmental reports and value-added statements, particularly industries in which environmental factors are significant and when employees are regarded as an important user group.

This chapter discusses these additional reports and statements that form part of corporate annual reports. These include reports required under Companies Act, 2013; Listing Agreement with Stock Exchanges; Accounting Standards and information provided voluntarily by companies.

10.2 Notes to Accounts

Every corporate annual report contains a separate schedule on "Notes to Accounts." Notes to accounts are an integral part of financial statements. These facilitate the understanding of financial statements and analyze the impact of treatment of transactions in a particular manner on the financial performance and financial position of a company.

According to Indian Accounting Standard (Ind AS) 1 "Presentation of Financial Statements", a complete set of financial statements comprises: (i) a balance sheet as at the end of the period (including statement of changes in equity which is presented as a part of the balance sheet); (ii) a statement of profit and loss for the period; (iii) a statement of cash flows for the period; (iv) notes, comprising a summary of significant accounting policies and other explanatory information and (v) a balance sheet as at the beginning of the earliest comparative period when an entity applies an accounting policy retrospectively or makes a retrospective restatement of items in its financial statements, or when it reclassifies items in its financial statements.

Under Section 134(7) of the Companies Act, 2013, a signed copy of every financial statement, shall be issued, circulated or published, among other reports, with a copy of any notes annexed to or forming part of such financial statement.

The notes provide further sub-classifications of line items presented in the Balance Sheet, and additional line items, headings and subtotals in the statement of profit and loss, when such presentation is relevant to an understanding of the entity's financial performance. These notes form part of the form of Financial Statements prescribed under Schedule III to the Companies Act, 2013 and have been detailed in Chapter 8.

The notes also (a) present information about the basis of preparation of financial statements and specific accounting policies; (b) disclose information required by Ind AS that is not presented elsewhere in the financial statements; and (c) provide information that is not presented elsewhere in the financial statements, but is relevant to an understanding of any of them.

An entity is required to present notes in a systematic manner and has to cross-reference each item in the balance sheet, in the statement of changes in equity which is a part of the balance sheet and in the statement of profit and loss, and statement of cash flows to any related information in the notes.

The notes comprise a summary of significant accounting policies and other explanatory information.

10.2.1 Significant Accounting Policies

Besides details of line items in the Balance Sheet and Profit and Loss account, an entity is also required to disclose a summary of significant accounting policies, which includes: (a) the measurement basis (or bases) used in preparing the financial statements, (b) the other accounting policies used that are relevant to an understanding of the financial statements and (c) judgments that management has made in the process of applying the entity's accounting policies and that have the most significant effect on the amounts recognized in the financial statements. Significant accounting policies appearing in the annual report of Asian Paints Limited for the year ended March 31, 2016 are given in Exhibit 10.1.

Exhibit 10.1

Asian Paints Limited: Notes to Financial Statements for the Year Ended March 31, 2017

Company Background

Asian Paints Limited (the 'Company') is a public limited Company domiciled and incorporated in India under the Indian Companies Act, 1913. The registered office of the Company is located at 6A, Shantinagar, Santacruz East, Mumbai, India. The Company is engaged in the business of manufacturing, selling and distribution of paints, coatings, products related to home decor, bath fittings and providing related services.

1 Significant Accounting Policies

1.1 Basis of Preparation of Financial Statements

These financial statements are the separate financial statements of the Company (also called standalone financial statements) prepared in accordance with Indian Accounting Standards ('Ind AS') notified under Section 133 of the Companies Act, 2013, read together with the Companies (Indian Accounting Standards) Rules, 2015.

For all periods up to and including the year ended 31st March, 2016, the Company had prepared its financial statements in accordance with Accounting Standards notified under the Section 133 of the Companies Act, 2013, read together with Rule 7 of the Companies (Accounts) Rules, 2014 ('Previous GAAP'). Detailed explanation on how the transition from previous GAAP to Ind AS has affected the Company's balance sheet, financial performance and cash flows is given under Note 31.

These financial statements have been prepared and presented under the historical cost convention, on the accrual basis of accounting except for certain financial assets and financial liabilities that are measured at fair values at the end of each reporting period, as stated in the accounting policies set out below. The accounting policies have been applied consistently over all the periods presented in these financial statements.

1.2 Current/Non-current Classification

Any asset or liability is classified as current if it satisfies any of the following conditions:

(a) the asset/liability is expected to be realized/settled in the Company's normal operating cycle;
(b) the asset is intended for sale or consumption;
(c) the asset/liability is held primarily for the purpose of trading;
(d) the asset/liability is expected to be realized/settled within 12 months after the reporting period;
(e) the asset is cash or cash equivalent unless it is restricted from being exchanged or used to settle a liability for at least 12 months after the reporting date;
(f) in the case of a liability, the Company does not have an unconditional right to defer settlement of the liability for at least 12 months after the reporting date.

All other assets and liabilities are classified as non-current.

For the purpose of current/non-current classification of assets and liabilities, the Company has ascertained its normal operating cycle as 12 months. This is based on the nature of services and the time between the acquisition of assets or inventories for processing and their realization in cash and cash equivalents.

1.3 Summary of Significant Accounting Policies

(a) Business Combinations

Business combinations are accounted for using the acquisition method. At the acquisition date, identifiable assets acquired and liabilities assumed are measured at fair value. For this purpose, the liabilities assumed include contingent liabilities representing present obligation and they are measured at their acquisition date fair values irrespective of the fact that outflow of resources embodying economic benefits is not probable. The consideration transferred is measured at fair value at acquisition date and includes the fair value of any contingent consideration. However, deferred tax asset or liability and any liability or asset relating to employee benefit arrangements arising from a business combination are measured and recognized in accordance with the requirements of Ind AS 12, 'Income Taxes' and Ind AS 19, 'Employee Benefits', respectively.

Where the consideration transferred exceeds the fair value of the net identifiable assets acquired and liabilities assumed, the excess is recorded as goodwill. Alternatively, in case of a bargain purchase wherein the consideration transferred is lower than the fair value of the net identifiable assets acquired and liabilities assumed, the difference is recorded as a gain in other comprehensive income (FVTOCI) and accumulated in equity as capital reserve. The costs of acquisition excluding those relating to issue of equity or debt securities are charged to the Statement of Profit and Loss in the period in which they are incurred.

In case of business combinations involving entities under common control, the above policy does not apply. Business combinations involving entities under common control are accounted for using the pooling of interests method. The net assets of the transferor entity or business are accounted at their carrying amounts on the date of the acquisition subject to necessary adjustments required to harmonize accounting policies. Any excess or shortfall of the consideration paid over the share capital of transferor entity or business is recognized as capital reserve under equity.

(b) Goodwill

Goodwill is an asset representing the future economic benefits arising from other assets acquired in a business combination that are not individually identified and separately recognized. Goodwill is initially measured at cost, being the excess of the consideration transferred over the net identifiable assets acquired and liabilities assumed, measured in accordance with Ind AS 103, 'Business Combinations'.

Goodwill is considered to have indefinite useful life and hence is not subject to amortization but tested for impairment at least annually. After initial recognition, goodwill is measured at cost less any accumulated impairment losses.

For the purpose of impairment testing, goodwill acquired in a business combination, is from the acquisition date, allocated to each of the Company's cash generating units (CGUs) that are expected to benefit from the combination. A CGU is the smallest identifiable group of assets that generates cash inflows that are largely independent of the cash inflows from other assets or group of assets. Each CGU or a combination of CGUs to which goodwill is so allocated represents the lowest level at which goodwill is monitored for internal management purpose, and it is not larger than an operating segment of the Company.

A CGU to which goodwill is allocated is tested for impairment annually, and whenever there is an indication that the CGU may be impaired; by comparing the carrying amount of the CGU, including the goodwill, with the recoverable amount of the CGU. If the recoverable amount of the CGU exceeds the carrying amount of the CGU, the CGU and the goodwill allocated to that CGU is regarded as not impaired. If the carrying amount of the CGU exceeds the recoverable amount of the CGU, the Company recognizes an impairment loss by first reducing the carrying amount of any goodwill allocated to the CGU and then to other assets of the CGU pro rata based on the carrying amount of each asset in the CGU. Any impairment loss on goodwill is recognized in the Statement of Profit and Loss. An impairment loss recognized for goodwill is not reversed in subsequent periods.

On disposal of a CGU to which goodwill is allocated, the goodwill associated with the disposed CGU is included in the carrying amount of the CGU when determining the gain or loss on disposal.

(c) Property, Plant and Equipment

(i) Measurement at recognition: An item of property, plant and equipment that qualifies as an asset is measured on initial recognition at cost. Following initial recognition, items of property, plant and equipment are carried at its cost less accumulated depreciation and accumulated impairment losses.

The Company identifies and determines cost of each part of an item of property, plant and equipment separately, if the part has a cost which is significant to the total cost of that item of property, plant and equipment and has useful life that is materially different from that of the remaining item.

The cost of an item of property, plant and equipment comprises of its purchase price, including import duties and other nonrefundable purchase taxes or levies, directly attributable to the cost of bringing the asset to its working condition for its intended use and the initial estimate of decommissioning, restoration and similar liabilities, if any. Any trade discounts and rebates are deducted in arriving at the purchase price. Cost includes cost of replacing a part of a plant and equipment if the recognition criteria are met. Expenses directly attributable to new manufacturing facility during its construction period are capitalized if the recognition criteria are met. Expenditure related to plans, designs and drawings of buildings or plant and machinery is capitalized under relevant heads of property, plant and equipment if the recognition criteria are met.

Items such as spare parts, standby equipment and servicing equipment that meet the definition of property, plant and equipment are capitalized at cost and depreciated over their useful life. Costs in nature of repairs and maintenance are recognized in the Statement of Profit and Loss as and when incurred.

(ii) Capital work in progress and capital advances: Cost of assets not ready for intended use, as on the Balance Sheet date, is shown as capital work in progress. Advances given towards acquisition of fixed assets outstanding at each Balance Sheet date are disclosed as Other Non-Current Assets.

(iii) Depreciation: Depreciation on each part of an item of property, plant and equipment is provided using the Straight Line Method based on the useful life of the asset as estimated by the management and is charged to the Statement of Profit and Loss as per the requirement of Schedule II of the Companies Act, 2013. The estimate of the useful life of the assets has been assessed based on technical advice which considers the nature of the asset, the usage of the asset, expected physical wear and tear, the operating conditions of the asset, anticipated technological changes, manufacturers warranties and maintenance support, etc. The estimated useful life of items of property, plant and equipment is mentioned as follows:

	Years
Factory buildings	30
Buildings (other than factory buildings)	60
Plant and equipment (including continuous process plants)	10–20
Scientific research equipment	8
Furniture and fixtures	8
Office equipment and vehicles	5
Information technology hardware	4

Freehold land is not depreciated. Leasehold land and leasehold improvements are amortized over the period of the lease.

The Company, based on technical assessment made by technical expert and management estimate, depreciates certain items of property plant and equipment (as mentioned below) over estimated useful lives which are different from the useful lives prescribed under Schedule II to the Companies Act, 2013 (Schedule III). The management believes that these estimated useful lives are realistic and reflect fair approximation of the period over which the assets are likely to be used.

The useful lives of certain plant and equipment are estimated in the range of 10–20 years. These lives are different from those indicated in Schedule II.

Scientific research equipments are depreciated over the useful estimated life of 8 years which is higher than the life prescribed in Schedule II.

Vehicles are depreciated over the useful estimated life of 5 years which is lower than the life prescribed in Schedule II.

Information technology hardware are depreciated over the useful estimated life of 4 years which is higher than the life prescribed in Schedule II.

The useful lives, residual values of each part of an item of property, plant and equipment and the depreciation methods are reviewed at the end of each financial year. If any of these expectations differ from previous estimates, such change is accounted for as a change in an accounting estimate.

(iv) **Derecognition:** The carrying amount of an item of property, plant and equipment is derecognized on disposal or when no future economic benefits are expected from its use or disposal. The gain or loss arising from the Derecognition of an item of property, plant and equipment is measured as the difference between the net disposal proceeds and the carrying amount of the item and is recognized in the Statement of Profit and Loss when the item is derecognized.

(d) Intangible Assets

(i) **Measurement at recognition:** Intangible assets acquired separately are measured on initial recognition at cost. Intangible assets arising on acquisition of business are measured at fair value as at date of acquisition. Internally generated intangibles, including research cost, are not capitalized and the related expenditure is recognized in the Statement of Profit and Loss in the period in which the expenditure is incurred.

Following initial recognition, intangible assets are carried at cost less accumulated amortization and accumulated impairment loss, if any.

(ii) **Amortization:** Intangible Assets with finite lives are amortized on a Straight Line basis over the estimated useful economic life. The amortization expense on intangible assets with finite lives is recognized in the Statement of Profit and Loss. The estimated useful life of intangible assets is mentioned as follows:

	Years
Purchase cost, user license fees and consultancy fees for Computer Software (including those used for scientific research)	4
Acquired trademark	5
Acquired brand (bath fitting brand – Ess Ess)	2

The amortization period and the amortization method for an intangible asset with finite useful life is reviewed at the end of each financial year. If any of these expectations differ from previous estimates, such change is accounted for as a change in an accounting estimate.

(iii) **Derecognition:** The carrying amount of an intangible asset is derecognized on disposal or when no future economic benefits are expected from its use or disposal. The gain or loss arising from the Derecognition of an intangible asset is measured as the difference between the net disposal proceeds and the carrying amount of the intangible asset and is recognized in the Statement of Profit and Loss when the asset is derecognized.

(e) Impairment

Assets that have an indefinite useful life, for example goodwill, are not subject to amortization and are tested for impairment annually and whenever there is an indication that the asset may be impaired.

Assets that are subject to depreciation and amortization and assets representing investments in subsidiary and associate companies are reviewed for impairment, whenever events or changes in circumstances indicate that carrying amount may not be recoverable. Such circumstances include, though are not limited to, significant or sustained decline in revenues or earnings and material adverse changes in the economic environment.

An impairment loss is recognized whenever the carrying amount of an asset or its CGU exceeds its recoverable amount. The recoverable amount of an asset is the greater of its fair value less cost to sell and value in use. To calculate value in use, the estimated future cash flows are discounted to their present value using a pre-tax discount rate that reflects current market rates and the risk specific to the asset. For an asset that does not generate largely independent cash inflows, the recoverable amount is determined for the CGU to which the asset belongs. Fair value less cost to sell is the best estimate of the amount obtainable from the sale of an asset in an arm's length transaction between knowledgeable, willing parties, less the cost of disposal.

Impairment losses, if any, are recognized in the Statement of Profit and Loss and included in depreciation and amortization expense. Impairment losses are reversed in the Statement of Profit and Loss only to the extent that the asset's carrying amount does not exceed the carrying amount that would have been determined if no impairment loss had previously been recognized.

(f) Revenue

Revenue is recognized when it is probable that economic benefits associated with a transaction flows to the Company in the ordinary course of its activities and the amount of revenue can be measured reliably. Revenue is measured at the fair value of the consideration received or receivable, net of returns, trade discounts and volume rebates allowed by the Company.

Revenue includes only the gross inflows of economic benefits, including excise duty, received and receivable by the Company on its own account. Amounts collected on behalf of third parties, such as sales tax and value-added tax, are excluded from revenue.

(i) **Sale of products:** Revenue from sale of products is recognized when the Company transfers all significant risks and rewards of ownership to the buyer, while the Company retains neither continuing managerial involvement nor effective control over the products sold.

(ii) **Rendering of services:** Revenue from services is recognized when the stage of completion can be measured reliably. Stage of completion is measured by the services performed till Balance Sheet date as a percentage of total services contracted.

(iii) **Interest, royalties and dividends:** Interest income is recognized using effective interest method. Royalty income is recognized on an accrual basis in accordance with the substance of the relevant agreement. Dividend income is recognized when the right to receive payment is established.

(g) Government Grants and Subsidies

Recognition and measurement: The Company is entitled to subsidies from government in respect of manufacturing units located in specified regions. Such subsidies are measured at amounts receivable from the government which are non-refundable and are recognized as income when there is a reasonable assurance that the Company will comply with all necessary conditions attached to them. Income from subsidies is recognized on a systematic basis over the periods in which the related costs that are intended to be compensated by such subsidies are recognized.

The Company has received refundable government loans at below-market rate of interest which are accounted in accordance with the recognition and measurement principles of Ind AS 109, 'Financial Instruments'. The benefit of below-market rate of interest is measured as the difference between the initial carrying value of loan determined in accordance with Ind AS 109 and the proceeds received. It is recognized as income when there is a reasonable assurance that the Company will comply with all necessary conditions attached to the loans. Income from such benefit is recognized on a systematic basis over the period of the loan during which the Company recognizes interest expense corresponding to such loans.

(i) **Presentation:** Income from subsidies are presented on gross basis under Revenue from Operations. Income arising from below-market rate of interest loans are presented on gross basis under Other Income.

(h) Inventory

Raw materials, work-in-progress, finished goods, packing materials, stores, spares, components, consumables and stock-in-trade are carried at the lower of cost and net realizable value. However, materials and other items held for use in production of inventories are not written down below cost if the finished goods in which they will be incorporated are expected to be sold at or above cost. The comparison of cost and net realizable value is made on an item-by-item basis.

In determining the cost of raw materials, packing materials, stock-in-trade, stores, spares, components and consumables, weighted average cost method is used. Cost of inventory comprises all costs of purchase, duties, taxes (other than those subsequently recoverable from tax authorities) and all other costs incurred in bringing the inventory to their present location and condition.

Cost of finished goods and work-in-progress includes the cost of raw materials, packing materials, an appropriate share of fixed and variable production overheads, excise duty as applicable and other costs incurred in bringing the inventories to their present location and condition. Fixed production overheads are allocated on the basis of normal capacity of production facilities.

(i) Financial Instruments

A financial instrument is any contract that gives rise to a financial asset of one entity and a financial liability or equity instrument of another entity.

(i) **Financial assets:** Initial recognition and measurement:

The Company recognizes a financial asset in its Balance Sheet when it becomes party to the contractual provisions of the instrument. All financial assets are recognized initially at fair value, plus in the case of financial assets not recorded at fair value through profit or loss (FVTPL), transaction costs that are attributable to the acquisition of the financial asset.

Where the fair value of a financial asset at initial recognition is different from its transaction price, the difference between the fair value and the transaction price is recognized as a gain or loss in the Statement of Profit and Loss at initial recognition if the fair value is determined through a quoted market price in an active market for an identical asset (i.e. level 1 input) or through a valuation technique that uses data from observable markets (i.e. level 2 input).

In case the fair value is not determined using a level 1 or level 2 input as mentioned above, the difference between the fair value and transaction price is deferred appropriately and recognized as a gain or loss in the Statement of Profit and Loss only to the extent that such gain or loss arises due to a change in factor that market participants take into account when pricing the financial asset.

However, trade receivables that do not contain a significant financing component are measured at transaction price.

Subsequent measurement: For subsequent measurement, the Company classifies a financial asset in accordance with the following criteria:

1. The Company's business model for managing the financial asset and
2. The contractual cash flow characteristics of the financial asset.

Based on the above criteria, the Company classifies its financial assets into the following categories:

1. **Financial assets measured at amortized cost:** A financial asset is measured at the amortized cost if both of the following conditions are met:
   (a) The Company's business model objective for managing the financial asset is to hold financial assets in order to collect contractual cash flows and
   (b) The contractual terms of the financial asset give rise on specified dates to cash flows that are solely payments of principal and interest on the principal amount outstanding.

   This category applies to cash and bank balances, trade receivables, loans and other financial assets of the Company (Refer Note 29 for further details). Such financial assets are subsequently measured at amortized cost using the effective interest method.

   Under the effective interest method, the future cash receipts are exactly discounted to the initial recognition value using the effective interest rate. The cumulative amortization using the effective interest method of the difference between the initial recognition amount and the maturity amount is added to the initial recognition value (net of principal repayments, if any) of the financial asset over the relevant period of the financial asset to arrive at the amortized cost at each reporting date. The corresponding effect of the amortization under effective interest method is recognized as interest income over the relevant period of the financial asset. The same is included under other income in the Statement of Profit and Loss.

   The amortized cost of a financial asset is also adjusted for loss allowance, if any.

2. **Financial assets measured at FVTOCI:** A financial asset is measured at FVTOCI if both of the following conditions are met:
   (a) The Company's business model objective for managing the financial asset is achieved both by collecting contractual cash flows and selling the financial assets, and
   (b) The contractual terms of the financial asset give rise on specified dates to cash flows that are solely payments of principal and interest on the principal amount outstanding.

This category applies to certain investments in debt instruments (Refer Note 29 for further details). Such financial assets are subsequently measured at fair value at each reporting date. Fair value changes are recognized in the Other Comprehensive Income (OCI). However, the Company recognizes interest income and impairment losses and its reversals in the Statement of Profit and Loss.

On Derecognition of such financial assets, cumulative gain or loss previously recognized in OCI is reclassified from equity to Statement of Profit and Loss.

Further, the Company, through an irrevocable election at initial recognition, has measured certain investments in equity instruments at FVTOCI (Refer Note 29 for further details). The Company has made such election on an instrument by instrument basis. These equity instruments are neither held for trading nor are contingent consideration recognized under a business combination. Pursuant to such irrevocable election, subsequent changes in the fair value of such equity instruments are recognized in OCI. However, the Company recognizes dividend income from such instruments in the Statement of Profit and Loss.

On Derecognition of such financial assets, cumulative gain or loss previously recognized in OCI is not reclassified from the equity to Statement of Profit and Loss. However, the Company may transfer such cumulative gain or loss into retained earnings within equity.

3. **Financial assets measured at FVTPL:** A financial asset is measured at FVTPL unless it is measured at amortized cost or at FVTOCI as explained above. This is a residual category applied to all other investments of the Company excluding investments in subsidiary and associate companies (Refer Note 29 for further details). Such financial assets are subsequently measured at fair value at each reporting date. Fair value changes are recognized in the Statement of Profit and Loss.

   Derecognition: A financial asset (or, where applicable, a part of a financial asset or part of a group of similar financial assets) is derecognized (i.e. removed from the Company's Balance Sheet) when any of the following occurs:

   (a) The contractual rights to cash flows from the financial asset expires.

   (b) The Company transfers its contractual rights to receive cash flows of the financial asset and has substantially transferred all the risks and rewards of ownership of the financial asset.

   (c) The Company retains the contractual rights to receive cash flows but assumes a contractual obligation to pay the cash flows without material delay to one or more recipients under a 'pass-through' arrangement (thereby substantially transferring all the risks and rewards of ownership of the financial asset).

   (d) The Company neither transfers nor retains substantially all risk and rewards of ownership and does not retain control over the financial asset.

In cases where the Company has neither transferred nor retained substantially all of the risks and rewards of the financial asset, but retains control of the financial asset, the Company continues to recognize such financial asset to the extent of its continuing involvement in the financial asset. In that case, the Company also recognizes an associated liability. The financial asset and the associated liability are measured on a basis that reflects the rights and obligations that the Company has retained.

On Derecognition of a financial asset, (except as mentioned in the second point above for financial assets measured at FVTOCI), the difference between the carrying amount and the consideration received is recognized in the Statement of Profit and Loss.

Impairment of financial assets: The Company applies expected credit losses (ECL) model for measurement and recognition of loss allowance on the following:

(a) Trade receivables and lease receivables

(b) Financial assets measured at amortized cost (other than trade receivables and lease receivables)

(c) Financial assets measured at FVTOCI

In case of trade receivables and lease receivables, the Company follows a simplified approach wherein an amount equal to lifetime ECL is measured and recognized as loss allowance.

In case of other assets (listed as ii and iii above), the Company determines if there has been a significant increase in credit risk of the financial asset since initial recognition. If the credit risk of such assets has not increased significantly, an amount equal to 12-month ECL is measured and recognized as loss allowance. However, if credit risk has increased significantly, an amount equal to lifetime ECL is measured and recognized as loss allowance.

Subsequently, if the credit quality of the financial asset improves such that there is no longer a significant increase in credit risk since initial recognition, the Company reverts to recognizing impairment loss allowance based on 12-month ECL

ECL is the difference between all contractual cash flows that are due to the Company in accordance with the contract and all the cash flows that the entity expects to receive (i.e. all cash shortfalls), discounted at the original effective interest rate.

Lifetime ECL are the expected credit losses resulting from all possible default events over the expected life of a financial asset. 12-month ECL are a portion of the lifetime ECL which result from default events that are possible within 12 months from the reporting date.

ECL are measured in a manner that they reflect unbiased and probability weighted amounts determined by a range of outcomes, considering the time value of money and other reasonable information available as a result of past events, current conditions and forecasts of future economic conditions.

As a practical expedient, the Company uses a provision matrix to measure lifetime ECL on its portfolio of trade receivables. The provision matrix is prepared based on historically observed default rates over the expected life of trade receivables and is adjusted for forward-looking estimates. At each reporting date, the historically observed default rates and changes in the forward-looking estimates are updated.

ECL impairment loss allowance (or reversal) recognized during the period is recognized as income/expense in the Statement of Profit and Loss under the head 'Other expenses'.

Financial Liabilities

Initial recognition and measurement: The Company recognizes a financial liability in its Balance Sheet when it becomes party to the contractual provisions of the instrument. All financial liabilities are recognized initially at fair value minus, in the case of financial liabilities not recorded at FVTPL, transaction costs that are attributable to the acquisition of the financial liability.

Where the fair value of a financial liability at initial recognition is different from its transaction price, the difference between the fair value and the transaction price is recognized as a gain or loss in the Statement of Profit and Loss at initial recognition if the fair value is determined through a quoted market price in an active market for an identical asset (i.e. level 1 input) or through a valuation technique that uses data from observable markets (i.e. level 2 input).

In case the fair value is not determined using a level 1 or level 2 input as mentioned above, the difference between the fair value and transaction price is deferred appropriately and recognized as a gain or loss in the Statement of Profit and Loss only to the extent that such gain or loss arises due to a change in factor that market participants take into account when pricing the financial liability.

Subsequent measurement: All financial liabilities of the Company are subsequently measured at amortized cost using the effective interest method (Refer Note 29 for further details).

Under the effective interest method, the future cash payments are exactly discounted to the initial recognition value using the effective interest rate. The cumulative amortization using the effective interest method of the difference between the initial recognition amount and the maturity amount is added to the initial recognition value (net of principal repayments, if any) of the financial liability over the relevant period of the financial liability to arrive at the amortized cost at each reporting date. The corresponding effect of the amortization under effective interest method is recognized as interest expense over the relevant period of the financial liability. The same is included under finance cost in the Statement of Profit and Loss.

Derecognition: A financial liability is derecognized when the obligation under the liability is discharged or cancelled or expires. When an existing financial liability is replaced by another from the same lender on substantially different terms, or the terms of an existing liability are substantially modified, such an exchange or modification is treated as the Derecognition of the original liability and the recognition of a new liability. The difference between the carrying amount of the financial liability derecognized and the consideration paid is recognized in the Statement of Profit and Loss.

(j) Derivative Financial Instruments and Hedge Accounting

The Company enters into derivative financial contracts in the nature of forward currency contracts with external parties to hedge its foreign currency risks relating to foreign currency denominated financial liabilities measured at amortized cost.

The Company formally establishes a hedge relationship between such forward currency contracts ('hedging instrument') and recognized financial liabilities ('hedged item') through a formal documentation at the inception of the hedge relationship in line with the Company's Risk Management objective and strategy.

The hedge relationship so designated is accounted for in accordance with the accounting principles prescribed for a fair value hedge under Ind AS 109, 'Financial Instruments'.

Recognition and measurement of fair value hedge: Hedging instrument is initially recognized at fair value on the date on which a derivative contract is entered into and is subsequently measured at fair value at each reporting date. Gain or loss arising from changes in the fair value of hedging instrument is recognized in the Statement of Profit and Loss. Hedging instrument is recognized as a financial asset in the Balance Sheet if its fair value as at reporting date is positive as compared to carrying value and as a financial liability if its fair value as at reporting date is negative as compared to carrying value.

Hedged item (recognized financial liability) is initially recognized at fair value on the date of entering into contractual obligation and is subsequently measured at amortized cost. The hedging gain or loss on the hedged item is adjusted to the carrying value of the hedged item as per the effective interest method and the corresponding effect is recognized in the Statement of Profit and Loss.

Derecognition: On Derecognition of the hedged item, the unamortized fair value of the hedging instrument adjusted to the hedged item is recognized in the Statement of Profit and Loss.

(k) Fair Value

The Company measures financial instruments at fair value in accordance with the accounting policies mentioned above. Fair value is the price that would be received to sell an asset or paid to transfer a liability in an orderly transaction between market participants at the measurement date. The fair value measurement is based on the presumption that the transaction to sell the asset or transfer the liability takes place either:

1. In the principal market for the asset or liability or
2. In the absence of a principal market, in the most advantageous market for the asset or liability

All assets and liabilities for which fair value is measured or disclosed in the financial statements are categorized within the fair value hierarchy that categorizes into three levels, described as follows, the inputs to valuation techniques used to measure value. The fair value hierarchy gives the highest priority to quoted prices in active markets for identical assets or liabilities (Level 1 inputs) and the lowest priority to unobservable inputs (Level 3 inputs).

Level 1: Quoted (unadjusted) market prices in active markets for identical assets or liabilities

Level 2: Inputs other than quoted prices included within Level 1 that are observable for the asset or liability, either directly or indirectly

Level 3: Inputs that are unobservable for the asset or liability

Business overview statutory repo: For assets and liabilities that are recognized in the financial statements at fair value on a recurring basis, the Company determines whether transfers have occurred between levels in the hierarchy by re-assessing categorization at the end of each reporting period and discloses the same.

(l) Investment in Subsidiary and Associate Companies

The Company has elected to recognize its investments in subsidiary and associate companies at cost in accordance with the option available in Ind AS 27, 'Separate Financial Statements'. The details of such investments are given in Note 4. Impairment policy applicable on such investments is explained in note 1.3(e) above.

(m) Foreign Currency Translation

Initial recognition: On initial recognition, transactions in foreign currencies entered into by the Company are recorded in the functional currency (i.e. Indian Rupees), by applying to the foreign currency amount, the spot exchange rate between the functional currency and the foreign currency at the date of the transaction. Exchange differences arising on foreign exchange transactions settled during the year are recognized in the Statement of Profit and Loss.

Measurement of foreign currency items at reporting date: Foreign currency monetary items of the Company are translated at the closing exchange rates. Non-monetary items that are measured at historical cost in a foreign currency are translated using the exchange rate at the date of the transaction. Non-monetary items that are measured at fair value in a foreign currency are translated using the exchange rates at the date when the fair value is measured.

Exchange differences arising out of these translations are recognized in the Statement of Profit and Loss.

(n) Income Taxes

Tax expense is the aggregate amount included in the determination of profit or loss for the period in respect of current tax and deferred tax.

Current tax: Current tax is the amount of income taxes payable in respect of taxable profit for a period. Taxable profit differs from 'profit before tax' as reported in the Statement of Profit and Loss because of items of income or expense that are taxable or deductible in other years and items that are never taxable or deductible under the Income Tax Act, 1961.

Current tax is measured using tax rates that have been enacted by the end of reporting period for the amounts expected to be recovered from or paid to the taxation authorities.

Deferred tax: Deferred tax is recognized on temporary differences between the carrying amounts of assets and liabilities in the financial statements and the corresponding tax bases used in the computation of taxable profit under Income Tax Act, 1961.

Deferred tax liabilities are generally recognized for all taxable temporary differences. However, in case of temporary differences that arise from initial recognition of assets or liabilities in a transaction (other than business combination) that affect neither the taxable profit nor the accounting profit, deferred tax liabilities are not recognized. Also, for temporary differences, if any, that may arise from initial recognition of goodwill, deferred tax liabilities are not recognized.

Deferred tax assets are generally recognized for all deductible temporary differences to the extent it is probable that taxable profits will be available against which those deductible temporary difference can be utilized. In case of temporary differences that arise from initial recognition of assets or liabilities in a transaction (other than business combination) that affect neither the taxable profit nor the accounting profit, deferred tax assets are not recognized.

The carrying amount of deferred tax assets is reviewed at the end of each reporting period and reduced to the extent that it is no longer probable that sufficient taxable profits will be available to allow the benefits of part or all of such deferred tax assets to be utilized.

Deferred tax assets and liabilities are measured at the tax rates that have been enacted or substantively enacted by the Balance Sheet date and are expected to apply to taxable income in the years in which those temporary differences are expected to be recovered or settled.

Presentation of current and deferred tax: Current and deferred tax are recognized as income or an expense in the Statement of Profit and Loss, except when they relate to items that are recognized in OCI, in which case, the current and deferred tax income/expense are recognized in OCI.

The Company offsets current tax assets and current tax liabilities, where it has a legally enforceable right to set off the recognized amounts and where it intends either to settle on a net basis, or to realize the asset and settle the liability simultaneously. In case of deferred tax assets and deferred tax liabilities, the same are offset if the Company has a legally enforceable right to set off corresponding current tax assets against current tax liabilities and the deferred tax assets and deferred tax liabilities relate to income taxes levied by the same tax authority on the Company

(o) Provisions and Contingencies

The Company recognizes provisions when a present obligation (legal or constructive) as a result of a past event exists and it is probable that an outflow of resources embodying economic benefits will be required to settle such obligation and the amount of such obligation can be reliably estimated.

If the effect of time value of money is material, provisions are discounted using a current pre-tax rate that reflects, when appropriate, the risks specific to the liability. When discounting is used, the increase in the provision due to the passage of time is recognized as a finance cost.

A disclosure for a contingent liability is made when there is a possible obligation or a present obligation that may, but probably will not require an outflow of resources embodying economic benefits or the amount of such obligation cannot be measured reliably. When there is a possible obligation or a present obligation in respect of which likelihood of outflow of resources embodying economic benefits is remote, no provision or disclosure is made.

(p) Measurement of EBITDA

The Company has opted to present Earnings Before Interest (finance cost), Tax, Depreciation and Amortization (EBITDA) as a separate line item on the face of the Statement of Profit and Loss for the period. The Company measures EBITDA based on profit/(loss) from continuing operations.

(q) **Cash and Cash Equivalents**

Cash and Cash equivalents for the purpose of Cash Flow Statement comprise cash and cheques in hand, bank balances, demand deposits with banks where the original maturity is 3 months or less and other short-term highly liquid investments.

(r) **Employee Benefits**

Short-term employee benefits: All employee benefits payable wholly within 12 months of rendering the service are classified as short-term employee benefits and they are recognized in the period in which the employee renders the related service. The Company recognizes the undiscounted amount of short-term employee benefits expected to be paid in exchange for services rendered as a liability (accrued expense) after deducting any amount already paid.

Post-Employment Benefits:

I. **Defined contribution plans:** Defined contribution plans are employee state insurance scheme and Government administered pension fund scheme for all applicable employees and superannuation scheme for eligible employees.

Recognition and measurement of defined contribution plans: The Company recognizes contribution payable to a defined contribution plan as an expense in the Statement of Profit and Loss when the employees render services to the Company during the reporting period. If the contributions payable for services received from employees before the reporting date exceeds the contributions already paid, the deficit payable is recognized as a liability after deducting the contribution already paid. If the contribution already paid exceeds the contribution due for services received before the reporting date, the excess is recognized as an asset to the extent that the prepayment will lead to, for example, a reduction in future payments or a cash refund.

II. **Defined Benefit Plans:**

Provident fund scheme: The Company makes specified monthly contributions towards Employee Provident Fund scheme to a separate trust administered by the Company. The minimum interest payable by the trust to the beneficiaries is being notified by the Government every year. The Company has an obligation to make good the shortfall, if any, between the return on investments of the trust and the notified interest rate.

Gratuity scheme: The Company operates a defined benefit gratuity plan for employees. The Company contributes to a separate entity (a fund), towards meeting the Gratuity obligation.

Pension scheme: The Company operates a defined benefit pension plan for certain specified employees and is payable upon the employee satisfying certain conditions, as approved by the Board of Directors.

Post-retirement medical benefit plan: The Company operates a defined post-retirement medical benefit plan for certain specified employees and is payable upon the employee satisfying certain conditions.

Recognition and measurement of defined benefit plans: The cost of providing defined benefits is determined using the Projected Unit Credit method with actuarial valuations being carried out at each reporting date. The defined benefit obligations recognized in the Balance Sheet represent the present value of the defined benefit obligations as reduced by the fair value of plan assets, if applicable. Any defined benefit asset (negative defined benefit obligations resulting from this calculation) is recognized representing the present value of available refunds and reductions in future contributions to the plan.

All expenses represented by current service cost, past service cost, if any, and net interest on the defined benefit liability/(asset) are recognized in the Statement of Profit and Loss. Remeasurements of the net defined benefit liability (asset) comprising actuarial gains and losses and the return on the plan assets (excluding amounts included in net interest on the net defined benefit liability/asset), are recognized in OCI. Such remeasurements are not reclassified to the Statement of Profit and Loss in the subsequent periods.

The Company presents the above liability/(asset) as current and non-current in the Balance Sheet as per actuarial valuation by the independent actuary; however, the entire liability towards gratuity is considered as current as the Company will contribute this amount to the gratuity fund within the next twelve months.

Other long-term employee benefits: Entitlements to annual leave and sick leave are recognized when they accrue to employees. Sick leave can only be availed while annual leave can either be availed or encashed subject to a restriction on the maximum number of accumulation of leave. The Company determines the liability for such accumulated leaves using the Projected Accrued Benefit method with actuarial valuations being carried out at each Balance Sheet date.

(s) Lease Accounting

Leases are classified as finance leases whenever the terms of the lease transfer substantially all the risks and rewards of ownership to the lessee. All other leases are classified as operating leases.

In respect of assets taken on operating lease, lease rentals are recognized as an expense in the Statement of Profit and Loss on straight line basis over the lease term unless

(1) another systematic basis is more representative of the time pattern in which the benefit is derived from the leased asset or

(2) the payments to the lessor are structured to increase in the line with expected general inflation to compensate for the lessor's expected inflationary cost increases

(t) Research and Development

Expenditure on research is recognized as an expense when it is incurred. Expenditure on development which does not meet the criteria for recognition as an intangible asset is recognized as an expense when it is incurred.

Items of property, plant and equipment and acquired Intangible Assets utilized for Research and Development are capitalized and depreciated in accordance with the policies stated for Property, Plant and Equipment and Intangible Assets.

(u) Borrowing Cost

Borrowing cost includes interest, amortization of ancillary costs incurred in connection with the arrangement of borrowings and exchange differences arising from foreign currency borrowings to the extent they are regarded as an adjustment to the interest cost.

Borrowing costs, if any, directly attributable to the acquisition, construction or production of an asset that necessarily takes a substantial period of time to get ready for its intended use or sale are capitalized, if any. All other borrowing costs are expensed in the period in which they occur.

(v) Segment Reporting

Operating segments are reported in a manner consistent with the internal reporting provided to the Chief Operating Decision Maker (CODM) of the Company. The CODM is responsible for allocating resources and assessing performance of the operating segments of the Company.

(w) Events after Reporting date

Where events occurring after the Balance Sheet date provide evidence of conditions that existed at the end of the reporting period, the impact of such events is adjusted within the financial statements. Otherwise, events after the Balance Sheet date of material size or nature are only disclosed.

(x) Non-Current Assets held for sale

The Company classifies non-current assets as held for sale if their carrying amounts will be recovered principally through a sale rather than through continuing use of the assets and actions required to complete such sale indicate that it is unlikely that significant changes to the plan to sell will be made or that the decision to sell will be withdrawn. Also, such assets are classified as held for sale only if the management expects to complete the sale within 1 year from the date of classification.

Non-current assets classified as held for sale are measured at the lower of their carrying amount and the fair value less cost to sell. Non-current assets are not depreciated or amortized.

(y) Recent Accounting Pronouncements

Standards issued but not yet effective: In March 2017, the Ministry of Corporate Affairs issued the Companies (Indian Accounting Standards) (Amendments) Rules, 2017, notifying amendment to Ind AS 7, 'Statement of cash flows'. This amendment is in accordance with the recent amendments made by International Accounting Standards Board (IASB) to IAS 7, 'Statement of cash flows'. The amendment is applicable to the Company from April 1, 2017.

Amendments to Ind AS 7: The amendments to Ind AS 7 requires the entities to provide disclosures that enable users of financial statements to evaluate changes in liabilities arising from financing activities, including both changes arising from cash flows and non-cash changes, suggesting inclusion of a reconciliation between the opening and closing balances in the Balance Sheet for liabilities arising from financing activities to meet the disclosure requirement.

The Company is evaluating the requirements of the amendment, and the effect on the financial statements is being evaluated.

(Source: Asian Paints Annual Report 2016–2017)

10.2.2 Contingent Liabilities

According to Ind AS 37 "Provisions, Contingent Liabilities and Contingent Assets", a contingent liability is: (a) a possible obligation that arises from past events and whose existence will be confirmed only by the occurrence or non-occurrence of one or more uncertain future events not wholly within the control of the entity; or (b) a present obligation that arises from past events but is not recognized because: (i) it is not probable that an outflow of resources embodying economic benefits will be required to settle the obligation; or (ii) the amount of the obligation cannot be measured with sufficient reliability.

A contingent liability is not a real liability but a potential liability that depends on an uncertain future event. Contingent liabilities are commonly associated with legal proceedings, tax disputes, guarantees for loans.

For example, if a company provides a guarantee for a bank loan taken by its subsidiary, the holding company has a contingent liability. If the subsidiary makes its loan payments and pays off the loan, the holding company will have no liability. If the subsidiary fails to make the payments, the holding company will have a liability.

Company A which is into pharmaceutical business is sued by company B for a patent infringement. In this case, company A has a contingent liability. If company A is found guilty, it will have a liability. However, if company A is not found guilty, the company will not have an actual liability.

An entity does not recognize a contingent liability. It just discloses the contingent liability in "notes to accounts." If the possibility of an outflow of resources embodying economic benefits is remote, no disclosure is required.

Whenever disclosure of contingent liability is required, an entity shall disclose for each class of contingent liability at the end of the reporting period a brief description of the nature of the contingent liability and, where practicable: (a) an estimate of its financial impact, (b) an indication of the uncertainties relating to the amount or timing of any outflow; and (c) the possibility of any reimbursement.

An extract from CIPLA Ltd.'s Annual Report for the year ended March 31, 2014, related to contingent liabilities and commitments is reproduced in Exhibit 10.2.

Exhibit 10.2

CIPLA Ltd.: Contingent Liabilities and Commitments for the Year Ended March 31, 2014

	(Rs. in Million)	
	2014	2013
Contingent Liabilities		
Claims against the company not acknowledged as debt	48.2	65.1

(Continued)

	(Rs. in Million)	
	2014	2013
Guarantees (refer note)	1,523.8	27,506.6
Letters of credit	93.2	115.9
Refund of technical know-how and licensing fees on account of non-compliance of certain obligations as per respective agreements	29.5	25.4
Income tax	1002.9	1,917.8
Excise duty/service tax	809.3	298.5
Sales tax	54.6	39.9
	3,561.5	29,969.2
Commitments		
Estimated amount of contracts unexecuted on capital account	2008.8	1718.9
Other commitments	6,443.3	8,248.5
	8,452.1	9,967.4
	12,013.6	39,936.6

Note: Guarantees disclosed under contingent liabilities during the previous year include counter indemnity/guarantees furnished by the company in an aggregate amount of ZAR 4520 million (approximately Rs. 26,670 Million) in relation to the acquisition of Cipla Medpro South Africa (Pty) Ltd.

10.3 Directors' Report

Under Section 134(3) of the Companies Act, 2013, every company is required to attach a report by the Board of Directors to its financial statements presented in a general meeting. This report is required to include the following:

1. The extract of the annual return as provided under sub-section(3) of Section 92. Under Section 92(3), every company is required to prepare a return (called the annual return) in the prescribed form.
2. The number of meetings of the Board.
3. Directors' Responsibility Statement.
4. A statement on declaration given by independent directors under sub-section(6) of Section 149. Under Section 149(6), every independent director is required to give a declaration stating that he/she meets the criteria of independence. This declaration is to be given by the independent director at the first meeting of the Board in which he/she participates as a director and thereafter at the first meeting of the

Board in every financial year or whenever there is any change in the circumstances which may affect his/her status as an independent director.

5. In the case of a company covered under sub-section(1) of Section 178, the company's policy on directors' appointment and remuneration, including criteria for determining qualifications, positive attributes, independence of a director and other matters provided under sub-section(3) of Section 178. Under Section 178, the Board of Directors of every listed company and such other class or classes of companies, as may be prescribed shall constitute the Nomination and Remuneration Committee.
6. Explanations or comments by the Board on every qualification, reservation or adverse remark or disclaimer made—(i) by the auditor in his/her report and (ii) by the company secretary in his/her secretarial audit report.
7. Particulars of loans, guarantees or investments under Section 186. Section 186 imposes restrictions on loans, guarantees and investments made by companies.
8. Particulars of contracts or arrangements with related parties referred to in sub-section(1) of Section 188 in the prescribed form.
9. The state of the company's affairs.
10. The amounts, if any, which it proposes to carry to any reserves.
11. The amount, if any, which it recommends should be paid by way of dividend.
12. Material changes and commitments, if any, affecting the financial position of the company, which occurred between the end of the financial year of the company to which the financial statements relate and the date of the report.
13. The conservation of energy, technology absorption, foreign exchange earnings and outgo, in such manner as may be prescribed.
14. A statement indicating development and implementation of a risk management policy for the company, including identification therein of elements of risk, if any, which in the opinion of the Board may threaten the existence of the company.
15. The details of the policy developed and implemented by the company on corporate social responsibility initiatives taken during the year.
16. In case of a listed company and every other public company having such paid-up share capital as may be prescribed, a statement indicating the manner in which the formal annual evaluation has been made by the Board of its own performance and that of its committees and individual directors.
17. Such other matters as may be prescribed.

10.3.1 Directors' Responsibility Statement

The Directors' Responsibility Statement referred to in clause (c) of sub-section(3) of Section 134 shall state that:

1. In the preparation of the annual accounts, the applicable accounting standards had been followed along with proper explanation relating to material departures.
2. The directors had selected such accounting policies and applied them consistently, and made judgments and estimates that are reasonable and prudent so as to give a true and fair view of the state of affairs of the company at the end of the financial year and of the profit and loss of the company for that period.

3. The directors had taken proper and sufficient care for the maintenance of adequate accounting records in accordance with the provisions of this Act for safeguarding the assets of the company and for preventing and detecting fraud and other irregularities.
4. The directors had prepared the annual accounts on a going concern basis.
5. The directors, in the case of a listed company, had laid down internal financial controls to be followed by the company and that such internal financial controls are adequate and were operating effectively.

   Explanation: For the purposes of this clause, the term "internal financial controls" means the policies and procedures adopted by the company for ensuring an orderly and efficient conduct of its business, including adherence to company's policies, safeguarding of its assets, prevention and detection of frauds and errors, accuracy and completeness of accounting records, and the timely preparation of reliable financial information.
6. The directors had devised proper systems to ensure compliance with the provisions of all applicable laws and that such systems were adequate and operating effectively.
7. The Board's report and any annexures thereto under sub-section(3) shall be signed by the chairperson of the company if he/she is authorized by the Board and where he/she is not so authorized, shall be signed by at least two directors, one of whom shall be a managing director, or by the director where there is only one director.
8. A signed copy of every financial statement, including consolidated financial statement, if any, shall be issued, circulated or published along with a copy each of: (a) any notes annexed to or forming part of such financial statement; (b) the auditor's report and (c) the Board's report referred to in sub-section(3).

10.4 Independent Auditors' Report

The accounts of a company are required to be audited by an independent outside auditor. An audit is the examination of a company's accounting system, controls, accounting records and the financial statements resulting there from.

Section 134(2) of the Companies Act, 2013 requires that the auditors' report shall be attached to every financial statement.

Section 143(2) of the Companies Act, 2013 provides that the auditor shall make a report to the members of the company on the accounts examined by him/her and on every financial statement required by or under this Act to be laid before the company in the general meeting.

The report shall after taking into account the provisions of this Act, the accounting and auditing standards and matters which are required to be included in the audit report and to the best of his/her information and knowledge, the said accounts, financial statements give a true and fair view of the state of the company's affairs as at the end of its financial year and profit or loss and cash flow for the year and such other matters as may be prescribed.

The auditor's report shall also state:

1. Whether he/she has sought and obtained all the information and explanations which to the best of his/her knowledge and belief were necessary for the purpose of his/her audit and if not, the details thereof and the effect of such information on the financial statements.

2. Whether, in his/her opinion, proper books of account as required by law have been kept by the company so far as appears from his/her examination of those books and proper returns adequate for the purposes of his/her audit have been received from branches not visited by him/her.
3. Whether the report on the accounts of any branch office of the company audited by a person other than the company's auditor has been sent to him/her and the manner in which he/she has dealt with it in preparing his/her report.
4. Whether the company's balance sheet and profit and loss account dealt with in the report are in agreement with the books of account and returns.
5. Whether, in his/her opinion, the financial statements comply with the accounting standards.
6. The observations or comments of the auditors on financial transactions or matters which have any adverse effect on the functioning of the company.
7. Whether any director is disqualified from being appointed as a director under sub-section(2) of Section 164.
8. Any qualification, reservation or adverse remark relating to the maintenance of accounts and other matters connected therewith.
9. Whether the company has adequate internal financial controls system in place and the operating effectiveness of such controls.
10. Such other matters as may be prescribed.

Where any of the matters required to be included in the audit report under this section is answered in the negative or with a qualification, the report shall state the reasons thereof.

Besides a report on the matters mentioned above, Companies (Auditor's Report) Order, 2003 (CARO) requires the auditors to comment on certain other matters. Important matters covered by CARO are as follows:

1. Maintenance of proper records and physical verification of fixed assets and inventory.
2. Loans taken from or granted to companies and firms in which directors are interested.
3. Adequacy of internal control systems.
4. Transactions (other than loans) with companies and firms in which directors are interested.
5. Compliance with legal requirements relating to acceptance of public deposits.
6. Existence of adequate internal audit system in specified companies.
7. Maintenance of cost records.
8. Record of payment of statutory dues.
9. Default in repayment of loans.

10.4.1 Forming an Opinion and Reporting on Financial Statements

The auditor shall express an unmodified opinion when the auditor concludes that the financial statements are prepared, in all material respects, in accordance with the applicable financial reporting framework. In order to form that opinion, the auditor shall conclude as to whether the auditor has obtained reasonable assurance about whether the financial statements as a whole are free from material misstatement, whether due to fraud or error.

10.4.1.1 Modifications to the Opinion in Independent Auditors' Report

If the auditor concludes that, based on the audit evidence obtained, the financial statements as a whole are not free from material misstatement or is unable to obtain sufficient appropriate audit evidence to conclude that the financial statements as a whole are free from material misstatement, the auditor shall modify the opinion in the auditors' report.

10.4.1.2 Types of Modifications in the Opinion

Clean opinion means when there is no qualification or reservation in the Auditors' Report. The auditor may modify his/her opinion as follows:

1. **Qualified opinion:** This type of opinion occurs when the auditor, either on the basis of evidence obtained or otherwise, concludes that misstatements are material but not pervasive to the financial statements. An example of a qualified opinion in respect of Kingfisher Airlines Ltd. Financial Statements for the year ended March 31, 2013 is presented in Exhibit 10.3.

Exhibit 10.3

Qualified Auditor Opinion – Kingfisher Airlines Ltd.

Attention is invited to note 48 forming parts of the Financial Statements ("Notes") regarding the method of accounting of costs incurred on major repairs and maintenance of engines of aircrafts taken on operating lease of Rs. 664.22 lakhs (year ended March 31, 2012, Rs. 28,480.24 lakhs) (aggregate expenditure up to March 31, 2013 after eliminating expenditure on returned/redelivered assets Rs. 25,020.97 lakhs), which have been capitalized and amortized over the estimated useful life of repairs. In our opinion, this treatment is not in accordance with generally accepted accounting standards prevalent in India and ought to have been recognized in the Statement of Profit and Loss as and when incurred.

2. **Adverse opinion:** An adverse opinion is issued when the effect of a disagreement is so material and pervasive to the financial statements with appropriate audit evidence that the auditor concludes that a qualification of the report is not adequate to disclose the misleading or incomplete nature of the financial statements. An example of an adverse opinion in respect of Victory Paper and Boards (India) Limited Financial Statements for the year ended March 31, 2013 is presented in Exhibit 10.4.

Exhibit 10.4

Adverse Audit Opinion – Victory Paper and Boards (India) Ltd.

"We believe that the audit evidence we have obtained is sufficient and appropriate to provide a basis for our *adverse* audit opinion."

Basis for Adverse Opinion

1. The company is the manufacturer of different varieties of paper. The details of inventory valuation are not available with the company. Also, inventory records in respect of raw material, finished goods, consumables, stores and spares and semi-finished goods were not

made available for verification. Hence, we are unable to verify the compliance of Accounting Standard – 2, Valuation of Inventories.
2. The company has made a scrap sale of Rs. 9,760,080 during the year. The nature and description of items sold as scrap was not available. Hence, we are unable to verify the correctness of these transactions.
3. The company has paid electricity charges and interest thereon, amounting to Rs. 432.46 lakhs to Kerala State Electricity Board and shown under "other receivables", which in our opinion should have been charged as a revenue expenditure in the year it was incurred. (See note no. 9 of the notes forming part of accounts.)
4. According to our opinion, trade receivable of Rs. 21,330,153 and Advance for Fixed Assets of Rs. 674,923 is long outstanding and is doubtful of recovery.
5. Debtors, creditors and loans and advances are subject to confirmation and reconciliation.

3. **Disclaimer opinion:** A disclaimer opinion is expressed when the possible effect of a limitation on scope is so material and pervasive that the auditor has not been able to obtain sufficient appropriate audit evidence and is, accordingly, unable to express an opinion on the financial statements. For example, if the accounts are seized by the Central Excise department, the company will not furnish any record. In such a case, disclaimer opinion will be expressed by the auditor.

10.4.2 Form of Independent Auditors' Report

The independent auditors' report has the following distinct heads:

1. Report on the financial statements
2. Management's responsibility for the financial statements
3. Auditor's responsibility
4. Opinion
5. Report on other legal and regulatory requirements
6. Annexure to the independent auditors' report

It should be noted that the auditor expresses only an opinion as to whether the financial statements present a true and fair view of the financial position and performance of the company. A favorable report by the auditors does not preclude minor errors in the financial statements. While a favorable report implies that investors and creditors can rely on the financial statements, they need to use financial statements with caution in the case of a qualified report.

10.5 Segment Information

The financial statements follow the entity concept and reveal the financial performance and financial position of the enterprise as a whole. An enterprise may be engaged in multiple business activities, each of which generates revenues and incurs expenses. The operating results of these distinct activities may be reviewed regularly by the management to decide on resource allocation to these activities and to assess their performance. To make the financial statements more useful to the users, Ind AS 108, "Operating Segments" requires that:

> *An entity shall disclose information to enable users of its financial statements to evaluate the nature and financial effects of the business activities in which it engages and the economic environments in which it operates.*

An entity is required to report separately information about each operating segment that is identified based on specified criteria.

10.5.1 Operating Segments

An operating segment is a component of an entity:

1. that engages in business activities from which it may earn revenues and incur expenses (including revenues and expenses relating to transactions with other components of the same entity),
2. whose operating results are regularly reviewed by the entity's chief operating decision maker to make decisions about resources to be allocated to the segment and assess its performance, and
3. for which discrete financial information is available.

10.5.2 Segment Information

An entity is required to disclose the following for each period for which a statement of profit and loss is presented:

10.5.2.1 General Information

1. Factors used to identify the entity's reportable segments, including the basis of organization (e.g., whether the management has chosen to organize the entity around differences in products and services, geographical areas, regulatory environments, or a combination of factors and whether operating segments have been aggregated).
2. Types of products and services from which each reportable segment derives its revenues.

Reportable segments are those operating segments that meet the requirements of quantitative thresholds provided in Ind AS 108 "Operating Segments."

10.5.2.2 Information about Profit or Loss, Assets and Liabilities

An entity shall report a measure of profit or loss for each reportable segment.

An entity shall report a measure of total assets and liabilities for each reportable segment if such amounts are regularly provided to the chief operating decision maker.

An entity shall also disclose the following about each reportable segment if the specified amounts are included in the measure of segment profit or loss reviewed by the chief operating decision maker, or are otherwise regularly provided to the chief operating decision maker, even if not included in that measure of segment profit or loss:

1. revenues from external customers;
2. revenues from transactions with other operating segments of the same entity;
3. interest revenue;
4. interest expense;

5. depreciation and amortization;
6. material items of income and expense disclosed in accordance with paragraph 97 of Ind AS 1 "Presentation of Financial Statements";
7. the entity's interest in the profit or loss of associates and joint ventures accounted for by the equity method;
8. income tax expense or income; and
9. material non-cash items other than depreciation and amortization.

An entity shall report interest revenue separately from interest expense for each reportable segment unless a majority of the segment's revenues are from interest and the chief operating decision maker relies primarily on the net interest revenue to assess the performance of the segment and make decisions about resources to be allocated to the segment. In such a situation, an entity may report that segment's interest revenue, net of its interest expense and disclose that it has done so.

An entity shall disclose the following about each reportable segment if the specified amounts are included in the measure of segment assets reviewed by the chief operating decision maker or are otherwise regularly provided to the chief operating decision maker, even if not included in the measure of segment assets:

1. the amount of investment in associates and joint ventures accounted for by the equity method, and
2. the amount of additions to non-current assets other than financial instruments, deferred tax assets, post-employment benefit assets and rights arising under insurance contracts.

10.5.2.3 Reconciliations

An entity shall provide reconciliations of all of the following:

1. The total of the reportable segments' revenue to the entity's revenue.
2. The total of the reportable segments' measures of profit or loss to the entity's profit or loss before tax expense (tax income) and discontinued operations. However, if an entity allocates to reportable segments items such as tax expense (tax income), the entity may reconcile the total of the segments' measures of profit or loss to the entity's profit or loss after those items.
3. The total of the reportable segments' assets to the entity's assets.
4. The total of the reportable segments' liabilities to the entity's liabilities.
5. The total of the reportable segments' amounts for every other material item of information disclosed to the corresponding amount for the entity.

Exhibit 10.5 presents segment information provided by ACC Ltd. in its annual report for the year ended December 31, 2014.

Exhibit 10.5

Segment Information in ACC Annual Report for the Year Ended December 31, 2014

The company has disclosed Business Segment as the primary segment. Segments have been identified taking into account the nature of products, the differing risks and returns, the organization structure and internal reporting system. The company's operations predominantly relate to the manufacture of cement and ready mix concrete. The export turnover is not significant in the context of the total turnover of the company. Further, the risk and returns are not significantly different from that of India. As such there is only one geographic segment.

Inter-Segment Transfers

Inter-Segment Transfer Pricing Policy – Cement supplied to ready mix concrete activity and ready mix concrete supplied to cement activity are based on current market prices. All other inter-segment transfers are at cost (Table 10.1).

Table 10.1 ACC Ltd. – Information about primary business segments

(Rs. in Million)

	Cement		Ready Mix Concrete		Total	
	2014	2013	2014	2013	2014	2013
Revenue						
External sales	107,203	102,332	7,608	6,559	114,811	108,891
Other operating revenue	2,484	2,512	88	94	2,572	2,606
Inter-segment sales	1,225	1,150	90	62	1,315	1,212
	110,912	105,994	7,786	6,715	118,698	112,709
Less: Elimination	1,225	1,150	90	62	1,315	1,212
Total Revenue	**109,687**	**104,844**	**7,696**	**6,653**	**117,383**	**111,497**
Result						
Segment Result	9,414	10,729	162	19	9,576	10,748
Unallocated corporate income					336	395
Operating profit					**9,912**	**11,143**
Finance cost					(828)	(1,136)
Interest and dividend income					2,268	2,262
Income taxes					331	(1,312)
Profit After Tax					11,683	10,957
Other Information						
Segment assets	101,720	88,969	2,711	2,310	104,431	91,278
Unallocated corporate assets					22,282	29,658
Total Assets					**126,713**	**120,936**
Segment liabilities	27,990	24,335	1,497	1,133	29,487	25,468
Unallocated corporate liabilities					14,870	17,219
Total Liabilities					**44,357**	**42,687**
Capital expenditure	15,711	9,503	170	150	15,881	9,653
Depreciation and amortization	5,391	5,562	185	177	5,576	5,739
Impairment loss recognized	---	119	---	---	---	119
Other non-cash expenses	331	43	60	90	391	133

10.6 Related Party Transactions

Related party relationships are a normal feature of commerce and business. For example, entities frequently carry on parts of their activities through subsidiaries, joint ventures and associates. In such circumstances, the entity has the ability to affect the financial and operating policies of the investee through the presence of control, joint control or significant influence.

A related party relationship could have an effect on the profit or loss and financial position of an entity. Related parties may enter into transactions that unrelated parties would not. For example, an entity that sells goods to its parent at cost might not sell on the terms to another customer. Also, transactions between related parties may not be made at the same amounts as between unrelated parties.

The profit or loss and financial position of an entity may be affected by a related party relationship even if related party transactions do not occur. The mere existence of the relationship may be sufficient to affect the transactions of the entity with other parties. For example, a subsidiary may terminate relations with a trading partner on acquisition by the parent of a fellow subsidiary engaged in the same activity as the former trading partner. Alternatively, one party may refrain from acting because of the significant influence of another—e.g., a subsidiary may be instructed by its parent not to engage in research and development.

For these reasons, knowledge of an entity's transactions, outstanding balances, including commitments and relationships with related parties may affect the assessment of its operations by users of financial statements, including assessment of risks and opportunities facing the entity.

Ind AS 24 "Related Party Disclosures" provide for disclosures relating to related party transactions. The objective of this Standard is to ensure that an entity's financial statements contain disclosures necessary to draw attention to the possibility that its financial position and profit or loss may have been affected by the existence of related parties and by transactions and outstanding balances, including commitments with such parties.

To enable users of financial statements to form a view about the effects of related party relationships on an entity, it is appropriate to disclose the related party relationship when control exists, irrespective of whether there have been transactions between related parties. This is because the existence of control relationship may prevent the reporting entity from being independent in making its financial and operating decisions. The disclosure of the name of the related party and the nature of the related party relationship where control exists may sometimes be at least as relevant in appraising an entity's prospects as are operating results and the financial position presented in its financial statements. Such a related party may establish the entity's credit standing, determine the source and price of its raw materials and determine to whom and at what price the product is sold.

10.6.1 Related Party

A *related party* is a person or an entity that is related to the entity preparing its financial statements (the reporting entity).

1. A person or a close member of that person's family is related to a reporting entity if that person:
   - **(a)** has control or joint control over the reporting entity;
   - **(b)** has significant influence over the reporting entity; or
   - **(c)** is a member of the key management personnel of the reporting entity or of a parent of the reporting entity.

2. An entity is related to a reporting entity if any of the following conditions apply:
   - **(i)** The entity and the reporting entity are members of the same group (which means that each parent, subsidiary and fellow subsidiary is related to the others).
   - **(ii)** One entity is an associate or joint venture of the other entity (or an associate or joint venture of a member of a group of which the other entity is a member).
   - **(iii)** Both entities are joint ventures of the same third party.
   - **(iv)** One entity is a joint venture of the third entity and the other entity is an associate of the third entity.
   - **(v)** The entity is a post-employment benefit plan for the benefit of employees of either the reporting entity or an entity related to the reporting entity. If the reporting entity is itself such a plan, the sponsoring employers are also related to the reporting entity.
   - **(vi)** The entity is controlled or jointly controlled by a person identified in step (1) of the above list.
   - **(vii)** A person identified in step (1a) of the above list has significant influence over the entity or is a member of the key management personnel of the entity (or of a parent of the entity).

Control is the power to govern the financial and operating policies of an entity so as to obtain benefits from its activities. *Joint control* is the contractually agreed sharing of control over an economic activity.

Key management personnel are those persons having authority and responsibility for planning, directing and controlling the activities of the entity, directly or indirectly, including any director (whether executive or otherwise) of that entity.

Significant influence is the power to participate in the financial and operating policy decisions of an entity, but is not the control over those policies. Significant influence may be gained by shared ownership, statute or agreement.

10.6.2 Related Party Transaction

A *related party transaction* is a transfer of resources, services or obligations between a reporting entity and a related party, regardless of whether a price is charged.

10.6.3 Disclosures

Relationship between a parent and its subsidiaries shall be disclosed, irrespective of whether there have been transactions between them.

An entity shall disclose the name of its parent and, if different, the ultimate controlling party.

If neither the entity's parent nor the ultimate controlling party produces consolidated financial statements available for public use, the name of the next most senior parent that does so shall also be disclosed.

An entity shall disclose key management personnel compensation in total and for each of the following categories:

1. short-term employee benefits;
2. post-employment benefits;
3. other long-term benefits;
4. termination benefits; and
5. share-based payment.

If an entity has had related party transactions during the periods covered by the financial statements, it shall disclose the nature of the related party relationship and information about those transactions and outstanding balances, including commitments, necessary for users to understand the potential effect of the relationship on financial statements. At a minimum, disclosures shall include:

1. the amount of transactions;
2. the amount of outstanding balances, including commitments, and:
   (a) their terms and conditions, including whether they are secured, and the nature of the consideration to be provided in settlement; and
   (b) details of any guarantees given or received;
3. provisions for doubtful debts related to the amount of outstanding balances; and
4. the expense recognized during the period in respect of bad or doubtful debts due from related parties.

The disclosures required shall be made separately for each of the following categories:

1. the parent;
2. entities with joint control or significant influence over the entity;
3. subsidiaries;
4. associates;
5. joint ventures in which the entity is a venture;
6. key management personnel of the entity or its parent; and
7. other related parties.

The following are examples of transactions that are disclosed if they are with a related party:

1. purchases or sales of goods (finished or unfinished);
2. purchases or sales of property and other assets;
3. rendering or receiving of services;
4. leases;
5. transfers of research and development;
6. transfers under license agreements;
7. transfers under finance arrangements (including loans and equity contributions in cash or in kind);
8. provision of guarantees or collateral;
9. commitment to do something if a particular event occurs or does not occur in the future, including executory contracts (recognized and unrecognized);
10. settlement of liabilities on behalf of the entity or by the entity on behalf of the related party;
11. management contracts including for deputation of employees.

10.7 Corporate Governance Report

Under Clause 49 of the listing agreement, listed companies need to have a separate section on Corporate Governance in the Annual Report, with a detailed compliance report on Corporate Governance. The compliance report includes both mandatory and non-mandatory requirements. Non-compliance of any mandatory requirement with reasons thereof and the extent to which the non-mandatory requirements have been adopted should be specifically highlighted.

10.7.1 Mandatory Requirements

The following is the list of mandatory requirements to be included in the report:

1. A brief statement on the company's philosophy on code of governance.
2. **Board of directors:**
   - (a) Composition and category of directors, e.g., promoter, executive, non-executive, independent non-executive, nominee director, which institution represented as lender or as an equity investor.
   - (b) Attendance of each director at the Board meetings and the last AGM.
   - (c) The number of other Boards or Board Committees in which he/she is a member or Chairperson.
   - (d) The number of Board meetings held, dates on which they were held.
3. **Audit committee:**
   - (a) Brief description of terms of reference
   - (b) Composition, name of members and Chairperson
   - (c) Meetings and attendance during the year
4. **Remuneration committee:**
   - (a) Brief description of terms of reference
   - (b) Composition, name of members and Chairperson
   - (c) Attendance during the year
   - (d) Remuneration policy
   - (e) Details of remuneration to all the directors
5. **Shareholder's committee:**
   - (a) Name of non-executive director heading the committee
   - (b) Name and designation of compliance officer
   - (c) Number of shareholders' complaints received so far
   - (d) Number of complaints not solved to the satisfaction of shareholders
   - (e) Number of pending complaints
6. **General body meetings:**
   - (a) Location and time, where the last three AGMs were held.
   - (b) Whether any special resolutions were passed in the previous three AGMs.
   - (c) Whether any special resolution was passed in the previous year through postal ballot – details of voting pattern.
   - (d) Person who conducted the postal ballot exercise.
   - (e) Whether any special resolution is proposed to be conducted through postal ballot.
   - (f) Procedure for postal ballot.
7. **Disclosures:**
   - (a) Disclosures on materially significant related party transactions that may have potential conflict with the interests of company at large.
   - (b) Details of non-compliance by the company, penalties, strictures imposed on the company by Stock Exchange or SEBI or any statutory authority, on any matter related to capital markets, during the last 3 years.

(c) Whistle blower policy and affirmation that no personnel has been denied access to the audit committee.
(d) Details of compliance with mandatory requirements and adoption of non-mandatory requirements for this clause.

8. **Means of communication:**
   (a) Quarterly results
   (b) Newspapers wherein results are normally published
   (c) Any website, where the results are displayed
   (d) Whether it also displays official news releases
   (e) The presentations made to institutional investors or to the analysts
9. **General shareholder information:**
   (a) AGM: Date, time and venue
   (b) Financial year
   (c) Date of Book closure
   (d) Dividend Payment date
   (e) Listing on Stock Exchanges
   (f) Stock code
   (f) Market Price Data: High, Low during each month in the last financial year
   (h) Performance in comparison to broad-based indices such as BSE Sensex, CRISIL index, etc.
   (i) Registrar and transfer agents
   (j) Share transfer system
   (k) Distribution of shareholding
   (l) Dematerialization of shares and liquidity
   (m) Outstanding GDRs/ADRs/Warrants or any convertible instrument, conversion date and likely impact on equity
   (n) Plant locations
   (o) Address for correspondence

10.7.2 Non-Mandatory Requirements

1. **The board:** A non-executive Chairman may be entitled to maintain a Chairman's office at the company's expense and also allowed to reimburse expenses incurred in performing his/her duties. Independent Directors may have a tenure not exceeding, in the aggregate, a period of 9 years, on the Board of a company. The company may ensure that the person who is being appointed as an independent director has the requisite qualifications and experience which would be of use to the company and which, in the opinion of the company, would enable him/her to contribute effectively to the company in his/her capacity as an independent director.
2. **Remuneration committee:**
   (a) The board may set up a remuneration committee to determine on their behalf and on behalf of the shareholders with agreed terms of reference, the company's policy on specific remuneration packages for executive directors, including pension rights and any compensation payment.

(b) To avoid conflicts of interest, the remuneration committee, which would determine the remuneration packages of the executive directors may comprise of at least three directors, all of whom should be non-executive directors, the Chairman of committee being an independent director.

(c) All the members of the remuneration committee could be present at the meeting.

(d) The Chairman of the remuneration committee could be present at the Annual General Meeting, to answer the shareholder queries. However, it would be up to the Chairman to decide who should answer the queries.

3. **Shareholder rights:** A half-yearly declaration of financial performance, including a summary of significant events in the last 6 months, may be sent to each household of shareholders.
4. **Audit qualifications:** The company may move towards a regime of unqualified financial statements.
5. **Training of board members:** A company may train its Board members in the business model of the company and the risk profile of the business parameters of the company, their responsibilities as directors, and the best ways to discharge them.
6. **Mechanism for evaluating non-executive board members:** The performance evaluation of non-executive directors could be done by a peer group comprising the entire Board of Directors, excluding the director being evaluated; and Peer Group evaluation could be the mechanism to determine whether to extend/continue the terms of appointment of non-executive directors.
7. **Whistle blower policy:** The company may establish a mechanism for employees to report to the management concerns about unethical behavior, actual or suspected fraud or violation of the company's code of conduct or ethics policy. This mechanism could also provide for adequate safeguards against victimization of employees who avail the mechanism and also provide for direct access to the Chairman of the Audit committee in exceptional cases. Once established, the existence of the mechanism may be appropriately communicated within the organization.

10.8 Management Discussion and Analysis Report

Management Discussion and Analysis (MD&A) Report is a requirement of the listing agreement of the company with the stock exchange. This requirement, therefore, applies to a listed company only.

Clause 49 of the listing agreement provides that as part of the directors' report or as an addition thereto, a MD&A report should form part of the Annual Report to the shareholders. This MD&A should include discussion on the following matters within the limits set by the company's competitive position:

1. Industry structure and developments
2. Opportunities and threats
3. Segment-wise or product-wise performance
4. Outlook
5. Risks and concerns
6. Internal control systems and their adequacy
7. Discussion on financial performance with respect to operational performance
8. Material developments in human resources/industrial relations front, including the number of people employed

MD&A report provides useful insights about the industry in which a company operates, its competitive position in the industry, future prospects of the company and the risks facing the company.

10.9 Business Responsibility Report

Under Clause 55 of the Listing Agreement, listed entities are required to submit *Business Responsibility Report* as part of their Annual Reports, describing the initiatives taken by them from an environmental, social and governance perspective in the suggested format. The requirement is applicable to top 100 listed companies based on Market Capitalization at BSE as on March 31, 2012 and shall be effective from the financial year ending on or after December 31, 2012.

"Responsible Business" conduct refers to the commitment of businesses to operating in an economically, socially and environmentally sustainable manner while balancing the demands of shareholders and other interest groups. It is about managing risks and impacts, which affect business' ability to meet its objectives.

The report is prepared in five sections: section A to section E:

1. Section A requires general information about the company: name, address, businesses, locations, markets, etc.
2. Section B requires financial details of the company: paid up capital, turnover, profit, spending on corporate social responsibility (CSR) activities, etc.
3. Section C requires information about the participation of subsidiary companies, suppliers and distributors in the business responsibility (BR) activities of the company.
4. Section D requires details about directors and head responsible for BR, existence or non-existence of principle-wise [as provided by National Voluntary Guidelines (NVG) on Social, Environmental and Economic responsibilities of business] BR policies, and governance related to BR.

10.9.1 National Voluntary Guidelines

India's National Voluntary Guidelines on Social, Environmental and Economic Responsibilities of Business, released by the Ministry of Corporate Affairs (MCA), have been formulated with the objective of creating positive framework conditions to advance the role of business in economic growth, which is socially and environmentally sustainable, while also ensuring enhanced competitiveness and integration into the global markets. The NVGs are a set of the following nine principles:

- **Principle 1:** Businesses should conduct and govern themselves with ethics, transparency and accountability.
- **Principle 2:** Businesses should provide goods and services that are safe and contribute to sustainability throughout their life cycle.
- **Principle 3:** Businesses should promote the wellbeing of all employees.
- **Principle 4:** Businesses should respect the interests of, and be responsive towards all stakeholders, especially those who are disadvantaged, vulnerable and marginalized.
- **Principle 5:** Businesses should respect and promote human rights.
- **Principle 6:** Businesses should respect, protect and make efforts to restore the environment.
- **Principle 7:** Businesses, when engaged in influencing public and regulatory policy, should do so in a responsible manner.
- **Principle 8:** Businesses should support inclusive growth and equitable development.
- **Principle 9:** Businesses should engage with and provide value to their customers and consumers in a responsible manner.

Section E requires information on the company's performance on each of the above nine principles.

Some disclosures are made voluntarily by companies. Two of these disclosures that are quite common are the value added statement and economic value added (EVA).

10.10 Value Added Statement

Value added statement is a statement that shows how much value has been created by an entity in an accounting period through utilization of various inputs such as materials, capital, manpower and other resources and how it is allocated among different stakeholders (employees, lenders, shareholders, government, etc.).

Value added statement is different from the profit and loss account as the latter reveals the value generated for the shareholders after meeting the claims of other stakeholders. Exhibit 10.6 presents the value added statement included by the Steel Authority of India Limited in its annual report for the year ended March 31, 2014.

Exhibit 10.6

Value Added Statement – Steel Authority of India Limited

For the year	2013–14		2012–13	
Value of own production	518, 250		523,800	
Other revenue	13,440		15,710	
		531,690		539,510
Less: Cost of raw materials	192,720		212,020	
Stores and spares	31,790		31,120	
Power and fuel	49,420		48,300	
Excise duty	56,770		53,890	
Freight outward	9,760		9,530	
Other operating cost	36,340		44,370	
		376,800		399,230
Total value added		154,890		140,280
Establishment cost		95,790		86,370
Financing cost		9,680		7,480
Dividend provision		8,340		8,260
Corporate income tax		6,080		10,700
Dividend tax		1,420		1,350
Income retained in business				
Depreciation	17,170		14,030	
Retained in business	16,410		12,090	
		33,580		26,120
Total value added		154,890		140,280

10.11 Economic Value Added Statement

Economic value added (EVA) statement measures the economic profit earned by an entity. Economic profit is the profit earned in excess of the required return of the company's investors (being shareholders and debt holders). It is calculated by deducting the cost of financing the firm's capital from the profit earned by the firm. A firm is considered to create value when the return on the capital employed by a firm is greater than the cost of that capital. Exhibit 10.7 presents the economic value added statement included by ACC Limited in its annual report for the year ended December 31, 2014.

Exhibit 10.7

Economic Value Added Statement – ACC Limited

(Rs. in Million)

Year ended December 31	2014	2013	2012	2011	2010
Capital employed	87,710	83,670	80,630	82,210	73,550
Average capital employed	85,690	82,150	81,420	77,880	71,440
Net operating profit after taxes*	11,680	10,960	12,880	13,250	11,200
Cost of capital	11,050	10,840	9,810	9,500	8,210
Value added	630	120	3,070	3,750	2,990
Return on Capital employed (%)	13.63	13.34	15.82	17.01	15.68
Weighted average cost of capital (%)	12.90	13.20	12.05	12.20	11.49
Value added/capital employed (%)	0.73	0.14	3.77	4.81	4.19
Market capitalization (as at December 31	262,870	208,060	268,360	213,450	201,940
Add: Debts		350	1,630	5,110	5,240
Less: Cash and cash equivalents	16,860	26,210	31,370	29,320	23,880
Enterprise value	246,010	182,200	238,620	189,240	183,300
Enterprise value/Year end capital employed (Times)	2.80	2.18	2.96	2.30	2.49

*Net operating profit excludes exceptional item and tax impact on the same.

Summary – Review of Learning Objectives

1. **Understand the information provided in the annual reports of companies.** Typically, annual reports include detailed notes to accounts and significant accounting policies; directors' report; auditors' report; corporate governance report; management discussion

and analysis report; business responsibility report, segment data; related party disclosures; value added statement, etc.

2. **Understand the topics to be covered under Notes to Accounts that form part of financial statements of a company.** The notes provide further sub-classifications of the line items presented in the Balance Sheet, and additional line items, headings and subtotals in the statement of profit and loss, when such presentation is relevant to an understanding of the entity's financial performance. The notes also: (a) present information about the basis of preparation of the financial statements and the specific accounting policies; (b) disclose the information required by Ind AS that is not presented elsewhere in the financial statements; and (c) provide information that is not presented elsewhere in the financial statements, but is relevant to the understanding of any of them.
3. **Understand the contents of Directors' Report, Independent Auditors' Report, Corporate Governance Report, Management Discussion and Analysis and Business Responsibility Report.** Each of these reports have detailed requirements relating to their content. An entity is required to include the Directors' Report and Auditors' Report in its Annual Report under the provisions of the Companies Act, 2013. Corporate Governance Report and Management Discussion and Analysis are required under Clause 49 of the Listing Agreement, and the Business Responsibility Report is required under Clause 55 of the Listing Agreement.
4. **Understand the difference between a Clean Audit Report and a Modified Audit Report.** Clean opinion means when there is no qualification or reservation in the Auditors' Report. The auditor shall express an unmodified opinion when the auditor concludes that the financial statements are prepared, in all material respects, in accordance with the applicable financial reporting framework. If the auditor concludes that, based on the audit evidence obtained, the financial statements as a whole are not free from material misstatement or is unable to obtain sufficient appropriate audit evidence to conclude that the financial statements as a whole are free from material misstatement, the auditor shall modify the opinion in the auditors' report.
5. **Understand the different kinds of modifications in Independent Auditors' Report.** *Qualified opinion* occurs when the auditor, either on the basis of evidence obtained or otherwise, concludes that misstatements are material but not pervasive to the financial statements. An *Adverse opinion* is issued when the effect of a disagreement is so material and pervasive to the financial statements that the auditor concludes that a qualification of the report is not adequate to disclose the misleading or incomplete nature of financial statements. A *Disclaimer* opinion is expressed when the possible effect of a limitation on the scope is so material and pervasive that the auditor has not been able to obtain sufficient appropriate audit evidence and is, accordingly, unable to express an opinion on the financial statements.
6. **Understand the requirements of Indian Accounting Standards relating to disclosure of information pertaining to Operating Segments and transactions with Related Parties.** An entity is required to report separately information about each operating segment that is identified based on specified criteria. The information primarily relates to profit/loss, assets and liabilities of these segments.

   Further, if an entity has had related party transactions during the periods covered by the financial statements, it shall disclose the nature of the related party relationship and information about those transactions and outstanding balances, including commitments, necessary for users to understand the potential effect of the relationship on the financial statements.

7. **Understand the Value Added Statement and the Economic Value Added Statement that are provided voluntarily by many companies as part of their annual reports.** Value Added Statement shows how much value has been created by an entity in an accounting period through utilization of various inputs such as materials, capital, manpower and other resources and how it is allocated among different stakeholders (employees, lenders, shareholders, government, etc.).

   Economic Value Added (EVA) statement measures the economic profit earned by an entity. Economic profit is the profit earned in excess of the required return of the company's investors (being shareholders and debt holders). It is calculated by deducting the cost of financing the firm's capital from the profit earned by the firm. A firm is considered to create value when the return on the capital employed by a firm is greater than the cost of that capital.

Glossary

- **Contingent liability** is not a real liability but a potential liability that depends on an uncertain future event. Contingent liabilities are commonly associated with legal proceedings, tax disputes, guarantees for loans.
- **Value added** is the difference between the value of output and the cost of inputs required to produce that output.
- **Economic value added (EVA)** is the difference between the profit earned by the firm and the cost of financing the firm's capital.
- **Operating segment** is a component of an entity that engages in business activities from which it may earn revenues and incur expenses; whose operating results are regularly reviewed; and for which discrete financial information is available.
- **Related party** is a person or entity that is related to the entity that is preparing its financial statements (the reporting entity) in the manner specified by Ind AS 24 "Related Party Disclosures."

Multiple Choice Questions

1. Annual reports of companies contain information required by ________.
   a. companies Act, 2013
   b. indian accounting standards
   c. listing agreement with stock exchanges
   d. all of the above

2. Which of the following is not a part of the complete set of financial statements under Ind AS1 "Presentation of Financial Statement"?
   a. Balance sheet
   b. Profit and loss account
   c. Notes to accounts
   d. Value added statement

3. National voluntary guidelines on social, environment and economic responsibility have a set of ________ principles.
   a. six
   b. eight
   c. seven
   d. nine

4. A contingent liability is a liability that creates ________.
   a. a possible obligation
   b. a real obligation
   c. a current obligation
   d. no obligation

5. The value added statement reveals the value created for ________.
   a. shareholders
   b. employees
   c. directors
   d. stakeholders
6. Economic value added (EVA) statement measures ________.
   a. operating profit
   b. gross profit
   c. economic profit
   d. net profit
7. Which of the following terms is not associated with the independent auditors' report?
   a. accounting system
   b. corporate governance
   c. controls
   d. accounting records
8. Directors' responsibility statement is a part of ________.
   a. directors' report
   b. auditors' report
   c. corporate governance report
   d. business responsibility report
9. Business responsibility report has ________ sections.
   a. four
   b. eight
   c. five
   d. six
10. The auditor believes that the financial statement do not give a true and fair view, and the effect is so material that a disclosure is required to the extent that financial statement may be misleading or incomplete in nature, the auditor should issue ________.
   a. a disclaimer of opinion
   b. a qualified opinion
   c. an adverse opinion
   d. an unqualified opinion, but include a reference to this matter in the audit report

Review Questions

1. An entity does not recognize a contingent liability. It just discloscs it. Do you agree? Explain.
2. What is included in the complete set of financial statements under Ind AS1 "Presentation of Financial Statements"?
3. Briefly explain a contingent liability.
4. How is a value added statement different from profit and loss account?
5. Explain the term economic value added statement.
6. An audit is only the examination of accounting records of an entity. Comment.
7. When does an auditor form an "unmodified" opinion about the financial statements of an entity?
8. Briefly explain the different types of modified opinion that an auditor can give on the financial statements of an entity.
9. Mention the different heads under which the independent auditor submits the auditors' report.
10. What is the main objective of the business responsibility report?
11. Define an operating segment.
12. Who is a related party under Ind AS 24 "Related Party Disclosures"?
13. What is the difference between value added and economic value added?

Answers to Multiple Choice Questions

1. (d)
2. (d)
3. (d)
4. (a)
5. (d)
6. (c)
7. (b)
8. (a)
9. (c)
10. (c)

Statement of Cash Flows

11

LEARNING OBJECTIVES

After reading this chapter, you will be able to:

- Understand the purpose of preparing the cash flow statement.
- Understand the classification of cash flows from different activities.
- Understand the difference between direct and indirect methods of computing cash flows from operating activities.
- Understand how to deal with certain special items such as income taxes, foreign currency cash flows, cash flows from interest and dividend, etc., in preparing the cash flow statement.
- Understand how to deal with financing and investing activities that do not involve any cash flow.

11.1 Introduction

An entity earning handsome profits may face shortage of cash due to the presence of accruals, deferrals and non-cash items in its income statement. The entity needs sufficient amount of cash to sustain its operations and to meet its obligations towards creditors and investors. Cash flow statement is a statement that shows the flow of cash during a period. Flow here means change or movement in cash. Transactions which increase cash are classified as cash inflows, and transactions which decrease cash are classified as cash outflows. Information contained in the cash flow statement is of particular significance to investors and creditors as they can use past cash flows to project future cash flows and form an opinion about the ability of the entity to honor its obligations towards them.

11.2 Cash and Cash Equivalents

Cash includes cash (cash on hand, demand deposits with bank) and cash equivalents. Cash equivalents are short-term, highly liquid investments that are readily convertible into known amounts of cash, and are subject to an insignificant risk of changes in value, for example, securities with a maturity period of 3 months or less from the date of acquisition (acquisition of debt or preference shares shortly before redemption, bank deposits with a short maturity period).

Two accounting standards AS-3 "Cash Flow Statement" and Indian Accounting Standard 7 (Ind AS-7) "Statement of Cash Flows" issued by the Institute of Chartered Accountants of India, contain guidelines for the preparation of cash flow statement. Ind AS-7 is applicable to certain specified companies. Ind AS-7 includes bank overdrafts that are repayable on demand as a part of cash and cash equivalent, whereas the existing AS-3 is silent on this aspect.

11.3 Purposes of Cash Flow Statement

Cash flow statement provides information about the cash flows associated with the period's operations and also from the entity's investing and financing activities. Both the accounting standards require that the cash flow statement should report cash flows during the period, classified into cash flows from operating, investing and financing activities. Using the cash flow statement, shareholders, lenders and other users can assess:

1. Whether the entity will be able to generate positive cash flows in the future.
2. Whether the entity will be able to meet its obligations and pay dividends.
3. Whether the entity needs to raise more funds.
4. Why there is a difference between the amount of net income and related net cash flows from operating activities.
5. The effect of entity's investing and financing activities on its cash and other accounts.
6. The reasons behind change in the beginning and ending balance of cash and cash equivalents.

11.4 Operating Activities

Operating activities are the principal revenue producing activities of an enterprise, and include activities that are not investing or financing activities. Cash flows from operating activities include cash effects of those transactions and events that determine the net profit or loss (except profit or loss on sale of fixed assets). Some examples of cash flows from operating activities are:

1. Cash receipts from sale of goods or rendering of services.
2. Cash receipts from royalties, fees, commission and other revenue.
3. Cash payment to suppliers for goods and services.
4. Cash payment to and on behalf of employees.
5. Cash receipts and cash payments of an insurance entity for premiums and claims, annuities and other policy benefits.
6. Cash payment or refund of income taxes unless they can be specifically identified with financing and investment activities.
7. Cash receipts and payments from contracts held for dealing or trading purposes.

11.5 Investing Activities

Investing activities include acquisition and disposal of long-term assets and other investments not included in cash equivalents. Some examples of investing activities are:

1. Cash payments to acquire property, plant and equipment, intangibles and other long-term assets. These payments include those relating to capitalized development costs and self-constructed property, plant and equipment.
2. Cash receipts from sale of property, plant and equipment, intangibles and other long-term assets.
3. Cash payments to acquire equity or debt instruments of other entities and interests in joint ventures (other than payments for those instruments considered to be cash equivalents or those held for dealing or trading purposes).
4. Cash receipts from sale of equity or debt instruments of other entities and interests in joint ventures (other than receipts for those instruments considered to be cash equivalents and those held for dealing or trading purposes).
5. Cash advances and loans made to other parties (other than advances and loans made by a financial institution).
6. Cash receipts from repayment of advances and loans made to other parties (other than advances and loans of a financial institution).
7. Cash payments for future contracts, forward contracts, option contracts and swap contracts except when the contracts are held for dealing or trading purposes, or the payments are classified as financing activities.
8. Cash receipts from future contracts, forward contracts, option contracts and swap contracts except when the contracts are held for dealing or trading purposes, or the receipts are classified as financing activities.

11.6 Financing Activities

Financing activities are activities that result in changes in the size and composition of the owner's capital (including preference share capital in case of a company) and borrowings of an enterprise. Examples of financing activities are:

1. Cash proceeds from issuing shares or other equity instruments.
2. Cash payments to owners to acquire or redeem the entity's shares.
3. Cash proceeds from issuing debentures, loans, notes, bonds, mortgages and other short- or long-term borrowings.
4. Cash repayments of amounts borrowed.
5. Cash payments by a lessee for the reduction of outstanding liability relating to a finance lease.

11.7 Reporting Cash Flows from Operating Activities

Cash flows from operating activities can be calculated using either the *direct method* or the *indirect method.*

11.7.1 Direct Method

In the case of direct method, gross cash receipts and gross cash payments are shown under major classes. Cash receipts include cash sales, receipts from debtors, commission and fee received and interest. Cash payments include payments for purchases, payments to and for employees, operating expenses, interest payments and direct tax payments.

The format for calculating cash flows from operating activities using the *direct method* is given as follows:

Cash Flows from Operating Activities	
Cash receipts from customers	---
Cash paid to suppliers and employees	(---)
Cash generated from operations	---
Income taxes paid	(---)
Cash flows before extraordinary items	---
Extraordinary items	---
Net cash flows from operating activities	---

Cash receipts from customers include receipts from cash sales and receipts from debtors in respect of credit sales. To calculate the cash receipts from debtors, credit sales need to be adjusted for change in the balance of debtors during the accounting period. If the balance of debtors increases during the accounting period, the cash receipts from credit sales will be less than the amount of credit sales. The inverse will be the case when the balance of debtors decreases during the accounting period. The relationship between credit sales and cash receipts from credit sales is given by

Cash receipts from credit sales = Beginning balance of debtors + Credit sales – Ending balance of debtors

Cash paid to suppliers includes payment for cash purchases and payments to creditors in respect of credit purchases. To calculate the cash payment to suppliers, credit purchases need to be adjusted for change in the balance of creditors during the accounting period. If the balance of creditors increases during the accounting period, the cash payment for credit purchases will be less than the amount of credit purchases. The inverse will be the case when the balance of creditors decreases during the accounting period. The relationship between credit purchases and cash paid to suppliers is given by

Cash paid to suppliers = Beginning balance of creditors + Credit purchases – Ending balance of creditors

When the information relating to credit purchases or credit sales is not available, the entire sales or purchases are assumed to be on credit basis.

Sometimes, the amount of purchases is embedded in the amount of cost of sales. In such a case, the amount of cost of sales has to be adjusted for change in the amount of inventories during the accounting period. The amount of closing inventories is added to the cost of sales and the amount of beginning inventories is deducted from the resulting sum. The relationship between cost of sales and purchases is given by

Cost of sales = Beginning inventories + Purchases – Ending inventories

Payments to employees also need to be adjusted for prepayments and outstanding amounts. For example, the expense on salaries and wages during an accounting period is Rs. 100,000. An amount of Rs. 10,000 has been paid as advance salary while an amount of Rs. 15,000 has not been paid at the end of the accounting period. The payment to employees in this case is Rs. 95,000 (Rs. 100,000 + Rs. 10,000 – Rs. 15,000).

Illustration 11.1

A company registers sales of Rs. 250 million in a year. The debtors at the beginning and at the end of the year were Rs. 46 million and Rs. 84 million, respectively. Cash receipts from customers can be calculated in the following manner.

Statement Showing Cash Receipts from Customers

	(Rs. in Million)
Sales	250
Add: Debtors at the beginning	46
	296
Less: Debtors at the end	84
Cash receipts from customers	212

The company in the above example reports its cost of sales during the year at Rs. 160 million. The inventories at the beginning and at the end of the year were Rs. 14 million and Rs. 18 million, respectively. Creditors at the beginning and at the end of the year were Rs. 33 million and Rs. 30 million, respectively. Cash payments to suppliers can be calculated in the following manner.

Statement Showing Cash Payments to Suppliers

	(Rs. in Million)	
Cost of sales		160
Add: Creditors at the beginning	33	
Stock at the end	18	
		51
	(Rs. in Million)	
Less: Creditors at the end	30	
Stock at the beginning	14	
		44
Cash paid to suppliers		167

Based on the above information the cash generated from operating activities using the direct method can be calculated as follows:

Cash Flows from Operating Activities	
Cash receipts from customers	212
Cash paid to suppliers and employees	(167)
Cash generated from operations	45

11.7.2 Indirect Method

Under the indirect method, the net profit or loss disclosed by the income statement is adjusted for:

1. Non-cash items such as depreciation, provisions and unrealized foreign exchange gains or losses.
2. change in current assets and current liabilities.
3. Any deferrals or accruals of past or future operating cash receipts or payments.
4. All other items that affect investing or financing cash flows.

The format for calculating cash flows from operating activities using the *indirect method* is given as follows:

Cash Flows from Operating Activities

Net profit before tax and extraordinary items	---
Adjustment for:	
Depreciation	---
Non-cash items	---
Non-operating items (dividend, interest income)	---
Operating profit before working capital changes	---
Working capital adjustment	---
Cash generated from operations	---
Income taxes paid	(---)
Cash flows before extraordinary items	---
Extraordinary items	---
Net cash flows from operating activities	---

Illustration 11.2

Following information is available from the books of a company.

(Rs.)

	2014	2015
Net profit		500,000
Depreciation		25,000
Income received in advance	1,000	1,200
Prepaid expenses	3,200	2,800
Debtors	210,000	230,000
Creditors	116,000	110,000
Outstanding expenses	5,000	4,000
Accrued income	3,000	2,400

Cash flow from operating activities can be calculated using the indirect method as follows:

Net profit	500,000
Add: Depreciation	25,000
Operating profit before working capital changes	525,000
Increase in income received in advance	200
Decrease in pre-paid expenses	400
Increase in debtors	(20,000)
Decrease in creditors	(6,000)
Decrease in outstanding expenses	(1,000)
Decrease in accrued income	600
Cash generated from operations	499,200

Ind AS-7 "Statement of Cash Flows" encourages entities to report cash flows from operating activities using the direct method. The direct method provides information that may be useful in estimating future cash flows and is not available under the indirect method.

11.8 Reporting Cash Flows from Investing Activities

Cash flows from investing activities arise from purchase and sales of fixed assets and financial assets. These also include receipt of dividends and interest. Cash flows from investing activities are calculated from the changes in the balance of fixed assets and investments. The cash effect of any transactions related to these assets during the accounting period is also considered.

Illustration 11.3

Following information is available from the books of a company:

Particular	As on March 31, 2014	As on March 31, 2015
Fixed assets:		
Land	80,000	160,000
Building and equipment	600,000	900,000
Accumulated depreciation on building and equipment	190,000	210,000
Dividend received		10,000
Interest received		20,000

- Depreciation provided during 2014–15 was Rs. 96,000.
- Cost of equipment sold was Rs. 115,000.
- Profit on sale of equipment was Rs. 19,000.

To build up cash flows from investing activities, we need to find out the cash flows associated with the purchase and sale of fixed assets.

From the given information, we can find out that the company has spent Rs. 80,000 (= Rs. 160,000 – Rs. 80,000) on purchase of land.

We can also find out the amount spent by the company on purchase of building and equipment as the balances given are at cost and also the cost of equipment sold is given. This is equal to the ending balance of building and equipment + Cost of equipment sold – Beginning balance of building and equipment. This is Rs. 415,000 (Rs. 900,000 + Rs. 115,000 – Rs. 600,000)

To find out the amount of cash received from sale of equipment, we need to know the amount of accumulated depreciation for the equipment that has been sold. For this purpose, we prepare the accumulated depreciation account as follows:

Accumulated Depreciation Account

		(Rs.)			(Rs.)
	To Building and Equipment A/c (Dep on equipment sold)	76,000	2014 April 1	By Balance b/d	190,000
2015 March 31	To Balance c/d	210,000	2015 March 31	By Profit and Loss A/c (provision for the year)	96,000
		286,000			286,000

We can now find out the cash received from the sale of equipment by preparing the building and equipment account.

Building and Equipment Account

		(Rs.)			(Rs.)
2014 April 1	To Balance b/d	600,000		By Accumulated Dep A/c (Dep on equipment sold)	76,000
	To Bank A/c (purchase of equipment)	415,000		By Bank A/c (sale of equipment)	58,000
	To Profit and Loss A/c (profit on sale of equipment)	19,000	2015 March 31	By Balance c/d	900,000
		1,034,000			1,034,000

Cash flow from investing activities can now be worked out as follows:

Cash Flows from Investing Activities

	(Rs.)
Purchase of land	(80,000)
Purchase of building and equipment	(415,000)
Sale of equipment	58,000
Dividend received	10,000
Interest received	20,000
Net cash outflow from investing activities	(407,000)

11.9 Reporting Cash Flows from Financing Activities

Cash flows from financing activities arise from issue and redemption of capital and loans. These also include payment of dividends and interest. Cash flows from financing activities are calculated from the changes in the balance of shareholders' funds and borrowings. The cash effect of any transactions related to these items during the accounting period is also considered.

Illustration 11.4

Following information is available from the books of a company:

Particular	As on 31.3.2014 (Rs.)	As on 31.3.2015 (Rs.)
Equity sharc capital	9,330,000	15,300,000
Preference share capital	2,530,000	2,930,000
Loans	116,500,000	115,200,000
Dividend paid		4,660,000

Cash flow from investing activities can now be worked out as follows:

Cash Flows from Financing Activities

Issue of share capital	5,970,000
Issue of preference capital	400,000
Repayment of loans	(1,300,000)
Dividend paid	(4,660,000)
Net cash inflow from financing activities	410,000

11.10 Treatment of Special Items

11.10.1 Foreign Currency Cash Flows

An entity should record cash flows arising from transactions in a foreign currency in the entity's functional currency by applying to the foreign currency amount the exchange rate between the functional currency and the foreign currency on the date of cash flow. Functional currency is the currency of the primary economic environment in which the entity generates and expends cash. The cash flows of a foreign subsidiary should be translated at the exchange rate between the functional currency and the foreign currency on the dates of cash flows.

11.10.2 Interest and Dividend

Cash flows from interest and dividends received and paid should be disclosed separately. Cash flows arising from the interest paid, and interest and dividends received in the case of a financial enterprise should be classified as cash flows arising from operating activities. In the case of other enterprises, cash flows arising from interest paid should be classified as cash flows from financing activities, while interest and dividends received should be classified as cash flows from investing activities. Dividends paid should be classified as cash flows from financing activities.

International Financial Reporting Standards (IFRS) allow a company to classify the interest paid and dividend paid as either an operating or financing activity. Under the US GAAP, interest expense paid to providers of debt capital must be classified as part of cash flow from operations (as is interest income), and payment of dividends to providers of equity capital classified as a financing activity.

11.10.3 Taxes on Income

Cash flows arising from taxes on income are to be separately disclosed, and need to be classified as cash flows from operating activities unless they can be specifically identified with financing and investing activities.

11.10.4 Investment in Subsidiaries, Associates and Joint Ventures

An entity can use equity or cost method to account for an investment in an associate or a subsidiary. In either case, the investor reports only the cash flows between itself and the investee in its cash flow statement, for example, to dividends and advances.

An entity which reports its interest in a jointly controlled entity using the proportionate consolidation should include its proportionate share of the jointly controlled entity's cash flows in its consolidated statement of cash flows.

An entity which reports its interest in a jointly controlled entity using the equity method should include in its statement of cash flows the cash flows in respect of its investment in the jointly controlled entity, and distributions and other payments or receipts between it and the jointly controlled entity.

11.10.5 Changes in Ownership Interests in Subsidiaries and Other Businesses

When an entity obtains or loses control of subsidiaries or other businesses, it should separately show the aggregate cash flows arising from investing activities. In addition, it should disclose the total consideration paid or received; the portion of the consideration consisting of cash and cash equivalents; the amount of cash and cash equivalents in the subsidiaries or other businesses over which control is obtained or lost; and the amount of assets and liabilities other than cash or cash equivalents in the subsidiaries or other businesses over which control is obtained or lost.

11.10.6 Non-Cash Investing and Financing Transactions

Investing and financing transactions that do not require the use of cash or cash equivalents should be excluded from the cash flow statement. Such transactions should be disclosed elsewhere in the financial statements in a way that provides all the relevant information about the investing and financing activities.

Examples of non-cash transactions are:

1. The acquisition of assets by assuming directly related liabilities or by means of a finance lease.
2. The acquisition of an enterprise by means of issue of shares.
3. The conversion of debt to equity.

11.10.7 Reporting Cash Flows on Net Basis

An entity is generally required to report gross cash receipts and gross cash payments arising from different activities. However, cash flows arising from the following operating, investing or financing activities may be reported on a net basis:

1. Cash receipts and payments on behalf of customers when the cash flows reflect the activities of the customer rather than those of the entity.
2. Cash receipts and payments for items in which the turnover is quick, the amounts are large, and the maturities are short.

Examples of cash receipts and payments referred to in point (1) above are:

(a) The acceptance and repayment of demand deposits of a bank.
(b) Funds held for customers by an investment entity.
(c) Rents collected on behalf of, and paid over to, the owners of properties.

Examples of cash receipts and payments referred to in point (2) above are advances made for, and the repayment of:

(a) Principal amounts relating to credit card customers.
(b) The purchase and sale of investments.
(c) Other short-term borrowings, for example, those which have a maturity period of three months or less.

Cash flows arising from each of the following activities of a financial institution may be reported on a net basis:

1. Cash receipts and payments for the acceptance and repayment of deposits with a fixed maturity date.
2. The placement of deposits with and withdrawal of deposits from other financial institutions.
3. Cash advances and loans made to customers and the repayment of those advances and loans.

11.10.8 Components of Cash and Cash Equivalents

An entity is required to disclose the components of cash and cash equivalents and to present a reconciliation of the amounts in its statement of cash flows with the equivalent items reported in the balance sheet.

An entity also has to disclose the policy which it adopts in determining the composition of cash and cash equivalents and the effect of any change in the policy for determining components of cash and cash equivalents. For example, a change in the classification of financial instruments previously considered to be part of an entity's investment portfolio.

11.10.9 Other Disclosures

An entity is required to disclose, together with a commentary by management, the amount of significant cash and cash equivalent balances held by the entity that are not available for use by the group. There are various circumstances in which cash and cash equivalent balances held by an entity are not available for use by the group. Examples include cash and cash equivalent balances held by a subsidiary that operates in a country where exchange controls or other legal restrictions apply when the balances are not available for general use by the parent or other subsidiaries.

11.11 Format of Cash Flow Statement (Direct Method)

A. Cash flows from operating activities	
Cash receipts from customers	---
Cash paid to suppliers and employees	(---)
Cash generated from operations	---
Income taxes paid	(---)
Cash flows before extraordinary items	---
Extraordinary items	---
Net cash flows from operating activities	---
B. Cash flows from investing activities	
Purchase of fixed assets	(---)
Purchase of investments	(---)
Sale of fixed assets	---
Sale of investments	---
Interest received	---
Dividend received	---
Net cash flows from investing activities	---
C. Cash flows from financing activities	
Proceeds from issue of share capital	---
Proceeds from long-term borrowings	---
Repayment of long-term borrowings	(---)
Dividend paid	(---)
Net cash flows from financing activities	---

(Continued)

Net increase (or decrease) in cash and cash equivalents (A + B + C)	---
Cash and cash equivalents as at ------ (opening)	--
Cash and cash equivalents as at ------ (closing)	---

11.12 Format of Cash Flow Statement (Indirect Method)

A. Cash flows from operating activities	
Net profit before tax and extraordinary items	---
Adjustment for:	
Depreciation	---
Non-cash items	---
Non-operating items (dividend, interest income)	---
Operating profit before working capital changes	---
Working capital adjustment	---
Cash generated from operations	---
Income taxes paid	(---)
Cash flows before extraordinary items	---
Extraordinary items	---
Net cash flows from operating activities	---
B. Cash flows from investing activities	
Purchase of fixed assets	(---)
Purchase of investments	(---)
Sale of fixed assets	---
Sale of investments	---
Interest received	---
Dividend received	---
Net cash flows from investing activities	---
C. Cash flows from financing activities	
Proceeds from issue of share capital	
Proceeds from long-term borrowings	---
Repayment of long-term borrowings	(---)
Dividend paid	(---)
Net cash flows from financing activities	---
Net increase (or decrease) in cash and cash equivalents (A + B + C)	---
Cash and cash equivalents as at ------ (opening)	---
Cash and cash equivalents as at ------ (closing)	---

The cash flow statement of Asian Paints Limited for the year 2015–16 is presented in Exhibit 11.1.

Exhibit 11.1

Cash Flow Statement of Asian Paints Limited for the Year Ended 31st March, 2016

(Rs. in Crores)

	Year 2015–16		Year 2014–15	
(A) Cash flow from operating activities				
Profit before prior period item, tax and after exceptional item	2,377.75		1,933.57	
Adjustments for:				
Depreciation, amortization & exceptional item	238.36		225.52	
Interest income	(11.53)		(5.19)	
Dividend income	(70.30)		(71.27)	
Finance costs	23.40		27.13	
Provision for doubtful debts and advances	3.34		1.59	
Bad debts written off	1.98		1.09	
Net unrealised foreign exchange (gain)/loss	(10.98)		8.27	
Profit on sale of long term investments (net)	(24.70)		(27.54)	
Profit on sale of short term investments (net)	(3.81)		(2.07)	
Profit on sale of fixed assets (net)	(10.37)		(0.33)	
Provision/(Reversal of provision) for diminution in value of long term investments	65.35		(14.04)	
Operating profit before working capital changes	2,578.49		2,076.73	
Adjustments for:				
(Increase) in trade receivables*	(34.91)		(8.66)	
(Increase) in other receivables*	(79.65)		(82.53)	
(Increase)/Decrease in loans and advances	(25.94)		32.28	
Decrease/(Increase) in inventories*	192.06		(130.79)	
Increase/(Decrease) in trade and other payables*	161.45		(165.92)	
Increase in provisions	15.15		11.64	
Cash generated from operating activities	2,806.65		1,732.75	
Income tax paid (net of refund)	(760.96)		(589.15)	
Net cash generated from operating activities		2,045.69		1,143.60
* Previous year figures are after adjustments pursuant to acquisition of net current assets which are classified as investing activities				

	Year 2015–16		Year 2014–15	
(B) Cash flow from investing activities				
Purchase of fixed assets	(686.72)		(336.28)	
Sale of fixed assets	12.22		1.49	
Loans to subsidiary	(0.20)		(0.28)	
Repayment of loan from subsidiaries	-		0.40	
Purchase of front end sales business from Ess Ess Bathroom Products Private Limited (Refer Note 47)	-		(36.48)	
Purchase of long-term investments - Subsidiaries	(143.17)		(0.50)	
Purchase of long-term investments - others	(282.33)		(242.00)	
Purchase of short-term investments	(70.04)		(0.04)	
Sale of long-term investments	209.70		330.53	
Sale/(Purchase) of short-term investments - others	19.04		(87.00)	
Proceeds from sale of short-term investments (net)	3.81		2.07	
Interest received	4.61		4.55	
Dividend received from subsidiaries	3.05		2.41	
Dividend received from others	67.25		68.86	
Net cash used in Investing activities		(862.78)		(292.27)
(C) Cash flow from financing activities				
Proceeds from long-term borrowings	5.90		0.06	
Repayment of long-term borrowings	(7.48)		(8.17)	
Proceeds from short-term borrowings*	-		19.92	
Repayment of short-term borrowings#	-		(39.84)	
Finance costs paid	(19.76)		(29.69)	
Dividend and dividend tax paid	(749.72)		(672.95)	
Net cash used in financing activities		(771.06)		(727.67)
#Previous year figure includes repayment of borrowings taken over pursuant to acquisition (Refer note 47).				
*Previous year figure is after adjustment pursuant to acquisition of short-term loan which is classified as investing activity (Refer note 47).				
(D) Net increase/(decrease) in cash and cash equivalents		411.85		123.66
Add: Cash and cash equivalents as on April 1		862.69		739.03
Cash and cash equivalents as on March 31		1,274.54		862.69

Notes:

(a) The above cash flow statement has been prepared under the "Indirect Method" as set out in the Accounting Standard 3 (AS-3) on cash flow statement.

(Rs. in Crores)

		31.03.2016	31.3.2015
(b)	Cash and cash equivalents comprises of		
	Cash on hand	0.06	0.05
	Balances with bank:		
	- Current accounts	2.13	22.58
	- Cash credit account	6.42	1.60
	- Deposits with banks with maturity less than 3 months	43.51	-
	Cheques on hand	24.63	30.40
	Cash and cash equivalents (Refer note 16)	76.75	54.63
	Add: Investment in liquid mutual funds [Refer note 13B (1)]	1.197.79	808.06
	Cash and cash equivalents in cash flow statement	1,274.54	862.69
(c)	Previous year's figures have been regrouped, wherever necessary		

(Source: Asian Paints Annual Report 2015–16)

11.13 Analysis of Cash Flow Statement

We can now examine the cash flow statement of Asian Paints Limited given in Exhibit 11.1 to clarify the points we referred to under the purposes of the cash flow statement in Section 11.3. It should, however, be kept in mind that for a proper analysis of the cash flow statement, the information contained in the cash flow statement has to be supplemented by information contained in other financial statements as well as historical financial data.

1. **Whether the entity will be able to generate positive cash flows in the future:** We observe that the company has generated positive cash flow of Rs. 1,144 crore in 2014–15 and Rs. 2,046 crore in 2015–16 from operating activities. These cash flows more than offset the net cash outflows from investing and financing activities and there is a net increase in the balance of cash and cash equivalents in both the years. We also observe a similar pattern in the years 2013–14 and 2012–13. The revenue of the company has been consistently growing over the past many years. It also has significant income (Rs. 75 crore in 2015–16) from interest and dividend. It is, therefore, reasonable to expect that the company will be able to generate positive cash flows in the future.
2. **Whether the entity will be able to meet its obligations and pay dividends:** The company has been earning handsome operating profits over the years. The interest cost is very low as the company is a low debt company (debt-to-equity ratio 0.01 in 2015–16). The company is, therefore, unlikely to face any problem in meeting its interest and principal repayment obligations. The ability of a company to pay dividends depends on its *free cash flows.* Free cash flows are cash flows available after the company has met the requirements for additional investment in working capital and fixed assets. We observe that in 2015–16, the company generated Rs. 2046 crore after meeting its working capital requirements.

The company spent a net amount of Rs. 675 crore on fixed assets. That leaves Rs. 1,371 crore with the company for payment of dividend of 750 crore (dividend percent 750%). In 2014–15 also, the company had free cash flow of Rs. 808 crore to pay a dividend of Rs. 673 crore (dividend percent 610%). The company has been a high dividend payer and is expected to maintain the current level of dividend or only to marginally increase it. With increasing fresh investment in fixed assets, the company's free cash flows are only expected to increase in the future. We can, therefore, be reasonably confident of the company's ability to meet its obligations and to pay dividends.

3. **Whether the entity needs to raise more funds:** This question is important since it is not easy for every company to raise external funds by way of equity or debt. Debt funds are not easily available to companies that do not have a good track record of profitable performance. Raising money through equity is quite costly.

   We have seen that the company has been generating enough cash flows from its operations to meet its requirements of capital expenditure, interest and dividend payments. In addition, the company has Rs. 1,433 crore in current investments and Rs. 1,006 crore in non-current investments as on March 31, 2016 which the company can liquidate at the time of need. It does not appear that the company would need to raise more funds.

4. **Why is there a difference between the amount of net income and related net cash flows from operating activities:** The difference arises because the amount of profit before tax (Rs. 2,378 crore) is adjusted for:
   (a) *Non-cash items*: Depreciation, amortization, provision for doubtful debts, bad debts, unrealized foreign exchange gains and provision for diminution in the value of long-term investments (Rs. 298 crore).
   (b) *Non-operating items*: Interest income, dividend income, finance costs, profit on sale of long-term and short-term investments and profit on sale of fixed assets (–Rs. 97 crore).
   (c) *Change in working capital (Rs. 228 crore)*: There is a significant reduction of investment in receivables (Rs. 192 crore) and increase in credit from suppliers (Rs. 161 crore). Receivables and advances have increased by Rs. 141 crore and provisions have increased by Rs. 15 crore.
   (d) Actual amount paid for income tax (–Rs. 761 crore).
   (e) Net cash generated from operating activities is Rs. (2,378 + 298 – 97 + 228 – 761) = Rs. 2,046 crore.

5. **The effect of entity's investing and financing activities on its cash and other accounts:** There is a net cash outflow of Rs. 863 crore on account of the company's investing activities. These comprise of purchase and sale of fixed assets; purchase and sale of long-term and short-term investments; and income from dividend and interest. There is a net cash outflow of Rs. 771 crore on account of the company's financing activities which comprise of change in long-term borrowings, payment of interest on borrowings and payment of dividend. These two activities together account for a net cash outflow of Rs. 1,634 crore in 2015–16. There was a cash inflow of Rs. 2,046 crore from operating activities. The net increase in the cash balance during 2015–16 is, therefore, Rs. 412 crore (= Rs. 2,046 crore – Rs. 1,634 crore).

6. **The reasons behind change in the beginning and ending balance of cash and cash equivalents:** The balance of cash and cash equivalents was Rs. 863 crore on April 1, 2014. It has changed to Rs. 1,275 crore as on March 31, 2015. There is a net increase of Rs. 412 crore in the balance. This is the combined effect

of cash flows from three types of business activities: operating activities (cash inflow Rs. 2,046 crore), investing activities (cash outflow of Rs. 863 crore), and financing activities (cash outflow of Rs. 771 crore).

7. **The overall picture:** The company is in good financial health with high positive cash flows from operating activities which are more than sufficient to meet the company's requirement of reinvestment for growth, meet its obligations to its lenders and pay a handsome dividend to its shareholders. Investors can expect the company to keep growing as it has been making substantial investments in new assets year after year.

Summary – Review of Learning Objectives

1. **Understand the purpose of preparing the cash flow statement.** The purpose of the cash flow statement is to provide information about the company's ability to generate positive cash flows in future periods; the company's ability to meet its obligations and pay dividends; the company's need for external financing; reasons for difference between the amount of net income and related net cash flows from operating activities; both the cash and non-cash aspects of company's investing and financing activities; and causes of the change in the amount of cash and cash equivalents between the beginning and end of the accounting period.
2. **Understand the classification of cash flows from different activities.** Cash flow statement should report cash flows during the period from operating, investing and financing activities. Operating activities are the principal revenue producing activities of the enterprise and other activities that are not investing or financing activities. Investing activities are the acquisition and disposal of long-term assets and other investments not included in cash equivalents. Financing activities are the activities that result in changes in the size and composition of the owners' capital (including preference share capital in case of a company) and borrowings of an enterprise.
3. **Understand the difference between direct and indirect methods of computing cash flows from operating activities.** Cash flows from operating activities can be calculated using either the direct method or the indirect method. In case of direct method, gross cash receipts and gross cash payments are shown under major classes such as cash sales, receipts from debtors, commission and fee received and interest received, payments for purchases, payments to and for employees, operating expenses, interest payments and direct tax payments.

   Under the indirect method, the net profit or loss disclosed by the income statement is adjusted for non-cash items such as depreciation, provisions and unrealized foreign exchange gains or losses; change in current assets and current liabilities; and all other items for which the cash effects are on investing or financing cash flows.
4. **Understand how to deal with certain special items such as income taxes, foreign currency cash flows, cash flows from interest and dividend, etc. in preparing the cash flow statement.** An entity should record cash flows arising from transactions in a foreign currency in the entity's functional currency by applying to the foreign currency amount the exchange rate between the functional currency and the foreign currency on the date of the cash flow.

   Cash flows arising from interest paid and interest and dividends received in the case of a financial enterprise should be classified as cash flows arising from operating activities. In the case of other enterprises, cash flows arising from interest paid should be classified as cash flows from financing activities, while interest and dividends received should be classified as cash flows from investing activities. Dividends paid should be classified as cash flows from financing activities.

Cash flows arising from taxes on income are to be separately disclosed and need to be classified as cash flows from operating activities unless they can be specifically identified with financing and investing activities.

5. **Understand how to deal with financing and investing activities that do not involve any cash flow.** Investing and financing transactions that do not require the use of cash or cash equivalents should be excluded from the cash flow statement. Such transactions should be disclosed elsewhere in the financial statements in a way that provides all the relevant information about these investing and financing activities.

Glossary

- **Cash** includes cash (cash on hand, demand deposits with bank) and cash equivalents.
- **Cash equivalents** are short-term, highly liquid investments that are readily convertible into known amounts of cash, and are subject to an insignificant risk of changes in value.
- **Cash inflows** are transactions which increase cash.
- **Cash outflows** are transactions which decrease cash.
- **Financing activities** are activities that result in changes in the size and composition of the owner's capital (including preference share capital in case of a company) and borrowings of an enterprise.
- **Functional currency** is the currency of the primary economic environment in which the entity generates and expends cash.
- **Investing activities** include the acquisition and disposal of long-term assets and other investments not included in cash equivalents.
- **Operating activities** are the principal revenue producing activities of the enterprise and other activities that are not investing or financing activities.

Solved Problems

1. From the income statement and the balance sheet of Strong Ltd. (Tables 11.1 and 11.2), you are required to prepare a cash flow statement using: (i) direct method and (ii) indirect method.

Table 11.1 Income statement and reconciliation of earnings for the year ended March 31, 2015 **(Rs.)**

Net sales		4,032,000
Less: Cost of sales	3,168,000	
Depreciation	96,000	

(*Continued*)

Table 11.1 (Continued)

		(Rs.)
Salaries and wages	384,000	
Operating expenses	128,000	
Provision for taxation	140,800	
		3,916,800
Net operating profit		115,200
Non-recurring income (profit on sale of equipment)		19,200
Profit for the year		134,400
Retained earnings (balance in profit and loss account b/f)		242,880
		377,280
Dividend declared and paid during the year		115,200
Profit and loss account balance as on March 31, 2015		262,080

Table 11.2 Comparative balance sheets

(Rs.)

Particulars	As on March 31, 2014	As on March 31, 2015
Fixed assets:		
Land	76,800	153,600
Building and equipment	576,000	921,600
Current Assets:		
Cash	96,000	115,200
Debtors	268,800	297,600
Stock	422,400	153,600
Advances	12,480	14,400
	1,452,480	1,656,000
Capital	576,000	710,400
Surplus in profit and loss A/c	242,880	262,080
Sundry creditors	384,000	374,400
Outstanding expenses	38,400	76,800
Income-tax payable	19,200	21,120
Accumulated depreciation on building and equipment	192,000	211,200
	1,452,480	1,656,000

The cost of equipment sold was Rs. 115,200.

Solution: See Tables 11.3–11.9.

Table 11.3 Statement showing cash receipts from customers

	(Rs.)
Sales	4,032,000
Add: Debtors at the beginning	268,800
	4,300,800
Less: Debtors at the end	297,600
Cash receipts from customers	4,003,200

Table 11.4 Statement showing cash payments to suppliers and employees

	(Rs.)	(Rs.)
Cost of goods sold		3,168,000
Add: Operating expenses		128,000
Salaries and wages		384,000
		3,680,000
Add: Creditors at the beginning	384,000	
Outstanding expenses at the beginning	38,400	
Stock at the end	153,600	
Advances at the end	14,400	
		590,400
		4,270,400
Less: Creditors at the end	374,400	
Outstanding expenses at the end	76,800	
Stock at the beginning	422,400	
Advances at the beginning	12,480	
		886,080
Cash paid to suppliers and employees		3,384,320

Table 11.5 Income tax payable account

	(Rs.)		(Rs.)
To income tax A/c (tax paid)	138,880	By balance b/d	19,200
To balance c/d	21,120	By profit and loss A/c	140,800
	160,000		160,000

Table 11.6 Accumulated depreciation account

	(Rs.)		(Rs.)
To building and equipment A/c	76,800	By balance b/d	192,000
(Dep on equipment sold)		By profit and loss A/c	96,000
To balance c/d	211,200	(provision for the year)	
	288,000		288,000

Table 11.7 Building and equipment account

	(Rs.)		(Rs.)
To balance b/d	576,000	By accumulated dep A/c	76,800
To bank A/c	460,800	(dep on equipment sold)	
(purchase of equipment)		By bank A/c (sale of equipment)	57,600
To profit and loss A/c	19,200	By balance c/d	921,600
(profit on sale of equipment)			
	1,056,000		1,056,000

Table 11.8 Cash flow statement of Strong Ltd. for the year ended March 31, 2015 (direct method)

	(Rs.)
Cash flows from operating activities	
Cash receipts from customers	4,003,200
Cash paid to suppliers and employees	(3,384,320)
Cash generated from operations	618,880
Income tax paid	(138,880)
A. Net cash inflow from operating activities	480,000
Cash flows from investing activities	
Purchase of land	(76,800)
Purchase of building and equipment	(460,800)
Sale of equipment	57,600
B. Net cash outflow from investing activities	(480,000)
Cash flows from financing activities	
Issue of share capital	134,400
Dividend paid	(115,200)
C. Net cash inflow from financing activities	19,200
Net increase in cash and cash equivalents during the year (A + B + C)	19,200
Cash and cash equivalents at the beginning of the year	96,000
Cash and cash equivalents at the end	115,200

Table 11.9 Cash flow statement of Strong Ltd. for the year ended March 31, 2015 (indirect method)

	(Rs.)
Cash flows from operating activities	
Net profit before taxation and extraordinary items	256,000
Adjustment for	
Depreciation	96,000
Operating profit before working capital changes	352,000
Increase in debtors	(28,800)
Decrease in stock	268,800
Increase in advances	(1,920)
Decrease in creditors	(9,600)
Increase in outstanding expenses	38,400
Cash generated from operations	618,800
Income tax paid	(138,800)
A. Net cash inflow from operating activities	480,000
Cash flows from investing activities	
Purchase of land	(76,800)
Purchase of building and equipment	(460,800)
Sale of equipment	57,600
B. Net cash outflow from investing activities	(480,000)
Cash flows from financing activities	
Issue of share capital	134,400
Dividend paid	(115,200)
C. Net cash inflow from financing activities	19,200
Net increase in cash and cash equivalents during the year (A + B + C)	19,200
Cash and cash equivalents at the beginning of the year	96,000
Cash and cash equivalents at the end	115,200

2. From the summarized cash account of S Ltd. (Tables 11.10 and 11.11), prepare the cash flow statement for the year ended March 31, 2015 in accordance with Ind AS-7 using direct method.

Table 11.10 Summarized cash account

	(Rs. in '000)		(Rs. in '000)
Opening balance	50	Payment to suppliers	2,000
Issue of share capital	300	Purchase of fixed assets	200
Received from customers	2,800	Overhead expenses	200

(*Continued*)

Table 11.10 (Continued)

	(Rs. in '000)		(Rs. in '000)
Sale of fixed assets	100	Wages and salaries	100
		Tax paid	250
		Dividend paid	50
		Bank loan	300
		Closing balance	150
	3,250		3,250

Solution:

Table 11.11 Cash flow statement for the year ended March 31, 2015

		(Rs. in '000)
Cash flow from operating activities		
Cash received from customers		2,800
Less: Cash paid to suppliers	2,000	
Cash paid for overhead expenses	200	
Cash paid for wages and salaries	100	
		2,300
		500
Less: Income tax paid		250
Net cash generated from operating activities		250
Cash flow from investing activities		
Sale of fixed assets	100	
Less: Purchase of fixed assets	200	
Net cash used in investing activities		(100)
Cash flow from financing activities		
Received from issue of share capital	300	
Less: Payment of bank loan	300	
Payment of dividend	50	
	350	(50)
Net cash used in financing activities		
Net increase in cash and equivalents		100
Add: Cash and equivalents at the beginning of the year		50
Cash and equivalents at the end of the year		150

3. Prepare the cash flow statement of Gamma Ltd. for the year ended March 31, 2015 from the following information:

1. Sales for the year: Rs. 1.35 billion, out of which 60% was cash sales.
2. Purchases for the year amounted to Rs. 550 million, out of which 80% was credit purchase.
3. Administrative and selling expenses amounted to Rs. 180 million, and salary paid was Rs. 220 million.
4. The company redeemed debentures of Rs. 200 million at a premium of 10%. Debenture holders were issued equity shares of Rs. 150 million towards redemption and the balance was paid in cash. Debenture interest paid during the year was Rs. 15 million.
5. Dividend paid during the year amounted to Rs. 100 million. Dividend distribution tax was paid @ 17%.
6. Investments costing Rs. 120 million were sold at a profit of Rs. 24 million.
7. Rs. 80 million was paid towards income tax during the year.
8. A new plant costing Rs. 210 million was purchased in part exchange for an old plant. The book value of the old plant was Rs. 120 million, but the vendor took over the old plant at a value of Rs. 100 million only. The balance was paid to the vendor in cash.
9. Closing debtors were higher than opening debtors by Rs. 50 million.
10. Trade creditors on March 31, 2015 exceed the outstanding on March 31, 2014 by Rs. 20 million.
11. Cash in hand and at Bank on March 31, 2014 was Rs. 60 million.

Solution:

Cash Flow Statement of Gamma Limited for the Year Ended March 31, 2015

Direct Method	(Rs. in Million)	(Rs. in Million)
Cash flow from operating activities:		
Cash receipt from customers (sales)	1,300	
Cash paid to suppliers and expenses (530 + 180 + 220)	(930)	
Cash flow from operation	370	
Less: Tax paid	(80)	
Net cash from operating activities		290
Cash flow from investing activities:		
Purchase of fixed assets (210 – 100)	(110)	
Sale of investments	144	
Net cash from investing activities		34
Cash flow from financing activities:		
Dividend paid	(117)	
Redemption of debentures (220 – 150)	(70)	
Interest on debentures	(15)	
Net cash from financing activities		(202)
		122
Add: Opening balance of cash in hand and at bank		60
Cash in hand and at bank on March 31, 2015		182

Working Notes

(a) Calculation of cash receipt from sales

Cash sales (1,350 × 60%)	810
Cash collection from credit sales (1,350 × 40%) – 50 (increase in debtors)	490
	1,300

(b) Calculation of cash paid for purchases

Cash purchases (550 × 20%)	110
Cash payment for credit purchases (550 × 80%) – 20 (increase in creditors)	420
	530

4. Prepare the cash flow statement from investing activities of Creative Furnishings Ltd. for the year ended March 31, 2015.

	(Rs.)
Plant acquired by issue of 8% debentures	156,000
Claim received for loss of plant in fire	49,600
Unsecured loans given to subsidiaries	485,000
Interest on loan received from subsidiary companies	82,500
Pre-acquisition dividend received on investment made	62,400
Debenture interest paid	116,000
Term loan repaid	425,000
Interest received on investment (TDS of Rs. 8,200 was deducted on the above interest)	68,000
Book value of plant sold (loss incurred Rs. 9,600)	84,000

Solution:

Cash Flow Statement of Creative Furnishings Ltd. for the Year Ended March 31, 2015

Cash flows from investing activities	
Unsecured loans given to subsidiaries	(485,000)
Interest on loan received from subsidiary companies	82,500
Pre-acquisition dividend received on investment made	62,400
Interest received on investment	68,000
Sale of plant	74,400
Cash used in investing activities before extraordinary items	(197,700)
Claim received for loss of plant in fire	49,600
Net cash flow from investing activities	(148,100)

5. The summarized balance sheets of X Ltd. as on March 31, 2014 and 2015 are given in Table 11.12.

Table 11.12 Summarized balance sheet of X Ltd. as on March 31, 2014 and 2015

Liabilities	As on March 31, 2014 (Rs.)	As on March 31, 2015 (Rs.)
Equity share capital	1,000,000	1,250,000
Capital reserve	---	10,000
General reserve	250,000	300,000
Profit and loss A/c	150,000	180,000
Long-term loan from the bank	500,000	400,000
Sundry creditors	500,000	400,000
Provision for taxation	50,000	60,000
Proposed dividends	100,000	125,000
	2,550,000	2,725,000
Assets		
Land and building	500,000	480,000
Machinery	750,000	920,000
Investment	100,000	50,000
Stock	300,000	280,000
Sundry debtors	400,000	420,000
Cash in hand	200,000	165,000
Cash at bank	300,000	410,000
	2,550,000	2,725,000

Additional information:

1. Dividend of Rs. 100,000 was paid during the year ended March 31, 2015.
2. Machinery purchased during the year for Rs. 125,000.
3. Machinery of another company was purchased for a consideration of Rs. 100,000, payable in equity shares.
4. Income tax provided during the year is Rs. 55,000.
5. Company sold some investment at a profit of Rs. 10,000, which was credited to capital reserve.
6. There was no sale of machinery during the year.
7. Depreciation written off on land and building is Rs. 20,000.

From the above particulars, prepare a cash flow statement for the year ended March 31, 2014 as per Ind AS-7 (indirect method).

Solution:

Cash Flow Statement for the Year Ended March 31, 2015

	(Rs.)	(Rs.)
I. Cash flows from operating activities		
Net profit made during the year (W.N.1)	260,000	
Adjustment for depreciation on machinery (W.N.2)	55,000	
Adjustment for depreciation on land and building	20,000	
Operating profit before change in working capital	335,000	
Decrease in stock	20,000	
Increase in sundry debtors	(20,000)	
Decrease in sundry creditors	(100,000)	
Income tax paid	(45,000)	
Net cash from operating activities		190,000
II. Cash flows from investing activities		
Purchase on machinery	(1,25,000)	
Sale of investments	60,000	
		(65,000)
III. Cash flows from financing activities		
Issue of equity shares (2,50,000 – 1,00,000)	1,50,000	
Repayment of long-term loan	(1,00,000)	
Dividend paid	(1,00,000)	
		(50,000)
Net increase in cash and cash equivalent		75,000
Cash and cash equivalents at the beginning of the period		500,000
Cash and cash equivalents at the end of the period		575,000

Working Notes:

(i) Net profit made during the year ended March 31, 2015

	(Rs.)
Increase in P & L (Cr.) balance	30,000
Add: Transfer to general reserve	50,000
Add: Provision for taxation made during the year	55,000
Add: Provided for proposed dividend during the year	1,25,000
	2,60,000

(ii) Calculation of depreciation on machinery:

	(Rs.)	(Rs.)
Machinery (beginning balance)	750,000	
Purchase of machinery for cash	125,000	
Purchase of machinery against shares	100,000	
		975,000
Less: Machinery (ending balance)		920,000
Depreciation charged during the year		55,000

(iii) Calculation of income tax paid

Beginning balance in the provision for taxation account	50,000
Add: Provision made during the year	55,000
	105,000
Less: Ending balance in the provision for taxation account	60,000
Tax paid during the year	45,000

(iv) Calculation of dividend proposed for the year

Ending balance in the proposed dividend account	125,000
Add: Dividend paid during the year	100,000
	225,000
Less: Beginning balance in the proposed dividend account	100,000
Dividend proposed for the year	125,000

Multiple Choice Questions

1. Interest received on long-term investments is shown under ________.
   - **a.** operating activities
   - **b.** financing activities
   - **c.** investing activities
   - **d.** none of the above

2. What information would you find in a statement of cash flow that you would not be able to get from the other two primary financial statements?
   - **a.** Cash provided by or used in financing activities
   - **b.** Cash balance at the end of the period
   - **c.** Total liabilities due to creditors at the end of the period
   - **d.** Net income

3. A company had a net income of Rs. 165,000 during 2015. It provided for a depreciation of Rs. 75,000 during the year. During the year, accounts receivable increased by Rs. 55,000 and accounts payable increased by Rs. 25,000. The company's cash flow from operating activities was ________.

a. Rs. 320,000
b. Rs. 170,000
c. Rs. 210,000
d. Rs. 120,000

4. During 2015, a company raised Rs. 5,000,000 by issuing shares, and repaid a loan of Rs. 750,000. It received dividend of Rs. 40,000 and interest of Rs. 50,000 from its investments. It also paid a dividend of Rs. 60, 000 to its shareholders and interest of Rs. 75, 000 on its loans. Its cash flow from financing activity was ________.
   a. Rs. 4,115,000
   b. Rs. 4,225,000
   c. Rs. 4,230,000
   d. Rs. 4,865,000

5. During 2015, a company purchased land for Rs. 3,750,000. The company also sold a building for Rs. 950,000. The company's cash flow from investing activity was ________.
   a. Rs. 46,50,000
   b. Rs. 28,50,000
   c. Rs. 28,00,000
   d. Rs. 35,50,000

6. Dividend paid is always classified as a/an ________.
   a. operating activity
   b. investing activity
   c. financing activity
   d. none of the above

7. Decrease in the amount of creditors results in ________.
   a. increase in cash
   b. decrease in cash
   c. decrease in assets
   d. no change in assets

8. Which of the following is **not** a financing activity in the cash flow statement of a non-finance company?
   a. Issue of shares
   b. Payment of dividends
   c. Receipt of dividends
   d. Borrowing money from a bank

Review Questions

1. What is a cash flow statement?
2. What are the main purposes of preparing a cash flow statement?
3. Describe the three kinds of activities used for reporting cash flows in the cash flow statement, giving examples of cash flows from different activities.
4. Financing and investing activities also involve certain non-cash transactions. Give some examples of such transactions and state how these transactions are disclosed.
5. Describe the direct method of determining cash flows from operating activities.
6. State the adjustments made to the income figure for arriving at the cash flows from operating activities under the indirect method.
7. Define cash equivalents. Give three examples.
8. Describe the treatment of interest and dividend income and expense in the cash flow statement prepared by financial enterprises and other enterprises.

Practice Problems

1. Rupal Products Ltd. presents to you the following balance sheets and profit and loss account (Tables 11.13 and 11.14).

Table 11.13 Balance sheet of Rupal Products Ltd.

	As on March 31, 2014 (Rs.)	As on March 31, 2015 (Rs.)
Liabilities		
Equity share capital	2,500,000	2,500,000
Profit and loss account	2,075,000	2,365,000
14% Debentures	1,500,000	1,250,000
Sundry creditors	256,250	304,250
Expenses outstanding	54,500	68,500
Provision for bad debts	20,000	22,500
	6,405,750	6,510,750
Assets		
Fixed assets	6,000,000	6,500,000
Less: Provision for depreciation	2,000,000	2,450,000
	4,000,000	4,050,000
Investments	625,000	250,000
Stock	1,033,250	1,267,750
Sundry debtors	400,000	450,000
Cash at bank	335,500	483,500
Preliminary expenses	12,000	9,000
	6,405,750	6,510,750

Table 11.14 Profit and loss account for the year ended March 31, 2015

	(Rs.)		(Rs.)
To: Opening stock	1,033,250	By sales	9,100,500
Purchases	4,884,500	Closing stock	1,267,750
Gross profit	4,450,500		
	10,368,250		10,368,250
To: Operating expenses	1,958,750	By gross profit	4,450,500
Provision for bad debts	2,500	Law sult compensation	125,000
Provision for depreciation	450,000	Interest on investment	65,000
Preliminary expenses written off	3,000	Profit on sale of investment	18,750
Interest on debentures	192,500		
Income tax paid	821,000		
Net profit	1,231,500		
	4,659,250		4,659,250

You are required to prepare the cash flow statement for the year ended March 31, 2015 using: (i) direct method and (ii) indirect method.

2. Magnus Technologies Ltd. presents to you the following balance sheets and profit and loss account (Table 11.15).

Table 11.15 Balance sheet of Magnus Technologies Ltd.

	As on March 31, 2015 (Rs.)	As on March 31, 2014 (Rs.)
Liabilities		
Equity share capital	600,000	450,000
8% Preference share capital	180,000	225,000
General reserve	75,000	60,000
Profit and loss account	72,000	45,000
Proposed dividend	75,000	63,000
Sundry creditors	94,500	67,500
Expenses outstanding	54,000	45,000
Provision for taxation	75,000	60,000
	1,225,500	1,015,500
Assets		
Goodwill	120,000	150,000
Land and building	255,000	300,000
Plant and machinery	300,000	120,000
Investments	45,000	30,000
Sundry debtors	300,000	240,000
Stock	163,500	115,500
Cash in hand	15,000	22,500
Cash at bank	12,000	15,000
Preliminary expenses	15,000	22,500
	1,225,500	1,015,500

The additional information is as follows:

1. An interim dividend of Rs. 30,000 has been paid in 2014–15.
2. A machine was sold for Rs. 15,000. The written-down value of the machine was Rs. 18,000. Depreciation of Rs. 15,000 is charged on plant and machinery in 2014–15.
3. Depreciation charged on building is Rs. 7,500 for the year.

You are required to prepare a cash flow statement for the year ended March 31, 2015. Explain why the company's cash balance decreased despite the company earning a profit during the year.

3. The information given in Table 11.16 is available from the books of Standard Company Ltd.

Table 11.16 Extracts from books of account of Standard Company Ltd.

(Rs.)

	2014	2015
Profit made during the year		250,000
Income received in advance	500	600
Prepaid expenses	1,600	1,400
Debtors	105,000	115,000
Creditors	58,000	55,000
Outstanding expenses	2,500	2,000
Accrued income	1,500	1,200

Calculate cash flow from operations.

4. From Table 11.17, calculate cash from operations.

Table 11.17 Profit and loss account for the year ended March 31, 2015

	(Rs.)		(Rs.)
To Salaries	50,000	By gross profit	250,000
Rent	10,000	Profit on sale of land	50,000
Depreciation	20,000	Income tax refund	30,000
Loss on sale of plant	10,000		
Goodwill written off	40,000		
Proposed dividend	50,000		
Provision for tax	50,000		
Net profit	100,000		
	330,000		330,000

5. Ms. Jyoti of Star Oils Limited has collected the information given in Table 11.18 for the preparation of cash flow statement for the year 2015. Prepare the cash flow statement for the year 2015.

Table 11.18 Extracts from books of accounts of Star Oil Mills for the year 2015

	(Rs. in Million)
Net profit	2,500
Dividend (including dividend tax) paid	853.5
Provision for income tax	500

(Continued)

Table 11.18 (Continued)

	(Rs. in Million)
Income tax paid during the year	424.8
Loss on sale of assets (net)	4
Book value of assets sold	18.5
Depreciation charged to profit and loss account	2,000
Amortization of capital grant	0.6
Profit on sale of investments	10
Carrying amount of investments sold	2,776.5
Interest income on investments	250.6
Interest expenses	1,000
Interest paid during the year	1,052
Increase in working capital (excluding cash and bank balance)	5,607.5
Purchase of fixed assets	1,456
Investment in joint venture	385
Expenditure on construction work-in-progress	3,474
Proceeds from calls-in-arrear	0.2
Receipt of grant for capital projects	1.2
Proceeds from long-term borrowings	2,598
Proceeds from short-term borrowings	2,057.5
Opening cash and bank balance	500.3
Closing cash and bank balance	698.8

6. Balance sheets of XYZ Ltd. as on December 31, 2014 and 2015 are given in Table 11.19.

Table 11.19 Balance sheet of XYZ Ltd.

	As on December 31, 2014 (Rs.)	As on December 31, 2015 (Rs.)
Liabilities		
Equity share capital	450,000	450,000
General reserve	300,000	310,000
Profit and Loss account	56,000	68,000
Sundry creditors	168,000	134,000
Mortgage loan	----	270,000
Provision for taxation	75,000	10,000
	1,049,000	1,242,000

(Continued)

Table 11.19 (Continued)

	As on December 31, 2014 (Rs.)	As on December 31, 2015 (Rs.)
Assets		
Fixed assets	400,000	320,000
Investments	50,000	60,000
Sundry debtors	210,000	455,000
Stock	240,000	210,000
Cash at bank	149,000	197,000
	1,049,000	1,242,000

The additional information is as follows:

1. Investments costing Rs. 8,000 were sold during the year 2015 for Rs. 8,500.
2. During the year, a part of fixed assets costing Rs. 10,000 was sold for Rs. 12,000 and the profit was included in the profit and loss account.
3. Provision for tax made during the year was Rs. 9,000.
4. Dividend paid during the year amounted to Rs. 40,000.

You are required to prepare a cash flow statement for the year ended December 31, 2015.

7. From the information as contained in income statement and balance sheet of Ril Ltd. (Tables 11.20 and 11.21), you are required to prepare a cash flow statement using: (i) direct method and (ii) indirect method.

Table 11.20 Income statement for the year ended March 31, 2015

	(Rs. in Million)	(Rs. in Million)
Net sales		203,010
Less: Cost of sales	159,840	
Depreciation	25,340	
Salaries and wages	3,750	
Operating expenses	8,910	
Provision for tax	570	
		198,410
Net operating profit		4,600
Add: Other income	6,450	
Profit on sale of asset	420	6,870
Profit for the year		11,470

(Continued)

Table 11.20 (Continued)

	(Rs. in Million)	(Rs. in Million)
Add: Balance of profit and loss account b/f		111,830
		123,300
Less: Dividend declared	4,200	
Tax on dividend	460	
		4,660
		118,640
Add: Share premium account		7,720
Profit and loss account as on March 31, 2015		126,360

Table 11.21 Comparative balance sheets

	As on March 31, 2015		As on March 31, 2014	
	(Rs. in Million)	(Rs. in Million)	(Rs. in Million)	(Rs. in Million)
Assets:				
Fixed assets:				
Land		10,290		9,010
Buildings and equipment		236,340		211,870
Gross block		246,630		220,880
Less: Accumulated depreciation		92,140		66.920
Net block		154,490		153,960
Investments		60,670		42,950
Current assets:				
Cash	1,0820		4,8980	
Debtors	8420		4570	
Stock	18,230		1,4090	
Advances	40,590		1,6760	
Other current assets	480		250	
		78,540		84,650
Liabilities:		293,700		281,560
Equity capital		1,0530		9,330
Preference capital		2,930		2,530
Reserves and surplus		126,360		111,830
Loans		115,200		116,500

(Continued)

Table 11.21 (Continued)

	As on March 31, 2015		As on March 31, 2014	
	(Rs. in Million)	(Rs. in Million)	(Rs. in Million)	(Rs. in Million)
Sundry creditors		2,9590		33,450
Provision for tax		2,660		5,440
Other liabilities		6,430		2,480
		293,700		281,560

Cost of equipment sold was Rs. 400 million.

8. From the information as contained in income statement and balance sheet of XYZ Ltd. (Tables 11.22 and 11.23), you are required to prepare a cash flow statement using the indirect method.

Table 11.22 Income statement for the year ended December 31, 2015

	(Rs. in Million)
Net sales	10,000
Cost of sales	(5,300)
Operating expenses	(3,520)
Net operating profit	1,180
Loss on sale of equipment	(40)
Profit before tax	1,140
Income taxes	(480)
Net income	660

Table 11.23 Comparative balance sheets

	As on December 31, 2015		As on December 31, 2014	
	(Rs. in Million)	(Rs. in Million)	(Rs. in Million)	(Rs. in Million)
Sources of funds:				
Shareholders' funds				
Share capital	1,400		1,400	
Retained earnings	1,100		920	
Loan funds		2,500		2,320
Bonus payable		1,350		400
		3,850		2,720

(Continued)

Table 11.23 (Continued)

	As on December 31, 2015		As on December 31, 2014	
	(Rs. in Million)	(Rs. in Million)	(Rs. in Million)	(Rs. in Million)
Application of funds:				
Fixed assets:				
Plant and equipment	4,300		3,090	
Less: Accumulated depreciation	(2,180)		(1,940)	
		2,120		1,150
Investments		600		750
Current assets:				
Cash	260		100	
Debtors	1,800		2,700	
Stock	2,050		1,600	
Prepaid expenses	170		200	
	4,280		4,600	
Less: Current liabilities & provisions:				
Sundry creditors	2,300		3,100	
Provision for tax	150		80	
Accrued liabilities	700		600	
	3,150		3,780	
		1,130		820
		3,850		2,720

Additional information:

(a) Dividends of Rs. 480 million were paid in 2015.

(b) The loss on sale of equipment of Rs. 40 million reflects the transaction in which the equipment with an original cost of Rs. 120 million and accumulated depreciation of Rs. 50 million was sold for Rs. 30 million in cash.

9. Balance sheets of Anupama Trading Company as on January 1, 2015 and December 31, 2015 are given in Table 11.24.

Table 11.24 Balance sheets of Anupama Trading Company

	As on January 1, 2015 (Rs.)	As on December 31, 2015 (Rs.)
Liabilities		
Equity share capital	1,250,000	1,530,000
Sarika's loan	250,000	
Loan from bank	400,000	500,000
Creditors	400,000	440,000
	2,300,000	2,470,000
Assets		
Machinery	800,000	550,000
Land	400,000	500,000
Building	350,000	600,000
Sundry debtors	300,000	500,000
Stock	350,000	250,000
Cash at bank	100,000	70,000
	2,300,000	2,470,000

The additional information is as follows:

(a) Provision for depreciation against machinery as on January 1, 2015 was Rs. 250,000 and on December 31, 2015 was Rs. 400,000.

(b) During the year, a machine costing Rs. 100,000 (total depreciation written off Rs. 30,000) was sold for Rs. 50,000.

(c) Net profit made during the year was Rs. 450,000.

You are required to prepare a cash flow statement for the year ended December 31, 2015.

10. From the information given in Table 11.25 related to Bright Ltd., prepare the cash flow statement for the year ended on March 31, 2015.

Table 11.25 Comparative balance sheets of Bright Ltd.

	As on March 31, 2014 (Rs.)	As on March 31, 2015 (Rs.)
Liabilities		
Equity share capital	300,000	350,000
18% Preference share capital	200,000	100,000
14% debentures	100,000	200,000
Reserves and surplus	110,000	270,000

(Continued)

Table 11.25 (Continued)

	As on March 31, 2014 (Rs.)	As on March 31, 2015 (Rs.)
Creditors	70,000	145,000
Provision for doubtful debts	10,000	15,000
	790,000	1,080,000
Assets		
Fixed assets (net)	510,000	620,000
10% Investments	30,000	80,000
Sundry debtors	100,000	210,000
Stock	100,000	90,000
Cash at bank	40,000	75,000
Discount on debentures	10,000	5,000
	790,000	1,080,000

You are informed that during the year:

(a) A machine with a book value of Rs. 40,000 was sold for Rs. 25,000.
(b) Depreciation charged during the year was Rs. 70,000.
(c) Preference shares were redeemed on March 31, 2015 at a premium of 5%.
(d) An interim dividend of 15% was paid on equity shares on March 31, 2015. Preference dividend was also paid on March 31, 2015.
(e) New shares and debentures were issued on March 31, 2015.

You are required to prepare a cash flow statement for the year ended March 31, 2015.

11. From the information given in Table 11.26, prepare the cash flow statement for Smile Ltd.

Table 11.26 Extracts from books of accounts of Smile Ltd.

	As on March 31, 2014 (Rs. in '000)	As on March 31, 2015 (Rs. in '000)
Equity and liabilities		
Shareholders' funds:		
Share capital	1,800	2,000
Reserves and surplus:		
General reserve	50	30
Profit and loss account	140	160

(Continued)

Table 11.26 (Continued)

	As on March 31, 2014 (Rs. in '000)	As on March 31, 2015 (Rs. in '000)
Non-current liabilities:		
Loan on mortgage @ 8% (taken on July 1, 2014)	---	50
Current liabilities:		
Bank overdraft	115	114
Trade payables	22	40
Short-term provisions:		
Provision for final dividend	90	80
	2,217	2,474
Assets		
Non-current assets:		
Freehold building	1,000	1,160
Machinery and plant	340	490
Furniture and fittings	7	6
Goodwill	150	130
Investment in shares	100	120
Preliminary expenses	15	5
Current assets:		
Inventories	440	422
Trade receivables	160	134
Prepaid expenses	4	5
Cash in hand	1	2
	2,217	2,474

Additional information:

(a) Depreciation on freehold building @ 2½% on cost Rs. 12,00,000; on machinery and plant @ 10% on cost Rs. 5,00,000; on furniture and fitting @ 5% on cost Rs. 10,000.
(b) Dividend received Rs. 6,000 was used in writing down the book value of investment in shares.
(c) Goodwill was written off out of the general reserve.
(d) The proposed dividend for the year ended March 31, 2014 was paid off and the interim dividend of Rs. 60,000 was paid out of profit and loss account.

12. Prepare a cash flow statement from the particulars given in Table 11.27 relating to Comfort Hotel Ltd. Also explain why does the company's cash balance decreased inspite of the company earning a profit during the year.

Table 11.27 Comparative balance sheets of Comfort Hotel Ltd.

	As on March 31, 2014 (Rs.)	As on March 31, 2015 (Rs.)
I. Equity and liabilities		
(1) Shareholders' funds		
(a) Share capital	800,000	800,000
(b) Reserves and surplus	900,000	953,600
(2) Non-current liabilities		
(a) Debentures	300,000	330,000
(b) Provision for depreciation	320,000	470,000
(3) Current liabilities		
(a) Trade payables	282,000	229,000
(b) Income tax payable	28,000	41,000
Total	2,630,000	2,823,600
II. Assets		
(1) Non-current assets		
(a) Fixed assets	1,500,000	1,780,000
(b) Investments	220,000	205,000
(2) Current assets		
(a) Inventories	650,000	614,000
(b) Trade receivables	205,000	216,000
(c) Cash	15,000	7,000
(d) Bank	40,000	1,600
Total	2,630,000	2,823,600

Additional information:

(a) Fixed assets for Rs. 200,000 were purchased during the year for cash.
(b) Fixed assets costing Rs. 40,000, with accumulated depreciation of Rs. 17,000, were sold for Rs. 10,000 during the year.
(c) Debentures of the face value of Rs. 1,20,000 were issued in exchange for fixed assets during the year.
(d) Debentures of Rs. 90,000 were redeemed during the year at par.
(e) Investments for Rs. 45,000 were purchased during the year.
(f) Some investments costing Rs. 60,000 were sold for Rs. 86,000 during the year.
(g) Interest on investments received during the year was Rs. 8,000.
(h) Debenture interest paid during the years was 42,000.
(i) Dividend @15% was paid on share capital along with Rs. 12,000 for dividend tax.

13. A company has provided you the details given in Table 11.28.

Table 11.28 Balance sheet as on December 31, 2014 and December 31, 2015

	December 31, 2014 (Rs.)	December 31, 2015 (Rs.)
Liabilities		
Share capital	70,000	74,000
Debentures	12,000	6,000
Reserve for doubtful debts	700	800
Trade creditors	10,360	11,840
Profit and loss a/c	10,040	10,560
	103,100	1,03,200
Assets		
Cash	9,000	7,800
Debtors	14,900	17,700
Stock	49,200	42,700
Land	20,000	30,000
Goodwill	10,000	5,000
	103,100	103,200

Additional information:

(a) Dividend paid is Rs. 3,500.
(b) Land purchased for Rs. 10,000.

Prepare a cash flow statement as per Ind AS-7.

14. Raj Ltd. gives you the following information for the year ended March 31, 2015:

(a) Sales for the year Rs. 4,800,000. The company sold goods for cash only.
(b) Cost of goods sold was 75% of sales.
(c) Closing inventory was higher than the opening inventory by Rs. 50,000.
(d) Trade creditors on March 31, 2006 exceed the outstanding on March 31, 2005 by Rs. 100,000.
(e) Tax paid during the year amounts to Rs. 150,000.
(f) Amounts paid to trade creditors during the year Rs. 3,550,000.
(g) Administrative and selling expenses paid Rs. 360,000.
(h) One new machinery was acquired in December, 2005 for Rs. 600,000.
(i) Dividend paid during the year Rs. 1,20,000.
(j) Cash in hand and at Bank on March 31, 2006 was Rs. 70,000.
(k) Cash in hand and at Bank on April 1, 2005 was Rs. 50,000.

Prepare the cash flow statement for the year ended March 31, 2006 as per the prescribed accounting standard.

15. The following figures have been extracted from the books of X Limited for the year ended on March 31, 2015. You are required to prepare a cash flow statement.

(a) Net profit before considering income tax and income from law suits, but after taking into account the following items was Rs. 2 million.

  (i) Depreciation on fixed assets: Rs. 500,000.

  (ii) Discount on issue of debentures written off: Rs. 30,000.

  (iii) Interest on debentures paid: Rs. 350,000.

  (iv) Book value of investments: Rs. 300,000 (sale of investments for Rs. 320,000).

  (v) Interest received on investments: Rs. 60,000.

  (vi) Compensation received Rs. 90,000 by the company in a suit filed.

(b) Income tax paid during the year: Rs. 1,050,000.

(c) 15,000, 10% preference shares of Rs. 100 each were redeemed on March 31, 2015 at a premium of 5%. Further the company issued 50,000 equity shares of Rs. 10 each at a premium of 20% on April 2, 2014. Dividend on preference shares were paid at the time of redemption.

(d) Dividends paid for the year 2013–2014 Rs. 500,000 and interim dividend paid Rs. 300,000 for the year 2014–2015.

(e) Land was purchased on April 2, 2014 for Rs. 240,000 for which the company issued 20,000 equity shares of Rs. 10 each at a premium of 20% to the land owner as consideration.

(f) Current assets and current liabilities in the beginning and at the end of the years are given in Table 11.29.

Table 11.29 Current assets and current liabilities

	As on March 31, 2014 (Rs.)	As on March 31, 2015 (Rs.)
Stock	1,200,000	1,318,000
Sundry debtors	208,000	213,100
Cash in hand	196,300	35,300
Bills receivable	50,000	40,000
Bills payable	45,000	40,000
Sundry creditors	166,000	171,300
Outstanding expenses	75,000	81,800

16. Balance sheet of Raman Ltd. is given in Table 11.30.

Table 11.30 Balance sheet of Raman Ltd.

(Rs. in '000)

Liabilities	March 31, 2014	March 31, 2015	Assets	March 31, 2014	March 31, 2015
Share capital	500	500	Land & building	300	300
9% Debentures	200	160	Machinery	164	180

(Continued)

Table 11.30 (Continued)

(Rs. in '000)

Liabilities	March 31, 2014	March 31, 2015	Assets	March 31, 2014	March 31, 2015
Sundry creditors	230	216	Stock-in-trade	200	228
Profit and loss A/c	40	54	Sundry debtors	170	162
Depreciation fund	80	88	Cash and bank balances	120	110
Contingency reserve	140	110	Current investment	262	190
Outstanding expenses	30	48	Pre-paid expenses	4	6
	1,220	1,176		1,220	1,176

The following information is furnished:

(a) An old machinery costing Rs. 30,000 was sold for Rs. 10,000. The accumulated depreciation in respect of the said machinery amounts to Rs. 16,000.
(b) A new machinery was acquired for Rs. 46,000.
(c) 9% Debentures were redeemed at a discount of 4% of their face value.
(d) Dividend at 12% was declared and paid in cash.
(e) Income tax liability of Rs. 30,000 paid was debited to contingency reserve.

You are required to prepare a cash flow statement in accordance with the Accounting Standard 3.

Answers to Multiple Choice Questions

1. (c)
2. (a)
3. (c)
4. (a)
5. (c)
6. (c)
7. (b)
8. (c)

Analysis of Financial Statements

12

LEARNING OBJECTIVES

After reading this chapter, you will be able to:

- Understand the objectives of financial analysis.
- Describe and perform horizontal, vertical and trend analysis.
- Understand and compute ratios used in analyzing profitability, efficiency in asset utilization, financial position and market standing of a company.
- Understand how to analyze financial statements of banking companies.
- Understand limitations of ratio analysis.
- Understand the concept of sustainable income.
- Understand the concept of quality of earnings.

12.1 Introduction

Information contained in financial statements of an entity is used for decision making by three major users of such information: investors, lenders and management. Investors are interested in earning a fair return on their investment. Lenders are interested in the ability of the entity to pay interest and repay loans. Management of the entity, besides being concerned with the aforementioned issues, is also interested in the efficient use of resources, generation of adequate cash flows to pay operating expenses and improvement in the overall performance of the entity. Financial statement analysis is used by all these users for taking appropriate decisions.

Financial statement analysis is the study of relationships between the elements of the same statement or different financial statements and the trend of these elements. The purpose of financial statement analysis is to determine the meaning and significance of the data contained in the statements so that a forecast can be made of the prospects for future earnings, expected dividends and the ability of the business to pay interest and debt as it matures. It provides useful information that supplements the information contained in financial statements.

Financial statement analysis involves rearrangement of financial information, comparison, analysis and interpretation of information. It can be external or internal; horizontal or vertical; and intra-firm or inter-firm.

Analysis done by the management to assess the financial health of the organization and its operational efficiency is called *internal analysis*. Analysis carried out by parties external to the organization, such as investors, credit rating agencies, government agencies, etc., is called *external analysis*. *Horizontal analysis* compares financial data over a number of years to analyze the trend. *Vertical analysis* is based on the financial data of a particular year. *Inter-firm analysis* compares financial variables of two or more firms to understand their relative competitive position. *Intra-firm analysis* compares the performance of different units of the same firm.

12.2 Techniques of Financial Analysis

The following techniques can be used for analyzing the financial statements:

1. Horizontal analysis
   (a) Comparative financial statements
   (b) Trend percentages
2. Vertical analysis (common size financial statements)
3. Ratio analysis
4. Quality of earnings
5. Sustainable income

12.3 Comparative Financial Statements

The figures of two or more periods are placed side by side. Comparison of absolute and percentage change in the figures over the periods is made to derive meaningful conclusions. An illustration of comparative balance sheets is given in Exhibit 12.1 and of comparative income statements in Exhibit 12.2.

Exhibit 12.1

Comparative Balance Sheets

	2013 (Rs.)	2014 (Rs.)	Rupee Change Increase (Decrease)	% Change Increase (Decrease)
Equity share capital	10,000,000	12,500,000	2,500,000	25.0
Reserves and surplus	4,825,000	6,250,000	1,425,000	29.5
Long-term loans	2,000,000	2,500,000	500,000	25.0
Accounts payable	1,250,000	1,500,000	250,000	20.0
Taxes payable	850,000	1,000,000	150,000	17.6
Total current liabilities	2,100,000	2,500,000	400,000	19.0

(Continued)

	2013 (Rs.)	2014 (Rs.)	Rupee Change Increase (Decrease)	% Change Increase (Decrease)
Total liabilities and stockholders' equity	18,925,000	23,750,000	48,25,000	25.5
Land	4,375,000	5,000,000	625,000	14.3
Property, plant and equipment	2,375,000	5,375,000	3,000,000	126.3
Accumulated depreciation	(2,000,000)	(2,625,000)	(625,000)	(31.3)
Long-term investments	1,875,000	2,750,000	875,000	46.7
Cash	2,750,000	3,250,000	500,000	18.2
Accounts receivable	3,000,000	3,250,000	250,000	8.3
Inventory	5,375,000	5,625,000	250,000	4.7
Prepaid expenses	1,175,000	1,125,000	(50,000)	(4.3)
Total current assets	12,300,000	13,250,000	950,000	7.7
Total assets	18,925,000	23,750,000	4,825,000	25.5

Exhibit 12.2

Comparative Income Statements

	2013	2014	Rupee Change Increase (Decrease)	% Change Increase (Decrease)
Sales revenue	16,250,000	17,500,000	1,250,000	7.7
Cost of goods sold	11,375,000	12,500,000	1,125,000	9.9
Gross profit	4,875,000	5,000,000	125,000	2.6
Employee benefit expenses	1,056,250	1,250,000	193,750	18.3
Other administrative expenses	1,175,000	1,200,000	25,000	2.1
Depreciation	375,000	875,000	500,000	133.3
Total expenses	2,606,250	3,325,000	718,750	27.6
Operating income	2,268,750	1,675,000	(593,750)	(26.2)
Interest expense	(125,000)	(175,000)	(50,000)	40.0
Other income	1,250,000	1,875,000	625,000	50.0
Net income before tax	3,393,750	3,375,000	(18,750)	(0.06)
Tax	(1,006,250)	(1,000,000)	6,250	(0.06)
Net income	2,387,500	2,375,000	(12,500)	(0.05)

12.4 Trend Percentages

Trend percentages are useful for making a comparative study of the financial statements over a number of years. The earliest year used for comparison is treated as the base year. The base year figure for each item of the financial statement is taken as 100. The figures for the subsequent years are expressed as percentages of the base year figure. An illustration of trend percentages is given in Exhibit 12.3.

Exhibit 12.3

Trend Percentages

	Amount (Rs. in Million)				Trend Percentage			
	2011	2012	2013	2014	2011	2012	2013	2014
Income statement								
Net sales	94,300	111,300	108,890	114,810	100.0	118.0	115.5	121.7
Operating EBITDA	19,210	21,960	16,290	15,070	100.0	114.3	84.8	78.4
Profit before tax	15,400	14,510	12,270	11,350	100.0	94.2	79.7	73.7
Profit after tax	13,250	10,610	10,960	11,680	100.0	80.0	82.7	88.2
Balance sheet								
Shareholders' funds	71,920	73,830	78,250	82,360	100.0	102.7	108.8	114.5
Borrowings	5,110	1,630	350	0	100.0	31.9	6.8	0
Net fixed assets	65,730	61,750	63,240	75,130	100.0	93.9	96.2	114.3
Cash	29,320	31,370	26,210	16,860	100.0	107.0	89.4	57.5
Current assets	36,910	30,980	34,760	34,850	100.0	83.9	94.2	94.4
Current liabilities	37,680	38,630	37,260	39,000	100.0	102.5	98.9	103.5
Capital employed	82,210	80,630	83,670	87,710	100.0	98.1	101.8	106.7

12.5 Common-Size Financial Statements

All figures of a financial statement are expressed as a percentage of a common base, which is taken as 100. This common base is the sales figure in the case of statement of profit and loss and the total of assets or of liabilities in case of balance sheet. Common-size balance sheets are shown in Exhibit 12.4 and common-size income statements in Exhibit 12.5.

Exhibit 12.4

Common-Size Balance Sheets

	2013 (Rs.)	Percent	2014 (Rs.)	Percent
Equity share capital	10,000,000	52.8	12,500,000	52.7
Reserves and surplus	4,825,000	25.5	6,250,000	26.3
Long-term loans	2,000,000	10.6	2,500,000	10.5
Accounts payable	1,250,000	6.6	1,500,000	6.3
Taxes payable	850,000	4.5	1,000,000	4.2
Total current liabilities	2,100,000	11.1	2,500,000	10.5
Total liabilities and stockholders' equity	18,925,000	100.0	23,750,000	100.0
Land	4,375,000	23.1	5,000,000	21.1
Property, plant and equipment	2,375,000	12.6	5,375,000	22.6
Accumulated depreciation	(2,000,000)	(10.6)	(2,625,000)	(11.1)
Long-term investments	1,875,000	9.9	2,750,000	11.6
Cash	2,750,000	14.5	3,250,000	13.7
Accounts receivable	3,000,000	15.9	3,250,000	13.7
Inventory	5,375,000	28.4	5,625,000	23.7
Prepaid expenses	1,175,000	6.2	1,125,000	4.7
Total current assets	12,300,000	65.0	13,250,000	55.8
Total assets	18,925,000	100.0	23,750,000	100.0

Exhibit 12.5

Common-Size Income Statements

	2013 (Rs.)	Percent	2014 (Rs.)	Percent
Sales revenue	16,250,000	100.0	17,500,000	100.0
Cost of goods sold	11,375,000	70.0	12,500,000	71.4
Gross profit	4,875,000	30.0	5,000,000	28.6
Employee benefit expenses	1,056,250	6.5	1,250,000	7.1
Other administrative expenses	1,175,000	7.2	1,200,000	6.9
Depreciation	375,000	2.3	875,000	5.0

(Continued)

	2013 (Rs.)	Percent	2014 (Rs.)	Percent
Total expenses	2,606,250	16.0	3,325,000	19.0
Operating income	2,268,750	14.0	1,675,000	9.6
Interest expense	(125,000)	(0.8)	(175,000)	(1.0)
Other income	1,250,000	7.7	1,875,000	10.7
Net income before tax	3,393,750	20.9	3,375,000	19.3
Tax	(1,006,250)	(6.2)	(1,000,000)	(5.7)
Net income	2,387,500	14.7	2,375,000	13.6

12.6 Ratio Analysis

Ratio analysis makes use of financial ratios for financial analysis. Financial ratios are relationships between two financial variables appearing in financial statements. According to J. Batty, "The term accounting ratios is used to describe significant relationships which exist between figures shown on a balance sheet, in a profit and loss account, in a budgetary control system or in any other part of the accounting organization." A ratio is thus a numerical relationship between two variables which are connected with each other in one way or the other. A ratio may be expressed as a number, a fraction, a percentage or a proportion.

Ratio analysis is a technique of establishing meaningful relationships between significant variables of financial statements, and interpreting the relationships to form judgment regarding the financial affairs of the unit. Ratio analysis is usually employed to assess the profitability, efficiency and financial condition of an enterprise. Depending on the purpose they serve, ratios may be classified as follows:

1. Measures of profitability
2. Tests of efficiency in investment utilization (efficiency ratios)
3. Tests of financial position
4. Ratios involving share information

Ratios are illustrated using the information contained in the following financial statements of Asian Paints Ltd. given in Exhibits 12.6 and 12.7 and additional information.

Exhibit 12.6

Statement of Profit and Loss of Asian Paints Ltd. for the Year Ended March 31, 2014

	Rs. (in Million)	Rs. (in Million)
Net sales and other operating revenue		104,187
Other income		1,737
		105,924

(Continued)

	Rs. (in Million)	Rs. (in Million)
Less: Expenses		
Cost of materials consumed	57,587	
Purchase of stock-in-trade	2,566	
Changes in inventories of F.G., WIP and stock-in-trade	(753)	
Employee benefit expenses	4,824	
Other expenses	22,191	
		86,415
EBITDA		19,509
Depreciation and amortization		2,123
Finance cost		261
Profit before exceptional items		17,125
Exceptional items		100
Profit before tax		17,025
Less: Tax expense		5,335
Profit after tax		11,690

Raw material purchased by the company during the year ended March 31, 2014 amounted to Rs. 58,531 million.

Exhibit 12.7

Balance Sheet of Asian Paints Ltd. as on March 31, 2014

(Rupees in Million)

	March 31, 2014	March 31, 2013
Equities and liabilities		
Shareholders' funds		
Share capital	959	959
Reserves and surplus	35,050	29,263
	36,009	30,222
Non-current liabilities		
Long-term borrowings	395	463
Deferred tax liability (net)	1,771	1,433
Long-term provisions	803	771
	2,969	2,667

(Continued)

	March 31, 2014	March 31, 2013
Current liabilities		
Trade payables	14,988	12,141
Other current liabilities	7,475	7,194
Short-term provisions	5,375	4,237
	27,838	23,572
Total	**66,816**	**56,461**
Assets		
Non-current assets		
Fixed assets	19,732	20,749
Tangible assets	390	270
Intangible assets	379	525
Capital work-in-progress	20,501	21,544
Non-current investments	5,482	3,597
Long-term loans and advances	946	911
Other non-current assets	63	—
Current Assets		
Current investments	4,820	1,050
Inventories	16,650	14,808
Trade receivables	7,124	6,339
Cash and bank	7,454	5,515
Short-term loans and advances	2,015	1,627
Other current assets	1,761	1.070
	39,824	30,409
Total	**66,816**	**56,461**

Additional Information:

Share capital of the company consists of 959 million shares of Re. 1 each. The company paid a dividend of Rs. 5.30 per share for the year ended March 31, 2014. The total amount paid as dividend was Rs. 5,084 million, and the company paid Rs. 820 million as dividend distribution tax. Cash flows from operating activities for the year ended March 31, 2014 was Rs. 13,688 million. The closing price of the share on the Bombay Stock Exchange as on March 31, 2014 was Rs. 546.50.

12.6.1 Profitability Measures

The profitability ratios are used to check if the company is generating an acceptable return for its owners. Both creditors and investors are interested in the profit-making ability of a company. Lack of adequate profitability adversely affects the liquidity of the company, its ability to raise external financing and its growth prospects. Widely used measures of profitability include profit margins, earnings per share (EPS), return on capital employed (ROCE), return on assets (ROA) and return on equity (ROE).

12.6.1.1 Profit Margin

Profit margins are used to analyze the profit made per unit of sales. Three kinds of profit margins are generally used: gross profit margin, operating profit margin and net profit margin.

Gross profit margin is calculated as follows:

$$\text{Gross profit ratio} = \frac{\text{Gross profit}}{\text{Sales}} \times 100$$

Gross profit is the difference between sales value and cost of goods sold. The cost of goods sold is not directly provided in the statement of profit and loss and needs separate computation.

Profitability of operations and efficiency of the management have a bearing on gross profit. Companies enjoying a monopoly in the market have a high gross profit ratio.

Operating profit is the profit before interest and tax and does not include other income. Net profit is the profit after tax.

$$\text{Operating profit ratio} = \frac{\text{Profit before interest and tax}}{\text{Sales}} \times 100$$

For Asian Paints, the operating profit margin for the year ended March 31, 2014 is

$$\text{Operating profit ratio} = \frac{19{,}509 - 2{,}123}{104{,}187} \times 100 = 16.69\%$$

and the net profit margin for the year ended March 31, 2014 is

$$\text{Net profit ratio} = \frac{\text{Net profit}}{\text{Sales}} \times 100 = \frac{11{,}690}{104{,}187} \times 100 = 11.22\%$$

A meaningful interpretation of the profit margin requires its comparison with other firms in the industry and with earlier time periods. Low margins compared to competing firms may mean one or more of the following:

1. Company's products fall in a lower margin category.
2. Company may have been following a marketing strategy of high volume and low margin.
3. Company may have been charging a lower price to increase its market share.
4. Company's costs are relatively higher.

Changes in the margin from year to year may also be due to the above reasons. The analyst must always keep in mind the fact that companies can have different profit margins simply because they follow different accounting practices or they belong to different industries.

12.6.1.2 Earnings per Share

Earnings per share are the net income available per equity share. It is calculated as

$$\text{Earnings per share} = \frac{\text{Net profit} - \text{Preference dividend}}{\text{Number of equity shares}} = \frac{11{,}690}{959} = \text{Rs.}\,12.19$$

Listed companies are required to report two versions of EPS: basic EPS and diluted EPS.

Basic EPS is calculated by dividing the net profit or loss for the period available to equity shareholders by the weighted average number of equity shares outstanding during the period.

Diluted EPS also takes into account the dilution of EPS in the future due to obligations entered into by the company such as warrants and stock options. The diluted EPS is calculated under the assumption that the conversion rights or options are exercised on the first day of the accounting period.

This ratio helps in evaluating the prevailing market price of the share. Higher earnings per share translate into a higher market price because it indicates better performance and prospects of the company.

12.6.1.3 Return on Capital Employed

Return on capital employed measures the returns generated by the business on the amount invested in the business. Capital employed refers to total of owners' funds and non-current liabilities, and hence represents funds entrusted to a concern for relatively long periods of time. It can also be calculated by adding net working capital to fixed assets. This ratio is calculated as

$$\text{Return on capital employed} = \frac{\text{Profit before interest and tax}}{\text{Average (Long-term liabilities} + \text{Owner's equity)}} \times 100$$

For Asian Paints, ROCE for the year ended March 31, 2014 is

$$\text{ROCE} = \frac{17{,}386}{(36404 + 30685)/2} \times 100 = \frac{17{,}386}{33{,}545} \times 100 = 51.8\%$$

Interest is added back to the net profit for calculating these ratios because the objective is to determine how well the sources of funds, including the borrowed funds, have been used. If the interest is deducted for calculating the net profit, the resulting figure will understate the earnings generated by using the different sources of funds.

Profit being the overall objective of a business enterprise, ROCE is a barometer of the enterprise's performance. This is a key ratio and all other ratios can be linked to this. This ratio can be used to judge the enterprise's borrowing policy and whether the funds have been usefully deployed in the business. If an enterprise having the ROCE of 11% borrows at 12%, it would indicate that the enterprise has not made efficient use of funds, it could have avoided borrowing and that it had been borrowing at a rate higher than its earning rate.

ROCE becomes difficult to interpret when the total capital is low; the profits are volatile; new capital has been raised during the year and only used for part of the year; and the assets are at historic values and are out of date.

A variant of this ratio is ROA. This ratio relates profit to investment in the enterprise and shows how much the firm has earned on the investment of all the financial resources, that is, owners' equity, long-term liabilities and current liabilities. It is also expressed as a percentage. ROA is often used by the top management to evaluate the performance of divisional managers in the use of assets. The divisional manager has a significant influence over the use of assets, but little control on how these assets are financed. ROCE is a better measure for those division managers who have a significant influence on asset acquisition, purchasing and production schedules, credit policy, cash management and the level of current liabilities.

$$\text{Return on assets} = \frac{\text{Profit before interest and tax}}{\text{Average total assets}} \times 100$$

For Asian Paints, ROA for the year ended March 31, 2014 is

$$\text{ROA} = \frac{17{,}386}{(56{,}461 + 66{,}816)/2} \times 100 = 28.2\%$$

12.6.1.4 Decomposing Return on Capital Employed

The ROCE can be decomposed into two ratios:

1. **Asset utilization (turnover) ratio:** It reflects the efficiency with which assets are utilized, and is calculated as

$$\text{Asset utilization ratio} = \frac{\text{Sales revenue}}{\text{Average (Shareholder's funds + Long-term debt)}}$$

For Asian Paints, the asset utilization ratio for the year ended March 31, 2014 is 104187/33,545 = 3.1.

2. **Profit margin (or return on sales) ratio:** It reflects the profits made per unit of sales, and is calculated as

$$\text{Profit margin} = \frac{\text{Profit before interest and tax}}{\text{Sales revenue}}$$

For Asian Paints, the profit margin for the year ended March 31, 2014 is 17,386/104,187 = 0.1669 or 16.69%.

ROCE is the product of the above two ratios:

$$\text{ROCE} = 3.1 \times 16.69\% = 51.8\%$$

Companies selling undifferentiated products (e.g. fast moving consumer goods) generally work on low margins and high turnover. On the contrary, companies selling differentiated products (e.g. customized furniture) work on high margins and low turnover. The decomposition of ROCE into profit margin and asset utilization ratio, also called the *Du-Pont Analysis*, helps analysts to understand the reason underlying the change in ROCE among different companies during a time period and for the same company over a period of time. Comparison of profit margin and turnover usually is meaningful only in evaluating firms in the same industry. Cross-industry comparison of these two ratios is often meaningless and can even be misleading.

12.6.1.5 Return on Equity

The return on equity relates profits to owners' equity, and is expressed as a percentage. Equity stands for owners' funds and includes equity share capital, general reserves, capital reserves, balance in share premium account and other reserves available to shareholders. However, accumulated losses and fictitious assets to be written off should be deducted from equity. The term *profit* here means the profits to which the shareholders are entitled to after meeting all expenses, including interest on loans and income tax. Also non-operating incomes such as interest income on investment are included in profit. The ratio is calculated as under:

$$\text{Return on equity} = \frac{\text{Profit after interest and tax} - \text{Preference dividend}}{\text{Average equity}} \times 100$$

For Asian Paints, ROE for the year ended March 31, 2014 is

$$\text{ROE} = \frac{11{,}690}{(36{,}009 + 30{,}222)/2} \times 100 = 35.3\%$$

This ratio may be used for declaration of dividend and building up of reserves. It also indicates the efficiency with which funds are deployed in the business. For example, if the rate of return on equity is 10% and the interest available on bank deposits is 12%, it would indicate that the funds are not profitably deployed and the investors would not be willing to invest in that enterprise.

12.6.1.6 Decomposition of ROE

To understand the factors affecting a firm's ROE, particularly its trend over time and its performance relative to competitors, analysts often "decompose" ROE into the product of a series of ratios. Each component ratio is in itself meaningful, and the process serves to focus the analyst's attention on separate factors influencing performance.

A useful decomposition of ROE is

$$\text{ROE} = \underset{(1)}{\frac{\text{Profit after tax}}{\text{Sales}}} \times \underset{(2)}{\frac{\text{Sales}}{\text{Assets}}} \times \underset{(3)}{\frac{\text{Assets}}{\text{Equity}}}$$

$$\Rightarrow \text{ROE} = \text{Margin} \times \text{Turnover} \times \text{Leverage}$$

Factor 1, the firm's *profit margin* or *return on sales* (ROS) and Factor 2, *asset utilization ratio* have been shown above as factors that explain the variation in a company's ROCE. For explaining variation in ROE for a company or companies, a third factor plays an important role.

Factor 3, the ratio of assets to equity, is a measure of the firm's degree of financial leverage. It is called *leverage ratio* and is equal to 1 plus the total debt-to-equity ratio. Financial leverage helps boost ROE if ROCE is greater than the interest rate on the firm's debt.

For Asian Paints, profit margin for the year ended March 31, 2014 is 11.22% (= 11,690/104,187), asset utilization ratio is 1.69 [= (104,187/61,639); here the value 61,639 is average of total assets] and leverage ratio is 1.86 [= (61,639/33,116); here the value 33, 116 is average equity]. ROE is the product of these three ratios, which is given by

$$\text{ROE} = 11.22\% \times 1.69 \times 1.86 = 35.3\%$$

In calculating ROCE and ROE, the figure in the numerator relates to the accounting period and the figure in the denominator relates to the end of the accounting period. To bring about consistency in the figures, wherever possible, the average value of assets or equity should be used. The average is calculated using the values at the beginning and at the end of the accounting periods.

Exhibit 12.8 provides a comparison of Asian Paint's profitability ratios for the year ended March 31, 2014 with its peers and Exhibit 12.9 shows the company's profitability ratios over the 5-year period from 2010 to 2014.

Exhibit 12.8

Profitability Measures of Asian Paints and Its Peers for the Year Ended March 31, 2014

Profitability Measure	Asian Paints	Akzo Nobel	Berger Paints	Kansai Nerolac
Operating profit ratio (%)	16.70	8.64	10.69	9.75
Net profit ratio (%)	11.22	6.33	6.92	6.55
Earnings per share (Rs.)	12.19	32.18	6.76	38.33
Return on capital employed (%)	51.80	22.04	31.54	20.45
Return on equity (%)	35.30	17.72	20.70	14.51

Asian paints profitability is better than its peers on all counts. However, Akzo Nobel and Kansai Nerolac have better EPS.

Exhibit 12.9

Profitability Measures of Asian Paints for the Period March 31, 2010 to March 31, 2014

Profitability Measure/ Year Ended	March 31, 2010	March 31, 2011	March 31, 2012	March 31, 2013	March 31, 2014
Operating profit ratio (%)	21.3	18.0	17.5	17.2	16.7
Net profit ratio (%)	15.1	12.3	12.0	11.7	11.2
Earnings per share (Rs.)	80.8	78.1	99.9	109.5	12.2*
Return on capital employed (%)	78.2	62.1	61.0	55.1	51.8
Return on equity (%)	58.5	43.9	43.0	38.1	35.3

*Face value of share reduced from Rs. 10 to Re. 1.

All profitability measures of Asian Paints, except the EPS, show a decline over the years.

12.6.2 Tests of Efficiency in Investment Utilization (Efficiency Ratios)

The efficiency ratios measure the effectiveness with which a concern uses the resources or assets at its disposal. These ratios are usually calculated on the basis of sales or cost of sales, and are expressed in number of times rather than as a percentage. Such ratios should be calculated separately for each type of asset. The greater the ratio, the more will be the efficiency of asset usage. A lower ratio will show underutilization of resources available to the concern. Following sections mention the important efficiency ratios usually calculated by a concern.

12.6.2.1 Inventory Turnover Ratio

The inventory turnover ratio relates the cost of goods sold to the average inventory. It measures how many times the average inventory is sold during the year. Average inventory is the mean of the opening inventory and closing inventory. The ratio is calculated as

$$\text{Inventory turnover ratio} = \frac{\text{Cost of goods sold or Sales}}{\text{Average inventory}}$$

For Asian Paints, the inventory turnover ratio for the year ended March 31, 2014 is

$$\text{Inventory turnover ratio} = \frac{104{,}187}{(14{,}808 + 16{,}650)/2} = \frac{104{,}187}{15{,}729} = 6.62$$

The cost of goods sold can either be calculated as

$$(\text{Sales} - \text{Gross profit})$$

or as

$$(\text{Opening stock} + \text{Purchases} + \text{Manufacturing expenses} - \text{Closing stock})$$

This ratio reflects the efficiency of inventory management. A higher ratio is a sign of higher efficiency and vice versa. However, there is a need to balance between a very high or a very low ratio. A very high ratio resulting from extremely low level of inventory may result in loss of sales in future due to the inability to deliver goods promptly.

Efficiency in inventory management can also be determined by calculating another ratio, the number of days' inventory held. Number of days' inventory indicates how long the inventory is held by the company on an average.

This ratio is calculated as follows:

$$\text{Number of days' inventory} = \frac{\text{Average inventory}}{\text{Cost of goods sold or Sales}} \times 365$$

or as

$$\text{Number of days' inventory} = \frac{365}{\text{Inventory turnover ratio}}$$

For Asian Paints,

$$\text{Number of days' inventory} = \frac{15{,}729}{104{,}187} \times 365 = 55 \text{ days}$$

Alternatively,

$$\text{Number of days' inventory} = \frac{365}{6.62} = 55 \text{ days}$$

This figure can be used to compare the efficiency in inventory management with other units in the same industry.

12.6.2.2 Debtors' Turnover Ratio

The debtors' turnover ratio shows the relation between sales and outstanding amount due from the debtors to whom goods were sold on credit. The ratio is calculated as follows:

$$\text{Debtors' turnover ratio} = \frac{\text{Net credit sales}}{\text{Average debtors}}$$

For Asian Paints,

$$\text{Debtors' turnover ratio} = \frac{104{,}187}{(6{,}339 + 7{,}124)/2} = \frac{104{,}187}{6{,}732} = 15.48$$

For the calculation of this ratio, debtors include sundry debtors and trade bills receivables. It is preferable to take the average of the value of the debtors in the beginning and the end. If the company sells goods both for cash and on credit, only credit sales figure should be used to calculate debtors' turnover ratio. Since the information on credit sales is not available in the financial statements of the company, the ratio may be calculated with reference to the total sales figure. Though the ratio becomes distorted, it still may be useful to compare the ratio of an entity over time if the proportion of credit and cash sales remains constant from year to year.

A high debtors' turnover ratio shows prompt collection of bills, and a low ratio shows that the enterprise is having difficulty in collection of dues from debtors. Debtors' turnover ratio can be used to calculate the average collection period. Average collection period shows the accounts receivables in terms of the number of days of credit sales during a particular period. This is a measure of the average length of time taken for debtors to settle their balance. Average collection period can be calculated as follows:

$$\text{Average collection period} = \frac{365}{\text{Debtors' turnover ratio}}$$

For Asian Paints,

$$\text{Average collection period} = \frac{365}{15.48} = 24 \text{ days}$$

It can also be calculated as

$$\text{Average collection period} = \frac{\text{Average debtors}}{\text{Net credit sales}} \times \text{Number of days in a period}$$

$$= \frac{6{,}732}{104{,}187} \times 100 = 24 \text{ days}$$

The average collection period shows how the credit policy of the concern is enforced. For example, if a company allows 30 days' credit to its customers and the collection period is 45 days, it means collection from debtors is not efficient.

12.6.2.3 Creditors' Turnover Ratio

The creditors' turnover ratio shows the relation between purchases and outstanding amount due to the creditors from whom goods were purchased on credit. The ratio is calculated as follows:

$$\text{Creditor's turnover ratio} = \frac{\text{Credit purchases}}{\text{Average creditors}}$$

For Asian Paints,

$$\text{Creditor's turnover ratio} = \frac{58{,}531 + 2{,}566}{(12{,}141 + 14{,}988)/2} = \frac{61{,}097}{13{,}565} = 4.5$$

For the calculation of this ratio, creditors include sundry creditors and trade bills payables. It is preferable to take the average of the value of the creditors in the beginning and at the end. If the company purchases goods both for cash and on credit, only credit purchases figure should be used to calculate creditors' turnover ratio. Since the information on credit purchases is not available in the financial statements of the company, the ratio may be calculated with reference to the total purchases figure. Though the ratio becomes distorted, it still may be useful to compare the ratio of an entity over time if the proportion of credit and cash purchases remains constant from year to year.

Creditors' turnover ratio can be better interpreted by converting it into average payment period.

The average payment period shows the average number of days of credit that the company has from its suppliers. It can be calculated as follows:

$$\text{Average payment period} = \frac{365}{\text{Creditor's turnover ratio}} = \frac{365}{4.5} = 81 \text{ days}$$

It can also be calculated as

$$\text{Average payment period} = \frac{\text{Average creditors}}{\text{Credit purchases}} \times \text{Number of days in a period}$$

$$= \frac{13{,}565}{61{,}097} \times 365 = 81 \text{ days}$$

A high creditors' turnover ratio means that the company takes a long time to pay for credit purchases. This may be due to the company's ability to obtain a long credit period from its suppliers. A long credit period is always good for a company's cash flow.

12.6.2.4 Cash-to-Cash Operating Cycle

Cash-to-cash operating cycle measure the length of time between purchase of inventory and collection of cash from sales. It is the sum of number of days' inventory and the average collection period.

$$\text{Cash-to-cash operating cycle} = \text{Number of days' inventory} + \text{Average collection period}$$

For Asian Paints,

$$\text{Cash-to-cash operating cycle} = 55 \text{ days} + 24 \text{ days} = 79 \text{ days}$$

In the year ended March 31, 2014, it took Asian Paints 79 days on an average to convert purchased inventories into cash.

Exhibit 12.10 provides a comparison of Asian Paint's investment-utilization ratios for the year ended March 31, 2014 with its peers and Exhibit 12.11 presents the company's asset-utilization ratios over the 5-year period 2010–2014.

Exhibit 12.10

Tests of Efficiency of Investment Utilization of Asian Paints and Its Peers for the Year Ended March 31, 2014

Measure of Efficiency of Investment Utilization	Asian Paints	Akzo Nobel	Berger Paints	Kansai Nerolac
Inventory turnover ratio (times)	6.62	7.42	5.66	5.35
Number of days' inventory (days)	55	49	64	68
Debtors' turnover ratio (times)	15.48	8.48	9.56	7.21
Average collection period (days)	24	43	38	51
Creditors' turnover ratio (times)	4.50	2.85	4.45	4.85
Average payment period (days)	81	128	82	75
Cash-to-cash operating cycle (days)	79	92	102	119

In utilization of investment in inventories, only Akzo Nobel performs slightly better than Asian Paints. Asian Paints also manages investment in receivables better than others in the industry. Kansai Nerolac has a better payable management than Asian Paints. Asian Paints has the lowest cash-to-cash operating cycle.

Exhibit 12.11

Tests of Efficiency of Investment Utilization of Asian Paints for the Period March 31, 2010 to March 31, 2014

Measure of Efficiency of Investment Utilization/Year ended	March 31, 2010	March 31, 2011	March 31, 2012	March 31, 2013	March 31, 2014
Inventory turnover ratio (times)	7.8	6.9	6.8	6.5	6.6
Number of days' inventory (days)	47	53	54	56	55

(Continued)

Measure of Efficiency of Investment Utilization/Year ended	March 31, 2010	March 31, 2011	March 31, 2012	March 31, 2013	March 31, 2014
Debtors' turnover ratio (times)	16.0	18.1	18.4	15.8	15.5
Average collection period (days)	23	20	20	23	24
Creditors' turnover ratio (times)	6.5	4.8	5.5	4.8	4.5
Average payment period (days)	56	77	66	77	81
Cash-to-cash operating cycle (days)	70	73	74	79	79

Number of days' inventories and receivables has been increasing over the years resulting in an increase in the duration of cash-to-cash operating cycle from 70 days in 2010 to 79 days in 2014. However, the company has been able to offset the requirement for additional cash resources by increasing the average payment period to its creditors from 56 days to 81 days over the same period.

12.6.3 Tests of Financial Position

Tests of financial position include tests of both short-term and long-term solvency of the business. Tests of short-term solvency focus on the liquidity position of the company. While a business should be profitable, profit, by itself, is not sufficient to ensure survival of the business. A company must have sufficient liquid assets to meet its short-term obligations. A company could be forced into liquidation in the absence of sufficient liquid funds. Two important ratios used to measure short-term liquidity are current ratio and quick ratio. These two ratios are commonly called *liquidity ratios.*

Tests of long-term solvency focus on the ability of the company to pay interest and repay principal of its long-term borrowings. The main ratios in this category are debt–equity ratio and interest coverage ratio. These ratios are commonly called *solvency ratios.*

12.6.3.1 Current Ratio

Current ratio is the relation of a company's current assets to its current liabilities. This ratio establishes the ability of the business to meet its short-term obligations and is therefore of particular significance to short-term creditors. Current assets are "cash and other assets that are expected to be converted into cash or consumed in the production of goods or rendering of services in the normal course of business." These include cash in hand, cash at bank, sundry debtors, bills receivables, loans and advances, inventory, prepaid expenses, accrued income and short-term investments in the form of marketable securities.

A current liability is a "liability including loans, deposits and bank overdraft which fall due for payment in a relatively short period, normally not more than 12 months." Current liabilities include bank overdraft, short-term loans, bills payable, sundry creditors, provision for taxation, proposed dividend and outstanding expenses.

The current ratio is calculated as follows:

$$\text{Current ratio} = \frac{\text{Current assets}}{\text{Current liabilities}}$$

For Asian Paints, from 2013 to 2014,

$$\text{Current ratio} = \frac{39{,}824}{27{,}838} = 1.43$$

and from 2012 to 2013,

$$\text{Current ratio} = \frac{30{,}409}{23{,}572} = 1.29$$

A low current ratio (less than 1) may indicate that a company would have difficulty in paying bills as they become due without selling some long-term assets. A high current ratio may not always be good as it may indicate too much money being tied up in inventory, receivables and unproductive cash balances. It is difficult to specify a normal level of current ratio as this level differs from one industry to another. It is advisable to compare a company's current ratio with the industry average and to observe its trend over a number of years.

12.6.3.2 Quick Ratio

Quick ratio is a more precise measure of liquidity than the current ratio. This ratio is also known as *acid test ratio* or *liquid ratio*. Quick ratio relates quick current assets to current liabilities. Quick current assets are those current assets, which are convertible into cash rather early such as cash, marketable securities, debtors and bills receivables. Inventory is not treated as a quick current asset as it is not likely to be realized early. Quick ratio is calculated as follows:

$$\text{Quick ratio} = \frac{\text{Current assets} - \text{Inventories}}{\text{Current liabilities}}$$

For Asian Paints, from 2013 to 2014,

$$\text{Quick ratio} = \frac{(39{,}824 - 16{,}650)}{27{,}838} = 0.83$$

and from 2012 to 2013,

$$\text{Quick ratio} = \frac{(30{,}409 - 14{,}808)}{23{,}572} = 0.66$$

This ratio shows the ability of the firm to pay its obligations without relying on the sale and collection of inventories. In a business, a 1:1 ratio of quick current assets to current liabilities is treated as a satisfactory relation.

12.6.3.3 Debt–Equity Ratio

The debt–equity ratio relates debt to equity or owners' funds. Debt here means long-term liabilities that mature after 1 year and include long-term loans from financial institutions and banks, public deposits and debentures. Equity means owners' funds and includes equity share capital, preference share capital, general reserves, capital reserves, share premium and other reserves available to equity shareholders. Accumulated losses and fictitious assets such as preliminary expenses, discount on issue of shares or debentures, which are yet to be written off, should be deducted from the equity. The debt–equity ratio is calculated as follows:

$$\text{Debt–equity ratio} = \frac{\text{Debt}}{\text{Equity}}$$

For Asian Paints, from 2013 to 2014,

$$\text{Debt–equity ratio} = \frac{395}{36{,}009} = 0.01$$

and from 2012 and 2013,

$$\text{Debt–equity ratio} = \frac{463}{30{,}222} = 0.01$$

Asian Paints has a very small amount of debt in its capital structure. This ratio indicates the degree of protection enjoyed by long-term lenders. The lower the ratio, the higher will be the degree of protection to the lenders. A debt–equity ratio of 2:1 is considered satisfactory. For capital-intensive industries such as ship-building, power units, cement units, etc., a higher ratio is allowed.

12.6.3.4 Interest Coverage Ratio

The interest coverage ratio relates interest obligations to profits before interest and tax and indicates the number of times interest obligation is covered by the profits for the period. It is always desirable to have profits more than the interest payable; otherwise the position of the lenders is unsafe. This ratio is calculated as follows:

$$\text{Interest coverage ratio} = \frac{\text{Profit before interest and tax}}{\text{Interest}}$$

For Asian Paints, from 2013 to 2014,

$$\text{Interest coverage ratio} = \frac{17{,}386}{261} = 66.7 \text{ times}$$

and from 2012 to 2013,

$$\text{Interest coverage ratio} = \frac{15{,}464}{306} = 50.5 \text{ times}$$

Asian Paints has a very healthy interest coverage ratio that has improved in 2013–14 over 2012–13.

Since interest is a charge on profit and is allowed as deduction for tax purposes, profit in the numerator is profit before interest and tax. This ratio is expressed as a number and not as a percentage.

Exhibit 12.12 provides a comparison of Asian Paint's financial position ratios for the year ended March 31, 2014 with its peers and Exhibit 12.13 presents the company's financial position ratios over the 5-year period from 2010 to 2014.

Exhibit 12.12

Tests of Financial Position of Asian Paints and Its Peers as on March 31, 2014

Measure of Financial Position	Asian Paints	Akzo Nobel	Berger Paints	Kansai Nerolac
Current ratio (times)	1.43	1.23	1.36	1.79
Quick ratio (times)	0.83	0.94	0.73	0.84
Debt–equity ratio (times)	0.01	0.10	0.01	0.06
Interest coverage ratio (times)	66.7	136.6	10.6	681.7

Short-term liquidity position of Asian Paints is comparable with its peers. All the major companies in the paints industry employ a very small amount of debt in their capital structure. Interest coverage ratio of Asian Paints is quite high though Akzo Nobel and Kansai Nerolac have a much higher ratio.

Exhibit 12.13

Tests of Financial Position of Asian Paints for the Period March 31, 2010 to March 31, 2014

Measure of Financial Position	March 31, 2010	March 31, 2011	March 31, 2012	March 31, 2013	March 31, 2014
Current ratio (times)	0.92	0.99	1.29	1.29	1.43
Quick ratio (times)	0.40	0.38	0.69	0.66	0.83
Debt–equity ratio (times)	0.04	0.03	0.02	0.01	0.01
Interest coverage ratio (times)	79.4	74.2	45.2	50.6	66.7

The trend of the current ratio and the quick ratio shows an improved liquidity position of the company. The solvency position of the company is strong as it has a very low amount of debt. This is also reflected in a high interest coverage ratio.

12.6.4 Ratios Involving Share Information

Investors in equity shares are more interested in the return from their investment in the form of dividend and price appreciation. Ratios such as dividend payout, dividend yield and price–earnings ratio that capture the relationship among dividend, earnings and market price of share are of particular interest to existing and potential investors in a company's shares.

12.6.4.1 Dividend Payout Ratio

The dividend payout (D/P) ratio measures the relationship between the earnings belonging to equity shareholders and the dividend paid to them. It can be calculated in one of the following two ways:

1. $$\text{Dividend payout ratio} = \frac{\text{Total dividend paid to equity shareholders}}{\text{Total net profit belonging to equity shareholders}} \times 100$$

   For Asian Paints,

   $$\text{Dividend payout ratio} = \frac{5{,}084}{11{,}690} \times 100 = 43.5\%$$

2. $$\text{Dividend payout ratio} = \frac{\text{Dividend per equity share (DPS)}}{\text{Earnings per share (EPS)}} \times 100$$

   For Asian Paints,

   $$\text{Dividend payout ratio} = \frac{5.30}{12.19} \times 100 = 43.5\%$$

This ratio reflects the dividend policy followed by the company, and the extent to which profits are retained in the business (which can be determined by deducting the D/P ratio from 100). The D/P ratio is likely to be low for a growth company as such a company would require large amount of funds for reinvestment. A mature company that has not many profitable investment opportunities is likely to have a higher D/P ratio.

12.6.4.2 Dividend Yield

The dividend yield ratio indicates the percentage return provided by the dividend on the market price of the share and is calculated as follows:

$$\text{Dividend yield} = \frac{\text{Dividend per share}}{\text{Market price per share}} \times 100$$

For Asian Paints, the dividend yield for an investor who purchases the share on March 31, 2014 for Rs. 546.50 is

$$\text{Dividend yield} = \frac{\text{Rs. } 5.30}{\text{Rs. } 546.50} \times 100 = 0.97\%$$

A low dividend yield may mean that either the investors expect the dividends to grow rapidly or the share is overpriced. A high dividend yield may indicate that investors consider investment in the company's share to be a risky investment or the share is underpriced. Dividend yield should not be interpreted as expected return from the share. There is another component of returns from investment in a share: the change in price over the holding period.

12.6.4.3 Price–Earnings Ratio (P/E Ratio)

Market price of the share incorporates everything the market knows about the company. Earnings are the net profit available to equity shareholders. Relating the market price to the earnings gives an insight into how the investors judge the performance of the concern.
It is calculated as follows:

$$\text{Price–Earnings ratio} = \frac{\text{Market price per share}}{\text{Earnings per share}}$$

For Asian Paints, P/E ratio for 2013–14 is Rs. 546.50/Rs. 12.19 = 44.83.

The earnings per share used in the denominator can be last year's figure or the forecasted figure for the next year.

A high P/E ratio suggests that the share is an attractive investment in the eyes of investors. The attractiveness may arise out of the belief that the share carries a low risk or that the earnings are expected to grow quickly in the future. An unduly high P/E ratio relative to companies with similar risk-return profile may mean that the share is overpriced.

This measure is not under the direct control of the company. But if there is a decline in the P/E ratio of a company without a general decline in the stock market prices, it becomes a cause of concern for the management.

Exhibit 12.14 provides a comparison of Asian Paint's market-related ratios for the year ended March 31, 2014 with its peers and Exhibit 12.15 presents the company's market-related ratios over the 5-year period from 2010 to 2014.

Exhibit 12.14

Ratios Involving Share Information of Asian Paints and Its Peers for the Year Ended March 31, 2014

Ratio	Asian Paints	Akzo Nobel	Berger Paints	Kansai Nerolac
Dividend payout ratio (%)	43.5	239.2	32.5	28.7
Dividend yield (%)	0.97	8.36	0.96	0.94
Price–earnings ratio (times)	44.8	27.9	33.9	30.5

Akzo Nobel shows very high dividend payout and dividend yield ratios as it declared a special dividend of Rs. 60 per share for the year ended March 31, 2014. If the effect of this special dividend is taken out, Asian Paints shows an overall better performance.

Exhibit 12.15

Ratios Involving Share Information of Asian Paints for the Period March 31, 2010 to March 31, 2014

Ratio	March 31, 2010	March 31, 2011	March 31, 2012	March 31, 2013	March 31, 2014
Dividend payout ratio (%)	33.4	39.6	44.0	42.0	43.5
Dividend yield (%)	1.32	1.27	1.24	0.94	0.97

The company has steadily increased its dividend payout ratio. However, the dividend yield shows a decline over the 5-year period due to more than 2.5 times appreciation in the company's share price during this period.

12.6.5 Limitations of Ratio Analysis

Ratio analysis fails to take into account many qualitative factors that affect a company's performance and future prospects. For example, ratios do not capture the size effect. Large companies have better bargaining power and enjoy economies of scale. Notes to the accounts contain important information which is not reflected in ratios. For example, contingent liabilities and commitments faced by the company.

Different accounting policies followed by companies in respect of depreciation, inventory valuation and other matters can distort comparison among companies. Ratio analysis also ignores the effect of industry characteristics on profitability.

Some companies deliberately manipulate financial statements by creative accounting and window-dressing. Ratio analysis becomes useless in such cases.

12.7 Analyzing Financial Statements of Banking Companies

Financial statements of banks can also be analyzed using bank specific measures and ratios. The analysis can be done from the perspective of liquidity, solvency, profitability and market performance.

12.7.1 Liquidity

Liquidity of assets is very important for banks. The importance of liquidity for banks was highlighted during the credit crisis of 2007 when many banks suffered due to lack of liquidity.

Under the Basel III norms, banks are required to have sufficient liquid assets. The sufficiency of liquidity is measured using two ratios: liquidity coverage ratio and net stable funding ratio. These are described as follows:

1. **Liquidity coverage ratio:** Designed to make sure that the bank can survive a 30-day period of acute stress. It is the ratio of high quality liquid assets to net cash outflow for acute 30-day stress period.

$$\text{Liquidity coverage ratio} = \frac{\text{High quality liquid assets}}{\text{Cash outflow for acute 30-day stress period}}$$

   This ratio is required to be at least equal to 1. The circumstances that the banks need to consider as stressful include a 3-notch downgrade in the bank's credit rating, partial loss of deposits, loss of unsecured wholesale funding, increased haircuts on secured funding, increased collateral requirements, drawdown on lines of credit, etc.

2. **Net stable funding ratio:** It is a longer term measure designed to ensure that stability of funding sources is consistent with the permanence of the assets that have to be funded by a bank. It is the ratio of the amount of stable funding to the required amount of stable funding for a period of longer term stress.

$$\text{Net stable funding ratio} = \frac{\text{Amount of stable funding}}{\text{Required amount of stable funding}}$$

   This ratio is also required to be at least equal to 1. Basel III norms prescribe two types of factors for calculation of this ratio. The first type of factor is available stable funding factors (ASF). Each source of available funds (capital, deposits, etc.) is multiplied by the relevant ASF to calculate the numerator of the ratio.

   The prescribed level of ASF factors is presented in Exhibit 12.16.

Exhibit 12.16

Available Stable Funding Factors Under Basel III

ASF Factor	Category
100%	Tier 1 and Tier 2 capital Preferred stock and borrowing with remaining maturity greater than 1 year
90%	Stable demand deposits and term deposits
80%	Les stable demand deposits and term deposits
50%	Wholesale demand deposits
0%	All other liability and equity categories

The second type of factor is required stable funding factor (RSF). Each category of required funding (assets, off-balance sheet exposures, etc.) is multiplied by the relevant RSF to calculate the denominator of the ratio. The prescribed level of ASF factors is presented in Exhibit 12.17.

Exhibit 12.17

Available Stable Funding Factors Under Basel III

RSF Factor	Category
0%	Cash and short-term instruments (<1 year)
5%	Claims on sovereign governments with a risk weight = 0% (>1 year)
20%	Corporate bonds rating AA or higher (>1 year) Claims on sovereigns with risk weight = 20%
50%	Gold, equities, and bond rated A
65%	Residential mortgages
85%	Loans to retail and small business (<1 year)
100%	All other assets

12.7.2 Profitability

In addition to the usual measures of profitability such as return on assets (ROA), return on capital employed (ROCE) and return on equity (ROE), two widely used measures of bank's profitability are net interest margin (NIM) and cost-to-income ratio.

12.7.2.1 NIM

A bank accepts deposits paying a certain rate of interest on such deposits. It lends this money to borrowers charging a certain rate of interest. NIM is the difference between interest income and interest expenses of the bank as a percentage of average interest earning assets.

Higher the net interest margin, higher is the profitability of the bank.

$$\text{NIM} = \frac{\text{Net interest income}}{\text{Average interest earning assets}}$$

Here, net interest income (NII) is the difference between interest income and interst expense. Average interest earning assets are loans/advances given to borrowers by the bank. Average of the beginning to end of the period is considered for prudent calculation.

Illustration 12.1

Assume that the interest income of a bank during a year is Rs. 900 million and the interest expense during the same period is Rs. 480 million. The interest earning assets at the beginning and at the end of the year are Rs. 12 billion and Rs. 14 billion, respectively.

$$\text{NIM} = \frac{(\text{Rs. 900 million} - \text{Rs. 480 million})}{(\text{Rs. 12,000 million} + \text{Rs. 14,000 million})/2} = \frac{\text{Rs. 420 million}}{\text{Rs. 13,000 million}} = 3.23\%$$

The NIM earned by the three prominent Indian banks during the year ended March 31, 2016 is presented in Exhibit 12.18.

Exhibit 12.18

NII and NIM of the Three Indian Banks for the Year Ended March 31, 2016

Name of Bank	Net Interest Income (Rs. Billion)	Net Interest Margin (%)
State Bank of India	568.82	2.96
HDFC Bank	275.92	4.30
ICICI Bank	212.20	3.49

Out of the three banks, HDFC has the highest NIM and is more profitable than the other banks.

12.7.2.2 Cost-to-Income Ratio

Cost-to-income ratio is the ratio of a bank's operating expenses to its total income. Operating expenses include employee salaries, rent, administrative expenses, advertising expenses, etc. Total income is the sum of net interest income and non-interest income (fee-based income).

$$\text{Cost-to-income ratio} = \frac{\text{Operating expenses}}{(\text{NII} + \text{Non-interest income})}$$

Lower the ratio, higher the profitability of the bank.

The cost-to-income ratio of the three prominent Indian banks during the year ended March 31, 2016 is presented in Exhibit 12.19.

Exhibit 12.19

Cost-to-Income Ratio of the Three Indian Banks for the Year Ended March 31, 2016

Name of Bank	Cost-to-Income Ratio (%)
State Bank of India	49.13
HDFC Bank	44.30
ICICI Bank	34.70

Out of the three banks, ICICI bank has the lowest cost-to-income ratio and is more profitable than other banks on this count.

12.7.3 Solvency

Solvency is related to the ability of the bank to meet its long-term obligations. The solvency of the bank depends on the relative amounts of the bank's assets and long-term liabilities. Two important measures of a bank's solvency are non-performing asset (NPA) ratio and capital adequacy ratio (CAR).

12.7.3.1 Non-Performing Asset (NPA) Ratios

The concept of non-performing assets has already been dealt with in Chapter 9. The NPA ratios reflect the quality of the bank's loans and can have a major influence on the future profitability and survival of the bank. Two NPA ratios are generally used: Gross NPA ratio and the net NPA ratio. These are defined as follows:

$$\text{Gross NPA Ratio} = \frac{\text{Gross NPA}}{\text{Gross Advances}}$$

$$\text{Net NPA Ratio} = \frac{(\text{Gross NPA} - \text{Specific Loan Loss Provisions})}{\text{Net Advances}}$$

A higher NPA ratio represents a lower quality of assets.

The NPA ratios of the three prominent Indian banks during the year ended March 31, 2016 are presented in Exhibit 12.20.

Exhibit 12.20

NPA Ratios of the Three Indian Banks for the Year Ended March 31, 2016

Name of Bank	Gross NPA Ratio (%)	Net NPA Ratio (%)
State Bank of India	6.50	3.81
HDFC Bank	0.90	0.30
ICICI Bank	5.14	2.67

Out of the three banks, HDFC has the lowest NPA ratio indicating higher safety of capital.

12.7.3.2 Capital Adequacy Ratio (CAR)

Capital adequacy ratio is the ratio of capital funds to the risk-weighted assets where capital funds consist of Tier I and Tier II capital. As explained in Chapter 9, CAR is prescribed by banking regulatory authorities to ensure that banks have the necessary capital to absorb unexpected losses. Though the minimum level of CAR prescribed by the RBI for Indian banks is 9%, most banks have their CAR in excess of 9%.

The CAR is further divided into Tier 1 and Tier 2 capital. Tier I capital represents the core capital and is more permanent than Tier 2 capital.

The CAR of the three prominent Indian banks during the year ended March 31, 2016 is presented in Exhibit 12.21.

Exhibit 12.21

CAR of the Three Indian Banks for the Year Ended March 31, 2016

Name of Bank	CAR (%)	
	Tier 1 (%)	Tier 2 (%)
State Bank of India	9.92	3.20
HDFC Bank	13.20	2.30
ICICI Bank	13.09	3.55

Out of the three banks, ICICI bank has the highest CAR indicating its higher capacity to absorb unexpected losses.

12.7.4 Ratios Involving Share Information

The ratios in this category – dividend yield ratio, dividend payout ratio and price-to-earnings ratio – are used for banking companies in the same manner as in the case of other business entities.

12.8 Quality of Earnings

The term quality of earnings is used in the context of making accounting choices. It is the degree to which managers, when faced with a choice of items that have a high impact on earnings, choose items that result in income recognition that is more likely to lead to recurring patterns of income. The more likely an item of income is to recur, the higher its quality will be. To generate confidence of investors and lenders in financial reports and to make capital markets efficient, it is necessary that the earnings reported by companies are of high quality.

Quality of earnings suffers when earnings are managed. Earnings management is planned timing of revenues, expenses, gains and losses to smooth the net income. The following ways are generally used to manage earnings:

1. Use of one-time items such as sale of investments or fixed assets.
2. Inflate revenues in the short-run by providing sales incentives to achieve higher sales at the end of the year. These goods might be returned by the customers in the subsequent year.
3. Use of improper adjusting entries, for example, recognizing revenue on multi-year contracts too quickly and treating operating expenses as capital expenditure.

A quality of earnings analysis involves adjusting the net income or EBITDA for revenue or expenses that are judged to be non-recurring, to develop an adjusted or pro forma EBITDA, reflecting a normalized picture of EBITDA. Although a quality of earnings analysis begins with historical results, the adjustments are based on judgments about revenue and expenses that are non-recurring or discretionary in nature.

Exhibit 12.22 provides some examples of how companies play with accounting policies to their advantage.

Exhibit 12.22

Earnings Management by Companies

Indosolar, a Delhi-based solar cell manufacturer had a Rs. 3,570 million IPO. The company already had a policy in place to amortize preliminary expenses, of which a few million rupees were still outstanding at the time of the IPO. But it suddenly changed the policy when accounting for the IPO expenses of Rs. 335.8 million. It decided to charge them to its share premium account.

This meant that the total outstanding expenses, some Rs. 362.7 million, would be set off on the balance sheet, and not in the profit and loss account, for 2010–11. The company was neck-deep in losses (Rs. 570 million in March 2011). The decision to charge IPO expenses to the share premium account prevented losses of a few more millions from going on the books.

Suzlon Energy, Asia's third-largest wind turbine maker, decided not to align the revenue recognition policy of its overseas subsidiary, RE power, with its own for the financial year 2010–11, although it had been doing so earlier under the Indian GAAP. Suzlon had been facing rough weather since 2008, because of the global recession and concerns over the quality of its turbine blades. "RE power's revenues were earlier computed by applying Suzlon's milestones for revenue recognition," says Suzlon's Chief Financial Officer Robin Banerjee. According to the company, the nature and level of customization of contracts of RE power and Suzlon are different, and maintains that there is no change in the group's revenue recognition policy. "The change is in the process of consolidation of revenues," explains Banerjee. The result of this consolidation is that Suzlon's revenue for 2010–11 is higher by Rs. 9,740 million, and net profit by Rs. 1095.7 million. So Suzlon's first glimmer of good news in a while came in 2010–11, but with remarks from the auditors, SNK & Co. and S.R. Batliboi & Co.

Under IFRS, companies will have to follow the same revenue recognition policy for the parent and subsidiaries. Differential accounting treatment under the Indian GAAP leaves substantial room for subjectivity, and gives companies the license to twist accounting policies to suit their convenience.

Another example of questionable accounting practices is the way in which some *pharmaceutical companies* treat *research expenses*. Under both the Indian GAAP and IFRS, research expenses are capitalized only after the company is certain that the new drug is ready for the market, and after it applies for the approval of the drug regulatory authority. And yet, many Indian companies capitalize research expenses even before clinical trials are over. When capitalized, expenditure goes directly on the assets side of the balance sheet, with no impact on the profit and loss account. If it is not capitalized, it appears on the profit and loss account and lowers profits. In the case of biotechnology firm, **Panacea Biotec**, auditors S.R. Batliboi have inserted a qualification with regard to capitalization of expenditure on clinical trials, which added up to nearly Rs. 600 million for

2010–11. The management justifies it by saying it is confident that the products in trials will be commercially viable.

Consider the case of Kolkata-based **Dhunseri Petrochem & Tea**. In March 2011, a fire broke out at the raw material storage facility of Dhunseri Petrochem & Tea's plant in Haldia, West Bengal, disrupting operations, and causing the loss of inventory, fixed assets and production. Dhunseri filed an insurance claim for Rs. 650 million, and wanted to include this amount under "other income" for the financial year ending March 31, 2011.

Dhunseri's auditors Lovelock & Lewes insisted on a qualification, because the amount approved by the insurance company was not received. The claim remained unsettled beyond the end of the financial year. But Dhunseri's audit committee, which included the independent directors and Executive Chairman C.K. Dhanuka, insisted the money be shown as other income for 2010–11, on the grounds that other companies had done similar things before. Another reason given was that if the insurance claims were not shown as income, profits for 2010–11 would be depressed, and the next year's profits inflated. By accounting for the unrealized claim in 2010–11, Dhunseri increased its other income from Rs. 810 million to Rs. 1,460 million, and its profits, from Rs. 760 million to Rs. 1,270 million.

(Source: Business Today, September 18, 2011)

12.9 Sustainable Income

For forecasting future cash flows, analysts need to ensure that current earnings do not include irregular items. Net income adjusted for irregular items is called *sustainable income.* It is the most likely level of income to be achieved in the future. It differs from the actual net income by the amount of irregular revenues, expenses, gains and losses.

Two major irregular items are as follows:

1. Discontinued operations
2. Extraordinary items

Discontinued operations refer to the disposal of a significant part of the business or an activity. As the results of discontinued operations will not be a part of an entity's results in the future, the entity is required to report the profit and loss from discontinued operations net of tax.

Exhibit 12.23 provides an illustration of disclosure of profit and loss from discontinued operations.

Exhibit 12.23

Discontinuing Operations

On December 7, 2012, the management of Claris Life Sciences Limited entered into a certain agreement with Otsuka Pharmaceutical Factory, Inc., Japan ('Otsuka') and Mitsui & Co. Ltd., Japan ('Mitsui') for the transfer of its Infusion Business to Claris Otsuka Limited on a 'slump sale' basis.

The financial results of this business appear as profit from *discontinuing operations* in the financial statements of the company as shown below:

Claris Life Sciences Limited

Statement of Profit and Loss for the year ended on December 31, 2013

	Rs. (in Million)
Profit after tax	812.19
Profit after tax comprises of:	
(a) Profit from continuing operations (after tax)	392.13
(b) Profit from discontinuing operations (before tax)	295.86
(c) Profit on disposal of infusion business under slump sale	150.60
(d) *(Add)/Less*: Tax expense/(reversal) of discontinuing operations	
(i) Tax expense of discontinuing operations	88.45
(ii) Tax on disposal of infusion business under slump sale	
(net of reversal of deferred taxes of Rs. 2,885.18 lakhs)	(62.04)
X. Earnings per share (basic and diluted)	
(nominal value per equity share of Rs. 10)	
(a) Continuing operations	6.14
(b) Total operations	12.73

Extraordinary items are events and transactions that are both unusual in nature and occur infrequently, for example, loss caused by a natural calamity that is not usual in a particular area. However, loss to crop due to weather is not an extraordinary item as it is not infrequent. Other examples of extraordinary items are expropriation of property by a foreign government, and effect of a newly elected law.

The following are not extraordinary items:

1. Effect of major natural calamities common to an area.
2. Write-down of inventories or receivables.
3. Losses attributable to labor strikes.
4. Gains or losses from sale of property, plant or equipment.

Exhibit 12.24 provides an illustration of disclosure of extraordinary items.

Exhibit 12.24

Extraordinary Items

The audited financial results of Alstom India Limited for the year ended March 31, 2014 contain the following statement about an extraordinary item:

> The Board of Directors of the Group at its meeting held on 15 January 2014, has approved the sale and transfer of its transportation system undertaking (the Transport business of the

Company) to a group company, ALSTOM Transport India Limited as a going concern on a slump sale basis, for a lump sum consideration without values being assigned to individual assets and liabilities. As per the agreement dated 6 March 2014, the transfer of transport business became effective from end of business hours of 31 March 2014. The agreed total consideration for slump sale of Rs. 28.69 million against the net assets value of Rs. 17.0 million as on 31 March 2014 has resulted in capital gain to the Group of Rs. 11.69 million, reported as profit on sale of Transport business in the statement of profit and loss as an *extraordinary item*. As a result Balance Sheet figures are not comparable with the previous year.

Summary – Review of Learning Objectives

1. **Understand the objectives of financial analysis:** The purpose of financial statement analysis is to determine the meaning and significance of the data contained in the statements so that a forecast may be made of the prospects for future earnings, expected dividends and the ability of the business to pay interest and debt as it matures. It provides useful information that supplements the information contained in financial statements.
2. **Describe and perform horizontal, vertical and trend analysis.** Horizontal analysis compares financial data over a number of years to analyze the trend. Comparative balance sheets and comparative profit and loss statements are used to perform horizontal analysis. Vertical analysis is based on the financial data of a particular year. It is carried out by preparing common-size balance sheet and common-size income statement. Each item in the balance sheet is expressed as percent of total assets and each item in the income statement is expressed as percent of sales. In trend analysis, all items in the base year financial statements are expressed as 100 and items in subsequent years' financial statements are expressed as percentages of the base year figures.
3. **Understand and compute ratios used in analyzing profitability, efficiency in asset utilization, financial position and market standing of a company.** The profitability ratios are used to check if the company is generating an acceptable return for its owners. Widely used measures of profitability include profit margins, earnings per share (EPS), return on capital employed (ROCE), return on assets (ROA) and return on equity (ROE).

   Ratios used to measure efficiency in asset utilization measure the effectiveness with which a concern uses the resources or assets at its disposal. Main ratios in this category include debtors' turnover ratio, inventory turnover ratio, creditors' turnover ratio, and cash-to-cash operating cycle.

   Tests of financial position include tests of both short-term and long-term solvency of the business. Tests of short-term solvency focus on the liquidity position of the company. Two important ratios used to measure short-term liquidity are current ratio and quick ratio. Tests of long-term solvency focus on the ability of the company to pay interest and repay principal of its long-term borrowings. The main ratios in this category are debt–equity ratio and interest coverage ratio.

   The market standing of the company is reflected in the market price of the share. Market price is partly influenced by the returns that the investors get in the form of dividend, and partly by the perception of investors about the prospects of the company. Ratios such as dividend payout, dividend yield and price–earnings ratio capture the relationship among dividend, earnings and market price of share.

4. **Understand how to analyze financial statements of banking companies.** Financial statements of banks can also be analyzed using bank specific measures and ratios. These include liquidity coverage ratio, net stable funding ratio, net interest margin, cost-to-income ratio, NPA ratios and capital adequacy ratios.
5. **Understand limitations of ratio analysis.** Ratio analysis fails to take into account many qualitative factors that affect a company's performance and future prospects. These include the size and contingent liabilities of the company. Different accounting policies followed by companies in respect of depreciation, inventory valuation and other matters can distort comparison among companies. Ratio analysis also ignores the effect of industry characteristics on profitability. Some companies deliberately manipulate financial statements by creative accounting and window-dressing. Ratio analysis becomes useless in such cases.
6. **Understand the concept of sustainable income.** Net income adjusted for irregular items is called sustainable income. It is the most likely level of income to be achieved in the future. Two major irregular items are: discontinued operations and extraordinary items. Discontinued operations refer to the disposal of a significant part of the business or an activity. Extraordinary items are events and transactions that are both unusual in nature and occur infrequently.
7. **Understand the concept of quality of earnings.** Quality of earnings indicates the degree to which full and transparent information is provided to the users of financial statements. Quality of earnings suffers when earnings are managed. Earnings management is the planned timing of revenues, expenses, gains and losses to smooth the net income.

Glossary

- **Asset turnover ratio** reflects the efficiency with which assets are utilized. It is calculated by dividing the sales by sum of shareholders' funds and long-term debt.
- **Average collection period** shows the accounts receivables in terms of number of days of credit sales during a particular period. It is calculated dividing 365 days by debtors' turnover ratio.
- **Average payment period** shows the average number of days of credit that the company has from its suppliers. It is calculated dividing 365 days by creditors' turnover ratio.
- **Basic EPS** is calculated by dividing the net profit or loss for the period available to equity shareholders by the weighted average number of equity shares outstanding during the period.
- **Capital adequacy ratio** is the ratio of capital funds to the risk-weighted assets where capital funds consist of Tier I and Tier II capital.
- **Cash-to-cash operating cycle** measure the length of time between the purchase of inventory and collection of cash from sales. It is the sum of number of days' inventory and the average collection period.
- **Common-size financial statements** are financial statements in which all items are expressed as a percentage of a common base which is taken as 100.
- **Comparative financial statements.** Figures of two or more periods are placed side by side. Comparison of absolute and percentage change in the figures over the periods is made to derive meaningful conclusions.
- **Cost-to-income ratio** is the ratio of a bank's operating expenses to its total income.
- **Creditors' turnover ratio** shows the relation between purchases and outstanding amount due to the creditors from whom goods were purchased on credit.

- **Current ratio** is the relation of a company's current assets to its current liabilities. This ratio establishes the ability of the business to meet its short-term obligations.
- **Days' inventory** measures the average number of days' inventory is held. It is calculated by dividing 365 days by the inventory turnover ratio.
- **Debt–equity ratio** relates debts to equity or owners' funds, and measures the ability of the business to meet its long-term obligations.
- **Debtors' turnover ratio** shows the relation between sales and outstanding amount due from the debtors to whom goods were sold on credit.
- **Discontinued operations** refer to the disposal of a significant part of the business or an activity.
- **Diluted EPS** takes into account the dilution of EPS in the future due to obligations entered into by the company such as warrants and stock options.
- **Dividend payout ratio** measures the relationship between the earnings belonging to equity shareholders and the dividend paid to them.
- **Dividend yield** indicates the percentage return provided by the dividend on the market price of the share, and is calculated dividing dividend per share by market price per share.
- **Earnings per share** is the net income available per equity share.
- **External analysis** is the analysis carried out by parties external to the organization such as investors, credit rating agencies, government agencies, etc.
- **Extraordinary items** are events and transactions that are both unusual in nature and occur infrequently.
- **Financial statement analysis** is the study of relationships between the elements of the same statement or different financial statements and the trend of these elements.
- **Gross non-performing assets ratio** is the ratio of gross non-performing assets to gross advances.
- **Gross profit** is the difference between sales value and cost of goods sold.
- **Horizontal analysis** compares financial data over a number of years to analyze the trend.
- **Interest coverage ratio** relates interest obligations to the profits before interest and tax and indicates the number of times interest obligation is covered by the profits for the period.
- **Inter-firm analysis** compares financial variables of two or more firms to get an idea of their relative competitive position.
- **Internal analysis** is the analysis done by the management to assess the financial health of the organization and its operational efficiency.
- **Intra-firm analysis** compares the performance of different units of the same firm.
- **Inventory turnover ratio** relates the cost of goods sold to the average stock. It measures how many times the average stock is sold during the year.
- **Leverage ratio is** the ratio of assets to equity. It is a measure of the firm's degree of financial leverage.
- **Liquidity coverage ratio** is designed to make sure that the bank can survive a 30-day period of acute stress. It is the ratio of high quality liquid assets to net cash outflow for acute 30-day stress period.
- **Net interest margin** is the difference between interest income and interest expenses of the bank as a percentage of average interest earning assets.
- **Net non-performing assets ratio** is the ratio of net non-performing assets to net advances. Net non-performing assets are gross non-performing assets minus specific loan loss provisions.
- **Net profit** is the profit after tax.
- **Net stable funding ratio** is the ratio of the amount of stable funding to the required amount of stable funding for a period of longer-term stress.
- **Operating profit** is the profit before interest and tax and also does not include other income.
- **Price–earnings (P/E) ratio** compares the market price per share to the earnings per share. It is calculated as the market price per share divided by earnings per share.
- **Profit margin** is used to analyze profit made per unit of sales. Three kinds of profit margins are

generally used: gross profit margin, operating profit margin and net profit margin.

- **Quality of earnings** indicates the degree to which full and transparent information is provided to the users of financial statements.
- **Quick ratio** is a more precise measure of liquidity than the current ratio. Quick ratio relates quick current assets to current liabilities. Quick current assets are current assets minus inventories. Quick ratio is also known as *acid test ratio* or *liquid ratio.*
- **Ratio analysis** is a technique of establishing meaningful relationships between significant variables of financial statements and interpreting the relationships to form judgment regarding the financial affairs of the unit.
- **Return on assets** relates profit to investment in all the financial resources, that is, owners' equity, long-term liabilities and current liabilities.
- **Return on capital employed** measures the returns generated by the business on total of owners' funds and non-current liabilities.
- **Return on equity** relates profits to owners' equity.
- **Sustainable income** is the most likely level of income to be achieved in the future. It differs from the actual net income by the amount of irregular revenues, expenses, gains and losses.
- **Vertical analysis** is based on the financial data of a particular year and is carried out by expressing each item in the financial statement as a percentage of a base amount.

Solved Problems

1. A company earns a profit before tax of Rs. 50 million and declares a dividend of Rs. 4 per share. The company's share capital consists of 5 million shares of Rs. 10 each. The price of the share is Rs. 200 on the stock exchange. The tax rate applicable to the company is 30%.

Calculate (a) earnings per share, (b) dividend payout ratio, (c) dividend yield and (d) price–earnings ratio.

Solution:

(a) Earnings per share = Profit after tax/Number of equity shares $= 50(1-0.30)/5 =$ Rs. 7

(b) Dividend payout ratio = Dividend per share/Earnings per share = Rs. 4/Rs. 7 = 0.57 or 57%

(c) Dividend yield = Dividend per share/Market price per share = Rs. 4/Rs. 200 = 2%

(d) Price earnings ratio = Market price per share/Earnings per share = Rs. 200/Rs. 7 = 28.6 times

2. The following ratios are given for a company:

Debt–equity ratio	2:3
Return on equity	20%
Current ratio	1.50
Inventory turnover ratio (based on sales)	20 times
Net profit margin ratio	5%
Interest on long-term loan	10%

Complete the following statements:

Income Statement

	(Rs. in 000's)
Sales	
Cost of goods sold	
Gross profit	
Operating expenses	850
EBIT	
Interest	90
Profit before tax	
Tax provision (50%)	
Profit after tax	

Balance Sheet

		(Rs. in 000's)
Liabilities	Assets	
Equity	Fixed assets	
Long-term debt	Current assets	
Accounts payable	Cash	
	Receivables	60
	Inventory	
	Total current assets	540
Total	Total	

Solution:

Income Statement

	(Rs. in 000s)
Sales	5,400
Cost of goods sold	3,920
Gross profit	1,480
Operating expenses	850
EBIT	630
Interest	90
Profit before tax	540
Tax provision (50%)	270
Profit after tax	270

Balance Sheet

(Rs. in 000's)

Liabilities		Assets	
Equity	1,350	Fixed assets	2,070
Long-term debt	900	Current assets	
Accounts payable	360	Cash	210
		Receivables	60
		Inventory	270
		Total current assets	540
Total	2,610	Total	2,610

Working Notes

Long-term debt = Interest amount/Rate of interest = 90/10% = 900.

Current ratio = 1.50 = Current assets/Accounts payable; Accounts payable = 540/1.50 = 360.

Debt–equity ratio = 2:3.

Equity = 900 × 3/2 = 1,350.

Return on equity = 20% of 1,350 = 270.

Net profit = 270.

Net profit = 5% of sales.

Sales = 270/0.05 = 5,400.

Inventory = Sales/20 = 5,400/20 = 270.

3. The following information relates to ABC Ltd. for the two years to 31 March 2014 and 2015 (Tables 12.1 and 12.2).

Table 12.1 Profit and loss account of ABC Ltd.

(Rs. in Million)

	2013–14	2014–15
Sales	2,250	2,850
Cost of goods sold		
Beginning inventory	120	150
Add: Purchases	1,500	2,100
	1,620	2,250
Less: Ending inventory	150	300
Cost of goods sold	1,470	1,950
Gross profit	780	900
Other expenses	375	525
Net income	405	375

Table 12.2 Balance sheet of ABC Ltd.

	2014	2015
	Rs. (in Million)	Rs. (in Million)
Assets		
Fixed assets	870	690
Current assets		
Stock	150	300
Trade debtors	560	1,200
Bank	40	0
Total current assets	750	1,500
Current liabilities		
Bank overdraft	0	15
Trade creditors	120	300
Net current assets	630	1,185
Total	1,500	1,875
Capital and reserves		
Capital	1,350	1,350
Profit and loss account	150	525
Total	1,500	1,875

Analyze the company's performance for the year ended March 31, 2015. Make use of accounting ratios to support your analysis.

Solution: See Table 12.3.

Table 12.3 Accounting ratios

	2014	2015
Gross profit ratio	780/2,250 × 100 = 34.7%	900/2,850 × 100 = 31.6%
Net profit ratio	405/2,250 × 100 = 18.0%	375/2,850 × 100 = 13.2%
Return on capital employed	405/1,500 × 100 = 27.0%	375/1,875 × 100 = 20%
Stock turnover	1,470/150 = 9.8 times	1,950/300 = 6.5 times
Current ratio	750/120 = 6.25:1	1,500/315 = 4.8:1
Debtor collection period	(560/2,250) × 365 = 91 days	(1,200/2,850) × 365 = 154 days
Creditor payment period	(120/1,500) × 365 = 29 days	(300/2,100) × 365 = 53 days

Comments: The sales of the company have increased by Rs. 600 million (26.7%) in 2015. However, the gross profit has increased by only 15.4%. The company seems to have reduced its profit margin to increase its sales. This is reflected in the gross profit ratio declining from 34.7% in 2014 to 31.6% in 2015.

Other expenses have also increased disproportionately by 40%, bringing down the net profit by 7.4%. The net profit ratio is down from 18% to 13.2%.

The current ratio has declined from 6.25 in 2014 to 4.8 in 2015. The liquidity position is, however, still healthy. Both the debtor collection period and creditors' payment period have increased substantially. A part of it could be due to increased sales. But such a significant increase in turnover ratios appears to be due to poor working capital management which is also reflected in the deterioration of cash position, with the company having an overdraft by the end of 2015.

With a precarious cash position, the company will find it difficult to survive unless it improves its cash flows.

4. Amba Limited commenced business on April 1, 2014 with an equity capital of Rs. 2,000,000 in shares of Rs. 10 each. The following details were gathered from the accounting records of the company for the year ended March 31, 2015.

Sales to net fixed assets	5 times
Gross profit margin	25%
Net profit margin	8.5%
Interest coverage ratio	4
Provision for income tax	30%
Proposed dividend (assume that it is not taxable)	10%
Administrative expenses	Rs. 150, 000
WDV depreciation rate (depreciation not yet provided)	25%

You are required to prepare a profit and loss statement for the year ended March 31, 2015.

Solution:

Statement of profit and loss is given below:

Amba Limited

Statement of profit and loss for the year ended March 31, 2015

	(Rs.)
Revenue	
Sales	7,000,000
Less: Cost of goods sold	5,250,000
Gross profit	1,750,000
Expenses	
Depreciation	466,667
Administrative expenses	150,000
Interest	283,333
Profit before tax	850,000
Tax	255,000
Profit after tax	595,000

(*Continued*)

	(Rs.)
Less: Dividend	200,000
Retained profit	395,000

Working Notes

Let sales be Rs.	X
Net fixed assets (Sales/5)	0.20X
Depreciation = 0.25 × (Net fixed assets + depreciation)	
0.75 Depreciation = 0.25 (0.20 X)	
Depreciation	(0.2/3) X
Gross profit	0.25X
Less: Administrative expenses	150,000
Less: Depreciation	(0.2/3) X
Profit before interest and tax	(0.55/3) X − 150,000
Interest coverage ratio or PBIT/Interest (I)	4
(0.55/3 X − 150000)/I = 4 or	
I = (0.0.55/3 X − 150000)/4 =	(0.55/12) X − 37,500

$$
\begin{aligned}
\text{Profit after tax} &= \text{PBIT} - \text{Interest} - \text{Tax} \\
&= \text{PBIT} - \text{Interest} - 0.3\ (\text{PBIT} - \text{Interest}) \\
&= 0.7\ (\text{PBIT} - \text{Interest}) \\
&= 0.7\big[(0.55/3\ X - 150{,}000) - (0.55/12\ X - 37{,}500)\big] \\
&= 0.7\ (1.65/12\ X - 112{,}500)
\end{aligned}
$$

Also, PAT = 0.085 X

That is, 0.085 X = 1.155/12 X − 78,750 or X = 7,000,000

Multiple Choice Questions

1. Given that earnings per share = Rs. 50, dividend payout ratio = 40%, dividend yield = 3.2%. The price of ordinary shares implied by the above data is ________.
   - **(a)** Rs. 78
   - **(b)** Rs. 625
   - **(c)** Rs. 1,563
   - **(d)** Rs. 3,906

2. Which of the following would normally be included in the calculation of debt–equity ratio?
   - **(a)** Debentures
   - **(b)** Preference shares
   - **(c)** Bank overdraft
   - **(d)** All of the above

3. If X = (Current assets – Stocks)/(Current liabilities), X is known as ______.
   - **(a)** quick ratio
   - **(b)** acid test ratio
   - **(c)** current ratio
   - **(d)** both options (a) and (b)

4. Which of the following ratio is considered to assess the likely growth prospects of the company and whether the company is a low risk investment?
   (a) Earnings per share
   (b) Diluted earnings per share
   (c) Price–earnings ratio
   (d) Dividend yield
5. Financial analysis of a business may not be able to achieve any one of the following issues:
   (a) Improve the profitability of the project.
   (b) Delineate the risks involved in the project.
   (c) Highlight the salient factors that lead to the greatest uncertainty.
   (d) Possibly suggest methods by which the risks might be reduced.
6. The debt collection period may increase (decrease) between one period and another for a number of reasons except for any one of those mentioned below:
   (a) If credit is given to unsatisfactory customers.
   (b) Earlier the business had a zero debt collection period.
   (c) Credit terms to an existing customer changes.
   (d) If there is no consistent follow-up of overdue debts.
7. The current ratio of a company depends on a number of factors listed below except one of the following options:
   (a) Volatility of the working capital requirement.
   (b) Nature of company's business.
   (c) Imminence of current liabilities.
   (d) Long-term investments of the company.
8. Which of the following financial ratios will be affected by an error in recording the value of inventory in the financial statement?
   (i) Inventory turnover ratio
   (ii) Current ratio
   (iii) Earnings per share
   (iv) Interest coverage ratio

   (a) Option (i) only
   (b) Options (i) and (ii)
   (c) Options (i), (ii) and (iii)
   (d) All of the above

Review Questions

1. List the possible reasons for high P/E ratio of a share.
2. Distinguish between inter-firm and intra-firm comparisons.
3. Explain the difference between horizontal and vertical analyses.
4. Which of the profitability ratios is the most reliable for analysis and why?
5. Explain the limitations of financial ratio analysis in the interpretation of the financial statements of a company.
6. Explain how P/E ratio and dividend yield ratio can be used in formulating appropriate equity investment recommendations.
7. Define current ratio and quick ratio. Briefly explain the reasons for calculating these ratios.
8. When are the earnings of an entity considered to be of good quality?
9. Out of a mature and a growth company, which company is likely to have a higher dividend payout ratio and why?
10. Define debtors' turnover ratio and inventory turnover ratio and explain their use.

Practice Problems

1. The following figures are taken from a company's published accounts for the year 2014–15.

	(Rupees in Million)
Equity share capital (75 million shares of Rs. 10 each)	750
10% Preference share capital (2.25 million shares of Rs. 100 each)	225
Reserves	1,050
12% Debentures	300
Current liabilities	210
	2,535
Profit before interest and tax	465

Calculate the return on capital employed and the interest coverage ratio.

2. The following information is available from the accounting records of a company.

Annual sales	Rs. 1,800,000
Current liabilities	Rs. 750,000
Days sales outstanding (DSO) (360-day year)	40
Inventory turnover ratio	5
Current ratio	1.5
Gross profit margin	25%

The company's current assets consist of cash, inventories and accounts receivable. Calculate the amount of cash the company is carrying.

3. The information given in Table 12.4 is taken from the accounts of XYZ Ltd. for 2014 and 2015.

Table 12.4 Accounts of XYZ Ltd. for 2014 and 2015

	2014 (Rs.)	2015 (Rs.)
Sales	1,200,000	1,500,000
Net profit before tax and interest	120,000	180,000
Long-term loans	150,000	450,000
Share capital	150,000	180,000
Reserves	75,000	120,000

Calculate the return on capital employed (ROCE) for the two years. Comment on the change in ROCE using its decomposition into profit margin ratio and asset utilization ratio.

4. The ratios in Table 12.5 have been calculated from financial statements of two companies of similar size and same industry.

Table 12.5 Comparative profitability ratios

	X Ltd.	Y Ltd.
Gross profit ratio	30%	15%
Net profit ratio	20%	10%
Return on capital employed	7.5%	10.5%

Explain which of the two companies is more profitable and why.

5. Construct the balance sheet of XYLO Industries as on March 31, 2015 based on the information provided below:
Asset cover [(Total assets – Current liabilities – Intangible assets)/Loans] = 2
Debt to total assets ratio [Loans/(Loans + Equity)] = 0.4
Quick ratio = 1.12
Current ratio = 3
Other information as on March 31, 2015:

   1. Current liabilities are Rs. 90,000.
   2. 10% debentures are Rs. 200,000.
   3. Intangible assets are Rs. 100,000.
   4. Current assets comprise of only cash and inventories.
   5. Loan capital and equity share capital constitute equal proportion of balance sheet.

6. Complete the balance sheet by using the following information and ratios.

Long-term debt to shareholders' funds	1:2
Sales to total assets	5 times
Debtor turnover period	36 days
Inventory turnover ratio	9 times
Gross profit margin	20%
Quick ratio	1 to 1

(Assume 360 days in a year.)
Projected balance sheet format is given in Table 12.6.

Table 12.6 Format of projected balance sheet

	(Rs.)		(Rs.)
Payables	600,000	Cash	?
Long-term debt	?	Debtors	?
Equity shares	200,000	Stock	?
Profit	200,000	Plant	?
Total liabilities and equity		Total assets	

7. The current ratio of a company is 1.5:1. State with reasons which of the following would improve, reduce or not change the ratio:
   (a) Repayment of long-term debts.
   (b) Bills receivable drawn on debtors for 2 months.
   (c) Sale of goods for cash Rs. 30,000 (cost Rs. 35,000).
   (d) Purchase of computer for accounts section on credit, allowed by the vendor for two months.
8. The following figures have been extracted from the records of a company (Table 12.7).

Table 12.7 Extracts from financial statements

Particulars	2014 (Rs.)	2015 (Rs.)
Sales	1,350,000	2,700,000
Gross profit	337,500	540,000
Current assets	450,000	675,000
Current liabilities	225,000	375,000

The CEO of the company is of the opinion that the CFO is very efficient as there is an increase in profit from Rs. 337,500 to Rs. 540,000 by his efforts. Again the current assets have increased from Rs. 450,000 to Rs. 675,000 whereas current liabilities have increased by only Rs. 150,000 and thus the short-term financial position is also becoming strong.

Do you agree with him? State yes/no. Give reasons for your answer.

9. Tyco Industries Ltd. currently has sales of Rs. 1,500 million. It is expecting an increase of 10% in sales over the next year. Its latest balance sheet as on March 31 is summarized in Table 12.8.

Table 12.8 Balance sheet of Tyco Industries Ltd. as on March 31

Liabilities	Rs. (in Million)	Assets	Rs. (in Million)
Equity capital	440	Net fixed assets	480
Retained earnings	180	Marketable securities	40
Long-term debt	45	Debtors	225
Sundry creditors	165	Inventory	255
Bank loan	50		
Other current liabilities	120		
	1,000		**1,000**

If the company expects to maintain its previous year's total asset turnover (based on sales) ratio, determine the expected level of total assets, and the extent of additional funds required to finance the incremental asset.

10. The CFO of a company is developing a financial plan for the company. He obtains the following estimates:

	Year				
	0	1	2	3	4
Sales (Rs. in Million)		450	540	675	945
Net non-current assets (Rs. in Million)		360	430	495	560
Equity share capital (Rs. in Million)	270				
Long-term debt (Rs. in Million)	125				

For planning purposes, he has also made the following estimates and assumptions:

Cost of goods sold (% of sales)	60
Return on sales (after tax) (%)	15
Dividend payout ratio (%)	40
Turnover (times) based on year-end sales values	
Cash and debtors	3
Inventory	2
Required current ratio	1.5:1
Required ratio of long-term debt to equity	0.4

Considering that the above assumptions are correct, determine how much additional equity capital, if any, the company will have to issue each year.

11. From the balance sheet given in Table 12.9, calculate: (i) current ratio, (ii) quick ratio and (iii) debt–equity ratio.

Table 12.9 Balance sheet

Liabilities	Amount (Rs.)	Assets	Amount (Rs.)
Equity share capita	1,000,000	Goodwill	500,000
6% Preference share capital	500,000	Plant and machinery	600,000
General reserve	100,000	Land and building	700,000
Profit and loss a/c	400,000	Furniture	100,000
Provision for tax	176,000	Stock-in-trade	600,000
Bills payable	124,000	Bills receivable	30,000
Bank overdraft	20,000	Debtors	150,000
Creditors	80,000	Bank	200,000
12% Debentures	500,000	Marketable securities	20,000
	2,900,000		2,900,000

12. From the statement of profit and loss given in Table 12.10, calculate: (i) gross profit ratio, (ii) net profit ratio, and (iii) operating profit ratio.

Table 12.10 Statement of profit and loss

	Amount (Rs.)	Amount (Rs.)
Sales		1,600,000
Raw material consumed	680,000	
Manufacturing expenses	400,000	
Cost of goods sold		1,080,000
Gross profit		520,000
Selling, general and administrative expenses		(280,000)
Value of furniture lost by fire		(8,000)
Compensation for land acquisition		48,000
Net profit		280,000

13. The data in Tables 12.11 and 12.12 are taken from the records of ABC Ltd.

Table 12.11 ABC Ltd. – Comparative balance sheet as on March 31

	2015	2014
	(Rs.)	(Rs.)
Assets		
Current assets	600,000	400,000
Property, plant and equipment	1,000,000	1,000,000
Other assets	160,000	200,000
Total assets	1,760,000	1,600,000
Liabilities		
Current liabilities	440,000	500,000
Long-term liabilities	240,000	100,000
Share capital	600,000	600,000
Retained earnings	480,000	400,000
Total liabilities	1,760,000	1,600,000

Table 12.12 ABC Ltd. — Comparative income statement for the year ended March 31

	2015 (Rs.)	2014 (Rs.)
Sales	5,300,000	4,480,000
Cost of goods sold	3,720,000	3,380,000
Gross margin on sales	1,580,000	1,100,000
Operating expenses	1,020,000	680,000
Operating income	560,000	420,000
Interest expense	40,000	20,000
Income before taxes	520,000	400,000
Income taxes	130,000	120,000
Net income	390,000	280,000

Compute the following ratios for 2015 and 2014:

(a) Current ratio
(b) Debt–equity ratio
(c) Debt (debt-to-assets) ratio
(d) Fixed assets turnover
(e) Interest coverage ratio
(f) Return on sales

14. The summarized statement of profit and loss of Rajasthan Product Ltd. for the year ended March 31, 2015 and balance sheet on that date is given in Tables 12.13 and 12.14.

Table 12.13 Statement of profit and loss

	Amount (Rs.)	Amount (Rs.)
Sales		1,000,000
Raw material consumed	200,000	
Manufacturing expenses	300,000	
Cost of goods sold		500,000
Gross profit		500,000
Selling, general and administrative expenses		(100,000)
Value of furniture lost by fire		(55,000)
Interest		(10,000)
Profit on sale of investment		50,000

(Continued)

Table 12.13 (Continued)

	Amount (Rs.)	Amount (Rs.)
Profit before tax		385,000
Provision for tax		154,000
Profit after tax		231,000

Table 12.14 Balance sheet

Liabilities	Amount (Rs.)	Assets	Amount (Rs.)
Equity share capital (10,000 shares of Rs. 10 each)	100,000	Fixed assets	250,000
10% Preference share capital	100,000	Stock-in-trade	250,000
General reserve	100,000	Sundry debtors	100,000
5% Debentures	200,000	Cash at bank	50,000
Bills payable	50,000		
Creditors	100,000		
	650,000		650,000

The current market price of the company's share is Rs. 225.
Examine the profit and loss account and balance sheet given in Tables 12.13 and 12.14 and calculate the following ratios:

(i) Gross profit ratio
(ii) Current ratio
(iii) Debt–equity ratio
(iv) Inventory turnover ratio
(v) Liquid ratio
(vi) Debt to total assets ratio
(vii) Working capital turnover ratio
(viii) Debtors turnover ratio
(ix) Operating profit ratio
(x) Interest coverage ratio
(xi) Return on capital employed
(xii) Return on equity
(xiii) Earnings per share
(xiv) Price–earnings ratio

15. A company's stock turnover is five times; stock at the end is Rs. 10,000 more than that at the beginning; sales (all credit) are Rs. 4,00,000; rate of gross profit on cost is 1/4; current liabilities are Rs. 1,20,000; acid test ratio is 0.75. Calculate its current assets.

Answers to Multiple Choice Questions

1. (b)
2. (d)
3. (d)
4. (c)
5. (a)
6. (b)
7. (d)
8. (d)

Financial Reporting Standards

13

LEARNING OBJECTIVES

After reading this chapter, you will be able to:

- Understand the meaning and importance of accounting standards.
- Know the existing accounting standards issued by Institute of Chartered Accountants of India.
- Understand the International Financial Reporting Standards (IFRS) and advantages of adopting them.
- Understand the applicability of new Indian Accounting Standards (Ind AS) notified by the Ministry of Corporate Affairs of India and the roadmap for their implementation.
- Understand the key differences between Indian GAAP, IFRS and Ind AS with respect to important accounting transactions and events.

13.1 Introduction

Accounting standards are pronouncements made by accounting bodies specifying the accounting requirements for different transactions and events. Entities prepare their financial statements based on accounting standards. Financial statements based on accounting standards are expected to make a fair presentation of an entity's financial performance, financial position and cash flows to different users of financial statements. Accounting standards also bring about uniformity in financial reporting and make financial statements of different entities comparable.

13.2 Accounting Standards Issued by ICAI

Accounting bodies in different countries are responsible for formulating the accounting standards applicable to that country. In India, accounting standards are formulated by the Council of the Institute of Chartered Accountants of India (ICAI) through its Accounting Standards Board. Thereafter, these accounting standards are considered by the National Advisory Committee on Accounting Standards (NACAS) of the Ministry of Corporate Affairs, which recommends the Standards to the Central Government for notifying under the Companies Act. The Government, on accepting the recommendation of the Committee, notifies the Standards under the Companies Act by publishing them in the Official Gazette. Currently, the following accounting standards, also commonly known as the Indian GAAP (generally accepted accounting standards), have been notified.

- AS 1 – Disclosure of Accounting Policies
- AS 2 – Valuation of Inventories
- AS 3 – Cash Flow Statement
- AS 4 – Contingencies and Events Occurring after the Balance Sheet Date
- AS 5 – Net Profit or Loss for the Period, Prior Period Items and Changes in Accounting Policies
- AS 6 – Depreciation Accounting
- AS 7 – Construction Contracts (revised 2002)
- AS 8 – Accounting for Research and Development (AS 8 is no longer in force since it was merged with AS 26)
- AS 9 – Revenue Recognition
- AS 10 – Accounting for Fixed Assets
- AS 11 – The Effects of Changes in Foreign Exchange Rates (revised 2003)
- AS 12 – Accounting for Government Grants
- AS 13 – Accounting for Investments
- AS 14 – Accounting for Amalgamations
- AS 15 – Employee Benefits (revised 2005)
- AS 16 – Borrowing Costs
- AS 17 – Segment Reporting
- AS 18 – Related Party Disclosures
- AS 19 – Leases
- AS 20 – Earnings Per Share
- AS 21 – Consolidated Financial Statements
- AS 22 – Accounting for Taxes on Income
- AS 23 – Accounting for Investments in Associates in Consolidated Financial Statements
- AS 24 – Discontinuing Operations
- AS 25 – Interim Financial Reporting
- AS 26 – Intangible Assets
- AS 27 – Financial Reporting of Interests in Joint Ventures
- AS 28 – Impairment of Assets
- AS 29 – Provisions, Contingent Liabilities and Contingent Assets
- AS 30 – Financial Instruments: Recognition and Measurement and Limited Revisions to AS 2, AS 11 revised 2003), AS 21, AS 23, AS 26, AS 27, AS 28 and AS 29
- AS 31 – Financial Instruments: Presentation
- AS 32 – Financial Instruments: Disclosures, and limited revision to Accounting Standard

The detailed contents of the above accounting standards are available at the website of the Institute of Chartered Accountants of India.

13.3 International Financial Reporting Standards (IFRS)

As the business world becomes closer in its financial and trade ties, many countries are moving towards International Financial Reporting Standards (IFRS). IFRS are common accounting rules for financial reporting. IFRS comprise the following:

1. **Two series of standards:** Those explicitly called International Financial Reporting Standards and the older series of International Accounting Standards (IAS).
2. **Two series of interpretations:** Those issued by the former Standing Interpretations Committee (SIC) and those issued by the existing International Financial Reporting Interpretations Committee (IFRIC) of the International Accounting Standards Board (IASB).

13.4 Advantages of Adopting IFRS

Adoption of IFRS has many advantages. Investors can compare financial statements of companies located in different countries and decide where to invest money. It becomes easier for companies to raise money outside their home country and for countries to attract foreign investment. As IFRS are principle-based rather than rule-based, these can be adapted to specific business conditions in a country.

13.5 Indian Accounting Standards

IFRS have many advantages, and hence many countries have adopted them as their national standard. India has decided to converge its accounting standards with IFRS instead of adopting IFRS. In a move towards convergence with IFRS, in 2007 the ICAI commenced the process of developing a complete set of accounting standards that are "converged with" IFRS. These are known as Indian Accounting Standards or Ind AS. Indian Accounting Standards have certain modifications to IFRS to reflect "Indian conditions."

Implementing the new accounting standards, the Ministry of Corporate Affairs (MCA) of India has notified 'lhe Companies (Indian Accounting Standards) Rules, 2015. The following Indian Accounting Standards have been notified under this.

Indian Accounting Standard (Ind AS) 101	First-Time Adoption of Indian Accounting Standards
Indian Accounting Standard (Ind AS) 102	Share-Based Payment
Indian Accounting Standard (Ind AS) 103	Business Combinations
Indian Accounting Standard (Ind AS) 104	Insurance Contracts
Indian Accounting Standard (Ind AS) 105	Non-Current Assets Held for Sale and Discontinued Operations
Indian Accounting Standard (Ind AS) 106	Exploration for and Evaluation of Mineral Resources
Indian Accounting Standard (Ind AS) 107	Financial Instruments: Disclosures
Indian Accounting Standard (Ind AS) 108	Operating Segments
Indian Accounting Standard (Ind AS) 109	Financial Instruments
Indian Accounting Standard (Ind AS) 110	Consolidated Financial Statements

Indian Accounting Standard (Ind AS) 111	Joint Arrangements
Indian Accounting Standard (Ind AS) 112	Disclosure of Interests in Other Entities
Indian Accounting Standard (Ind AS) 113	Fair Value Measurement
Indian Accounting Standard (Ind AS) 114	Regulatory Deferral Accounts
Indian Accounting Standard (Ind AS) 115	Revenue from Contracts with Customers
Indian Accounting Standard (Ind AS) 1	Presentation of Financial Statements
Indian Accounting Standard (Ind AS) 2	Inventories
Indian Accounting Standard (Ind AS) 7	Statement of Cash Flows
Indian Accounting Standard (Ind AS) 8	Accounting Policies, Changes in Accounting Estimates and Errors
Indian Accounting Standard (Ind AS) 10	Events After the Reporting Period
Indian Accounting Standard (Ind AS) 12	Income Taxes
Indian Accounting Standard (Ind AS) 16	Property, Plant and Equipment
Indian Accounting Standard (Ind AS) 17	Leases
Indian Accounting Standard (Ind AS) 19	Employee Benefits
Indian Accounting Standard (Ind AS) 20	Accounting for Government Grants and Disclosure of Government Assistance
Indian Accounting Standard (Ind AS) 21	The Effects of Changes in Foreign Exchange Rates
Indian Accounting Standard (Ind AS) 23	Borrowing Costs
Indian Accounting Standard (Ind AS) 24	Related Party Disclosures
Indian Accounting Standard (Ind AS) 27	Separate Financial Statements
Indian Accounting Standard (Ind AS) 28	Investments in Associates and Joint Ventures
Indian Accounting Standard (Ind AS) 29	Financial Reporting in Hyperinflationary Economies
Indian Accounting Standard (Ind AS) 32	Financial Instruments: Presentation
Indian Accounting Standard (Ind AS) 33	Earnings per Share
Indian Accounting Standard (Ind AS) 34	Interim Financial Reporting
Indian Accounting Standard (Ind AS) 36	Impairment of Assets
Indian Accounting Standard (Ind AS) 37	Provisions, Contingent Liabilities and Contingent Assets
Indian Accounting Standard (Ind AS) 38	Intangible Assets
Indian Accounting Standard (Ind AS) 40	Investment Property
Indian Accounting Standard (Ind AS) 41	Agriculture

The detailed contents of the above accounting standards are available at the website of the Ministry of Corporate Affairs, Government of India.

13.6 Applicability and Roadmap for Implementation of Ind AS

From April 1, 2016, Ind AS will be mandatorily applicable to the following companies:

1. Companies whose equity and/or debt securities are listed or are in the process of listing on any stock exchange in India or outside India and having net worth of Rs. 500 crore or more.
2. Companies having networth of Rs. 500 crore or more, other than those covered in the above point.
3. Holding, subsidiary, joint venture or associate companies of the above companies.

From April 1, 2017, Ind AS would be mandatory for

1. Companies – whose equity and/or debt securities are listed or are in the process of being listed within India or outside India – having a net worth of less than Rs. 500 crore.
2. Other companies, that are unlisted having a net worth of Rs. 250 crore or more but less than Rs. 500 crore.

Holding, subsidiary, joint venture or associate companies of these entities would have to comply with this deadline.

Companies whose securities are listed or in the process of listing on SME exchanges would not be required to apply Ind AS. Such companies shall continue to comply with the existing accounting standards unless they choose otherwise.

Ind AS norms can be followed by companies on a voluntary basis from April 1, 2015. Ind AS, once applied voluntarily, cannot be revoked.

An Indian company's overseas subsidiary, associate, joint venture and other similar entities can prepare their standalone financial statements in accordance with requirements of the concerned jurisdiction. However, such companies are required to prepare their consolidated financial statements in accordance with the Ind AS.

Companies which are not required to follow Ind AS would continue to follow accounting standards as prescribed in Companies (Accounting Standards) Rules, 2006. These are the earlier accounting standards formulated by ICAI.

Ind AS are also not applicable to banking, insurance and non-banking finance companies.

13.7 Comparison of Indian GAAP, IFRS and Ind AS

Ind AS norms are converged with the IFRS, but those are not IFRS-equivalent. Further, some companies in India will follow the old accounting standards (Indian GAAP) while others follow Ind AS. It would be of interest to see the key differences between the requirements of Indian GAAP, IFRS and Ind AS. These differences in respect of some important types of accounting transactions and events are presented in Table 13.1.

Table 13.1 Comparison of Indian GAAP, IFRS and Ind AS

Presentation of Financial Statements	Indian GAAP	IFRS	Ind AS
Components of financial statements	The requirements for the presentation of financial statements are set out in Statutes that govern the entity. For instance, Schedule III to the Companies Act, 2013 sets out financial statement requirements in the case of companies;	A complete set of financial statements comprises of a statement of financial position, a statement of comprehensive income, a statement of changes in equity, a statement of cash flows and notes to	A complete set of financial statements under Ind AS 1 comprises of a balance sheet at the end of the period (including statement of changes in equity which is presented as a part of the balance sheet), statement

(*Continued*)

Table 13.1 (Continued)

Presentation of Financial Statements	Indian GAAP	IFRS	Ind AS
	Schedule III to the Banking Regulation Act, 1949 (for banks) sets out financial statement requirements in the case of banks. In general, the financial statements comprise of balance sheet; statement of profit and loss; cash flow statement, if applicable and notes to the financial statements including summary of accounting policies. A statement of comprehensive income is not required to be prepared. A statement of changes in equity is not required. Movement in share capital, retained earnings and other reserves are presented in the notes to the financial statements.	the financial statements including summary of accounting policies.	of profit and loss, a statement of cash flows and notes including summary of accounting policies and other explanatory information.
Presentation of consolidated financial statements	Only listed entities with one or more subsidiaries are required to present consolidated financial statements.	Entities with one or more subsidiaries are required to present consolidated financial statements unless specific criteria are met.	Unlike IFRS, Ind AS do not mandate which entities are required to prepare consolidated financial statements as the requirements to present consolidated or separate financial statements is regulated by governing statutes in India.

(*Continued*)

Table 13.1 (Continued)

Presentation of Financial Statements	Indian GAAP	IFRS	Ind AS
Comparatives	Comparative information is required for the preceding period only.	Similar to Indian GAAP; however, entities making prior period adjustment or reclassifications or applying accounting policy retrospectively should present a statement of financial position as at the beginning of the earliest comparative period.	Similar to IFRS
Formats	Schedule III prescribes mandatory formats for presentation of balance sheet and statement of profit and loss. However, the same stand modified, if any change is required for compliance with the requirements of the Companies Act including Accounting Standards.	Only illustrative formats for presentation of financial statements have been given.	Ind AS 1 does not include any illustrative formats for the presentation of financial statements though Ind AS 27 does set out the form in which consolidated financial statements are to be presented.
Definition of "material"	Financial statements should disclose all "material" items, the knowledge of which might influence the decisions of the user of the financial statements.	Omissions or misstatements are material if individually or collectively they could influence the economic decisions that users take on the basis of financial statements.	Similar to IFRS
Fair presentation	Fair presentation requires compliance with the applicable requirements of the Companies Act, 2013 and other regulatory requirements, and the application of the qualitative characteristics of the Accounting Standards Framework.	Fair presentation requires faithful representation of the effects of the transactions, other events and conditions in accordance with the definitions of and recognition criteria for assets, liabilities, income and expenses set out in the framework.	Similar to IFRS

(Continued)

Table 13.1 (Continued)

Presentation of Financial Statements	Indian GAAP	IFRS	Ind AS
	Departures from Accounting Standards or Companies Act, 2013 are prohibited unless permitted by other regulatory framework.	In extremely rare circumstances, in which management concludes that compliance with requirements of a Standard or interpretation is so misleading, it may depart from the Standard or the interpretation.	
Classification of financial liabilities under refinancing arrangements	There is no guidance in the existing standards. Schedule III specifies that financial liabilities shall be classified as current, where the company does not have an unconditional right to defer settlement of the liability for at least 12 months after the reporting date.	A financial liability is classified as current if the agreement to refinance or reschedule payments on a long-term basis is completed after the end of the reporting period and before the financial statements is authorized for issue.	Similar to IFRS
Classification of financial liabilities on breach of covenants	There is no guidance in the existing standards.	A financial liability is classified as non-current if the lender has agreed before the end of the reporting period to provide a grace period of a minimum 12 months after the reporting period within which the breach can be rectified and the lender cannot demand immediate repayment.	Similar to IFRS
Classification of expenses	Expenses are classified by nature.	Expenses are classified by either nature or function. Certain additional disclosures are required in the notes to the financial statements depending on the presentation choice selected by the entity.	Entities should present an analysis of expenses recognized in profit or loss using a classification based only on the nature of expense.

(Continued)

Table 13.1 (Continued)

Presentation of Financial Statements	Indian GAAP	IFRS	Ind AS
Profit or loss attributable to non-controlling shareholders	Profit or loss attributable to non-controlling shareholders is disclosed as a deduction from the profit or loss for the period as an item of income or expense.	Profit or loss attributable to non-controlling interest holders and equity holders of the parent entity is disclosed as an allocation of profit or loss and total comprehensive income for the period.	Similar to IFRS
Presentation of other comprehensive income (OCI)	There is no concept of OCI. All incomes, expenses, gains and losses are presented in the income statement except certain items that are required to be directly recognized in reserves. For example, revaluation surplus and foreign currency translation reserve.	Other comprehensive income items may be presented in a single statement of comprehensive income or a separate statement.	An entity is required to present all items of income and expense, including components of other comprehensive income in a period in a single statement of profit and loss.
Extraordinary items	Extraordinary items are disclosed separately in the statement of profit and loss and are included in the determination of the net profit or loss for the period.	Entities are not permitted to present any item of income or expense as extraordinary.	Similar to IFRS
Reclassification	A disclosure is made in the financial statement that comparative amounts have been reclassified to conform to the presentation in the current period without additional disclosures for the nature, amount and reason for reclassification.	When comparative amounts are reclassified, the nature, amount and reason for reclassification are disclosed.	Similar to IFRS

(Continued)

Table 13.1 (Continued)

Presentation of Financial Statements	Indian GAAP	IFRS	Ind AS
Statement of changes in equity	A statement of changes in equity is not required. Movements in share capital, retained earnings and other reserves are to be presented in the notes to accounts.	A statement of changes in equity is presented showing: (a) the total comprehensive income for the period, (b) effects of retrospective application or restatement of each component of equity, (c) for each component of equity, a reconciliation between opening and closing balances, separately disclosing changes resulting from: (i) profit or loss, (ii) each item of other comprehensive income and (iii) transactions with owners in their capacity as owners, showing separately contributions by and distributions to owners and changes in ownership interests in subsidiaries that do not result in a loss of control.	A statement of changes in equity is presented as part of the balance sheet. The statement of changes in equity contains information which is similar to that under IFRS.
Estimation uncertainty and critical judgment	No specific requirement	Entities should disclose the key sources of estimation uncertainty and judgments made in applying entity's critical accounting policies in the financial statements.	Similar to IFRS
Capital	AS 1 does not require an entity to disclose information that enables users of its financial statements to evaluate the entity's objectives, policies and processes of managing capital.	Requires disclosure of information about the management of capital and compliance with capital requirements.	Similar to IFRS

(Continued)

Table 13.1 (Continued)

Inventories	Indian GAAP	IFRS	Ind AS
Scope	Commodity inventories are not excluded from the scope. Excludes producers' inventories of livestock, agricultural and forest products, and mineral oils, ores and gases to the extent they are measured at net realizable value, in accordance with well-established practice in these industries. Work-in-progress arising in the normal course of business of service providers is excluded.	Inventories held by commodity broker-traders, who measure their inventories at fair value minus costs to sell, producers of agricultural and forest products, agricultural produce after harvest, minerals and mineral products to the extent they are measured at the net realizable value, in accordance with well-established practices in those industries do not come under measurement requirements of IAS 2. Changes in fair value minus costs to sell/changes in net realizable value are recognized in profit or loss in the period of change.	Similar to IFRS
Reversal of write-down of inventory	No specific guidance in AS 2 for reversal of write-down of inventories.	Reversal of write-down of inventories is allowed up to the amount of original write-down.	Similar to IFRS
Classification of inventories	Inventories need to be classified as raw materials, work-in-progress, finished goods, etc.	No requirement to specific classification.	Similar to IFRS
Statement of Cash Flows	**Indian GAAP**	**IFRS**	**Ind AS**
Bank overdrafts	Considered as financing activities.	Included as cash and cash equivalents if they form an integral part of an entity's cash management.	Similar to IFRS
Cash flows from extraordinary items	Classified as operating, financing or investing activities and separately disclosed.	No items of cash flows is shown as extraordinary as presentation of items as extraordinary is not permitted.	Similar to IFRS

(Continued)

Table 13.1 (Continued)

Statement of Cash Flows	Indian GAAP	IFRS	Ind AS
Interest and dividend	For financial enterprises, interest paid and interest received are classified as operating activities; dividend paid is classified as financing activity. For other enterprises, interest and dividends received are classified as investing activities. Interest and dividends paid are classified as financing activities.	Allows classification as operating, investing or financing activities in a manner consistent from period to period.	Similar to Indian GAAP
Acquisition and disposal of properties	No specific guidance	Entities may sell items of property, plant and equipment held by them for rental to others. Cash payments/receipts in respect of acquisition/disposal of such assets are classified as operating activities.	Similar to IFRS
Changes in ownership interest	No specific guidance	Changes in ownership interest in a subsidiary without loss of control are treated as financing activities.	Similar to IFRS
Investing activities	No specific guidance	Only expenditures resulting in a recognized asset in the statement of financial position should be classified as investing activities.	Similar to IFRS
Income Taxes	**Indian GAAP**	**IFRS**	**Ind AS**
Deferred taxes	Deferred taxes are computed for timing difference in recognition of profit or loss for the purpose of financial reporting and income tax.	Deferred taxes are computed for temporary differences between the carrying amount of an asset or liability in the statement of financial position and its tax base.	Similar to IFRS

(Continued)

Table 13.1 (Continued)

Income Taxes	Indian GAAP	IFRS	Ind AS
Recognition of deferred tax assets and liabilities	Deferred taxes are generally recognized for all timing differences.	Deferred taxes are recognized for all temporary differences between accounting and tax base of assets and liabilities with some exceptions.	Similar to IFRS
Recognition of taxes on items recognized in other comprehensive income or directly in equity	No specific guidance in AS 22.	Tax on items recognized in other comprehensive income or directly in equity is also recognized in other comprehensive income or in equity, as appropriate.	Similar to IFRS
Recognition of deferred tax assets	Deferred tax asset for unused tax losses and unabsorbed depreciation is recognized only to the extent that there is virtual certainty supported by convincing evidence that sufficient future taxable income will be available against which such deferred tax assets can be realized. Deferred tax asset for all other unused credits/timing differences is recognized only to the extent that there is a reasonable certainty that sufficient future taxable income will be available against which such deferred tax assets can be realized.	Deferred tax asset is recognized for carry forward unused tax losses and unused tax credits to the extent it is probable that future taxable profit will be available against which the unused tax losses and tax credits can be utilized.	Similar to IFRS
Investments in subsidiaries, branches and associates, and interests in joint ventures	No deferred tax liability is recognized.	Deferred tax liability for all taxable temporary differences is recognized except to the extent specified in certain cases.	Similar to IFRS

(Continued)

Table 13.1 (Continued)

Income Taxes	Indian GAAP	IFRS	Ind AS
Deferred tax in respect of business combinations	No specific guidance.	Goodwill is reduced with the amount of the acquiree's income tax loss carry forward or other deferred tax assets. If the carrying amount of goodwill is 0, these benefits are recognized in profit or loss. All other deferred tax benefits are recognized in profit or loss (or if IAS 12 so requires, outside profit or loss).	Similar to IFRS
Deferred tax on unrealized intra-group profits	Deferred tax is not recognized	Deferred tax on unrealized intra-group profit is recognized at the buyer's rate.	Similar to IFRS
Classification	Schedule III requires net deferred tax assets and net deferred tax liabilities to be presented as part of non-current assets and non-current liabilities, respectively.	Always classified as non-current if current and non-current classification is presented.	Similar to IFRS
Disclosure	Certain additional details as required under IFRS, not required.	Additional disclosures required include either a numerical or a tax-rate reconciliation, details of tax holidays and expiry, and unrecognized deferred tax liability on undistributed earnings of subsidiaries, branches, associates and joint ventures.	Similar to IFRS
Tax benefits related to share-based payments	No specific guidance	Deferred tax benefit is calculated based on the tax deduction for the share-based payment under the applicable tax law (e.g., intrinsic value).	Similar to IFRS

(Continued)

Table 13.1 (Continued)

Income Taxes	Indian GAAP	IFRS	Ind AS
Recovery of revalued non-depreciable assets	Revaluation is considered as permanent difference and there is no deferred tax effect.	Measurement of deferred tax liability or asset arising from revaluation is based on the tax consequences from the sale of asset rather than through use.	Similar to IFRS
Recovery of investment property measured under fair value model	Not applicable as investment property cannot be measured using fair value.	In the case of investment property measured using the fair value model, for measuring deferred taxes; there is a rebuttable presumption that the carrying amount will be recovered through sale.	Similar to Indian GAAP
Changes in tax status of an entity or its shareholders	No specific guidance	Current and deferred tax consequences are included in the profit or loss for the period of change unless the consequences relate to transactions or events recognized outside profit or loss either in other comprehensive income or directly in equity in the same or a different period.	Similar to IFRS
Property, Plant and Equipment	**Indian GAAP**	**IFRS**	**Ind AS**
Scope	There is no exemption from AS 10 for property under development for future use as investment property.	Property under construction or development for future use as investment property is excluded from the scope of IAS 16 and is within the scope of IAS 40 – Investment Property.	Similar to IFRS

(Continued)

Table 13.1 (Continued)

Property, Plant and Equipment	Indian GAAP	IFRS	Ind AS
Replacement cost	Replacement cost of an item of property, plant and equipment is generally expensed when incurred. Only expenditure that increases the future benefits from existing asset beyond its previously assessed standard of performance is capitalized.	Replacement cost of an item of property, plant and equipment is capitalized if replacement meets the recognition criteria. Carrying amount of items replaced is derecognized.	Similar to IFRS
Cost of major inspections	Costs of major inspections are generally expensed when incurred.	Costs of major inspections and overhauls are recognized in the carrying amount of property, plant and equipment.	Similar to IFRS
Revaluation	No specific requirement on frequency of revaluation.	If an entity adopts the revaluation model, revaluations are required to be made with sufficient regularity to ensure that the carrying amount does not differ materially from that which would be determined using the value at the end of the reporting period.	Similar to IFRS
Depreciation	Fixed assets are not required to be componentized and depreciated separately, though AS 10 states that such an approach may improve the accounting for an item of fixed asset. Schedule XIV to the Companies Act, 1956 specifies the minimum depreciation rates to be used for different categories of assets.	Property, plant and equipment are componentized and depreciated separately. There is no concept of minimum statutory depreciation under IFRS.	Similar to IFRS

(*Continued*)

Table 13.1 (Continued)

Property, Plant and Equipment	Indian GAAP	IFRS	Ind AS
Compensation for impairment	No specific requirement. In practice, compensation is offset against replaced items of property, plant and equipment.	Compensation from third parties for impairment or loss of items of property, plant and equipment are included in the profit or loss when the compensation becomes receivable.	Similar to IFRS
Transfers from revaluation reserve	Transfers may be done through statement of profit and loss.	Transfers from revaluation reserve to retained earnings are made directly and not through profit or loss.	Similar to IFRS
Residual value	Estimates of residual value are not required to be updated.	Estimates of residual value need to be reviewed at least at the end of each year.	Similar to IFRS
Reassessment of useful life and depreciation method	Not currently required.	Requires annual reassessment of useful life and depreciation method.	Similar to IFRS
Change in the method of depreciation	Requires retrospective re-computation of depreciation. Any excess or deficit on such re-computation is required to be adjusted in the period in which such change is affected. Such a change is treated as a change in accounting policy and its effect is quantified and disclosed.	Changes in depreciation method are considered as change in accounting estimate, and applied prospectively.	Similar to IFRS
Presentation of capital advances	Schedule III requires capital advances to be presented separately under the head "long-term loans and advances" as part of non-current assets.	No specific guidance, though usually included in capital work-in-progress.	Similar to IFRS

(Continued)

Table 13.1 (Continued)

Property, Plant and Equipment	Indian GAAP	IFRS	Ind AS
Routine sale of some properties	No such requirement as in IFRS.	Entities might routinely sell items of property, plant and equipment that they have previously held for rental to others. The proceeds from sale of such assets should be recognized as revenue in accordance with IAS 18.	Similar to IFRS
Changes in existing decommissioning, restoration and similar liabilities	No specific guidance	Provisioning for decommissioning, restoration and similar liabilities that have previously been recognized as part of the cost of an item of property, plant and equipment are adjusted for changes in the amount or timing of future costs and for changes in market-based discount rates.	Similar to IFRS
Revenue	**Indian GAAP**	**IFRS**	**Ind AS**
Definition	Revenue is the gross inflow of cash, receivables or other consideration arising in the course of ordinary activities from the sale of goods, from the rendering of services, and use by others of enterprise resources yielding interest, royalty and dividends.	Revenue is the gross inflow of economic benefits during the period arising in the course of ordinary activities of an entity when these inflows result in increases in equity, other than increases relating to contributions from equity participants.	Similar to IFRS

(Continued)

Table 13.1 (Continued)

Revenue	Indian GAAP	IFRS	Ind AS
Principal versus agent	No specific guidance	Amounts collected on behalf of third parties such as sales, service taxes and value added taxes are excluded from revenues. Guidance on whether an entity acts as a principal or as an agent is included in the accompanying illustrative examples (but not forming part of IAS 18).	Similar to IFRS
Measurement	Revenue is recognized at the nominal amount of consideration receivable. On AS 30 becoming effective, there will be no difference between AS 9 and IAS 18 "Revenue."	Fair value of revenue from sale of goods and services when the inflow of cash and cash equivalents is deferred is determined by discounting all future receipts using an implied rate of interest. The difference between the value and nominal amount of consideration is recognized as interest income using the effective interest method.	Similar to IFRS

(*Continued*)

Table 13.1 (Continued)

Revenue	Indian GAAP	IFRS	Ind AS
Financial service fees	Financial service fee is recognized as revenue depending on whether the service has been provided "once for all" or on a continuing basis. Loan origination and arrangement fees are recognized as revenues when the loan has been originated. On AS 30 becoming effective, there will be no difference between AS 9 and IAS 18 "Revenue."	Fees that are an integral part of the effective interest rate of a financial instrument, for example, loan origination and arrangement fees are deferred and recognized as an adjustment to the effective interest rate. However, when the financial instrument is measured at fair value with changes in fair value recognized in profit or loss, the fees are recognized as revenue when the instrument is initially recognized.	Similar to IFRS
Interest	Interest is recognized on a time proportion basis taking into account the amount outstanding and the rate applicable. On AS 30 becoming effective, there will be no difference between AS 9 and IAS 18 "Revenue."	Interest income is recognized using the effective interest method.	Similar to IFRS
Dividend recognition in separate financial statements	Dividend income declared out of post-acquisition profits should be recognized in the statement of profit and loss. Dividend declared out of pre-acquisition profits will go to reduce the cost of the investment.	Entire dividend income should be recognized in the profit or loss, irrespective of whether it is declared out of pre-acquisition or post-acquisition profits, though it may, in some situations be necessary to test the investment for impairment.	Similar to IFRS
Exchange transactions	No specific guidance.	The accounting treatment depends on whether the exchange transaction involves goods and services of similar nature and value.	Similar to IFRS

(*Continued*)

Table 13.1 (Continued)

Revenue	Indian GAAP	IFRS	Ind AS
Services rendered	Completed service contract method or proportionate completion method permitted. Revenues from installation fees and production commission are recognized when installation and production are completed unless the installation is incidental to sale.	Requires recognition using percentage of completion method. Revenues from installation fees and production commission are recognized with reference to stages of completion, unless the installation is incidental to sale.	Similar to IFRS
Barter transactions involving advertising services	No specific guidance in AS 9. However, the Guidance Note on Accounting for Dot.com companies provides guidance for advertising barter transactions which is similar to IFRS.	Fair value of services provided is measured with reference to non-barter transactions that occur frequently, representing a substantial number of transactions. Consideration involves cash or other securities that have a reliable measure of fair value and do not involve transactions with the same counterpart to the barter transaction.	Similar to IFRS
Customer loyalty programs	No specific guidance.	Award credits are accounted for as a separate identifiable component of a sales transaction, with the consideration allocated between the awards credit and the other components of sale.	Similar to IFRS

(Continued)

Table 13.1 (Continued)

Related Party Disclosures	Indian GAAP	IFRS	Ind AS
Definition of close member of the family	No definition of close member of the family. Instead the term relative has been defined.	Close members of the family of a person are those family members who may be expected to influence, or be influenced by, that person in their dealings with the entity and include: (a) That person's children and spouse or domestic partner. (b) Children of that person's spouse or domestic partner. (c) Dependents of that person or that person's spouse or domestic partner.	Close members of the family of a person are persons specified within the meaning of "relative" under the Companies Act, 2013 and that person's domestic partner, children of that person's domestic partner and dependents of that person's domestic partner.
Post-employment benefit plans	Not considered as related parties.	Unlike Indian GAAP, considered as related party.	Similar to IFRS
Exemptions	Entities are exempt from disclosures if such disclosures would conflict with an entity's duties of confidentiality as specifically required in terms of a statute or by any regulator or similar component authority.	No such exemption. Certain minimum disclosures should be made by government-related entities.	Disclosures which conflict with confidentiality requirements of statute/ regulation are not required to be made.
Key management personnel compensation	Entities under the control of Government are not required to disclose related party relationship and transactions with other Government controlled entities.	Unlike Indian GAAP, disclosed in total and analyzed by component.	Similar to IFRS
Items to be disclosed	Generally disclosed in aggregate. Disclosure of the volume of transactions with related parties, either as an amount or as an appropriate proportion and amounts or appropriate proportions of outstanding items.	The amount of transactions with related parties and the amount of outstanding balances including commitments.	Similar to IFRS

(*Continued*)

Table 13.1 (Continued)

Earnings Per Share	Indian GAAP	IFRS	Ind AS
Disclosure in financial statements	AS 20 requires disclosure of basic and diluted EPS information, both in separate and consolidated financial statements of the Parent.	When an entity presents both separate and consolidated financial statements, EPS is required to be presented only in the consolidated financial statements. An entity may disclose EPS in its separate financial statements voluntarily.	EPS is required to be presented both in consolidated and separate financial statements.
Additional disclosures	No specific disclosures are required in respect of discontinued operations and instruments that could potentially dilute earnings per share in the future.	Separate basic and diluted earnings per share are disclosed for discontinued operations. Disclosure is also required for instruments that could potentially dilute earnings per share in the future, but were not included in the calculation of diluted earnings per share because they are anti-dilutive for the periods presented.	Similar to IFRS
Extraordinary items	EPS with and without extraordinary items should be presented.	There is no concept of extraordinary item.	Similar to IFRS
Mandatorily convertible instrument	No specific requirement.	Ordinary shares to be issued on conversion of a mandatorily convertible instrument are included in the calculation of basic EPS from the date the contract is entered into.	Similar to IFRS
Shares issuable after a passage of time	No specific guidance.	Ordinary shares that are issuable solely after a passage of time are not treated as contingently issuable shares because passage of time is a certainty.	Similar to IFRS

(Continued)

Table 13.1 (Continued)

Earnings Per Share	Indian GAAP	IFRS	Ind AS
Contingently returnable shares	No guidance.	Outstanding ordinary shares that are contingently returnable are not treated as outstanding and are ignored in the calculation of basic EPS until the shares are no longer subject to recall.	Similar to IFRS
Segments	**Indian GAAP**	**IFRS**	**Ind AS**
Determination of segments	Requires an enterprise to identify two sets of segments (business and geographical), using risks and rewards approach, with the enterprise's system of internal financial reporting to key management personnel serving only as the starting point for the identification of such segments.	Operating segments are identified based on the financial information that is regularly reviewed by the chief operating decision maker in deciding how to allocate resources and in assessing performance.	Similar to IFRS
Operating segments – Measurement	Segment information is prepared in conformity with the accounting policies adopted for preparing and presenting financial statements of the enterprise as a whole. Segment revenue, segment expense, segment result, segment asset and segment liability are defined. A reconciliation is presented between the information disclosed for reportable segments and the aggregated information in the entity's financial statements.	Segment profit or loss is reported on the same measurement basis as that used by the chief operating decision maker. No requirement to disclose information about liabilities unless such a measure is regularly provided to the chief operating decision maker. Requires reconciliation of segment performance measures and segment assets and liabilities with the corresponding amounts reported in the financial statements.	Similar to IFRS

(Continued)

Table 13.1 (Continued)

Segments	Indian GAAP	IFRS	Ind AS
Operating segments – entity wide disclosures	Disclosures are required based on the classification of segments as primary or secondary.	Requires disclosure of: (a) revenues from external customers from each product or service, (b) revenues from external customers in the country of domicile and from foreign countries, and (c) geographical information on certain non-current assets located in the country of domicile and foreign countries. Information on major customers, including total revenues from each major customer is disclosed if revenue from such a customer is 10% or more of an entity's revenues.	Similar to IFRS

Summary – Review of Learning Objectives

1. **Understand the meaning and importance of accounting standards.** Accounting standards are pronouncements made by accounting bodies that specify the accounting requirements for different transactions and events. When financial statements are based on accounting standards, these are expected to make a fair presentation of an entity's financial performance, financial position and cash flows to different users of financial statements. Accounting standards also bring about uniformity in financial reporting and make financial statements of different entities comparable.
2. **Know the existing accounting standards issued by Institute of Chartered Accountants of India.** ICAI has issued 32 Accounting Standards (AS) which are also commonly known as Indian GAAP.
3. **Understand the International Financial Reporting Standards and advantages of adopting them.** IFRS comprise two series of standards and two series of interpretations. By adopting IFRS, investors can compare financial statements of companies located in different countries and decide where to invest money. It becomes easier for companies to raise money outside their home country and for countries to attract foreign investment. IFRS are also more flexible.
4. **Understand the applicability of new Indian Accounting Standards (Ind AS) notified by the Ministry of Corporate Affairs of India**

and the roadmap for their implementation. Ind AS can be voluntarily adopted by companies with effect from April 1, 2015. These have to be mandatorily applied by one category of companies from April 1, 2016 and the second category of companies from April 1, 2017. Further some companies shall continue to comply with the existing accounting standards unless they choose otherwise.

5. **Understand the key differences between Indian GAAP, IFRS and Ind AS with respect to important accounting transactions and events.** Ind AS are more or less converged with IFRS. There are major differences in the Indian GAAP and the Ind AS with respect to the presentation of financial statements, inventory accounting, presentation of cash flows, revenue recognition, etc. Once implemented, Ind AS are expected to increase the relevance and reliability of financial statements for both domestic and international investors and lenders.

Glossary

AS Accounting Standards
GAAP Generally Accepted Accounting Practices
IAS International Accounting Standards
IFRIC International Financial Reporting Interpretations Committee
IFRS International Financial Reporting Standards
Ind AS Indian Accounting Standards
SIC Standing Interpretations Committee

Review Questions

1. What are accounting standards? Why are these necessary for the preparation and presentation of financial statements?
2. What advantage can Indian companies derive by preparing and presenting their financial statements in accordance with IFRS?
3. Is Ind AS exactly similar to IFRS? Comment.
4. Some categories of companies have been exempted from adoption of Ind AS. Name these categories.

Index